Ernst Kapp · Ausgewählte Schriften

Ernst Kapp

Ernst Kapp

Ausgewählte Schriften

Walter de Gruyter & Co.

Berlin 1968

Herausgegeben von HANS und INEZ DILLER

Archiv-Nr. 36 43 681

©

1968 by Walter de Gruyter & Co., vormals G. J. Göschen'sche Verlagshandlung — J. Guttentag,
Verlagsbuchhandlung — Georg Reimer — Karl J. Trübner — Veit & Comp., Berlin 30
Alle Rechte des Nachdrucks, der photomechanischen Wiedergabe, der Übersetzung, der Herstellung
von Mikrofilmen und Photokopien, auch auszugsweise, vorbehalten.
Satz und Druck: Walter de Gruyter & Co., Berlin — Printed in Germany

Inhalt

Besprechung:

Wolfgang Schadewaldt, Die Geschichtschreibung des Thukydides
Ein Versuch

1930

Thukydides' Werk sollte den als Einheit gefaßten Krieg der Jahre 431—404 bis zur Endkatastrophe Frühjahr 404 erzählen; das steht 5, 26, 1, und wenn die Darstellung faktisch im Sommer 411 sozusagen mitten im Satz abbricht, so war es der bis zur Albernheit formalistischen Betrachtungsweise des Dionysios von Halikarnaß vorbehalten, deswegen den Verf. in Widerspruch mit sich selbst bringen zu wollen und die Möglichkeit seines trotz nicht kurzen Lebens vorzeitigen Todes zu | ignorieren. Was das Ende von Th.' Schriftstellerei betrifft, liegen die Dinge gerade wegen der Äußerung 5, 26, 1 nur zu eindeutig; dagegen bedeutet sein Selbstzeugnis über deren Anfang für jede Betrachtung eine Schwierigkeit. 27 Jahre hat der ‚Krieg der Peloponnesier und Athener' gedauert, dessen Ende Th. natürlich erst seit 404 übersehen konnte, aber ihn zu beschreiben ‚angefangen hat er gleich zu Beginn' (1, 1, 1), d. h. gleich 431 oder allenfalls in den ersten Jahren nach 431. Was und wie er in der beinahe ein Menschenalter erreichenden Dauer des Krieges an dem Werk gearbeitet hat, dafür bleibt der Phantasie ein unangenehm großer Spielraum. Denn das, was allein die Möglichkeit streng einheitlicher Interpretation gewährleistete und wozu man aus Bequemlichkeitsgründen am liebsten griffe, daß sich Th. während dieser ganzen langen Zeit auf Vorarbeiten beschränkt und mit der eigentlichen Ausarbeitung des Werkes erst nach 404 begonnen hätte, ist von vornherein gerade das Unwahrscheinliche. Daß wir in unserem Text Sätze und ganze Abschnitte lesen, die von Th. geraume Zeit vor der Katastrophe 404, und solche, die nachher geschrieben sind, daran zweifelt heute wohl niemand, und damit eröffnen sich Möglichkeiten der Interpretation, die grundsätzlich zu leugnen niemandem zugestanden werden kann. Wieweit aber die Interpretation gezwungen ist, auf diese Möglichkeiten einzugehen, und was sich dabei für Th.' Arbeit an seinem Werk ergibt, daran reichen grundsätzliche Erwägungen nicht heran. Wohl aber muß man sich prinzipiell noch über weitere Möglichkeiten im klaren sein. Th. hat sein Werk unfertig hinterlassen, keine Spur davon, daß er selbst auch nur Teile herausgegeben hätte, also müssen wir mit einem Herausgeber rechnen, und die Möglichkeit besteht, daß dieser Herausgeber auch in unserem Text gelegentlich die Hand im Spiele hat. Wer will grundsätzlich diese Möglichkeit bestreiten? Und endlich, wenn das Werk im ganzen unfertig war, dann ist es möglich, daß auch im einzelnen Unfertigkeiten vorliegen, die der Herausgeber nicht hat beseitigen können oder wollen, die aber Th. selbst hätte beseitigen müssen und würde beseitigt haben, wenn er noch dazu gekommen wäre. Auch dieser fatalen Diagnose, daß Th. in diesem oder jenem Falle ,hätte müssen', und der aus anderen Partien geschöpften Zuversicht, er ,würde haben', läßt sich kein prinzipieller Widerstand, sondern höchstens der Zweifel an unserer Fähigkeit, dann noch ins Reine zu kommen, entgegensetzen; äußerlich möglich ist vielerlei, und die Wissenschaft hat mit bequemen und unbequemen Möglichkeiten dieser Art in gleicher Weise zu rechnen, ohne sich auf das eine oder andere etwas zugute zu tun.

Der Krieg, der 431 begonnen hatte, kam 421 zum formalen Abschluß. Th., der sich gleich zu Beginn vorgenommen hatte, ihn zu beschreiben, lebte damals schon in der Verbannung, die ihn in die Lage| setzte, die Geschehnisse in größerer Ruhe als die unmittelbar Beteiligten aufzufassen (5, 26, 5). Man darf daran zweifeln, ob er den Friedensenthusiasmus der Athener (Aristoph. *Frieden*) auch nur von ferne mitgemacht hat. Aber daß seine Unbefangenheit so weit gegangen wäre, daß er dem Frieden von vornherein zu wenig getraut hätte, um schon mit einer endgültig gedachten Ausarbeitung zu beginnen, das wäre eine, wenn auch schließlich mögliche, doch recht gewagte Hypothese. Möglich ist auch die Annahme, er habe freilich schon zu schreiben angefangen und das Geschriebene auch später verwertet, aber so überarbeitet, daß es für uns praktisch darauf hinausliefe, als wäre alles erst nach 404 verfaßt, Wie gesagt, das sind Möglichkeiten, nur läßt sich auf dieser Grundlage vieles namentlich in den beiden ersten Büchern nicht interpretieren. Das hat Ullrich (Beiträge zur Erklärung des Thukydides, Programm Hamburg 1846) bewiesen; und es gibt hier, so vieles im einzelnen noch strittig bleiben mag, kein Kompromiß und keine Gegensätzliches aufhebende Synthese.

Vieles in den ersten beiden Büchern läßt sich nur verstehen, wenn es bald nach 421 und jedenfalls vor dem Ausgange des großen Krieges geschrieben ist. Ullrich wollte, möglichst einfach konstruierend, sie und dazu das 3. Buch und von dem 4. bis etwa 4, 48 ganz der ersten Periode von Th.' Schriftstellerei zuweisen und ließ nur im 2. Buch das sich offen als nach 404 geschriebene gebende Kapitel 2, 65 und außerdem die Erwähnung des Archelaos 2, 100, 2 ungern als ausnahmsweise nachgetragene späte Einfügungen gelten. Die Frage, ob der Geschichtschreiber „vielleicht noch eine nachbessernde Durchsicht seines Werkes beabsichtigt" haben sollte, warf er auf, um sie zu verneinen; die Möglichkeit, daß es zu einer wirklichen Überarbeitung der ersten Bücher gekommen wäre, schied für ihn ganz aus. Es hat sich gezeigt, daß sein Standpunkt insoweit unhaltbar war. Man muß mit zahlreicheren späteren Zusätzen rechnen als er wollte, und vor allem heben sich aus dem Zusammenhang der ersten beiden Bücher umfangreiche geschlossene Partien heraus, an deren Abfassung nach 404 heute nicht mehr gezweifelt wird, so im ersten Buch mindestens die Erzählung vom Mauerbau und die Pentekontaetie (1, 88—118, 2) und dazu der § 1, 23, 6 und die Pausanias- und Themistoklesepisode (1, 128—138), und im zweiten Buch mindestens noch die letzte Periklesrede (2, 59—64).

Für die beiden ersten Bücher kann wenigstens die Problemlage als geklärt angesehen werden. Es gibt genügend feste Anhaltspunkte für die beiden durcheinandergehenden Schichten, und die Aufgabe, sie, die im Bewußtsein des Schriftstellers durch die Erfahrungen der sizilischen Expedition und des sog. dekeleischen Krieges getrennt waren, in ihrer notwendig großen Verschiedenheit zu erfassen, muß weithin lösbar sein, mag nun Th. mit seiner Überarbeitung fertig geworden sein | oder nicht, und mag im letzteren Fall ein Herausgeber eingegriffen haben oder nicht.

Weniger klar läßt sich zur Zeit die Frage für das dritte und vierte Buch und für 5, 1—24 stellen. Hier muß — unter Vorbehalt der Möglichkeit eines teilweisen Übereinanderliegens — mit dem Aneinanderstoßen zweier verschiedenen Abfassungsperioden angehöriger Partien (im vierten oder dritten Buch) gerechnet werden, und zu den beiden zeitlichen Möglichkeiten, die für die ersten beiden Bücher gegeben sind, ist hier noch eine dritte: bald nach 412, in Betracht gezogen worden, die für jene wohl ausscheidet.

5, 25. 26 beginnt die Darstellung der Zeit nach dem ersten zehnjährigen Kriege mit dem nach 404 geschriebenen sog. zweiten Prooimion, dessen fundamentale Bedeutung für die Entstehungsgeschichte des ganzen Werkes fast allgemein anerkannt ist. Es hätte auch nie geleugnet werden dürfen, daß es von Th. für die Stelle, an der es steht, und für die Funktion, die es nun hat, geschrieben worden ist. Aber natürlich ist damit nicht, wie Ullrich annahm, das Urteil über alles Folgende bereits festgelegt. Auch was nach 5, 26 in unserem Text steht, kann ganz oder partienweise vor 404 geschrieben sein. Aber wir sind hier für die Unterscheidung in wesentlich ungünstigerer Lage als für die beiden ersten Bücher. Denn wenigstens in den Büchern 6—8 ist nichts vor dem katastrophalen Ausgang der sizilischen Expedition geschrieben, und dieser Ausgang ist, wenn Th.' Darstellung nicht ein-

fach falsch ist, in ganz Griechenland von vornherein als das Ende der
athenischen Macht aufgefaßt worden. Das war freilich eine starke
Unterschätzung der athenischen Kraft, wie derselbe Th. betont, aber
den allgemeinen Eindruck, daß der Lauf der Geschehnisse eine für
Athen lebensgefährliche Wendung genommen hatte (8, 24, 5), wird
dieser ruhige Beurteiler schwerlich auch nur zeitweise ganz haben vergessen können. Dann aber ist der Abstand der Situation in den ersten
Jahren nach 413 und der Wirkung, die sie notwendig auf das Denken
des Schriftstellers ausüben mußte, von der nach 404 bei weitem nicht
so groß wie der der ersten Jahre nach 421, wo Athen sich trotz aller
nach Th.' Meinung begangenen Fehler mit seinen Ansprüchen gegen
Sparta durchgesetzt zu haben schien. Unter diesen Umständen ist es
nicht wunderbar, daß die bisherigen Behandlungen der Bücher 5—8,
gerade soweit sie auf der Analogie der im Anschluß an Ullrich für die
ersten beiden Bücher gewonnenen Vorstellungen ruhten, vergleichsweise unsichere Ergebnisse erzielt haben, und der Versuch Schade-
waldts[1], zunächst aus den | Büchern 6 und 7, der als verhältnismäßig
geschlossen anerkannten Darstellung des sizilischen Unternehmens,
mit neuer, freilich die Ergebnisse der sog. Analyse mit Auswahl vor-
aussetzender Methode Neues zu gewinnen, darf sich mit Recht des leb-
haften Interesses der für Th. interessierten Philologen rühmen.

Man hat die Unstimmigkeiten und Unfertigkeiten, die man in der
Erzählung der Ereignisse von 421—416 (5, 27—5 Schluß) und der
Jahre 412/11 (Buch 8) festzustellen meinte, als notwendige Eigentümlichkeiten einer bald nach den Ereignissen niedergeschriebenen Skizze,
der zur Endgültigkeit eben die Kenntnis des noch im Ungewissen
liegenden Ausganges fehlte, geglaubt fassen zu können. Wenn sich
aus dieser Umgebung die sizilische Expedition als schon künstlerisch
geformte Einheit, mit Anfang, Mitte und Ende, heraushob, so ließ
sich geltend machen, daß dieses Geschehen, innerhalb des einen großen
Krieges freilich ein Teilgeschehen, doch als solches des dramatischen
Schlusses schon 413 nicht entbehrte (s. Schwartz, Das Geschichtswerk
des Th.[2] Bonn 1929, 211f.). Gewonnen war dann jedenfalls, auch wenn
man Cwiklinskis unhaltbare Hypothese einer ursprünglichen Mono-
graphie über den sizilischen Krieg[2] fallen ließ, daß man Th. nicht so gar

---

[1] Das Buch enthält auf den ersten 40 Seiten den im Mai 1928 auf der Fachtagung
der klassischen Altertumswissenschaft in Weimar gehaltenen Vortrag, ,,ausgebaut
und sparsam durch Anmerkungen ergänzt", dazu zwei Beilagen: 1. Das Prooimion
des Thukydides (S. 43—67), 2. Die Exkurse des Thukydides (67—99) und auf
S. 100 als Nachtrag Wilamowitz' Interpretation von Thuk. 6, 15, 3. 4.

[2] Hermes 12, 1877, 23ff. Dagegen genügt ein Satz von Schwartz (S. 7): ,,Für Th.
war die Geschichte des Krieges, den er erlebte, spätestens nach seiner Verbannung
der Inhalt seines Lebens geworden, den er so wenig teilen konnte, wie sein Leben
selbst."

lange (415—404) in der Ausarbeitung dessen, was uns vorliegt, brauchte pausieren zu lassen, um ihn auf Materialsammlung und sonstiges für uns ungreifbares Vorarbeiten zu beschränken. Dieser horror vacui bei der Konstruktion der äußeren Entstehungsgeschichte wird noch begreiflicher, wenn von der jetzigen Darstellung des ersten 10jährigen Krieges nicht nur der Schluß des 4. und der Anfang des 5. Buches Kennzeichen später Entstehung tragen, sondern darüber hinaus noch mindestens die sizilischen Ereignisse (beginnend 3, 86) von vornherein auf das spätere große Unternehmen der Athener orientiert, also schwerlich zu ganz anderer Zeit als die Bücher 6 und 7 geschrieben sind. Ist auch das alles nach 404 abgefaßt und dazu noch die durch die Analyse der ersten beiden Bücher erkannten Partien, dann bleibt nicht viel übrig, was Th. während seiner 20jährigen Verbannung an auch zuletzt noch brauchbarer schriftlicher Fixierung fertig bekommen hätte. Indessen, es bedarf nur des Aussprechens, um das Uferlose solcher Erwägungen zu merken und um sich davon frei zu machen, sie vorweg | für die Richtung, in der man seine Ergebnisse sucht, bestimmend werden zu lassen. Schwerlich wird sich von hier aus etwas Stichhaltiges einwenden lassen gegen eine mit den durch die zwischenliegende Forschung nötig gewordenen Kautelen versehene Rückkehr zu Ullrichs einfacher chronologischer Konstruktion (Niederschrift der ersten nicht vollendeten Fassung der Geschichte des 10jährigen Krieges nach 421, Abbrechen etwa 415, erneute Vorarbeiten, Aufnahme der endgültigen Ausarbeitung der Geschichte des ganzen Krieges 404), die man als das äußere Ergebnis der vorliegenden neuen Untersuchung bezeichnen kann. Aber diese äußeren Dinge bestimmen weder die Methode noch das Ziel der Arbeit Sch.s. Er macht sich die Bahn frei durch grundsätzliche Erwägungen anderer Art.

Allseitig ist zugestanden, daß die Darstellung des sizilischen Unternehmens im ganzen und fast durchweg auch im einzelnen wenigstens im Vergleich mit allem Übrigen bei Th., wo Unfertigkeiten und was uns so vorkommt, immer wieder die Schwierigkeit für den Interpreten bilden, und insbesondere im Gegensatz zu den umgebenden Büchern 5 und 8, so ziemlich alle Epitheta verdient, die die Erfüllung unserer Ansprüche an vollendete Darstellung eines großen historischen Geschehens bedeuten. Schadewaldt bestreitet grundsätzlich, daß für die Qualität der Darstellung die Qualität des Ereignisses und seine unmittelbare Wirkung auf den Mitlebenden den zureichenden Grund abgeben könne; weder lasse sich die Einheit der Form aus der Einheit des Geschehens erklären, das gebe es überhaupt nicht, noch für die Wirkungskraft des Wortes die Unmittelbarkeit des Erlebens verantwortlich machen, das gebe es höchstens in moderner Zeit seit Goethe. Nun ist letzteres für Th. so weder von Schwartz noch von Wilamowitz, gegen die Sch. sich wendet, behauptet worden, beide erklären ausdrücklich die Eindringlichkeit der künstlerischen Gestaltung aus der bereits erreichten schriftstellerischen Meisterschaft („die durch lange Übung kühn gewordene Kraft des Schilderns", Schwartz 212, „und er stand auf dem Gipfel seines Könnens", Wilamowitz, Platon 2, 14), und dagegen gibt es grundsätzlich nichts einzuwenden. Die Frage war aber, was gegebenenfalls Th. schon bald nach 413 veranlassen konnte, von dieser Meisterschaft im Falle der sizilischen Expedition Gebrauch zu machen, und da setzten allerdings beide den unmittelbaren Eindruck dieses radikal abgeschlossenen Einzelgeschehens ein. Hier kam Wilamowitz der von Sch. bekämpften Erlebnistheorie vielleicht etwas näher als Schwartz, sofern nach ihm direkt das Positive, der Entschluß zur Fortsetzung der ursprünglich beabsichtigten Darstellung nur des 10jährigen Krieges, geweckt wird, während Schwartz wie Ullrich zunächst das Negative, das vorläufige Abbrechen jener Darstellung um der nun | selbstverständlich gewordenen Darstellung des ganzen Krieges willen hervorhebt, um dann sekundär die Anziehungskraft der abgeschlossenen Tragödie auf den Schaffensdrang des Geschichtschreibers wirken zu lassen. Gewiß kann man beiden Gelehrten Zweifel entgegensetzen, aber die Begründung dafür wird sich schwerlich in dem Rahmen vorläufiger Erwägungen über Form und Stoff, Erlebnis und Pathos der Darstellung halten können.

Gegen die andere grundsätzliche Bemerkung Sch.s, über die Einheit der Form, muß der Rezensent aussprechen seinerseits grundsätzliche Bedenken zu haben. Daß geistige Einheit aus dem Geist und nicht aus dem Stoff kommt, gilt für alles Geistige, nicht bloß für die Stufe der geistig-künstlerischen Formwerdung. Jedem der interessierten Mitlebenden, der Gelegenheit zu hören und die Fähigkeit zu denken hatte, schlossen sich die Berichte über das sizilische Unternehmen, auch wenn sie „ihm zu verschiedenen Zeiten, auf verschiedene Einzelfakta bezüglich ungeordnet zukamen", zu einer einheitlichen, mehr oder weniger richtigen und mehr oder weniger eindrucksvollen Vorstellung von dem Gesamtverlauf des Unternehmens zusammen; das wird auch bei Th. nicht erst nachträglich, sondern unmittelbar und vermutlich gut funktioniert haben. Warum das überhaupt erwähnen, um dann die „psychologisch-denktechnische Leichtigkeit der Formung dieser bequemeren Materie" zuzugestehen? Das für die diskutierte Frage an der psychologisch-denktechnischen *Leistung* Wesentliche vollzieht sich spontan und ist von etwaigen gedanklichen Schwierigkeiten des reflektierenden Historikers zu unterscheiden. Man sollte nicht grundsätzlich wegreden wollen, daß das historiographische Objekt von Bedeutung sein *kann* sowohl für die Gestaltungsmöglichkeiten wie für den Gestaltungswillen. Und dann bleibt auch von dem Satz,

daß die schließlich erreichte Form „dem Geiste des Gestalters, nicht
dem Stoffe angehört", nur eine Selbstverständlichkeit übrig.

Grundsätzlich kann man sich nur über Möglichkeiten unterhalten,
der Möglichkeiten sind meist mehrere, und die Möglichkeit, die Sch.
seinerseits vorweg hinstellt, ist ohne weiteres als solche anzuerkennen.
Es kann sein, daß Th. für die Darstellung der sizilischen Expedition
alle ihm zu Gebote stehenden Mittel eingesetzt hat nicht nur deshalb,
weil es eine erschütternde Tragödie darzustellen gab, sondern weil dies
Geschehen ihm in der Rückschau den entscheidenden Anfang vom
Ende der athenischen Macht bedeutete. Natürlich sind dann die Bücher 6 und 7 nach 404 geschrieben. Dem Rezensenten leuchtet diese
Möglichkeit um so mehr ein, als es ihm nach 404 gar nicht einmal einer
besonders „energischen geistigen Durchdringung" des großen Gegen-
standes zu bedürfen scheint, um nunmehr das sizilische Unternehmen |
wieder so einzuschätzen, wie man es nach Th.' eigener Darstellung vor-
schnell, gewiß, bereits 413/12 in ganz Griechenland getan hatte. Aber
es wird sich empfehlen, über diese Differenz hinwegzugehen, weil es
sonst wieder Auseinandersetzungen über Form und Stoff geben könnte, darüber nämlich, wieweit es erlaubt ist, im Falle der Katastrophe
von 404 der Materie bestimmenden Einfluß zuzugestehen[3].

Zur Sache. „Die entscheidende Frage ist: gibt es in Buch 6 und 7
handgreifliche, objektive Indizien für die Spätdatierung nach 404?"
(Sch. 8.) Entscheidend ist diese Frage, solange derartige Indizien
nicht auch für die versuchte Frühdatierung beigebracht werden —
bisher ist das nicht geschehen — und jene anderen sich nicht als
spätere Einschübe beseitigen lassen — auch das ist bisher nicht gelungen. Denn dann bleibt nichts übrig, als für die Bücher 6 und 7 mit
der Zweischichtentheorie zu brechen. Sch. bejaht das Vorhandensein
solcher Indizien, und sein Versuch, für diese Bücher das Recht einheit-
licher Interpretation auf der Grundlage der Abfassungszeit nach 404
wiederzugewinnen und fruchtbar zu machen, erscheint nach der ganzen
Lage der Dinge wohl gegründet. Sehr zu begrüßen ist, daß der Verfasser
es über sich gewonnen hat, auch in der gedruckten Veröffentlichung

---

[3] Anmerkungsweise sei daran erinnert, daß Schwartz für die nach ihm vor 404 geschriebene, in dem Enthaltenen noch weithin wiederzuerkennende Skizze der Geschichte des Krieges von 421—411 eine Zwischenzeit suchte, in der Th. „meinte,
ein baldiges Ende des Krieges vorauszusehen, und dem Reiz nicht widerstehen
konnte, zunächst einmal zu skizzieren, wie furchtbar jener Schlag" — die sizilische
Katastrophe — „Athen traf und wie wunderbar es ihm trotzdem Stand hielt", und
die Vermutung wagte, „daß Th. vielleicht schon vor, jedenfalls nach der Schlacht
bei Kyzikos erwartete, daß es . . . zum Frieden kommen werde" (229. 230). Sicher
würde das, wenn sich innerhalb der Bücher 6 und 7 Spuren der Erwartung fänden,
daß das attische Reich diesen Schlag auf die Dauer doch würde überleben können.
Ich finde dergleichen nirgends, nur das Gegenteil.

die für ihn selbst zunächst bestimmenden Beobachtungen herauszustellen. Das kann der gewünschten weiteren Erörterung nur förderlich sein; und dem Referenten, der keine eigene Untersuchung zu führen hat, sei gestattet, die Besprechung auf die von Sch. hervorgehobenen besonders beweisenden Fälle zu beschränken.

Der Katalog der schließlich im Kampf um Syrakus gegeneinander versammelten Städte und Stämme (7, 57—59, 1) ist wegen der zwanglosen Erwähnung der Ägineten, ‚die damals Ägina besaßen‘, auf die Zeit nach 405, d. h. praktisch nach 404 festgelegt. Schwartz, dessen Idiosynkrasie gegen gedankliche Inkongruenz der Thukydidesinterpretation hoffentlich für immer die Lust zum oberflächlichen Dochverstehenwollen nimmt und sie durch die auf dem Boden von Wilamo-| witz’ alter Herausgeberhypothese (vgl. jetzt SBBerl. 1919, 934) gebotene Rücksichtslosigkeit des Aufdeckens zu neuer Tiefe da zwingt, wo diese Hypothese nicht befriedigt, Schwartz hatte auf gedankliche Unstimmigkeiten hingewiesen, die bei der Einfügung des Katalogs in den jetzigen Text passiert sind und die er als des Th. unwürdig dem Herausgeber zuschob. Sch. begegnet dem glücklich mit dem Hinweis auf eine über Herodot (7, 59ff.) zu dem *B* der Ilias zurückführende „historiographische Tradition“, die es ausschließt, das Auftreten des Kataloges an dieser Stelle der Erzählung als Zufallsprodukt zu verstehen.

In der Tat, hier kommt man auf festen Boden. Damit ist so viel gewonnen[4], daß man verzeihen möge, wenn ich den entgegenstehenden Schwierigkeiten ein paar Worte gönne, obwohl Sch. in der Ökonomie seines Vortrages kürzer darüber hinweggeht. Daß Schwartz in dem διενοοῦντο κλήσειν 7, 56, 1 (~ διενοοῦντο . . . ἀποπέμπειν 7, 27, 1) gegenüber dem ἔκλῃον οὖν 59, 3 (~ εὐθὺς ἀπέπεμπον 29, 1) nicht das Ungeschick des Herausgebers, sondern ein verschiedentlich wiederkehrendes stilistisches Mittel des Th. charakterisiert hat, bemerkt Sch. selbst an anderer Stelle (S. 83). — 7, 56, 3 hat der Gedanke einen doppelten Knick. Die Syrakusaner haben alle Aussicht bekommen, die Athener und ihre Bundesgenossen zu Lande und zu Wasser zu überwältigen. Und das ist für sie eine große Sache, denn es bedeutet das Ende der Herrschaft der Athener, und davon werden die Syrakusaner den Ruhm haben. Und abgesehen davon sind sie im Begriff, nicht nur der Athener selbst Herr zu werden, sondern auch ihrer vielen Bundesgenossen, und wiederum sie selbst nicht allein, sondern auch — mit denen, die ihnen zu Hilfe gekommen sind: das ist so ein unmöglicher Gedanke. Mindestens das zweite ‚sondern auch‘ steuert gar zu direkt auf den Katalog hin, der ja auch die Bundesgenossen der Syrakusaner bringen sollte. „Der Herausgeber hat das gefühlt und die Ungereimtheit dadurch zu mildern gesucht, daß er den Syrakusiern inmitten ihrer Bundesgenossen eine Vorzugsstellung zuschreibt, ohne Erfolg; denn er muß zugeben, daß sie die Führung mit den Korinthern

---

[4] „Geschrieben ist“ die Völkertafel „wegen der Äginetenerwähnung nach 405. Also stammt der Zusammenhang, in dem sie steht, aus dieser späten Zeit. Diesen kann man bis ans Ende des 7. Buches und weit zurück bis ins 6. Buch verfolgen: gelegentlich zwar eine ungeglättete Stelle, aber nirgends ein Bruch, alles aus einem Guß'' (S. 11).

und Spartanern teilten" sagt Schwartz (204). Mit Recht wendet Sch. ein: ,,Neben den dorischen Vormächten Sparta und Korinth an der Spitze vieler Bundesgenossen zu stehen, ist für den Kolonialstaat Syrakus ruhmvoll" (S. 10, 1). Die Reparatur des Gedankens ist so fein wie nur möglich, und es ist sicher verfehlt, von Th. etwas Glatteres zu verlangen, falls er den Katalog gerade für diese Stelle geschrieben hat. Daran kann aber überhaupt kein Zweifel sein, denn es läßt sich für den Katalog aller Bundesgenossen weder vorher noch hinterher ein passender Platz ausfindig machen, und daß der Schriftsteller ganz bewußt verfuhr, beweisen die Schlußworte 7, 59, 1 καὶ τότε ἤδη πᾶσαι (sc. αἱ ἐπικουρίαι) ἀμφοτέροις παρῆσαν καὶ οὐκέτι οὐδὲν οὐδετέροις ἐπῆλθεν. Nicht ganz so leicht ist mit dem andern, worauf Schwartz aufmerksam gemacht hat, fertig zu werden. Man erwartet in | erster Linie die Masse der Teilnehmer am Entscheidungskampf zur Anschauung gebracht zu finden, und Einleitungs- und Schlußsatz (57, 1. 59, 1) bestätigen diese Erwartung. Statt dessen drängt sich in der Aufzählung der athenischen Bundesgenossen ein an sich interessanter, aber wirklich überschießender Gedanke vor, daß es sich nämlich hier nicht um eine natürliche, sondern eine mehr oder weniger zufällige, auf Augenblicksinteressen oder Zwang gegründete Koalition handelt, und Zahlen werden nirgends genannt. Sch. beruft sich auch hierfür auf die ,,historiographische Tradition". Im *B* der Ilias und bei Herodot neben der Haupttendenz Genealogisches, Ethnographisches: ,,Auch Th. behält die Verbindung zweier Absichten in der einen Katalogform bei, wenn er, was ohne Not Bedenken erregt hat, neben dem Motiv von Zahl und Menge die Lösung der alten Stammesbindungen und die vom Zufall regierten neuen Mächtegruppierungen betont" (S. 10). Ich denke, das ist ebenso eine leichte Überspannung des Gedankens der traditionellen und formalen Bindung, wie wenn dann Versuche gemacht werden, die Analogien der Orte, an welchen die Kataloge bei Homer, Herodot und Th. stehen, in eine identische Funktion einzufangen. Der Schiffskatalog steht vor den Kampferzählungen der Ilias, der Katalog Herodots vor dem Einmarsch in Europa, man mag von beiden sagen, sie stehen kurz vor dem Beginn der großen Ereignisse: das paßt nicht auf Th. Die Kampferzählungen der Ilias gelten den letzten Kämpfen vor Troja, Th.' Katalog steht vor der letzten Seeschlacht: das ist bedenklich, und jedenfalls gibt es dazu keine Analogie bei Herodot. Und was bei Herodot besonders charakteristisch ist, die Musterung und Ordnung von Heer und Flotte vor Beginn der Kriegshandlungen und vor dem Katalog, das gibt es auch bei Th., aber es steht 6, 42f. Schon die Tatsache eines andersgearteten Kataloges der πρώτη παρασκευή der Athener weist auf besondere Bedingungen hin, unter denen Th. 7, 56ff. schrieb. Von den sukzessive anwachsenden Streitmassen hatte er sukzessive erzählen müssen, und es war selbstverständlich, daß er diese Erzählung mit den ihm jeweilig zu Gebote stehenden Zahlenangaben und sonstigen Spezifizierungen ausstattete. So ist das für den Katalog 7, 57f. vorweggenommen, der abgesehen von der erst hier erfolgenden Aufzählung der teilnehmenden attischen Kolonisten und der Zwangsbundesgenossen Athens kaum die eine oder andere neue Einzelheit bringen kann. Daß Th. die Zahlenangaben nicht wiederholen wollte, ist an sich begreiflich, schon deshalb, weil sie, namentlich für die Syrakusanischen Bundesgenossen, lückenhaft ausfallen mußten. Wollte er überhaupt noch einen Katalog bringen — warum er das wollen konnte, ja mußte, hat Sch. erklärt —, dann blieb entweder eine kahle Aufzählung der Städte- und Völkernamen[5], womit der Zweck ganz sicher nicht erreicht worden wäre, oder er mußte gedanklicher Erweiterung in irgendeiner Rich-

---

[5] Also wie das Kapitel 9 des 2. Buches, das Aly (RhM. 1928, 361ff.) mit dem *B* und der Herodotstelle vergleicht. Aber wenn, wie er anzudeuten scheint, das ,,Prinzipielle der Formfrage" über die starken Unterschiede zwischen 2, 9 und 7, 57f. hinwegzusehen gestattet, so wird von hier aus der Streit der Meinungen nicht zur Ruhe kommen.

tung Raum geben. Für die syrakusanische Seite waren in traditioneller Weise geographische Erläuterungen möglich und sehr passend die Betonung der unbestimmt großen Zahl der Sikelioten und insbesondere wieder der Syrakusaner; für die athenischen Bundesgenossen wäre Geographisches meist eine Lächerlichkeit gewesen und auch nur eine zusammenfassende Zahlenangabe (die Zahl 40000 steht erst 7, 75, 5) trotz der mannigfachen vorhergehenden Einzelangaben nicht genau | zu geben hätte auch für den Zweck nicht gereicht. Also ein Gedanke war dringend erwünscht, und wenn es an sich ein interessanter und des Th. würdiger Gedanke ist, so werden wir uns nun nicht wundern, daß er nach Möglichkeit gestreckt und ziemlich gesucht durchgeführt ist. Voraussetzung für das Verständnis ist aber allerdings Sch.s These, daß die ganze Völkertafel „nur von Th. selbst, nur für diese Stelle gedacht und geschrieben" ist.

Die zweite Stelle, an der Sch. ansetzt, ist das Kapitel 6, 15. Schon Ullrich hatte es gelegentlich seiner Untersuchung mit 2, 65 kombiniert und gestützt darauf und auf die Umrahmung der Pisistratidenepisode (6, 53, 3. 6, 60, 1) hervorgehoben, daß Th. den gänzlichen Untergang Athens in den Jahren 415—404 nicht von den Nachwirkungen der Verluste des ersten Krieges herleitet, „auch nicht so sehr von dem Unglück in Sizilien, noch auch von dem Vorschub, welchen die Perser den Peloponnesiern durch Hilfsgelder geleistet; vorwaltend von der unseligen Bürgerentzweiung zu Athen selbst, welche, durch die Mißtrauen erweckende Persönlichkeit des sonst so hochbegabten Alkibiades hervorgerufen, schon in dem Hermokopidenprozeß ihren Anfang nahm, und erst mit dem Sturz der Dreißigmänner im zweiten Jahre nach dem peloponnesischen Kriege endete" (Beiträge 91). Ullrich deutete 6, 15, 3. 4 ὅπερ καὶ ὕστερον — ἔσφηλαν τὴν πόλιν noch unbefangen (= 2, 65, 12 Ende καὶ οὐ πρότερον — ἐσφάλησαν) auf 407—404; er zitierte dazu auch Aristoph. *Frösche* 1431. Schwartz, der natürlich sah, wie verhängnisvoll diese Paragraphen, so verstanden, für seine Konstruktion werden, falls man sich nicht entschließen kann, sie für einen späteren Zusatz zu erklären, leugnete radikal die Möglichkeit der Beziehung auf die Endkatastrophe und ging so weit, zu behaupten, „daß Th. niemals in so nachlässiger und undeutlicher Weise viel spätere, mit dem sizilischen Krieg nur sehr mittelbar zusammenhängende Vorgänge in ein Raisonnement hineingeflochten haben würde, das nach der Stelle, wo es eingeschaltet wurde, von jedem Leser nur auf den Krieg bezogen werden konnte, in dessen tragische Geschichte der Redekampf der beiden athenischen Protagonisten einführen sollte" (333). Unbedingt sei daran festzuhalten, „daß das gesamte Raisonnement sich nur um den sizilischen Krieg dreht". Hier war der Bogen überspannt. Schon die sich aufdrängende Erinnerung an die Parallelstelle über Brasidas 4, 81 ff. mit einem dem ὕστερον entsprechenden ἔς τε τὸν χρόνῳ ὕστερον πόλεμον und demselben τότε δ' οὖν hätte warnen können.

Freilich die Brasidasstelle ist unzweideutig, diese soll für den Fall der Beziehung auf viel Späteres mißverständlich und tadelnswert sein. Das Letztere jedenfalls nur, wenn der Autor auf Mißverständnisse gefaßt war und sich dagegen decken wollte: und das ist eben die Frage. Wenn er bei dem Satz ὅπερ καὶ καθεῖλεν ὕστερον τὴν τῶν Ἀθηναίων πόλιν οὐχ ἥκιστα an 404 dachte, dann brauchte ihm nicht bewußt zu werden, daß ein Interpret auch 413 | gemeint glauben könnte. Natürlich gilt auch das Umgekehrte. Und deswegen ist es vielmehr die Aufgabe sich zu überlegen, zu welchem der doch recht verschiedenen Inhalte der Ausdruck *ungezwungen* sich einstellen konnte. Diese Überlegung spricht wegen καθεῖλεν vorweg stark für 404, vgl. 5, 103, 1 ἐλπὶς δὲ κινδύνῳ παραμύθιον οὖσα τοὺς μὲν ἀπὸ περιουσίας χρωμένους αὐτῇ κἂν βλάψῃ οὐ καθεῖλε, einen Satz, den man auf die Katastrophe von 413, aber nicht auf die von 404 anwenden könnte. Aber mag das Wortklauberei sein und die Möglichkeit, an die ich nicht glaube, zugestanden werden, daß das sprachliche Gegenbild zu καθεῖλεν etwa 8, 97, 2 τοῦτο πρῶτον ἀνήνεγκε τὴν πόλιν wäre. Konnte denn sachlich aus der Situation von 415 heraus überhaupt bemerkt werden, dies, nämlich Alkibiades' noble Passionen, hätte später den Niedergang der Stadt verursacht, wenn mit ‚später' — was eigentlich gemeint ist: die Rückberufung 415 oder die Katastrophe 413 ? Beides zusammenfallen zu lassen, ist perspektivisch unmöglich — denn dann bedeutete ὕστερον zunächst die wenigen Monate bis zur Rückberufung, und demgegenüber der ganze Verlauf des sizilischen Krieges ein Nichts — und von einem von beiden für sich kann man so gar nicht sprechen. Und was für einen Zweck hätte dieses Vorgreifen innerhalb der Darstellung; das Kapitel 27 kam doch wahrhaftig schnell genug hinterher.

Mit Recht kehrt Sch., sich stützend auf den allgemeinen Eindruck und auf den Gebrauch des Wortes καθαιρεῖν, zu der Beziehung auf 404 zurück. Aber leider ist er auf halbem Wege stehengeblieben. Nach ihm geht zwar das anfängliche καθεῖλεν auf 404, dagegen bezieht er mit Schwartz das οὐ διὰ μακροῦ ἔσφηλαν τὴν πόλιν am Schluß auf 413. Dabei ist übersehen, daß der im § 4 charakterisierte Alkibiades nicht der des Anfangs von § 3 und des Jahres 415, sondern der des Jahres 407 ist, und daß die Folge von dessen Beseitigung nur die Katastrophe von 404 sein kann. Diese Interpretation des § 4, die für Ullrich eine Selbstverständlichkeit war, kann Sch. selbst auf S. 100 als Beitrag von Wilamowitz bringen, ohne sie, wie es scheint, für seine Person zu akzeptieren. Sie ist aber richtig. Denn wenn Schwartz behauptet hatte, das οὐ διὰ μακροῦ am Schluß könne nicht auf den Zeitraum 415—404 gehen, so ist demgegenüber Wilamowitz' Deutung auf 407—404 evident.

Nur so kommt die Perspektive in Ordnung; wenn von 415 weg auf das Ende des dekeleischen Krieges geblickt wird, dann rücken 407 und 405/4 zu einem οὐ διὰ μακροῦ zusammen. Von Gegenerwägungen bleibt vielleicht zu beachten, daß Schwartz eine deutliche Beziehung behauptete „zwischen ὡς τυραννίδος ἐπιθυμοῦντι und dem Verdacht der ξυνωμοσία ὀλιγαρχικὴ καὶ τυραννική (60, 1), der die Hermokopiden- und Mysterienprozesse so verhängnisvoll beeinflußte und zum Sturz des Alkibiades führte (61, 1. 4.)". Nun zieht das aber nur, wenn man mit Schwartz die Einordnung des Pisistratidenexkurses in das 6. Buch für unthukydideisch hält, oder auch dann nicht, denn das Wort τυραννικῇ neben ὀλιγαρχικῇ dient gar zu deutlich dieser Einordnung. Im übrigen aber würde Th. seine eigene Konstruktion der innerpolitischen Vorgänge des Jahres 415, aus der die Hermokopiden- und Mysteriensache und der Konkurrenzneid der ἐχθροί des Alkibiades nicht wegzudenken sind, ne|gieren, wenn er Alkibiades' persönliche Ansprüche an das Leben, zunächst sein nicht ganz integres Hauptmotiv, sich für das sizilische Unternehmen einzusetzen, zugleich als direkte Ursache für die 415 plötzlich einsetzende Sorge der Demokratie um ihren Bestand hinstellte.

Weiter bleibt die syntaktische Schwierigkeit: καὶ δημοσίᾳ κράτιστα διαθέντα τὰ τοῦ πολέμου ἰδίᾳ ἕκαστοι τοῖς ἐπιτηδεύμασιν αὐτοῦ ἀχθεσθέντες καὶ ἄλλοις ἐπιτρέψαντες οὐ διὰ μακροῦ ἔσφηλαν τὴν πόλιν.

Für die Deutung auf 415/3 auch eine sachliche Schwierigkeit, denn was wird gegebenenfalls 415 von Alkibiades auf andere übertragen? Daß von seiner Strategie direkt nicht die Rede sein darf, hat Schwartz gesehen und — von seinem Standpunkt aus sehr geschickt — die προστασία τοῦ δήμου hineinbringen wollen. An sich ist es freilich überflüssig, daß von der Prostasie geredet wird, und zusammengenommen sind die Worte ἰδίᾳ — ἀχθεσθέντες, ⟨τῆς προστασίας ἀπελάσαντες⟩ καὶ ἄλλοις ἐπιτρέψαντες eine recht vage Andeutung dessen, was 415 nach Th.' Darstellung wirklich passiert ist. Wie man ja auch das vorhergehende Satzglied nur mit schlechtem Gewissen Alkibiades' Leistungen von 415 entsprechen lassen kann. Für 407 ist nur sprachlich unbequem ,,καὶ ἄλλοις ἐπιτρέψαντες, das so kurz gesagt ist, daß man vorher die Absetzung einflicken wollte, er aber ertragen werden muß. Das paßt aber auf Sizilien gar nicht, denn da erhielt er keinen Nachfolger, wohl aber genau auf seinen Ersatz im Flottenkommando nach der Schlappe des Antiochos 407". So Wilamowitz, wobei unausgesprochen bleibt, ob ein anakoluthisches Schwebenlassen des überlieferten Akkusativs διαθέντα für möglich gehalten wird[6]. Aber jedenfalls, so sehr man beim Lesen in δημοσίᾳ κράτιστα διαθ. einen Objektivsakkusativ erwarten kann, so wenig konnte der Schriftsteller selbst, wenn er den aus den Dativen herausfallenden Akkusativ setzte, ihn dann vergessen und doch den von ihm abhängigen zweiten Akkusativ τὰ τοῦ πολέμου mit καὶ ἄλλοις ἐπιτρέψαντες aufnehmen. Nun hat freilich Schwartz' Polemik (332) mißtrauisch gemacht gegen die Verbesserung διαθέντι. Aber sie richtet sich gegen die allerdings ganz unmögliche Erklärung der Stelle im Classen-Steupschen Kommentar, derzufolge statt vor καὶ δημοσίᾳ hinter ἀχθεσθέντες zu interpungieren wäre, und die ich zu vergleichen bitten muß. Interpungiert man richtig nach καθέστασαν, und läßt man sich nicht durch den Einfall beirren, daß zu ἐπιτρέψαντες statt τὰ τοῦ πολέμου auch τὴν πόλιν gedacht werden könnte, so ergibt die Lesung διαθέντι m. E. etwas Vertrauenerweckendes. Ohne die Worte δημοσίᾳ und ἰδίᾳ—αὐτοῦ ist es nun glatt; gegen die Ergänzung des Gedankens durch ἰδίᾳ—ἀχθεσθέντες ist an sich auch nichts einzuwenden; und der einzig bleibende Anstoß, daß streng genommen statt der Antithese ἀχθεσθέντες doppelt stehen müßte, hebt sich für Th.' Stil selbst auf.

Wilamowitz' Beitrag sichert die Spätdatierung von 6, 15, denn sie befreit sie von einer unmöglichen Interpretation des § 4[7]. Nicht | gut aber steht es dann um die weitgehenden Folgerungen, die Sch. aus seiner Interpretation gezogen hatte. Sch. verkannte natürlich nicht,

---

[6] Vgl. jetzt Hermes 64, 1929, 476f., wo Wilamowitz ⟨ἔπαυσαν τῆς ἡγεμονίας⟩ ergänzt. Ich habe auf Wilamowitz' nun ausführlicher vorliegende Begründung hin nichts an meinen Bemerkungen zu 6, 15 geändert und erinnere nur, daß die von ihm hervorgehobene Bedeutung von προστασία die Voraussetzung für Schwartz' Ergänzungsvorschlag bildete, dessen Deutung auf 407 freilich falsch werden muß.

[7] Näher rückt freilich die Möglichkeit, ὅπερ—τότε δ᾽ οὖν als nachträgliche Einfügung zu beseitigen. Aber 6, 28, 2 setzt auch den § 15, 4 voraus, ohne doch, wie ich wohl aussprechen muß, Rückschlüsse für dessen Interpretation zu gestatten.

daß der Gedanke mit ἔσφηλαν τὴν πόλιν zu dem anfänglichen ὅπερ καὶ καθεῖλεν ὕστερον zurückkehrt. Und doch sollte das eine auf die Katastrophe von 413, das andere auf die von 404 gehen. Also hätte Th. beide Ereignisse gewissermaßen identifiziert. Sch. selbst betont das Auffallende dieses vermeintlichen Tatbestandes, verschiebt aber dabei die Lage des von ihm selbst geschaffenen Problems. Statt nämlich ernstlich die Möglichkeit der Identifikation zu diskutieren, auf die kein Leser gefaßt sein kann, bejaht er sie für den Fall, daß Th. einen „historisch notwendigen Zusammenhang" zwischen den beiden Katastrophen angenommen hätte, und wundert sich nur über letzteres, was, wenn man die Notwendigkeit und Unabwendbarkeit nicht in übertriebener und mit 2, 65 unvereinbarer Weise preßt, nach 404 doch gar nicht so wunderbar ist.

In dem Kapitel 6, 15 liegt keine Aufforderung, über das was dasteht hinaus geheimnisvollen ursächlichen Zusammenhängen zwischen 413 und 404 nachzugehen. Übrigens ist ja das, was offen dasteht, bemerkenswert genug, daß nämlich eben dasselbe Bedenkliche und Gefährliche in Alkibiades' Wesen, das ihn die Athener in die sizilische Expedition hineintreiben ließ, später, als er dank seiner überragenden Fähigkeiten der Retter Athens aus verzweifelter Lage geworden war, nicht zuletzt den Untergang mitverursachen sollte, weil es die Menge gegen ihn aufreizen mußte. Damit wird an passender Stelle etwas in helles Licht gerückt, wofür Th. nur einfache Worte und einfache Gedankenverbindungen zu Gebote stehen und wozu doch wir mit allem Aufwand moderner Wendungen nichts hinzutun können[8]. Im Dunkel aber bleibt an dieser Stelle die bald genug zu erzählende, nicht einfach von Alkibiades aus zu motivierende Rückberufung 415 und all das andere, was denn doch auch auf den in jeder Weise komplizierten Verlauf der sizilischen Expedition und des dekeleischen Krieges mitbestimmend wirkte; weder lag für den Schriftsteller eine Veranlassung vor, hier plötzlich „in gedrängten Worten" nach „den" Ursachen des Untergangs sowohl von 413 wie von 404 zu „forschen", noch werden wir folgen können, wenn der Versuch gemacht wird, aufzuzeigen, wie „alle Fäden im Kapitel 15" zusammenkommen. Daß die Bücher 6 und 7 nach 404 geschrieben sind, daß Th. nach 404 in der sizilischen Expedition die Krise des großen Krieges gesehen und sie entsprechend | dargestellt hat, und daß er der Persönlichkeit des Alkibiades einen hervorragenden Einfluß auf den Gesamtverlauf der Ereignisse eingeräumt hat, ist auch so glaublich und stimmt in der Tat zu den „klaren Worten" von 2, 65. Und gewiß ist es von primärer — ich

---

[8] Das genaue Gegenstück dazu ist die Brasidasstelle 4, 81, 2. 3, aus der wir auch nicht mehr und nicht weniger machen dürfen, als dasteht.

2*

würde nicht sagen von prinzipieller — Bedeutung für ein wirkliches
Verständnis und verdient alle Hervorhebung, wenn Th. vor der Darstellung der sizilischen Expedition das Jahr 404 erlebt hat.

Daß die Frage: vor 404 und vor 415? vor 404 aber nach 413?
nach 404? das Entscheidende ist für die Erschließung der verschiedenen Schichten in Th.' Geschichtswerk und der entsprechenden Epochen seiner Geschichtschreibung, das ist ja nicht neu. Aber ob prinzipiell neu oder nach Lage der Forschung selbstverständliche Konsequenz: jedenfalls ergibt sich die Aufgabe, den Th. von nach 404 gegen
den von nach 421, um der Einfachheit halber im Anschluß an Sch. nur
diese beiden Epochen in Betracht zu ziehen, auf Grund des neu gewonnenen Materials in anderer Weise abzuheben, als bisher geschehen
ist. Praktisch geht Sch. zur Lösung dieser Aufgabe — ich weiß es kurz
nicht anders zu charakterisieren — so vor: wir werden geneigt sein,
dem Th. von nach 404 alle Vollkommenheiten, die wir in seinem
Werke zu entdecken vermögen, zuzuschreiben, sehen wir also zu,
welche dieser Vollkommenheiten dem Th. von nach 421 noch fehlen,
dann wird sich das Weitere finden. Natürlich ist bei diesem Verfahren
die Versuchung groß, das Minus in der Leistung des früheren Th. zu
übertreiben. Alles hängt davon ab, ob dieser Versuchung wider-
standen ist.

Zur Charakteristik des Th. von nach 421 greift Sch. das Kapitel
1, 22 heraus[9]. Und aus diesem Kapitel sind es Anfang und Schluß,
die zunächst wichtig werden, der „Methodensatz" über die Reden
und die Äußerung über den Nutzen. Wohl bespricht Sch. ausführlich
auch das Mittelstück über die Ermittlung der ἔργα und das darin
bekundete „Streben nach garantierter Urkundlichkeit", wie er das
etwas anachronistisch nennt, aber dieses Streben erhält ja innerhalb
des Kapitels seinen Sinn erst durch den Schluß, und Sch. selbst meint
am Ende des Vortrages (S. 39), daß die nach ihm erst später erreichte
Stufe der historischen Wahrheit im Gegensatz zur historischen Richtigkeit schwerlich je im Bewußtsein des Historikers unterschieden
gewesen sein dürfte; vermutlich also würde dieser sich über die
angestrebte Wahrheit auch später nicht offen in Sch.s Sinn haben
äußern können[10]. Alles hängt an der Interpretation jener beiden
Stellen. |

---

[9] Das Recht dazu sichert ihm die ausgezeichnete Behandlung des Gesamtprooimions
in der ersten Beilage.

[10] „Aletheia, wie Th. die geschichtliche Objektivität nennt, bedeutet für die ausge-
reifte Geschichtschreibung soviel wie Sinngemäßigkeit des im Logos abgespiegelten
Bildes geschichtlicher Wirklichkeit" (S. 27). Auch daß das Vorkommen des
Wortes ἔργον 7, 87, 5 und von ἔργα 5, 26 direkt etwas für Th.' historiographisches
Bewußtsein beweise, will Sch. wohl selbst nicht sagen (S. 27f.).

Ich darf wohl für die Zwecke dieser Rezension als wahr unterstellen, daß das Kapitel 1, 22 dem früheren Th. gehört, finde auch nichts, was dagegen spräche. Aber was Sch. mit Pohlenz und anderen aus dem § 1 herausliest: „einmal, die Reden seien historisch nach Anlaß und Situation; ferner, für ihre Gesamttendenz wird annähernde Authentizität in Anspruch genommen" (S. 24), ist in seinem zweiten Teil falsch, das wird wohl noch öfter ausgesprochen werden müssen (vgl. Schwartz, diese Zeitschr. 2, 1926, 80). Man scheint sich in dem Ausdruck ἐχομένῳ ὅτι ἐγγύτατα τῆς ξυμπάσης γνώμης τῶν ἀληθῶς λεχθέντων von dem ἀληθῶς beeinflussen zu lassen, und doch scheint mir zunächst einleuchtend, daß, damit man herauslesen müßte, was man möchte, dieses ἀληθῶς nicht stehen dürfte. Denn dann hätten wir hier mit Sicherheit einfach die Gesamttendenz des Gesagten, die hoffentlich im Gegensatz zu dem genauen Wortlaut in den mehr oder weniger vagen Erinnerungen des Th. und seiner Gewährsmänner noch fest greifbar erhalten blieb, und das ὡς δ᾽ ἂν ἐδόκουν . . . ginge auf die möglichst entsprechende Ausfüllung dieser Umrisse mit Einzelheiten. Freilich Th. hätte in der Satzkonstruktion das Wichtigkeitsverhältnis umgekehrt und das ἐχομένῳ . . . erhielte limitativen Sinn. Und das soll das Bewußtsein gewesen sein, das Th. von seinem eigenen Verfahren hatte, wenn er einem Redner in einer bestimmten Situation das seiner Meinung nach Nötige in den Mund legte? Ich nehme bis auf weiteres an, daß das ὡς δ᾽ ἂν ἐδόκουν . . . sein ganzes Verfahren bei der Abfassung von Reden beschreibt und das ἐχομένῳ . . . die Art und Weise dieses Verfahrens erläutert. Wie verfuhr er? Er hielt sich möglichst an die Gesamttendenz. Und woher nahm er die? Konnte sich die Gesamttendenz dessen, was faktisch geredet war, aus der *ganzen* Situation ergeben, oder ergab sich die Gesamttendenz *ausschließlich* aus seiner und seiner Gewährsmänner[11] vagen Erinnerung an den faktischen Wortlaut? Nur wenn man letzteres für möglich und ersteres für unmöglich hält, ist die Ausnutzung des ‚Methoden|satzes' für die Chronologie der Reden eine weittragende Entdeckung. Andernfalls darf man ein Streben nach möglichster ‚Wirklichkeitstreue' in den Reden für keine Zeit behaupten, und es bleibt höchstens, daß so etwas wie die Einführung der Athenerrede 1, 72, falls, wie es scheint, die

---

[11] Nebenbei: Der Gegensatz des die ἔργα betreffenden § 2: οὐκ ἐκ τοῦ παρατυχόντος πυνθανόμενος ἠξίωσα γράφειν οὐδ᾽ ὡς ἐμοὶ ἐδόκει beweist, daß Th. sich für die Reden bei der Prüfung dessen, was er etwa von ἄλλοθέν ποθεν ἀπαγγέλλοντες (§ 1) erfuhr, nicht lange aufhielt. Und daß hier deutlich herauskommt, daß er die Reden im Gegensatz zu den ἔργα schrieb: ὡς ἐμοὶ ἐδόκει, kann keine Logik in das Gegenteil der „strengsten Wirklichkeitstreue auch soweit möglich bei den Reden" (Sch. 24) verkehren. Über die richtige Beziehung von μέν und δέ darf ich wohl schweigen.

athenische Gesandtschaft Fiktion ist, und etwa der Melierdialog, den Sch. nennt, in dem ‚Methodensatz' nicht schon berücksichtigt ist¹².

„Aber weiter: Th. beabsichtigt in 1, 22 mit seinem Werke nur ein ὠφέλιμον zu erzielen, ‚brauchbar' soll es sein, ein Besitzstück von bleibendem Nutzwert" (S. 28). — „Th. ... lehnt es ab, zu gefallen, wenn er nur nütze. So bleibt der Geschichtschreibung nur mehr der einzige karge Wert des ὠφέλιμον, der freilich zu imposanter Großartigkeit gesteigert wird; ihre Bedeutung geht fast auf in dem einzigen Zweck der Techne für den Politikos" (S. 29)¹³. Also fast nur zum Zwecke der praktischen Nutzanwendung in künftigen ähnlichen Fällen hätte dieser Th. geschrieben. Es sei mir erlaubt, vorerst auf eine Stelle aus der Beschreibung der Pest einzugehen. Die Pest trat plötzlich in Athen auf, zuerst im Piräus, wo es denn hieß, die Peloponnesier hätten die Brunnen vergiftet, Wasserleitungen gab es damals dort noch nicht. Später aber kam sie auch in die obere Stadt, und jetzt ging das Sterben erst recht an. Über die Ursachen, die so etwas Großes plötzlich zu bewirken imstande sind, mögen Arzt und Laie ihre verschiedenen Vermutungen hegen und sagen. ‚Ich aber werde sagen, wie es dabei herging, und werde mit der Darstellung einem Betrachter für den möglichen Fall der Wiederholung die Mittel in die | Hand geben, etwas vorherzuwissen und nicht nichtzuwissen (προειδὼς μὴ ἀγνοεῖν 2, 48, 3); ich habe die Krankheit selbst gehabt und sie an anderen gesehen'. Ist nun die Pestbeschreibung um der praktischen Nutzanwendung willen geschrieben?¹⁴ Für Ärzte oder für den Hausgebrauch? — Die Menschen starben und starben, ‚und es gab sozusagen überhaupt kein

---

¹² Nicht ganz verständlich ist mir, was Sch. (S. 24) von Anachronismen sagt: „Die kühnen Anachronismen des Epitaphios, der dritten und letzten Rede des Perikles lassen es (nämlich die gewünschte Anwendbarkeit des ‚Methodensatzes') uns am besten erkennen: Perikles redet hier nicht aus dem Wissen und in der Absicht des Politikers von 429, sondern aus dem Wissen und in der Absicht des Historikers von nach 404." Es scheint wirklich gemeint zu sein, daß der Historiker von nach 421 derartige Anachronismen vermieden haben würde; denn daß sie nicht so kühn sein konnten, versteht sich von selbst. Beispielsweise ist der nicht festsitzende Satz 1, 144, 1 (vgl. Sch. 71, 3) von dem Historiker von nach 404 geschrieben deshalb, weil der Historiker von nach 421 nicht vom ἀρχὴν μὴ ἐπικτᾶσθαι, sondern nur vom Vermeiden einer Landschlacht (unmittelbar vorher) sprechen zu lassenVeranlassung hatte. Aber natürlich hatte auch er schon die Gedanken, die er in den Reden vorbringen ließ, nach dem, was hinterher faktisch eingetreten war, gewählt und gesiebt.
¹³ Darauf vorbereitend die Paraphrase S. 23, in der τῶν μελλόντων—ἔσεσθαι wiedergegeben ist mit „was in Zukunft sich wieder so oder annähernd so gestalten kann" (statt ‚wird', und wo bleibt κατὰ τὸ ἀνθρώπινον?), und wo vorgeschlagen wird, zu κτῆμα ἐς ἀεί dem Sinne nach zu ergänzen χρῆσθαι, wodurch der ‚Nutzwert' herauskommen soll.
¹⁴ „Der Methodiker und Praktiker spricht, wenn Th. es ablehnt, ungewisse Vermutungen über die Ursachen der Pest zu äußern, sondern lieber zu Nutz der Nachwelt aufzeichnet, was er mit eigenen Augen gesehen und an eigenem Leibe erfahren

Mittel, durch dessen Anwendung man hätte nützen (ὠφελεῖν) können, denn was dem einen half, schadete dem andern, und ob einer kräftig oder schwächlich war, keiner war sicher, alle ergriff die Krankheit, einerlei wie sie lebten. Und das Entsetzlichste war die Verzweiflung, die den packte, der die Krankheit spürte, und daß sie sich bei der Pflege ansteckten und wie die Schafe starben' (51, 2—4). Das Unheil ist zu groß, man wird gleichgültig auch gegen die nächsten Verwandten. Am meisten Mitleid mit Sterbenden und Leidenden haben schließlich die, die die Krankheit überstanden haben, weil sie vorherwissen (διὰ τὸ προειδέναι 51, 6[15]). — Darf man mit dem zitierten § 2, 48, 3 den § 1, 22, 4 vergleichen, dann ist dessen Sinn etwa: ,Und so zum Anhören wird wohl das Fehlen alles Unterhaltungsmäßigen einen wenig freundlichen Eindruck machen. Solchen Beurteilern aber, die von dem, was geschehen ist und, nach den Gesetzen des Menschlichen, so und so ähnlich sich wiederholen wird, das Unverfälschte werden sehen wollen, etwas ihrem Urteil nach Nützliches gegeben zu haben, wird mir genug sein. Ein Buch für immer, kein Vorlesungsstück für den Moment des Hörens habe ich verfaßt.' Was steht hier absolut und nicht relativ, das σαφές oder das ὠφέλιμον? Und wenn es, wie nicht zu bestreiten, den Beurteilern, für die Th. schreibt, um das σαφές geht, ist es das der Methode oder das des Objekts, wollen sie unverfälschte Wissenschaftlichkeit, oder unverfälschtes Wissen? Und wenn, wie ebenfalls nicht zu bestreiten, letzteres, wird es nicht einigermaßen gefährlich, gegen den Wortlaut in betont utilitaristischem | Sinn weiterzufragen, warum und wozu? Man muß interpretieren wie Lukian (πῶς δεῖ ἱστ. σ. § 42), um gerade von hier aus an den ,,historisierenden Sophisten" (S. 30) zu glauben, der ,,sich selbst wesentlich als Bringer einer neuen garantierten geschichtlichen Wirklichkeitsermittlung gegeben" ist (dies S. 36) und viel davon hält im Hinblick auf ,,die Nützlichkeit" (so, absolut, in der Paraphrase S. 23). — Nur dem Th. von nach 404 gesteht Sch. zu, nicht bloß ,Brauchbares' und wenn ,Nützliches', dann jedenfalls in einem nun neuen höheren Sinn zu schreiben (S. 29). An einer Stelle des Vortrages, auf die ich ausdrücklich verweisen muß, denn ich unterschlage den Zusammenhang, heißt es: ,,Der zehnjährige

---

hat (2, 48, 3)." Um Sch. nicht Unrecht zu tun, muß ich bemerken, daß in seinem Zusammenhang (S. 31) der Ton nicht auf den ,,Nutz der Nachwelt", sondern auf das ,Prinzip der Urkundlichkeit' fällt Aber auch im Nebenton kann man sich vergreifen.

[15] Und weil sie selbst sich nun sicher fühlen, denn zum zweiten Male wurde man jedenfalls nicht lebensgefährlich krank. Und das waren die Beneideten. ,Man kann nicht helfen, höchstens sich anstecken' ist die einzige Nutzanwendung, die die ganze grauenhafte Schilderung gestattet. So gleich 2, 47, 4, wo τὸ πρῶτον θεραπεύοντες ἀγνοίᾳ bedeutet, daß die Ärzte anfangs aus Unkenntnis zu kurieren versuchten, was sie später, sofern sie noch lebten, aufgaben — διὰ τὸ προειδέναι.

archidamische Krieg war nicht der Gegenstand, an dem der Geschichtschreiber erwachsen und sich vollenden konnte" (S. 37). ,,Thukydides
geht aus dem ersten Kriege im wesentlichen als derselbe hervor, der
in den Krieg hineingegangen war" (ebendort). Jenes für die Vollen-
dung zugegeben: kann dies in irgendeinem Sinne richtig sein?

Th. glaubte zu Beginn des Krieges an Perikles' Staatskunst, und er ist diesem
Glauben bekanntlich treu geblieben bis nach 404. Zu Beginn des Krieges mußte er
erwarten, daß der Krieg den entsprechenden Verlauf nähme, und er hat schwerlich
schon damals damit gerechnet, daß der Lauf der Dinge *dumm* (ἀμαθῶς) gehen kann,
ebensogut wie das Denken des Menschen (1, 140, 1). Ich möchte weder mit Schwartz
noch mit Schadewaldt darüber streiten, was ein ,reifer Mann' ist; jedenfalls glaube
ich nicht, daß Th. sieben Jahre vor seiner Strategie[16] schon weit erhaben war über
die Stimmung der Jungen, die in den Krieg eintraten οὐκ ἀκουσίως ὑπὸ ἀπειρίας
(2, 8, 1). Aber es kam die Pest πρᾶγμα μόνον δὴ τῶν πάντων ἐλπίδος κρεῖσσον
γεγενημένον (2, 64, 1, geschrieben nach 404). An der Pest starb Perikles, und was
kam dann nicht alles, die Fehler der athenischen Kriegführung, Kleons absurder
Triumph und Thukydides' persönliches Fiasko und die Verbannung. Schließlich
fällt der bewunderte Brasidas, und so gibt es für Athen den verhältnismäßig günstigen
Frieden. Gewiß, wer das erlebt hat, hat damit noch nicht 415—404[17] erlebt, aber er
hat | etwas erlebt und wird auch etwas zu ,sehen' gelernt haben. Den Th. von 431
kennen wir nicht, mögen ihm also ungefährdet ein nicht groß genug vorzustellendes
Vertrauen auf für den Krieg vorweg mitgebrachte rational-kritische Mittel zu-
sprechen. Aber in manchen Worten des Th. von 421, den wir kennen, hören wir einen
volleren Ton. Ein Satz wie 3, 82, 2 γιγνόμενα μὲν καὶ ἀεὶ ἐσόμενα, ἕως ἂν ἡ αὐτὴ
φύσις ἀνθρώπων ᾖ enspringt nicht dem sophistischen Unterricht, nicht dem Glauben
an die Nützlichkeit und nicht dem Glauben an die Unfehlbarkeit (vgl. 1, 22, 3) der
eigenen Methode. Ein ,,Staatsethiker" spricht freilich auch nicht so, nach meinem
Dafürhalten auch keiner, der es werden konnte.

Es hat keinen Zweck, die schon lang gewordene Besprechung des
inhaltreichen Vortrags fortzusetzen, ehe hier Übereinstimmung er-
reichbar scheint, und ich höre auf, um die wertvollen Beilagen nicht
ganz zu kurz kommen zu lassen.

Die erste führt, und das ist nichts Geringes, unter Berücksichtigung
früherer Arbeiten, aber unabhängig in fast durchweg zum Verständnis
des nicht an der Oberfläche Liegenden zwingender Interpretation den

---

[16] Will man Alkibiades vergleichen, dann übersehe man nicht 5, 43, 2 die Einschränkung ὡς ἐν ἄλλῃ πόλει, zu der Th. doch Veranlassung gehabt haben muß.

[17] Das ist eine Selbstverständlichkeit, aber auf ihr ruht alles, was sich an dem Th.
von nach 404 Neues beobachten und verstehen läßt. Wenn der Krieg 431—421
nicht der Gegenstand war, an dem der Geschichtschreiber sich vollenden konnte,
so war es das Geschehen von vor 431 bis 404, zumal es vorweg das Erleben des
Menschen bestimmt hatte. Das kommt bei Sch. etwas hintennach (S. 35): ,,Das
angedeutete Phänomen einer geistigen Entfaltung, so sehr es sich dabei um eine
rein geistige Problematik handeln mag, es schließt doch das geistige Schicksal
eines Menschen ein und wird somit weiter zum menschlichen Problem." Wenn
ich recht verstehe, wird dann in Sch.s Terminologie jenes zum Logos und dieses zum
Mythos. Ich kann das Bedenken nicht unterdrücken, daß man aus seinen Wendungen
eine Konzession herauslesen könnte, die die Wissenschaft nicht zu machen braucht.

Nachweis, daß „das Gesamtprooimion (1, 1—1, 23, 5) einmalig konzipiert und einmalig geschrieben ist", und dann natürlich nicht erst nach 404.

Drei Fragen waren nach dem Stande der wissenschaftlichen Diskussion zu behandeln; Sch. macht es dem, der folgen will, bequem (S. 44):

„1. Ist zwischen 1, 1 und 1, 2 wirklich mit Pohlenz und Schwartz eine Lücke anzusetzen und in ihr die Erwähnung der Troika (Schwartz) oder der Medika (Pohlenz) zu fordern?"

„2. Steht 22 zu 20/21 wirklich in keinem ursprünglichen Zusammenhang?"

„3. Hat 23 mit dem Zusammenhang 20/21 und 1, 2—19 ursprünglich nichts zu tun?"

Alle drei werden verneint, die erste in schlechthin erschöpfender Behandlung, für die zweite und dritte wird die Untersuchung zum mindesten soweit vorgetragen, daß die Wissenschaft aus der gewiesenen Richtung nicht mehr wird abirren dürfen.

Nur zwei Bemerkungen. Mit sicherem Griff ist die alles umfassende Bedeutung der interpretatorischen Frage nach der Zerlegung der προγεγενημένα (1, 1) in τὰ πρὸ αὐτῶν und τὰ ἔτι παλαιότερα (1, 2) erfaßt und die Frage selbst in der Hauptsache erledigt. Aber wenn Th. von beiden sagt, ein σαφῶς εὑρεῖν sei wegen der Länge der vergangenen Zeit unmöglich gewesen, so kann man ihm freilich nicht verwehren, die 50 Jahre zurück bis zu den Perserkriegen ein χρόνου πλῆθος zu nennen (S. 51); aber es bleibt der Anstoß, daß in der Kürze der Zerlegung und gleichzeitigen Zusammenfassung der Anschein erweckt wird, als beständen für die Einschätzung der Größe der Perserkriege ähnliche Schwierigkeiten wie für die des troischen Krieges, was Sch. selbst mit Recht verneint (S. 58). Ich möchte glauben, daß dies einer der nicht seltenen Fälle ist, in denen Th. einem komplizierten Gedanken oder Sachverhalt nicht die genügende Zahl von Worten oder Sätzen gönnt, um allen logischen Komplikationen im Ausdruck | gerecht zu werden. — Und dann: Warum klappt das Kapitel 23 nach? Sch. kombiniert dies richtig mit der Frage, warum 20, 1 nur die παλαιά (= τὰ ἔτι παλαιότερα 1, 2) genannt sind, obwohl der letzte Teil der Archäologie (18. 19) sogar über die Perserkriege hinaus bis unmittelbar an den Anfang des peloponnesischen Krieges geführt hatte. Und er macht anschaulich, wie sich in Th.' Gedankenführung die beabsichtigten methodischen Bemerkungen über die eigene Darstellung zusammenfinden konnten mit einer abschließenden Bemerkung nur über die παλαιά, für die Th. im Gegensatz zu den Perserkriegen und gar der späteren Entwicklung gehalten gewesen war, „die Wirklichkeit zu rekonstruieren, ehe er überhaupt zu einem Vergleich mit der ihm gegebenen Wirklichkeit seines Krieges schreiten konnte" (S. 58). Und sicher ist richtig, daß, da der in Kapitel 1 in Aussicht gestellte Vergleich mit den Perserkriegen weder in der Archäologie noch innerhalb der Kapitel 20/21 *ausgesprochen* wird, Kapitel 23 folgen mußte. Aber eine der Bedingungen, die das für uns zunächst Verwirrende ermöglichen, scheint mir nicht ganz erfaßt. Sch. setzt ein, daß Th. für den Vergleich mit den Perserkriegen unverhältnismäßig viel leichteres Spiel hatte als für den troischen Krieg (S. 57). Das gilt natürlich für die Ermittlung der faktischen Größe des Vergleichsobjektes, aber für den Vergleich selbst, so wie er im Kapitel 23 durchgeführt wird, gilt es zugestandenermaßen nicht. Wenigstens nahm man es bisher als Argument für die frühe Abfassungszeit, daß nur weil es sich um den 10 jährigen Krieg handelt, in diesem Kapitel so offenbar rhetorisch αὔξησις geübt werden muß, und ich sehe nicht, daß Sch. anderer Meinung wäre. Wenn man den Blick auf die Ereignisse richtet, dann ist es wirklich nicht so selbstverständlich, daß die Perserkriege kleiner waren als der archidamische Krieg. Aber unter einem anderen Gesichtpunkt erübrigte es sich allerdings, den Vergleich direkt auszusprechen, nämlich unter dem der wachsenden Machtmittel. Unter diesem Gesichtspunkt gesehen erscheinen aber die Perserkriege in Kap. 18/19, und die Darstellung gipfelt nicht umsonst in dem implicite die Perserkriege übertrumpfenden Satz ,Und es wurde ihnen (den Lakedämoniern und den Athenern) bis zu diesem Krieg hin je die eigene Rüstung größer als wie sie einst bei unversehrter Bundesgenossenschaft am stärksten geblüht hatten' d. h. größer als die gemeinsame Macht, die notorisch den Persern überlegen war. An diesem Punkte mußte der Schriftsteller abbrechen, mußte er zurückgreifen, wenn er überhaupt vor Eintritt in seine Erzählung noch etwas zu bemerken hatte. Und ich meine, es ist klar, daß *wenn* abgesetzt wurde, dies in einer gedanklichen Situation geschieht, die zunächst alles andere, nur nicht den Gedanken an den in diesem Moment implicite erledigten Größenvergleich des peloponnesischen Krieges mit dem Perserkrieg aktuell werden lassen mußte; und ebenso klar ist, daß nachträglich dann unter dem Gesichtspunkt der ἔργα (21, 2) der Vergleich doch noch fehlte, und nun am Schluß, wie wieder Sch. richtig bemerkt, auch die ,,erwünschte Möglichkeit'' bot, ,,zur Sache selbst zu gelangen (23, 4): ἤρξαντο δὲ αὐτοῦ . . .'' (S. 59). — Daß Th. schon bei 20, 1 τὰ μὲν οὖν παλαιά der keinesfalls mehr auf dieses μὲν zurückgreifende Anfang von 23 τῶν δὲ πρότερον ἔργων vorschwebte, scheint mir unter den dargelegten Umständen nicht nötig, es ist ja auch sprachlich kaum möglich. Die ganze Archäologie schildert eine Aufwärtsbewegung, aber bis Kap. 17 einschließlich gewissermaßen unter negativem Vorzeichen, indem immer wieder die noch nicht erreichte Größe betont wird, 18/19 dagegen positiv eine rapide Emporentwicklung bis an ,diesen Krieg' selbst heran. Wird an diesem Punkt auf das demonstrandum, daß alles verhältnismäßig klein war, zurückgegriffen, so hatte der Gedanke am unmittelbar Vorhergehenden | keinen Halt, und wenn er bis auf Kapitel 17 zurückglitt, dann ergab sich ohne weiteres τὰ μὲν οὖν παλαιά.

Beilage 2. Die Exkurse des Thukydides. Sch. hatte es innerhalb der Bücher 6 und 7 neben der Völkertafel 7, 56 ff. noch mit zwei Exkursen zu tun, denen die Analyse den Platz, an dem sie stehen, hatte verbieten wollen (7, 27. 28 und 6, 54—59). Ich bin überzeugt, daß es seiner Interpretationskunst gelungen ist, in diesen und anderen Fällen die ,,Ketzerei'' gegen Übergriffe der Analyse als das Richtige zu erweisen.

Aber der Vortrag unternahm es, weit über jede Begrenzung der Aufgabenstellung hinausgreifend, eine Gesamtanschauung von zwei Hauptepochen der Geschichtschreibung des Th. zu geben, derart, daß die frühere in ihrer Beschränktheit gegenüber der späteren, und diese allein als repräsentativ für den vollendeten Historiker erscheint. Diesem eindrucksvollen Versuch konnte mein auf der niedrigeren Ebene kritischer Bemerkungen gehaltenes Referat nicht gerecht werden; um so mehr bin ich verpflichtet, auszusprechen, daß Sch.s Betrachtungsweise sich als besonders fruchtbar erweist, wenn er jetzt in umfassender Erörterung die im Vortrag notgedrungen nur kurz begründete These durchführt, daß der erste Entwurf wohl Anmerkungen, die ein Faktum des Berichts sichern sollen, aber keinen eigentlichen Exkurs enthielt, zu dessen Wesen es gehört, „daß er von der Haupterzählung abführt zu einem fernliegenden Stoff, der um seiner selbst willen erstrebt wird" (S. 33). Entsprechend seiner Gesamtanschauung ordnet sich ihm auch diese Tatsache in das Bild der Stufe geistiger Entwicklung, die erst dem Th. von nach 404 zu erreichen gegeben war und die es diesem ermöglicht, früher nach Form und Inhalt Abgelehntes aufzunehmen und zugleich die von je herrschende Ratio „in einer höheren, reiferen, universalen Geistesform" aufzuheben (S. 34).

Ich taste nichts an und nehme nur zu dem Schlußstein, der Behandlung der Pentekontaetie (S. 95—99), und nur zu einer allerdings wichtigen Einzelheit das Wort. Die Pentekontaetie ist nicht nur überhaupt der wichtigste aller thukydideischen Exkurse, sicher nach 404 geschrieben, sondern sie ist auch deshalb bemerkenswert, weil in diesem Fall Th., nachdem er im Anschluß an die Erzählung vom Mauerbau und die Übernahme der Hegemonie im Perserkriege durch die Athener den Gegenstand angekündigt hat, selbst von ‚Exkurs' spricht (ἐκβολὴ τοῦ λόγου 1, 97, 2) und ihn motiviert. Zwei Gründe gibt er an; davon reicht der erste, die Mangelhaftigkeit der Arbeit des einzigen Vorgängers, so interessant es ist, daß Th. sich nunmehr doch selbst in die Reihe stellt, nicht zu, denn er rechtfertigt zwar die Neudarstellung, aber nicht die Einfügung in dieses Werk. Um so wichtiger ist der zweite: ἅμα δὲ καὶ τῆς ἀρχῆς ἀπόδειξιν ἔχει τῆς τῶν Ἀθηναίων ἐν οἵῳ τρόπῳ κατέστη. Um ihm sein volles Gewicht zu geben, zieht Sch. den sicher erst gleichzeitig geschriebenen § 1, 23, 6 an, durch den Th. auf den Inhalt des Exkurses vorbereitet, ohne ihn gleich da folgen zu lassen, wo man ihn um der zeitlichen Reihenfolge willen und vor allem wegen des durch den Ausdruck ἀληθεστάτη πρόφασις gekennzeichneten Rangverhält|nisses der Kriegsursachen erwarten könnte. So erhebt sich die alte Frage, warum Th. die Pentekontaetie überhaupt als Exkurs geschrieben hat. Die allerdings etwas subalterne Erwägung, daß Th. dann die ganze frühere Darstellung hätte umschreiben müssen und daß er das vermeiden wollte, verbietet Sch. Er meint, weniger einfach, auf der erreichten letzten Entwicklungsstufe sei sich der Historiker zwar bewußt, mit einem tieferen Wirklichkeitsbegriff zu arbeiten, aber doch nicht genügend sicher bewußt, um in einen aus der früheren Stufe vorliegenden, nur geschichtliche Richtigkeit enthaltenden Logos die geschichtliche Wahrheit anders als in der Form einer ‚Ekbole' hineinbauen zu können. Schwerlich exakt. Zunächst gilt es einen eigentümlichen Sprachgebrauch festzustellen. Die Unterscheidung von äußeren Anlässen und innerem Grund, die noch heute zum handwerksmäßigen und weltanschaulichen eisernen Bestand gehört, wenn zu einem Kriege, ‚der doch kommen mußte', Stellung genommen werden soll, hat ihren Ursprung fraglos in dem § 1, 23, 6. Weniger fraglos aber ist es, ob bei Th. auch im Ausdruck, wie Sch. sagt, „der Superlativ deutlich von der Wirklichkeit eine ‚eigentliche Wirklichkeit', von der Objektivität eine ‚eigentliche Objektivität' zu scheiden" sucht. Die Worte ἀληθεστάτη πρόφασις finden sich bei Th. noch einmal, 6, 6, 1, wo das wahre Motiv der Athener, das sie zu dem sizilischen Unternehmen treibt, abgehoben wird von den vorzeigbaren Gründen, die an Parallelstellen ihrerseits als solche durch das Wort πρόφασις gekennzeichnet werden (6, 8, 4. 6, 33, 2. 6, 76, 2 vgl. 3, 86, 4); insbesondere durch den Ausdruck 6, 33, 2 πρόφασιν μὲν . . ., τὸ δὲ ἀληθὲς Σικελίας ἐπιθυμίᾳ wird deutlich, daß es sich in der Wortverbindung ἀληθεστάτη πρόφασις nur um ein rein ausdrucksmäßiges, übrigens leicht erklärliches[18] Umspringen des Wortes πρόφασις handelt, das im Falle der Antithese

---

[18] πρόφασις ‚der Grund, den man angeben kann': 1, 133, 1. 3, 9, 2. 3, 13, 1. 3, 40, 6.

eigentlich auf die andere Seite gehört (vgl. Dem. 18, 156. 158, wo das Wort zugleich auf beiden Seiten erscheinen kann, ohne daß doch die für solchen Zusammenhang ursprüngliche Bedeutung ‚Vorwand' ganz verloren wäre). Nicht anders ist es 1, 23, 6; und der Vergleich mit 1, 118, 1. 126, 1. 146, 1, Stellen, in denen das Wort auf seiner ursprünglichen Seite steht[19], macht nun nicht die mindeste Schwierigkeit. Dann aber ist die Unterscheidung, die Th. 1, 23, 6 *ausspricht*, alles andere als ge-danklich belastet, bedeutet gerade keinen tieferen Wirklichkeitsbegriff, sondern etwas, was der Schriftsteller auch im Bewußtsein der Handelnden voraussetzt, daß es nämlich wahre Beweggründe gibt, von denen man aber wohlweislich nicht viel spricht, und solche, die man offen ausspricht, die aber weniger wahr zu sein pflegen. Es ist eine grobe Unterscheidung, die man nicht zu fein anfassen darf[20]. — Sodann mag man vielleicht sagen, der frühe Th. habe in der unmittelbaren Vorgeschichte die Ursachen des Krieges suchen | zu müssen geglaubt. Dazu stimmt z. B. die Kunst, mit der in der Erzählung der Schlacht bei den Sybotainseln die Rolle der athenischen Schiffe herausgearbeitet ist (1, 45ff.). Aber man kann nicht ohne weiteres sagen: „Der späte Th. sah tiefer, forschte nach der ‚wirklichen Ursache', der ἀληθεστάτη πρόφασις", wenn diese das Wachsen der Macht Athens ist. Gegen die Annahme eines völligen Bruches in „Th.' Anschauungen über die Ursachen und die Vorgeschichte des Krieges" hat sich mit Recht Pohlenz (GGN. 1919, 99ff.) gewandt und richtiger gemeint, es handele sich um eine „Verschiebung in der subjektiven Wertung gege-bener Fakta". ‚Die Lakedämonier wollen ja doch den Krieg aus Furcht vor Athen' und ‚Der Krieg kommt ja doch', das ließ die erste Fassung die Kerkyräer schon vor 431 ausspielen (1, 33, 3. 1, 36, 1, vgl. 1, 42, 2), und darauf haben die einen in Athen wohl gleich 431 und ganz sicher zur Selbststärkung nach 429 sich berufen, wenn die anderen meinten: ‚Hätten wir doch nur das megarische Psephisma gestrichen'. Wie die ἀληθεστάτη πρόφασις mit ‚eigentlich wirkliche', ‚nicht offenkundige' Ursache falsch übersetzt ist, da Th. von dem wahren, nicht offen gesagten Grund spricht, so kommt man auch sachlich nicht durch, wenn man Th. das Wachsen der athenischen Macht als die Voraussetzung für den zum Krieg führenden Gegensatz Sparta-Athen erst nachträglich erforschen und finden läßt. — Sch. legt Wert darauf, daß die an-geblich neu gesehene Ursache den Nachweis einer jahrzehntelangen Entwicklung ver-langte, also eine Erzählung. Da nun aber die kausalen Beziehungen nicht neu ent-deckt zu werden brauchten, so reduziert sich dies auf das Plus dieser Erzählung in der neuen Bearbeitung. Sicher ist, daß die frühere Darstellung des zehnjährigen Krieges mit den Ursachen einsetzte, die innerhalb des bestehenden 30jährigen Frie-dens zum Kriege führten, und daß sie ein weiteres Ausholen in der Erzählung nicht beabsichtigte. Nach 404 war die Aufgabe der Darstellung ‚dieses' Krieges von selbst zu der Aufgabe geworden, den Niedergang der athenischen Macht von höchster Blüte zum gänzlichen Untergang zu schildern. Es hat etwas unmittelbar Einleuchtendes, daß ein Komplement, das den Aufstieg zeigte, Bedürfnis wurde: man braucht zu ἅμα δὲ καὶ τῆς ἀρχῆς ἀπόδειξιν ἔχει τῆς τῶν Ἀθηναίων ἐν οἵῳ τρόπῳ κατέστη nichts hinzuzutun. — Aber es bleibt die Frage, auf die Th. sich begreiflicherweise nicht

---

[19] Zu 1, 141, 1 mag man sich am ehesten der medizinischen Terminologie erinnern, von der 2, 49, 2 in der Tat abhängig sein wird. Aber für 1, 23, 6 darf man nicht behaupten, daß Th. „für die Ursache, die als die wirkliche angeführt werden muß, das Wort gebraucht, mit dem die ionische Physik und Medizin den wissenschaft-lichen Kausalitätsbegriff ausdrückt" (Schwartz 250).

[20] Dionysios von Hal. (περὶ Θ. c. 10f.) brauchte nur wenig zu vergröbern, um das Problem der Disposition nicht nur aufreizender, sondern auch treffender zu for-mulieren als die Modernen; freilich brauchte er nicht zu verstehen, sondern wollte einfach tadeln.

einläßt, warum die Ergänzung als Exkurs steht. Man sage ruhig: Hätte Th. das Komplement vorausschicken wollen, dann hätte er alles Frühere zerstören und umschreiben müssen. Und dazu hatte er keine Veranlassung, denn er hatte von dem κτῆμα ἐς ἀεί nichts zurückzunehmen, wohl aber hatte er zu ergänzen, hier wie in den Reden. Andererseits gesteht der § 1, 23, 6 offen ein, daß für die Ergänzung der Anfang in Frage kam, sonst stände er nicht da. Auf die Ergänzung an späterer Stelle vorzubereiten, nicht Rechenschaft von neuen kausalen Erwägungen zu geben, ist zunächst seine Funktion. Nur dazu eignet sich die Unterscheidung mit πρόφασις, dazu aber auch hervorragend gut, denn der Beweggrund, von dem man nicht spricht, braucht in der Erzählung erst im entscheidenden Moment wieder hervorgeholt zu werden. Aber etwas schießt über, was Pohlenz gut ins Licht gerückt hat durch den Hinweis darauf, daß „noch der Nikiasfriede zu beweisen schien, daß der Dualismus an sich nicht notwendig zu einer gewaltsamen Lösung drängte": die Spartaner gehen gezwungen in den Krieg. Dies aber kann man nicht trennen von der Einführung des großen Exkurses an der Stelle, auf welche diese vorausweist.

Untergebracht ist die Ergänzung hinter der entscheidenden Versammlung in Sparta, wo die Motive der Lakedämonier zur Sprache kommen konnten. | 1, 88 wird der Übergang mit einer Wendung gefunden, die erstaunlich sein würde, wenn die Absicht nicht zu deutlich wäre. Nicht auf die Reden der Bundesgenossen hin (für den Leser praktisch = Korintherrede 68—71, aus dem ersten Entwurf; das von Schwartz festgestellte Zeitverhältnis zu der Korintherrede 120—124 hätte Pohlenz nicht versuchen dürfen umzukehren), sondern aus Furcht vor der wachsenden Macht der Athener fassen die Lakedämonier den entscheidenden Entschluß. Dabei haben die Korinther faktisch ziemlich alles auseinandergesetzt, was die Lakedämonier bestimmen kann, von ihrer bisherigen Langsamkeit abzugehen (schon das schließt m. E. aus, daß diese Korintherrede gleichzeitig mit 1, 88 entstanden wäre, aber nicht, daß sie stehen bleiben sollte) ; und daß die Lakedämonier erst in diesem Moment ihre traditionelle Langsamkeit aufgeben, dabei bleibt es auch nach der neuen Wendung: das steht ausdrücklich 118, 2, zum Abschluß der großen Einfügung 89—117. Es wird an der alten Konstruktion des historischen Herganges nicht das Mindeste geändert, bis auf das Eine: Die Lakedämonier taten, was sie taten, nicht so sehr überredet, wie von sich aus. Das ist wiederum zunächst ein Griff des Schriftstellers, der sich zu helfen weiß und es ausnutzt, daß er ursprünglich die Motive, die Sparta jetzt zum Entschluß treiben mußten, den Korinthern in den Mund gelegt hatte. Aber ich gebe gern zu: hinter dieser einen, dazu noch in einen Moment verlegten Nuance: ‚nicht überredet' (‚gezwungen', wenn man 1, 23, 6 hinzunimmt) verbirgt sich alles, was nach 404 dem Historiker die weitere Vorgeschichte des großen Krieges darstellenswert erscheinen lassen mußte.

Das äußerlich Auffallende an dem freilich nach Wichtigkeit, Inhalt und Form doch für sich stehenden großen Exkurs 1, 88—118 könnte man also, glaube ich, mehr aus der äußeren schriftstellerischen Situation von nach 404 erklären, ohne zu verkennen, daß dieser äußeren Situation eine innere, geistige entspricht. Ihrer sich unmittelbar zu bemächtigen, ging Sch. die βασιλικὴ ἀτραπός seines Vortrags. Alle Bedenken dagegen dürfen zurückstehen, wo soviel Wichtiges zur Sprache gebracht und soviel Boden gewonnen wird wie in seinem Buch.

Besprechung:

Hermann Langerbeck, ΔΟΞΙΣ ΕΠΙΡΥΣΜΙΗ.
Studien zu Demokrits Ethik und Erkenntnislehre

1936

Auf den Sinn, den das vorliegende Buch seinem Obertitel gibt, kann man erst gegen Ende der Betrachtung zu sprechen kommen; für den scheinbar weniger fragwürdigen Untertitel aber müssen wir gleich aus Seite 2 der Einleitung entnehmen, daß der Verfasser ihn lieber mit zwei Paar Anführungszeichen würde haben drucken lassen, wenn sich das für einen Titel schickte. In dieser Einleitung wird vorweg ohne weiteres „die Unmöglichkeit, die Ziele vorsokratischen Denkens unmittelbar auf den Sinnzusammenhang modernen Sprechens und Denkens zu beziehen", „die Inkommensurabilität vorsokratischen und modernen Denkens", der vom Verf. angestrebte „Verzicht auf unmittelbares Einordnen der Ergebnisse des demokritischen Denkens in modernes Denken", deren „radikales Anderssein", das Bemühen des Verf. „um Herausarbeitung des ἕτερον[1] des antiken und besonders des vorsokratischen Denkens" und somit die „Aufgabe, das ganz Andere in seinem Anderssein doch zu verstehen" derartig gehäuft und stark betont, daß sich beim Verf. selbst die Frage anmeldet, ob dies wissenschaftliche Vorurteil der neuen philologischen Untersuchung nicht den „Verzicht auf lebendige Wirkung auf modernes philosophisches Denken" und damit Ungeschütztheit gegen den „Vorwurf eines unfruchtbaren Historismus, der seinen Gegenstand der lebendigen Wirklichkeit beraubt", mit sich bringe. Der Verf. beruhigt den Leser, den er sich, vielleicht mit Recht, weniger um die Richtigkeit als um die Wirksamkeit der wissenschaftlichen Ergebnisse besorgt vorstellt, mit einem Hinweis auf das „Bemühen um einen vorstandpunktlichen Ausgangspunkt der Philosophie". Diesem Bemühen könne es dienen, wenn sich aufzeigen ließe, wie es für den Standpunkt Demokrits weder ein Er-

---

[1] Was soll das griechische Wort? Immerhin kann dadurch in diesem Falle zum Sinn nichts hinzugetan und von ihm nichts fortgenommen werden; unerfreulicher ist schon etwa das Auftauchen von τὰ ἐφ᾽ ἡμῖν in einem Zusammenhang, der durch die generelle Bedeutung des aristotelischen Terminus leidet (59), und dem Verf. selbst wird es unerfreulich sein, daß ihn seine Vorliebe für überflüssige griechische Wörter zu der nur durch Cicero zu belegenden, eigentlich aber widersinnigen Wortbildung ἀπολιτικός verführt hat (19).

kenntnisphänomen in modernem Sinne, noch ein Phänomen des Sitt-
lichen habe geben können. „Die Frage, ob überhaupt ‚Erkenntnis‘ und
‚Sittlichkeit‘ echte Phänomene vor aller Standpunktlichkeit oder viel-
leicht schon als Wort *Deutungen* von tiefer liegenden echten Phäno- |
menen sind, die sich jeder möglichen Benennung entziehen, müßte vor
die Quaestio facti[2], die nach dem ‚Was‘ von ‚Erkenntnis‘ und ‚Sittlichkeit‘ fragt, treten.“ Die Anführungszeichen bei den Worten Erkenntnis und Sittlichkeit (kurz vorher: Demokrits ‚Ethik‘) wird jeder
für die Sache Interessierte beifällig aufnehmen, aber was im übrigen
über Philologie und Philosophie angedeutet wird, kann auch als Andeutung nicht genügen. Mit dem Aufzeigen des radikalen Andersseins
der „vorsokratischen, speziell demokritischen Spekulation“ kann man
dem modernen Philosophen höchstens dazu behilflich sein, seine moderne Auffassung nicht für die einzig mögliche, unmittelbar sach-
gegebene zu halten, falls er das nötig hat. Aber damit wäre höchstens
der Weg zur Standpunktlosigkeit gewiesen, von der der Verf. selbst
nichts hält (S. 5: „die Gleichung: Unphilosophisch = Vorurteilslos
dürfte ja auch in der Philologie nicht mehr zeitgemäß sein“). Was er
die Philosophie als Ausgangspunkt suchen läßt, sind „echte Phänomene vor aller Standpunktlichkeit“, „echte Phänomene, die sich jeder
möglichen Benennung entziehen“. Dem Rezensenten erscheint, was in
diesen Wendungen ausgesprochen wird, wie das Messer ohne Klinge,
dem der Griff fehlt; und er zweifelt daher daran, daß die Philosophie,
wenn sie wirklich dies sucht, es jemals zu greifen bekommt. Aber das
ist wohl nur Kritik der gewählten Ausdrücke; mit der Richtung, in
der der Ausgangspunkt eines sachlichen Philosophierens gesucht wird,
kann man sich dabei einverstanden fühlen, zugleich aber in der Betonung der Ansprüche der Philologie weiter gehen. Es gibt zwei Möglichkeiten: entweder die älteren Denker dachten im Vergleich mit den
moderneren Denkern abstrus, oder sie dachten zwar noch nicht so
viele Gegenstände, aber ihre wenigeren Gegenstände dachten sie verhältnismäßig einfach und natürlich. Im ersten Falle könnte man überhaupt und auch als Philologe etwas Besseres tun, als Geschichte der
antiken Philosophie treiben; im zweiten Fall aber identifiziert sich das
Interesse der Philosophie an sachgegebenen Ausgangspunkten mit gewissen Interessen der klassischen Philologie gerade im Wesentlichen,
so daß es keiner Apologie für die letztere bedarf. Höchstens kann man
der klassischen Philologie den Vorwurf machen, sie arbeite für die Bedürfnisse der modernen Philosophie und des modernen Lebens nicht

---

[2] Der echte Gegensatz zur Frage quid facti ist die Frage quid iuris (der Rezensent
war gewissenhaft genug, die Stelle bei Kant nachzuschlagen). In unserm Text
aber scheint nur der Gegensatz zwischen einer mehr und einer weniger befangenen
quaestio facti gemeint, den man nicht so ausdrücken sollte.

schnell und nicht systematisch genug. Darauf kann dann die Philologie entweder mit dem hesiodeischen ὅσῳ πλέον oder, höflicher, mit dem Zugeständnis antworten, daß sie es unter den gegebenen Umständen | der Philosophie auch gar nicht verdenke, wenn diese sich die Geschichte der antiken Philosophie, die sie zu brauchen glaubt, systematischer und schneller selbst schreibt.

Über diese Dinge wird es unter Philologen schwerlich echte Differenzen geben, und wenn, so wird dadurch die philologische Arbeit, soweit sie ungezwungen und ehrlich getan wird, nicht beeinflußt. Die klassische Philologie ist zu fest mit der für jeden Gebildeten gegebenen Wirklichkeit verbunden, um sich durch allgemeine Erwägungen irgendwelcher Art deduzieren oder durch praktische Erwägungen irgendwelcher Art vom Wege abbringen zu lassen. Nachdem der Verf. von dem aus dieser Selbstsicherheit der Philologie genommenen Recht, selbständig zu denken, zu unserer Freude gleich zu Anfang ziemlich energischen Gebrauch gemacht hat, wendet er sich zu den innerphilologischen „Vorfragen sachlicher und methodischer Art", die er vor der eigentlichen Interpretation glaubt klären zu müssen. Auf die gedankliche Konstruktion solcher Dinge pflegt neuerdings wieder besondere Mühe verwendet zu werden, und wenn man dementsprechend darauf gefaßt ist, in der Einleitung die neue Arbeit zum mindesten als Synthesis von wissenschaftlicher Thesis und Antithesis präsentiert zu bekommen, so läßt man es sich gern gefallen, wenn der Verf. nur rasch die bisherigen Behandlungen sowohl der Ethik wie der Erkenntnislehre Demokrits als in hoffnungsloser Gegensätzlichkeit befindlich hinstellt, um demgegenüber seinerseits den „archimedischen Punkt" anzugeben. Aber dann wird es doch recht kompliziert; der Referent versucht, kurz zu bleiben. Wirklich schlimm ist es mit dem radikalen Anderssein des antiken Denkens nur bei den Vorsokratikern. Hier sind wir Modernen, wenn wir gewisse Fragmente und sonstige Zeugnisse unmittelbar zu verstehen glauben und uns einbilden, es sei da von Dingen wie „Erscheinung, Wahrnehmung, Empirie, absolutem Sein, reinem Denken, Wissenschaft", von erkennendem Subjekt und zu erkennendem Objekt, oder auch nur von ‚Wahrheit'[3] die Rede, ganz sicher auf dem Holzweg, denn all das ist erst mit der nach Aristoteles' sicherem Zeugnis nicht vor Platon entdeckten οὐσία κατὰ τὸν λόγον in die Welt gekommen, wo wir Modernen von nun an schon eher unmittelbar Fuß fassen können. Aber vorher und insbesondere bei Demokrit dürfen wir nicht etwa das eine oder andere vermeintlich unmittelbar an-

---

[3] Dies kommt allerdings erst auf S. 41, dafür um so kräftiger: „Anders gesagt: Man wird auf die Anwendung des Wortes ‚Wahrheit' zur Deutung vorsokratischer Doktrinen schlechthin verzichten müssen. Erst durch Platon wird ἀλήθεια zur ‚Wahrheit'."

sprechende Fragment oder Zeugnis zum Halt nehmen, sondern der
einzige feste Punkt ist, daß „jedenfalls das ideale Sein für Demokrit |
von vornherein ausgeschlossen ist". Die gegenwärtige wissenschaftliche
Situation macht übrigens eins zu drei (S. 8: „die drei entscheidenden
Punkte"): 1. Nach Jaeger ist Aristoteles „überall da, wo er den Pla-
tonismus als Ganzes gegen alle Früheren abgrenzt, über jeden Verdacht eines ,Mißverständnisses' erhaben"; 2. Stenzel „sah die wesen-
hafte Verbindung von ἀρετή und εἶδος und bewies somit die Transzendenz gerade der ursprünglichsten Form der Idee"; 3. „K. Reinhardt
bewies an der δόξα des Parmenides die Unvollziehbarkeit eines wirklichen Subjektivismus für das archaische Denken". Lassen wir Punkt
3 wie Platon *Theaet.* 183e beiseite und vergröbern wir 1 und 2 um der
Kürze willen über das von L. für sich in Anspruch genommene und erlaubte Maß hinaus, so bleibt, daß erheblich viel mehr Wissenschaft-
lichkeit von Platon und seinem primär ethisch gerichteten Denken ab-
hängt, als man gemeinhin annimmt. Nachdem der Versuch, auf solcher
Grundlage zu arbeiten, für die Geschichte der Mathematik zurück-
gewiesen worden ist (siehe Kurt v. Fritz, Platon, Theaetet und die
antike Mathematik, Philol. 87, 1932, 40ff., 136ff.), sieht man ungern,
wie sich der Verf. für die Geschichte der Naturphilosophie von vornherein darauf festlegt und Ähnliches für die Geschichte der Medizin an-
kündigt[4]. Für die Ethik ergibt sich keine eigentlich neue Grundlage, dementsprechend fühlt sich L. da zunächst im Negativen sicherer als im Positiven, entschließt sich aber gerade deswegen, die Behandlung der ethischen Fragmente voranzustellen. Damit ist die Disposition des Haupt-
teiles der Arbeit (52—118) „Demokrit" in der Hauptsache bestimmt;
vorausgeschickt wird auf S. 14—51 ein bei den Absichten des Verf. allerdings unerläßlicher erster Teil „Protagoras", der dem Zweck gewidmet
ist, „wenigstens die Möglichkeit einer Deutung des homo-mensura-Satzes
ohne Annahme einer ,Erkenntnisrelation' für Protagoras anzugeben";
endlich folgt S. 119—129 ein kurzer dritter Teil über die Demokriteer.

Vom ersten Teil greift diese Rezension nur „I. Die Protagoras-
abschnitte des Theaetet" heraus[5]. |

---

[4] S. 9f. Dies allerdings unfreiwillig. L. ist gezwungen, zu behaupten, in einer ganzen
Reihe von hippokratischen Schriften mache sich nachplatonisches Denken breit
(Beweis: „Wie stark man mit der Einwirkung platonischen Denkens auf Teile
des C. Hippocr. rechnen muß, zeigt ja (!) Περὶ τέχνης"), sonst wackelt der „archi-
medische Punkt". Wessen wir uns zu versehen haben, zeigt eine gelegentliche Behauptung S. 23: „Der Empiriebegriff entsteht im *Gorgias* — ... — erst als Gegen-
begriff zum platonischen τέχνη-Begriff."

[5] Das Kapitel enthält weiter: II. Die Protagorasabschnitte des Protagoras. III. Protagoras bei Aristoteles und Sextus Empiricus. Anhang zum ersten Teil: 1. Literatur. 2. Lexikalische Übersicht über αἰσθάνεσθαι, νοεῖν und Synonyme bei den
Vorsokratikern.

Aus der ‚Form' weiß heute die Kunst der Interpretation verblüffende Dinge hervorzuzaubern. Im vorliegenden Falle scheint Form die Tatsache zu sein, daß Platon im Theaetet einen Knaben zum Hauptgesprächspartner des Sokrates gewählt hat — weiter nichts —, und hervorgeholt wird für das Verständnis des Dialogs in zwölf Zeilen, daß es sich im Gespräch mit dem Knaben „keinesfalls um die kritische Prüfung geläufiger Antworten auf eine geläufige Frage handeln kann" — darüber läßt sich noch reden — „sondern um Neuschöpfung eines ganzen geistigen Kosmos auf dem fruchtbaren Boden der Entdeckung eines Problems" — das geht zu weit.

S. 41 wird Friedländer zunächst gelobt, weil in seinem Platonwerk „wirklich einmal Ernst damit gemacht wird, den Gehalt eines platonischen Dialogs primär von der Form aus zu verstehen", aber zum Schluß S. 44 hören wir: „Damit aber bleibt trotz allem, was zur Begründung der Einführung Theaetets als Gesprächspartner gesagt wird, nach meinem Empfinden die Stellung Theaetets schief und ungeschickt: Er bleibt Vertreter irgendeiner communis opinio, nicht Mitentdecker einer neuen Wahrheit." Platon selbst wählt freilich die Form, könnte man sagen, daß zum Schluß gesagt wird, mit allem, was zur Sprache gekommen wäre, wäre keine Wahrheit entdeckt und mehr als das zu beurteilen vermöchte Sokrates' Hebammenkunst nicht; und Platon selbst nutzt die Tatsache, daß Theaetet noch ein Kind ist, in anderer Weise für den Gang des Dialoges aus: aber diese Selbstverleugnung der Form erklärt vermutlich nur, warum es „immer noch nicht zur Selbstverständlichkeit geworden ist, einen platonischen Dialog auch gerade in seinem philosophischen Gehalt von der Form her zu verstehen" (14).

Lassen wir das auf sich beruhen; der Verf. hätte es gar nicht nötig gehabt. Er hätte auch nicht nötig gehabt, den Terminus διαίρεσις und was dazu gehört, unbekümmert darum, ob Platon selbst ihn verwendet, und ohne Rücksicht auf die jeweiligen dialektischen Nuancen dem Platontext aufzudrängen.

Der einfachen Fragestellung πότερον ταὐτὸν ἢ ἕτερον entspricht bei Platon die einfache Bestimmung des Ergebnisses *Theaet.* 186e/187a. Ich will nicht hersetzen, wie das bei L. aussieht. — In dem Beispiel *Theaet.* 147d ergibt die Dichotomie nicht unmittelbar den gesuchten Begriff, sondern nach ihrer Ausführung läßt sich der gesuchte Begriff als auf den einen Teil der Dichotomie bezüglich ohne weiteres definieren. Damit ist kein Verfahren angegeben, sondern ein Beispiel für die gewünschte Lösung. Man braucht es nicht allzu ernst zu nehmen, wenn aus dem harmlosen Eifer des jungen Mathematikers ein Nebensinn herauszuhören ist, den nur τῶν κρειττόνων τις hineingelegt haben kann; aber man wird den Spaß gelten lassen müssen, denn es stimmt: ohne Bezugnahme auf die zugeordneten Erkenntnisobjekte läßt sich für Platon die ἐπιστήμη nicht bestimmen. Im *Theaetet* selbst ist vergleichbar der antiplatonische Lösungsversuch 201eff. Die platonische Lösung wird im *Staat* entwickelt und noch im *Timaeus* 27d zugrunde gelegt, obwohl es bei Platon inzwischen komplizierter geworden war. Im *Theaetet* konnte sie nicht kommen. Denn wohin der *Theaetet* als Ganzes dialektisch gehört, sagt eindeutig der *Parmenides*, auf den nicht umsonst Bezug genommen wird. Es handelt sich darum, ob | die für Vieles unentbehrliche Ideenlehre gegen die Angriffe zu halten ist. Sokrates, dem es ‚noch' an dialektischer Übung fehlt, ist unsicher geworden und wird belehrt: wenn man eine

Hypothese macht, muß man nicht nur die aus der Position, sondern auch die aus der Negation sich ergebenden Konsequenzen prüfen (135e), mit anderen Worten: man muß nicht nur bei den Schwierigkeiten der Ideenlehre verweilen, sondern auch prüfen, wohin man gerät, wenn man sie nicht gelten läßt. Übungshalber und beispielsweise wird das dann auf einem Niveau, das als unter der Ideenlehre liegend längst und ausdrücklich gekennzeichnet ist, allseitig vorgemacht (160b stoßen die beiden Teile der großen Übung zusammen). Was in dem ganzen Dialog offen bleibt und zunächst gefordert wird, ist nicht etwa eine direkte Verteidigung der Ideenlehre gegen die Angriffe — Platon gibt im Alter mehr und mehr zu, daß man sie in Worten nicht geben kann, denkt aber nicht daran zu kapitulieren — sondern, um es noch einmal zu sagen, die Betrachtung der Schwierigkeiten, in die man gerät, wenn man ohne Ideenlehre auskommen will. Genau das ist der *Theaetet*, der übrigens eine einfachere Methode ᾗ αὖ οὐχ οὕτως ἔχει im Kleinen anzuwenden weiß (161a). Je näher man zusieht, um so lebendiger und vielgestaltiger sind die Varianten der Dialektik; nur gerade die διαίρεσις-Methode ist ein wenig natürliches Gebilde, das allein im *Sophistes* recht am Platz ist.

Das für seine Zwecke Wesentliche sucht der Verf. gleich aus einer Interpretation des Abschnittes *Theaet.* 152a—c zu gewinnen. Dort heißt es nach Einführung des Satzes des Protagoras und Erläuterung dessen, was damit behauptet wird: ‚Es ist anzunehmen, daß ein so weiser Mann keinen Unsinn redet; folgen wir ihm also.‘

Was jetzt kommt, muß also dartun, daß die Behauptung des Protagoras keinen Unsinn darstellt. Zunächst steht die Frage da: ‚Kommt es nicht vor, daß beim Wehen eines und desselben Windes der eine von uns friert, der andere nicht?‘ Natürlich wird sie bejaht. Nur soweit läßt L. Platon etwas von Protagoras übernehmen: ‚‚Dann aber setzt die elenktische Frage ein: πότερον οὖν τότε αὐτὸ ἐφ᾽ ἑαυτοῦ τὸ πνεῦμα ψυχρὸν ἢ οὐ ψυχρὸν φήσομεν; damit ist φαίνεσθαι und εἶναι auseinandergerissen. Zugleich mit der Konstituierung des ‚Dinges an sich‘ tritt notwendig auch der Gegenbegriff der ‚Erscheinung‘ oder auch des ‚Scheins‘ auf‘‘ usw. S. 15f. Diese Interpretation ist falsch. Der Satz πότερον tritt nicht als elenktische Frage auf, sondern als Aufzeigen einer Sinnlosigkeit, die in diesem Falle zwingt, dem Protagoras recht zu geben, ὅτι τῷ μὲν ῥιγῶντι ψυχρόν, τῷ δὲ μὴ οὔ. Wir sind noch durchaus bei der Bemühung, Protagoras zu folgen; und es kann keine Rede davon sein, daß wir statt dessen vielmehr die Konstituierung des Dinges an sich und zugleich der Gegenbegriffe Erscheinung oder Schein miterleben sollten, und daß damit die Diskussion auf eine neue Ebene verschoben werden sollte. Man kann vielleicht zweifeln — der Rezensent tut es aber ebensowenig wie der Verf. —, ob das Beispiel vom wehenden Wind von Protagoras übernommen ist; man kann aber nicht daran zweifeln, daß, wenn Protagoras es gebraucht hat, daß er dann die Alternative so gestellt hat, wie Platon es tut, daß es ihm also schon möglich war, die Behauptung, der Wind für sich selbst wäre kalt, bewußt zu negieren. Genau dieselbe Alternative steht im *Kratylos* 385e, auch da ist nach Platons Darstellung der Sinn von Protagoras' Satz identisch mit der Negierung des anderen Teiles der Alternative. Es ist allerdings ein Unterschied zwischen den beiden Stellen: im *Kratylos* erscheint die Behauptung des Protagoras als paradox, im *Theaetet* dagegen | als einleuchtend, was an der allgemeinen Fassung im *Kratylos* und an dem im *Theaetet* gewählten besonderen Beispiel liegt.

Richtig sagt der Verf.: ‚‚Der homo-mensura-Satz wird nicht als Beleg des Sensualismus zitiert‘‘; Platon macht es in der Tat deutlich, daß er den Satz nicht als Behauptung über die αἴσθησις vorfand. Dagegen gibt der besprochene Abschnitt keinen Anlaß, von „Heraklitismus" des Protagoras zu reden. Platon gibt den Satz als Behauptung περὶ ἐπιστήμης, und was er, so gefaßt, bedeutet, darüber können wir uns leicht im *Euthydem* orientieren: jeder Mensch hat immer ohne weiteres ein untrügliches Wissen über das, was ist und was nicht ist. Bei der im *Theaetet* vorweggestellten Identifikation von ἐπιστήμη und αἴσθησις denkt sich der Knabe Theaetet nicht allzuviel, aber der Dialektiker Platon hat seine ganze Dialogführung darauf aufgebaut, und was zunächst erreicht wird, ist dies, daß der Satz des Protagoras von vornherein auf den Geltungsbereich eingeschränkt auftritt, wo er einen guten Sinn hat. L. sagt richtig, das Ziel des Abschnittes sei gar nicht, den Protagoras zu widerlegen; wenn er aber fortfährt „sondern vielmehr mit seiner Hilfe den Satz des Theaetet in Beziehung zu einer bestimmten Seinsvorstellung zu bringen, ihn so in seiner Geltung zu beschränken und dabei freilich gänzlich umzugestalten", so muß man in diesen Worten den „Satz des Theaetet" und den des Protagoras miteinander vertauschen und die gänzliche Umgestaltung mildern, dann wird es richtig. Nicht der Satz des Theaetet — der ist es von vornherein —, sondern der des Protagoras erscheint am Schluß des Abschnittes auf ein bestimmtes Sein beschränkt, das ist aber etwas, von dessen Bedeutung Protagoras selbst nichts wußte oder nichts wissen wollte; sein Satz lautete allgemein.

So haben wir das berühmte moderne Problem, was der Satz des Protagoras eigentlich bedeutet, in einer neuen Form. Er hat seinen guten Sinn auf dem Gebiet der αἴσθησις, und trotzdem geschieht ihm offenbar Gewalt, wenn er darauf eingeschränkt gedacht wird. Früher hieß es meist: Der Satz des Protagoras ergäbe einen guten Sinn, wenn wir bei ‚Mensch‘ an Mensch überhaupt denken dürften und nicht gerade an die individuellen Verschiedenheiten, aber dem stehe vor allem Platons Zeugnis in *Kratylos* und *Theaetet* entgegen, also könne der Satz nur bedeuten, es gäbe kein allgemeines, sondern nur ein individuelles Wissen. Sonderbar ist dann aber wieder, daß Protagoras, wenn er eigentlich meinte, es gäbe kein Maß, das angäbe, wofür man sich bei gegeneinander stehenden Ansichten zu entscheiden hätte, dies so ausdrückte, das Maß wäre der Mensch. Über diese Schwierigkeiten scheint mir die nicht kühne Hypothese hinwegzuhelfen, daß Protagoras seinen Satz beweisen wollte. Wenn man behaupten will, es hätte keinen Sinn, sich Sein und Nichtsein der Dinge anders denken zu wollen, als die Menschen es tun, so kann man das für die Gattung zunächst nur behaupten; aufzeigen, daß es wirklich keinen Sinn hat, kann man nur an den Individuen, zunächst wenigstens. Es hat keinen Sinn, der Person A, der die Zugluft kalt ist, beibringen zu wollen, sie wäre es nicht, weil | sie es der Person B nicht ist; genau so wenig Sinn hat es, den Menschen überhaupt einreden zu wollen, es wären Dinge, die ihnen nicht sind, und es wären Dinge nicht, die ihnen sind: wenn das ein möglicher Gedanke ist, dann scheint mir für das historische Verständnis von Protagoras‘ Satz alles gewonnen. Denn die ganze Naturphilosophie wenigstens der damaligen Zeit und auch Heraklit leben von der Behauptung, ‚die Menschen‘ dächten Seiendes und Nichtseiendes falsch und es wäre ganz anders. Wenn demgegenüber der Mensch als Maß der Dinge ausgespielt wird, so ist das Ablehnung jeder sich den ‚Menschen‘ gegenüber wichtig machenden besonderen

Spekulation, im Sinne des gesunden Menschenverstandes, als dessen hervorragender
Vertreter Protagoras in Platons *Protagoras* sich so vertrauenerweckend mit allem,
was für den harmlosen Menschen *ist*, zu identifizieren weiß, — schon beinahe Isokrates.
Nur, Protagoras hatte einen wirklichen Gedanken, der negativ gewendet und auf
die Grenzen der menschlichen Erkenntnis bezogen eine Binsenwahrheit geworden
ist. Aber geistreicher war die positive Verwendung zur Verteidigung des Menschen-
wissens gegen die Spekulation. Man vergleiche Kapitel 3 der Schrift περὶ ἀρχαίης
ἰητρικῆς, in der man sich überhaupt auf Schritt und Tritt an Protagoras erinnert
fühlt. Dem Sinne nach steht dort: Die Beobachtung, daß gesunden und kranken
Menschen nicht dasselbe zuträglich ist, hat zur Aufstellung einer spezifischen Kran-
kendiät, d. h. der Medizin geführt. Gerade so hat in einer früheren Periode die Beobachtung, daß den Menschen nicht dasselbe zuträglich ist wie den Tieren, zur Aufstellung einer spezifischen Menschendiät geführt. Es wäre richtig, auch diese Er-
findung ἰητρική zu nennen, ὅτι γε εὕρηται ἐπὶ τῇ τοῦ ἀνθρώπου ὑγιείῃ τε καὶ σωτηρίῃ
καὶ τροφῇ, ἄλλαγμα ἐκείνης τῆς διαίτης, ἐξ ἧς οἱ πόνοι καὶ νοῦσοι καὶ θάνατοι ἐγένοντο.
Wollte man dieser Aufstellung mit derselben Verständnislosigkeit begegnen, wie
dem Protagoras, so könnte man einwenden, daraus, daß den verschiedenen Menschen
Verschiedenes zuträglich wäre, könnte man höchstens erschließen, daß es keine
generelle Medizin geben könne. Und doch ist weder die Analogie dumm noch der
Satz, der die Gattungsmedizin konstituiert, indem er in einem Atem ausspricht,
was sich nur gesondert entweder vom individuellen oder vom Gattungsmenschen
denken läßt. Mit demselben Doppelsinn verbietet der Satz des Protagoras, es dem
Menschen gegenüber besser wissen zu wollen. Losgelöst von seinem historischen Be-
ziehungspunkt läuft er, um seines Beweises willen, darauf hinaus, daß es dem be-
liebigen Einzelmenschen gegenüber kein Besserwissen geben könne. So aufgefaßt
erscheint er schon in Platons *Euthydem*, und ebenso dann im *Kratylos* und *Theaetet*,
ist dann aber wehrlos gegen Argumente ad hominem.

Bei dem Abschnitt *Theaetet* 152c—161e kommt es L. nur darauf
an, zu zeigen, „daß Platon die Umgestaltung des heraklitischen Seins-
begriffes zum Relativismus als *Deutung*, nicht als Bericht gibt".
M. E. handelt es sich darum, daß dem wenig durchgreifenden Relativismus der Beweisstücke des Protagoras mit Hilfe der extremsten
heraklitisierenden Flußlehre das Äußerste an Konsequenz zur Seite gegeben werden soll. Der Versuch fällt ganz glänzend aus, wirkt aber,
worauf man achte, auf Theaetet nicht sonderlich überzeugend (157c),
und Sokrates steigert bis 158e nur noch seine Unsicherheit. Dann
jedoch verteidigt Sokrates das Feine durch das Grobe, über dessen
Unzulänglichkeit man, nachdem die Möglichkeit unendlich feinerer |
Ausgestaltung aufgezeigt ist, willig hinwegsieht, und der Erfolg ist ein
ganz solider und echter Eindruck (160d). In dieser Partie haben wir
es, wenn wir von verbindenden Schnörkeln zum Vorhergehenden ab-
sehen, wieder wie in dem Beispiel vom kalt und nicht kalt empfundenen
Wind mit einem sehr greifbaren Relativismus zu tun: auf der einen
Seite Sokrates, der entweder gesund oder krank sein kann, und auf der
anderen Seite ein und derselbe Wein, der dem gesunden Sokrates süß
und dem kranken Sokrates bitter ist. Einleuchtend wird aufgezeigt,
daß zwischen wahrnehmendem Ich und wahrgenommenem Süß oder

Bitter eine unaufhebbare und stets die Wahrheit liefernde Relation
besteht, die gleichbedeutend mit Wissen sein müsse. Einen Relativismus dieser Art für Protagoras zu bestreiten, sehe ich nach Platons
Darstellung weder eine Veranlassung noch eine Möglichkeit. Freilich
war es ein reichlich primitiver Relativismus, der kräftiger Nachhilfe
bedurfte, um im 2. Viertel des 4. Jh. überhaupt noch diskutabel zu sein.
Aber allgemein gedacht war er — falls Protagoras kein Sensualist war,
sondern Kalt und nicht Kalt, Süß und Bitter ausspielte, um nach deren
Analogie Sein und Nichtsein der Dinge überhaupt bemessen sein zu
lassen.

Damit glaube ich die Besprechung des Protagorasteiles in L.s Buch
und in Platons Dialog beschließen zu können. Nur wenn Platon sich
unwahrscheinlicherweise eine allmähliche Erschließung dessen, was der
historische Protagoras wirklich gemeint hätte, mit zur Aufgabe gestellt
haben sollte, würden wir hoffen dürfen, durch eine weitere Interpretation des Dialogs über denjenigen Sinn des Protagorassatzes hinauszukommen, der von vornherein zugrunde gelegt wird. Diesen Sinn zu bestimmen, ist nicht so schwer, wie man nach den Bemühungen L.s annehmen könnte, wenn man *Euthydem* und *Kratylos* zu Hilfe nimmt.
Natürlich besteht die Aufgabe, über diesen nicht nur sachlich, sondern
auch historisch unhaltbaren Sinn hinauszukommen, aber L. sucht in
verkehrter Richtung. Schon aus dem *Euthydem* können wir lernen, daß
Protagoras' Satz von Hause aus ungeschützt war gegen das φορτικὸν
ἐρώτημα, das 287a unvermutet kommt: τίνος διδάσκαλοι ἥκετε. Nach
L.s Theaetetinterpretation wäre umgekehrt der Satz geraden Wegs entstanden aus dem Anspruch, „den einzelnen ungeschulten Menschen
und die Gesamtheit der πόλις von ihren Übeln zu befreien wie der Arzt
den Kranken". Dann könnten wir allerdings alles andere wegwerfen.

Im Hauptteil des Buches behandelt L., was ihn bei Demokrit vor
allem interessiert; wir wissen, es ist die Frage, ob bei Demokrit von
Ethik und Erkenntnislehre in modernem Sinne die Rede sein könne.
Er ist vorweg geneigt, die Frage zu verneinen, weil Demokrit Vor-
sokratiker bzw. Vorplatoniker ist. Besprochen werden alle Fragmente |
und Zeugnisse, die für die Fragestellung etwas auszugeben scheinen,
dabei, wie es sich gehört, besonders solche Stellen, die für den modernen
Leser der negativen These des Verf. entgegenzustehen scheinen. Wenn
die Kritik das „Nachplatonische" in Überlieferung und moderner Darstellung beseitigt hat, wird versucht, das echt „Vorsokratische", das
eigentlich da war, aufzuzeigen. Zur Sprache kommen reichlich ein
Drittel der Fragmente Demokrits, darunter fast alle wichtigen, und
eine beschränktere Zahl Testimonien. Gern erkennt man an, daß der
Verf. in der Einzelerklärung selbständig und mehrfach so treffsicher
und glücklich vorgeht, daß hier ein dauernder Gewinn außer Frage

steht. Aber die Rezension kann sich nach diesem Hinweis nur noch mit dem beschäftigen, was der Verf. grundsätzlich Wichtiges und Neues zu bringen glaubt, und auch dies nur in Beschränkung auf den Teil des reichlich ausgebreiteten und in dem neuen Sinn behandelten Materials, der eine verhältnismäßig einfache und eindeutige Entscheidung verlangt und trägt.

Es ist das Vorurteil des Verf., daß das archaische Denken ein für uns Moderne eigentümlich schwieriges Denken gewesen sei, und es ist das Vorurteil des Rezensenten, daß man das archaische Denken so lange nicht als Denken verstanden habe, als es sich nicht als ein einfaches und natürliches Denken auch für uns erwiesen hat. Gut läßt sich der daraus entspringende Unterschied der Auffassungen sogleich an der Lehre von den Götter-εἴδωλα aufzeigen, mit der L. beginnt. Demokrits Lehre gebe ich mit L.s Worten (52): „frg. 166: ‚Gewisse Bilder nahen sich den Menschen und von diesen sind die einen Gutes, die anderen Übles wirkend‘. Die εἴδωλα sind nicht ‚Abbilder‘, sondern Bilder, Erscheinungen, die selbst etwas wirken. Sie selbst sind groß und übergewaltig und schwer zu zerstören, aber nicht unzerstörbar. Sie kündigen den Menschen die Zukunft, indem sie erscheinen und Stimmen hören lassen (vgl. A 78).“ In dieser Lehre nun gab es für Epikur und die hellenistische Akademie Schwierigkeiten (A 74). Sie bestand nach L. „in der Gleichsetzung der Imagines selber mit den Göttern, während für sie die Imagines nur die Funktion einer Übermittlung vom transzendenten Gott zum menschlichen Erkenntnisvermögen haben. Daraus folgt für Demokrit die Vergänglichkeit der Götter, während Epikur an ihrer Unvergänglichkeit festhalten kann.“ Alles wunderschön. Nur: merkt der Verf. eigentlich nicht, daß er hier das Wort ‚transzendent‘ in einem fast so groben Sinn gebraucht, wie ihn das Wort εἴδωλον von jeher in sich schließt? Und diese Sorte Transzendenz soll Demokrit nicht haben denken können, wohl aber Epikur und Ciceros Akademiker? Die Schwierigkeit für Epikur lag ganz anderswo. Sie zu erfassen, brauchen wir uns nicht in ein dem modernen Empfinden paradoxes | archaisches Denken hineinzuzwingen; wohl aber müssen wir versuchen, den Denkgegenstand möglichst in derjenigen Ansicht zu fixieren, die den antiken Denkern den Anlaß zu ihren Gedankenbildungen bot. Die Aufgabe ist in diesem Fall nicht so schwer, wie sie aussieht. Wozu ist die Poesie in der Welt? δ 795 kommt der Athene ein Gedanke. Sie macht ein εἴδωλον, das ganz der Schwester der Penelope gleicht, und schickt es zu der um ihren Sohn besorgten, aber nun schlafenden Penelope, um sie zu beruhigen. Das εἴδωλον kündet der Penelope ‚Dein Sohn wird wiederkommen‘, Penelope hält es zunächst für die in der Ferne wohnende Schwester und antwortet in diesem Sinn, da gibt sich das εἴδωλον als Bote der Athene zu erkennen. Damit

ist es für Penelope ‚Gott und Überbringer göttlicher Botschaft' (δ 831),
sie möchte nun Auskunft über Odysseus, das εἴδωλον antwortet nichtssagend und entschwindet am Türschloß vorbei ἐς πνοιὰς ἀνέμων. Für
seine Götterlehre fand also Demokrit in der von der Poesie mitge-
formten Welt der gewöhnlichen Vorstellung reale, innerhalb gewisser
Grenzen selbständig agierende, dünne, flüchtige Gebilde vor, für die
weder die geschlossene Tür noch die geschlossenen Augen ein Hindernis
waren. Solche Gebilde konnte nun seine Naturphilosophie ohne weiteres aus Atomen und Leerem zustande kommen lassen. Es brauchte kein
Gott sie zu bilden und zu schicken und es brauchte kein Vorbild da
zu sein, nach dem sie sich formten: lebendig waren sie ja gerade ohne
dies. Übrigens genügte das faktische Vorkommen und Auftreten solcher Gebilde im Traum und ähnlichen Zuständen vollkommen, um
den gewöhnlichen Glauben an die Götterwelt zu erklären[6]; für die ver-
hältnismäßige Einheitlichkeit dieser Welt reichte die Hilfsannahme,
daß die εἴδωλα lange lebten; bloß ad hoc wie bei dem Dichter des δ, der
mit einem Minimum von Transzendenz sogar in dieser Hinsicht auskommt (anders das B der Ilias), dafür aber die formende Göttin hatte,
durften sie ohnehin nicht sein. Auf diese Weise leugnete Demokrit die
gewöhnlich geglaubte Transzendenz der Götterwelt, das war für ihn
leicht; für die gewöhnlichen Traumerscheinungen, die nach unserer
Ansicht auf Reminiszenzen beruhen, konnte er sie nicht leugnen, und
das war für ihn schwer. Glücklicherweise haben wir hier einmal bei
Plutarch einen Bericht (A 77), der alles gibt, was wir nur wünschen
können und auf den ich angelegentlich verweisen kann.

      Anders sahen die Dinge für Epikur aus. Denkt man sich nämlich
die εἴδωλα der Göttererscheinungen und der Traumerscheinungen
nach | Analogie der epikureischen Wahrnehmungstheorie als tote
Häutchen, dann ergibt sich für beide dieselbe Schwierigkeit: wie können sie selbständig agieren? Für Demokrit handelte es sich um selbständige Atomgebilde mit soviel selbständigem Eigenleben, wie sie
eben zeigten, und schwierig war nur, nicht daß Bilder agierten, sondern
daß bei den gewöhnlichen Träumen dies Agieren oft stark im Sinne
des ursprünglichen Wesens sich vollzieht, daß sie also über die äußere
Ähnlichkeit hinaus auch davon etwas mitbekommen haben mußten.
Epikur geriet durch den mechanistischen Ausgleich in seiner Lehre in
eine viel verzweifeltere Lage. Es bedurfte eines gewaltigen Aufwandes
an, wie wir heute zugeben müssen, glücklicher technischer Phantasie
(Lucr. 4, 768—776) und an ebenfalls recht modern anmutender Theo-

---

[6] Irreführend, von einem „religiösen Verhältnis" Demokrits zu den εἴδωλα zu reden,
   das gibt der Ausdruck bei Sextus Emp. ἔνθεν καὶ εὔχετο εὐλόγχων τυχεῖν εἰδώλων
   nicht her. Dort wird ‚um' die Eidola gebeten, oder wenn wir dem Sperrdruck eine
   Konzession machen, gebetet, nicht ‚zu' ihnen.

rie der Aufmerksamkeit (4, 788—815), um sich ihr gewachsen zu zeigen. Dabei stellt sich für die Götter der nur für sie von Demokrit geleugnete Glaube an ihre Sonderexistenz den Erscheinungen gegenüber einfach wieder her, wenn auch in der nun nötigen Sublimierung.

„Noch krasser", fährt L. auf S. 53 fort, „tritt für jedes spätere Empfinden dieselbe Paradoxie in frg. 119 auf: ,Auf Grund ihrer eigenen Ratlosigkeit haben die Menschen das Bild der Tyche gebildet.' Und unmittelbar darauf ist die Tyche doch wieder als in der Realität wirkend vorgestellt. Sie kämpft mit der Phronesis. Das ist dieselbe ἀβουλίη, aus der bei Parmenides die reale Welt entstand (vgl. Parm. B 6, 5)." Diels übersetzte B 119 harmlos und im wesentlichen richtig: ,Die Menschen haben sich ein Idol des Zufalls gebildet zur Beschönigung ihrer eigenen Ratlosigkeit. Denn nur in seltenen Fällen wirkt der Zufall der Klugheit entgegen: das meiste im Leben weiß ein wohlverständiger Scharfblick ins Gerade zu richten.' Aber das konnte L. nicht brauchen, weil, wie wir der nun folgenden Behandlung von B 297 entnehmen, Vorsokratiker „eine rein innerpsychische Vorstellung deutlich gegen die Realität abzusetzen" nur dann „die innere Möglichkeit" haben, wenn diese „durch die Form der Aussage über die Zukunft gegeben" wird. „Jede Voraussage hat etwas rein Subjektives." Aber das ist Ausrede. Im Fragment 297 ist von den erlogenen Hadesvorstellungen die Rede. Die Lügengebilde über das Leben nach dem Tode gehen gar nicht speziell auf die Zukunft, nur die Angst des Einzelnen, die durch sie begründet wird. Allgemein ist zu bemerken, daß die erfolgreiche Lüge schon früh, und nicht wohl anders gedacht werden konnte als so, daß der Lügner eine Lüge, der Wahrheit ähnlich, bildet, und daß diese Lüge dann im Belogenen als eine „rein innerpsychische Vorstellung", als etwas „rein Subjektives" da ist, das für den die Sachlage Überschauenden selbstverständlich deutlich gegen die Realität abgesetzt ist. Damit war die äußere Möglichkeit gegeben, nach dieser | Analogie sehr vielerlei zu denken und zu benennen, und wie der Anwendungsbereich des Wortes ψεῦδος zeigt, hat man nicht lange auf die innere Möglichkeit gewartet. Daß aber gar jemand, der, um eine geistige Sachlage zu beschreiben, von einem künstlich gebildeten εἴδωλον einer Sache im Gegensatz gegen die Sache selbst spricht, diese beiden nicht deutlich voneinander habe absetzen können, dafür ist fr. 119 ein denkbar schlechter Beleg. Es ist zu interpretieren, wie es die Bedeutungen der Worte und der Satzzusammenhang verlangen, und nicht gegen Sinn und Verstand so, daß nach Demokrits Meinung die τύχη, die manchmal wirklich mit der φρόνησις kämpft und auf deren beschränkte Wirksamkeit die äußere und innere Verlogenheit der Menschen sich viel zu oft beruft, durch die Ausrede mitgebildet wäre. Das ist Unsinn an Stelle von meisterhaft knapper und treffender Anschau-

lichkeit, für deren Verständnis wir noch gewinnen, wenn wir εἴδωλον
so einfach wie möglich nehmen, nicht als falsches Bild einer wirkenden
Macht, sondern als Ersatzstück im Einzelfall, wo das Wesen — das
kein Gott zu sein braucht — in Wahrheit gar nicht da ist (z. B. *E* 449).
Diese Fälle sind hier zahlreich, da die wirklich vernunftwidrige τύχη
selten ist. |

In dem Kapitel über die ‚Ethica' ist es L. m. E. am wenigsten geraten, in wissenschaftlicher Darstellung seine Ergebnisse der langen
Reihe der besprochenen Fragmente abzugewinnen; L. weiß, worauf er
hinaus will, der Leser kann vor Formulierung der jeweiligen „Ergebnisse" höchstens halb verstehen und gerät in eine unbehagliche Stimmung,
wenn unerwartet — denn vieles ist gut — an klar scheinender Überlieferung in zunächst unkontrollierbarer Weise heruminterpretiert
wird, während zugleich in unklarer, vieldeutiger, wenn nicht korrupter
Überlieferung Dinge gefunden werden, die sich in der klaren Überlieferung nicht ausgesprochen finden. Auf diese Weise ist das Kapitel gegen
eine kurze wissenschaftliche Kritik geschützt. Ein kurzes Referat kann
nur die sich deutlich abhebenden Ergebnisse zur Sprache bringen. Das
wichtigste steht gegen Schluß (75): „In der Ethik Demokrits wird
kein Problem aufgeworfen. Es wird überhaupt nicht gefragt, sondern
ein vorbildhaftes Sein von allen Seiten schildernd eindrucksvoll gestaltet. Um es auf eine antithethische Formel zu Platon zu bringen:
Sie ist rein protreptisch, nie elenktisch." Das Erste ist richtig. Demokrit hat nichts in petto, was das ganze Leben umgestalten würde und
worüber ein junger Mensch wie der Kallikles in Platons *Gorgias* und
der noch nicht alte Platon, der hinter dem Sokrates des *Gorgias* steht,
leidenschaftlich disputieren würde. Demokrit spricht als Erfahrener,
und wenn ein solcher das Wort nimmt in ethischen Dingen, dann versteht sich so gut wie alles von selbst, aber: οὐκ οἰκεῖος ἀκροατὴς ὁ νέος[7].
Die Jugend muß erzogen werden, das meint auch Demokrit. Wozu,
übersieht nur das Alter, und wie, darüber hat das Alter seine eigenen
Gedanken, auch Demokrit. — Das Gegensatzpaar protreptisch-elenk-
tisch, das bei L. zu einer beachtenswerten Bemerkung über die verschiedene Form der schriftstellerischen und gedanklichen Disposition
bei Platon und Aristoteles einerseits und bei Demokrit andererseits
überleitet, ist terminologisch unglücklich gewählt, weil es treffender
einen Gegensatz *innerhalb* der sokratischen Reden und der davon
beeinflußten Literatur bezeichnet. Sehen wir davon ab, so bleibt: „es

---

[7] Denn der ist unerfahren und leidenschaftlich. So Aristoteles in der *Nikomachischen
Ethik*. In der *Eudemischen Ethik* schloß sich der Ethiker immerhin noch in das
praktische Ziel der ethischen Betrachtungen ein: οὐ γὰρ εἰδέναι βουλόμεθα, τί ἐστιν
ἀνδρεία, ἀλλ᾽ εἶναι ἀνδρεῖοι, οὐδὲ τί ἐστι δικαιοσύνη, ἀλλ᾽ εἶναι δίκαιοι. Wie ganz
anders es aber im *Protreptikos* geklungen hatte, wissen wir auch.

wird ein vorbildhaftes Sein gestaltet". Wo wird gestaltet? „In der |
Ethik Demokrits", die eine bestimmte literarische Form hat, d. h. also
für uns: in Demokrits ethischen Fragmenten. Wie wird gestaltet?
Unmittelbar vorher hieß es von einer Reihe von Fragmenten (74):
„Es handelt sich nicht um . . ., sondern immer nur um die schlichte
Darstellung des wachsenden Assimilationsprozesses an die ἀγαθά,
dessen Ergebnis der φρόνιμος oder εὔθυμος oder αὐτάρκης ist." Von
einer anderen Reihe von Fragmenten wird auf S. 63 gesagt: „Immer
steht im Hintergrund die erzieherische Mahnung, durch ἄσκησις die
ἕξις zu *gestalten* (von L. gesperrt), die den Menschen dem μεταπίπτειν
und dem κίνδυνος enthebt." Dazu nehme man noch etwa (68): „Neben
der διδαχή, der Belehrung, ist von besonderer Wichtigkeit für die Ge-
staltung der φύσις die Gewöhnung (vgl. frg. 279), besonders die Gewöhnung durch das Vorbild, also die μίμησις (vgl. frg. 228). Die
μίμησις ist die unerläßliche Vorstufe des vollendeten ἀγαθός (vgl.
frg. 39). Das μιμεῖσθαι τοὺς κακούς ist dagegen χαλεπόν (vgl. frg.
79"[8]; kurz vorher (66): „Zusammenfassend kann man feststellen, daß
auch hier der Blick auf den ἀγαθὸς ἀνήρ, nicht auf das ἀγαθόν gerichtet ist (vgl. auch frg. 229). Erst die spezifisch Sokratisch-Platoni-
sche Frage zog die ‚Versachlichung' des ethischen Denkens mit Notwendigkeit nach sich." Etwas weiter fällt das Wort ‚Vorbild-Ethik'
(von L. selbst in Anführungszeichen gesetzt). Was ist Vorbild-Ethik?
Formal, wie es uns scheinen muß, ein Durcheinander von im engeren
Sinne pädagogischen Behauptungen, Mahnungen zur Selbstgestaltung
und schlichter Darstellung des wachsenden Assimilationsprozesses.
Und wie sieht das Vorbild aus? Hier kommen wir von hinten herum
zu dem von L. schon auf S. 56 gebrachten „zentralen Punkt des Demokritischen Denkens, der Überwindung des κίνδυνος, der Gewinnung
der ἀσφάλεια". Und hier wird es unerfreulich. Denn eine sachliche
Ethik kann sachlich Gefahr und Sicherheit aufzeigen, ohne sich einem
Lächeln auszusetzen, aber eine Vorbild-Ethik, in der das Sich-nicht-
in-Gefahr-begeben — im gewöhnlichen Sinne — und die Mahnung, den
Blick nach unten und *nicht* nach oben zu richten, eine solche Rolle
spielt wie in dem einzigen großen Fragment 191[9], hat nichts Gewinnen-
des. | Es sei denn, Demokrit habe das da befürwortete Verhalten nicht

---

[8] Der Verf. läßt gelegentlich die Absicht erkennen, „die Nuancierung im ganzen
richtig zu treffen" (63). Wie grausam dabei mit der Nuancierung im einzelnen
umgegangen wird, davon kann man sich überzeugen, wenn man jedes einzelne
der hier zitierten Fragmente nachschlägt.

[9] L. verkennt die doch nachgerade bekannte archaische Gedankenführung, die sich
schrittweise vom Ausgangspunkt entfernt, um schrittweise zu ihm zurückzukehren.
Daß 6 Zeilen vor dem Ende das εὐθυμέεσθαι einmal im Innern der Gedanken-
entwicklung auftaucht, hat seinen guten Grund. διόπερ τὰ μὲν μὴ δίζεσθαι χρεών:

so sehr als vorbildlich, wie vielmehr als das sachlich einzig Richtige hinstellen und begründen wollen. Aber das kann man nicht einfach „auf eine antithetische Formel zu Platon bringen".

Das als Überleitung zur Erörterung der Naturphilosophie bzw. der Erkenntnislehre Demokrits sich gebende Kapitel „Psychologische Vorstellungen" (75—83) bringt als Kernstück eine für Demokrit richtige Interpretation von Ar. *de an.* 404a 1—16, 27—31, 405a 8—13. Obwohl Aristoteles 405a 9, um Demokrits Ansicht darzustellen, sagt: ψυχὴν μὲν γὰρ εἶναι ταὐτὸ καὶ νοῦν, kann Demokrit selbst dies weder als Behauptung noch gar als Prämisse aufgestellt haben, und wahrscheinlich gilt Ähnliches von dem Satz 404a 28 τὸ γὰρ ἀληθὲς εἶναι τὸ φαινόμενον.

Aber dem Aristoteles tut L. Unrecht. S. 81: „Es ergibt sich, daß Aristoteles aus einem sorgfältig exzerpierten Zusammenhang Schlüsse zieht, diese Schlüsse dann wiederum ohne weiteres als Beleg für die Ansicht des zitierten Philosophen verwendet (so 405a 9 den Satz: ψυχὴν . . . νοῦν), ja sogar ausdrücklich die Eindeutigkeit der so gewonnenen Ergebnisse dem Autor zuschreibt (404b 1: διασαφεῖ, 404a 28: ἁπλῶς). Wie sollte es auch für den Logiker anders sein, als daß ihm die Vollständigkeit der Prämissen völlig genügt, um den Schluß als eindeutig gegeben anzusehen." Um mit dem Letzten zu beginnen, sei spaßeshalber erwähnt, daß nicht einmal der Logiker Aristoteles so entfernt von aller psychologischen Wirklichkeit war: *An. pr.* 2, 67a 33—37, geschweige der über Vorgänger referierende Philosoph, der kein schlechter Leser und ein klarer Denker war. 404a 25 ist der Zusammenhang: Ähnlich auch Anaxagoras, aber nicht ganz so wie Demokrit. Bei Demokrit ist ψυχή und νοῦς einfach dasselbe . . . dagegen Anaxagoras ist weniger eindeutig über diese Dinge usw. Das bedeutet nicht, daß A. im Gegensatz zu D. weniger eindeutige Beweise über diese Dinge gehabt hätte, sondern daß er sich widerspruchsvoll über sie geäußert hätte, während es bei Demokrit einfach ist. 405a 8—13 genau zu interpretieren übersteigt die Erfordernisse und Möglichkeiten dieser Rezension. Hier genügt soviel: Wie Z. 13 ‚Anaxagoras scheint zu differenzieren‘ vorausgeschickt werden muß, nicht als Prämisse des Anaxagoras, sondern damit man das Folgende nicht falsch versteht, so erscheint Z. 9 die Identifizierung nicht als Prämisse aus Demokrits Gedankengang, sondern um darauf aufmerksam zu machen, daß bei diesem Gedankengang nicht von νοῦς im besonderen Sinne die Rede ist. Aristoteles kann sogar sich ausdrücken: ‚sie sagen, es wäre dasselbe‘, wo er faktisch meint: ‚sie denken sich das Eine, als wäre es das Andere‘; Beweis: *de an.* 427a 21f. = 427a 26f., und in diesem Fall, wo es sich um νοεῖν, φρονεῖν = αἰσθάνεσθαι handelt, merkt man, woher wir diesen für die Diskussion praktischen Gebrauch, die Unfähigkeit oder den Mangel der Absicht, zu differenzieren, als positive These eines Früheren zu formulieren, schon kennen: aus Platons *Theaetet* (vgl. S. 36). Dort, 152a, wird auch dieses sonderbare ‚Sagen‘, das kein Aussprechen und kein direktes Behaupten ist, in aller Ausführlichkeit und Unmißverständlichkeit entwickelt. Somit bleibt unbewiesen, daß das | aus der Dialektik hervorgegangene logische Bewußtsein des Aristoteles sein psychologisches und historisches Bewußtsein in dem Grade getrübt hätte, wie L. es für das Natürliche hält.

das ist das Gewöhnliche, verneint; aber vom Gegenteil kann nun nicht gesagt werden, man solle es erstreben, sondern nur, man solle es als Mittel zum A und O des Gedankens — unweigerlich der εὐθυμίη — benutzen.

Das wichtigste Kapitel des Buches „IV. Μορφή und Σχῆμα" (83 bis 100)[10] verdankt seinen Titel Demokrits Satz: ἄνθρωπός ἐστιν ὃ πάντες ἴδμεν (B 165), über den sich Sextus Empiricus lustig macht, indem er ihn als Definitionsversuch nimmt. Aristoteles 640b 30 nimmt ihn ernst — natürlich nicht als Definition — und weist darauf hin, daß hier für Demokrit Wissen um den Menschen gleich Bekanntschaft mit seiner äußeren μορφή (= σχῆμα + χρῶμα) gewesen sei — einleuchtend, mehr können wir nicht sagen. Der Zweck, zu dem Aristoteles den Satz verwendet, ist, anschaulich zu machen, daß so, zwar nicht im Falle eines toten Machwerkes (der κλίνη), wohl aber im Falle des Lebewesens das Allerwesentlichste, Lebendigkeit und organische Struktur, unter den Tisch falle, welche Versäumnis, so gut es ging, nachzuholen Epikur vorbehalten blieb (frg. 310 Us.): ἄνθρωπός ἐστι τὸ τοιουτονὶ μόρφωμα μετ' ἐμψυχίας.

L. stellt das etwas anders dar, gewinnt aber jedenfalls richtig: Demokrit ‚bestimmte' ein Lebewesen noch nicht durch εἶδος (für Aristoteles in diesem Falle gleich ψυχὴ ἢ ψυχῆς μέρος ἢ μὴ ἄνευ ψυχῆς 641a 18) und οὗ ἕνεκα, sondern „noch durch die μορφή, die zweimal durch die Verbindung von τῷ τε σχήματι καὶ τῷ χρώματι als im Bereich der αἴσθησις verbleibend charakterisiert wird." Zu betonen ist nur, daß Aristoteles, dem wir diese Charakteristik verdanken, mit seinem Interesse ausschließlich bei der wissenschaftlichen Behandlung der beseelten Lebewesen ist, nicht bei der allgemeinen Physik und nicht bei der Erkenntnislehre. Wenn L. nun doch den Satz in Zusammenhang bringt mit einem der bekannten Zeugnisse für die Atomtheorie (85f.), so scheint damit zunächst noch nichts besonders Neues behauptet zu werden, und jedenfalls hat er vollkommen recht und gerät hoffentlich mit niemandem in Konflikt[11], wenn er darauf aufmerksam macht, daß was die Atomtheorie selbst betrifft, „die Relation zum Subjekt dabei nicht die geringste Rolle spielt, sondern nur von durchaus realen μεταβολαί die Rede ist, um das Problem des τὸ αὐτὸ ἐναντίον δοκεῖν ἄλλῳ καὶ ἄλλῳ zu erklären". |

Überrascht ist man erst, wenn man im Weiterlesen erfährt, daß inzwischen etwas Wichtiges für Demokrits Erkenntnislehre klar geworden sein soll, nämlich was es mit der von Aristoteles für Demokrit behaupteten Gleichsetzung von ἀληθῆ und φαινόμενα auf sich hat: nach

[10] Diese Besprechung nimmt „VI. Die ‚Erkenntnislehre'" (112—118) gleich hinzu, muß aber darauf verzichten, „V. Die 'Αἴσθησις'-Lehre" (100—112) und den 3. Teil „Die Demokriteer" (119—129) noch einzubeziehen.

[11] Es müßte schon ein Kantianer Kants Leistung so sehr verkennen, daß er Demokrit deswegen zum erkenntnistheoretischen Vorgänger Kants machen wollte, weil seine Naturphilosophie wie geschaffen ist, um Kants Erkenntnistheorie darauf anzuwenden, was anzunehmen man sich trotz manchmal bedenklicher Ausdrucksweise schwer entschließen wird.

Demokrit ist ‚Mensch' u. dgl. gleich der durch σχῆμα und χρῶμα bestimmten μορφή, damit allgemein einsichtig und Grundlage weiterer Erkenntnis, für Aristoteles ist die μορφή einerseits ein φαινόμενον[12], andererseits durch den, der auf sie eine Erkenntnis basiert, damit für ἀληθής erklärt. Erst aus den aristotelischen Zutaten soll sich für uns der Schein ergeben, daß es bei den Atomisten zu einer „betonten Auseinandersetzung" mit der αἴσθησις gekommen wäre: das aber hält L. für ausgeschlossen.

Seine eigene Deutung ist in dem Protagoraskapitel vorbereitet. Dort S. 21 las man für Protagoras und Xeniades: „Die Möglichkeit, zwischen ἀλήθεια und ψεῦδος zu scheiden, leugnen sie beide. Diese Möglichkeit gewinnt erst Platon, indem er das heraklitische Sein als nur bezügliches Sein auf die αἰσθητά einschränkt, so Raum für das unveränderliche Sein, das zugleich ὂν καθ᾽ αὑτό ist[13], gewinnt, und die ἀλήθεια auf die Erkenntnis, die dieses ὂν καθ᾽ αὑτό zum Gegenstand hat, bezieht." Auch war schon angedeutet: „Im ἀληθές lag zweifellos vom Anfang an die Bedeutung des ‚Konstanten, Zuverlässigen' mit darin." Jetzt hören wir es ganz ähnlich. Die gewöhnlichste Täuschung hat uns alle genarrt. ἀλήθεια ist ein Homonym, und der starke Bedeutungsunterschied ist aus dem jeweiligen Gegensatz — entweder ψεῦδος, oder ἄδηλον — zu erfassen. S. 91: „Innerhalb des Gegensatzpaares ἀλήθεια — ψεῦδος entspricht sie der ‚Wahrheit' gleich Richtigkeit, als Gegenbegriff zum ἄδηλον ist sie beinahe synonym mit σαφήνεια". Springen wir gleich zum Schluß! Für Demokrit ist Wahrheit das Klare, Feste, Zuverlässige — die Atome und das Leere, demgegenüber ist das Unklare, Wandelbare, Unzuverlässige nicht etwa nicht richtig aufgefaßt, sondern im Gegenteil gerade adäquat aufgefaßt. Aber empfehlenswerter ist ja wohl das Feste, Zuverlässige. Wie kommen wir dahin? Nach B 11 und S. 115: in „kontinuierlichem Fortschritt der Erkenntnis vom Groben zum Feinen". Freilich ist nach S. 118 die Antwort in B 11 nur angedeutet. „Über die Art und Weise aber, | wie dies ἐπὶ-λεπτότερον-Gehen der γνώμη vor sich geht, bleiben wir auch da im unklaren." Vermutlich, meint L., war es ähnlich wie in der ‚Ethik', wo „alle Fragmente auf das Erreichen der ἀμετάπτωτος βεβαιότης" tendierten, wenn auch nach S. 10 das Positive der Inter-

---

[12] Das ist in diesem Fall richtig, aber nur in einem besonderen Sinn, der bei L. nicht herauskommt und mit dem er auch nichts würde anfangen können. Bei einem Lebewesen genügen nämlich Gestalt und was sonst zu sehen ist, wirklich nicht zur Bestimmung dessen, was es ist. Das liegt einfach an der Nichtwahrnehmbarkeit der Seele, aber nicht an dem Gegensatz τί — ποῖον (84) und ebenfalls nicht an dem von Ding an sich und Erscheinung.

[13] Auf die Verwechslung, der L. zum Opfer gefallen ist, werden wir noch zu sprechen kommen, s. S. 49.

pretation „durchaus an der Übereinstimmung mit den Zielen des ‚erkenntnistheoretischen' Denkens" hing. Jedenfalls handelt es sich bei letzteren „überhaupt nicht um das Problem der Transzendenz als vielmehr um die allerdings nicht voll lösbare Aufgabe, das μετα-πίπτειν zu überwinden, von der δόξις = ἐπιρυσμίη zu dem ἐτεῆ ὄν zu kommen. ... die γνῶμαι unterscheiden sich nicht als Anschauung und Denken nach ihrer Form, sondern nach ihrer Sicherheit und Deutlichkeit."

Um endlich einmal zu dem Titel des Buches zu kommen: er stammt aus B 7. L. verwirft die Übersetzung ἐπιρυσμίη ‚Zustrom' mit Recht und vermutet seinerseits nach ἐπιρρυθμίζειν Pl. *Leg*. 802b ‚umgestalten' (nicht korrekt, hier ist ἐπικορrelat zu ὅτι δ᾽ ἂν ἐνδεές, also nicht ‚um-', sondern ‚hinzu-') etwa ‚Umformung, Umgestaltung' (113). „Wir erhalten dann den klaren Gegensatz der konstanten σχήματα, der ῥυσμοί, und der variablen ἐπιρυσμίαι, von denen die letzteren der δόξις zugeordnet sind[14]." Aber es ist unerlaubt, das ‚Variable' im Gegensatz zum Konstanten in das Wort ἐπιρυσμίη hineinzudeuten. Für den Wechsel mußte Demokrit Worte wie ἀμειψιρυσμίη, ἀμειψιρυσμεῖν (‚ἀλλάσσειν τὴν σύγκρισιν ἢ μεταμορφοῦσθαι'), ἀμειψικοσμίη bilden (B 8a, 139, 138). Und wie ἀμειψιρυσμεῖν entweder bedeutet ‚den ῥυσμός, d. h. die Gesamtgestalt wechseln' oder ‚die ῥυσμοί, d. h. die Atome wechseln', so kann ἐπιρυσμίη eigentlich nur entweder einen zu dem, was da ist, hinzukommenden ῥυσμός oder etwas, was zu den ῥυσμοί hinzukommt, bedeuten. Aber ich ziehe vor, auf die Deutung zu verzichten, um nicht etwas zu Wichtiges aus einer zu schwierigen Stelle herauszuholen.

Es braucht nicht ausgeführt zu werden, daß die neue Demokritauffassung mit dem Augenschein aller wichtigen Fragmente und fast aller wichtigen Zeugnisse in Widerspruch steht; das will sie ja gerade auf Grund der modernen Ergebnisse „in den zentralen Problemen der Geschichte der antiken Philosophie: Platon und Aristoteles" (7). Und wenn sich die Arbeit für Protagoras auf das Problem Platon stützte, so ist sie für Demokrit auf Aristotelesinterpretationen angewiesen; die Rezension muß eine Probe bringen.

Zweckmäßig halten wir uns an die beiden Stellen der *Metaphysik*, die nach L. „ja auch sachlich die konzentrierteste Darstellung des ‚Erkenntnisproblems' bei Demokrit sind" (89). In der Erwähnung 1009a 27 findet L. den entscheidenden Nachweis, „daß die Früheren, und unter ihnen Demokrit, aus Unkenntnis des ὄν αὐτὸ καθ᾽ αὐτό notwendig zu dem Ergebnis der Koinzidenz der Gegensätze kommen mußten. Nach Einführung des ὄν αὐτὸ καθ᾽ αὐτό, d. h. der Substanz, muß man das ὄν der παλαιοί als **nur** φαινόμενον oder αἰσθητόν | beschreiben." Die Darstellung ist mehr als ungenau. 1009a 6ff. sagt Aristoteles zwar, daß die Leugnung des Satzes vom Widerspruch und der Satz des Protagoras sich wechselseitig voneinander ableiten lassen und insofern von derselben Art zu denken zeugen, und macht dann den Unterschied zwischen eristischen und ehrlichen Denkanstrengungen; aber diese beiden Unterscheidungen kreuzen sich wechselseitig, und mit dem Übergang 1009a 22f. sind wir bei ehrlichen Herakliteern, zu denen Anaxagoras und Demokrit nicht

---

[14] Weiter: „Daß die ἐπιρυσμίη keineswegs *nur* Folge der Relation zum Subjekt ist, beweist B 9: κατά τε — ἀντιστηριζόντων". Das von mir gesperrte „nur" nimmt diesem Satz alle Bedeutung; niemand behauptet ja das Gegenteil.

ohne weiteres gehören, sondern nur, wenn man Aristoteles' Darstellung genau so geistreich sein läßt, wie sie ist[15]. Weder von Anaxagoras noch von Demokrit konnte gesagt werden, sie wären zu dem Ergebnis der Koinzidenz der Gegensätze gekommen, wohl aber konnte in ihrer naturphilosophischen Konstruktion etwas aufgezeigt werden, was dem hinter dem ehrlichen Heraklitisieren steckenden Gedanken entsprach: eben das tut Aristoteles 1009a 26—30. Dann kommt er mit seiner eigenen Lösung durch δυνάμει — ἐντελεχείᾳ. Durch sie wird das Heraklitisieren unmittelbar in Ordnung gebracht; A. und D. aber werden durch sie deswegen betroffen, weil sie die Materie unveränderlich und bis ins Kleinste exakt durchkonstruiert denken wollen, was Aristoteles für einen Fehler hielt. Endlich 1009a 36 ἔτι δ᾽ ἀξιώσομεν αὐτοὺς ὑπολαμβάνειν καὶ ἄλλην τινὰ οὐσίαν εἶναι τῶν ὄντων, ᾗ οὔτε κίνησις ὑπάρχει οὔτε φθορὰ οὔτε γένεσις τὸ παράπαν. Damit wird Anerkennung für ein weites erst von Platon entdecktes Gebiet gefordert, auf dem die Behauptung des Widerspruchs von vornherein gar nicht aufkommen kann, das aber A. und D. mit ihren naturphilosophischen Konstruktionen direkt gar nicht betreten haben; wieder werden sie nicht primär betroffen. Aus dem ganzen Abschnitt können wir für Demokrit nichts weiter lernen, als was wir auch sonst wissen, daß Demokrit nämlich die Welt aus Atomen und Leerem zustandekommen ließ und dadurch in Konflikt mit Aristoteles' ὕλη-Begriff kam. Von ὂν αὐτὸ καθ᾽ αὑτό und „nur" φαινόμενον zu sprechen besteht bisher ebensowenig Veranlassung wie für Aristoteles selbst, denn zu dem Satz des Protagoras kommt Aristoteles erst wieder mit 1009b 1 ὁμοίως δὲ καὶ ἡ περὶ τὰ φαινόμενα ἀλήθεια ἐκ τῶν αἰσθητῶν ἐλήλυθεν. ἡ περὶ τὰ φ. ἀλ. bedeutet den Satz des Protagoras in der Formulierung πάντα τὰ φαινόμενα ἀληθῆ εἶναι. Es folgen die aus dem *Theaetet* bekannten Beweise für den Satz, die handgreiflich ἐκ τῶν αἰσθητῶν hergeholt sind, mit dem Ergebnis 1009b 9 ποῖα οὖν τούτων ἀληθῆ ἢ ψευδῆ, ἄδηλον· οὐδὲν γὰρ μᾶλλον τάδε ἢ τάδε ἀληθῆ, ἀλλ᾽ ὁμοίως. In dem einleitenden Satz bedeutet ἐνίοις nicht, daß andere von einer anderen Grundlage aus zu dem Satze gekommen wären, sondern daß nur ‚Einige' — eben Protagoras und wer sonst den Satz ganz in seinem Sinne brauchte — die Konsequenz gezogen haben (vgl. *de an.* 427b 3, wo in freilich nur verwandtem Zusammenhang der Satz ebenfalls als mögliche Konsequenz, die Einige— wieder Protagoras — gezogen haben, bezeichnet wird). Die Konsequenz, die diese Einigen ziehen, ist (1009a 9), es sei nicht zu bestimmen — auf dem Gebiet der αἰσθητά—, was wahr oder falsch sei, vielmehr sei alles in gleicher Weise wahr. L. | weist mit Recht darauf hin, daß die φαινόμενα offenbar der umfassendere Begriff sind. In der Tat, Aristoteles' Darstellung wäre sinnlos, wenn die περὶ τὰ φ. ἀλήθεια von ihren Urhebern nicht allgemein, sondern auf die αἰσθητά beschränkt gewesen wäre. Aber ihr gutes Gewissen für die allgemeine Behauptung leitet sich aus den an Hand der αἰσθητά geführten Beweisen her. Genau so stellt Platon die Sache im Theaetet hin. —Solche Beweise traut L. freilich weder dem Protagoras noch irgendeinem Vorsokratiker zu. Erst durch Aristoteles hätten die älteren Lehren den Anschein erhalten, „eine bereits sehr ausgebildete Form des Kriterienstreites vorauszusetzen" (90). Indessen der Wind, den an und für sich kalt oder nicht kalt zu denken, und der Wein, den an und für sich süß oder bitter zu denken, nach Protagoras Unsinn ist, und das γλυκύ, μηδενὶ δὲ γλυκύ und allgemein das αὐτὸ ἐφ᾽ αὑτοῦ

---

[15] Ungern unterdrücke ich den Vergleich mit dem *K*, den uns Jaeger leicht gemacht hat. Dort 1062b 12ff. ist es noch einfach, ohne die geistreichen Erweiterungen. Freilich, wenn aus 1062b 21f. herausgelesen wird, „daß es über die Entstehung des homo-mensura-Satzes zwei verschiedene Theorien gab", womit L. (37f.) nicht allein steht, statt daß das auch sprachlich einzig Mögliche erkannt wird, daß nämlich die gerade in eins genommene ὑπόληψις nun wieder in ihre beiden ursprünglichen Bestandteile zerfällt, dann ist wenig zu gewinnen.

τι, das denken zu wollen er den Menschen verbietet, sind als ganz handfeste Einzeldinge gedacht, sie sind in einem ganz groben Sinne transzendent und haben mit dem platonischen αὐτὸ ὃ ἔστι und dem aristotelischen τί ἦν εἶναι ursprünglich nichts zu schaffen, verdanken also die Möglichkeit, gedacht werden zu können, nicht „der" sokratischen Frage. Bei L. liegt eine Verwechslung vor, die die philologische Interpretation dauernd stört und es zu einem ernsthaften philosophiegeschichtlichen Ergebnis überhaupt nicht kommen läßt. Fahren wir in der genaueren Interpretation fort. Sie zwingt, Schritt für Schritt vorzugehen und anzuerkennen, daß im folgenden Demokrit zweimal vorkommt. Zunächst im unmittelbaren Anschluß an den oben zitierten Satz 1009 b 9—11. Danach hätte es keinen Sinn, auf dem Gebiet, von dem Protagoras seine Beweise hernahm, die eine Behauptung wahrer als die andere finden zu wollen. διὸ Δημόκριτός γέ φησιν ἤτοι οὐδὲν εἶναι ἀληθὲς ἢ ἡμῖν γ᾽ ἄδηλον. Hier meint L.: „Eigentlich doch ein sonderbarer Beleg für die These, daß ihnen ἀληθές = φαινόμενον gewesen sei" und geht dann ganz in die Irre. Das Einfache ist: Demokrit gehört nicht zu „ihnen", zu den ἔνιοι, die den Satz des Protagoras sagen, sondern er zieht auf Grund derselben Voraussetzungen eine Konsequenz, bei der sich der Ausdruck umkehrt. Damit wird unverkennbar, daß Demokrits Wahrheitsbegriff grob transzendent, auf die Dinge selbst bezogen ist, so wie Protagoras' Satz eine grobe Leugnung dieser Transzendenz war. ‚Entweder es ist nichts wahr, oder *uns* ist die Wahrheit *nicht* offenbar' ist, wie übrigens auch das γε bei Demokrits Namen andeutet, direkt Opposition zu dem Satze πάντων χρημάτων μέτρον ἐστὶν ἄνθρωπος, und der korrelate positive Sinn ist: Nur wenn man die Wahrheit als etwas den Menschen nicht Offenbares ansetzt, kann von ihr die Rede sein. Man lese die Fragmente B 6—10, und man wird zugeben, daß bei Aristoteles 1009 b 9—12 Demokrit auf Protagoras nicht nur in logischer, sondern in der ursprünglichen historischen Bezogenheit folgt; es ist also auch kein Zufall, daß von allen Vorsokratikern an dieser Stelle allein Demokrit steht.

Danach setzt Aristoteles mit einem ὅλως δὲ zu einer neuen Betrachtung an, in der nun Demokrit mit Empedokles und so gut wie ‚allen' — genannt werden noch Parmenides, Anaxagoras und Homer, den nach *de an.* 404 a 29 Demokrit selbst in diesen Zusammenhang gebracht hat — in einer Gruppe erscheint. Die Betrachtung schließt wirkungsvoll mit der Verzweiflung an der Möglichkeit der Wahrheitssuche, ‚wenn die größten Wahrheitssucher solche Meinungen von der Wahrheit haben und solche Behauptungen über sie aufstellen'. Was für Meinungen? Zuerst (b 12ff.) sehen sie protagoreisch aus, zuletzt (b 32ff.) heraklitisch und in dieser Richtung geht es dann 1010 a 1ff. weiter bis zum unfreiwillig komischen Extrem. Uns interessiert hier nur der | Anfang 1009 b 12—15. Kann von Demokrit gesagt werden: er begreift Wahrheitserfassung (φρόνησις) als identisch mit der sinnlichen Wahrnehmung, diese ist für ihn körperliche Veränderung, folglich sagt er, was in der Sinneswahrnehmung erscheint, ist zwangsweise wahr? Selbstverständlich kann Demokrit das sagen und muß es sogar ziemlich ausführlich gesagt haben[16], aus dieser Sachlage zog er ja die Schlüsse B 6—10, wie wir soeben gesehen haben. Man kann sagen, hier wäre das Problem der Transzendenz nicht gesehen, und es wäre unerlaubt und tadelnswert, das hier nicht zu sehen, aber man sollte nicht leugnen wollen, daß die Transzendenz der Dinge über unsere subjektive Auffassung hinweg in diesem Gedankenzusammenhang selbstverständliche primitive Voraussetzung ist. Darüber ist nicht einmal Aristoteles erhaben, vgl. die Auseinandersetzung 1010 b 30ff. Gewiß, es ist ziemlich primitiv. Und das soll erst Platon in die Welt gesetzt haben? Platon, der im *Theaetet* von einem im Gespräch nur durch den Hinweis auf ‚Parmenides' verratenen Stand-

---

[16] Natürlich nicht wörtlich. Wortwidersprüche, auf die nichts ankäme, bei Demokrit selbst nachzuweisen reicht unser Material nicht aus.

punkt aus das ihm fremde Bornierte und das weniger fremde Radikale mit gleicher Überlegenheit nebeneinander hinstellt? — Platon hat etwas anderes getan. Er hat mit seiner Ideenlehre das Denken und seine Objekte aus der Welt der sinnlichen Wahrnehmung herausgehoben; und er hat im ersten Teil des *Theaetet* die Verwirrung, die entsteht, wenn man Denken und sinnliche Wahrnehmung theoretisch vermengt, aufgezeigt. Das nimmt Aristoteles immer wieder auf, hat sich aber seinerseits eine Theorie der αἴσθησις gebildet, die auch diese über das Niveau der körperlichen Veränderung erhebt, und diese spielt er 1009 b 13 sachgemäß mit aus.

Auf den Vergleich mit *de an.* 427a 17ff. einzugehen muß der Rezensent sich versagen. Dort paßte Demokrit aus bestimmten Gründen nicht hinein. Dafür steht er speziell *de an.* 404a 27, mit dem Homerzitat. Hier haben wir für Demokrit dasselbe wie *Met.* 1009 b 15—30, aber *ohne* die Gleichung αἴσθησις — ἀλλοίωσις, die hier in περὶ ψυχῆς Aristoteles auch noch nicht bringen konnte, weil er die entsprechende Theorie noch nicht entwickelt hat. Es ist von νοῦς und φρονεῖν die Rede, ohne daß im besonderen an αἴσθησις gedacht würde und ohne daß darauf etwas ankäme. Weil für Demokrit das Wahre das Erscheinende ist, lobt er als guten Ausdruck das homerische ‚Andersdenken‘ für ‚Irredenken‘. Daraus wird aber nicht der Schluß gezogen: Also ist für Demokrit das Denken zwangsweise wahr (was doch *Met.* 1009 b 14 vom φαινόμενον κατὰ τὴν αἴσθησιν behauptet werden kann), sondern umgekehrt: also gebraucht Demokrit den νοῦς nicht als Vermögen der Wahrheit. Fragt man, woher die Möglichkeit dieses entgegengesetzt klingenden Schlusses? so ist zunächst darauf aufmerksam zu machen, daß hier nicht steht: für Demokrit ist alles Erscheinende wahr; für wen das gilt, der braucht nicht zu suchen; das ist Protagoras und nicht Demokrit. Dagegen läßt der Satz: das Wahre ist das Erscheinende, Spielraum für die Bedeutung, Demokrit sucht das Wahre in der Erscheinung (und nicht wo Platon und Aristoteles es suchen), und die ist richtig, vgl. 315b 9 ἐπεὶ δ᾽ ᾤοντο τἀληθὲς ἐν τῷ φαίνεσθαι, was auch gerade nicht bedeutet, daß Leukipp und Demokrit sich bei den φαινόμενα beruhigten. Sodann ist auch die Konsequenz, die gezogen wird, nicht Konsequenzmacherei, sondern ehrliche Auslegung: Demokrit kann wirklich keinen νοῦς und kein φρονεῖν geglaubt haben, denen die Wahrheit unmittelbar zugänglich wäre.

Das Denken hat keinen eigenen Weg zur Wahrheit, die Wahrheit liegt im φαίνεσθαι, aber das Denken beruhigt sich nicht ohne weitere Umstände bei den φαινόμενα, sondern es hat an ihnen mancherlei auszusetzen (315b 10), und es ist erst zufrieden, wenn es etwas gemacht hat (315b 7 ποιήσαντες τὰ σχήματα usw.), was seinen Ansprüchen genügt und zu den φαινόμενα stimmt (325a 23). So gibt Aristoteles die Sache wieder, wenn er schildert, wie es bei Leukipp und Demokrit aussah. Daß diese einfache und natürliche Schilderung einen Kantianer zur Begeisterung bringen kann, braucht uns doch nicht zu bestimmen, sie zu verschmähen. Denn erkenntnistheoretische Bedenken oder Gedanken machte sich Demokrit, soviel wir wissen, in diesem Punkte allerdings nicht. Was es da bei ihm gab, war einmal, allgemein-theoretisch, ein harmloser Ärzteglaube an das normale Denken, den uns Theophrast, wo er das ‚Homer‘-Zitat im ursprünglichen Zusammenhang bringt (*de sens.* § 58), glücklicherweise erhalten hat, und zum andern, in eigener Sache, war es der für seine Zeit gerechtfertigte Glaube, daß die Atomlehre durch die φαινόμενα ‚bewiesen‘ würde. Darauf muß hier zum Schluß noch eingegangen werden.

Nach Sextus Emp. 7, 140 (Vors. 59 B 21a) hat Demokrit den Anaxagoras gelobt wegen seines Ausspruches ὄψις τῶν ἀδήλων τὰ φαινόμενα. Einen weiten Überblick über den Anwendungsbereich dieses Satzes verdanken wir Hans Diller (Hermes 67, 1932, 14—42). Diller verneint die Möglichkeit, Beweisformen, ,,deren Grundzug weder analogisch, noch semeiotisch im ärztlichen Sinn, sondern logisch und eristisch ist", in den Anwendungsbereich einzubeziehen. Ursprung (Melissos) und Eigenart auch dieser dritten Argumentationsweise werden in dem Aufsatz anschaulich geschildert, und es ist keine Frage, daß das von Aristoteles angegebene Gesamtverfahren der Atomistik ihr verwandt ist, und so scheint nach Dillers Aufsatz auch dies Gesamtverfahren nicht in den Anwendungsbereich zu gehören. An L.s Einwand (48) ist soviel richtig, daß der Satz dann nicht charakteristisch für Anaxagoras und Demokrit sein würde. L.s eigene Deutung, die durch eine m. E. sinnstörende Sperrung ,,*Sehen* des Unsichtbaren" herausbringen will, was nicht herauszubringen ist, braucht nicht mehr diskutiert zu werden. Ich selbst finde eigentlich keine Schwierigkeit für die Anwendung des Satzes gerade auf Demokrits Gesamtverfahren. Der Fortschritt der Atomistik über Melissos hinaus macht aus dessen Beweisverfahren das Umgekehrte und mehr. Bei Melissos ein versuchsweises Sichidentifizieren mit dem Augenschein, Konsequenzmacherei und daraufhin Widerspruch gegen den Augenschein; bei der Atomistik steht der Widerspruch am Anfang, dann schöpferisches Denken (das Denken ,macht' etwas), und dann kann der Augenschein bleiben, wie | er ist, ja eventuell zur Bestätigung dienen. Für Anaxagoras dürfen wir Ähnliches ansetzen, und dann hätten wir die Situation, die sein Wort voraussetzt. Es braucht nämlich nur die Möglichkeit in Zweifel gezogen zu sein, über Dinge, die unterhalb oder außerhalb der Wahrnehmungsgrenzen liegen, sichere Behauptungen aufzustellen, weil man die ja nicht verifizieren könnte, dann ist dem Rechtfertigungsversuch der Denkfaulheit mit dem Satze die einzig schlagende Antwort erteilt. Gegen solches Verifizieren durch die φαινόμενα kann allerdings der Logiker — ausnahmsweise wirklich nur der Logiker — einwenden: ja, wenn es nicht das ἐκ ψεύδους ἀληθὲς δεῖξαι gäbe (Ar. 78a 6—10)! Aber das ist erst eine Klarstellung der aristotelischen Logik, auf die Aristoteles mit Recht stolz war. Hiergegen kann die Wissenschaft das Experiment setzen: dies, kompliziert durch die Rolle der Mathematik, die hier beiseite bleiben muß: dann wird die Sache modern. Dabei muß noch auf den folgenreichen Unterschied zwischen Anaxagoras (Empedokles) und Demokrit hingewiesen werden, der darin besteht, daß Demokrit den Satz des Protagoras soweit annahm, daß das Unerklärliche an den ,sekundären Qualitäten' nicht etwa für unerklärlich erklärt, sondern einfach aus der wissenschaftlichen Be-

trachtung eliminiert wurde[17], die es nun viel leichter hatte, wissen-
schaftlich zu sein. — Einfacher geht es mit ,,vorsokratisch" — ,,nach-
platonisch". Man versucht es mit der Behauptung (95), ,,daß den
Vorsokratikern überhaupt der Rekurs auf eine objektive Instanz ganz
fernlag". Und Xenophanes B 34? Hatte der nicht gewisse — unbe-
friedigte oder befriedigte, darauf kommt es hier nicht an — Bedürfnisse
in dieser Richtung? Keine Spur! ,,Ein Gegensatz zwischen γνώμη
und ὄψις ist nirgends angedeutet" hören wir auf S. 45. Und περὶ
ἀρχαίης ἰητρικῆς Kap. 1: διὸ οὐκ ἠξίουν αὐτὴν ἔγωγε καινῆς ὑποθέσιος
δεῖσθαι, ὥσπερ τὰ ἀφανέα τε καὶ ἀπορεόμενα, περὶ ὧν ἀνάγκη, ἤν τις
ἐπιχειρῇ τι λέγειν, ὑποθέσει χρῆσθαι, οἷον περὶ τῶν μετεώρων ἢ τῶν
ὑπὸ γῆν· ἃ εἴ τις λέγοι καὶ γινώσκοι ὡς ἔχει, οὔτ' ἂν αὐτῷ τῷ λέγοντι
οὔτε τοῖς ἀκούουσι δῆλα ἂν εἴη, εἴτε ἀληθέα ἐστὶν εἴτε μή· οὐ γὰρ ἔστι,
πρὸς ὅτι χρὴ ἀνενέγκαντα εἰδέναι τὸ σαφές. ἰητρικῇ δὲ πάλαι πάντα
ὑπάρχει . . .? — Das ist nachplatonisches Denken, werden wir zu hören
bekommen; das steht schon in der Einleitung (9f.). |

Der Referent glaubt nicht an das abgekürzte Verfahren. Und doch
geschähe dem Verf. des Buches Unrecht, wenn man sein Bemühen als
unwissenschaftlich bezeichnen wollte. Er wirft keine überflüssigen
Fragen auf, wo die Wissenschaft die zu fordernde Antwort schon gegeben hätte. Auf die Frische der wissenschaftlichen Orientierung und
der wissenschaftlichen Fragestellung einzugehen, kann der Wissenschaft nur gut tun. Deswegen hat sich der Rezensent viele Mühe gegeben, deutlich zu machen, worum es sich handelt, auf die Gefahr hin,
sehr deutlich zu werden und viel Gutes zu unterschlagen. Es geschah,
um das Beste an dem Buch, die berechtigten wissenschaftlichen Forde-
rungen, nicht zu unterschlagen.

---

[17] Vom erkenntnistheoretischen νόμῳ zu sprechen hat der Rezensent keine Gelegenheit, weil L. sie nicht gibt. L. spricht viel vom νόμος auf politischem und ethischem Gebiet und beruft sich für seine Auffassung auf Stier, der sich auf Reinhardt beruft. Das würde für das erkenntnistheoretische νόμῳ bedeuten, was wir
von Reinhardt gelernt haben. Hoffentlich hat L. nicht beabsichtigt, es preis-
zugeben. ,,Jetzt" werden wir auf eine Leipziger philosophische Dissertation von
1933 verwiesen (112 Anm.), in der dem Demokrit möglichst wenig zuleide getan
werden soll und wo man unmöglich finden kann, was man nach L.s Verweisung
suchen müßte.

Πισθέταιρος

1929

„Unerträglich, daß der ‚Treufreund' immer wieder spukt. Wem ist er denn treu, wem Freund?" (U. v Wilamowitz-Moellendorff, Lesefrüchte 234, Hermes 63, 1928, 372 Anm. 1). Und doch tut die Rüge wenigstens Schroeders Ausgabe der *Vögel* Unrecht. Freilich die Bemerkung zum Personenverzeichnis: „Für | Goethes ‚Treufreund' (‚guter Kamerad', die Zuverlässigkeit selber!) fällt ins Gewicht, daß dem ‚geriebenen Fuchs' (430) in der Selbstvorstellung (644) die Biedermannsmiene besonders gut steht" scheint nur das alte Bedenken, ‚Treufreund' passe nicht zum *Charakter*, wenig zwingend in das Gegenteil verkehren zu wollen; aber im Kommentar zu 644 heißt es: „Der Name Pisth. wächst hier unmittelbar aus dem Gang der Handlung heraus (545ff. 637), nur für den Augenblick ersonnen, wenn auch später als Rufname (ohne Nebenklang) bequem". Das Richtige würde vielleicht noch klarer herausgekommen sein, wenn insbesondere auf die Verse 629—635 hingewiesen wäre.

Wie müßte man 644 ‚Peithetairos' deuten? Gewiß, der Athener hat die Vögel für seinen Plan zu gewinnen vermocht, aber solange er ihnen gegenüber das πείθειν üben mußte, waren er und sie noch nicht Genossen, sie mußten es erst werden (627); dann aber ordnen sich die Vögel ihm als Haupt der Verschwörung so selbstverständlich unter (636f.), daß künftig ein πείθειν sich erübrigt. Auf das Verhältnis zu den Vögeln paßt dieser Name als Ganzes weder so noch so. Wer also für die Form Πειθ- oder Πεισέταιρος eintritt, kann die Wahl des Namens nur auf das Verhältnis zu ‚Euelpides' beziehen und wird sich dafür auf V. 339f. berufen, wo wir es ja gern hinnehmen, daß derjenige von den beiden Athenern, der im Stück selbst erst mit dem φεῦ φεῦ 162 deutlich die führende Rolle übernehmen kann, nun von jeher so zu dem Gefährten gestanden haben soll. Aber 339 hat er den Namen noch gar nicht (so auch Wilamowitz, Ar. Lysistrate 1927, 127f.), und in der Situation 644 entbehrt das Verhältnis der beiden Athener zueinander jeder Aktualität.

Wir würden so ziemlich das Wichtigste preisgeben, was wir über das Wesen der alten Komödie zugelernt haben, wollten wir uns dazu verstehen, gleichwohl die erst für die Verse 644f. gebildeten Namen der beiden Athener unabhängig von der momentanen Situation des

Stückes aus ihren differenzierten „Charakteren" zu erklären. Die Situation ist hier aber die, daß die Vögel 629 ff. in ihrer Begeisterung das Gelingen des Plans einzig und allein von der einen Bedingung abhängig fühlen:

> ἐὰν σὺ παρ' ἐμὲ θέμενος ὁμόφρονας λόγους
> δίκαιος ἄδολος ὅσιος ἐπὶ θεοὺς ἴῃς
> ἐμοὶ φρονῶν ξυνῳδά . . . (631 ff.).

Wie soll nun der heißen, auf dessen ehrliches Mittun somit alles ankommt? Leicht zu sagen (643): Πισθέταιρος. Auch der Name ‚Euelpides' wirkt in diesem Zusammenhang lediglich als gutes Omen. —

In einer Zeit, in der man die Orthographie πιστος-επεισθην *lernen* mußte, war für einen mit πισθ- beginnenden Namen die | Schreibung -ει- geradezu vorbestimmt, womit nicht bestritten werden soll, daß an sich Entstehung aus der Variante πειθ- und πεισ- auch denkbar wäre.

The Theory of Ideas in Plato's Earlier Dialogues

Nach 1942

I. Plato's Original View of Ideas

There is no need for a special justification if this book attempts to contribute to a solution of the much discussed problems of Plato's theory of ideas by taking first things first. To-day, we are entitled to deal separately with the theory of ideas such as it is presented in Plato's earlier dialogues and may well try to determine Plato's original view of ideas as opposed to a later stage of development. For from Plato's self-testimony in *Parmenides* (130a ff.) we know now that in its initial form the theory of ideas was not yet concerned seriously with as many things as later on. Accordingly, with regard to the problem of what kind of ideas were, chronologically, first in Plato's mind, we do not depend any longer on guesswork and genetic constructions entirely our own.

Scholars found themselves in a different and rather desperate situation before reasonable methods of observation of style and language had established a reliable relative chronology between three main groups of the Platonic writings. It is true that a mechanical handling of "stylometry" or "Sprachstatistik" still threatens to obscure the clear result of the observations of Campbell, Dittenberger, Blass and some others; nevertheless we may take it for granted that the *Sophistes, Politicus, Timaeus, Critias, Philebus*, some genuine *Letters* and the *Laws* were written later than all the other genuine Platonic dialogues, and that the *Republic, Phaedrus, Parmenides* and *Theaetetus* form a middle group, whereas the *Apology* and the remaining dialogues belong to an earlier period of Plato's literary work[1]. Thanks to this discovery of the relative chronology of groups of Plato's writings we see now that at the comparatively late time of the *Parmenides* Plato himself was aware of an early and a later form of the theory of ideas, and fortunately it is easy now to trace their difference in the comparatively early and late dialogues.

The passage of the *Parmenides* that has become so important runs as follows, in Jowett's translation (*Parm.* 130a).

---

[1] It is practically certain, too, although not merely for external reasons — that this first stylistic period ended with the *Phaedon, Symposion, Lysis* and *Cratylus*.

(Socrates, who is described as still a very young man, after listening to a lecture of Zeno, has offered the theory of ideas as a solution of the Eleatic problems.)

"While Socrates was speaking, Pythodorus thought that Parmenides and Zeno were not altogether pleased at the successive steps of the argument; but still they gave the closest attention, and often looked at one another, and smiled as if in admiration of him. When he had finished, Parmenides expressed their feelings in the following words: —

"Socrates, he said, I admire the bent of your mind towards philosophy; tell me now, was this your own distinction between ideas in themselves and the things which partake in them? and do you think that there is an idea of likeness apart from the likeness which we possess, and of the one and the many, and of the other things which Zeno mentioned?"

"I think that there are such ideas, said Socrates."

"Parmenides proceeded: And would you also make absolute ideas of the just and the beautiful and the good, and of all that class?"

"Yes, he said, I should."

"And would you make an idea of man apart from us and from all other human creatures, or of fire and water?"

"I am often undecided, as to whether I ought to include them or not."

"And would you feel equally undecided, Socrates, about things of which the mention may provoke a smile? — I mean such things as hair, mud, dirt, or anything else which is vile and paltry; would you suppose that each of these has an idea distinct from the actual objects with which we come into contact, or not?"

"Certainly not, said Socrates; visible things like these are such as they appear to us, and I am afraid that there would be an absurdity in assuming any idea of them, although I sometimes get disturbed, and begin to think that there is nothing without an idea; but then again, when I have taken up this position, I run away, because I am afraid that I may fall into a bottomless pit of nonsense, and perish; and so I return to the ideas of which I was just now speaking, and occupy myself with them."

"Yes, Socrates, said Parmenides; that is because you are still young; the time will come, if I am not mistaken, when philosophy will have a firmer grasp of you, and then you will not despise even the meanest things; at your age, you are too much disposed to regard the opinions of men." — — — And then, suddenly, Parmenides raises his objections against the doctrine of ideas. These objections (*Parm.* 130e—134e) anticipate some of Aristotle's famous arguments, which we probably should accept as final, if the dialogue *Parmenides* did not show that they were familiar to Plato himself without, however, shaking his belief in 'ideas' (see *Parm.* 135a—136a).

From the passage quoted above in Jowett's translation we learn, firstly, that at the time of the *Parmenides* Plato distinguished between a limited theory of ideas applied only to predications like similar, one, many and so on, just, beautiful, good and so on, and a more universal theory applied also to things like man, fire, water and even hair, mud, dirt and so on. Secondly, the distinction was not made by Plato merely from a systematic point of view, but it has chronological importance. The first set of ideas pointed out in the *Parmenides* corresponds exactly to the doctrine that is set forth or presupposed in the *Phaedo*, the *Symposion*, and in parts of the *Republic*, whereas ideas of things like man, fire, water and so on were discussed not earlier than in the *Parmenides* itself, in the *Timaeus* and the *Philebus*, all of which are later than the *Phaedo* and the *Republic*. Thirdly, and this is most important for our present purpose, it is clearly stated that a daring universal theory of ideas including things like man, fire, water is much more entangled with difficulties and exposed to objections than the more modest and diffident theory of the first stage.

As to the objections raised by the Parmenides of the dialogue, Julius Stenzel cleared the way for a consistent interpretation[2]. Are the objections meant as an attack on the early limited form? According to the preceding part of the dialogue we might, indeed, expect just this. But such an attack ought to be entirely different from what we really read. The distinction between probable and improbable ideas made by the young Socrates ought to have been stressed and discussed; and the result would have been either that the timid halfhearted thesis had to be abandoned or that it had to be transformed into a universal theory. But, instead of discussing Socrates' temporary convictions and scruples, Parmenides simply predicts a universal theory of ideas for the future, and his argument is concerned with difficulties that, as Stenzel has seen, could become actual and all-important only after this development had taken place. Thus, the objections do not represent the reasons that compelled Plato to

---

[2] Studien zur Entwicklung der platonischen Dialektik, Breslau, 1917. The main thesis of this book, according to which a Platonic idea is originally dependent on and almost an equivalent to an intuition of *arete* has become part of the creed of the so-called 'third humanism'. An English translation made from the second German edition of 1931 appeared 1940 at the Clarendon Press, Oxford; the English title is: Plato's Method of Dialectic.

transform his earlier theory, as some interpreters[3] would like to make us believe; on the contrary, the objections point out difficulties Plato had to face when his earlier theory, which was confined mainly to objects of ethical or moral interest, already had been changed and extended to different kinds of things and especially to objects of natural science.

There seems to be no doubt, then, that in Plato's sight the original stage of the theory of ideas had been the easier one to understand, at least for the beginner; and accordingly a modern reader or interpreter might well expect to find comparatively little difficulty in trying to understand or explain the original theory of ideas first. But if we think so, we have to quit Stenzel's company and from now on to go our own way. Stenzel believed that the history of Greek philosophy was characterized by a very slowly but continuously proceeding disentanglement of formal logic from the mythical and metaphysical ingredients of the primitive attitude of the human mind[4], and thus we find him stating on the very first page of his 'Studien' as follows (English edition p. 23): "The most important result of such an inquiry will be that Plato's discovery of the concept comes at the end rather than at the beginning of his evolution" ("Als wichtigstes Ergebnis stellt sich hierbei heraus, daß der 'Begriff' nicht am Anfang, sondern am Ende der platonischen Entwicklung steht"); "the view which finds in the theory of Ideas a consistent and comprehensive doctrine of the Concept must be rejected as a survival of the obsolete treatment of Plato as a systematic philosopher in the modern sense of the word — equally whether the concepts are held to be *substantialized*, or are interpreted as 'rules of method'" ("die Ideenlehre im Sinne einer einheitlichen, allgemeinen — gleichviel ob 'hypostasierten' oder 'methodischen' — Begriffslehre ist demnach als ein Rudiment überwundener Ansichten vom platonischen 'System' anzusehen"). On page 29 (Engl. p. 55) we are informed (concerning the problems of the *Parmenides*): "Plato does not ha e to fight his way to the Idea — that comes naturally to his spirit — but to something that seems to the modern mind vastly simpler — to the concept" ("Er ringt — nicht um die Idee, die ist seinem Geiste gemäß — sondern er ringt um den uns so viel einfacher erscheinenden Begriff"), and on page 14 the term "archaisches Denken" occurs (the English translation has

---

[3] Esp. H. Jackson, whose series of articles on "Plato's Later Theory of Ideas" in the Journal of Philology (10. 11. 13. 14. 16, 1882—1888) has certainly given a new impulse to Platonic studies.

[4] See Stenzel's article "Logik" in Pauly-Wissowa RE XIII, 1927, 991 ff. and E. Kapp's article "Syllogistik", RE IV A, 1931, 1046 ff.

only 'ancient thinkers', p. 38)[5]. We see, Stenzel was convinced that at the beginning of Plato's philosophical work our simplest logical notions were as strange to his mind as "Ideas" seem to be to the modern mind and that accordingly what is the easiest thing to us was the most difficult to Plato and vice versa.

At the moment I have to oppose to this approach to Plato's ideas merely a prejudice of my own. I do not believe that thinking can be done by different means, and on principle I profess a preference for any explanation of Plato that does not require a suspension of plain logic in order to understand imaginary ways of archaic thought. Of course, an appeal to a prejudice does not mean a decision, but in this case it makes at least a clear issue; the point in question will be simply, whether we shall be able to come to a direct and comparatively easy understanding of Plato's original assumption of 'ideas' or not.

It is fairly certain to-day which of the dialogues we have to search in the first place for a comparatively easy aspect of 'ideas' because of chronology and contents: the *Symposion* and the *Phaedo*. Both of them are earlier than the *Republic*, and the *Cratylus*, which, indeed, has to be mentioned here, obviously presupposes some passages of the *Symposion* and the *Phaedo* and on the other hand is presupposed in the tenth Book of the *Republic*.

As is well known, the *Symposion* deals only with one Idea, the Idea of the Beautiful; but it might seem, as if at once we get a strictly negative reply to our naive questioning; for when Diotima comes to speak about the Beautiful in its purity, she doubts whether Socrates will be able to follow her words, because the thing is so very difficult to grasp. This famous passage of the *Symposion* would induce even me to try the methods of our modern historians of Mind, if the *Phaedo*, which certainly was almost contemporaneous with the *Symposion*, did not present the matter under quite a different aspect.

This dialogue mentions again and again a multitude of Ideas, and amongst them the Idea of the Beautiful — beside the Ideas of the Just and the Good 'and so on' — but the doctrine is not referred to as if it were something new or difficult to understand. On the contrary, all

---

[5] In his article "Logik", which appeared ten years later than the "Studien", Stenzel summarized his opinion as follows (Col. 1005, 1. 41—52): „Das Formal-Logische, überhaupt der Begriff, steht am Ende der platonischen Entwicklung; am Anfange sind die logischen Mittel, mit denen Platon arbeitet und die ihm entgegentretenden Fragen zu bewältigen sucht, höchst komplizierte Gebilde gestalthaften Charakters; die Idee, weit entfernt davon, hypostasierter Begriff zu sein, ist im Gegenteil ein archaischer Denktypus von ganz bestimmter, mit unsern modernen Denkmitteln — am wenigsten mit einer vagen modernen Intuition — nicht ohne weiteres zu erfassender und zu beschreibender logischer Funktion."

who are present on the day of Socrates' death are acquainted with it and need only to be reminded of it, when Socrates takes it as a basis for some of his arguments for the immortality of the soul.

The following passages illustrate the way in which the *Phaedo* refers to the doctrine of ideas:

Phd. 65d (first mention of ideas): "And what about this: Do we assume something that is the just itself or do we not assume such a thing ?" — "Certainly we do, by God." — "And again something that is beautiful in this sense and good ?" — "Of course."

Phd. 74a: "And shall we proceed a step further, and affirm that there is such a thing as equality (φαμέν πού τι εἶναι ἴσον) not of one piece of wood or stone with another, but that, over and above this (παρὰ πάντα ταῦτα), there is an absolute equality (ἕτερόν τι, αὐτὸ τὸ ἴσον) ? Shall we say so ?" — "Say so, yes, replied Simmias, and swear to it, with all the confidence in life. —"

Phd. 77a: "There is nothing which to my mind is so patent" (replies one of Socrates' interlocutors) "as that beauty (καλόν), goodness (ἀγαθόν), and the other notions of which you were just now speaking, have a most real and absolute existence."

Phd. 100b: "first of all I assume that there is an absolute beauty (τι καλὸν αὐτὸ καθ' αὐτό) and goodness (ἀγαθόν) and greatness (μέγα), and the like; grant me this, and I hope to be able to show you the nature of the cause, and to prove the immortality of the soul." — Cebes said: "You may proceed at once with the proof, for I grant you this."

Phd. 102a: "After all this had been admitted, and they had agreed that ideas exist (εἶναί τι ἕκαστον τῶν εἰδῶν), and that other things (τἄλλα) participate in them and derive their names from them, Socrates, if I remember rightly, said: — . . .[6]"

We should be at a loss to reconcile the different views of ideas in the *Symposion* and in the *Phaedo*, if Plato himself had not stated expressly that the method of Ideas followed in the *Phaedo* was a particularly modest, cautious and safe way of explaining things, and by no means must be confounded with the question of the ultimate cause of what is good in the physical as well as in the moral world (*Phd.* 99d—102a). Now, while in the *Phaedo* Socrates' anticipation of a science founded on cognition of the ultimate cause is strictly distinguished from the doctrine of Ideas, this distinction does not

---

[6] In the same way 'ideas' are mentioned at the end of the dialogue *Cratylus*: *Crat.* 439c: "There is a matter, master Cratylus, about which I often dream, and I should like to ask your opinion: Tell me, whether there is or is not any absolute beauty or good (τι . . . αὐτὸ καλὸν καὶ ἀγαθόν) or any other absolute existence ? — Certainly, Socrates, I think so."

appear any longer in Plato's treatment of the ultimate source of beauty in the *Symposion* and of the ultimate source of goodness in the *Republic*; and in consequence here the cognition of either the Idea of the beautiful or the Idea of the good is said to be the greatest and most difficult task to which the human mind may aspire (*Symp.* 210a—212a, *Rep.* 505a). Thus, then, we may be sure that it is the *Phaedo* which presents the doctrine of Ideas in a less complicated, easier and earlier form, and that it is *this* form of the doctrine which we have to consider, if we want to understand Plato's original view of 'ideas'.

The fundamental thesis of Plato's theory of ideas consists from the very beginning in the assertion that a single idea as such is something apart and different from all the many subjects which occur in common life and which may take, in the common usage of language, the name of the Idea as their proper predicate. I have to quote again the passage *Phd.* 74a, which begins one of the most striking sections in the *Phaedo*; but this time it seems necessary to replace Jowett's translation by a more exact and simpler one: " Do we not assume" asks Socrates "that there is something equal, not a piece of wood to another piece of wood or a stone to another stone and the like, but beside all these things something else, the equal itself (ἀλλὰ παρὰ ταῦτα πάντα ἕτερόν τι, αὐτὸ τὸ ἴσον) ?" — "Certainly we do assume this, most decidedly." — "And do we know it what it is ?" — "Absolutely." There can be no doubt that Plato wrote the *Phaedo* in the conviction that he possessed striking evidence for certain 'ideas' separate from the common things called by the names of these ideas; and on the other hand, there can also be no doubt that it was just this being something else beside the many things, this being παρὰ ταῦτα πάντα ἕτερόν τι, that was rejected by Aristotle not only as inconceivable but as quite superfluous for the purpose of thinking and of arguing about the things of the real world and real life. This is the locus classicus in Aristotle's *Second Analytica* (77a 5): "That there be Ideas or the one beside the many things (εἴδη μὲν οὖν εἶναι ἢ ἕν τι παρὰ τὰ πολλά), is not necessary for the sake of argumentation; what is necessary is only that it may be true to predicate one thing *of* many things (ἓν κατὰ πολλῶν). For otherwise there will be no universal predication (τὸ καθόλου), and if this is not, there will be no terminus medius, and, failing this, there will be no demonstration."

Now, fortunately, just these two expressions of which Aristotle makes use in order to signify what he himself judges to be the necessary logical conditions of all sound demonstrations, the ἓν κατὰ πολλῶν and the καθόλου, appear in that Platonic dialogue which as a whole comes nearest to the doctrines of the *Phaedo* without yet having established a theory of Ideas: the *Meno*[7]. The ἓν κατὰ πολλῶν we find in 73d: "What else could virtue be but the power of governing mankind, if you are looking for something that is one and the same and applies to all of them (sc. all men who may be called ἀγαθοί) — εἴπερ ἕν γέ τι ζητεῖς κατὰ πάντων". And the καθόλου we find a little later in the *Meno* (77a). "And now, in your turn, you are to fulfill your promise, and tell me what virtue is in the universal" (literally, 'telling me about virtue as a whole what it is' — κατὰ ὅλου εἰπὼν ἀρετῆς πέρι ὅτι ἐστίν). Without going into further detail I venture to assert that all the *Meno*'s examples of definitions and attempts at definitions do not presuppose anything but the simplest rules of plain logic. Certainly there is nothing in the *Meno* to indicate that the object of a question like: what is a bee, what is color, what is virtue, is a mysterious something, apart and different from the many common things called bees, colors, virtues and so on. There are no postulates in the *Meno* regarding definitions and their objects that Aristotle or we ourselves should hesitate to accept; on the contrary, it seems very probable that Aristotle's and our own notions of an orderly definition are derived to a large extent directly from the *Meno* and the one or other closely related Platonic dialogues, like the *Laches* or *Charmides*.

This very simple statement of the presence of plain logic and of the absence of the specific characteristic of the Platonic theory of ideas in the early dialogues concerned with the definition of human virtue or virtues, viz. the *Meno*, the *Laches* and the *Charmides*, to which we may add the *Protagoras* also, is important because of the scientific situation created by Stenzel's Studies. According to Stenzel the logical means which Plato applied, in the beginning, when he attempted a solution of the logical questions occurring to him, were not the simple rules of plain elementary logic, but "höchst komplizierte Gebilde gestalthaften Charakters"; the meaning of this is that not only the first examples of Platonic ideas were complex entities like the virtues of men or other beings or things, but that such complex structures dominated even the method of Plato's early reasonings and argumentations. Now, this is simply not true. The logical means applied by Plato throughout the earlier dialogues concerned with human virtue are not different from the simple rules of Aristotelian and our own logic; it is just because these rules are set forth and applied that human virtue becomes a grave problem. On the one hand, for instance, it is evident that before discussing questions like whether

---

[7] In *Phd.* 72e Plato refers so openly to what had been said in the *Meno* that there can be no doubt about the relative chronology of these two dialogues.

virtue is teachable, one should have an answer to what virtue itself is; and, on the other hand, after a little elementary logical training, unexpected difficulties of ascertaining what virtue is arise.

Obviously, it is neither true nor does it make sense to say that these problems resulted from applying archaic logical means that were essentially identical with and specially adapted to the virtues under discussion; and yet this is implied in Stenzel's theory of the development of Plato's dialectic. — The difficulty of finding an answer to the question of wherein human virtue consists was not a result of Plato's having no notion of a plain concept and therefore putting his questions in an archaic way — which he did not do — but, as we may learn from the *Republic*, this difficulty was created merely by the very complicated nature of the subject. In order to give a reply to the question of what human virtue is, or human virtues are, Plato found it necessary to write large parts of his main work, where he had to build up a whole picture of human society and to construct the human soul out of its different parts and, finally, even to explain his theory of ideas. But there is no need of recurring to 'ideas' (instead of concepts), if we want to understand the method of questioning in the early dialogues concerned with the problem of human virtue; on the contrary, the closer one clings to the Platonic texts, the clearer one will see that the thing to be derived from this kind of dialectic is not more and not less but just the elementary notion of a 'concept' and the correct definition. —

Beside the problem of the possibility of teaching virtue the *Meno* raises the question of the possibility of enlarging human knowledge by research. As is well known, Plato's reply in the *Meno* is strictly in the affirmative; he demonstrates the fact of acquiring new knowledge by means of the mathematical episode with the young slave of Meno, and he shows a way of explaining this fact by his famous theory of anamnesis; but, again, in the *Meno* he does not recur to the characteristic of Ideas, viz. of being something apart from all things of the sensible world. Only the *Phaedo*, while quoting directly the earlier doctrine of the *Meno*, introduces as a new argument for the pre-existence of the soul that Ideas are not found in this world of the senses nor are merely abstracted from sensible things and that accordingly they must have been accessible to the mind in a previous state of life. The primitive doctrine of anamnesis, as given in the *Meno*, would not even have been compatible with urging a fundamental difference between the knowledge carried along by the soul into this life and the data of the senses that occur to it during this life.

If now we turn back to *Phaedo*, the difficulty is that this dialogue does not demonstrate but rather presupposes some kind of theory of ideas. But the thesis itself is given repeatedly with fair clearness and strictness of terminology. One may formulate it briefly thus: We are convinced that words like equal, big, small, one, two, and so on, and words like good, beautiful, just, pious, and so on, have a meaning of their own, and that what is meant by them has an existence each of its own, and that it is not only allowed but necessary for all dialectical purposes to distinguish this meaning or this entity from all the subjects of common life that may take those words as predicates. The distinction is expressed by an additional "itself", as for instance: the equal itself (and not an equal stone or piece of wood), the beautiful itself (and not a beautiful face, man, horse or garment), the just itself (and not a certain just action). In order to point out this difference of 'ideas' from common things more explicitly Plato coined the formula ὃ ἔστιν, of which a translation is scarcely possible. As is shown by certain passages, the ὃ ἔστιν was first merely the correlate of the dialectical question τί ἐστιν; and in this case it signifies that which makes a thing what it is and accordingly is involved in the knowledge of the thing and belongs to its definition[8]. But already in the *Phaedo* the ὅ is occasionally taken not as predicate noun equivalent but as subject of the clause, for instance αὐτὸ τὸ ὃ ἔστιν ἴσον (*Phd.* 74d) instead of αὐτὸ τὸ ἴσον ὃ ἔστιν (74b), and then we have to acknowledge the very peculiar and captious signification of an entity that *is* a certain predicate absolutely as a definiendum *is* its definition[9].

It is by no means asserted that every participant of the dialogue might be able to give a satisfying answer to all the questions implied in this terminology, for instance to the question of what the just is by itself; on the contrary, there is a hint (76b) that after the death of Socrates perhaps no man would be left who could do this in an effective way; the participants agree unanimously only upon this that we are bound to assume separate entities corresponding to such questioning. This is exactly what Cratylus at the end of the dialogue *Cratylus* concedes without hesitation to Socrates[10] and what in the dialogue *Euthydemus* may even serve as basis for a cheap paralogism (not, indeed, without an unmistakable hint at the real philosophical

---

[8] 65d λέγω περὶ πάντων . . . τῆς οὐσίας ὃ τυγχάνει ἕκαστον ὄν, cf. *Meno* 72c ἐκεῖνο δηλῶσαι, ὃ τυγχάνει οὖσα ἀρετή. — *Phd.* 74b ἦ καὶ ἐπιστάμεθα αὐτὸ ὃ ἔστιν [sc. αὐτὸ τὸ ἴσον].

[9] *Phd.* 75b: πάντα τὰ ἐν ταῖς αἰσθήσεσιν ἐκείνου ὀρέγεται τοῦ ὃ ἔστιν ἴσον (but immediately following εἰληφότας ἐπιστήμην αὐτοῦ τοῦ ἴσου ὅτι ἔστιν). *Crat.* 389b οὐκοῦν ἐκεῖνο δικαιότατ' ἂν αὐτὸ ὃ ἔστι κερκὶς καλέσαιμεν; The next step is the outspoken statement that the ὃ ἔστιν means absolute, independent existence: *Rep.* 597a.

[10] See p. 60 n. 6.

importance of the distinction between the many beautiful things and the beautiful itself)[11].

As far as I can see only so much can be found in the text of the *Phaedo* concerning the original assumption of separate ideas; for, the repeated statement that such ideas cannot be perceived with the senses of the body is obviously an addition to the original view, made up and stressed in connection with the new arguments for the immortality of the soul. So we have to look elsewhere for a mental situation, from which the fundamental conviction that we are bound to state separate ideas may be derived. In the whole of Plato's written work I have found only two dialogues which may be said to bridge the gap between an earlier stage of his philosophy and the theories of the *Phaedo*, viz. the *Euthyphro* and the *Major Hippias*. I restrict myself to a consideration of the decisive passage of the *Euthyphro* for the sake of brevity and clearness, and also because the question of the authenticity of the *Hippias* is as yet by no means settled. Incidentally, the *Euthyphro* seems to be hinted at by Plato himself; in one of the most important passages of the *Phaedo* (75c) — and similarly once in the *Republic* (479a) — the ὅσιον is named expressly beside the usual trinity of Good, Beautiful and Just.

In the *Euthyphro* Socrates pretends to be eager for the sake of his defence in his future trial against Meletus to learn from the theologian Euthyphro, what kind of thing it is, the pious and the impious, τὸ εὐσεβὲς καὶ τὸ ἀσεβές or τὸ ὅσιον and τὸ ἀνόσιον. Euthyphro gives as an instance of what is pious a very exceptional action and apparently he is very proud of being perhaps the only man in the world who is able to see that the predicate pious is appropriate to this action. But Socrates, far from being impressed, remarks soberly that it would not do for him to be given one or two instances of pious actions; what he wants is something to consider and to take as guidance, if a certain action is given and the question arises whether such an action is pious or the opposite. *Euthyphro* 6d: "Remember that I did not ask you to give me two or three examples of piety, but to explain the general idea[12] which makes all pious things to be pious.

---

[11] *Euthyd.* 300e: "Why, Socrates, said Dionysodorus, did you ever see a beautiful thing ? — Yes, Dionysodorus, I replied, I have seen many. — Where they other than the beautiful, or the same as the beautiful ? — Now I was in a great quandary at having to answer this question, and I thought that I was rightly served for having opened my mouth at all: I said however, They are not the same as absolute beauty (ὅμως δὲ ἕτερα ἔφην αὐτοῦ γε τοῦ καλοῦ) but they have beauty present with each of them." (And so on).

[12] The Greek text has ἀλλ' ἐκεῖνο αὐτὸ τὸ εἶδος 'that idea *itself*' the reference is to 5d: "I adjure you to tell me the nature of piety and impiety, which you said that you knew so well; . . . Is not piety in every action always the same ? and impiety,

Do you not recollect that there was one idea which made the impious impious, and the pious pious? — I remember. — Tell me what is the nature of this idea[13], and then I shall have a standard to which I may look, and by which I may measure actions, whether yours or those of any one else, and then I shall be able to say that such and such an action is pious, such another impious."

In order to see the importance of this passage it will be necessary to compare it closely with the corresponding situation at the beginning of the *Meno*. Socrates' interlocutor, Meno, wants to know whether virtue is teachable or not. Socrates in his reply confesses that he knows nothing at all about virtue (*Meno* 71b): "and when I do not know the 'quid' (τί ἐστιν) of anything how can I know the 'quale' (ὁποῖόν τι)? How, if I knew nothing at all of Meno, could I tell, if he was fair, or the opposite of fair; rich and noble, or the reverse of rich and noble? Do you think that I could? — No, indeed. — Then they try to get, as we may call it, the common notion or the 'concept'[14] of virtue." Meno gives a list of different kinds of virtues, but Socrates is not satisfied. (*Meno* 72a) "When I ask you for one virtue, you present me with a swarm of them, which are in your keeping. Suppose that I carry on the figure of the swarm, and ask of you, What is the nature of the bee? and you answer that there are many kinds of bees, and I reply: But do bees differ as bees, because there are many and different kinds of them; or are they not rather to be distinguished by some other quality" (the Greek text has 'something else'), "as for example beauty, size or shape? How would you answer me? — I should answer that bees do not differ from one another, as bees. — And if I went on to say: That is what I desire to know, Meno; tell me what is *the quality*" (the Greek text has simply 'what is that') "in which they do not differ, but are all alike; — would you be able to answer? — I should. — And so of the virtues, however many and different they may be, they all have a common nature which makes them virtues; and on this he who would answer the question, 'What is virtue?' would do well to have his eye fixed: Do you understand? — I am beginning to understand ..."

At first sight these two passages quoted here from the *Euthyphro* and the *Meno* do not look so very different. In both cases Socrates introduces the question "What is ...?" and seeks a definition in

---

again —, is it not always the opposite of piety, and also the same with itself, having, as impiety, one notion which includes whatever is impious?"

[13] Ταύτην τοίνυν με αὐτὴν δίδαξον τὴν ἰδέαν τίς ποτέ ἐστιν — 'this idea *itself*' (not one or two of the many pious things) 'what it is'.

[14] I use the word 'concept' as it was defined by D. G. Allen (pref. p. VI) for the purpose of his translation of Stenzel's Studien: "The concept is that which we comprehend, when we know a definition."

order to be able to decide whether a certain predicate (teachable —
pious) is or is not fitting a certain subject (virtue — certain actions).
And yet the presumptions implied in the dialectical proceeding of
the two dialogues are opposite of one another. In the *Meno* the presumption runs this way: in order to tell whether Meno is fair or not,
one ought to know first who Meno is; whereas the presumption of the
Euthyphro would be (if formulated correspondingly): in order to tell,
whether Meno is fair, one ought to know first, what 'fair' is, or, in
other words, the *Meno* is interested in the definition of the subject
of its problem (Is virtue teachable?), but in the *Euthyphro* Socrates
seeks the definition of something that is essentially the predicate of a
problem (Is this action pious?). In the *Meno* the thing sought is
simply the καθόλου of the particular or individual cases of virtue, and
there is not the slightest hint that, for instance, the universal 'bee'
should be understood as something beside the many bees. On the other
hand, from the point of view of the *Euthyphro*, it becomes strikingly
evident that predicates like pious and impious (and we may as well
take the famous triad just and unjust, fair and foul, good and evil)
are different from their many possible but very often problematic
subjects, and that their essence cannot be adequately expressed in
terms of such subjects. In a very simple way they *are* something
beside the subjects and it is easy to understand that in order to know
what they are we must take them by themselves and not confound
them with their usual or possible subjects.

It will be sufficient to quote again the beginnings of the first two
sections of the *Phaedo* that deal with ideas, in order to show that the
original 'ideas' were predicates like 'the pious' in the *Euthyphro*. "Do
we assume something that is the just itself or do we not assume such a
thing?" (*Phd.* 65 d). "Do we not assume that there is something equal,
not a piece of wood to another piece of wood or a stone to another stone
and the like, but beside all these things something else, the equal itself?" (*Phd.* 74 a). It is a result of the discussions of the *Phaedo* that
the terminological 'itself' comes to denote something superior to the
many things of the sensible world and perceptible by mind only; but
in passages like the two ones just quoted, where the additional views
of the *Phaedo* are obviously not yet implied, the 'itself' has an easier
understanding. Originally the 'itself' denoted the meaning of one and
the same predicate adjective in opposition to the many subjects of
which it might become predicate, and it is not by chance that the two
main groups of ideas which the *Phaedo* discusses—the moral ones and the
mathematical ones — are primarily adjectival, apt to become predicates
rather than subjects of sentences referring to the world of common life, and
certainly not 'concepts' of the subjects that may take them as predicates.

5*

So long as the theory of ideas remained founded on the consideration of certain predicates, the 'separation', stigmatized by Aristotle
(*Metaph.* 1078b 3. 1086b 4), but fondly discussed by modern interpreters of Plato, did not involve any mystery. The 'separation' of
such predicates from their possible subjects is even simpler to understand than that 'separation' with which the German philosopher
Hermann Lotze began the first Chapter of the First Book of his *Logik*[15]
and which, according to the famous second Chapter of the Third Book,
would also have been the true basis of Plato's doctrine of Ideas. In
this latter chapter Lotze explained his view of what "at the outset",
was essential for the doctrine of Ideas in the following way[16]:

"Perception shows us the things of sense undergoing changes in their qualities. But
while black becomes white and sweet sour, it is not blackness itself which passes into
whiteness, nor does sweetness become sourness; what happens is that these several
qualities, each remaining identical with itself, succeed each other in the thing, and the
conceptions through which we think these things have themselves no part in the muta-
bility which we attribute on account of their changes to the things of which the qualities
are the predicates, and even he who attempted to deny this would be affirming it
against his will, for he could not represent sweetness as passing into sourness, without
separating the one property from the other, and determining the first for his own
thought in an idea which will always mean something different from the second into
which it is supposed to have changed. It is a very simple and unpretending, but yet
a very important thought to which Plato here gives expression for the first time."

These and similar passages describe and explain admirably the
selfsameness and immutability that distinguished Platonic Ideas from
the very start of the theory; yet, "at the outset", namely in the
Euthyphro, Plato did not oppose the 'pious itself' to the quality 'pious'
perceived in a thing (and perhaps succeeded by the opposite quality
in the same thing), but he opposed it simply to one or two, or any
number of, definite actions; and in the *Phaedo* he opposed the 'equal
itself' and the 'beautiful itself' not to the perceptions of 'equal' and
'beautiful' produced by the things, but again simply to equal stones,
pieces of wood, and to beautiful people, horses, garments respecti-
vely[17]. In Lotze's account this does not seem to make much difference,
because according to him the turning of any "affection of our sen-
sibility into an independent objective content" (p. 435) is sufficient

---

[15] p. 11 of the English translation, edited by B. Bosanquet, Oxford 1884: ,,As soon as
we give the name of green or red to the different movements which waves of light
produce through our eyes, we have separated something before unseparated, our
sensitive act from the sensible matter to which it refers."

[16] L. c. p. 435.

[17] As *Phd.* 102 d ff. shows, Plato was quite able to distinguish between things "having"
a certain predicate and that which being actually present in the things of our sensible
world entitles them to the predicate, when this distinction served his purpose. But
when he was concerned with establishing the legitimacy of positing the 'equal *itself*'
and the 'just *itself*', to introduce this distinction would have obscured the issue

to make an Idea with definite and eternally valid relations to other parts of the "World of Ideas"[18], and because in his Chapter on Plato's Ideas he failed to discuss cases in which the claim of things to certain predicates is controversial or in some way obscured or puzzling. In such cases obviously the Idea cannot be understood as an objectification of the perception involved, and the issue is not the relation of the perception, but the relation of the *thing* as subject to the predicate. Now, it may be safely stated that, in the beginning, Plato was almost exclusively interested in cases of this latter kind[19] and that there is no trace in the earlier dialogues that his original approach to Ideas could have been based on observations similar to those which Lotze had "had occasion" to expound at the beginning of his first Chapter of Logic. Lotze's examples, red and green, or black and white, sweet and sour, would not have helped Plato to establish his theory of Ideas.

The fact that the original Ideas were supposed to furnish *predicates* to subjects that belong to our external world easily explains their "separation" and Plato's technical use of the "itself" in his earliest discussions of Ideas. Yet, as the unfitness of Lotze's examples may show, even then Plato's Ideas were not merely predicates.

That strong conviction in favor of separate ideas — a 'beautiful' *itself*, an 'equal' *itself* — which again and again is uttered by the Socrates of the *Phaedo* and his interlocutors is obviously based on more than the purely logical aspect. In order to trace it to its ultimate source, we shall have to consider apart each of the two major groups of 'ideas', which the *Phaedo* discusses.

As to mathematical 'ideas', things are curiously complicated. The mathematical 'knowledge' elicited in the *Meno* by Socrates from the 'memory' of the young uneducated slave is related to a quadrangle and its diameter, and it is just the 'quadrangle itself' and the 'diameter itself' that in the *Republic* (510d) are chosen as examples of objects of

---

hopelessly. This may be seen from *Phd.* 103b 3—5, where the 'itself' in opposition to the 'thing' refers not only to the idea (τὸ ἐν τῇ φύσει) but also to τὸ ἐν ἡμῖν, and where, accordingly, in order to signify the idea, Plato was forced to replace his usual αὐτό by the rather unexpected expression τὸ ἐν τῇ φύσει.

[18] Cp. p. 436: "If the current of the outer world had brought before us only once in a transient appearence the perception of two colours or two sounds, our thought would immediately separate them from the moment of time at which they appeared and fix them and their affinities and their contrasts as an abiding object of inner contemplation, no matter whether they were ever presented to us again in actual experience or not."

[19] *Euthyphro* 76ff. (cf. *Phdr.* 263a), *Phd.* 74b, 78d/e, 101a/b, 102b-d, *Rep.* 479a-d, 523e—525a. As to the absolutely not controversial case of things in the narrow sense with respect to their own name (*Phdr.* 263a, *Rep.* 523c/d) see p. 112n. 82

mathematical thought. And it may also be said that the predicates
'equal', 'larger', 'smaller', which are outstanding among the mathematical 'ideas' of the *Phaedo* are of fundamental importance in the
problem and the demonstration of the *Meno*. Indeed, this is the evidence on which John Burnet based an hypothesis about the origin
of the theory of ideas. I quote from his note in *Phd.* 65d (Plato's
Phaedo, Oxford 1925): "The geometer makes a number of statements about 'the triangle', as, for instance, that its interior angles are
equal to two right angles, and we know that his statements are true.
Of what is he speaking? Certainly not of any triangle which we can
perceive by our senses (for all these are only approximately triangles)
nor even of any we can imagine. He is speaking of what is 'just a
triangle' (αὐτὸ τρίγωνον) and nothing more. Now, if geometry is true,
that triangle must be the true triangle. It is from this consideration
that the theory seems to have arisen. The next step is to extend it to
such things as 'right' (δίκαιον) and 'beautiful' (καλόν) . . ."

In close adherence to Burnet's views A. E. Taylor (Socrates, 1933,
p. 160) ventured a kind of general definition of what Burnet and he
prefer to call 'Forms' instead of Ideas: "If we would avoid . . . misunderstandings, it is best to say simply that the Form is that — whatever it may be — which we mean to denote whenever we use a signi-
ficant 'common name' as the subject of a strictly and absolutely true
proposition, the object about which such a proposition makes a true
assertion." To be sure, if I may make use of Burnet's words (l. c.):
"there is nothing in the doctrine here set forth which should be un-
intelligible to any one who understands a few propositions of Euclid".
Unfortunately, this is not the doctrine set forth by Plato in the *Phaedo*.
It is only the *Phaedo*'s commentator Burnet who occasionally sup-
plants the *Phaedo*'s mathematical 'ideas', namely the predicates equal,
larger, smaller, one, two etc. by illustrations from a subject of mathematical propositions like the triangle, and there is nothing in the
Phaedo to make us believe that a Form "simply" corresponds to the
subject of a propostition, and there is no reference at all to the strictly
and absolutely true propositions of science. There is not even any
mention of mathematical objects in the narrower sense, except in 73a/b,
in an undisguised quotation of the mathematical episode of the *Meno*.

The *Meno* shows that mathematics had from the beginning an
important influence on Plato's theory of knowledge, and it is scarcely
possible to underrate this influence in the developped theory of the
Republic; but the evidence of the *Phaedo* is decidedly unfavorable to
the view that pure mathematics should have had the leading part
in the establishment of that initial stage of the doctrine of 'ideas'
which the *Phaedo* presupposes.

Now for the *moral* 'ideas'. The following list shows, where such 'ideas' are named[20] in the *Phaedo*:

65d just — beautiful — good[21],
75c beautiful — good — just — pious,
76d beautiful — good,
77a beautiful — good,
78d beautiful,
100b beautiful — good.

In common language the meaning of these adjectives varies greatly according to the diversity of their subjects; but if we regard them as a homogeneous group, all the four of them turn to decidedly moral signification. Even then there are two possibilities: they may be said of *man* (as a source of action), and in this case the adjectives designate human *virtue* or *virtues*; in the other case they are immediately predicated of human *actions*. We have already seen that in earlier Platonic dialogues virtue und virtues are discussed as general concepts and not as something beside the respective subjects (not as an 'idea'), and we have also seen that the τί ἐστιν-question which originally led to 'ideas' must have been logically identical with that of the *Euthyphro*, which is concerned with a standard of *actions*. Moreover the group good, fair, just, pious would be a very inexact and incomplete list of human virtues, whereas it comprises exhaustively the one side of those moral alternatives, with which *judgements on actions* are concerned: just or unjust, fair or foul, good or bad, pious or impious[22]. We may, then, definitely reject the modern attempt (Stenzel, 'third humanism') to regard *virtue* as the prototype of 'ideas'[23] and turn our attention exclusively towards the field of moral action.

By an ingenious trick Plato in the *Euthyphro* manages to discuss the three main moral alternatives immediately after Socrates has set

---

[20] In the Greek text always by adjectives, whereas mathematical 'ideas' are frequently spoken of by nouns (ἰσότης, μέγεθος, σμικρότης etc). There is nowhere an indication that the number of ideas might be limited, usually the exemplifications are marked by an "et cetera".

[21] With regard to Plato's strict distinction (99c/d) the appearance of 'good' (and its superlatives and comparatives) in the picture of an optimistical explanation of the world 97b—99c (and of βέλτιον, βέλτιστον, δικαιότερον and κάλλιον in the analogy taken from human action 98e—99b) had to be left out of the list.

[22] 'Pious' and 'impious', the just and unjust in man's relation to the gods, are usually not registered apart.

[23] This view would be more consistent with Aristotle's unhistorical construction, according to which 'ideas' were at the beginning universals; and, as *Metaph.* 1078 a 17 ("Socrates dealt with the moral virtues and first sought universal definitions concerning them") and an interesting chapter of the *Eudemian Ethics* (older than the *Nicomachean Ethics*), 1216b 3—1216b 25, illustrate, Aristotle himself certainly was not far from it.

the terms for a definition of 'the pious'. Euthyphro tries to give a for-
mally correct definition, it is the definition of theology (*Euthyphro*
6 e ff.): "'Pious' is that which is dear to the gods." Now, the author
of the dialogue had carefully prepared (5 e—6 b) a temporary assumption, which is deservedly abandoned later on (9 c/d): "And further,
Euthyphro" Socrates is entitled to ask at this moment "the gods were
admitted to have enmities and hatreds and differences? — Yes, that
was also said." . . . (Differences about numbers and figures create no
ill-will because they can be settled by a sum or by a weighing machine.)
. . . "But what differences are there which cannot be thus decided, and
which therefore make us angry and set us at enmity with one another?
I dare say the answer does not occur to you at the moment, and therefore *I* will suggest that these enmities arise when the matters of
difference are the just and unjust, good and evil, honorable and dishonorable (τό τε δίκαιον καὶ τὸ ἄδικον καὶ καλὸν καὶ αἰσχρὸν καὶ
ἀγαθὸν καὶ κακόν). Are not these the points about which men differ,
and about which when we are unable satisfactorily to decide our
differences, you and I and all of us quarrel? — Yes, Socrates, the nature
of the differences about which we quarrel is such as you describe. —
And the quarrels of the gods, noble Euthyphro, when they occur, are
of a like nature? — Certainly they are. — They have differences of
opinion, as you say, about good and evil, just and unjust, honorable
and dishonorable: there would have been no quarrels among them,
if there had been no such differences — would there now? — You are
quite right. — Does not every man love that which he deems noble
and just and good (καλὰ καὶ ἀγαθὰ καὶ δίκαια), and hate the opposite
of them? — Very true. — But, as you say, people regard *the same
things*, some as just and others as unjust, — about these they dispute;
and so there arise wars and fightings among them. — Very true."

I had to quote so much because of the following parallel in the
— as far as the doctrine of ideas is concerned — most important
section of the *Phaedo*: "Do not sometimes equal pieces of wood and
stone, *the same things*, appear to one man equal and to another man
unequal? — Certainly (74 b)."

In the *Phaedo* this statement leads up to the assertion that equal
things like equal stones and pieces of wood fall short of being so
perfectly equal as the 'equal itself' (which never even appears to be
unequal). In the *Euthyphro* the surprising result is that the same
things that are dear to the gods are also hated by the gods, and that,
then, Euthyphro has not answered the question which Socrates asked.
"For" says Socrates "I certainly did not ask you to tell me what action
is both pious and impious: but now it would seem that what is loved-
by-the-gods is also hated-by-the-gods (ὃ τυγχάνει ταὐτὸν ὂν ὅσιόν τε

καὶ ἀνόσιον)." In this case the context of the dialogue does not compel us to take so very seriously the thing that is at once pious and impious and therefore not fit to satisfy Socrates. But then it is really puzzling to meet it again in an impressive passage of the *Republic*, where Plato is not jesting (479a): "Of all these many beautiful things is there one which will not be found ugly; or of the just, which will not be found unjust; or of the holy (τῶν ὁσίων), which will not also be unholy (ἀνόσιον)? — No; the beautiful will in some point of view be found ugly; and the same is true of the rest."

In what point of view?

The answer seems easy in the case of the beautiful, if we do not understand it in a moral sense; this is certainly permitted, because even the *Phaedo* occasionally opposes the changing bodily qualities of the many beautiful men or horses or garments "etc." to the one unchanging beautiful itself (78d/e). So there is not much to object to Burnet's explanation (note in *Phaedo* 65d 4): "We have never had experience of a perfectly beautiful thing, yet we judge things by their greater or less conformity to what is 'just beautiful' (αὐτὸ καλόν)." Only if one sticks very closely to Plato's words, one may feel a little uneasy.

But in Burnet's note this comment on 'the beautiful' is only a doublet of the preceeding one on 'the just': "We have never had experience of a perfectly right action, yet we judge actions by their greater or less conformity to what is 'just right' (αὐτὸ δίκαιον)." This would make wonderful sense, if we were free to interpret either Plato or Burnet on the basis of Kantian philosophy but that is out of the question. As it is, we get into serious trouble.

As the example of the triangle (above p. 70) shows, according to Burnet it would have been implied in Plato's doctrine of ideas that a real human action is never entirely straight, but can be only approximately so and that it is always at least a little crooked, too. To raise in a certain situation the simple question: Is this what I am advised to do, just or not just, as Socrates does in the *Crito* (48b), would be a sign of moral naiveté — the correct question would be: is it more just than unjust, or comes it more or less near the standard? On the other hand, obviously this theoretical knowledge that anyway my action cannot be perfectly right would be practically valueless (if not worse). — There is no sign anywhere in Plato's writings that he ever intended to teach such a theoretical (if not practical) relativism with regard to real moral *action*[24]; on the contrary, we have every

---

[24] As, indeed, he did with regard to the real just *man* and the real good *city*, *Rep.*472b to 473b.

reason to believe that just this would have appeared to him running over to the enemy.

Little, however, seems to be gained, if we restrict ourselves more cautiously to what is said in the passages quoted above (p. 70f.) from the *Euthyphro* and the *Phaedo*. The 'just' and the 'unjust' are of those points "about which men differ"; one and the same thing may appear just to me and not just to others (which the 'just itself' could not do). And so, in a way, there will be no real just action "which will not be found unjust" too. But of course this is true of any just action, and especially of an exceptional and outstanding one, and cannot be of any practical moral relevance; certainly, it should not (*Crito* 48a!).

It is very fortunate, then, that we may know without conjecturing what Plato was thinking of when in the 5th Book of the *Republic* he opposed to the one idea of "the" just and "the" pious[25] the many just and pious things that according to him were unjust as well as just and impious as well as pious. At the end of the 7th Book of the *Republic* the educational question arises at what age the best young men of the 'good city' will be sufficiently mature to be led up by dialectic to the whole philosophic truth. Plato — who, incidentally, when he wrote this, was scarcely much more than 50 years old — believes that an age of less than thirty years would be too dangerous. His reason is this (*Rep.* 538c): "You know that there are certain principles about justice and honour (δόγματα . . . περὶ δικαίων καὶ καλῶν), which were taught us in childhood, and under their parental authority we have been brought up, obeying and honouring them. — That is true. — There are also opposite maxims and habits of pleasure which flatter and attract the soul, but do not influence those of us who have any sense of right, and they continue to obey and honour the maxims of their fathers. — True. — Now, when a man is in this state, and the questioning spirit asks what is fair or honourable (τί ἐστι τὸ καλόν) and he answers as the legislator has taught him, and then arguments many and diverse refute his words, until he is driven into believing that nothing is honourable any more than dishonourable, or just or good any more than the reverse, and so of all the notions which he most valued, do you think that he will still honour and obey them as before? — Impossible. — And when he ceases to think them honourable and natural as heretofore, and he fails to discover the true, can he be expected to pursue any life other than that which flatters his

---

[25] As always, things are more complicated in the case of the καλόν ('beautiful' and 'honorable') and of the 'good', but if at the present we confine our *investigation* to their moral meaning, there is no extra problem.

desires? — He cannot. — And from being a keeper of the law he is converted into a breaker of it? — Unquestionably." And so on[26]. There could not be a more vivid illustration of the way in which we learn from early childhood those 'principles about justice and honour' than in the following passage from Protagoras' big speech in the *Protagoras* (*Prot.* 325d): "Education and admonition commence in the first years of childhood, and last to the very end of life. Mother and nurse and father and tutor are vying with one another about the improvement of the child as soon as ever he is able to understand what is being said to him: he cannot say or do anything without their setting forth to him that this is just and that is unjust; this is honorable and that is dishonorable; this is holy, that is unholy; do this and abstain from that. And if he obeys, well and good; if not, he is straightened by threats and blows, like a piece of bent or warped wood. At a later stage they send to him teachers . . ." Of course all these many 'this' and 'that' are indications of certain actions, definite so far that they are easy to understand and to apply in a single case. It is not difficult to see what will happen when the 'questioning spirit' (in the Greek text it is the personified question itself that comes and asks) asks his question: the prescriptions of the educators will prove insufficient because they are too particular and at the same time so vague that exceptions are unavoidable. How typical this dialectical situation appeared to Plato is well illustrated by the fact that the whole discussion of the *Republic* is started by an example of exactly this kind of questioning and answering (*Rep.* 331c): "Well said, Cephalus, I replied, but as concerning justice, what is it? — to speak the truth and to pay our debts — no more than this? And even to this are there not exceptions? Suppose that a friend when in his right mind has deposited arms with me and he asks for them when he is not in his right mind, ought I to give them back to him? No one would say that I ought or I should be right in doing so, any more than they would say that I ought always to speak the truth to one who is in his condition. — You are quite right, he replied. — But then, I said, speaking the truth and paying your debts is not a correct definition of justice." Here the old man Cephalus, who would not be a fit inter-

---

[26] Gifted young men certainly would not have followed the historical Socrates as eagerly as they did, if he had acted according to the pedagogical caution here recommended. On the other hand, on the part of Plato, this whole section (537d—539d) is almost an admission that Socrates was capable of corrupting young men. Elsewhere the social and political conditions at Athens are made responsible for cases like that of Alcibiades and Socrates (*Rep.* 494e). But here we are planning the educational system of the 'good city', where bad influences are anxiously kept away from boys and young men!

locutor, hands over the argument to his son Polemarchus, who is more than willing to defend against Socrates what he has learnt; of course the result of this first phase of the dialogue is the confession of not knowing what to say (336a).

In the important section at the end of the 5th Book (474bff.), from which I quoted one statement above (p. 73), the rare philosopher, who is able to see the ideas of the beautiful (honorable), just etc., is opposed to the average man, who is not only not able but not willing to acknowledge ideas instead of the many beautiful, just etc. things in which he believes. It is true, these 'many' honorable, just and holy things are, in a way, human actions, but they are not considered immediately as such, but as the only (unstable) substance of the moral *beliefs* of the many, that which they have to answer, if asked for "the" just, pious etc., halfway between truly being "the" honorable, just etc. and not being it at all. In other words, in the moral field the one idea and the many things are opposed not as the standard of conduct and the single human actions, but as the standard, which is reached and seen by the philosopher alone, object and source of his knowledge, and the primitive many substitutes of a standard, which are impressed on the minds of the many by common education, custom and law and which form their 'opinion', something between knowledge and absolute ignorance[27]. Or to say it as briefly as possible in Plato's own words: what is opposed to the 'idea' are "the many things in which the 'many' *believe* about beautiful (honorable) and so on" (τὰ τῶν πολλῶν πολλὰ δόγματα καλοῦ τε πέρι καὶ τῶν ἄλλων *Rep.* 479d).

In the *Phaedo* the true meaning of the 'many' moral things which are opposed to each moral idea is obscured because on account of its special problems the dialogue is not immediately interested in the difference of opinion (of the 'many') from knowledge (of the knowing man), but in the by no means equivalent difference of body and soul, sense-perception and mind-perception. In this connection the equal stones and pieces of wood and the beautiful men, horses and garments are much better examples than could be found in the moral field, where mere sense-perception scarcely means anything[27a]. But then, it is only the more important that, in a very peculiar way, even the *Phaedo* acknowledges that the moral ideas and a knowledge of them that is only found with the true philosopher are at the bottom of the doctrine of ideas.

---

[27] An exceptional man like Euthyphro may have opinions of his own, but as long as there is no knowledge of the idea, he is in the same spot with the 'many', no matter how much he may despise (*Euthyphro* 3b) them.

[27a] Cf. Ch. III p. 113. n.83. *Theaet.* 185bff. the confusion of δόξα and αἴσθησις is corrected.

In order to demonstrate the pre-existence of the soul Plato has to stress two points: 1) that men *have* a knowledge of ideas, 2) that ideas cannot have become known to us through the senses of the body The second point is a matter of logical analysis, but of course it would be illusory without the first point being granted. Now, in the case of the 'equal itself', our knowledge of it is — and may be — simply assumed (74b). But as far as the moral ideas are concerned, Plato's proceeding is more complicated. First, indeed, he emphasizes that what is true of the 'equal' — viz. that we must have had a prenatal knowledge of it — is also true of the beautiful (honorable) itself and the good itself and the just and the pious etc. (75c/d). But then the question arises, whether we are born with an actual knowledge of ideas or only later gain it back, being reminded of the ideas by sensible things (*Phd.* 76a). "And which alternative, Simmias, do you prefer? had we the knowledge at our birth, or did we recollect the things which we knew previously to our birth? — I cannot decide at the moment. — At any rate you can decide whether he who has knowledge will or will not be able to render an account of his knowledge? what do you say? — Certainly, he will. — But do you think that every man is able to give an account of these very matters about which we are speaking? — Would that they could, Socrates, but I rather fear that to-morrow, at this time, there will no longer be any one alive who is able to give an account of them such as ought to be given. — Then you are not of opinion, Simmias, that all men know these things? — Certainly not." Is it not remarkable that at this moment the strength of the whole demonstration becomes dependent on the fact that of all living men only Socrates *is* able to give an account of what they are speaking of and accordingly *has* that knowledge the possession of which guarantees the pre-existence of the soul? Under a merely logical aspect this episode would weaken the force of the argument almost hopelessly. The only thing Socrates himself can do, if he wants to continue, is to ignore this rather perplexing reference to him, and so the demonstration comes to its intended conclusion. After that Socrates emphasizes that the proof of the pre-existence of the soul depends entirely on the assumption of that 'beautiful', 'good' etc. "of which we are always talking" (*Phd.* 76dff.), and it is this very basis of the demonstration that makes Socrates' interlocutor, Simmias, express his full conviction in the most positive way: "For there is nothing which to my mind is so patent as that beauty, goodness and the other notions of which you were just now speaking, have a most real and absolute existence; and I am satisfied with the proof." Of course the impression that we get here is exactly what Plato intended to impress on the mind of his readers, namely that the belief in the ideas 'beautiful (honorable)', 'good', 'just' and 'pious' is identical with the belief in what Socrates always had stood for, and obviously in Plato's sight the isolation of the unique man from the mental and moral capacity of all other living people does not weaken the argument but, on the contrary, makes it the more striking.

The questions of just or unjust, fair or foul, good or evil are discussed in Plato's early dialogues (*Apology, Crito, Gorgias*) with reference to Socrates' attitude and acting during and after his capital trial and as to the at once exceptional and exemplary part of Socrates, they are in complete agreement with the *Phaedo*; but in these dialogues the explanation of Socrates' standpoint is not given in the terms of the doctrine of ideas. Even in that passage of the *Phaedo*[28], where we are directly reminded of the subject of the *Crito* — that is of Socrates' decision to await death in prison according to his condemnation in a legal trial — there is no mention of ideas (*Phd.* 98e/99a): "the true cause . . . is, that the Athenians have thought fit (βέλτιον) to condemn me, and accordingly I have thought it better βέλτιον) and more right (δικαιότερον) to remain here and undergo my sentence"; . . . (flight would have been easy enough) . . . "if I had not chosen the better and nobler part (δικαιότερον καὶ κάλλιον), instead of playing truant and running away, of enduring any punishment which the state inflicts". In comparison with this clear and as it were self-evident statement the explanation of Socrates' general attitude according to the new doctrine of the *Phaedo* (see 63b—69e) looks curiously far-fetched and almost superfluous; not even the 'just itself' — the first 'idea' introduced to us in the *Phaedo* (65d) — seems necessary in order to make us understand the Socrates of the *Crito* and his unwillingness to 'run away'.

It is one of the most frequently discussed problems of the development of Plato's philosophy, whether, when he wrote his early dialogues, he had already in petto his doctrine of ideas or not. A solution will scarcely be reached as long as the doctrine of ideas is merely viewed as a theoretically advanced stage of dealing with certain problems in which Plato was interested from the beginning. At least until now, scholars have not been able to point out to each other convincingly how to distinguish between writing a dialogue from and writing it for an 'advanced' point of view. On the other hand, *if* it is possible to see a connection of the doctrine of ideas with some new experience of Plato and a change in his practical attitude which he could not or did not anticipate at an earlier time, the case is different. For, although a theory may be anticipated a long time before it is made public, it is

[28] Cp. p. 71 n. 21.

not very probable that it was anticipated at a time when there was no
need or desire for the theory. It is just such a lack of use for a doctrine
of 'ideas' (opposed to the 'opinions' of the many) at the time when
Plato wrote the *Apology*, the *Crito* and the *Gorgias* which I hope to be
able to demonstrate in the next chapter.

II. Apology, Crito and Gorgias

Encouraged by the incontestable success of Campbell's, Dittenberger's, and Blass's methods in separating three chronological groups
of the Platonic dialogues, other scholars have attempted to extend the
scope of 'stylometry' or 'Sprachstatistik'. Either by accumulating
indiscriminately as much alleged statistical material as possible
(Lutosławsky) or by seeking completeness of observation in a limited
field of allegedly important stylistic facts (v. Arnim) and by applying
in both cases mechanical statistical rules (of doubtful soundness), they
managed to end up with one continuous series of Platonic writings, the
chronological meaning of which was confidently assumed. It must be
said that the result has been a complete failure, owing to a misunderstanding of the reasons of the previous success. The original statistical
investigations were based on the observation of *startling* stylistic or
linguistic differences between two or three groups of Plato's writings
that called for an explanation and could only be accounted for by
introduction of the chronological factor. The success of these entirely
transparent methods is by no means a precedent for an unreasoned
belief in counting anything or everything for the sake of applying
statistical 'rules' that — whatever they may be — necessarily lead up
to *one* continuous sequence of the considered literary units. The only
effect of much labor in this direction has been a regrettable aspect of
uncertainty even where according to all rules of probability practical
certainty had been reached more than fifty years ago.

Of course there is still hope that new independent observations of
style and language or new exploitation of known facts may really
enlarge our outside evidence for the relative chronology of Plato's
writings, but for the time being this is only a hope. The lack of outside
data for the relative chronological order within each of the three
groups of Plato's writings is not so hampering as far as the second and
third group is concerned, because here at least the direction of development is known to us through our knowledge of the groups themselves.
But as for the initial period of Plato's literary work it would indeed be
very hard to get over the difficulties of chronology, if we did not have,
in this case, some valuable inside information of a kind that could only

be given by Plato himself. Thanks to Plato's autobiographical statements at the beginning of the *Seventh Letter* we know that even after Socrates' trial and death he continued to look out for a possibility to take his practical share in Athenian politics and that only at the end of the period between Socrates' death (399 B. C.) and Plato's so-called first voyage (about 389—387), when he was nearly 40 years of age, he lost all hope for an improvement of political conditions at Athens. Moreover — and this is equally important — we have Plato's own testimony that during this voyage he had a new experience which made an addition to his former political views (ταῦτα δὲ πρὸς τοῖς πρόσθε διανοούμενος 326d). In Italy and Sicily he became aware of an exclusively hedonistic way of life that was apt to spoil any individual educational achievements, and necessarily led to absolute political instability and insecurity and to open contempt of such political principles as justice and equality before the Law. "The men in power would not even stand to hear them named" (δικαίου δὲ καὶ ἰσονόμου πολιτείας τοὺς ἐν αὐταῖς δυναστεύοντας μηδ᾽ὄνομα ἀκούοντας ἀνέχεσθαι *Ep.* 7, 326d). Since isonomy was the catchword of democracy[29], this is a direct acknowledgement that at Athens the state of affairs was not so bad and it implies the confession that Plato had to go abroad before he could see the political life of his native city with that degree of tolerance and condescending appreciation of which the *Meno* and the *Menexenos* (certainly written in or soon after 386 B. C.) are our chief documents. This change of attitude towards the city which he had left in scorn and to which now he returned in order to settle down as leader of a philosophical and political school may at the beginning partly or even mainly have been conditioned by his practical aims, but it would not be sensible to doubt entirely of his sincerity, because we know that in the meantime he had also experienced that elsewhere it was not so safe for him as in Athens to propagate "what seemed to him to be best for mankind" (*Ep.* 7, 327a). In any case, the *Menexenos* shows that after Plato's return from his first voyage and at the beginning of his stay at Athens as a law-abiding private citizen, the political beliefs and ideals of the many at Athens were now to him an object worth of presentation for their own sake and in their own light.

Of all the writings of Plato only three, viz. the *Apology*, the *Crito* and the *Gorgias* can be attributed with practical certainty to the period between 399 and 389. Written without doubt after Socrates' death and concentrating exclusively upon his conflict with the Athe-

[29] Cp. Hdt. 3, 80: "The multitude ruling has firstly that best name of all, isonomy" πλῆθος δὲ ἄρχον πρῶτα μὲν οὔνομα πάντων κάλλιστον ἔχει, ἰσονομίην.

nian democracy they are interconnected in many respects, but they do not presuppose the contents of any of the other Platonic writings. Of the three, the *Apology* seems to have been written earlier than the *Crito*, and the *Crito*, in turn, earlier than the *Gorgias*. As to the *Gorgias*, there is a certain terminus post quem, viz. Plato's despair of personal political prospects at Athens, and an equally certain terminus ante quem, the so-called first voyage which resulted in a reconsideration of the political life of Athens; in other words, the *Gorgias* belongs certainly at the end of the first decade after Socrates' death. I do not know of any other Platonic dialogues that probably could have been written during this period[30].

In each of the three, in the *Apology*, the *Crito* and the *Gorgias*, the question at issue is one of just or unjust. The subject of the *Apology* is not so much the direct defence of Socrates against the charges of his opponents in the real trial[31], but rather the defence of his memory against the impression which the fact and the circumstances of his condemnation and execution necessarily must have made on the Athenian public. Nevertheless, the background of the discussion remains the question of whether Socrates was a criminal wrongdoer (18b, 24b); moreover, Plato chose to explain his provocative unyieldingness and seeming stubbornness during the trial as adherence to his rigid principle of never doing wrong (ἀδικεῖν) under conditions whatsoever (28bff., 35b/c, 37a/b, 38d/e). The problem of the *Crito* is mainly solved by an appeal to and by application of this principle; and the real subject of the *Gorgias* is the validity of the principle of not doing wrong even under such temporary conditions when only the alternative of suffering wrong is left[32].

---

[30] For exact substantiation this statement would require the decision of a large number of single questions of priority, but practically everything depends on the question whether the *Gorgias* or the *Protagoras* preceded in order of time. Now, both of them are certainly earlier than the *Meno*, and, whereas the *Gorgias* simply has no reference to the problems of the *Protagoras*, this latter dialogue disregards the views of the *Gorgias* concerning 'good' and 'pleasant' only ostensibly, but cannot be understood and has not been understood by anyone, who does not take or has not taken just these views of the *Gorgias* as the real convictions of the author of the *Protagoras*. This consideration places the *Protagoras* somewhere at the beginning of the second period of Plato's literary work, when he was going to establish or had established a 'school' of his own, and when in his ethical discussions the directly political and individually 'moral' point of view was superseded by an educational one.

[31] As it is indeed of Xenophon's *Apology* (and the corresponding parts of the *Memorabilia*). Xenophon — who was not present at the time of Socrates' trial—characterizes the accusation and its success as preposterous and not understandable, Plato, on the contrary, as only too well understandable.

[32] It is important to let this alternative have its original crude meaning. Whenever the alternative arises in real life, moral or political insincerity are inclined to simplify

According to *Apology*, *Crito*, and *Gorgias*, it is the rigidity with which Socrates sticks to the principle of never doing wrong that makes him different from other people, not a peculiar knowledge of right and wrong itself, as the theory of ideas would put it. The notion of just (not doing wrong — μὴ ἀδικεῖν) and unjust (= doing wrong — ἀδικεῖν) is nowhere part of the controversy; there is no question and no discussion of what ἀδικεῖν, and μὴ ἀδικεῖν means. On the contrary, Socrates' arguments would collapse or at least need reconsideration, if the notion of ἀδικεῖν itself were made to appear problematic. In the perspective of the *Apology* it is not a different view of what just and unjust are in themselves that will make Socrates lose his trial, but lack of time for convincing the judges of what Socrates' real business was (*Apol.* 19a, 24b, 37a). In the *Crito* not the idea of the just, but a well known topic of Attic public speeches is at the bottom of Socrates' reasoning, 50b: "Any one, and especially a clever rhetorician, will have a good deal to urge about the evil of setting aside the law which requires a sentence to be carried out", and in the *Gorgias* not Socrates, but his opponent Callicles challenges the common Athenian notions of just and unjust and Socrates turns out to be their defender and more than once quite seriously identifies his own view with that of the 'many'[33].

On the other hand, there are many passages where Socrates openly professes unqualified contempt of what the 'many' may be or say or believe or do. "I shall produce one witness only of the truth of my words, and he is the person with whom I am arguing; his suffrage

the problem by identifying the eventual object or subject of my doing or suffering wrong, so that the object of my wrongdoing would be himself at least an intentional wrongdoer. But this case of more or less prospective self-defence is by no means the problem of the *Gorgias*. — Incidentally, even if wrongdoing is taken in the sense of harming entirely innocent and innocuous people, common sense becomes remarkably ruthless and anti-Platonic, as soon as political danger from abroad is considered. Isocrates, the Athenian high priest of common sense, said with reference to the ruthless way in which the Athenian empire was founded: "They preferred all the unpleasant things to submission to the rule of Sparta. For, as the choice was between two things, both of them not nice, they thought it better to do dreadful things to others and have an empire in a way that was not just than to avoid this blame and be enslaved undeservedly to the Spartans. All men who are in possession of their sense would choose this way and be resolute about it, only a few of those who pretend to be wise, would say 'no!' if they were asked the question". (Isocr. 12, 117/118).

[33] *Gorg.* 488e: "And are not the many of opinion, as you were lately saying, that justice is equality, and that to do is more disgraceful than to suffer injustice? — is that so or not? Answer, Callicles, and let no modesty be found to come in the way; do the many think, or do they not think thus?" *Gorg.* 491d: "What do you mean by 'ruling over himself'? — A simple thing enough; just what is commonly said (οὐδὲν ποικίλον, ἀλλ' ὥσπερ οἱ πολλοί), that a man should be temperate and master of himself, and ruler of his own pleasures and passions."

I know how to take; but with the many I have nothing to do, and do not even address myself to them" (*Gorg.* 474a). Socrates brought to trial will be in the position of a physician who "would be tried in a court of little boys at the indictment of the cook" (*Gorg.* 521e, cp. 464d): "a competition in which children were the judges, or men who had no more sense than children". And it is the heaviest blow Socrates deals at Callicles — the only passage, indeed, where the advocate of 'Herrenmoral', Callicles, admits of being hit — when Socrates shows that the only way to satisfy Callicles' political ambitions is to "become as like as possible to the Athenian people" (*Gorg.* 513a—c)[34]. In the *Crito* Socrates refers to the principle of not caring what the many — in opposition to the knowing man — will say and what they believe as to one of those unchangeable convictions which he and his friends always have maintained (46cff.), and even in the *Apology* the representatives of the many, the 'men of Athens' — whom, incidentally, Socrates avoids calling judges (see 40a) — have to stand frank words like these: "I am certain, o men of Athens, that if I had engaged in politics, I should have perished long ago, and done no good either to you or to myself. And do not be offended at my telling you the truth: for the truth is, that no man who goes to war with you or any multitude, honestly striving against the many lawless and unrighteous deeds which are done in a state, will save his life; he who will fight for the right, if he would live even for a brief space, must have a private station and not a public one" (*Apol.* 31e).

The notions of just and unjust, on which the Socrates of the *Apology*, the *Crito*, and the *Gorgias*, bases his arguments are well known by the many and quite understandable to them; but the many do not get the slightest credit for it in Socrates' account, because privately they do not feel bound by these their own notions of just and unjust and not even in public life by their own laws and political or legal decisions. It is true, in the *Crito* their opinions in matters of just and unjust, honest and dishonest, good and evil are being opposed to the knowledge of the knowing man and truth itself (47aff.), but that does not mean — as according to Plato's later theory it would — that the many lack knowledge of a transcendent idea of the just and therefore are not capable of distinguishing correctly between right and wrong, but that they do not care for the consequences of unjust actions and take their decisions rather from other points of view, and even this

---

[34] The whole passage is very remarkable. Quite unexpectedly the reader has to face the revelation that there is no effective art of impressing the many by imitating their ways, but that in order to become a true demagogue one has to develop in oneself exactly that degree of genuine meanness which characterizes the 'many' who are to be led (οὐ γὰρ μιμητὴν δεῖ εἶναι ἀλλ' αὐτοφυῶς ὅμοιον τούτοις).

without consistency. *Crito* 48c: (For Socrates the question of his trying to escape from prison is simply the question of whether it will be just or not —) "but those considerations, which you mention, of money and loss of character and the duty of educating one's children, are, I fear, Crito, indeed view-points of these people, who readily kill a man and who would restore him to life, too, if only they could, without any sense, of these 'many'." Inconsiderateness, laxity and fickleness rather than ignorance of what only the philosopher could know make them unworthy of regard and of logical address. In private life theirs is the attitude that was stigmatized almost 30 years before Socrates' death in Euripides' famous lines (*Hippolytus* 375ff.):

> How oft, in other days than these, have I
> Through night's long hours thought of men's misery,
> And how their life is wrecked! And to mine eyes
> Not in man's knowledge, not in wisdom lies
> The lack that makes for sorrow. Nay, we scan
> And know the right — for wit has many a man —
> But will not to the last end strive and serve.
> For some grow too soon weary, and some swerve
> To other paths, setting before the right
> The diverse far-off image of Delight;
> And many are delights beneath the sun . . .[35]
>
> (Translation by Gilbert Murray).

As to the political sphere, the following paragraph in the anonymous reactionary pamphlet on the Government of Athens, which must have been written almost exactly at the same time as Euripides' *Hippolytus* (428 B. C.), points out another peculiar combination of knowledge and disregard of 'virtue' as one of the characteristics of the Athenian demos:

[35] The ethos of these lines is entirely different from that of Medea's tragic words: "I know full well the horrors I shall dare / but passion is stronger than my sober will, / passion the cause of direst woes to mortals" (Eur. *Med.* 1078—80, transl. by A. T. Murray). For the above quoted lines of Phaedra's speech do not represent her own attitude, but that of common people, which at the moment of the speech she is determined not to let overcome her better insight ("This is the truth I saw then and see still / Nor is there any magic that can stain / That white truth for me, or make me blind again"). Tragedy begins when her clear-sighted philosophy to which Socrates scarcely could have added anything and which probably was derived by Euripides from the Socratic *source*, proves powerless against passion and seduction. In Euripides' view Phaedra was certainly not one of the careless 'many', the 'we' who are characterized in her speech; both, the poet and his tragic heroine, know of philosophy; but it was the poet's conviction that not only the common notion of right and wrong but even deliberate philosophy makes a weak stand against passion. In 428, when Socratic (moral) philosophy just began to influence intellectual circles at Athens, Euripides' position seems to have been a rather advanced one; a little more than a generation later Plato was entitled to identify just this view with that of the mob (*Prot.* 352b).

"I say then, that the people of Athens know very well, which of the citizens are good and which are bad; but, while knowing this, they love those who are of use and advantage to themselves, even though they be bad, and rather entertain dislike for the better sort, for they do not think that the merit which is in them is for the good of the people in general but for their harm"[36](2, 19, transl. by J. S. Watson, 1891).

Both passages, the modern poet's and the reactionary politician's, were possibly influenced by Socrates' philosophizing; certainly they demonstrate that the more or less contemptuous characterization of the 'many' that we found in Plato's *Apology*, *Crito*, and *Gorgias*, was current in Athens as early as the twenties of the fifth century B. C. For a reactionary by family tradition and by experience like Plato, there was no need to waste thoughts or words on it, as long as it agreed with his own views. As Alcibiades put it talking in Sparta about Athenian democracy (Thuc. 6, 89, 6): "But about admitted madness (ἄνοια, cf. that οὐδενὶ ξὺν νῷ) *Crito* 48c; Hdt. 3, 81 . . . ἄνευ νόου . . .) there could not be said anything new."

This traditional view of the 'mad' attitude of the many in Plato's earliest writings furnishes a convenient background for Socrates' dialectic. There is no clearness and order in the concepts and no consistency in the thoughts of the many, but Socrates is able to do his arguing by picking up as it were immediately from their minds just those notions, principles and experiences which he needs for his purposes. Passages from the *Gorgias* are proof that this plain method leads with equal ease down to the lowest lows[37] and up to the highest heights[38] wherever its master chooses to proceed. There can be no doubt that this same astute exploitation of the abundant anomaly of the notions and principles of common life, and not an underlying method of unchanging 'ideas' or fixed concepts, was the simple secret of the dialectic invincibility of the historic Socrates. Xenophon's description of Socrates' dialectical power over his fellow-men seems fairly correct, only perhaps a little too credulous with regard to the solidity of the logical foundation: "If he himself was going to explain a thing, he started with premisses most likely to be agreed upon, be-

---

[36] The author continues: "On the other hand, some, who belong to the people by birth, are by no means of democratic disposition." This sentence has lately been discussed in some German dissertations and the result seems to be that the exception from the rule was indeed made for the sake of that man of the people who, as we all know, believed that virtue was in any case for the good of people and never for their harm, Socrates, of whose influence on reactionary circles this passage would be the oldest testimony. See Gnomon 15, 1939, p. 118.

[37] *Gorg.* 494e.

[38] *Gorg.* 508a: with a little support, indeed, from outside authority, we are led to see, all of a sudden, human virtue in cosmic perspective, to 'Weltanschauung' in the truest sense of the word

lieving this to be the surest way of reasoning, and therefore he was more successful in winning the consent of his hearers than any one I ever knew" (*Mem.* 4, 6, 15). It could not be said more briefly than in the phrase Xenophon uses *Mem.* 1, 2, 14, although it is not probable that he himself was aware of the pregnancy of his expression: (men like Alcibiades and Critias sought Socrates' company because they knew that he ...) τοῖς δὲ διαλεγομένοις αὐτῷ πᾶσι χρώμενον ἐν τοῖς λόγοις ὅπως βούλοιτο (it seems difficult to translate this plain Greek phrase, perhaps: 'and that in conversation he never failed to make of his interlocutors whatever he wished'; in German it would be: 'machte *mit* ihnen, was er wollte').

Socrates made of his interlocutors whatever he wished, but what he wished did not depend on his dialectical method; this method would have worked both ways in any case[39]. There is a rule in Aristotle's logic (which goes back to Plato's theory of knowledge by way of ideas), that the premisses of a scientific conclusion have to be more clear and certain, more 'true', than the conclusion itself. According to this rule historians of philosophy would have liked to identify the things Socrates stood for primarily in life and in philosophy with the *premisses* of such genuine Socratic discussions as we may imagine from some Platonic dialogues and some parts of Xenophon's writings. But it is in the nature of Socrates' dialectic that the premisses from which he started his discussions either furnished mere *argumenta ad hominem*[40] or, if they were of a more universal validity, even if collected and systematized, would be nothing more than a onesided and probably rather dull abstract of what may be presented to the average man as his own experience and as the rules of his own behavior in certain situations[41]. Plato's *Crito* is an exception. The *Crito* was written exclusively for the narrow circle of Socrates' intimate friends or followers[42] in

[39] Aristophanes' *Clouds* shows that people simply could not avoid seeing him as one of those who 'had it both ways' in their speeches (Ar. *Nub.* 112, and passim). How could they help it if the part of the devil's advocate agreed so well with him as Plato's *Minor Hippias* seems to indicate.

[40] In Plato's dialogues Socrates is a master of such argumentation. One of the finest specimens is the passage *Gorg.* 513a-c, quoted above p. 83. — In the *Cratylus* (386a) where Socrates's interlocutor is an exceedingly decent young man Socrates appeals against Protagoras' famous proposition to the fact that some men are good and others bad, in the *Euthydemus* to the teaching profession of the two ridiculed sophists (287a).

[41] We have a large *not* one-sided collection of such 'principles' in the first two books of Aristotle's *Rhetoric*, where this kind of 'psychology' is in place.

[42] 49d: "But I would have you consider, Crito, whether you really mean what you are saying. For this opinion has never been held, and never will be held, by any considerable number of persons; and those who are agreed and those who are not agreed upon this point have no common ground, and can only despise one another when they see how widely they differ."

order to show that Socrates could not but refuse to 'run away' if he wanted to stand by the convictions he had upheld all the time of his life[43]. Accordingly some propositions that in a normal Socratic dialogue would have been the *result* of an argument appear in the *Crito* as premisses of a moral deduction.

(*Crito* 48a/b) "You begin in error when you advise that we should regard the opinion of the many about just and unjust, good and evil, honorable and dishonorable. 'Well', someone will say, 'but the many can kill us'. — Yes, Socrates; that will clearly be the answer. — And it is true: but still I find that the old argument" — sc. against the importance of the opinion of the many — "is unshaken as ever. And I should like to know whether I may say the same of another proposition — that not life, but a good life, is to be chiefly valued? — Yes, that also remains unshaken. — And a good life is equivalent to a just and honorable one — that holds also? — Yes, it does. — From these premisses I proceed to argue the question whether I ought or ought not to try and escape without the consent of the Athenians . . .". Thus, the *Crito* is an exception that even better than anything else proves the rule that generally the things Socrates stood for made the conclusions and not the premisses of his discussions. But the *Crito* confirms the rule in a direct way, also. For the 'old argument' which led up to the first of the three 'premisses' according to the passage just quoted had been summarized in the *Crito* itself (46 d ff.); it was an induction that began with the deserved leadership of the knowing man, the expert[44], — and not the many — in questions of gymnastic training and health, and aimed at the leadership — against the many — of the expert in questions of 'just and unjust, fair and foul, good and evil'. Now, it is out of the question that genuinely felt opposition to the moral or political opinions of the 'many' should ever have originated from premisses and reasonings like those pointed out in this induction, and it is obvious that such an opposition or at least an inclination towards it must have existed already before it can be defended this way. And we may say that the same is true of the second and third 'premiss' of the *Crito*, because we know the kind of dialectic that is supposed to have led up to them from *Gorg.* 511 b ff. and 474 c ff.

---

[43] 46 d: "Were we right in maintaining this before I was condemned ? Or has the argument which was once good now proved to be talk for the sake of talking — mere childish nonsense ? That is what I want to consider with your help, Crito: — whether, under my present circumstances, the argument appears to be in any way different or not; and is to be allowed by me or disallowed" and so forth.

[44] The unusual meaning of ἐπιστάτης — 'knowing man, expert' (from ἐπίσταμαι) — instead of 'supervisor, chief' (from ἐφίσταμαι) must go back to an original Socratic pun, cp. *Prot.* 312 d, *Crat.* 390 b ff.

Thus the question arises whether such convictions or inclinations as represented by the three Socratic propositions of the *Crito* do at all presuppose primary, and more evident, 'truer', principles from which they have to be deduced logically in order to be acknowledged and fully understood, or whether they are an outgrowth of certain political and social conditions and a certain individuality, immediately understandable without any demonstration in the strict sense of the term. To put the question this way is to accept the second alternative. And it is not even necessary to stress the exceptional individuality of Socrates beyond certain limits. At least on the field of Athenian inner politics there must have been a strong affinity of Socrates' views to those of reactionary circles. We have Plato's report that after the catastrophe of the Peloponnesian War and the downfall of the then much abused democratic regime at Athens he — young as he was — believed that now, with his own friends and relatives as political leaders, life would turn from injustice to justice; and that to him the clash of his aged friend Socrates with the new regime came entirely unexpected (*Ep.* 7, 324c—325a). Moreover, any reading of the political pamphlet on the Government of Athens is apt to enliven and make surprisingly concrete many Socratic passages on virtue and meanness; and it is even easy to trace the social and political origin of the famous principle of the leadership of the knowing man — *and not the many* — in the Thucydidean dispute between Cleon and Diodotus (Thuc. 3, 37—48, see esp. 3, 43, 4).

Of course Socrates was not an ordinary reactionary. Plato's report in the *7th Epistle* and his *Gorgias* and *Crito* are convincing documents in this direction, too. But, on the other hand, Socrates had had to emancipate himself from being one of the many, and if not-belonging by birth to the oligarchic circles may have kept his eyes open for their peculiar weaknesses, his more intimate knowledge of his common fellow-Athenians may just as well have contributed to his notorious divergence from them[45] and to the profundity of his contempt for most of his social equals.

It may be said that Plato's oligarchic tendencies exaggerated the anti-democratic features in Socrates' picture, although there is no denying that Plato's aristocratic extraction could also work both ways. But for our present investigation it is not necessary to ponder over the dilemma, whether the peculiar nondemocratic attitude of the *Apology*, the *Crito*, and the *Gorgias*, was a more or less adequate picture of the historic Socrates. In any case it is a fact that in these three Platonic

---

[45] *Apol.* 34d: "Whether this opinion of me be deserved or not, at any rate the world has decided that Socrates is in some way superior to other men."

writings the democratic way of life is rejected as a way of injustice, offhand and almost unconcernedly, *not* because democracy does not know what justice is, but because it does not care for it, and, secondly, that in the defence of justice against Callicles' attack the defended notion of justice is simply that of the common man, that of the 'many'. No trace of an 'idea' of 'the' just, and not the slightest need of it in order to understand any of the moral and political convictions which here the Platonic Socrates is defending.

III. From Gorgias to Phaedo

On the basis of observation of style and language the dialogues *Republic*, *Phaedrus*, *Parmenides* and *Theaetetus* have been attributed to a chronological 'middle group' of Platonic writings, and from the point of view of contents it is probable that within this group the *Republic* was the earliest and the *Theaetetus* the latest work. Fortunately we have an absolute terminus post quem for each of these two dialogues. The *Republic*, especially its central part which is concerned with the education of the selected future leaders of the 'good city', cannot have been written before Plato himself had passed the age of fifty years which in his educational plan is considered as the beginning of the final stage of maturity (*Rep.* 540a)[46]; Plato reached that age in 377 B. C. The *Theaetetus* was written after 369, the year of a battle near Corinth in which the mathematician Theaetetus was fatally wounded.

In the case of the *Republic* and the *Phaedrus* we have, moreover, a kind of terminus ante quem. We happen to know that when Aristotle, at the age of seventeen years, in 366 B. C., came to Athens in order to study, he was for a short time a disciple of the "younger" Socrates[47] — known from Plato's dialogues *Theaetetus*, *Sophist* and *Statesman* — but that Socrates died soon and then Plato became Aristotle's teacher. Now, from a passage in Aristotle's *Metaphysics* (1036b 25) we learn that this Socrates was already quite familiar with ideas like the idea of 'animal' or 'man'. Thus we have a testimony that about the time of Aristotle's arrival at Athens and probably before Plato returned from his Second Sicilian Journey (366/5 B. C.) that stage of development of the theory of ideas when ideas like man, bull, fire, water, were seriously taken into consideration had already been reached and was common property of the members of the Academy. This is the stage which is

---

[4]- cf. Wilamowitz, Platon II 1919, 180.
[47] Pauly-Wissowa III A 1927, 890f., s. v. Sokrates 6; Philologues 79, 1924, 225ff.

presupposed in the *Parmenides*, but it is hardly believable that the discussion of 'ideas' had developed to this point when the relevant parts of the *Republic* and the *Phaedrus* were conceived by Plato[48]. Under these circumstances it seems fairly safe — for practical purposes — to assign the period between Plato's fiftieth birthday and his Second Sicilian Journey, that is the decade between the years 377 and 366, to the stylistic 'middle group', with the specification that *Republic* and *Phaedrus* would fall nearer the beginning and *Parmenides* and *Theaetetus* at the end of this period.

This chronological distribution leaves another decade[49] — the years 386 to 377 B. C. — for all Platonic writings of the first stylistic group that probably were written after Plato's return from the First Sicilian Journey (in 387 B. C.). They are the following, in alphabetical order: *Charmides, Cratylus, Euthydemus, Euthyphro, Hippias Minor*[50], *Io, Laches, Lysis, Menexenus, Meno, Phaedo, Protagoras, Symposium*. As to their relative chronology, first, there can be no doubt that the *Protagoras* preceded the *Meno*, because the *Meno* takes up the problem of whether virtue is teachable just where the *Protagoras* had left it; secondly, the *Meno* was written earlier than the *Phaedo*, because the *Meno* is openly referred to by Plato himself in the *Phaedo*. Furthermore, as we have seen in Chapter I, it is highly probable that the *Symposium* followed the *Phaedo*; and the conclusion of the *Cratylus* (439 a ff.) seems to presuppose both the *Phaedo* and the *Symposium*. An analysis of the *Lysis* would prove, in my opinion, that it was written later than the *Symposium*.

Of the other dialogues I should propose to insert the *Euthyphro*, *Euthydemus* and the *Charmides* between the *Meno* and the *Phaedo*[51] and to let the remainder form a chronological group with the *Protagoras* rather than with the *Meno*. A terminus post quem for the *Menexenus* is the 'peace of Antalcidas' (386 B. C., mentioned *Menex.* 245 e, curiously enough, in a speech that is laid in Socrates' mouth).

---

[48] See Chapter I (at the beginning).

[49] Or a year or even some years more, because the fifthieth birthday is only *terminus post quem* for the middle group, not a *terminus ante quem* for the first group.

[50] I prefer not to go into the problem of the genuineness of the *Hippias Maior*; but it should be possible to reach a decision from the point of view of the development of the theory of ideas.

[51] The *Euthyphro* for reasons set forth in Chapter I; the *Euthydemus* and *Charmides* mainly because of their advanced dealing with the old Socratic equation 'good' = 'knowledge', see the two specifically Socratic sections of the *Euthydemus* (278 e—282 d; 288 d—292 e) and the main part of the *Charmides* (164 c—175 d): which turns out to be a continuation of the discussion of the same problem, complicated by reference to the historical Socrates' 'knowledge' of knowledge and ignorance. The chronological relation of *Euthydemus* and *Charmides* is by no means convertible. The whole discussion is presupposed in *Rep.* 505 b.

B. C.

428/7	Plato's birth.	
400/399	Socrates' death.	
399—390:		
		Apology
		Crito
	Gorgias	

Plato's first journey.

386—377 (?):

	Protagoras	*Menexenus* (after 386)
		Hippias Minor
		Io
		Laches
	Meno	
		Euthydemus
		Charmides
		Euthyphro
	Phaedo	
		Symposium
		Lysis
		Cratylus

377 (?)—367:

	Republic	
		Phaedrus
	Parmenides	
		Theaetetus (after 369)

Plato's second Sicilian journey (366/5).

From Plato's survey of his political experiences during the first half of his life that is found at the beginning of the *Seventh Letter* (324b—326b), we learn that he did not stop waiting for an opportunity to become active in Athenian politics until shortly before his First Sicilian Journey. This statement is strongly confirmed by the *Apology* and the *Gorgias*; and fortunately the tragicomic picture of the always frustrated young would-be politician is interestingly enlivened by these two authentic documents of Plato's earlier political aspirations.

Apology 39c in the third part of the speech that pretends to be spoken after the death penalty has been pronounced: "And now, o men who have condemned me, I would fain prophesy to you; for I am about to die, and in the hour of death men are gifted with prophetic power. And I prophesy to you who are my murderers, that immediately after my departure punishment far heavier than you have inflicted on me will surely await you. Me you have killed because you wanted to escape the accuser, and not to give an account of your lives. But that will not be as you suppose: far otherwise. For I say that there will be more accusers of you than there are now: accusers whom hitherto I have restrained: and as they are younger they will be more inconsiderate with you, and you will be more offended with them. If you think by killing men you can prevent some one from censoring your evil lives, you are mistaken; that is not a way of escape which is either possible or honourable; the easiest and the noblest way is not to be disabling others, but to be improving yourselves. This is the prophecy which I utter before my departure to the judges who have condemned me."

It is clear that Plato, when he wrote this, was thinking of himself as one of those young men, who would be more 'inconsiderate' in dealing with the circle responsible for Socrates' death, and it is openly said that what is prophesied here will be different from the kind way of "a father or elder brother" described earlier in the *Apology* as something that the Athenians will never find again if they kill Socrates (30e—31b). So the 'prophecy' is an almost undisguised threat and an unmistakable hint at that kind of political activity for which Plato was looking during the first time after Socrates' execution. Neither can the 'prophecy' be understood as merely anticipating a somewhat more vigorous exhorting and scolding of private citizens by private citizens, nor as a political 'fight for the right' *within* the existing democracy, for such a fight had already been characterized as entirely hopeless, 31e: "the truth is, that no man who goes to war *with you or any other multitude*, honestly striving against the many lawless and unrighteous deeds which are done in the state, will save his life; he who will fight for the right, if he would live even for a brief space, must have a private station and not a public one."

We know that the political threat against democracy which seems to be implied in the 'prophecy' at the end of the *Apology* remained an empty gesture, and the *Seventh Letter* makes no secret of the main reason why it could not be carried into effect. Whereas the author of the *Apology* when he formulated his threat seems to have been sure of a considerable number of associates, the narration in the Seventh Letter simply lists Socrates' trial as the most unfortunate in the series of political disappointments in the young Plato's experiences, and then continues (in Harward's[52] translation):

Ep. VII 325c "As I observed these incidents and the men engaged in public affairs, the laws too and the customs, the more closely I

---

[52] The Platonic Epistles, Translated with Introduction and Notes by J. Harward, Cambridge 1932.

examined them and the farther I advanced in life, the more difficult it seemed to me to handle public affairs aright. For it was not possible to be active in politics without friends and trustworthy supporters; and to find these ready to my hand was not an easy matter, since public affairs at Athens were not carried on in accordance with the manners and practices of our fathers; nor was there any ready method by which I could make new friends. The laws too, written and unwritten, were being altered, and the evil was growing with startling rapidity." Even in this narration it is indicated that it took some time after Socrates' condemnation for Plato to realize that in politics he stood practically alone; obviously for a while Plato's practical hopes corresponded exactly to the 'prophecy' in the *Apology*. But then the prophecy proved wrong: Plato could not find the 'friends and trustworthy supporters' needed for his political aims: neither could he find them in his own social sphere — where he would have found them in the time "of our fathers" — nor were they to be found elsewhere.

As to the political aims themselves for which associates were wanted but not found, the *Seventh Letter* is rather vague; for a phrase like 'handle political affairs aright' would yield to any interpretation. The final crisis in Plato's attitude towards Athenian politics is described as follows:

Ep. VII 325e "The result was that, though at first I had been full of a strong impulse towards political life, as I looked at the course of affairs and saw them being swept in all directions by contending currents, my head finally began to swim; and, though I did not stop looking to see if there was any likelihood of improvement in these symptoms and in the general course of public life, I postponed action till a suitable opportunity should arise. Finally it became clear to me with regard to all existing communities, that they were one and all misgoverned. For their laws have got into a state that is almost incurable, except by some extraordinary reform with good luck to support it. And I was forced to say, in praise to true philosophy, that it is by this that men are enabled to see what justice in public and private life really is. Therefore, I said, there will be no cessation of evils for the sons of men, till either those who are pursuing a right and true philosophy receive sovereign power in the states, or those in power in the states by some dispensation of providence become true philosophers."

It is generally acknowledged by the modern interpreters and it cannot have been overlooked by any ancient reader that in the last two sentences (from "And I was forced to say") Plato deliberately makes use not only of the content but of the formulation of the startling thesis of the *Republic*, which is introduced there (472aff.) with "some fear and hesitation" as the most extraordinary proposal Socrates has to state and investigate. In the *Republic* the thesis is first formulated as follows (473c):

"Until philosophers are kings, or the kings and princes of this world have the spirit and power of philosophy, and political greatness and wisdom meet in one, and those commoner natures who pursue either to the exclusion of the other are compelled to stand aside, cities will never have rest from their evils, — no, nor the human race, as I believe, — and then only will this our state have a possibility of life and behold the light of day." It is referred to throughout the central part of this dialogue:

Rep. 487e: "Then how can you be justified in saying that cities will not cease from evil until philosophers rule in them, when philosophers are acknowledged by us to be of no use to them?"

Rep. 499a: "And this was what we foresaw, and this was the reason why truth forced us to admit, not without fear and hesitation, that neither cities nor states nor individuals will ever attain perfection, until the small class of philosophers whom we termed useless but not corrupt are providentially compelled, whether they will or not, to take care ot the state, and until a like necessity be laid on the state to obey them; or until kings, or if not kings, the sons of kings or princes, are divinely inspired with a true love of true philosophy."

Rep. 501e: "Then will they" — sc. the enemies of philosophy — "still be angry at our saying, that, until philosophers bear rule, states and individuals will have no rest from evil, nor will this our imaginary state ever be realized?"

Rep. 540d: "Well, I said, and you would agree (would you not?) that what has been said about the state and the government is not a mere dream, and although difficult not impossible, but only possible in the way which has been supposed; that is to say, when the true philosophers come into power, either one or more of them, in a state, despising the honours of this present world which they deem mean and worthless, esteeming above all things right and the honour that springs from right, and regarding justice as the greatest and most necessary of all things, whose ministers they are, and whose principles will be exalted by them when they set in order their own city?"

And finally *Rep.* 543a: "And so, Glaucon, we have arrived at the conclusion that in the perfect state wives and children are to be in common; and that all education and the pursuits of war and peace are also to be common, and the best philosophers and the bravest warriors are to be their kings? — That, replied Glaucon, has been acknowledged."

If we attend to the way in which the unexpectedness and paradoxy of the thesis is urged in the *Republic*, it is scarcely believable that the formula should have been coined and made public earlier and independently from the context in which it is found there; and certainly the author of the *Seventh Letter*, when he wrote "And I was forced to say . . .", could not expect, and consequently did not expect, to remind his readers of anything concerning his political and philosophical convictions but what he had said in his main work[53]. Under normal conditions this would lead to the conclusion that the *Republic* had already been conceived and published before Plato left Athens for his first journey, some time before his fortieth birthday. But, then, a considerable part of our fairly certain knowledge of the chronology of Plato's writing would be upset and, as far as the *Seventh Letter* is concerned, the conditions are not normal.

We need not be minute about the now much discussed exact date of its publication; at any rate it was written after Dion's death in 354 B. C., not before 353 B. C. (rather, in my opinion, a little later).

Regarding the general intention of this unique document of Plato's attitude toward practical politics, the results of recent studies are stated adequately in Harward's remarks (Translation p. 188ff.), from which I may quote a few sentences: "The 7th Epistle professes to be a reply to a request for help and counsel, addressed to Plato by friends of Dion at some time not long after his murder. By far the greater part of it is actually Plato's Apologia for himself. He describes and justifies his own career, so far as it brought him into contact with the political affairs of his day, his detachment from the politics of Athens and his intervention in those of Syracuse, his relation with Dionysios the Younger, and the failure of his attempts to influence that monarch for good in politics and philosophy. The justification of Dion is combined with his own; and clearly one of his objects in writing the letter was to raise a worthy memorial to his friend" (p. 189). — While we may assume that the *8th Epistle* "was actually sent to the Dionean party for circulation" (p. 192), the *7th Epistle* can only be understood if it "is regarded as a pamphlet intended for readers at Athens and in the Greek world generally" (p. 192), "not for Sicily" (p. 190).

Since the letter was written in the first place for Athens, its author does not bother with narrating and explaining what was well known to the Athenian public and for which obviously no 'Apologia' was

---

[53] Incidentally, even the phrase "I was forced to say" (λέγειν τε ἠναγκάσθην) reproduces the words "truth forced us to admit" (ἐλέγομεν, ὑπὸ τἀληθοῦς ἠναγκασμένοι) *Rep.* 499b.

intended, viz. the foundation of the Platonic school and Plato's scholarly and literary activities at Athens. So by means of one clever sentence that at first sight seems only to describe the effect of his teaching upon Dion (about 388 B. C.) he actually skips the whole time between his first Sicilian stay and the death of Dionysios I (in 367 B. C.) *Ep. VII* 327b: "The result was that *until the death of Dionysios* he lived in a way which rendered him somewhat unpopular among those whose manner of life was that which is usual in the courts of despots. *After that event ...*" This economy in dealing with the facts was obviously in accordance with the general purpose of the *7th Epistle*; but the practical consequence for its author was, that when Dion, in the course of the further narration, appealed to Plato's political convictions[54], on the one hand this appeal had to be based on what was known to the general public from Plato's *Republic* — for of course this dialogue was representative of his convictions at the time of Dionysios I's death —, but on the other hand, the details of the origin and the development of these convictions *could* not be stated correctly.

Under such conditions it is easy to understand that Plato chose to antedate the final formulation of his main political principle by about fifteen years, with a shift from some time after his fiftieth to some time before his fortieth birthday. For now, in the connection of thoughts that is presented to the reader of the *7th Epistle*, Dion may appeal to what Plato had taught him during his first stay at Syracuse, which in turn is apt to be explained by what Plato had been "forced to say" before he came to Italy and Sicily on his first visit. What mattered for the immediate purpose of the *7th Epistle* was that Dion's appeal to Plato's principle of philosopher rule should not come unexpectedly and unpreparedly, and this had to be managed somehow, since the actual conditions of the formulation and the publication of this principle — *after* Plato's return from the first journey to Athens — were to be skipped.

In order to get the facts behind the narration of the *7th Epistle* we must, first of all, remove the anachronism by which the 'Leitmotiv' of the central part of the *Republic* was antedated to a much earlier stage of the development of Plato's thoughts. If we do so, the main difficulty that is implied in the narration of the *7th Epistle* will also be found to be disappearing at once.

---

[54] *Ep.VII* 327e: "What opportunities, he said, shall we wait for, greater than those now offered to us by Providence. And he described . . . so that, now if ever, we should see the accomplishment of every hope that the same persons might actually become both philosophers and the rulers of great states. These were the appeals addressed to me and much more to the same effect."

According to this narration Plato's specifically *Athenian* experiences led up to a *universal* insight (*Ep. VII* 326a): "Finally it became clear to me with regard to *all existing communities*, that they were *one and all* misgoverned. For their *laws* have got into a state that is almost *incurable*, except by some extraordinary reform with good luck to support it. And I was forced to say ..." Then comes the first Italian and Sicilian journey and with it a new disappointment and a new experience (326b): "With these thoughts in my mind I came to Italy and Sicily on my first visit. My first impressions on arrival were those of strong disapproval—disapproval of the kind of life which was there called the life of happiness, stuffed full as it was with the banquets of the Italian Greeks and Syracusans, who ate to repletion twice every day, and were never without a partner for the night, and disapproval of the habits which this manner of life produces. For with these habits formed early in life, no man under heaven could possibly attain to wisdom — human nature is not capable of such an extraordinary combination. Temperance also is out of the question for such a man; and the same applies to virtue generally. No city could remain in a state of tranquillity *under any laws whatsoever*, when men think it right to squander all their property in extravagant excesses, and consider it a duty to be idle in everything else except eating and drinking and the laborious prosecution of debauchery. It follows necessarily that the constitutions of such cities must be constantly changing, tyrannies, oligarchies and democracies succeeding one another, while those who hold the power cannot so much as endure the name of any form of government which maintains justice and equality of rights. With a mind full of these thoughts, on the top of my previous convictions, I crossed over to Syracuse ..." In this passage the phrase "under any laws whatsoever" is in deliberate antithesis to the almost incurable state of the laws in "all existing communities" that was deplored in the preceding section. It is a very impressive and seemingly instructive antithesis; at Athens the perception of an almost incurable *state of laws* combined with a comparatively decent kind of life — comparatively decent, because otherwise Plato's "strong disapproval" of the Italian and Sicilian way would be without basis —, in Italy and Sicily the perception of an entirely hopeless *kind of life*, which would render unstable "any laws whatsoever" and actually resulted in a continuous change of tyrannies, oligarchies and democracies. So far it makes very good sense; but unfortunately, according to the narration of the *7th Epistle* Plato knew already before his journey to Italy that the state of laws in *all existing communities* was almost incurable, and, on the other hand, he knew also of the only possible cure in any case, namely the rule of philosophy. Under these condi-

7 Kapp, Ausgew. Schriften

tions — the conditions actually provided to the reader by the narration of the *7th Epistle* — the phrase in 326c "under any laws whatsoever" loses its point. Obviously philosopher-rule cannot be thought of as included in the "laws whatsoever"; on the contrary, that panacea would guarantee a decent kind of life. But then, since we know already that *all* existing communities are misgoverned because of the deplorable state of laws *everywhere*, there is no reason to discriminate between laws and laws, to expect more of one kind of laws than of another and to become disappointed; in other words, there is no reason for the phrase "under any laws whatsoever". This phrase makes sense only if we ignore the general formulation (326a) of the result of Plato's Athenian experience; for in that case it means that Plato learned now ("on the top of his previous convictions" 326d/e) that elsewhere, with laws different from those of Athenian democracy, there were nevertheless obstacles against "handling public affairs aright", obstacles for which Athenian democracy could not be held responsible and of which he had not even become aware in Athens.

Thus, a close interpretation of the text of the *7th Epistle* confirms the view that what Plato actually was "forced to say" at the end of the decade after Socrates' death as a result of his political experience at Athens, differed considerably from the universal formula of the *Republic* which the *7th Epistle* anticipates at this point of Plato's career.

Neither the precise nature of Plato's political aims, for which, during the first years after Socrates' death, he wanted but could not find associates (see above p. 93), nor, as we now have seen, the exact meaning of the following crisis in his political attitude can be determined immediately from the text of the *7th Epistle*, although without its autobiographical statements the task of getting at the important facts would be hopeless. But as soon as we see through the misleading quotation or adaptation of the thesis of the *Republic* in 326a, there can be no doubt where to turn in order to fill the resulting gap in our information. For this is where the *Gorgias* comes in[55].

In a way, already the *Gorgias* establishes the principle that only the philosopher is the true politician. When, toward the end of the dialogue (521d), Socrates, who never had had a hand in practical politics, proclaims himself as the only genuine politician in Athens, this is scarcely less provocative than the famous paradox of the philosopher king in the *Republic*. And from *Gorg.* 481cff. we know that this politician Socrates based everything he said or did on what philosophy had to say, and not on the pleasure of the people. So this

[55] Cp. Ch. II p. 80ff.

comes indeed very near to the first sentence which, according to *Ep.*
VII 326a, Plato 'was forced to say': "And I was forced to say, praising
true philosophy, that it is by this that men are enabled to see what
justice in public and private life really is". But as for the practical
prospects of the 'true politician', the *Gorgias* sees no way of winning
the people of the Athenian democracy for the dictates of philosophy,
and therefore — given the Athenian democracy with its laws and
traditions — the best way of saving one's soul, not for this life (because anything may happen in a city like Athens, 521c) but for
another life, will be not the life of an ordinary politician but that of a
philosopher who strictly confines himself to act as a philosopher should
(526c). All this is discussed with almost exclusive reference to Athenian
democracy, and no doubt is left that under its traditions the state of
things is by now hopelessly incurable.

In order to know more about Plato's finally frustrated political hopes
during the period after Socrates' death, we must ask against whom and
against what the fighting spirit of the 'new Archilochos'[56] was directed.
With the help of the dialogue *Gorgias* the answer is easy and revealing.

It is not the Athenian demos and its ways; as we have already seen
(Ch. II), Socrates declines to argue with the 'many'. Nor is it the art
of Rhetoric and its teachers: Rhetoric is obviously dealt with in the
Gorgias as being only a means toward an aim, and the problem at
issue is the aim and its contestants, not the means and its sellers. The
rhetoricians Gorgias and Polos are no more a match for 'Socrates'
than the many. The real fight is against politicians of Callicles' type
and their particular kind of politics[57].

---

[56] There seems to be no reason to doubt that this striking characterization of the author
of the *Gorgias* goes back to the historical Gorgias himself (Athenaeus 505d).

[57] We know nothing of the historical Callicles and too little of his political associates
(*Gorg.* 487c: Wilamowitz, Platon I 211; Taylor, Platon, the Man and his Work, ²1929,
105, 129n.) as to be able to decide why Plato chose him as Socrates' main opponent. At
any rate, it would not probably add much to the more intimate interpretation of the
dialogue, because whatever the political and moral convictions of the historical Callicles
may have been, they certainly could not be influenced by the unfavorable impression
that Socrates' trial and death must have made not only upon the enemies of the Socratic
circle (cf. *Crito* 45d, Crito speaking: "I am ashamed not only of you, but of us who
are your friends, when I reflect that the whole business will be attributed entirely
to our want of courage. The trial need never have come on, or might have been
managed differently; and this last act, or crowning folly, will seem to have occurred
through our negligence and cowardice, who might have saved you, if we had been
good for anything; and you might have saved yourself, for there was no difficulty
at all. See now, Socrates, how sad and discreditable are the consequences, both to
us and you"). The *Gorgias* openly presupposes just this impression, although,
of course, the conversation is supposed to be held at some more or less earlier date —
which "it is unusually difficult to determine" (Taylor, p. 104, cf. Wil. I 214, 2).

The 'Callicles' of the dialogue stands by no means for 'politics against philosophy' in general. In the first place, Plato draws a sharp line between his Callicles and the born demagogue who needs no artificial rhetoric[58] but is liked by the many because he is genuinely like them (513b). Callicles, who despises the demos, may be badly mistaken if he hopes to influence them while keeping his superiority[59], but obviously he is not that kind of a politician of which Aristophanes made Cleon the prototype.

Nietzsche has so effectively popularized Callicles' moral views that to-day interpreters need only to remind of Nietzsche and some of his slogans in order to have those views quite adequately understood[60]. But it must, secondly, not be ignored that Callicles develops his doctrine of immoralism merely in opposition to Socrates' thesis that suffering wrong is preferable to doing wrong (when there is no third way) and against Socrates' unpreparedness against political persecution *in Athens* (by perhaps "some miserable and mean person": Callicles' words, *Gorg.* 521c), and that the actual political activity for which he is training himself and calling up Socrates has little resemblance with that of "the men of action for action's sake, the Napoleons and Cromwells" (Taylor p. 116) or of a Caesar Borgia (Taylor p. 119). For although Callicles "fühlt sich als Herrenmensch" (Wilamowitz I 219), his scope is practically restricted to political life within the democratic state of Athens; far from being a partisan of the principle of aristocracy or oligarchy he is prepared to submit in everything to the pleasure of the demos, and it is exaclty this love and adulation of the demos that is slighted by Plato throughout the whole dialogue as contemptible parasitism.

As far as Callicles is concerned, the author of the *Gorgias* is much more interested in the special kind of politics that Callicles stands

---

[58] As Alcibiades, whom Plato puts in the same class with Callicles, did need and apply: Plutarch. *Alcib.* 10, 4.

[59] *Gorg.* 513b: "If you suppose that any man will show you the art of becoming great in the city, and yet not conforming yourself to the ways of the city, whether for better or worse, then I can only say that you are mistaken, Callicles; for he who would deserve to be the true natural friend of the Athenian Demos . . . must be by nature like them, and not an imitator only. He, then, who will make you most like them, will make you as you desire, a statesman and orator: for every man is pleased when he is spoken to in his own language and spirit, and dislikes any other".

[60] For instance, Taylor p. 116: "His morality, like Nietzsche's, may be an inverted one, but it is one with which he is in downright earnest"; p. 117: "When a really strong man — in fact, the *Übermensch* — appears, he will soon . . ."; p. 119: "Thus the ideal of Callicles, like that of Nietzsche, is the successfull cultivation of the *Wille zur Macht*, and his 'strong man', like Nietzsche's . . ."

for[61] than in the welfare of this man's individual soul. Why this passionate attack not on politics in general, nor on either of the two main factions at Athens whom Socrates had offended during the last years of his life (the simply democratic and the simply oligarchic faction[62]), but on a certain limited group of politicians who, according to Plato, were doomed to failure, not only spiritually, but practically, too, as he points out scornfully more than once (513b, 517a cf. 502a, 519a)?

Because these people were the only ones with whom, in Plato's sight, it was worth while to argue; they were from the classes where in earlier times he would have found political associates: really 'better' than the 'many', but now too discouraged by the oligarchic fiasco of 404/3 B. C., and, even worse, too disgusted with the pitiable spectacle of Socrates' trial and execution as to be accessible any longer to the political implications of Socrates' criticisms of Athenian life. They did not see, now, any practical possibility but deliberate and reckless compliance with the actual Athenian democracy[63].

As we have seen, Plato must have expected in the first time after Socrates' death quite a different reaction and hoped for a political development in the opposite direction. But then, disappointed, he turned radical in his way, and destroyed ruthlessly the ideological support of all 'good' and at the same time loyal citizens, namely the belief in the possibility of a democracy that is a democracy only by name, but in fact an aristocracy (Thuc. 2, 37, 1; 65, 9; Pl. *Menex.* 238c/d). And so, mutatis mutandis, i. e. under much more complicated historical, political and personal conditions, and with immensely refined literary means, the author of the *Gorgias* 'was forced to' ex-

---

[61] *Gorg.* 515b: "You are contentious, Socrates. — But it is not because of contentiousness that I ask you, but because I really want to know in what way you think that politics should be dealt with among us."

[62] There is reason to warn against confusion of Callicles' political attitude and that of truly oligarchic politicians like Critias. Critias did not profess immoralism (this is undeniably shown by *Ep. VII* 324d and strongly confirmed by Lysias *c. Erat.* § 5), and at least after 403 B. C., it would have been silly to explain his actions by "love of the Athenian Demos" which is the characteristic of Callicles. In Callicles there is nothing of the genuine anti-democratic spirit that, even after the downfall of the regime of the Thirty, could express itself so splendidly in the (of course, fictive) epigram

Σῆμα τόδ' ἐστ' ἀνδρῶν ἀγαθῶν, οἳ τὸν κατάρατον
Δῆμον 'Αθηναίων ὀλίγον χρόνον ὕβριος ἔσχον.

("This is the tomb of the brave men by whom the accursed Demos of Athens was checked in its insolence — for a short time"). Plato himself has more of that spirit.

[63] And its traditional imperialistic naval policy: *Gorg.* 519a. For, as Wilamowitz has seen (Platon I 235), written at the end of the first decade of the 4th century B. C., this passage condemns in fact the „Rückfall in die kriegerische Machtpolitik, jetzt bei dem Elend und der Armut im Innern so ganz aussichtslos".

press the same passionate antagonism to compromise with Athenian democracy that a generation ago had condensed itself in plainer words, thus: "I forgive the people themselves their attachment to a democracy, for it is pardonable in every one to study his own benefit; but whoever is not one of the people, and prefers to live under a democratic rather than an oligarchic form of government, is but meditating dishonesty, and knows that it is much easier for a knave to escape notice under a democracy than under an oligarchy" (Ps. Xen. *Rep. Ath.* 2, 20, Watson's translation). The difference, of course, is, that in the meantime "meditating dishonesty", in reaction against really or seemingly conventional phrases, had become a deliberate intellectual process and could not be fought any longer by merely calling its name. But here and there the same exclusiveness that addresses only "whoever is not one of the people", or, in the words of the *Gorgias*: "with the many I have nothing to do, and do not even address myself to them" (474a).

We know by now of what kind Plato's political views and aims were during the nineties of the 4th century B. C., and for what reasons he could not find associates where he sought them. But in order to know this we had to replace the quotation of the philosophical part of the *Republic* in the *7th Epistle* (326a) by the dialogue *Gorgias* which is in tendency much more like the venomous oligarchic pamphlet "Government of Athens" than like a philosophical treatise.

The theoretical and practical result of the *Gorgias* is very simple. Philosophy — doing in fact no more than to confirm by its dialectical arguments the common notions of just and unjust — insists that for decent people a decent life is preferable to injustice and indecency under any conditions whatsoever: and experience shows that a decent life is incompatible with political activity in Athens, as long as the 'better' men do not know better than to submit to the condition of Athenian democracy. Practically there is only the alternative of either living the private life of a philosopher "who does his own work" — like Socrates — or to leave the country.

From the *7th Epistle* we learn that Plato left the country for Italy and Sicily — and was strongly disappointed from the very beginning. At the end of his stay in Sicily he had trouble, because he had volunteered political advice at the court of a tyrant. On the other hand, in Dion he had found the best disciple of his ethical and political views he ever had.

The *7th Epistle* does not narrate Plato's return to Athens, and we have no testimony concerning the exact date of the foundation of the 'Academy'. But at the end of the period between the 'first' and the 'second' journey (387—367) Plato could be appealed to as the unique master of "words and power of persuasion", "enabling you to lead young men into the path of goodness and justice, and to establish in every case relations of friendship and comradeship among them" (328 d). And when he left Athens in 366 B. C., he was "leaving my own oc-cupations, which were certainly not discreditable ones, to put myself under a tyranny which did not seem to harmonize with my teaching or with myself" (329 b). In other words, at that time the 'Academy' must have existed as a well known institution, generally so much respected, that people simply could not understand the reasons for Plato's second departure.

Scanty as they are, these biographical data are nevertheless suf-ficient to explain the changes in Plato's attitude which we cannot fail to observe when we come from *Apology, Crito*, and *Gorgias*, to dialogues like *Menexenus, Protagoras*, and *Meno*. On this basis we established a provisional chronology of these dialogues in Chapter II, and, on the same basis, we extended, at the beginning of the present chapter, the chronology of Plato's writings to the so-called 'second' journey in 366 B. C. But as we have seen since, everything depends on an ade-quate interpretation of *Ep. VII* 326a.

Taylor (Plato, the Man and his Work[3], 1929, 20), who takes the chronological implications of this passage at their face value, comes to the following chronological distribution. According to him, "it should follow" that the "most philosophically advanced section of the *Republic* was already written in the year 388—7, with the consequence that the *Republic*, and by consequence the earlier dialogues in general, were completed at least soon after Plato was forty and before the actual foundation of the Academy". The *Theaetetus*, on the other hand — "the dialogue which seems to prelude to the later group" — is dated by Taylor exactly as we (and others) did, namely between 369 B. C. and 366 B. C. Result: All the Platonic dialogues listed by us above on p. 91, with the sole exception of the *Theaetetus*, the *Parmenides* and perhaps the *Phaedrus*, are crammed into a period between Socrates' death and "soon after Plato was forty and before the actual foundation of the Academy" ... "For twenty years after the foundation of the Academy Plato seems to have written nothing, unless the *Phaedrus*, a difficult dialogue to account for on any theory, falls early in this period. This is as it should be: the President of the Academy would for long enough after its foundation be far too busy to write. Then, pro-bably on the eve of the Sicilian adventure, after twenty years of work the Academy is sufficiently organized to leave its head, now a man of sixty years, leisure to write the *Theaetetus* and *Parmenides*" and so forth.

I have mentioned this eccentric arrangement because, if Taylor had not drawn these conclusions seriously, I should have had to propose them on my own in order to show the necessity of a more circumspect utilization of our main biographical source.

Of all Platonic writings the *Menexenus, Protagoras* and *Meno* make the greatest effort to show an appreciative and understanding attitude towards Athenian democracy, its institutions, its history and its leader. Since the *Menexenus* must have been written either in or soon after 386 B. C., it was immediately after Plato's return from his 'first' Italian and Sicilian journey that — in marked contrast to the *Gorgias* — this tendency prevailed.

Of course, Plato takes care not to identify himself completely with the favorable view of Athenian democracy: its praise is a praise of Athenians before an *Athenian* audience (*Menex.* 235d, twice quoted in Aristotle's *Rhetoric*); the justification of democratic education and institutions is laid in Protagoras' mouth, who, although he feels very superior to the 'many' (*Prot.* 317a, 352e, 353a), is nevertheless no more than they are able to indicate another standard of 'good' and 'evil' but pleasure and pain (354c, 354e/355a); and the *Meno*, in a famous passage at the end of the discussion, hints at a statesman whose virtue would be based on teachable knowledge and who, compared with ordinary statesmen, would be in virtue like the real thing beside shadows (100a).

Yet, a general tendency towards virtue is now, in a way, conceded to the Athenian commonwealth. The Athenian democracy is, in fact, an aristocracy — at least, intentionally: *Menex.* 238c—239a. The whole system of Athenian private education and public coercion is interpreted as a vast institution determined to produce justice and virtue in all citizens — in the speech of a teacher who is trying to sell advanced study in private and civic virtue: *Prot.* 320eff. In the *Meno*, the great historical leaders of Athenian democracy now get the credit of having been good men and good statesmen — although their virtue must have been of an unteachable kind, otherwise they certainly would have wanted to make others, too, and especially their sons good men and statesmen, which they were notoriously not able to do.

If we ask what would make the 'real thing in virtue', the *Menexenus* provides the hint that it might be different from what the 'many' believe[64]; according to the *Protagoras* it should be some kind of learning and knowledge[65] of which neither the 'many' nor Protagoras

---

[64] The Athenian democracy is, in fact, an aristocracy μετ᾽ εὐδοξίας πλήθους "based on what the multitude *believes* to be good" (238d); εὐδοξία is opposed to knowledge in *Meno* (99b); the people gives political authority and power to those" who are *reputed* the best men" (238d5) and so twice again: ὁ δόξας σοφὸς ἢ ἀγαθὸς εἶναι 238d8, ἀρετῆς δόξῃ καὶ φρονήσεως 239a4.

[65] Its Socratic nature is deliberately kept off the surface of the dialogue, but intimated by means of the misinterpretation of Simonides' poem, see especially 345a-e.

himself have an idea; the *Meno* suggests to conceive it in analogy to mathematical learning and as capable of being aroused by methodic questioning (85d plus 98a).

Menexenus, Protagoras and *Meno* are the writings of an author who is offering political education and political reform. As an educator he has to compete with other educators and as a reformer he has to point out the shortcomings of the practical politicians, without offending too much the notions of the ordinary citizen. This point of view has been expounded very ably by Wilamowitz in his interpretation of the *Menexenus* and the *Meno* (see the relevant chapters in his 'Platon'); but he failed to see that the *Protagoras* is an integral member of this group of dialogues. Yet in my opinion there can be no doubt about that. If the contents of the dialogue were not sufficient proof, it would be shown clearly by passages like *Meno* 91b—92d and *Rep.* 492a—493b. In the *Republic* one may read in outspoken words what the *Protagoras* had pictured, namely that, although the 'many' mistrust the 'sophists' and think of them as corrupters of the youth, these sophists are entirely bare of a political doctrine of their own and "that all those mercenary individuals, whom the many call Sophists and whom they deem to be their adversaries, do, in fact, teach nothing but the opinion of the many, that is to say the opinion of their assemblies; and this is their wisdom" (*Rep.* 493a)[66].

Beside practical politicians, who are opposed to professional teaching of their art (*Rep.* 488b, cp. Anytos in the *Meno*), and 'sophists' the *Republic* describes (495c—496a) a third group of men to be reckoned with in order to determine the actual position of philosophy in a democracy (i. e. the Athenian democracy): fake philosophers who are mainly responsible for "the harsh feeling which the many entertain towards philosophy" (500b). We know this type of 'philosophy' from the dialogue *Euthydemus*; the brothers Euthydemus and Dionysodorus correspond exactly to the general description[67] in *Rep.*

---

[66] In order to modernize the aspect of the 'sophists' Aristotle had to do nothing but to quote simply an arrogant passage of Isocrates (*Or.* 15, 79—83), which brilliantly exposes its author's incapacity for political theory (Arist. *EN* 1180b28—1181b12).

[67] *Rep.* 500c adds a specific feature: these 'philosophers' have a hateful way of insulting the many, always making persons instead of things the theme of their conversations. Since in the *Euthydemus* the two brothers do little in the line of personalities, this personally offensive attitude in addition to the futile dialectic method is obviously aimed at some certain contemporary (and who should it be but Antisthenes?). It is highly amusing to see that Isocrates, who, in fact, is bantered in 498d/e, understood the 'hateful way' (φιλαπεχθημόνως), too, as said of himself and complained bitterly of this undeserved insult (*Or.* 15, 260), although here (500c) Plato certainly did not mean him. Wilamowitz (Platon II 121) has seen this, but otherwise his interpretation is rather vague and not so useful as one should expect in this case of malicious

495c—496a, and their picture is presupposed here in the same way as the pictures of the 'sophist' in the *Protagoras* and of the average 'politician' in the *Meno* are presupposed in the relevant passages of the *Republic* about sophists and politicians. Thus, with regard to educational competition, the *Euthydemus* belongs to the group *Protagoras/Meno*; but from this point of view, too[68], it appears to have been written comparatively late. For while the other two dialogues point out the desirability and possibility of such a kind of education as Plato is offering, the *Euthydemus* deals with 'philosophy' as an already established separate educational profession and urges the necessity of discrimination within this profession.

In ChapterI I have dated the *Euthyphro* after the *Meno* and before the *Phaedo* because of the exclusive dependency of the doctrine of the *Phaedo* on τί ἐστι-questions put in the way of the *Euthyphro* (and not of the *Meno*). But it cannot be assumed that to prepare for the *Phaedo*'s doctrine of ideas was in the author's mind when he wrote the *Euthyphro*. Within this dialogue, the determination of the meaning of its τί ἐστι-question is merely intended to prepare a *logically* correct definition of 'the pious', and in this respect Socrates is completely satisfied without difficulty and without much delay (5c—7a). The main concern of the little dialogue is a material examination of the theological notion of piety[69] and its masterly elimination, once for all, from basic philosophical thought. Against attempts to attribute the *Euthyphro* to a time, early in Plato's career, when a defense of the historical Socrates' memory was his main object, it must be remarked that the undeniably important theoretical result of the dialogue has no reference to Socrates' alleged offense of the religious notions of ordinary citizens[70] which made part of the historical accusation, and that, on

polemic on the part of Plato; for he has failed to see (1) that, even if Isocrates called his own business philosophy, nevertheless Plato, if he had chosen to be outspoken about Isocrates, could have classified him only with the 'sophists' (as did Aristotle, see above n 66.), and (2) that "insulting the many" was part of playing the Socratic philosopher — outside, of course, the dignified Platonic school — cp. *Sympos.* 173d.

[68] For another point of view compare above p. 90n. 51.

[69] "Piety is that which is dear to the gods, and impiety is that which is not dear to them" is Euthyphro's Alpha (6e) and Omega (15b/c).

[70] Euthyphro is not one of them, on the contrary: "he instinctively takes the side of Socrates as soon as he has heard the nature of the charge against him, and classes Socrates and himself together as theologians exposed to the unintelligent derision of the 'vulgar'" (Taylor p. 147 following Burnet). With Burnet Taylor thinks it was "the natural inference" from what was known about Socrates, "that he was himself a sectary much of the same type as Euthyphro, as Euthyphro seems to suppose. It was a duty of piety to his memory to make it clear that his views on religion were very different . . .". But why, then, does Plato make a point of it that not only Socrates' views on religion, but his external attitude towards the Athenian people

the other hand, the clear perception of the secondary nature of 'being dear to the gods' as compared with 'justice itself'[71] is one of the foundations on which the whole structure of the *Republic* is built (363 a ff., 612 b ff.).

The *Euthydemus* and the *Euthyphro*, both of them in all probability composed later than the *Meno* and earlier than the *Phaedo*, mark logically and chronologically the beginning of that series of Platonic dialogues where in some way or other the 'one idea' is strictly opposed to the correspondent 'many things' as something different[72]. The relevant passage of the *Euthydemus* (300 e) indicates that at the time when this dialogue was written, Plato knew already so much of the philosophical importance of 'the beautiful itself' as the *Phaedo* presupposes; more cannot be said. But what about the *Euthyphro* ?

Both Taylor and Wilamowitz find something remarkable in it with respect to the doctrine of ideas.

Taylor p. 149: "It is noticeable that this common character of the "religiously right" is at the outset spoken of as a single ἰδέα (*Euthyphro* 5d) and subsequently as an εἶδος (6d) and as an οὐσία (11a). This is the language familiar to us as technical in the so-called Platonic 'theory of forms', but it is represented as understood at once by Euthyphro without any kind of explanation. It seems quite impossible to escape the conclusion that from the very first Plato represented Socrates as habitually using language of this kind and being readily understood by his contemporaries."

Wilamowitz I p. 208: "Vor allem fällt auf, daß der Name 'Idee des Frommen' erscheint, 'die Form an sich, durch welche alles Fromme

and the people's reaction were entirely different (3 c-e, 5 b/c) ? — Wilamowitz' interpretation of the introductory part of the dialogue (2 a-6 c) is more adequate to the text: according to him (I 204—208) it is Plato's choice (not a natural inference presupposed in the minds of the audience) to put Euthyphro and Socrates side by side: "Dieser Pfaffe ist die rechte Folie für Sokrates in dem, was er und wie er es tut" (205). But then, the theoretical part of the dialogue (16 pages against 7 of the introductory part) becomes almost superfluous for its main purpose („so, daß eigentlich die Gegenüberstellung des Pfaffen zur Rechtfertigung des Sokrates genügt", 204; „Zur siegreichen Verteidigung des Sokrates reicht diese Gegenüberstellung der Menschen und der Gesinnungen" — in the introductory part — „hin", 206), and, curiously enough, almost too important as to belong to an early time (206—208)!

[71] This 'itself' is different from the 'itself' of the doctrine of ideas; it simply opposes the thing justice to its possible consequences (not the predicate just to its possible subjects): *Rep.* 363 a 1, 612 b 2, c 10. In the *Euthyphro* Socrates complains that by answering 'dear to the gods' when asked what the pious is E. declines to make clear the essence of the thing, but only tells something that is happening to it (τὴν μὲν οὐσίαν μοι αὐτοῦ οὐ βούλεσθαι δηλῶσαι, πάθος δέ τι περὶ αὐτοῦ λέγειν, 11a).

[72] *Euthyphro, Euthydemus, Phaedo, Sympos., Lysis* (219 b—220 b), *Cratylus, Rep., Phaedr., Parm., Tim., Philebus.*

fromm wird' (6d). Damit ist mindestens der Gattungsbegriff logisch erfaßt[73], und es kostet einige Überwindung, nicht die ganze spätere Ideenlehre hereinzuziehen. Davor muß man sich doch hüten ... Denn mit Sicherheit läßt sich nicht mehr schließen, als daß Gedanken aufgestiegen sind, die einst die höchste Bedeutung erlangen sollten, aber jetzt nur eben aufblitzen."

It is amusing to see both scholars try their respective skeleton keys in order to come to an understanding of a wrongly antedated dialogue. But it is not necessary to assume with Taylor (or rather Burnet) that the "reality of the existence of 'forms' was already quite familiar to the historical Socrates", nor must we, with Wilamowitz, let Plato in his thirties anticipate his later thoughts in a wishful, uncertain and unsystematic way. What we need to do in order to understand the *Euthyphro* is simply to take seriously the theoretical discussion of 'piety' — that Plato himself did so is proved by the *Republic* — and to concede to its author and its audience so much logical training concerning definitions as e. g. *Laches* and *Meno* provide. For any one who knows so much of τί ἐστι-questioning will easily understand the logical proceeding of the *Euthyphro*: neither acquaintance with nor anticipation of the 'theory of forms' is required. In the *Euthyphro* it is the subject matter — moral predicates — that makes all the difference from the *Meno* and leads, by the way, to an important discovery: namely that the concepts of predicates (their 'τί ἐστι') like 'pious' and 'impious' should be conceived independently of their possible subjects, in order to get a definition. Such concepts were destined to become the prototypes of Platonic ideas, but there is no possibility of deciding how far Plato was already anticipating this later development when he wrote the *Euthyphro*[74].

---

[73] A very incorrect statement!

[74] Wilamowitz (II 157) has an interesting comment on *Euthydemus* 300e (see above p. 107 and Ch. I), where Socrates is compelled to answer: "The many beautiful things are not the same as the beautiful itself, but they have beauty present with each of them". Socrates' answer, Wilamowitz points out, „läuft nur darauf hinaus, daß καλόν hier nicht selbst erscheint, sondern nur als Prädikat von πρᾶγμα, also aussagt, daß dies ein Schönes (nicht das Schöne) an sich hat. Weiter als dies grammatisch logische Verhältnis liegt nichts darin. . . . An die Idee des Schönen, deren Zutritt, wie immer er auch zu erklären ist, das Einzelding schön macht, . . . zu denken, liegt durchaus keine Veranlassung vor. Dazu verführt, daß Dionysodor vom καλόν als etwas Gesondertem redet. Das führt den Leser Platons auf das αὐτὸ καλόν, die Idee. Soll Dionysodor die Ideenlehre kennen? Oder hat Platon versehentlich sie ihm geliehen? Ist es nicht vielmehr nur das Prädikat schön, ein sozusagen grammatischer Scherz . . . ?" Exactly; but is the very discovery of the 'separateness' of a predicate like beautiful — 'man' or 'bee' would not do, although they may occur as predicates grammatically — merely a joke ? Then, why becomes Socrates so embarassed ? "Now I was in a great quandary at having to answer this question and I thought that I was

The *Phaedo* is not only the first Platonic dialogue that urges the transcendence of ideas but also the first that proclaims unrestrained 'seeking after truth for the sake of knowledge'[75] as the real business of the philosopher. The fact that some few people[76] are such as to prefer thinking, learning and knowledge to any other activity or value, is assumed independently and previous to the first mention of 'ideas' in the dialogue (63e—64d). The tendency of the born philosopher towards knowledge is illustrated by the picture of a scientific and at the same time optimistic natural science and cosmology, desired but not found by the young Socrates, a picture in which ideas are not mentioned (96a—99c). After that we come with Socrates to the famous second-best, which is, if we read very carefully, the search for truth by way of dialectic in general (99d—100a), and only then, in continuance of the interrupted discussion of immortality, as a special case of dialectical procedure, recurrence is again made to the assumption of 'ideas' and application of this 'hypothesis' to the problem at issue[77].

The Socrates who seeks after truth by way of dialectic discussion rather than by physical observation is, of course, the 'old Socrates' whom everybody knows. It is easy to illustrate his dialectical method with passages of undoubtedly genuine 'Socratic' character.

With *Phaedo* 100a: "this was the method which I adopted: I first assume some principle (λόγος) which I judge to be strongest, and then I affirm as true whatever seems to agree with this — whether relating to the cause or to anything else — and that which disagrees I regard as untrue"

compare *Crito* 46b: "We ought to consider whether I shall or shall not do as you say. For I am and always have been such as not to obey anything but the principle (λόγος) which upon reflection appears to me to be the best . . ."

and *Gorgias* 509a: "My position has always been that I myself am ignorant how these things are, but that I have never met any one who

---

rightly served for having opened my mouth at all; I said however . . ." Obviously the author of the dialogue was aware of a serious problem.

[75] The expression ζητεῖν τὸ ἀληθὲς τοῦ γνῶναι χάριν does not occur in the *Phaedo* but is from *Rep.* 499a.

[76] Aristotle, not Plato, is responsible for the captious half-truth πάντες ἄνθρωποι τοῦ εἰδέναι ὀρέγονται φύσει (first sentence of the *Metaphysics*). Plato, in the *Philebus*, had only asserted in the negative, that a life without any kind of thinking would not be acceptable to anybody.

[77] Incidentally, in the following discussion 'ideas' are practically equivalent with what I should like to call 'predicative entities', and the introduction of ideas into this section of the dialogue (100bff.) is only a way of dealing with (non-transcendent!) qualities and attributes at a time when more suitable logical and ontological technical terms were not yet available.

could say otherwise, any more than you can, and not appear ridiculous. So then I affirm that these things are so. Now, if they are so, . . ."

The only difference is that in the *Phaedo* Socrates is going to apply his method of taking for granted what is conceded by the interlocutors (what appears to be the strongest logos) to a theoretical rather than a practical problem. But in the words of the *Phaedo* (70b/c), "no one, not even a Comic poet, could accuse him of talking idly in matters in which he had no concern", if he speculates about immortality on the day of his death.

As to the "account of the early development of Socrates" (*Phd.* 96a—99c), Burnet and Taylor are, in my opinion, quite right in rejecting "the preposterous suggestions that the narrative is meant as a description either of Plato's own mental development or of the development of a 'typical' philosopher" (Taylor p. 199/200). The details are too well adapted to the historical Socrates; Plato has without doubt "taken care that his story shall be in accord with historical probabilities". Yet I would not stress too much the 'strictly historical' quality of the account. For, (1) while the state of scientific opinion which is so ably criticized may indeed be that of the middle of the fifth century, the criticism itself seems to me late or post-Socratic rather than early or pre-Socratic, and, (2) although nobody would like to assume that the young Socrates was too dull or already too prejudiced as to be seriously interested in natural philosophy, yet one must realize that the surprisingly (96a θαυμαστῶς ὡς) onesided enthusiasm of the *Phaedo*'s 'young Socrates' for theoretical science is the only available means to force the impression that 'old Socrates' was *au fond* one of the born philosophers in the sense of the *Phaedo*. This born philosopher, who makes his first appearance in the *Phaedo* and of whom we have edifying pictures in the *Republic* and the *Theaetetus*, looks always more like a beloved disciple of Plato than anything else; and it is difficult to decide how much or how little literary art was needed to make the historical Socrates fit in.

But more important is the fact that this story of the early development of a 'born philosopher' is not the story of Plato's own development. Plato's own beginnings were the complete reverse of what later, as an educator, he thought desirable[78].

Phaedo 96a: Socrates speaking: "When I was young, Cebes, I had a prodigious desire to know that department of philosophy which is

---

[78] Cp. *Theaet.* 173c :"In the first place, the lords of philosophy"—as opposed to politicians — "have never, from their youth upwards, known their way to the Agora, or the dicastery, or the council, or any other political assembly; they neither see nor hear the laws or decrees of the state written or recited" and so forth; the whole passage is most instructive.

called the investigation of nature; to know the causes of things, and why a thing is and is created or destroyed appeared to me to be a lofty profession, and I was always agitating myself with the consideration of questions such as these: — Is the growth of animals the result of . . .".

Ep. VII 324b (Harward's translation): Plato speaking: "In my youth I went through the same experience as many other men. I fancied that if, early in life, I became my own master, I should at once embark on a political career. And I found myself confronted with the following occurences in the public affairs of my own city. The existing constitution being generally condemned, a revolution took place, and . . ."

Consequently, the domestic use of the principle: 'search of truth for the sake of knowledge' (instead of: 'search of knowledge for the sake of better practice') must have been discovered by Plato comparatively late; and it is consistent with everything we know of his career that the proclamation of this principle in the *Phaedo* should bear all the marks of a comparatively *new* discovery[79].

We are now prepared — and this I hope will justify the awkward slowness of our investigation so far — to raise, with regard to the *Phaedo*, a final question. What is, in the *Phaedo*, the main function[80] of that 'theory of ideas' which is so enthusiastically presupposed[81]?

The complete answer is implied in the first section after the first mention of 'ideas'.

Phaedo 65d: "There is another thing, Simmias; is there or is there not a 'just' itself? — Assuredly there is. — And a 'beautiful' and a 'good'? — Of course. — But did you ever behold any of such objects with your eyes? — Certainly not. — Or did you ever reach them with any other bodily sense? — and I speak not of these alone, but of greatness, and health, and strength and of the essence (what it is)

---

[79] *Euthyd.* and *Charmides* belong to the period in which it was made. In *Euthyd.* 290c Plato gives on purpose a glimpse of the primarily theoretical business of the philosopher; and the whole section of the dialogue, where this is found, (288d—292e) as well as the main part of the *Charmides* (164d—175d) are devoted to the puzzling revelation that, if knowledge is the only good which practically matters, then its highest form cannot exhaust itself in praising, propagating or scrutinizing knowledge, in other words, the business of the philosopher cannot be mere 'politics', not even in the sense in which 'politics' is taken in *Meno* 100a and *Gorg.* 521d. Cp. *Rep.* 505b.

[80] Not its original meaning. This I tried to explain in Chapter I.

[81] I have no other expression. Taylor (p. 149 n.) states "the reality of the existence of 'forms' is simply presupposed in the *Phaedo*, as elsewhere, without any explanation or justification" in support of Burnet's and his own pet presumption that the theory of forms was genuinely Socratic. But, why then, is it always cheered, whenever it is mentioned in the *Phaedo*?

of everything. Has the reality of them ever been perceived by you through the bodily organs? or rather, is not the nearest to the knowledge of each of them made by him who so orders his intellectual vision as to have the most exact conception of each object *itself* which he considers? — Certainly. — And he attains to the purest knowledge of them who goes to each with the mind alone, not introducing or intruding in the act of thought sight or any other sense together with reason, but with the very light of the mind in her own clearness searches into the very truth of each; he who has got rid, as far as he can, of eyes and ears and, so to speak, of the whole body, these being in his opinion distracting elements which when they infect the soul hinder her from acquiring truth and knowledge — who, if not he, is likely to attain to the knowledge of true being? — What you say has a wonderful truth in it, Socrates, replied Simmias."

This does not mean the truism that universal concepts are conceived in the mind and not perceived by the senses. For, in spite of the fact that here ideas seem to be stated of *everything* of which an essence (the 'what-is-it') may be sought and that the second group of examples (greatness, health and strength) has been taken from the *Meno* (72 d) — the *Meno*, which as we have seen in Chapter I, is indeed concerned with universal concepts —, the very selection of this group ('bee' e.g. would spoil everything) and the repeated addition of the pronoun 'itself' prevent us from concentrating upon anything but the essence of certain predicative entities[82].

---

[82] It is true that Plato never has been quite clear or quite frank about the difference of things in the narrow sense (bees, bulls, men, silver, fire, water, finger, hair) and predicative entities. nor about the dependence of his original theory of ideas on entities of the latter kind. But we have, fortunately, in *Rep.* 523 a ff. Plato's own statement that things like finger — in opposition to predications like great and small and so forth — are not apt to provoke speculation about their essence and accordingly not apt to arouse philosophical thinking: "Explain, he said. — I mean to say that objects of sense are of two kinds; some of them do not invite thought because the sense is an adequate judge of them; while in the case of other objects sense is so untrustworthy that further inquiry is imperatively demanded. — You are clearly referring, he said, to the manner in which the senses are imposed upon by distance, and by painting in light and shade. — No, I said, that is not at all my meaning. — Then what is your meaning? — When speaking of uninviting objects, I mean those which do not pass from one sensation to the opposite; inviting objects are those which do; in this latter case the sense coming upon the object, whether at a distance or near, gives no more vivid idea of anything in particular than of its opposite. An illustration will make my meaning clearer: — here are three fingers — a little finger, a second finger, and a middle finger. — Very good. — You may suppose that they are seen quite close: And here comes the point. — What is it? — Each of them equally appears a finger, whether seen in the middle or at the extremity, whether white or black, or thick or thin — it makes no difference; a finger is a finger all the same. In these cases the mind is not compelled to ask of thought the question

With regard to such entities, i. e. with regard to the moral predicates in the first place, a seemingly very simple truth is urged, namely, that thinking, pure intensive thinking[83], is required to be able to account for 'what they themselves' (not their subjects) 'are'. As we have seen in Chapter I, in the case of the moral predicates, it is merely the conviction *that* there are such objects of thought which is shared by all interlocutors, whereas the ability really 'to give an account of these matters' (*Phd.* 76b) is conceded only to Socrates.

More than any others, the moral alternatives, just or unjust, good or evil, honest or dishonest, pious or impious (with 'just' taking the lead as in *Phd.* 65d) have a primarily practical, not a theoretical significance. Therefore, even if 'pure intensive thinking' is required to account for them, the practical point of view might still prevail (as it does throughout the *Euthyphro*). But, on the other hand, the necessity of a purely theoretical dealing with these matters seems to be demonstrable at any rate; and we may presume that Plato, as an educator, insisted on it from the very beginning of 'Academic' instruction. What we know for certain is that after a period of about 20 years he was scared by the idea, that, in the field of politics, he might appear to himself "wholly and solely a mere man of words (λόγος μόνον)[84], one who would never of his own lay his hand to any act" (*Ep. VII* 328c, Harward's translation). We find a similar expression of dissatisfaction with a merely theoretical activity in *Rep.* 497a; and perhaps these two passages show better than more onesided ones the actual state of affairs in Plato's Academy. For elsewhere, first in the *Phaedo*, and then, in the *Symposium*, other passages of the *Republic*, in the *Phaedrus* and in the *Theaetetus*, he disposes of such scruples in the opposite way. With the doctrine of 'ideas', the doctrine of the just 'itself' (and not the single cases), the good 'itself' and so forth, it seems a little step to let the

---

what is a finger? for the sight never intimates to the mind that a finger is other than a finger. — True. — And therefore, I said, as we might expect, there is nothing here which invites or excites intelligence. — There is not, he said. — But is this equally true of the greatness and smallness of the fingers? can sight adequately perceive them? . . . " And *Phaedr.* 263a completes this statement by asserting a similar difference between the group 'iron', 'silver' on the one hand, and 'just', 'good' on the other hand.

[83] It seems obvious to me that in Plato's conception of 'purest knowledge' attained by him 'who goes to each with the mind alone, not introducing or intruding in the act of thought sight or any other sense together with reason' (*Phd.* 65e) there is a hopeless confusion between 'intensive reflection undisturbed by sensation' and 'senseless perception of transcendent objects'; in consequence of this confusion every theoretical effort comes on the side of 'pure thinking' (with transcendent objects), and every experience not found by 'thinking' on the side of sense-perception. Cp. Chapter I 76. Only in the *Theaet.* 185bff. the confusion of δόξα and αἴσθησις is lifted.

[84] Cp. *Rep.* 473a, where λέξις is opposed to πρᾶγμα as 'theory' to practice.

thing itself be what was wanted from the beginning, to let theory precede practice in valuation even in the practical field — and to pervert morals and moral instruction hopelessly.

In the *Phaedo* the impression that even in the field of morals (and politics) *theory* is wanted by the philosopher, is accomplished by a presumably unconscious but certainly most clever trick of arrangement: previous to the mention of ideas we hear of the abhorrence of the born philosopher from the pleasures and comforts of the body and his predilection for pure thinking (64 d—65 c)!

As an interpreter and defender of the historical Socrates Plato explained moral action simply and effectively as sticking to a felt and acknowledged definite obligation (not only in the *Apology* and the *Crito*, but, as we have already mentioned, even in the *Phaedo*, 98 e/99 a, see Chapter I conclusion). For the requirements of 'Academic' instruction morals were reconstructed differently. It is so easy (supposing we are born philosophers): if thinking and learning and their theoretical objects are our only real concern, then all the other 'so-called' values of life are either directly obstructive or 'not so important'; and thus, the philosopher gets, as it were, gratis all the so-called ordinary virtues: it cannot be worth while for him — as it is for ordinary people — to offend against the rules of common decency (*Phd.* 68 c—69 c, *Rep.* 485 a to 487 a). This, indeed, has become the moral attitude of the average Academician, and so there is probably some truth in it, especially so long as the Academician remains within the borders of Academical life and of scholastic Academical ambition and pride (*Theaet.* 172 c to 177 b).

It is a comfort to know that even in his later times Plato himself did not always feel and act according to the Academic way of life, which, as an educator, he had shaped for his best disciples.

To formulate, in conclusion, the result of this chapter: In the *Phaedo* it is the main function of the doctrine of ideas, that it provides separate, only theoretically perceivable objects to the theory of morals and politics, and thus, by stressing the theoretical character of accounting for moral predication, facilitates and, without necessarily implying it, corroborates[85] the Academic view that the whole business of the philosopher is primarily theoretical. Let practice come to the door of philosophy (*Rep.* 489 b/c), if it wants its guidance; philosophy does not care, at least not unconditionally; ideas are, anyway, more interesting than their application in practical life. —

---

[85] In a similar way the doctrine of ideas confirms — without necessarily implying it — the preconceived assumption of immortality (*Phd.* 73 b ff.). For a third, merely logical, use of the doctrine in the *Phaedo* see above p. 109 n. 77).

IV. Symposium

Although two of the best modern interpreters of Plato expressly declare the question of the relative chronology of the *Phaedo* and the *Symposium* to be an unsolvable one[86], I think my argument for the priority of the *Phaedo* (see Chapter I) is decisive. For while it is true that the discussions of the *Phaedo* lead up to a view on human life and the business of the philosopher which almost anticipates the revelation of the final aim of philosophy in Diotima's speech (*Symp.* 209e ff.), it is also true that the *Phaedo* does not *presuppose* anything like it in the minds of its readers; on the contrary, the confidence with which that minimum of a doctrine of ideas which *is* presupposed, is accepted by Socrates' interlocutors would be entirely out of place, if the author of the *Phaedo* could have thought of the possibility, that the mention of the 'good itself' and the 'beautiful itself' would remind his readers of a passage like *Symposium* 209e ff. And similarly, once a transcendent 'idea' had openly been put at the top of the *world* (*Symp.* 211a), the opposition between a daring optimistic cosmology and that cautious, simple and 'perhaps silly' (*Phd.* 100d) method of ideas which Socrates uses in the *Phaedo* could not be supposed to make sense in the minds of the readers; and the conclusion is, again, that at the time when the *Phaedo* was written, that unforgettable chapter of the *Symposium* did not yet exist.

On the other hand it seems clear to me, too, that Plato himself, when he wrote the *Phaedo*, was aware of a possible development of his doctrine of ideas in that very direction in which the Socrates of the *Phaedo* stated a gap in his own and other men's knowledge[87] and which was later on marked by the idea of the beautiful as it appears in the *Symposium*, the idea of the good in the *Republic*, and by the cosmology of the *Timaeus*. If, in the *Phaedo*, he refrained from actually indicating this way, he must have had some reason.

Theoretically there was no obstacle. It is true, at least according to my account of the origin of the doctrine of ideas, that 'ideas' were first thought of in the limited field of moral action; but already in the *Gorgias* Plato had confirmed the validity of the common moral postulates by a reference to the alleged cosmic validity of these same

---

[86] Wilamowitz, Platon, I 322: "in den beiden Dialogen, die er ziemlich gleichzeitig verfaßt haben muß, da sich trotz manchen Berührungen nicht erkennen läßt, welcher früher vollendet ist, . . . Phaidon und Symposion"; Taylor, Plato the Man and his Work, 175: "We cannot tell, for example, whether the *Phaedo* is earlier or later than the *Symposium*."

[87] *Phd.* 99c: "this is the principle which I would fain learn if any one would teach me. But as I have failed either to discover myself, or to learn of any one else, the nature of this principle, I will exhibit to you, if you like, what I have found to be the second best mode of enquiring into the cause."

principles[88]; and it is just the criticism of fifth century science in the
Phaedo which urges the necessity of one and the same final principle
of explanation for both cosmology and moral action. But why, then,
does the Socrates of the *Phaedo* avoid to speak of the ultimate source of
whatever is good in terms of the doctrine of ideas?

It takes a strong prejudice to declare (with Burnet) the account
of the early development of Socrates in the *Phaedo* 'strictly historical'
(Taylor l. c. p. 199) and, at the same time, to overlook or to mini-
mize the import of the statement that, as long as he lived, Socrates
himself was not able to discover or to learn of any one else the desired
principle of natural science, which, as we know, Plato was going to
identify with the transcendent 'idea' of the beautiful or of the good.
We are in no position to decide *a priori* and by ourselves what attitude
toward natural science was, in Plato's opinion, suitable to the Socrates
of the *Phaedo*, and what kind of attitude had to be avoided; but we
have the help of two well known passages of the *Apology*.

Apology 19c: "not that I mean to speak disparagingly of any one
who is a student of natural philosophy. I should be very sorry if
Meletus could bring so grave a charge against me" — sc. as to enforce
upon me such a concession. "But the simple truth is, o Athenians, that
I have nothing to do with physical speculations. Very many of those
here present are witnesses to the truth of this, and to them I appeal.
Speak then, you who have heard me, and tell your neighbours whether
any of you have ever known me hold forth in few words or in many
upon such matters . . . You hear their answer. And from what they
say of this part of the charge you will be able to judge of the rest."

Apology 26d: (Meletus:) "You are a complete atheist." (Socrates:)
"What an extraordinary statement! Why do you think so, Meletus?
Do you mean that I do not believe in the godhead of the sun or the
moon, like other men?" (Meletus:) "I assure you, judges, that he does
not: for he says that the sun is stone, and the moon earth." (Socrates:)
"Friend Meletus, you think that you are accusing Anaxagoras: and
you have but a bad opinion of the judges, if you fancy them illiterate
to such a degree as not to know that these doctrines are found in the
books of Anaxagoras the Clazomenian, which are full of them."
(Young men could easily buy the books and) "laugh at Socrates if he
pretends to father these views paradoxical as they are."

---

[88] *Gorg.* 508a: "And philosophers tell us, Callicles, that communion and friendship and
orderliness and temperance and justice bind together heaven and earth and gods
and men, and that this universe is therefore called Cosmos or order, not disorder or
disrule, my friend. But although you are a philosopher you seem to me never to have
observed that geometrical equality is mighty both among gods and men; you think
that you ought to cultivate inequality or excess, and do not care about geometry."

It is fairly in the line of this Socrates of the *Apology* to decline Anaxagoras' philosophy and to criticize its lack of the (Socratic) point of view 'what is best?', as Socrates does in the *Phaedo*; but to have him talk in this connection of the 'beautiful itself' (*Symposium*) or the 'idea of the good' (*Republic*) would have meant to let the historical Socrates raise — early in his life — the positive postulate of a transcendent basis of natural philosophy. We simply must accept the fact that Plato avoided to do this.

Plato's reserve, in the *Phaedo*, with regard to ideas as cosmic principles, does not only agree with the picture of Socrates' attitude in the *Apology*, but it is also entirely in harmony with the remarkable transitory sentence in Diotima's speech in the *Symposium*, where she doubts of Socrates' ability to follow her final steps (209e/210a).

Taylor, in consequence of Burnet's view that whatever Socrates utters in Plato's *Phaedo* and *Symposium* must be understood as an integral part of the philosophical experiences and convictions of the historical Socrates, tries to get rid of Diotima's doubt in the following way (Plato the Man and his Work, p. 229 n.): "Much infortunate nonsense has been written about the meaning of Diotima's apparent doubt whether Socrates will be able to follow her as she goes on to speak of the 'full and perfect vision' (τὰ τέλεα καὶ ἐποπτικά 210a 1). It has even been seriously argued that Plato is here guilty of the arrogance of professing that he has reached philosophical heights to which the 'historical' Socrates could not ascend. Everything becomes simple if we remember that the actual person speaking is Socrates, reporting the words of Diotima. Socrates is as good as speaking of himself, and naturally, as a modest man, cannot say anything that would imply that he has already 'attained perfection' or is assured of 'final perseverance'."

Even if it sounds not so very convincing that we have to understand Diotima's doubt as a mere contrivance to save the natural modesty of Socrates[89], yet it may seem difficult to disprove this 'simple' explanation. And the argument that Plato cannot have intended to disparage Socrates' abilities in comparison with his own philosophical ascent, might even be put in a stronger form. For since according to the conclusion of Diotima's speech only the vision of 'the beautiful itself' guarantees the birth of true virtue, even the latter would have been denied in Socrates, which of course is out of the question.

---

[89] It would be interesting to know whether it is the meaning of this interpretation that the 'historical' Socrates was bound always to disguise his most intimate thoughts in such a way, or whether only the Socrates of the *Symposium* had to display so much 'natural modesty'.

On the other hand, we have seen just now that in the *Phaedo* Plato had good reason not to let Socrates proceed of his own to what, in the *Symposium*, Diotima reveals in the final chapter of her speech, and the introductory sentence of this chapter seems rather to indicate that it is now not Socrates, but Plato, who is going to say what had never been said before in his writings or anywhere else. The question at issue may be stated in the following way: Did Plato write the final chapter of Diotima's speech on the ground that the historical Socrates had, during his lifetime, *said* enough of those things which Diotima reveals to make Plato's readers understand the chapter in Burnet's and Taylor's sense, namely, "to all intents and purposes . . . as a speech of Socrates" (Taylor p. 225), or, if not, is there any way of interpretation that lets the virtue of Socrates remain virtue of the true kind?

We may be sure to have formulated the issue correctly. For it is exactly in this form that the problem of the relation of Diotima's speech to the words and sayings of the historical Socrates has been anticipated and, once for all, answered by Plato himself. The comparison of Socrates with a Silenus bust, with which in the *Symposium* Alcibiades begins his praise of Socrates, has become one of the best known passages of the literature of all times (*Symp.* 215a): "And now, my boys, I shall praise Socrates in a figure which will appear to him to be a caricature, and yet I speak, not to make fun of him, but only for truth's sake. I say, that he is exactly like the busts of Silenus, which are set up at the statuaries' shops, holding pipes and flutes in their mouths; and they are made to open in the middle, and have images of gods inside them." But one of the diverse applications that Alcibiades makes of his comparison does not seem to have attracted enough attention; otherwise such a complete misunderstanding and misinterpretation of Plato's literary intentions in the *Phaedo* and the *Symposium* as is implied in Burnet's and Taylor's main thesis — that the doctrines put in the mouth of the Socrates of these dialogues were those actually maintained by the historical Socrates — would have been impossible. And yet this application comes at a conspicuous place and in the conspicuous form of a supplement, at the end of the whole speech (221c): "Many are the marvels which I might narrate in praise of Socrates; most of his ways might perhaps be paralleled in another man, but his absolute unlikeness to any human being that is or ever has been is perfectly astonishing. You may imagine Brasidas and others to have been like Achilles; or you may imagine Nestor and Antenor to have been like Pericles; and the same may be said of other famous men, but of this strange being you will never be able to find any likeness, however remote, either among men who now are or who ever have been — other than that which I have already suggested of Silenus and

the satyrs; and they represent in a figure *not only himself, but his words.*
For, although *I forgot to mention this to you before,* his words are like the
images of Silenus which open; they are ridiculous when you first hear
them, he clothes himself in language that is like the skin of the wanton
satyr — for his talk is of pack-asses and smiths and cobblers and
curriers, and he is always repeating the same things in the same words,
so that any ignorant or inexperienced person might feel disposed to
laugh at him; but he who opens the bust and sees what is within will
find that they are the only which have a meaning in them, and also the
most divine, abounding in fair images[90] of virtue, and of the widest
comprehension, or rather extending to the whole duty of a good and
honorable man. This, friends, is my praise of Socrates.''

I think it would be a waste of time to argue with anybody who
after carefully reading this epilogue of Alcibiades' portrait of the
historic Socrates (even in the dialogue Alcibiades knows nothing of
what Socrates had said before his entrance) would insist that the
historic Socrates must have *said,* or even *could* have said, things like
those the author of the *Symposium* makes him say in the 'report' of
Diotima's speech. The truth is that, according to Plato's *Symposium,*
the historic Socrates *lived* Diotima's words in his own unparalleled
way, although he never said anything like them; and the author has
done everything in his power to explain how that strange sort of thing
could be.

We have no reason to doubt Plato's sincerity when in Alcibiades'
speech he concentrated his literary art to produce the impression that
only an intimate understanding is needed in order to see the consistency of a lifelike portrait of the historical Socrates with the life in
philosophy that is described by Diotima, but all Plato's art is wasted
on us, if, beyond what Plato thought feasible, we try to put two and
two together and to complete either of the two pictures by single
features of the other.

The "Institute for Thinking" (φροντιστήριον) in Aristophanes'
Clouds and the discipline practised there (see esp. the scene 694ff.)
is sufficient proof that a certain inclination of Socrates for solitary
thinking was well known in Athens at a time when Plato was a
small boy. And, indeed, an extraordinary power of mental concentration is easily imagined to have been the natural complement to Socrates' dialectical invincibility. If we take Plato's dialogues, the author
is usually too preoccupied in letting Socrates make other people think
as to present him doing his own thinking. But in the *Phaedo,* where, as

---

[90] In Greek: ἀγάλματα, objects of religious veneration, as in 215a(quoted p. 118);
not εἴδωλα, incomplete semblances, as in 212a (quoted p. 120 n. 93).

we have seen, pure intensive thinking is stated to be the real business of the philosopher, we have twice the spectacle of Socrates meditating in silence[91]. Similarly, one would not say it could be by chance that in the *Symposium*, where self-forgetful contemplation of absolute beauty is revealed to be the consummation of the philosopher's desires, there is twice a picture of Socrates forgetting everything around him and becoming absorbed in concentrated thinking[92]. It cannot be chance, and yet Burnet and Taylor spoil everything by roughly identifying, when Plato's art, exploiting a certain identity of impression, had only hinted at a hidden identity without distorting the picture of the historical Socrates. For considered soberly, there is no identity. What Diotima describes in the final chapter of her speech is not a "rapt" or an "ecstasy" that may happen from time to time ("Plotinus four times, I, Porphyrius, once"), but the discovery of a new knowledge that, once it is reached, will guide the whole life of a man[93]. On the other hand, both cases of a trance-like state of intellectual concentration which are related of Socrates in the *Symposium* are interpreted by the narrators themselves as examples of Socrates' stubborn endurance in trying to solve a definite problem[94], and by no means as states of enraptured contemplation. Since Plato had no reason to *invent* essential differences, we may be sure that it was impossible to adapt the portrait of the historical Socrates in Alcibiades' speech closer to Diotima's description of the way to the end of philosophy than Plato has undertaken.

In general, the interrelation of these two subjects which are not simply identical, but certainly had close affinities in Plato's mind, has

---

[91] 84c: "When Socrates had done speaking, for a considerable time there was silence; he himself appeared to be meditating, as most of us were, on what had been said . . ."; 95e: "Socrates paused for quite a while, and seemed to be absorbed in reflection. At length he said . . . "

[92] *Symp.* 174d—175d; 220c/d.

[93] 212a: "In that communion only, beholding beauty with the eye of the mind, he will be enabled to bring forth, not images (cp. p. 119 n. 90) of beauty, but realities (for he has hold not of an image but of reality), and bringing forth and nourishing true virtue to become the friend of God and be immortal, if mortal man may. Would that be an ignoble life?"

[94] 175c: "At last when the feast was about half over — for the fit, as usual, was not of long duration — Socrates entered. Agathon . . . begged that he would take the place next to him; that 'I may touch you', he said, 'and have the benefit of that wise thought which came into your mind in the portico, and is now in your possession; for I am certain that you would not have come away until you had found what you sought'." 220c: "I have told you one tale and now I must tell you another, which is worth hearing, 'of the doings and sufferings of the enduring man' while he was on the expedition. One morning he was thinking about something which he could not resolve; he would not give it up, but continued thinking from early dawn until noon — there he stood fixed in thought; and at noon attention was drawn to him . . ." and so forth.

been stated so well by Wilamowitz that I am glad to be able to quote the following sentences (Wilamowitz, Platon I 387): "Wenn dem Sokrates auch die Lehre" — the doctrine contained in Diotima's final chapter — "fremd ist, so ist er doch Meister in dieser Erotik; seine die Seele emporführenden Reden werden durch die Berührung mit den schönen Knaben und Jünglingen erst geweckt, geboren, und so wird er der Führer der Jugend zum Schönen und Guten. Die Wirkung seiner Erotik zeigen uns zur Ergänzung die Geständnisse des Alkibiades. Aber diese bestätigen zugleich, daß Sokrates selbst die Werke der wahren Tugend zu üben weiß; er ist also selbst zum Anschauen des Ewig-Schönen gelangt, einerlei ob er jede Stufe des Weges beschritten hat. Dann wird er ein Ausnahmemensch sein, und so zeigt ihn auch das ganze Gemälde. Denn das Normale ist der Stufenweg, auf den so großer Wert gelegt wird, daß seine Stationen zweimal aufgezählt werden. Diesen Weg wird nicht nur der Liebende selbst gehen, sondern auch den Geliebten führen, durch die wahre Einsicht zur wahren Tugend und zum wahren Glück; aber der Weg ist nun zu einer Methode der Erziehung geworden, er ist nicht mehr sokratisch, sondern platonisch. Die Schule ist gegründet. Wir verspüren die inneren Erfahrungen und Erlebnisse des Lehrers Platon, der die Seinen immer höher steigen, immer weiter schauen lehrt; es klingen aber auch Erfahrungen und Erlebnisse seiner eigenen Jugend nach, seines Verkehres mit Sokrates und den Genossen seiner Jugend, älteren und jüngeren."

As far as Socrates is concerned, this is an adequate interpretation of Plato's intentions; moreover, it is not merely due to the difficulties of depicting unfamiliar experiences if, in Wilamowitz' words, the educational pathos and the claims of an in more than one sense perverted eroticism[95] sound a little hollow. A paraphrase of Plato's picture of the ascent from spiritual love of and spiritual begetting in beautiful bodies[96] through love of beauty in souls (resulting in the consideration and

---

[95] Wilamowitz in his chapter on the *Phaedrus* exclaims (I 469): „Was für eine Fratze hat man nicht aus der platonischen Liebe gemacht" and then he quotes Byron "O Plato Plato, you have paved the way . . ." and Wieland's Musarion in order to illustrate the modern misunderstandings „von denen das Altertum natürlich nichts weiß". But the difference between 'Platonic love' in the silly and insincere sense and in the genuine sense of the *Symposium* and the *Phaedrus* is simply that the latter was homosexual, and therefore less transparent in its motives and more yielding to educational interpretation; beside that it was — luckily, in this case — as 'Platonic' as possible. Even that seems to be too much for English decency; for in a remark to *Phaedrus* 253a—256d Taylor (p. 309) warns his readers: "The power and insight with which this account of the conflict between the spirit and the flesh is written should not mislead us into supposing that it must be concealed autobiography."

[96] As a matter of fact, only when he was a very old man Plato stigmatized homosexual eroticism as unnatural and as being not preliminary analogon of a higher kind of love but the opposite of what is desirable in human society (*Laws* 873aff.) The love of

talk of beautiful practices) and love of beauty in sciences (resulting in the creation of "many fair and noble thoughts and notions in boundless love of wisdom") to the vision (and, of course, love) of absolute beauty and the begetting of true virtue, is easy, if one sticks closely to Plato's expressions, as interpreters usually do. But such paraphrases lead at best to an account of the impression which Plato intended to produce and make one forget the decisive question, namely, whether the single stages of the ascent represent the single steps which actually had led Plato to the discovery of the doctrine of ideas.

Like most interpreters, Wilamowitz (I 388) takes for granted that personal experience is at the basis of 'Diotima's' final chapter. "Als Erlebnis müssen wir auch das Anschauen des Ewig-Schönen rechnen, also das Gefühl, das Ziel erreicht zu haben. Nur rückschauend vom Gipfel konnte er die Stationen des Weges in ihrer notwendigen Folge bezeichnen; er mochte manchen Irrweg getan haben, jetzt konnte er sicher führen." We have already heard — and in this we agree fully with Wilamowitz — that the *way* is not Socratic, but Platonic; now we are told of a *necessity* in the sequence of the single stations — but obviously Wilamowitz does not believe that Plato's previous personal experiences corresponded, or at least corresponded exactly, to that 'necessary sequence'. So the question arises what kind of necessity it is that Diotima prescribes

On the surface it is a pedagogical necessity, no doubt about that. Not only Wilamowitz talks pedagogy ("jetzt konnte er sicher führen" and the like), but Diotima too (e. g. 210a "if he be guided by his instructor aright"; or later, 211c "and the true order of going, or being led by another, to the things of love is to begin from . . ."). But while Wilamowitz chooses his explanatory phrases so highly serious as if the pedagogical jargon were the adequate expression of Plato's own educational intentions and experiences, Plato himself is non-committal. We have to take Diotima's pedagogical wisdom not on objective grounds but on Diotima's authority, and what kind of authority that is, is deliberately made rather doubtful. (e. g. 203b: "I was astonished at her words, and said: 'Is this really true, o thou wise Diotima?' And she answered with all the authority of the accomplished sophist: 'Of that, Socrates, you may be assured'. . ."). Wilamowitz would make us believe that Plato intended to express a pedagogical program as well as a kind of religious experience, but that he chose the form of Diotima's speech because he did not believe that "das Allerheiligste

---

"those who are pregnant in body only" and "*usually* betake themselves to women and beget children" has been dealt with beforehand (208eff.) and thus Diotima manages to speak not at all of homosexual love in the vulgar sense.

seines Herzens" (p. 383) was scientifically demonstrable. My objection to this is that in my opinion one may disguise almost anything under the mock form of an educational discipline, anything but the very thing itself, namely, one's own educational experience and convictions. The most useful German handbook of the history of ancient philosophy (Überweg-Prächter, 1926, p. 262) presents the single stages of the *way* prescribed by Diotima thus: "Wer sich nun der richtigen Erotik befleißigt, wird folgenden Stufengang einhalten (210aff.). Er wird als Jüngling schönen Leibern nachgehen, und zwar zunächst einem einzigen, um hier schöne Reden zu säen, dann, in der Erkenntnis, daß die Schönheit des einen Leibes derjenigen der anderen verschwistert ist, allen. Alsdann wird er seelische Schönheit höher zu schätzen lernen als leibliche, so daß ihn bei einem seelisch Tüchtigen schon geringe körperliche Blüte zum geistigen Zeugungswerk reizt. Diese Bildungstätigkeit nötigt ihn, das Schöne in den Gebräuchen und Gesetzen und — auf einer weiteren Stufe — in den Wissenschaften zu schauen, womit sich ihm ein weites Meer des Schönen eröffnet. Schließlich gelangt er . . .". This is fairly correct in a literal sense. But are we to understand it in this literal sense as Plato's pedagogical creed? There must be a less pedantic interpretation.

We know enough of the origin of the doctrine of ideas to be able to compare the single intellectual steps which actually have led up to the idea of the beautiful as it appears in the *Symposium*, with the allegedly 'necessary' sequence: beautiful bodies, beautiful practices, beautiful sciences, eternal unchanging beauty in itself. The 'beautiful (fair) itself' was first discovered as a moral predicate ('beautiful practices'), then it was interpreted as being in the same opposition to sensible things as mathematical predicates like the 'equal itself' (*Phd.* 74aff.; from the field of 'beautiful sciences'?) and this second step led to the acknowledgement of the 'beautiful itself' in an aesthetical rather than a moral sense, *Phd.* 78d: "Then now let us return to the previous discussion. Is that idea or essence, which in the dialectical process we define as essence or true existence — whether essence of equality, beauty, or anything else — are these essences, I say, liable at times to some degree of change? or are they each of them always what they are, having the same simple self-existent and unchanging forms, not admitting of variation at all, or in any way, or at any time? — They must be always the same, Socrates, replied Cebes. — And what would you say of the many beautiful — whether *men* or *horses* or *garments* or any other things which are named by the same names and may be called equal or beautiful, — are they all unchanging and the same always, or quite the reverse? . . ." and so forth. Here we are obviously in the field of "beautiful bodies". The next step, carefully prepared but not actually taken in the *Phaedo* (96a—99c, cp. above p. 109, 115ff.), acknowledgement of the "beautiful itself" (or, as the *Republic* has it, the idea of the good) as the source of natural and cosmic order, must be gathered from the climax in Diotima's description by negatives (211a): "And the beautiful will not appear to him as a face or hands or any other thing of bodily structure, or as an argument or as a knowledge, or existing in any external substratum, as for example in an *animal*, or in *earth*, or in *heaven* or anything else; but beauty absolute, separate, simple, and everlasting, which without diminution and without increase, or any change, is imparted to the evergrowing and perishing beauties of all other things." In the list of examples of things, which are not absolute beauty but to which beauty "is imparted" the beautiful face (cp. *Cratylus* 439d) and the beautiful hands belong to the "beautiful bodies" from which the way of the lover starts; next we have a beautiful argument and a beautiful knowledge, the latter certainly representing 'beautiful sciences'. 'Animal', 'earth' and 'heaven' circumscribe the objects of natural philosophy exactly as they do in *Phaedo* 96b: "When I was young, Cebes, I had a prodigious desire to know that department of philosophy which is called the investigation of nature; to know the causes of things, and why a thing is and is created or destroyed appeared to me to be a lofty profession; and I was always agitating myself with the consideration of questions such as these: — Is the growth of *animals* the result of ... and then I went on to examine ..., and then to the things of the *heaven* and the *earth*, and at last I concluded myself to be utterly and absolutely incapable of these enquiries". It is clear that in the passage of the *Symposium* absolute beauty takes the place of that principle of natural philosophy which, as we know from *Phaedo* 99c, Socrates "would fain learn if any one would teach" him. What love is concerned with in 'animal', 'earth' and 'sky' before that revelation is reached, is obviously not immediately their bodily beauty[97] but *knowledge* about them; this love is the desire described by Socrates in the just quoted

---

[97] Wilamowitz (I 385n.) failing to see the relation of the mention of *animal*, earth, and sky, to *Phd.* 96a—99c has a comment which begins entirely mistaken: "da kommt das Naturgefühl Platons heraus; daß ihn der gestirnte Himmel und der Sonnenglanz entzückt hat ... ergibt sich aus mehreren Äußerungen. Hier erkennen wir auch seine Empfänglichkeit für landschaftliche Schönheit, merken aber zugleich, wie wenig die Sprache noch befähigt war, diesen Empfindungen Ausdruck zu geben". Indeed, the simple word 'earth' is not very capable of expressing such sentiments as are lent to Plato by his interpreter. But even Wilamowitz adds: „Übrigens wollen wir uns hüten, Platons Natursinn zu überschätzen; es ist viel weniger Hingabe an das darin, was das Auge schaut, als die erzeugte Seelenstimmung, so im Eingang des Phaidros, und so wird er angesichts des Sternenhimmels vornehmlich Gedanken an die ewige Ordnung nachgehangen haben."

passage of the *Phaedo*. So, with 'animal, 'earth" and 'heaven' we are in the sphere of love of beautiful sciences, the last not the first of the three stages of love that precede the vision of the absolute (bodies, practices, sciences)[98].

In so far as the transcendence of the idea beyond natural and cosmic order comes as a climax, the *Symposium* is in complete agreement with the *Phaedo*, where the recognition of an 'idea' as the principle of natural philosophy is deliberately reserved for the future. But the single intellectual steps toward this end, which we are able to trace in the *Phaedo*, are incomparable with the single erotic stages of Diotima's discipline. The intellectual steps lead from moral subjects via mathematical ones to bodily beauty and natural and cosmic order, and in each case the intellectual discovery (that the idea is something apart) is as it were repeated, whereas in the erotic sequence one sudden discovery[99] follows the third stage, love of beautiful sciences. And the object of this third erotic stage, the sciences themselves, are not immediately found among those subjects from which, according to the *Phaedo*, ideas like the 'just itself' (not a just action), the 'equal itself' (not equal stones), the 'beautiful itself' (not a beautiful face), must be 'separated'.

Yet the incomparability of the intellectual steps in the discovery of ideas, as they are documented mainly by the *Phaedo*, with the erotic stages described in the *Symposium* ceases to be a puzzle, if, instead of attempting to find an analogy between the single steps and the single stages, we compare the third erotic stage with the *Phaedo* as a whole. For while in the *Phaedo* the sciences do not belong to those subjects which are differentiated from the ideas of their possible predicates — there is no mention there of the opposition of the beautiful itself to a beautiful science — it is one of the fundamental theses of the *Phaedo*, even more fundamental than what is *presupposed* of the doctrine of ideas, that *love* of pure knowledge (as opposed to weakness

---

[98] Unless 'argument' (logos), which in *Symp.* 211a is listed beside 'a knowledge', does include 'moral reason' — which is difficult to decide and certainly not clear — we miss the 'beautiful practices' among the examples of this passage. True virtue is too immediately connected with the idea as that a disparaging mention of human virtue (beauty in souls) would make good sense in the description of the idea. And, anyway, the explanation of the relation between the idea and true (Socratic) virtue is reserved for the end of the whole speech.

[99] It must, however, be noticed that only the beginning of the discovery is described as sudden (*Symp.* 210e "he . . . will suddenly perceive a nature of wondrous beauty"). In 211a the present stems of the verbs in the Greek words for "He who . . . begins to perceive that beauty" (ὅταν δή τις . . . ἐκεῖνο τὸ καλὸν ἄρχηται καθορᾶν) express even more precisely than the English phrase that time is required for the completion of the discovery.

for bodily pleasures or for riches or for honors, 68c) is *the* passion[100] of the philosopher.

We have seen in chapter III (p. 111) that the adoption of the principle 'search of truth for the sake of knowledge' came comparatively late in Plato's life and that, although the principle itself was old and well known at Athens[101], the personal experience must have been new when the *Phaedo* was published. The preceding period in Plato's life from the beginning of his literary career may well be characterized as dominated by a 'love of fairness' in the moral and political field, a love which resulted in corresponding discussions and dissertations (λόγοι). And the following passage in the *7th Epistle* (Harward's translation, 324c) is an eloquent document for such 'love of fairness' at an even earlier time (404/403 B. C.): "I found myself confronted with the following occurrences in the public affairs in my own city. The existing constitution being generally condemned, a revolution took place, and fifty-one men came to the front as rulers of the revolutionary government, namely ... Some of these were relatives and acquaintances of mine, and they at once invited me to share in their doings, as something to which I had a claim. The effect on me was not surprising in the case of a young man. I considered that they would, of course, so manage the state as to bring men out of a bad way of life into a good one. So I watched them very closely to see what they would do. And seeing, as I did, that in quite a short time they made the former government seem by comparison something precious as gold — for among other things they tried ... — seeing all these things and others of the same kind on a considerable scale, I disapproved of their proceedings, and withdrew from any connection with the abuses of the time."

---

[100] Erotic terminology in the *Phaedo* for instance 66e: "and then we shall attain the wisdom which we desire, and of which we say that we are lovers" (καὶ τότε ... ἡμῖν ἔσται οὗ ἐπιθυμοῦμέν τε καί φαμεν ἐρασταὶ εἶναι, φρονήσεως). 76e: "how inconsistent would they be if they trembled and repined, instead of rejoicing at their departure to that place where, when they arrive, they hope to gain that *which in life they desired — and that was wisdom —* ... " (οὗ διὰ βίου ἤρων τυχεῖν — ἤρων δὲ φρονήσεως — ...) What follows is a direct comparison of the 'love' of the philosopher with common love: "Many a man has been willing to go to the world below animated by the hope of seeing there an earthly love, or wife, or son, and conversing with them. And will he who is a true lover of wisdom (φρονήσεως δὲ ἄρα τις τῷ ὄντι ἐρῶν), and is strongly persuaded in like manner that only in the world below he can worthily enjoy her, still repine at death ?"

[101] In ancient philosophic literature Anaxagoras, who for some time lived at Athens, has become its outstanding representative, and Euripides praised this way of life in a once famous song (fr. 910, quoted by Wilamowitz I 77). To let the young Socrates be at first allured by theoretical science was at least not anachronistical, cp. above Ch. III p. 109.

Plato's literary work up to the time when he wrote the *Symposium*, and his autobiographical testimony in the *7th Epistle* contain more than enough documental proof that in his life the recognition of 'theory' as an aim (and not merely a means) had been preceded by a long period when love of 'fair practice' was the predominant factor in his activities. As to the lowest of the three erotical stages, 'love of beautiful bodies', we have no direct biographical document, but there is not the slightest reason to doubt that in this respect Plato's feelings had been normal according to Athenian — not our — notions, and that the natural complications in the erotic relations between two souls and two (male) bodies of different age were familiar to him. Wilamowitz remarks (I 388): "Für den Biographen ist es bitter, daß er die erotischen Erlebnisse aus Platons Jugend auch nicht von ferne erkennen kann, müssen sie doch die leidenschaftlichsten und folgenreichsten gewesen sein". But I do not think it would be so exceedingly interesting and important to know about these experiences, because average Athenian eroticism is all we need to understand even Plato's most subtle erotic doctrines; and of that, I should say, we know enough not to expect more enlightening revelations than we should do — *mutatis mutandis* — of average modern eroticism.

At any rate, when Plato wrote the *Symposium*, the three 'erotic' stages on the way to the 'end' (bodies, practices, sciences) must have been fairly distinguishable, to a retrospective view, in his own life. But of course they were not meant, at the same time, as a pedagogical program. It will not be necessary to compare in detail the educational chapters of the *Republic*; the main point is that, for higher education, Plato favored selection of the 'born philosophers', whom we know from the *Phaedo* and in whom, according to the *Republic* and the *Theaetetus*, love of science was supposed to be recognizable from the very beginning, and not as a third stage after love of bodies and love of practices.

Diotima's way toward the transcendent idea of fairness and beauty does not represent either an intellectual approach or an educational program. It contains undoubtedly some autobiographical truth, but Plato did not write the *Symposium* for the sake of his biography. And furthermore, since the approach to the supreme idea shown in the *Symposium* is not the intellectual one of the *Phaedo*, it would have been a preposterous disguise of the true intention, if the eroticism of the *Symposium* served merely the purpose of adding the last intellectual step by actually proclaiming the cosmic scope of the doctrine of ideas. But what, then, was in Plato's mind?

Interpreters are commonly generous in conceding to Plato the personal experience of such a vision of the idea of beauty as Diotima describes. Now, we might argue, if Plato really had this experience, it must have come to him as something beside or on top of his intellectual approach; for the intellectual approach could at best lead to the logical inference of a cosmic or hypercosmic function of an 'idea', but not to the vision of the idea actually exerting such a function. Hence the temptation for modern interpreters, even of Wilamowitz' rank, to understand Diotima's speech as Plato's confession that the doctrine of ideas culminates in religious rather than rational experience and conviction. Yet this distinction between a rational and a non-rational cognition of the idea is entirely un-Platonic. We know from the *Phaedo* that Plato believed the soul as such capable of seeing the objects of thought immediately — undisturbed by the organs of the body — "with the very light of the mind in her own clearness" (*Phd.* 66a). According to his views such an immediate awareness is the only truly rational and truly 'scientific' cognition[102]. Consequently, contrary to our logical and psychological conceptions, the assertion of the *possibility* of a full vision of the idea of beauty, which would reveal much more than the preceding intellectual approach could carry along, did not imply the slightest theoretical difficulty for Plato. But while there is no doubt that Plato could assert, without any of the modern epistemological scruples, the possibility of such a vision, and although Diotima's speech in the *Symposium* has opened the way for followers of Plato's philosophy and interpreters of his dialogues to talk of the possibility as of a fully actualized reality, the question remains whether Plato intended to intimate that he personally had experienced a completely satisfying vision of the idea. The answer is that Plato has done everything to prevent such a gross impression.

In Diotima's preliminary remarks philosophy is determined as a species of love and desire, namely a love and desire of wisdom, which is in the middle between ignorance and full possession of wisdom[103]. Diotima's speech itself is not concerned with wisdom — which may be a privilege of the Gods — but with philosophy considered as the

---

[102] The psychological basis of this theory of knowledge was, as we have seen, Plato's assuredness of autonomous standards of moral behaviour. In this field even we have no difficulty in reconstructing the experience of an immediate awareness of transcendent standards of our predications, no matter how we are to explain the experience
[103] *Symp.* 204a: "The truth of the matter is this: No god is a philosopher or seeker after wisdom, for he is wise already; nor does any man who is wise seek after wisdom. Neither do the ignorant seek after wisdom' . . . 'But who then, Diotima,' I said, 'are the lovers of wisdom, if they are neither the wise nor the foolish?' 'A child may answer that question,' she replied, 'they are those who are in the mean between the two . . .'" With regard to the idea of the good, which is an equivalent of the 'beautiful itself' of which Diotima speaks, we have the testimony of the *Republic* that Plato did not pretend to full 'wisdom'; for although the disclaimers made in *Rep.* 505a,

highest form of love and desire and with the procreation of true virtue as a result of this love. The sudden discovery of which she speaks (210e, cp. above p. 125 n. 99) is the discovery of a new knowledge and a new object of knowledge, but this discovery is expressly determined as a beginning and even the achievement to which it leads in the highest form of human life is still love and desire, and by no means that wisdom which would be in itself divine and beyond human capacity and human philosophy[104].

Since we know that in Plato's conception of knowledge there was no specific difference between intellectual or rational cognition and 'intuition', there is no reason to differentiate between the 'vision' of an idea as described by Diotima and the rational discovery of the doctrine of ideas. In any case, nobody can doubt that there must have been a moment in Plato's life when the scientific possibility of a doctrine of ideas with far-reaching consequences for any kind of knowledge appeared to his mind for the first time[105]. Such a moment contained an intellectual experience, which, as such, is fully understandable to any one who has the experience of a scientific hypothesis, and, on the other hand, is in absolute congruity with the sudden beginning of that vision which Diotima describes[106].

As far as the author is concerned, the *Symposium* does not mark a new step in the theoretical development of the doctrine of ideas,

---

506c-e fit, as confessions of ignorance, the historical Socrates, yet with reference to this subjet they represent Plato's, not Socrates' reserve. It is in Plato's school, not in Socrates' circle, that words like the following could actually be spoken: "you have often been told that *the idea of good is the highest knowledge*, and that all other things become useful and advantageous only by their use of this. You can hardly be ignorant that of this I was about to speak, concerning which, as you have often heard me say, we know so little . . ." (505a); and a book that contains them presupposes readers to whom the *Phaedo* and the *Symposium* are familiar.

[104] In *Rep.* 506c Adeimantos has pressed Socrates for his *opinion* concerning the idea of the good: "Do you not know, I said, that all mere opinions are bad, and the best of them blind? You would not deny that those who have any true notion without intelligence are only like blind men who feel their way along the road? — Very true. — And do you wish to behold what is blind and crooked, *when others will tell you what is bright and straight*?" With exactly the same mischievous irony *Symp.* 204a (see preceding note) had mentioned "another one who is wise" beside the god. Full 'wisdom' is precluded from human beings, according to Plato. But his reasons for the weakness and incompleteness of human knowledge must be looked for in the *Phaedo*, and not in modern epistemology.

[105] This moment lay chronologically earlier than the *Phaedo*, for, as we have seen, its author was obviously aware of the cosmological consequences, without communicating them openly to his readers.

[106] It would clear the way for an understanding of Plato, if one could silence interpreters who, on occasion of the *Symposium*, talk of 'intuition' in an hysterical way.

although the reader is, for the first time, openly confronted with its cosmic scope. Yet even in this respect the reader, if he is a good reader and has read the *Phaedo*, gets only what he could expect, and he gets it without further explanation.

The first task of an interpreter, that of determining the literal meaning of what is said about 'ideas' in the *Symposium*, is difficult only so long as we try, misled by certain modern epistemological prejudices, to understand something different from what our knowledge of the *Phaedo* should let us expect. But if, then, we shift to the question of what use is made, in the *Symposium*, of the doctrine of ideas, we grasp a real and historically most important development. For in the *Phaedo* the doctrine of ideas merely corroborated a preconception which was supposed to be leading in the mind of the born philosopher (the ideal student in Plato's Academy), namely, that intellectual study and thinking is the real business of life. But the *Symposium* proceeds to subordinate this, so to speak, naive stage of 'love of knowledge' to an allegedly highest form, which derives the justification of Academic study and Academic life not from the fact and the sincerity of a subjective inclination, but from the allegedly objective lovability of an allegedly transcendent object. Personal and typical experience furnished two convincingly lifelike 'lower' stages of 'love', and the exploitation of one of the most ingenious metaphors ever abused — 'childbirth in beauty', 206b, said of the male — provided a fascinating, though precarious, connection of 'theory for theory's sake' with practical life and Socratic morality (212a). The result is the impression of a sort of cosmic necessity for the Academic kind of life, deliberately communicated in a playful and, at the same time, highly artful and poetical way. This is not educational program, but, through contents and through its form, immediately effective in turning one's thoughts in the desirable direction, and thus, considered as a means to an end, rather easy to understand.

But there is not much hope. No less a scholar than Wilamowitz has the following sentences in his final section about Diotima's speech (I 391): "Wissenschaftliche Belehrung will das Symposion nicht geben; es fehlt ja die Dialektik, durch die sie allein erzielt wird. Dennoch gewinnt sich Platon durch kein anderes Werk so schnell einen Jünger, der sich ihm glaubend anvertraut. Denn aus dem eigenen inneren Erlebnis, aus Intuition, das ist eigentlich aus innerem Schauen, stammt, was er verkündet, und sein Eros führt über alles Intellektuelle hinaus eben zur Intuition, zur dauernden Befriedigung im reinen Anschauen. Hier macht er nicht den Vorbehalt, aber es war ihm wohl bewußt, was die Gläubigen zu vergessen sehr geneigt sind, daß er die Grenze des Wißbaren und Lehrbaren überflog, daß er zeigte, was unaussprechlich ist." One might remark that, according to Plato, a soul in a human body is far from reaching the limits of the knowable, and certainly in no danger of unconsciously trespassing.

V. Cratylus

In my provisional chronological survey at the beginning of chapter III I placed the *Lysis* and the *Cratylus* together with the *Symposium* between the *Phaedo* and the *Republic*. After this arrangement has been confirmed, as far as the *Symposium* is concerned, in chapter IV, it seems worth mentioning that in Dittenberger's statistical list (Hermes 16, 1881, 321 ff.) the *Symposium* and the *Lysis* got exactly the same position — after the *Phaedo*, at the beginning of Dittenberger's second stylistical group[107] — for reasons entirely independent of the contents of these dialogues[108]. But in the case of the *Cratylus* there seems to be no stylistic indication that it belonged to a group later than the *Phaedo*; and thus, while from this external point of view the chronological relation of the *Phaedo* and the *Cratylus* remains undetermined, Dittenberger's observations furnish an argument (though perhaps not a particularly strong one[109]) for letting the *Cratylus* precede the *Symposium* rather than follow it in the chronological series. Yet, from the point of view of contents, I must state that not only the chronological priority of the *Phaedo* to the *Cratylus* is, in my opinion, certain, but that even that of the *Symposium* to the *Cratylus* is at least more probable than the opposite relation.

In order to determine in a general way the development of the doctrine of ideas no special consideration of the contents of the *Lysis*

---

[107] *Symposium, Lysis, Phaedrus, Republic, Theaetetus.*

[108] Dittenberger's fundamental observation was the discovery of the fact that of the various combinations of the particle μήν with other particles which are familiar to us from late Platonic writings *three* do not at all occur in a certain group of dialogues. These three combinations are τί μήν; meaning a simple 'yes', γε μήν and ἀλλά . . . μήν; the dialogues in which none of them occur are the following: (*Apology*), *Crito, Gorgias, Protagoras, Hippias Minor, Laches, Meno, Euthydemus* (exception: one γε μήν), *Charmides, Euthyphro, Phaedo, Cratylus*. Now, it is a second fact deservedly emphasized by Dittenberger that in the other Platonic writings in which there is an equal chance for any of the three combinations (i. e. in the rest of the Platonic writings with the exception of the *Timaeus, Critias* and of course the *Epistles*) wherever one of the combinations is found, the other two occur also (,,Noch bezeichnender aber ist es, daß die drei doch in ihrem Wesen ganz verschiedenen Spracherscheinungen in der Weise miteinander connex sind, daß so gut wie überall, wo eine von ihnen auftritt, auch die beiden anderen vorkommen, und wo eine fehlt, auch keine der beiden anderen sich findet"). The dialogues which contain each all the three combinations are: *Phaedrus, Republic, Theaetetus, Parmenides, Philebus, Sophist, Statesman, Laws*. If we leave aside, as insignificant, the one γε μήν in the *Euthydemus*, the non-occurrence of a τί μήν; in the *Symposium*, and of a γε μήν in the *Lysis* (Dittenberger overlooked the τί μήν; in 219e) are the sole important exceptions of this rule, and they determine strictly the statistical position of the *Symposium* and the *Lysis* at the beginning of the second stylistic group, although, in this case, an equally strict chronological interpretation may not be indicated.

[109] See the preceding note.

and of its relation to the *Symposium* will be necessary; and also we may leave aside the question of the special relations between the *Cratylus* and the *Symposium*. The decisive issue, at this point, is the assumption that the *Cratylus* presupposes the contents of the *Phaedo* as present to the minds of its readers in the same way as the *Symposium* does, and that the chronological relation of the *Phaedo* and the *Cratylus* is therefore just as inconvertible as that of the *Phaedo* and the *Symposium*.

At the end of the dialogue, Plato leaves the question of the philosophical reliability of language alone for a moment and seizes the opportunity to oppose, as an alternative, his doctrine of ideas to the doctrine of Heraclitism favored by Cratylus. Heraclitism is interpreted in such a radical way that it precludes the possibility of naming or saying and of knowing a definite object (439d—440b). We learn from Aristotle's *Metaphysics* that it was the historical Cratylus who had finally drawn exactly these consequences (*Metaph.* 1010a 9—15)[110], and this enables us to understand the full meaning of the conclusion of the dialogue (440d/e), where in spite of Socrates' objections Cratylus shows a decided disinclination to abandon his conviction that Heraclitus is right. The doctrine of ideas does by no means appear as based on a partial compliance with Cratylus' Heraclitism (as Aristotle later interpreted, *Metaph.* 987a 29ff.), but it is supposed to be independently established and to open a way of getting rid of the disastrous consequences of Heraclitism, in so far as it teaches to take into account an unchanging 'beautiful itself', 'good itself' and so forth, instead of, for instance, the unstable and vanishing beauty of a beautiful body. The aspect of the doctrine of ideas is the same as in the *Phaedo* (especially one of its sections, 78cff.), and even the form of the first introduction is very similar:

Phaedo 65d: "Well, but there is another thing, Simmias: do we say there is a just itself or do we say none? — Assuredly we do. — And, again, a beautiful and good? — Of course."

Cratylus 439b/c: "There is another point ... For look, master Cratylus, what I often dream about. Shall we say that there is a beautiful itself and a good and so forth in each case? — Certainly, Socrates, I think so. — Then let us look at that (predicate) itself ...".

The sole difference is the extremely abridged form of the presentation of the doctrine of ideas in the *Cratylus*, which together with

---

[110] " ... the most extreme of the views above mentioned, that of the professed Heracliteans, such as was held by Cratylus, who finally did not think it right to say anything but only moved his finger, and criticized Heraclitus for saying that it is impossible to step twice into the same river; for *he* thought one could not do it even once."

Socrates' confession that he *often* has been dreaming about it, is equivalent to a reference by the author of the dialogue to a previous treatment of the subject, which in this case can only be found in the *Phaedo*, if not in both the *Phaedo* and the *Symposium*[111].

By comparing his own already established doctrine of ideas with the self-destructive tendencies of Heraclitism, Plato was able to throw a new light upon its philosophical advantages; but since the doctrine is here taken into consideration and left to further consideration exactly in the form in which it appears in the *Phaedo*, this is rather an act of consolidation than of theoretical progress. However, at an early stage of the same dialogue *Cratylus*, but in no apparent connection with this undoubtedly serious recommendation of the doctrine of the *Phaedo*, we find Plato actually extending his new doctrine or at least its terminology beyond the sphere of predicates. It is a first step in a dangerous direction, but it is extremely difficult for a reader to become aware of its importance, because Plato is obviously not in full earnest and because he continues playing in the only precisely corresponding passage found in his works, *Republic* 596a ff. In the *Cratylus* (386e ff., esp. 389b—390a) Socrates is backing up, for the sake of argument, the (in fact untenable) cause of a strict and universal natural relation between names and things named. In order to silence the most obvious objection he uses a remarkable fake, perhaps unique in the history of deliberate sophistry, namely the fictive notion of one and the same 'idea of name' which may (1) be adapted to any single case (and thus generate the whole vocabulary of a language, 389b—d) and (2) in any single case may be expressed in different syllabic material (and thus account for the existence of different vocabularies in different languages or dialects, 389d/e). This notion is elastic enough to serve all the momentary purposes and needs of the situation at the beginning of the dialogue, but is deservedly forgotten later on. While the 'idea of name' itself is but a curiosity in the history of the doctrine of ideas, we ought to consider closely that passage in the *Cratylus* which introduces the pattern after which the 'idea of a name' is counterfeited; it is most instructive. Socrates and his interlocutor have agreed with each other that instruments like a knife, a shuttle, an awl are physically predetermined by the nature of their respective functions; and now attention is called for a striking fact (389a):

---

[111] It is not conclusive, but the compendious phrase: "not asking whether a face is fair' or anything of that sort" (*Crat.* 439d) looks more like a recollection than an anticipation of the fuller expression in the "erotic" doctrine of the *Symp.* (211a): "the beautiful will not appear to him in the likeness of a face or of hands or anything of bodily nature"; the *Phaedo* in its corresponding passage (78d) has "men or horses or garments".

"To what does the carpenter look in making the shuttle? Does he not look to that which is naturally fitted to act as a shuttle? — Certainly. — And suppose the shuttle to be broken in making, will he make another, looking to the broken one? or will he look to that same form according to which he made the other (which he broke)? — To that same form, I should imagine. — Might not that be justly called *the true and ideal shuttle*[112]? — I think so. — And whatever shuttles are wanted, for the manufacture of garments, thin or thick, of flaxen, woollen, or other material, ought all of them have the form of the shuttle; and whatever is the shuttle best adapted to each kind of work, that ought to be the form which the maker produces in each case? — Yes. — And the same holds of other instruments: when a man has discovered the instrument which is naturally adapted to each work, he must express this natural form, and not others which he fancies, in the material, whatever it may be, which he employs; for example, he ought to know how to put into iron the forms of awls adapted by nature to their several uses? — Certainly. — And how to put into wood forms of shuttles adapted by nature to their uses? — True. — For the several forms of shuttles naturally answer to the several kinds of webs; and this is true of instruments in general. — Yes."

The fact to which Plato refers (being a fact of modern as well as of ancient technical practice) is quite familiar to us, and both the general description at the beginning, and the following specification agree well enough with our modern physical and technical notions to be understandable without difficulty. The only thing that needs an explanation is the Greek expression proposed by Plato as a technical term for the general pattern in the mind of the craftsman: "that itself which *is* shuttle" (and accordingly a little later, 389d; "that itself which *is* name"). We know both the terminological 'itself' and the terminological 'which-is- . . .'[113] from rather frequent occurrences in the *Phaedo*[114]; and as a result of our having proceeded step by step in our survey of Plato's writings we know furthermore that if the chronological priority of the *Phaedo* to the *Cratylus* should be denied, the quoted passage of the *Cratylus* would

---

[112] The Greek text has: "that itself which *is* shuttle" (αὐτὸ ὃ ἔστι κερκίς), where English syntax would require an indefinite article before 'shuttle'; but that would spoil everything because it is a point in Plato's doctrine that the 'itself' is *not* 'a' shuttle or 'a' bed (κλίνη τις, see *Rep.* 597a).

[113] Derived from a 'what it is', cp. Ch. I p. **64** and the following note.

[114] The 'itself' is found at the first mention of 'ideas' (*Phd.* 65d) and passim; as to the 'which-is . . . ' we must recollect that after having stated in *Phd.* 74a/b that there is 'an equal itself' and that 'we know it, what it is' Plato calls it in 74d 'the which-*is*-equal itself' and in 75b 'the which-*is*-equal', and that in 75d and in 92d he acknowledges expressly a general terminological use of the 'which-*is*'.

have been the earliest passage in Plato's works where he used the formula '(that) itself which *is* . . .'

In order to demonstrate the improbability of this latter assumption I should like to take advantage of a remark in Taylor's 'Plato'. Always eager to object to the notion of a development of the doctrine of ideas that would be traceable in Plato's earlier dialogues, Taylor comments on *Cratylus* 389a—390a as follows (Plato, the Man and his Work p. 81): "It should be noted that all through this passage the technical language of the doctrine of forms is used without explanation. Plato assumes that Hermogenes and Cratylus may be counted on to know all about it. To my own mind, it is just the frequency with which this assumption is made, apparently without any consciousness that it calls for any justification, which is the strongest reason for refusing to believe that the whole doctrine was 'developed' by Plato or any one after the death of Socrates."

This, I think, is a stimulating misstatement. The pattern in the mind of the craftsman is described by Plato as a fact of common knowledge, and so far as this fact as such is concerned any one may be counted on to be able to say 'yes' to Socrates' questions. Only this much is true that *one* of these questions presupposes a previous knowledge of the *technical language* of the doctrine of forms: "Might not that be *justly called* '(that) itself which *is* shuttle'?"; and not without reason this captious introduction of the doctrine of ideas pretends to be, not a question of fact, but a seemingly harmless question of terminology[115]. What really happens is this: Socrates' interlocutor, prepared by a clever presentation of an ordinary fact in ordinary language, yields to the suggestion that in a case like that of the making of a shuttle the use of the formula '(that) itself which *is* . . .' would be justified and that thus he opens his mind to further suggestions in that direction. A careful interpretation has to distinguish clearly between two clear alternatives:

Either, the formula and its introduction at this moment of the dialogue is fully understandable from the context of the *Cratylus* and fully 'justified' by this context alone, without any help from the out-

---

[115] The description of the making of a shuttle, an awl and so forth would lose nothing, if the allusion to the doctrine of ideas were cancelled. But Plato has to give some appearance of substance to the controversial issue of 'natural names'. Only if he is familiar with and reminded of 'ideas', a reader will be in a disposition to grant, what Plato needs at the moment, namely, that 'natural names' may be considered as *something apart* and *different* from the actual vocabularies of actual languages, in which a strict and immediate natural relation of names and things is too obviously missing.

side: in this case this passage of the *Cratylus* might of course be the earliest in Plato's writings where the formula is used, but since there would be no lack of explanation and no want of justification, there would also not be the slightest ground for such a reasoning as Taylor proposes.

Or, the introduction of the formula '(that) itself which *is* . . .' is not fully understandable without some outside help. In this case what is needed by the interpreter and what must have been presupposed by Plato in the minds of his audience is, of course, such a use of the formula as does not lack full explanation.

Now, as any reader of the *Phaedo* and the *Cratylus* may verify by himself, the use of the formula in the *Phaedo* is explained, and, to-day, can only be explained, by the context of the *Phaedo* itself, whereas, on the other hand, its occurrence in the *Cratylus*, to be understood, requires exactly so much acquaintance with the doctrine of ideas as may be got by reading the *Phaedo*. If, instead of drawing, for the second time now, the obvious conclusion that the *Cratylus* was written after the *Phaedo* had been published, we accepted Taylor's view, this would mean that, although 'all about' the doctrine of ideas that is necessary to understand the *Cratylus* was known to the Socratic circle before Socrates' death, Plato refrained from mentioning it for at least 15 years in at least a dozen of his works; but that nevertheless he could presuppose 'all about it' so clearly fixed in the minds of his readers that at the time when *Phaedo* and *Cratylus* were written it made no difference whether the first mention (cp. p. 134) looked like *Cratylus* 389 b or like the exposition of the doctrine of ideas in the *Phaedo*.

It might be objected that dialogues like the *Phaedo*, the *Symposium*, and the *Cratylus* were written for an audience acquainted with Plato's teachings and that therefore, even if the doctrine of ideas was developed not only after the death of Socrates but after Plato's return from his 'first' journey and after he had written the *Protagoras* and the *Meno* (as we have tried to demonstrate in chapters I to III), it is hazardous to presume that Plato was anxious not to write anything concerning ideas to which the key might not be found in some previous writing of his. On the contrary, one might argue, Plato himself has emphasized that writing books is a subordinate and secondary business and that "only a very simple person would believe that written books could do more than remind him *who already knows* what they are about" (*Phaedrus* 275 c); consequently it would have been a quite superfluous pedantry if in spite of this conviction he had written his dialogues as if everything depended on having studied his previous relevant publications[116].

---

[116] It is still necessary to read Schleiermacher's introduction to the *Phaedrus in extenso*, because otherwise it is impossible to judge for oneself of the impardonable sophistry

Yet there is another principle established by Plato in the same dialogue *Phaedrus*. Writing books may be mere pastime and play (276d), but if a book pretends to be a work of art it ought to be like "a living creature, having a body of its own and a head and feet; there should be a middle, beginning and end, adapted to one another and to the whole" (264c). There is such a thing as a 'bookwriter's necessity' (ἀνάγκη λογογραφική 264b) and, if anybody, Plato was entitled to speak of it. His dialogues, unless deliberately made parts of a trilogy or tetralogy, were conceived and written as independent and self-explanatory literary organisms, with an art that precluded any arbitrariness in the choice of the ingredients. In the case of the doctrine of ideas this fact may be stated with particular confidence, because through Aristotle's *Metaphysics* and other sources we know of Plato's oral teachings. Their difference from what we read in Plato's writings and the insufficiency and inadequateness of the latter to replace all that is lost of that orally propagated doctrine is a commonplace of ancient and modern interpreters, exploited for various purposes; but it cannot be denied and it should not be overlooked that while without the help of Plato's writings we would not even have the beginning of an understanding of the 'unwritten doctrine' (Taylor p. 503), there is as far as I know not the slightest evidence that Plato ever consciously presupposed a definite component of *unwritten* doctrine as an indispensible requisite for the understanding of any single passage in his writings. On the other hand, it is a fact that certain passages in certain dialogues that otherwise would be obscure are easily explained if cognizance of certain passages in other dialogues may be assumed. In some of these cases the chronological priority of the passage that is needed for an understanding is independently certain; no case is known to me in which the — unnatural — opposite chronological relation could be stated as a fact.

Trifling as these observations may seem, yet the facts are a little puzzling to account for, and, on the other hand, the consequences of their right interpretation are not negligible. Obviously a 'bookwriter's necessity' is involved; but while the requirement of organic structure is sufficient to explain, why a Platonic dialogue could not simply presuppose anything that so far was only known as part of Plato's oral teaching — such an ingredient would certainly not have made an organic part of the literary organism — the reason for the exception in the case that the subject had been treated in a preceding dialogue is not equally patent.

with which one of the most influential interpreters of Plato tried to derive the above mentioned pedantic point of view from the very principle that a book should never be taken too seriously.

Explanation would be easy, if Schleiermacher and his modern followers were right in considering not Plato's single dialogues as independent literary units with a "body and a head and feet of their own", but rather the whole of his literary work as the realization of one vast educational plan, a plan formed at the beginning of a literary career of more than fifty years. In this case, of course, an occasional reference to a previously written paragraph or chapter would be the natural thing. But this whole view is so completely incompatible not only with Plato's own utterances about books (cp. p. 136 ff.), but with the psychological possibilities, the biographical data and the contents of Plato's single works that the fact of occasional references from one dialogue to another is certainly not a sufficient support to maintain it any longer[117]. We had better look for a less controversial explanation.

We should not ask whether Plato, in spite of his declared contempt for people who take books too seriously, yet was arrogant enough to publish his own books for continuous study, but whether the audience which he must have had in mind when he wrote a single dialogue were likely to have read a certain already published dialogue (1) or not (2), or whether (3) some would be acquainted with it and others not[118]. When for some reason or other the particular dealing with a certain subject in one dialogue was to be taken up later in another, the procedure of the writer would be different under different circumstances. If the reader was not supposed to know or to remember the older passage, it was, of course, the natural thing to ignore it. For instance, when in the *Laws* (698 c—e) Plato told, for a second time, his version of the historical events of 490 B. C., it did not matter, so far as the reader was concerned, that about a generation ago he had used the same story in the *Menexenus* (240 a—e). But even such a repetition is exceptional in Plato's writings and, at any rate, conditions were different, if a characteristic feature of Platonic dialectic or doctrine was involved. There would always be at least part of the audience in

---

[117] Wilamowitz' critical remarks against v. Arnim (Schleiermacher, Shorey) hit the right nail on the head, although unfortunately they prelude to the chapter with Wilamowitz' worst chronological mistake (the *Protagoras* written before Socrates' death!); see his 'Platon' vol. I p. 124 ff. From a note p. 123 I should like to quote the following sentences: „Ich habe ja selbst in der Jugend diesen Irrgang mitgemacht, der den Anfänger Platon sich die Frage vorlegen ließ, vor die uns die Summe seiner fertigen Werke stellt. Es ist nichts anderes als Friedrich den Großen 1756 zu seinen Generalen sagen zu lassen ,heute fangen wir den siebenjährigen Krieg an'. Wir taten so, als hätte er seine Werke zugleich geschrieben und nicht geschrieben vor sich gehabt, statt sie jedes einzeln aus sich zu verstehen, wo sich dann eins auf dem andern aufbaut."

[118] To be accurate we must, in the third case, add a third group of those who needed reminding; cp. p. 139.

whose mind the older passage would be present. Although a Platonic dialogue is, on principle, an independent literary unit, simple consideration for the best part of his audience forbade to do the same thing twice (even if Plato the writer had inclined to self-plagiarism like Xenophon or Isocrates). Whether and in what way in such a case regard could be had for the other group of readers to whom the subject would be new, was a matter of discretion and literary skill. In a case like *Euthydemus* 282c a simple reminder that the question of whether virtue is teachable (the subject of the *Meno*) was not to be discussed now would do for both classes of readers; but sometimes the writer's dilemma required a more complicated solution. Most instructive is the passage of the *Phaedo* (72d) where the mathematical episode of the *Meno* is recalled. One of Socrates' two interlocutors remembers the thing clearly so that he can tell the other (who does not) what is necessary at the moment: this invention pays heed to all imaginable classes of readers[119]. — The fact that Plato had to consider different groups of readers is also, in my opinion, a help to the understanding of the much discussed introduction of the *Timaeus* with its deliberately incomplete recapitulation of the *Republic*. In this case even Taylor (p. 437) insists that we have an allusion to Plato's older book, and I agree completely with his suggestion (p. 438) "that the most likely explanation" . . . "is that which is also the simplest. Just so much of the *Republic*, and no more, is recalled as will be an appropriate basis for the story of the Athenian victory over Atlantis". Yet it would obviously be onesided to let Plato write the recapitulation *merely* in order to prevent his perfect readers, who had read everything and remembered everything, from recollecting too much. It cannot be by chance that, again, any imaginable kind of readers get what kind of help is possible for them from this remarkable introduction that manages to presuppose and *not* to presuppose knowledge of the dialogue *Republic*, at the same time and in more than one respect.

A literary device as used in the quoted passages of the *Phaedo* and at the beginning of the *Timaeus* is, of course, not practicable on every occasion; besides, the conditions are again different in dialogues that belong to exactly the same period and are written for exactly the same audience. In order to understand the central part of the *Republic*

---

[119] Readers to whom the episode of the *Meno* is present will be especially satisfied, readers with only a vague recollection will be grateful, and those without knowledge of the *Meno* will at least be enabled to follow the conversation with a clear understanding that some definite piece of doctrine is presupposed and of what kind it is. — Whoever denies or doubts that Plato's reference is directly to the *Meno*, denies in fact the reality of the first two groups of readers, who could not help being reminded of Plato's older dialogue in the first place.

(471c—541b) so much previous acquaintance with the doctrine of ideas is necessary as a reading of the *Phaedo* and the *Symposium* will furnish; if the *Republic* were composed as an absolutely independent literary unit, Plato would have had to insert into the dialogue some such presentation of his new doctrine as would completely replace the relevant parts of those other two dialogues, in other words, he would have had to fix the fundamentals of the doctrine of ideas for a second time in a literary form (as if he had not done it already), for an audience that most likely was acquainted with the older dialogues or at least could scarcely be unaware of their existence. In this case, the audience was also likely to know more or less about Plato's oral teachings; yet, I think, it is evident that only the existence of the *Phaedo* and the *Symposium* as literary realities caused Plato to abbreviate the first introduction of the doctrine of ideas in *Republic* 475e/476a to a minimum. And not only was Plato himself conscious of writing under certain conditions, but with that accuracy of communication which is one of his unrivalled literary accomplishments, he made Socrates say so in unmistakable words: "He said: Who then are the true philosophers? — Those, I said, who are lovers of the vision of truth. — That is also good, he said; but I should like to know what you mean? — To *another*, I replied, *I might have a difficulty* in explaining; but I am sure that *you* will admit a proposition which I am about to make . . ." (follows a condensed exposition of the doctrine of ideas in about six lines).

It happens that in the 10th Book of the *Republic* Plato again uses, for a special purpose, the 'idea' of an artificially made thing, which had appeared in the *Cratylus*; the examples are now a bed and a table. And again Plato needs, for his new purpose, the pattern in the mind of the craftsman according to which the single beds and the single tables are made; since we know, for external — statistical — reasons, that the *Cratylus* was chronologically prior to the *Republic*, we know consequently that in the latter Plato had to propose to his reader the same thing as in the *Cratylus* for a second time; and this is the way in which he did it (*Rep.* 596a/b): "Well then, shall we begin the enquiry" — concerning the nature of imitation — "*in our usual manner*: Whenever we have a common name for a number of individuals, *we are accustomed* to assume a corresponding idea or form: do you understand me? — I do. — Let us take any common instance; there are beds and tables in the world — plenty of them, are there not? — Yes. — But there are only two ideas or forms of them — one the idea of a bed, the other of a table. — True. — And *are we not also accustomed to say* that the maker of either of them is looking at the idea while making the beds or the tables for our use and that it is the same in similar

instances — for no artificer makes the ideas themselves: how could he?
— Impossible." Obviously Plato is anxious to avoid the impression as
if this were the first time that this subject is considered; and after our
survey of passages in which he acknowledges a previous literary
treatment of a certain subject, it is evident that now the reference is
to the passage of the *Cratylus* where the application of the doctrine of
ideas to the making of artificial things had been anticipated. The
difference between the two successive presentations of the same fact
is quite natural: after the *Cratylus* had expressly subordinated the
pattern in the mind of the craftsman to the doctrine of ideas ("Might
not that be justly called that itself which *is* shuttle?", see above p.
134), the passage of the *Republic* begins with a general formulation of the
doctrine of ideas and adds what is wanted as an already known special
consequence of the doctrine.

Perhaps no other couple of corresponding passages in Plato's
dialogues reveals with equal clearness the possibility as well as the
importance of a chronological interpretation of our literary documents. Taken by itself the passage in the tenth Book of the *Republic*
precludes any speculation concerning the development of the doctrine
of ideas because of the strictly general and extremely simple form in
which the doctrine is expressed. But considered in the light of its
chronological and literary relation to *Cratylus* 389a/b, the same passage
becomes unexpectedly a strong confirmation of our view that the general form of the doctrine of ideas was not there at the beginning, but
was the product of a secondary extension beyond the original field.
For, now, there is no doubt that this seemingly most simple and certainly too universal[120] formulation of the principle of the doctrine of
ideas was actually preceded and conditioned by a more original stage
of thought, in which nothing but the formula 'that itself which
is . . .' was presupposed so that the application of this formula to a thing
like a shuttle came as a surprising possibility rather than as a well
known implication.

We have come back to the passage which caused us to take up the
intricate problem of the dependence of one Platonic dialogue upon
another that was written earlier (above p. 136). It remains for us, in
conclusion of this chapter, to ask again, whether it is quite safe to

---

[120] "Whenever we have a common name for a number of individuals, we are accustomed
to assume a corresponding idea": this includes, of course, artificial things, of which,
however, according to Aristotle's testimony (*Metaph.* 991b 6, 1070a 18 and elsewhere), Plato's school did not recognize ideas. The restriction was inevitable, for
otherwise the simple craftsman would rank with the philosopher, as far as vision
of 'ideas' is concerned. In Plato's later dialogues there is no longer any mention of
'ideas' of artificial things.

assume the dependence of *Cratylus* 389 a/b upon the *literary* exposition of the doctrine of ideas in the *Phaedo*. At any rate it is certain that Plato in *Cratylus* 389 b supposes the reader to know the formula 'that itself which *is* . . .' from elsewhere, for in the case of a shuttle this formula is by no means so evidently 'justified' as it should be if nothing were presupposed (above p. 135 ff.). Now, in the meantime, we have seen that when Plato wrote the central part of the *Republic* he wrote for an audience that could not be supposed to be ignorant of the *Phaedo* and the *Symposium*, and that, in the tenth Book of the *Republic*, even the previous treatment of an 'idea' of an artificial thing in the *Cratylus* was deliberately acknowledged. We may conclude, then, that if the *Cratylus* was written intermediately between the *Phaedo* and the *Republic*, it is absolutely safe to assume that Plato wrote it for an audience that knew the *Phaedo*, for at this time a different audience is scarcely imaginable. Under such conditions, we may state now, he was not only entitled, but rather compelled to presuppose the knowledge of the formula 'that itself which *is* . . .', if he wanted to use it at all. In this case as in others the interrelation between the author and his audience enforced an exception from the rule which requires that a dialogue should be written as an independent literary unit. On the other hand, if the *Cratylus* had been written before the *Phaedo* was in the hands of Plato's readers, the same irregularity would have been without a reason and without an excuse.

VI. Later Dialogues

After we have definitively determined the position of the *Cratylus* as a literary document of the development of the doctrine of ideas, our chronological troubles have come to an end. For the dialogues that are left to consider belong to those two later groups of Plato's writings which have been distinguished from the earlier dialogues and from each other by observations of style and language. It is true that these observations furnish no evidence for the chronological placement of the single dialogues within their respective groups, but in the case of the earlier of these two groups (the so-called 'middle' stylistic group) comparison of the contents of the dialogues leaves scarcely any doubt that the chronological sequence was: *Republic, Phaedrus, Parmenides, Theaetetus*[121]; and as for the members of the latest — the 'third' —

---

[121] The psychological and mythical parts of the *Republic* and *Phaedrus* have been compared more than once with the certain result that the *Phaedrus* followed the *Republic*. The change of attitude towards the doctrine of ideas in the *Parmenides*

stylistic group, our knowledge that all of them, namely *Timaeus, Critias, Sophistes, Politicus, Philebus, Leges*, were certainly written later than the *Parmenides* and the *Theaetetus* is sufficient for our purpose.

Republic

The central part of the *Republic* (471c—541b) contains the most circumstantial, in fact, the only methodical literary presentation of the doctrine of ideas ever made by Plato. A detailed interpretation of this Platonic text is most urgently needed[122], but I cannot here go into that, and I shall confine myself to some remarks which are based on the results of our previous chronological investigation.

Although, as we have seen (above p. 140ff.), in the tenth Book of the *Republic* Plato made further use of the 'ideas' of artificial things, which were originally invented for the purposes of the *Cratylus*, no such ideas are considered in the serious presentation of the doctrine of ideas in the central part of the *Republic*. The ideas mentioned here are exclusively ideas of predicates; they are in the first place the moral triad: the good, the fair (beautiful), and the just; but for certain purposes the fair (beautiful) in the aesthetic sense comes in more handy, exactly as in the *Phaedo*, the *Symposium*, and in *Cratylus* 439d.

As to the doctrinal development, there are two important features:

(1) *Express acknowledgement of the exceptional and predominant position of the idea of the good as compared with other ideas and with the knowledge of ideas and things in general.* In order to understand this part of the doctrine, which makes dialectic the 'coping-stone' of sciences (*Rep.* 534e), it is necessary not only to consider the previous presentations of the doctrine of ideas in the *Phaedo* and the *Symposium* (taken side by side), but also the problem involved in the Socratic identification of 'good' and 'knowledge' as discussed in the *Euthydemus* and the *Charmides*[123]. The sublime ingenuousness of the captious com-

---

and the *Theaetetus* (as compared with *Symposium, Republic,* and *Phaedrus*) combined with the late absolute date of the *Theaetetus* (above Chapter III beginning) place these two dialogues later than *Republic* and *Phaedrus*; and regarding the relation of the *Parmenides* and the *Theaetetus* to each other it cannot and should not be denied that in *Theaet.* 183e/184a Plato acknowledges openly and deliberately that *Parmenides* is presupposed.

[122] Cp. K. v. Fritz, 'Platon, Theaetet und die Geschichte der Mathematik', Philologus 87, 1932, 40ff. 136ff.

[123] After what has been said in Chapter V concerning the literary situation resulting from the treatment of a certain subject in an older dialogue, it may safely be stated that in *Rep.* 505b/c we have a deliberate reference to *Euthyd.* 292d/e and *Charm.* 174b/c.

parison of 'the' good, truth, knowledge, and invisible objects with the sun, light, sight, and visible things is exempt from historical analysis; but, on the other hand, even in this case the chronological relations of our literary documents are strictly determined: no more and no less of the doctrine of ideas is *presupposed* in the central part of the *Republic* than had been literarily fixed in the earlier dialogues. This may seem a trifling remark, but I am not certain whether it is generally realized that the ideas taken into consideration are almost exclusively the moral *predicates* and that in the allegory of the den *their* essences are compared with the real things of the visible world so that a passage like *Rep.* 532a, where Plato speaks of 'sight' beholding after some training "the real animals and stars, and last of all the sun himself" (in the Greek text it is "the animals *themselves* and the stars *themselves* and last of all the sun *himself*"), is not at all intended to intimate a world of ideas containing the ideas of animals, stars etc. But for a reader familiar with *Timaeus* it is, indeed, almost impossible not to be reminded here of the intelligible world, as pictured in the *Timaeus*, i. e. the perfect animal comprehending all intelligible animals (*Tim.* 30c—31b); and it is only by sticking to the chronological facts that an ill-advised confusion of the realm of the idea of the good with that intelligible model of the visible world may securely be avoided.

(2) *The discrimination of mathematical thinking from purely intellectual dealing with ideas.* This is generally considered one of the most intricate problems of Plato's philosophy, and I agree that its aspect in Aristotle's *Metaphysics* is discouraging in the highest degree. But in the *Republic* we are at the beginning of the development of the doctrine in that direction and should not expect help from far-fetched explanations. The proper place to look for the direct meaning of Plato's words are his *preceding dialogues*, in this case, where mathematics is concerned, the *Meno* and the *Phaedo*.

In the *Meno* the easily verifiable power of the human soul to see the truth and reach knowledge in the mathematical field is pointed out in favor of the presumption that she has the same power in the educational and political field, too, and that accordingly even in politics knowledge instead of mere opinion should be sought, if the 'real thing' is wanted (*Meno* 100a, cp. above p. 104). Exactly the same parallel between easily verifiable mathematical knowledge with scarcely anywhere existing, yet *possible* knowledge in the moral-political field is exploited in *Phaedo* 74a—77a (see end of Chapter I). The difference from the *Meno* consists in the fact that now the 'knowledge' which is considered is determined as a knowledge of ideas, i. e. of certain predicates (the equal etc. — the just, the good, the fair etc.) the essence of which may be and ought to be asked for without regard for any of the subjects upon which the predicates may be observed in the practice of common life. According to the Platonic text it is an *obvious fact* that 'we know' the what-is-it of 'the equal itself' (74b); but while all the interlocutors are morally and logically certain that there must also be such entities as 'the fair itself, the good, just, pious itself etc'. (75c/d), it takes a Socrates to account for them in the proper way (76c).

The *Republic* teaches that mathematicians, *firstly*, do their speculating on the basis of such "hypotheses" as "the odd and the even and the figures and three kinds of angles and the like in their several branches of science; these are their hypotheses, which they and everybody are supposed to know, and therefore they do not deign to give any account of them either to themselves or others; but they begin with them, and go on until they arrive at last, and in a consistent manner, at their conclusion" (*Rep.* 510c/d). *Secondly*, we are informed, "although they make use of the visible forms and reason about them, they are thinking not of these, but of those objects which they resemble; not of the figures which they draw, but of the square itself and the diameter itself, and so on — the forms which they draw or make, and which have shadows and reflections in water of their own, are used by them as images, in turn, while they are really seeking to behold the things themselves, which can only be seen with the eye of the mind" (510d/e). In opposition to the practice of mathematicians philosophical thinking, *firstly*, does not take for granted the knowledge of its 'hypotheses', it uses "the hypotheses not as first principles, but only as hypotheses — that is to say as steps and points of departure into a world which is above hypotheses—in order that it may soar beyond them to the first principles of the whole; and clinging to this and then to that which depends on this, by successive steps it descends again" and it does so, *secondly*, "without the aid of any sensible object, from ideas, through ideas, and in ideas it ends" (511b/c).

In order to understand this, everything depends upon a resolute choice between two mutually exclusive possibilities in the case of mathematics. To which of the two ingredients of mathematical thinking does the 'equal itself' of the *Phaedo* belong? Does it belong to the 'hypotheses' the knowledge of which is simply presupposed by the mathematician, or to those intelligible objects of mathematical speculations and subjects of mathematical propositions, like the square 'itself', and the diameter 'itself', at which the work of the mathematician is aimed, although in practice he is forced to use visible models of them? We have already in our first chapter had occasion to protest against the tendency of some interpreters of the *Phaedo* to illustrate its doctrine by examples like 'the triangle' (above p. 70), and now we may add that it is equally impossible to substitute in *Rep.* 510d/e the notion of the 'equal itself' for that of the 'square itself' and the 'diameter itself'. Or has there ever been a mathematician who, instead of presupposing 'the equal' itself, did his reasoning for the sake of finding out something about *this* intelligible object and made use, for this purpose, of visible models of 'the equal' (equal stones, equal pieces of wood)?

If, then, 'the equal itself' can only rank with the 'hypotheses' in mathematical thinking of which the *Republic* speaks, the 'just itself', 'fair itself', 'good itself' as dealt with in the *Phaedo* will correspond to the 'hypotheses' of philosophical dialectic, and thus we get a surprisingly simple answer to one of the most vexed interpretative problems. What was in Plato's mind when in *Rep.* 510bff. he opposed the intellectual attitude of the philosopher to that of the mathematician? The mathematician, at least the mathematician of Plato's time, does not bother with questions like "what is 'the equal' itself?" for their own sake, but he takes the knowledge of an answer to such questions for granted, but in philosophy the raising of the question after the 'just itself' etc. and the acknowledgment of corresponding entities is exactly the starting-point, no more, for a purposely and allegedly entirely 'pure' reasoning concerning them the 'itself' preventing any recurrence to non-intelligible, sensible objects.

According to the *Meno* the mathematical parallel guarantees the possibility of knowledge elsewhere, too; according to the *Phaedo* the same parallel confirms the assumption of 'ideas' elsewhere, too; but the usefulness of the parallel might seem to vanish as soon as in the *Republic* the essential difference of the two respective kinds of 'knowledge' is exposed. But, fortunately, another characteristic of mathematical thinking takes over. Even if the dealing of the mathematician with his 'hypotheses' is decidedly unphilosophical, and even if he makes use of sensible models, it may safely be stated that his real interest is with intelligible objects, the square itself, the diameter itself, not with the arbitrarily chosen and drawn or formed models which he uses; and it sounds plausible, too, that being interested in intelligible objects of this kind[124] is a good preparation for the higher aims of the philosopher. Much has been made at all times of Plato's

---

[124] *Rep.* 532a-c (cp. 516a) shows that in the allegory of the den the objects of mathematical contemplation are represented by the *shadows* only of the real things outside the den and that, consequently, Plato did not think of them as of genuine 'ideas'. But the case of the 'equal itself' is different; as we have seen, it does not belong to that category. As an 'hypothesis' it is probably supposed to be *dealt with* differently by the mathematician and by the philosopher.

appreciation of the educational value of mathematics, but theoretically the educational point of view taken in the *Republic* serves only to obscure the fact that, after the discrimination of mathematical from philosophical thinking, the assumption of the possibility of a knowledge of ideas through 'pure' reasoning remains without any external support whatsoever.

In his writings Plato has never attempted to replace the epistemological arguments drawn (in the *Meno* and the *Phaedo*) from the fact of mathematical knowledge. For the famous allegory of the den (*Rep.* 514a1f., anticipated by the fantastical description of the divers regions of earth *Phd.* 108eff.) is by no means an equivalent. Although in a way the allegory condenses the whole doctrine of the *Phaedo*, the *Symposium* and the preceding parts of the *Republic* into one impressive picture, it cannot point out any of the distinctive features of knowledge in opposition to opinion (*Meno*) or of 'pure' intuition in opposition to sense-perception (*Phaedo*), since in the picture knowledge and intuition are represented by these very opposites. The function of the allegory is not to explain cognition of 'ideas' in terms of common experience, which would be impossible, but merely to illustrate the averseness of common experience from acknowledgement of 'ideas' and to point out the need of a methodical education towards that end.

In Plato's educational scheme (*Rep.* 521c—541b), the details of which we must leave aside, strong emphasis is laid on the study of mathematics as preparatory to entirely 'pure' intellectual activity; but the educational discussion of 'ideas' is postponed until after the carefully selected and trained disciples have reached their thirtieth year. Only then one "will have to prove them by the help of dialectic, in order to learn which of them is able to give up the use of sight and the other senses, and in company with truth to attain absolute being" (*Rep.* 537d). According to the preceding sections of the *Republic* the reason for the delay would seem to be that it takes so much time to train the mind intellectually for dialectic and 'pure' reasoning; but unexpectedly and with deliberate emphasis (537d: "And here, my friend, great caution is required") a different point of view is introduced. As in the *Phaedo*, the *Symposium*, the end of the *Cratylus*, and throughout the preceding parts of the *Republic* 'pure' thinking is supposed to be concerned in the first place with the *moral* predicates 'themselves' (the just, fair, good 'itself'); now, reasoning about them involves from the very beginning abandonment of the conventional rules of moral behaviour: therefore, we are told, a serious discussion of ideas requires a degree of maturity which is simply not to be found in younger men. It is probably no coincidence that Plato himself in his earlier twenties must have been one of those young people who were

mainly aware of the fun of the thing when they followed Socrates and
tried to imitate his dialectic (see *Apol.* 23c and 33c), and that only
when he was about thirty years old he can have reached that moral
maturity and understanding which enabled him to write the *Apology*
and the *Crito*. At any rate, this final chapter of the central part of the
Republic (537dff.), which is perhaps the most instructive document
of the original moral meaning of the doctrine of ideas (see Ch. I p.
75 n. 26 ff.), is also remarkable for the fact that Plato took occasion to
modify the overemphasis laid in the preceding sections on intellectual
training by the way in which the requirement of maturity of age is
introduced: obviously he did not believe in moral autonomy of
youngsters, even in the case of — most carefully guided and intellectually trained — born philosophers.

So much for the theoretical development of the doctrine of ideas
in the *Republic* and for the corresponding features of Plato's educational system.

As to the connection of Plato's political convictions with the
doctrine of ideas, it is out of the question to consider those convictions
dependent on the development of this doctrine. In fact, the political
theory and the practical attitude towards politics that are documented
in the *Republic* and in Plato's later writings can be adequately described without even mentioning any of the details of the doctrine of
ideas. The only thing provided by the new theory of knowledge is a
surprisingly simple theoretical foundation to Plato's antidemocratic
pretensions. In the *Gorgias* we have had the intriguing spectacle of a
Socrates defending the *common* notions of justice and decency and
spurning, at the same time, the *common* people who share these notions
(though they may not care for them); and in the *Meno* we have to
accept a tentative and by no means precise distinction between a 'true
opinion' of average good citizens and the 'real thing', namely a
postulated 'knowledge' of an imaginary super-politician. But now,
in the *Republic*, the inefficiency and undesirability of any form of
government by the people is easily deduced from the inability and
unwillingness of the masses to be impressed by questions like 'What
is the beautiful itself?' or 'the just itself'. We cannot argue with Plato
when with respect to the results of his teaching at Athens he took the
indifference and the disbelief of the masses for granted; he must have
known best. So, in his *Republic*, one simple question is sufficient to
eliminate, once and for all, democracy from theoretical competition
in the field of political theory (*Rep.* 493e): "Will the masses ever be
induced to believe in the beautiful itself rather than in the many
beautiful things, or in each kind itself rather than in the many of
each kind?" — "Certainly not".

On the other hand, since, for merely chronological reasons (if nothing else), this argument against democracy was not the beginning of Plato's anti-democratic attitude, we may state securely that it represents exactly that phase of this attitude which corresponded to his status as head of the Academy, in which the doctrine of ideas was taught and appreciated, while outsiders could not be expected to take it seriously.

Conclusion (*Timaeus, Phaedrus*)

I shall not try to describe the latest stage of the doctrine of ideas, of which the *Parmenides* is our earliest literary document (see Chapter I). The widespread opinion that in this latest period Plato modified his doctrine of ideas so as to come nearer to modern logical or epistemological conceptions is untenable; the *Timaeus* (see especially 51b—e) proves that, on the contrary, Plato was far from taking back anything that puzzles the modern mind equally as it did puzzle his contemporaries and his most eminent disciple, Aristotle. Yet it is also true that during this same period he was deeply interested in such plain logical procedures as were to supersede and to survive his doctrine of ideas in traditional logic under the headings 'definition' and 'classification'. I have ventured elsewhere (Greek Foundations of Traditional Logic, 1942, p. 36) the opinion that there was less genuine dependence between the logical part of Plato's philosophy and his developed doctrine of ideas than he himself believed; and I should like to conclude here with a passage of the *Phaedrus* that shows Plato starting to bridge the gap, though at least at the time when this dialogue was written (after the *Republic* but previously to the *Parmenides*) he was quite aware of the difference (never clarified in his later writings) between the requirements of ordinary human intercourse, which were to become the subject matter of Aristotelian logic, and the realm of those true objects of science or philosophy which (according to him) are accessible only to the Gods and to very few men (*Tim.* 51e).

The mythical part of the *Phaedrus* does not contain anything concerning ideas that would not be understandable after the exposition of the doctrine of ideas in *Phaedo, Symposium*, and *Republic*, and it is quite consistent that only the philosopher's soul has seen enough in her previous state of immortal life to be guided in this life to the highest achievement (248d ff.). But what is called 'dialectic' in the technical part of the dialogue is obviously also concerned with such logical methods as are useful not only in philosophy but in dealing with ordinary human beings and in common life. Under these conditions it is most instructive and helpful that in the mythical exposition of the *Phaedrus* Plato was considerate enough to explain, and discriminate at the same time, that modest part of intelligence which the average mortal shares with the philosopher and which corresponds fairly well to the Aristotelian notion of 'universals' and to the 'concepts' or the 'Begriffe' of traditional logic (*Phaedrus* 249 b—d): "The soul of a man may pass into the life of a beast, or from the beast return again into a man. But the soul which has never seen the truth will not pass into the human form. For a man must have intelligence of universals (δεῖ γὰρ ἄνθρωπον συνιέναι κατ᾽ εἶδος λεγόμενον) and be able to proceed from the many particulars of sense to one conception of reason (ἐκ πολλῶν ἰὸν αἰσθήσεων εἰς ἓν λογισμῷ συναιρούμενον); —this is the recollection of those things which our soul once saw while following God — when regardless of that which we now call being she raised her head up towards the true being. And therefore the mind of the philosopher alone has wings; and this is just, for he is always, according to the measure of his abilities, clinging in recollection to those things in which God abides, and in beholding which He is what He is. And he who employs aright these memories is ever being initiated into perfect mysteries and alone becomes truly perfect. But, as he forgets earthly interests and is rapt in the divine, the vulgar deem him mad, and rebuke him; they do not see that he is inspired."

It is a curiously twisted turn from the exigencies of common human understanding — via 'recollection' — to the mysteries patent, in this life, to the philosopher only; and I think this exposes the main reason, why it is so difficult to account for the latest stage of the doctrine of ideas. For obviously Plato is not only pointing out the difference between those exigencies and these mysteries, but is trying at the same time to convey to the mind of his reader the notion of some hidden identity.

Platon und die Akademie[1]

(Die Wissenschaft im Staat der Wirklichkeit)

1936

In einem einstündigen Vortrag einen Eindruck von der bleibenden Bedeutung Platons zu geben, so daß die ganze Notwendigkeit der Beschäftigung mit seinen Schriften und der Arbeit an ihrer Erklärung auf Schulen und Hochschulen eine des Gegenstandes würdige Darstellung fände, übersteigt die Kräfte eines Menschen; und es ist also nicht einmal Bescheidenheit, wenn ich für meinen Teil die durch das Thema mit Recht weit gespannten Erwartungen durch einleitende Bemerkungen stark einzuengen suche.

Eines Mittels zur Vereinfachung meiner Aufgabe möchte ich mich nämlich nicht bedienen. Man hört manchmal, jedes Land und jede Zeit könnte nur die eigenen Ideale in der Antike wiederfinden und wäre berechtigt, sie in ihr zu suchen; und deswegen wäre für jede Zeit und für jedes europäische Kulturgebiet die immer erneute Beschäftigung mit den Größen der antiken Literatur erforderlich. Aber wenn die Antike der jeweiligen Gegenwart nichts anderes zu bieten hätte, als was diese ohnehin schon in ihrem Bewußtsein hat, dann würde es schwerlich locken, die große Arbeit des Philologen zu tun, lediglich um vor Schülern und Studenten und zur eigenen Erbauung aufzeigen zu können, wie es dieses und jenes im Altertum auch schon, und meinetwegen vielleicht schon in klassischer Vorbildlichkeit gegeben habe. In meinem Falle könnte das z. B. bedeuten, daß ich etwa aufzeigte: Platon hat in klassischer Weise Wesen und Wert des gänzlich unprivaten Kasernenlebens geschildert (am Ende des dritten Buches | seines Staatswerkes); und er ist der klassische Forderer einer die Seelen der Menschen von vornherein ganz ausschließlich mit Staatsgesinnung erfüllenden staatlichen Erziehung; und er ist sich auch in klassischer Weise darüber klar gewesen, daß die Staatserziehung, soweit sie es mit Unmündigen zu tun hat, gewisser Fiktionen bedarf,

[1] Vortragsmanuskript für die auf den 28. August bis 2. September 1935 in die „Internationale School voor Wijsbegeerte" zu Amersfoort eingeladene Studienkonferenz, die der Bedeutung der klassischen Studien in der Gegenwart gewidmet war. Auf Einladung der Ortsgruppe Hamburg der Deutsch-Griechischen Gesellschaft wurde der Vortrag am 13. November 1935 auch in Hamburg gehalten.

also nach Platons Vorschlag etwa des Mythos von der gemeinsamen Abstammung aus dem gleichen Mutterboden, und von dem, allem irdischen Gold und Silber abholden, echten Gold und Silber in der Seele der zur Führung und zum Schutze des Staates Berufenen, dem in anderen Menschenseelen nur Eisen und Kupfer entspricht. Aus diesen und dergleichen Zügen könnte man natürlich ein aktuell sein sollendes Gesamtbild zusammenzustellen versuchen. Ein anderer würde andere Züge zu einem andern Bilde zusammenfügen können, und beide würden wir nach dieser Vorstellung von dem Verhältnis der Modernen zum klassischen Altertum vollkommen im Rechte sein können.

Einen solchen Weg möchte ich, wie gesagt, nicht gehen; denn ich halte eine vereinfachte Darstellung dieser Art nicht nur für wenig ersprießlich, sondern wo sie sich ihrer Einseitigkeit bewußt wird, für eine der Wissenschaft unwürdige Selbstverleugnung. Ich möchte nicht mißverstanden werden. Es liegt mir fern zu behaupten, wir Philologen könnten aus den Vorgängen unserer eigenen Zeit und unseres Landes nichts lernen; im Gegenteil: manche Seiten des antiken Lebens, über die man sonst hinwegsah, können plötzlich in ungeahnter Weise verständlich werden; aber hier lernen wir Philologen für die Erkenntnis des Altertums und bilden uns kaum ein, gerade damit die Gegenwart in wesentlicher Weise fördern zu können. Der Anspruch der klassischen Philologie, in unentbehrlicher Weise das Leben jeder europäischen Gegenwart zu bereichern und ihr Denken zu klären, kann sich schlechterdings nur auf diejenigen künstlerischen und gedanklichen Leistungen des Altertums gründen, von denen wir einerseits durch Tradition derart abhängig sind, daß ihr Nichtdagewesensein für den Gebildeten unvorstellbar wird, und zu denen andererseits der unmittelbare und natürliche Zugang nicht aus dem wechselnden Zeitbewußtsein heraus, sondern nur durch die ehrliche unzeitgemäßer Betrachtung fähige Arbeit der Philologie nach Menschenmöglichkeit sei es offen gehalten, sei es wiedergewonnen werden | kann. Nur wenn man möglichst vorurteilslos arbeitet[2], kann man dem Altertum diejenigen Dinge absehen,

---

[2] Ich habe nicht ohne Absicht das Wort ‚vorurteilslos‘ einfließen lassen, das heute etwas in Mißkredit gekommen ist, und ich habe ebenfalls absichtlich das Wort ‚unzeitgemäße Betrachtung‘ gebraucht, das, trotzdem es von einem Philologen stammt, schwerer in Mißkredit zu bringen ist, weil bekannt ist, daß dieser Philologe, Nietzsche, vorurteilslos genug war, den Betrieb seiner Wissenschaft nicht ohne weiteres als Weltanschauungsersatz gelten zu lassen. Es sollte aber auch bekannt sein, daß niemand weiter davon entfernt sein konnte als Nietzsche, vom Gelehrten als solchem das Verkünden eines alten oder neuen Glaubens zu erwarten. Dafür möge hier ein Stück aus der ersten unzeitgemäßen Betrachtung sprechen. Sie ist betitelt ,,David Strauss, der Bekenner und Schriftsteller‘‘, und von diesem Bekenner und Schriftsteller heißt es im dritten Abschnitt: ,,Sein Buch mit dem Titel

deren Darstellung der jeweiligen Gegenwart gerade deswegen nötig sein mag, weil sie in ihrem Bewußtsein nicht mehr obenauf liegen. Es ist vielleicht nur die Funktion des sich nicht trüben lassen wollenden Gedächtnisses, die wir Philologen für das Ganze ausüben und von der wir vor anderen Rechenschaft ablegen können — denn was wir für uns selbst von unserer philologischen Tätigkeit haben, geht | schließlich keinen Nichtphilologen etwas an; und das Humanistische an uns erscheint doch auch nur dann als etwas unentbehrlich Wertvolles, wenn wir uns selbst vor einen Spiegel stellen; die anderen wehren sich mit steigender und immer kompromißloserer Heftigkeit dagegen, gerade im Philologen den Begriff des Menschseins verkörpert finden zu sollen. Aber die Funktion des Gedächtnisses — mag sie nun eine hohe oder niedrige Schätzung finden, einerlei: wo überhaupt gedacht werden soll, ist die erste Voraussetzung, daß das Gedächtnis einigermaßen zuverlässig arbeitet.

Um nun zu meinem Thema und zu seiner bereits in Aussicht gestellten engen sachlichen Begrenzung zu kommen: es soll in diesem Vortrag nur von einem einzigen antiken Tatbestand die Rede sein, an den sich erinnern zu lassen der Gegenwart m. E. förderlich ist. Es soll nicht die Rede sein von Platons Kunst, und es soll auch von seiner Wissenschaft nur in einer ganz bestimmten Hinsicht die Rede sein, davon nämlich, welchen Platz er dieser Wissenschaft in einer für ihre Aufnahme nicht ohne weiteres eingerichteten Welt geschaffen hat. Daß von dieser Schöpfung, der Akademie, alle anderen Stätten unserer Welt abstammen, an denen das Wissen in seiner Freiheit und Selbstherrlichkeit gesucht und vermittelt wird, darf ich als zugestanden

,Der alte und der neue Glaube' ist einmal durch seinen Inhalt und sodann als Buch und schriftstellerisches Produkt eine ununterbrochene Confession; und schon darin, daß er sich erlaubt, öffentlich Confessionen über seinen Glauben zu machen, liegt eine Confession. — Das Recht, nach seinem vierzigsten Jahre seine Biographie zu schreiben, mag jeder haben, denn auch der Geringste kann etwas erlebt und in größerer Nähe gesehen haben, was dem Denker wertvoll und beachtenswert ist. Aber ein Bekenntnis über seinen Glauben abzulegen, muß als unvergleichlich anspruchsvoller gelten: weil es voraussetzt, daß der Bekennende nicht nur auf das, was er während seines Daseins erlebt oder erforscht oder gesehen hat, Wert legt, sondern sogar auf das, was er geglaubt hat. Nun wird der eigentliche Denker zu allerletzt zu wissen wünschen, was alles solche Straussennaturen als ihren Glauben vortragen, und was sie über Dinge in sich ,halbträumerisch zusammengedacht haben'" — dies ist Zitat aus Strauss und zeitbedingt — ,,über die nur der zu reden ein Recht hat, der von ihnen aus erster Hand weiß". Was nun kommt, ist nicht zeitbedingt: ,,Wer hätte ein Bedürfnis nach dem Glaubensbekenntnisse eines Ranke oder Mommsen, die übrigens noch ganz andere Gelehrte und Historiker sind, als David Strauss es war: die aber doch, sobald sie uns von ihrem Glauben und nicht von ihren wissenschaftlichen Erkenntnissen unterhalten wollten, in ärgerlicher Weise ihre Schranken überschreiten würden." Ich habe mich bemüht, in dieser wissenschaftlichen Unterhaltung die hier von Nietzsche für Klein und Groß gesetzten Schranken *nicht* in ärgerlicher Weise zu überschreiten.

unterstellen; und ich darf wohl auch ruhig noch weiter gehen und sagen: unsere Vorstellung von Wissenschaft als einer unpersönlichen und unabhängigen Macht, an die man in gewissen Dingen als höchste Instanz appellieren kann, findet ihre wesentlichste Stütze in dem Vorhandensein mehr oder weniger „akademischer" Institute; jedenfalls pflegen sich die heftigeren Angriffe auf Wissenschaft und wissenschaftliche Haltung weniger gegen die isolierte Person eines einzelnen Wissenwollenden zu richten als vielmehr gegen ihn als Angehörigen einer Gruppe, die sich in Fragen der Wissenschaft autonom dünkt.

Bei den Einzelheiten der platonischen Gründung können wir uns nicht lange aufhalten. Erfolgt muß sie sein nach Platons großer sogen. erster Reise, in den achtziger Jahren des 4. Jahrhunderts. Der Name stammt von der Örtlichkeit außerhalb der Stadt Athen, wo Platon in der Nähe eines großen öffentlichen Gymnasiums ein Grundstück für seine neuen Zwecke erwarb. Im | übrigen wissen wir gar nicht viel einzelnes, jedenfalls nicht so viel, um über die etwas vage Vorstellung wesentlich hinauszukommen, die wir uns aus den Nachwirkungen dieser Gründung auf spätere Zeiten bilden. Zu diesen Nachwirkungen gehört schon der Eindruck vom Betrieb der Akademie, den wir aus Cicero erhalten und der uns recht modern vorkommt. Bei Cicero zeigt sich übrigens der geistige Betrieb schon losgelöst von dem ursprünglichen Lokal, das man aber noch pietätvoll aufsuchen konnte; wie seit kurzer Zeit auch heute wieder, nicht ohne, wie man hört, sogar Reliquien aus echt platonischer Zeit noch verehren zu können.

In dieser ihrer eigenen Zeit scheint die Gründung Platons in Athen nichts besonders Aufregendes gehabt zu haben, was wohl den Absichten des Stifters selbst entsprach; auch aus dem finanziell und politisch ungefährdeten Dasein, das die Akademie in Athen weiterhin viele Jahrhunderte lang geführt hat, hat man wohl mit Recht auf ein beträchtliches Maß praktischer Klugheit geschlossen, das Platon bei der Gründung bewiesen hat. Während die Denkanstalt, das φροντιστήριον des Sokrates, eine groteske und unverschämte Komikererfindung der zwanziger Jahre des 5. Jahrhunderts war, wird gegen die Mitte des 4. Jahrhunderts die wirkliche Schule Platons von Isokrates und gleichzeitigen Komikern schon als etwas, was es in Athen nun einmal gab, wie andere Unterrichtsgelegenheiten auch, einfach hingenommen und verhältnismäßig harmlos bespöttelt oder kritisiert.

In der Tat, die Akademie war harmlos und galt als harmlos in Athen und für Athen, trotzdem Platons Philosophie dieses Athen mit seinen Institutionen und mit seiner Politik ziemlich radikal negierte und er es auch nicht etwa ängstlich vermied, daß von seinem politischen Urteil etwas ins große Publikum dränge. Hier bietet sich eigentlich neben dem Thema „Platon und die Akademie" noch das andere

„Athen und die Akademie", aber wir können, eben weil es zu Platons
Lebzeiten und auch späterhin zu keinem ernstlichen Konflikt zwischen
Platons Schule und dem athenischen Staat gekommen ist, kaum mehr
tun, als die Tatsache konstatieren und sie von Platon her und in seinem
Sinne zu begründen suchen; da haben wir Material genug. Dagegen lassen
wir die Frage, warum — mit fremden Augen angesehen — im | Athen
des 4. Jahrhunderts Platons Akademie trotz ihrer Lehre als ungefähr-
lich oder gar achtungswert galt, besser nur dahingestellt. Denn zu ihrer
Beantwortung würden wir uns, ohne greifbare Unterlagen, in eine
Unzahl untereinander wieder verschiedener, mehr oder weniger philo-
sophiefremder, wenn auch athenischer Seelen versetzen müssen.

Aber von Platon her sehend können wir die Stellung seiner Akademie in und zu Athen allerdings charakterisieren, und das soll nun versucht werden, natürlich auch dies ohne Anspruch auf Vollständigkeit,
sondern so, daß, was mir wesentlich scheint, mit wenigen — hoffentlich schlagenden — Zitaten belegt wird[3].

Daß Platon persönlich keine schlechten Erfahrungen mit seinen
Mitbürgern hinsichtlich der Schätzung seiner Person und der Achtung
seiner Tätigkeit gemacht hat, scheint schon eine Stelle im *Staat* zu
zeigen. Dort wird das Vorurteil der Menge gegen die Philosophie, das
den Gedanken der Philosophenherrschaft als absurd erscheinen läßt,
auf die Pseudophilosophen und die Unmöglichkeit für die wenigen
wirklichen Philosophen, sich in den jetzigen Staaten durchzusetzen,
zurückgeführt; und zum Schluß heißt es (499 d): „Möglich ist die
Philosophenherrschaft und damit der gute Staat; daß es schwer ist,
geben auch wir zu." — „So ist es, auch ich glaube es" sagt der Mit-
unterredner. „Aber die Vielen" sagt Sokrates, „die glauben es nicht,
wirst Du nun sagen." „Vielleicht" sagt der andere. — „Du, sei nicht
so überheblich in Deinem Urteil über die Vielen. Sie werden anderer
Meinung werden, wenn Du ihnen gut zuredest, ohne Rechthaberei,
und wenn Du sie, um ihr Mißtrauen gegen das Lernenwollen aufzu-
lösen, auf die Philosophen hinweist, die Du meinst, und ihnen erklärst,
was sie sind und was sie treiben, damit sie sie nicht mit denen verwechseln, die sie meinen. Oder glaubst Du, es könne jemand böse sein
auf das Nichtböse und neidisch auf das Neidfremde? Ich will Dir die
Antwort vorwegnehmen und sage: ich glaube, es gibt das in einigen
Wenigen, aber nicht in | der Menge, daß so böses Wesen entsteht." —
„Und ich glaube es mit."

---

[3] Die deutschen Wiedergaben machen keinerlei übersetzungskünstlerische oder
überhaupt stilistische Ansprüche. Vielfach mußte gekürzt, gelegentlich verein-
facht werden. Die antiken Gedanken bewußt nicht durch fälschende Nuancen
zu trüben, war allerdings Ehrensache.

Ist die Beziehung dieser Stelle auf wirkliche gute Erfahrungen Platons immerhin eine Ausdeutung, so haben wir eine ganz bestimmte Äußerung über seine Schultätigkeit in Athen im sogen. *7. Brief.* Er führt aus, was ihn zwang, im Jahre 367 dem Ruf seines Freundes Dion an den Hof Dionysios' II. zu folgen: „Ich konnte mich dem Ruf nicht entziehen", sagt er, „sondern ich ging konsequenterweise im Gefühl höchster Verantwortlichkeit, ging, indem ich aus solchen Gründen meine Beschäftigung verließ, die mir wahrlich keine Unehre machte, unter eine Tyrannis, die weder zu meiner Lehre noch zu meiner Person zu passen schien" (329b). καταλιπὼν τὰς ἐμαυτοῦ διατριβὰς οὔσας οὐκ ἀσχήμονας — diese einzige Litotes aus Platons Feder wiegt gewiß alles auf, was etwa Isokrates zur Herauskehrung der geachteten Stellung *seiner* Schule in Athen je geschrieben hat. Jedenfalls haben wir hier Platons eigenes Zeugnis, daß man ihm in Athen den Betrieb seiner Schule nicht nur nicht verdachte, sondern es im Gegenteil nicht verstehen konnte, daß er überhaupt noch für etwas anderes zu haben war.

Eine eigene direkte Theorie einer solchen Stätte der Philosophie, wie es die Akademie in Athen war, hat Platon nicht gegeben. Selbstverständlich dürfen wir uns ihren Betrieb nach Belieben ausmalen auf Grund der allgemeinen pädagogischen Schilderungen und Lehren in seinen Schriften und dessen, was wir von seinen intimen persönlichen Beziehungen zu den jungen Männern und den Männern seines Kreises direkt erfahren oder erschließen; an solchen Ausmalungen scheint mir heute kein Mangel zu sein. Aber die Theorie der Besonderheit eines akademischen, d. h. eines zur freien wissenschaftlichen Zusammenarbeit gegründeten Institutes in einem Staate, dessen Leitung nicht identisch ist mit der Leitung eben dieses Institutes, fehlt. Das ist kein Zufall. Denn die Theorie läuft bei Platon unweigerlich auf die Herrschaft der Wissenden hinaus; damit aber befinden wir uns in einer Welt, in der alle ernstlichen Konflikte zwischen Denken und Politik von vornherein ausgeschlossen sind und in der die schwersten Probleme des wirklichen Menschenlebens sich für den Einzelnen in geradezu lächerlich einfacher Weise lösen. |

Man muß sich einmal überlegen, was für eine Art von Lebensanschauung in Platons Idealstaat und im Staat seiner *Gesetze* für die Bürger zunächst mit allen Mitteln irrationaler Charakterbildung, die bei seiner pädagogischen Plänemacherei eine wichtige Rolle spielt, vorbereitet und dann ihnen nachträglich rational eingetrichtert werden soll. In einem Staate, in dem unter Leitung der Wissenden in allem und jedem mit freundlichem Zureden, oder aber, wenn das nicht hilft, mit rücksichtsloser Gewalt die Verwirklichung des Guten, Schönen und Gerechten durchgesetzt ist, ist es auch für den einzelnen nicht ratsam, aus der Rolle zu fallen und den unmotivierten Bösewicht zu spielen, vielmehr ist das geforderte Gegenteil nicht nur schöner, gerechter und besser, sondern auch wesentlich sicherer und angenehmer; mit anderen Worten, im verwirklichten Idealstaat läßt sich das vom Einzelnen zu fordernde Leben vollkommen zureichend auch hedonistisch begründen, wie das denn bei Platon für diesen Zweck auch einleuchtend geschieht. Ein Staat, der in seinem ganzen Betrieb nur das Gerechte, Schöne und Gute duldet, hat es spielend leicht, vor seinen angehenden Bürgern als Lehrer des Guten, Schönen und Gerechten aufzutreten; denn gefährdet wäre der Lehrerfolg nur bei einer etwaigen Diskrepanz zwischen politischem Leben und staatlichem Unterricht, aber die kommt ja im Idealstaat nicht vor.

Das wirkliche Leben, in das Platon hineingeboren war und in dem er die sein Leben und auch seine Schulgründung bestimmenden Erfahrungen machte, sah anders aus und führte ihn selbst zu einer ganz anderen, mit billiger Hedonistik schlechterdings nicht zu vereinigenden Lebensansicht. Um das klar zu erfassen, muß man geschieden sein lassen, was nicht auf dieselbe Ebene zu bringen ist, und seinen *Gorgias*, zusammen natürlich mit *Apologie* und *Kriton*, für sich allein nehmen ohne Rücksicht auf alle anderen platonischen Schriften und alle spätere platonische Theorie und Praxis, deren der *Gorgias* zu seiner Erklärung überhaupt nicht bedarf. Im *Gorgias* erscheint das ganze athenische Leben unter einem sehr düsteren Aspekt: das Unwürdige mittun, oder das Unwürdige erleiden, etwas Drittes gibt es nicht. Nicht, daß dies das Normale sein sollte: lieber würde man weder das eine noch das andere haben, aber in Athen gibt es zwangsläufig nur die eine oder die andere Wahl. Man sieht, das will überhaupt keine | allgemeingültige Ethik sein; es handelt sich um die unnatürlichen, ungesunden athenischen Zustände, aus denen der Prozeß des Sokrates allein erklärbar war; aber für sie wird mit so rücksichtsloser Schärfe in Sokrates' Sinne der Kampf des vornehmen Denkens gegen die Pöbelgesinnung fortgesetzt, daß es zunächst widersinnig scheint, daß sich gleichwohl späterhin dieses selbe Denken zu friedlichem Lehren in Athen würde ansiedeln können.

Und doch ist es so gekommen. Platon ist von der ersten großen Reise, die er etwa 40 Jahre alt unternahm, in der Haltung gegenüber seiner Vaterstadt geändert zurückgekehrt. Was diese Veränderung bewirkt hat, spricht er im *7. Brief* genügend deutlich aus. Er hatte die Hoffnung, in das praktische politische Leben Athens je hineinzukommen, aufgeben müssen und ging auf die Reise. In Italien und Sizilien aber lernte er eine derart kraß auf die rohesten Genüsse gerichtete Lebensführung kennen, daß dort die jeweiligen politischen Herren von Gerechtigkeit und bürgerlicher Gleichberechtigung im Staatsleben auch nicht einmal den Namen zu hören sich würden gefallen lassen:

„Das kam für mein Denken zu dem, was ich früher erfahren hatte, hinzu" — ταῦτα δὴ πρὸς τοῖς πρόσθε διανοούμενος u. s. w. (326 d). Darin liegt für die athenische Demokratie, deren Schlagwort die Isonomie war, eine ähnliche, das Wesentliche einmal bei Seite setzende, relative Anerkennung, wie man sie auch im *Menexenos* und *Menon* erkannt hat. Für uns ist das direkte Zeugnis, daß Platon im Ausland etwas Neues zur Beurteilung Athens kennen gelernt hat, natürlich wertvoll, wenn wir uns fragen, wie sich die Kampfansage in *Gorgias* und *Apologie* mit der späteren Schulgründung verträgt. Beides verträgt sich wirklich nicht; Platon hat, zwar nicht seine Theorie, soweit sie im *Gorgias* schon da war, wohl aber seine praktische Stellungnahme Athen gegenüber geändert.

Auf den *Kriton* bin ich in diesem Zusammenhang absichtlich nicht eingegangen. Man darf diese Schrift, in der Platon die innere Notwendigkeit von Sokrates' rätselhaftem und scheinbar widerspruchsvollem Verhalten in und nach seinem Prozeß sich selbst und dem intimen Kreis der Sokratiker nachträglich evident zu machen sucht, nicht zu einer allgemein gedachten und allgemeintheoretisch fundierten Anweisung für das Verhalten eines Staatsbürgers bei etwaigen Konflikten mit dem eigenen Staat oder | gar für das aktive staatsbürgerliche Verhalten überhaupt auswalzen. Als solche ist sie nicht geschrieben, und, weil der Fall des Sokrates viel zu exzeptionell war, auch schlecht zu gebrauchen, was diesen Gebrauch freilich auch schon im Altertum nicht gehindert hat. Soweit ist übrigens, soviel ich sehe, ernstlich kaum jemand gegangen, den *Kriton* speziell auf Platons eigenes bürgerliches Verhalten zugeschnitten sein zu lassen, was sich auch aus chronologischen Gründen nicht empfehlen würde.

Eine klare Rechtfertigung der eigenen politischen Haltung in Athen und zu Athen steht dagegen wieder im *7. Brief*. Platon setzt auseinander, unter welchen Bedingungen er zu politischer Raterteilung sich bereit hält, und führt aus (330c): „Wer einem Kranken, der ungesund lebt, einen Rat geben will, muß ihn zuerst zur Änderung seiner Lebensführung veranlassen und dann die weiteren Ratschläge geben. Will der Kranke die Diät nicht ändern, dann ist der, der die weitere Behandlung ablehnt, ein Mann und ein Arzt; wer sie gleichwohl übernimmt, ist kein Mann und kein Arzt. Ebenso" — ich kürze stark — „kann man nur einem Staat mit einigermaßen gesundem politischem Leben einen Rat geben; wo aber an ein ungesundes politisches Leben zu rühren bei Todesstrafe verboten ist und nur Helferdienste zu verächtlichen Zwecken gefordert werden, da ist der, der mittut, kein Mann; wer sich aber nicht dazu hergibt, der ist ein Mann. In diesem Sinne gebe ich im Privatleben, wenn der Ratholende ein einigermaßen ordentliches Leben führt und bereit ist, auf mich zu hören, einen ehrlichen Rat, und nicht nur, um ihn loszuwerden. Fragt er mich aber überhaupt nicht, oder ist es deutlich, daß er doch nicht auf mich hören wird, dann komme ich nicht als selbstgebetener Ratgeber, und mit Zwang nicht einmal, wenn er mein Sohn wäre. Einen Sklaven würde ich eventuell zwingen, Vater und Mutter aber mit Gewalt zu etwas zu zwingen, das scheint mir ein Vergreifen am Heiligen, es sei denn sie wären geisteskrank; sonst aber, wenn sie ein Leben führen, das ihnen gefällt, mir aber nicht, dann würde ich suchen, mich weder mit ihnen durch unnütze Vorwürfe zu verfeinden, noch aber auch zur Befriedigung von Begierden mich hergeben, die ich selbst nicht um den Preis des Lebens teilen möchte. Und so muß der Verständige auch über das Leben im eigenen Staat denken und | es danach einrichten: reden bei übeler Politik, wenn das Reden überhaupt Sinn hat und nicht die Todesstrafe darauf steht; Gewalt durch Revolution aber, wo die echte Besserung sich nicht ohne Verbannung und Tötung von Menschen erreichen läßt, dem Vaterland nicht antun, sondern dann Ruhe halten und das Gute wünschen, sich und der Stadt."

Das Letzte: βίαν δὲ πατρίδι πολιτείας μεταβολῆς μὴ προσφέρειν ὅταν ἄνευ φυγῆς καὶ σφαγῆς ἀνδρῶν μὴ δυνατὸν ᾖ γίγνεσθαι τὴν ἀρίστην klingt wohl nicht zufällig an Solons Verse an

$$εἰ\ δὲ\ γῆς\ ἐφεισάμην$$
πατρίδος, τυραννίδος δὲ καὶ βίης ἀμειλίχου
οὐ καθηψάμην μιάνας καὶ καταισχύνας κλέος,
οὐδὲν αἰδεῦμαι (fr. 23, 8—11 Diehl),

deren menschliche Großartigkeit freilich nicht zu erreichen war. Denn Solon brauchte wirklich nur die Hand auszustrecken nach dem Gewaltregiment, während es damit bei Platon, wie wir wissen, gute Wege hatte. Aber eine aufrechte männliche Haltung wahrt er sich doch.

Daß man der wirklichen Vaterstadt die gewöhnlichen Bürgerleistungen schuldet, ist nach der ausgeführten Analogie des Verhältnisses zu den Eltern selbstverständlich; aber im übrigen legt nun das politische Besserwissen keinerlei staatsbürgerliche Verpflichtungen auf. Dies kommt in voller Deutlichkeit und Nüchternheit an verschiedenen Stellen des *Staates* zum Ausdruck, von denen eine hier genügen möge (519b): „Brauchbar den Staat verwalten können weder die Ungebildeten, noch die Gebildeten, wenn man sie frei in ihrer Bildung verweilen läßt; die einen nicht, weil sie kein einheitliches echtes Ziel für das Handeln im Privatleben und im öffentlichen Leben haben; die andern nicht, weil sie freiwillig nicht in die Praxis gehen werden, da sie meinen, schon bei Lebzeiten das Wohnen auf den Inseln der Seligen gefunden zu haben. Also müssen wir die bestveranlagten Bürger zunächst zur höchsten Wahrheitserkenntnis hinaufführen, dürfen ihnen dann aber nicht erlauben, was ihnen jetzt erlaubt wird." — „Was denn nicht?" — „Dort zu bleiben und nicht an den Lasten und zweifelhaften Ehrungen des praktischen Lebens teilnehmen zu wollen." — „Ja, sollen wir ihnen denn Unrecht tun und sie, | trotzdem sie ein besseres Leben haben können, zwingen, schlechter zu leben?" — „Du vergißt, daß das Gesetz nie an den Vorteil eines einzelnen Standes, sondern immer nur an den gesamten Staatsverband denken kann. Und außerdem werden wir in unserem Staat den Philosophen bei uns auch gar kein Unrecht tun, sondern wir werden es ihnen selbst gegenüber rechtfertigen können, wenn wir sie zwingen, sich um die andern zu kümmern und sie zu bewahren. Nämlich, werden wir ihnen sagen, in den andern Städten nimmt, wer Philosoph wird, mit Recht nicht an den staatlichen Lasten teil. In ihnen erwachsen die Philosophen von sich aus, ohne Wissen und Willen des jeweiligen Regiments. Was aber von selbst gewachsen ist und niemandem die Aufzucht schuldet, das braucht sich auch keine Mühe zu geben, irgend wem Erziehungslohn zu zahlen. Euch aber ..." und nun kommt, was der Idealstaat im Gegensatz zu den andern Staaten für Erziehung, Bildung und Wissenschaft tut.

Daß das wirkliche Athen zu den andern Staaten gehört, ist keine Frage. Dann aber wird hier für den Philosophen in Athen ausdrücklich das geleugnet, daß er nämlich diesem Staat τροφεῖα schuldig wäre, woraus doch im *Kriton* die Verpflichtung des Sokrates hergeleitet wurde, den Tod im Gefängnis auf sich zu nehmen und abzuwarten. Das ist kein Widerspruch, weil es sich um verschiedene Dinge handelt, im einen Fall um den athenischen Bürger Sokrates, der nie etwas anderes hat sein wollen als ein athenischer Bürger, im anderen Fall um die Stellung der Philosophie in einem Staate, der von Philosophie und Wissenschaft nichts hält. Man darf solche Unterschiede aber auch nicht verwischen, wenn man Wesentliches gewinnen will.

Für unsere Frage ist das Wesentliche, daß Platon als Philosoph mit dem politischen Leben seiner Vaterstadt nichts zu tun haben will und sich durchaus nicht für verpflichtet hält, um ihretwillen sei es sich selbst, sei es einen andern zum Aufgeben des Lebens auf den Inseln der Seligen zu zwingen, was er doch um Dions willen über sich gewann. Schon seit längerer Zeit nimmt man es als „allbekannt, daß Platon die Ethik mit der Staats- und Gesellschaftslehre in den engsten Zusammenhang bringt und sich den tugendhaften Menschen nur als Bürger denken kann"[4]; aber | es pflegt in den Darstellungen zurückzutreten, was nicht zurücktreten darf, daß nämlich

1) der Bürger des Idealstaates die höchste Bürgerpflicht, das Mitregieren, notwendigerweise nur ungern auf sich nimmt, weil er ein besseres Leben gekostet hat, und daß

---

[4] H. v. Arnim, Die Kultur der Gegenwart, I Abt. V, Berlin und Leipzig 1909, 161.

2) der philosophische Bürger eines Staates wie Athen sich dieser höchsten Bürgerpflicht überhoben fühlt.

Nach dieser Vorbereitung sind wir, denke ich, imstande, uns eine platonische Ansicht von der Stellung der Akademie in Athen zu bilden. Es kann ja nur die des philosophischen Privatmannes sein, also — um eine andere vielzitierte Stelle des *Staates* (496 d e) zu benutzen — die Stellung desjenigen, der bei einem schweren Unwetter unter den Schutz einer Mauer beiseite tritt, zufrieden, sich selbst aus dem wüsten Treiben herauszuhalten. „Wahrlich nicht das Geringste, was ein Mensch erreichen kann!" sagt der Gesprächspartner. „Aber auch nicht das Höchste, denn es fehlt ihm der Staat, in dem er selbst noch wachsen und außer dem Eigenen das Gemeinwesen retten könnte", läßt Platon erwidern, für den diese Haltung aus theoretisch nicht restlos darzustellenden Gründen eine schwere Resignation bedeutet und bei dem die ernstgenommene Bereitschaft zum persönlichen Einsatz, wenn er Sinn hat, dahintersteht. Wer wollte dieser Haltung den Respekt versagen?

Aber das gilt nun eben doch nur für die Person Platons, nicht ohne weiteres auch für die Gemeinschaft, die er gegründet hat, und insbesondere nicht für die Männer, die berufen waren, die wissenschaftliche Arbeit fortzusetzen. Was Platon ihnen beschert hatte, war faktisch ein geistiges Leben auf den Inseln der Seligen, bei dem alle die lästigen Verpflichtungen wegfielen, die im Idealstaat immerhin auch dem zu Höchstem Berufenen obgelegen hätten. Und das haben die Klügsten und Ehrlichsten unter diesen Männern auch bewußt erfaßt. Die Lustlehre des Eudoxos ist doch nicht zufälligerweise von einem ernsthaften Gelehrten, der in Athen das Leben der Akademie mitlebte, aufgestellt worden. Und daß das Leben in Philosophie nicht nur das Edelste, Beste und Nützlichste, sondern auch bei weitem das Leichteste und Lustvollste und gleich dem Leben auf den Inseln der Seligen sei, verkündete | Aristoteles' *Protreptikos*; auch späterhin hat sich Aristoteles nie zu einer platten Bekämpfung des hedonistischen Standpunktes hergegeben. Freilich, was sich in diesen Männern bildete, war auch keine so bescheidene, auf eine kümmerliche Lust- und Unlustbilanz gegründete Lebensansicht, wie sie Platon für den idealen Durchschnittsbürger für hinreichend erachtete. Er selbst hat den Mitgliedern seiner Akademie, eines Kreises von scheinbar weltfremden Philosophen, das adlige Herrengefühl mitzuteilen gewußt, das darin besteht, unter keinen Umständen jemandes Bedienter sein zu müssen und allein recht zu wissen, was freies Leben heißt.

„Aber wir haben doch Zeit" beginnt ein berühmter Exkurs im *Theaetet* (172c), in dem dann aus diesem Zeithaben, zu denken und ruhig sich zu unterhalten, worüber man nur will, der Gegensatz des

freien Philosophen gegen den unfreien praktischen Gerichtsredner und
Politiker entwickelt wird. In seitenlangen Ausführungen wird gezeigt,
daß es durchaus mit rechten Dingen zugeht, wenn der Philosoph, in
die Praxis des Lebens gezogen, sich lächerlich macht, wie Thales vor
der thrakischen Sklavin. Umgekehrt aber, wenn der nur im politischen
Treiben Großgewordene sich einmal hinaufwagt in die Region des
freien Denkens und Redens, dann weiß er sich nicht zu helfen und
macht sich mit seinem verstiegenen Gestammel lächerlich, nicht vor
Thrakerinnen und vor keinem Ungebildeten, die merken es nicht, aber
vor jedem, der entgegengesetzt aufgewachsen ist wie ein Sklave (175 d).
Ich hebe aus der ganzen Partie, von der eigentlich jedes Wort her-
gehörte, nur einen Satz aus (175 d/e): ,,Das, Theodoros, ist die Art des
einen und des anderen, die eine die des wirklich in Freiheit und Frei-
zeit Aufgewachsenen, den Du den Philosophen nennst, der sich nichts
dabei vergibt, wenn er einfältig und ungeschickt scheint, wo es sich
um Sklavenverrichtungen handelt, gleichsam um Bettenmachen und
Essenkochen und Bedientenantworten geben; die andere die Art dessen, der alle solche Bedientenarbeit genau und flink verrichten kann,
aber nicht gelernt hat, wie ein anständiger Mensch den Mantel nach
rechts zu tragen und das Instrument der Rede zu nehmen, um ohne
falschen Ton einen Hymnus auf glücklicher Götter und Menschen
Leben anzustimmen." |

Es bedarf keines Beweises, daß hier die Freiheit der Philosophie
mit den Farben nicht der schlichten Bürgerfreiheit, sondern mit denen
der Zugehörigkeit zur gesellschaftlichen Aristokratie gemalt ist; und
es gibt keine bessere Illustration zu dem ἀναβάλλεσθαι ἐπιδέξια
ἐλευθερίως als die Szene in Aristophanes' *Vögeln* (1565ff.), wo der
vornehme Herr Poseidon zu seinem Leidwesen nicht nur mit dem
plumpen Herakles, sondern sogar mit einem Barbarengott, der nicht
einmal verständlich griechisch reden kann, in eine Gesandtschaft zu-
sammengewählt ist, und wo er gleich beim Auftreten mit dem letzteren
seine Last hat: ,,Du, was machst Du? So nach links trägst Du? Willst
Du nicht schleunigst den Mantel so wie ich nach rechts nehmen?
Was? Unglückswesen, bist Du denn verkehrt gewachsen? O Demokratie, wohin wirst Du uns noch bringen, wenn die Götter so einen
Kerl zum Gesandten wählen!"

Die gesellschaftlich aristokratische Auffassung des Philosophen-
daseins durch Platon und in Athen ist zum guten Teil vorbestimmt.
Denn für den Athener aus guter Familie ist es selbstverständlich, daß
er außer der gesellschaftlichen Konvention, wie man sich benimmt
und wie man sich kleidet, eine gewisse zweckfreie Bildung und geistige
Interessen von Hause aus mitbekommen hat, die sich der einfache Mann
nicht leisten kann, weshalb der Vorwurf der Unerzogenheit besonders

bitter empfunden wird und besonders bitter gemeint ist. Das ist der attische Sinn des Wortes παιδεία und des Gegensatzes zwischen πεπαιδευμένος und ἀπαίδευτος, zwischen Gebildet und Ungebildet, den wir Modernen ganz ähnlich, als gesellschaftliche Voraussetzung, auch ohne weiteres zur Hand haben.

In den Herrenallüren haben wir nun einen weiteren integrierenden Bestandteil des akademischen Lebens gleich bei Platon; und bilden konnte sich dieser Bestandteil allerdings nur in einer durch die Gunst oder Ungunst der Verhältnisse der praktischen Verantwortung überhobenen Sphäre. Der Stolz des Wissenschaftlers darauf, daß ihn niemand zwingen kann, weder zu dem, worüber er denkt, noch was er denkt, noch fertig zu sein, ehe er selbst es glaubt, ist bei rein theoretischen Gegenständen vielleicht erlaubt; aber soweit die Wissenschaft über Dinge des wirklichen Lebens überhaupt mitreden will, muß sie sich vorsehen. Solange sie sagt: Ich habe ein auch für die Praxis maßgebendes Wissen, | aber es ziemt sich, daß die Praktiker zu mir kommen, ich brauche ihnen nicht nachzulaufen (bei Platon sagt sie es *Staat* 489 c), solange ist ihr Anspruch auf Achtung kaum anfechtbar; aber in demselben Moment, wo sie sich aus dem Mangel ihres Mittuns in den dringenden Nöten der Praxis an sich ein Adelsgefühl zurecht macht, in demselben Moment gerät sie in Gefahr, sich ihres Anspruches auf Beachtung überhaupt zu begeben. Insbesondere aber ist es ein auf die Dauer unmöglicher Zustand, daß im freien Hochgefühl des Theoretikers Staatsphilosophie getrieben wird. Aber darauf will die *Theaetet*stelle selbst auch nicht hinaus, wenn sie betont, daß nur der Philosoph gute Gesellschaft ist. Sie führt nämlich bewußt hin 1. zu den Gedanken des *Phaidon* und 2. zu den Gedanken des *Gorgias*. Wie im *Phaidon* wird als die wahre Gesellschaft des Philosophen, die er sucht und der er sich angleicht, das Göttliche bestimmt; und wie im *Gorgias* wird gezeigt, daß, wer etwas Besseres und Vornehmeres sein will als die Vielen, das nie und nimmer so erreichen kann, daß er sich selbst auf die Ebene des verachteten Pöbels begibt.

Dagegen ist nicht viel einzuwenden. Nur wenn direkt an das Herrsein im Staate gedacht wird, verlieren bemerkenswerterweise für das nüchterne Denken die gesellschaftlichen Farben sofort jeden Glanz. Daß, wer eine staatliche Funktion ausüben will, gefälligst nicht an sich selbst, sondern an das Ganze zu denken hat, ist eine ganz primitive, aber auch primäre Wahrheit, die sofort erfaßt zu werden pflegt, sowie über das Wesen eines staatlichen Funktionärs überhaupt nachgedacht wird. Wer demgegenüber noch den Freiherrn spielen will, der kann es nur machen wie Aristipp bei Xenophon (*Mem.* 2, 1, 8) und darf für seine Person von staatlichen Funktionen nichts wissen wollen. Es ist der Mühe wert, die Begründung zu hören: ,,Es gehört schon ein großer

Mangel an Menschenverstand dazu, wo es schwer genug ist, sich selbst
das Nötige zu verschaffen, damit nicht genug zu haben, sondern sich
noch dazu aufzubürden, auch für seine Mitbürger, was die nötig haben,
zu besorgen. Und es sich selbst an vielem, was man möchte, fehlen zu
lassen, um sich als Staatsfunktionär, wenn man nicht alles erreicht,
was die Leute gern möchten, dafür zur Verantwortung ziehen zu lassen,
das ist die Höhe der Dummheit. Denn die Staaten verlangen (ἀξιοῦσιν)
in der Tat, einen solchen | Gebrauch von ihren Beamten zu machen,
wie ich von meinen Sklaven. Ich verlange, daß meine Bedienten mir
alles Nötige reichlich bereitstellen, ohne selbst etwas anzurühren, und
genauso, meinen die Staaten, müßten ihre Funktionäre ihnen alles
Gute in größter Menge beschaffen, sich selbst aber an nichts davon
vergreifen."

Diese Stelle habe ich ausgehoben, weil in ihr das Axiom, das ich
eine primitive, aber auch primäre Wahrheit genannt habe, ganz rein
herauskommt[5]. Selbstverständlich gilt dieses Axiom, daß der Staatsfunktionär immer nur an das Gemeinwohl und nicht an seine Person
zu denken hat, für Platons Staatsphilosophie; gerade er hat es theoretisch zu voller Geltung gebracht, übrigens auch die notwendige Ergänzung hinzugefügt, daß der Beamte so gestellt sein muß, daß er an
Privatnutzen nicht zu denken braucht. Aber auch in seinem großen
Werk über den *Staat* wird daneben an der Weltansicht des *Gorgias*
und an der des *Phaidon* durchaus festgehalten. Vereinigen lassen sich
alle drei Ansichten allenfalls in dem Wunschbild des Idealstaates,
übrigens auch da nicht so simpel, daß Philosophsein und gutes Staats-
bürger- oder Staatsschöpfersein einfach identisch würde; in die Welt
der Wirklichkeit aber ist auf diese Weise unter anderem auch die
akademisch-vornehmtuende Staatsphilosophie gekommen, die von
der Person ihres Stifters losgelöst ein Widerspruch in sich ist.

Dieser Fluch, daß die vornehme wissenschaftliche Haltung nicht
den Anschluß an die politische Wirklichkeit findet, mag sie auch noch
so viel davon in ihre Theorie aufzunehmen sich bemühen, ruht selbst
auf Aristoteles' Staatsphilosophie in ihrer spätesten Ausprägung.
Aristoteles hat das selbst empfunden und, spät genug, seine politischen
Theorien zwar nicht preisgegeben, wohl aber in ganz eigenartiger

---

[5] Ich füge noch einen von Athen unabhängigen Zeugen für dieselbe Wahrheit hinzu, Demokrit, den das Athen seiner Zeit nicht kannte und der seinerseits dieses
Athen nicht nötig hatte. Fragment 265 lautet in Diels' Übersetzung: „Die Menschen erinnern sich mehr an das Verfehlte als an das Gelungene. Und das ist ja
auch so ganz in der Ordnung. Denn wie nicht der Lob verdient, der anvertrautes
Gut zurückgibt, wohl aber der, der es nicht tut, übeln Ruf und Strafe, so steht es
auch mit dem Beamten. Denn er ist ja nicht dazu gewählt worden, seine Sache
schlecht zu machen, sondern gut".

Weise sich mit ihnen ins Privat|leben zurückgezogen. Am Schluß der *Nikomachischen Ethik* wird der gesuchte Übergang von der Ethik zur Politik in folgender Weise gefunden: ,,Die theoretische Erkenntnis der ethischen Dinge würde in sich abgeschlossen sein, wenn Tugend durch rationale Unterweisung allein erzeugt werden könnte. Aber das ist nicht der Fall; sondern Voraussetzung ist die rechte Gewöhnung des Irrationalen im Menschen. Von Ausnahmefällen abgesehen ist das beste Mittel dazu ein unpersönlich wirkender Zwang, wie ihn eigentlich nur der Staat und seine Gesetze ausüben können. Erzieherpflichten erkennt aber höchstens der spartanische Staat für sich an, die andern Staaten wollen sich um solche Dinge nicht kümmern, und es lebt ein jeder in ihnen wie er will, nach Kyklopenweise waltend über Weib und Kind (Hom. *Od. ι* 114). Das Beste wäre also eine rechte staatliche Fürsorge. Da nun aber die Dinge von Staatswegen vernachlässigt werden, so bleibt wohl nichts übrig, als jeden Einzelnen darauf angewiesen sein zu lassen, privatim für seine Kinder und Freunde zur Tugend beizusteuern, oder wenigstens es sich vorzunehmen. Und das wird er nach dem Gesagten am ehesten können, wenn er ein theoretischer Gesetzgeber wird, denn die Theorie der Sache bleibt dieselbe, auch wenn es sich um Privaterziehung handelt. Von wem lernt man nun die Gesetzgeberkunst? Eigentlich müßte man sie entweder von den Politikern oder von den Sophisten lernen. Aber die Politiker lehren nicht; und die Sophisten können nicht lehren, was sie versprechen. Da also alle Früheren das Werk der Gesetzgebung theoretisch unerledigt gelassen haben, so werden wir selbst zusehen müssen, über Gesetzgebung und überhaupt über Staatseinrichtung, damit die Philosophie über Menschendinge nach Möglichkeit ihre Vollendung finde" — und dann kommt ein kurzer Überblick über die *Politik*.

In diesen Ausführungen, die wohl das letzte sind, was wir überhaupt von Aristoteles über diese Dinge hören, steht einmal ganz klar, worauf eigentlich für ihn, genausogut wie für Platon, die theoretische Notwendigkeit einer Staatsphilosophie beruhte: nicht darauf nämlich, daß sie sich das menschliche Dasein *auch in ihren Wünschen* nur als Staatsbürgertum hätten denken können, was falsch ist (dazu noch eine letzte Stelle aus Platons *Staat*, 520e: ,,So ist es, mein Freund: nur wenn Du ein | Leben ausfindest, das besser ist als das Herrschen im Staat für diejenigen, die im Staat herrschen sollen, nur dann wird es möglich sein, daß Dir ein guter Staat entsteht"), sondern darauf, daß im Menschen etwas Niederes, Irrationales gegeben ist, das sich im allgemeinen höchstens durch staatlichen Zwang erziehen lassen will. Zum andern aber steht da: Die Staaten kümmern sich nicht um die ihnen von der Philosophie vorgezeichnete wichtigste Aufgabe; die Theorie bleibt richtig; aber ihre Anwendung wird sie wohl nur im

Privatleben finden; und um dieser Anwendung im Privatleben willen wollen wir uns denn nun zur Staatsphilosophie wenden, da sonst die Ethik eine Lücke hätte.

Hier sehen wir Aristoteles im Alter eine Privatansicht bilden, die zu kompliziert und zu resigniert ist, um als Allgemeingut weiterleben zu können: der Kampf um den Vorrang des βίος θεωρητικός oder πρακτικός innerhalb der peripatetischen Schule, der Streit zwischen Theophrast und Dikaiarch, steht unmittelbar bevor. Über ihn kann ich im Rahmen dieses Vortrags nicht mehr sprechen; ich weiß aber auch nichts Besseres über ihn zu sagen, als auf Werner Jaeger ,,Über Ursprung und Kreislauf des philosophischen Lebensideals" (Berl. Sitz.-Ber. 1928) zu verweisen.

Ich möchte schließen. Die Staaten kümmern sich nicht um die akademisch vorgetragene Staatsphilosophie, sie wenden sie nicht an, und andererseits vertragen sie vielfach ziemliche Kühnheiten, wenn sie eben akademisch bleiben. Aber es gibt Zeiten, in denen die Menschen jeden Respekt vor dem akademischen Treiben verlieren, weil die Wissenschaft zu vornehm ist, zu den unmittelbar dringenden politischen Fragen ernsthaft Stellung zu nehmen, trotzdem sie auch Staatswissenschaft sein zu wollen nicht aufhört. Durch solche Zeiten das akademisch-wissenschaftliche Hochgefühl hindurchzuretten ist schwer. Preisgegeben wird das Ziel, wenn die Wissenschaft selbst die Überzeugung aufgibt, entscheidende Instanz sein zu können und zu sollen, wo immer gedacht und mit Gründen gestritten wird. Zu diesem Verzicht hat sich die platonische Akademie selbst zeitweilig im Altertum entschlossen, und sie konnte dann, genausogut wie der Standpunkt Dikaiarchs, von der keineswegs ungroßartigen Lebensanschauung und Selbstbespiegelung des gebildetsten Römers und Redners annektiert werden, von dem wir alle abhängen, wenn wir uns Humanisten | nennen und uns als Humanisten fühlen; ich meine natürlich Cicero. Aber damit war die Wissenschaft nicht nur bei Seite geschoben, sondern tot.

Soll Wissenschaft und wissenschaftliche Haltung verteidigt werden, dann wird man mit der historischen Einsicht beginnen müssen, daß insonderheit für die Staatsphilosophie — aber Philosophie läßt sich schlecht teilen — das akademische Leben auf den Inseln der Seligen von Platon nur als Provisorium und nicht als selbstverständlicher Dauerzustand in die Welt gebracht werden konnte.

Theorie und Praxis bei Aristoteles und Platon

1938

Wenn man für die Ursprünge philosophischer Gedanken interessiert ist, bietet die Terminologie ein nur mit Gewalt zu beseitigendes Hindernis. Denn das Interesse für den Ursprung eines Gedankens setzt das Interesse für den Gedanken selbst voraus, und diesem Interesse werden, falls man nicht Philologe in einem kaum vorstellbar engen Sinne ist, moderne Anwendungsformen des Gedankens und eine moderne Ausdrucksweise entsprechen, die an den Ursprüngen nicht vorhanden gewesen zu sein brauchen. Denn derselbe Gedanke kann auf verschiedene Gegenstände angewendet werden, und er kann unter allen Umständen in sehr verschiedenen Worten ausgedrückt werden. Die damit gegebenen Schwierigkeiten sind bekannt und oft betont worden, sie müssen aber auch immer wieder besonders hervorgehoben werden, um einerseits sich und andern das Recht zu wahren, grundsatzlos das zweckmäßig Scheinende zu tun, andererseits aber an die Doppelgefahr zu erinnern, entweder durch willkürliche Terminologie wesentliche Unterschiede zu verwischen oder aber durch engherzige Terminologie Wohlbekanntes zu maskieren. In unserem Fall sind ,,Theorie und Praxis'' Schlagworte für ein uns Modernen geläufiges Problem, zu welchem, wenigstens im Bereich des Politisch-Ethischen, ursprüngliche Gedanken bei Platon und bei Aristoteles aufsuchen zu wollen nicht unerlaubt scheint; aber das gutgriechische Wortpaar gibt sich in gutem Griechisch zur Bezeichnung dieses Problems schlechterdings nicht her[1], und es hat auch keinen Zweck, nach echtgriechischen Ersatzbezeichnungen als Ausgangspunkten für die Behandlung des Problems bei Platon | und Aristoteles sich umzusehen. Um solche Ausgangspunkte zu liefern, dazu war die Sache damals noch nicht abgedroschen genug. Indessen, wenn die Hoffnung des Gräzisten, auf seinem Gebiet nicht nur in Worten Verhülltes und leere Worthülsen, sondern manchmal reine Körner zu finden, berechtigt ist, dann muß manches auch ohne und gegen das Sprachliche versucht werden.

Aber ich wäre in der Tat um einen Ausgangspunkt für das, was ich besprechen möchte, verlegen, wenn ich nicht in der glücklichen Lage

---

[1] Auf Griechisch sind der Theoretiker und der Praktiker in erster Linie durch die verschiedene Willensrichtung charakterisiert, während ,,Theorie und Praxis'' in unmittelbar sachlichen Konflikt zu geraten pflegen.

wäre, den Aufsatz von K. Kuypers „Recht und Billigkeit bei Aristoteles" bei den Lesern der Mnemosyne (1937, 5, 289 ff.) voraussetzen zu dürfen. Durch diesen Aufsatz sind zwar nicht den Worten, aber der Sache nach wesentliche Gedanken zu dem Problem „Theorie und Praxis" als wesentliche Bestandteile des Denkens des reifen Aristoteles aufgewiesen und, wie ich annehme, in den Vordergrund des Interesses jedes Lesers gerückt worden, so daß ich, den Aufsatz im Ganzen und in manchen Einzelheiten dankbar aufnehmend und voraussetzend, ohne weitere eigene Bemühung sofort zu meinen Bemerkungen übergehen kann.

Es handelt sich um die Sphären der Ethik und der Gesetzgebung. Für beide Sphären hat Aristoteles das Wort ὕλη geprägt (*E. N.* 1094 b 12, 1137 b 19), und diese ὕλη ist nach ihm im ersten Falle so, daß man von ihrer Behandlung keine exakt genauen wissenschaftlichen Bestimmungen erwarten darf, im zweiten Falle derart, daß unmöglich die doch für gesetzliche Bestimmungen notwendige allgemeine Fixierung für jeden Einzelfall das Richtige treffen kann. Offensichtlich haben wir hier in beiden Fällen denselben Gedanken und, was die ὕλη betrifft, sogar dieselbe Sache; aber andererseits gehört nur der Fall der Ethik unter unser Rubrum „Theorie und Praxis", denn nur hier, hier aber wirklich, haben wir etwas, das wir als „Theorie", wissenschaftliche Behandlung, bezeichnen müssen und als solches so der „Praxis" gegenüberstellen können, wie es Aristoteles mit seiner πολιτική τις μέθοδος und deren ὕλη macht. An der Identität des Gedankens ist aber trotz der hierdurch für uns gekennzeichneten Verschiedenheit der Anwendung natürlich nicht zu zweifeln. Gestützt auf diese Identität des Gedankens hat nun Kuypers die ihn zugrunde legende | Lehre von der Billigkeit, die in der *Nikomachischen Ethik* und manchmal, aber nicht durchweg, in der *Rhetorik* zu finden ist und die keinesfalls das ursprüngliche griechische Denken in seiner Unmittelbarkeit darstellt, aus der Gesamtentwicklung des Aristoteles zu dem grundsätzlichen Standpunkt der *Nikomachischen Ethik* hin zu erklären versucht[2]. Dabei kommt das Eigentümliche der aristotelischen Stellungnahme, daß nämlich trotz der Anerkennung der Unbestimmbarkeit der ὕλη und der daraus gezogenen Konsequenzen das Genauere im Ernste gerade doch nicht dem Ungefähr, der Lässigkeit und dem Belieben preisgegeben wird, zu so abgerundeter Darstellung, daß nichts zu zwingen scheint, die Ursprünge dieser Problematik außerhalb von Aristoteles' eigener Entwicklung zu suchen.

Aber bei genauerem Zusehen ergeben sich doch gedankliche Unstimmigkeiten, und zwar den Kern des Gedankens betreffend, was

---

[2] Ebenso eine gelegentlich in der *Politik* auftauchende entsprechende Empfehlung von Gesetzesänderungen (*Pol.* 1269 a 9).

immer ein sicheres Zeichen dafür ist, daß sein Ursprung noch nicht getroffen ist. Die *Nikomachische Ethik* führt an exponiertester Stelle 1094b 11ff. statt des auch ihr nicht unbekannten Gegensatzes von begründeter und unbegründeter Behauptung (*Eudemische Ethik* 1216b 35—1217a 17, *E. N.* 1095b 6, 1098a 33, 1143b 11) den Gegensatz genau — ungenau ein (τὸ ἀκριβές — παχυλῶς καὶ τύπῳ, ὡς ἐπὶ τὸ πολύ), und zwar ausdrücklich nicht nur für den empirisch und in der unwissenschaftlichen Vorstellung gegeben gedachten Gegenstand, sondern gerade für die wissenschaftlichen Ergebnisse, ethische Allgemeinheiten. Aber trotzdem sich Aristoteles dann auf das hohe Pferd des gebildeten Mannes setzt und nicht ohne gutes gesellschaftliches Empfinden, aber mit einer für den Wissenschaftler höchst zweideutigen Analogie (παραπλήσιον γὰρ φαίνεται μαθηματικοῦ τε πιθανολογοῦντος ἀποδέχεσθαι καὶ ῥητορικὸν ἀποδείξεις ἀπαιτεῖν) auf ethischem Gebiet gerade in der Akribologie einen Mangel an Erziehung sieht, wird unklar, wie er der theoretischen Konsequenz entgehen will, daß es in der ethischen Praxis im einzelnen nicht so genau darauf ankommen könne. Selbstverständlich gedenkt er diese Konsequenz nicht zu ziehen. Aber wer oder was soll nun eigentlich das Genaue liefern, wenn es sich dem Zugriff des Denkens entzieht? Ein theoretisch un|faßbares Gefühl als Primärquelle des Genauen ist für Aristoteles so ausgeschlossen[3] wie für Platon.

Im Falle der Gesetzgebung ist die Instanz, die das Genauere festsetzen soll und muß, äußerlich gegeben im Richter und jedem ihm analog vorgestellten Beurteiler eines andern. Aber es liegt auf der Hand, daß dieses Genauere gerade nicht das Lässigere, Mildere, Nachgiebigere zu sein braucht, trotzdem es Aristoteles so darstellt[4].

---

[3] Er kann, wenn er will und muß, das Schwere und Größte auf ethischem Gebiet und dessen griechisch gedachte Voraussetzungen sogar ganz ausgezeichnet definieren; aber man muß im 5. Buch der *Nikomachischen Ethik* suchen 1129b 11—1130a 14. — Dagegen Cicero appelliert gegen die Zweifel der Philosophen an das natürliche — römische — Rechtsgefühl. „*Huic igitur viro bono, quem Fimbria etiam, non modo Socrates noverat . . . Haec non turpe est dubitare philosophos, quae ne rustici quidem dubitent?*" (*de off.* 3, 77). Bei ihm sind beide Voraussetzungen gegeben, das Selbstgefühl des Römers und — die neue Akademie.

[4] Kuypers sucht das Ursprünglichere in dem Passus des 6. Buches der *E. N.* über die γνώμη, 1143a 19—24, und freut sich über den es scheinbar verratenden Zirkelbeweis ebensosehr, wie sich Greenwood (Aristotle, Nicomachean Ethics Book Six, 1909, 203) darüber geärgert hat. Richtig ist, daß in der Gerichtspraxis die Formel γνώμη τῇ ἀρίστῃ entweder in diesem milderen Sinne (Ar. *Rh.* 1375a 29) oder gerade umgekehrt (1375b 16) gedeutet wurde. Aber der Gedankengang zwingt, in Zeile 1143a 23 das Wort συγγνώμη mit Trendelenburg zu streichen. Dann ist die γνώμη, unparteiisch wie es sich gehört, von der συγγνώμη abgehoben als die κρίσις ὀρθή, und dies unterscheidende Wort bedeutet das Genaue, das „in einigen Fällen" — aber eben nicht in allen — zur συγγνώμη führt. Die συγγνώμη wird

Wir kommen mit unserer Untersuchung bei Aristoteles auf keinen Grund, auf dem wir selbst Fuß fassen könnten. Wenn wir den suchen, müssen wir uns entschließen, an Stelle der mehr summarischen Vorstellungen über das Verhältnis der aristotelischen zur platonischen Gedankenwelt, denen auch Kuypers sich anschließt (292), die jeweiligen Einzelheiten der erhaltenen platonischen und aristotelischen Schriften zu setzen. |

Nicht das Wort, wohl aber den Gedanken der sich dem technischen Erfassen entziehenden ὕλη der Gesetzgebung hat zuerst Platon für seine Zwecke ausgespielt. Warum gibt es etwas Besseres als die Herrschaft der Gesetze? ὅτι νόμος οὐκ ἄν ποτε δύναιτο τό τε ἄριστον καὶ τὸ δικαιότατον ἀκριβῶς πᾶσιν ἅμα περιλαβὼν τὸ βέλτιστον ἐπιτάττειν· αἱ γὰρ ἀνομοιότητες τῶν τε ἀνθρώπων καὶ τῶν πράξεων καὶ τὸ μηδέποτε μηδὲν ὡς ἔπος εἰπεῖν ἡσυχίαν ἄγειν τῶν ἀνθρωπίνων οὐδὲν ἐῶσιν ἁπλοῦν ἐν οὐδενὶ περὶ ἁπάντων καὶ ἐπὶ πάντα τὸν χρόνον ἀποφαίνεσθαι τέχνην οὐδ᾽ ἡντινοῦν *Politikos* 294a/b. Warum ist gleichwohl Gesetzgebung notwendig? Weil an das Bessere, nämlich an das durch kein Gesetz gebundene Urteil des denken könnenden königlichen Mannes nicht in jedem Einzelfall appelliert werden kann. Denn der ist nur ein Mensch, und zwar ein sehr seltener, und kann nicht überall dabeisitzen (295b). Die Konsequenz aus beidem ist, daß man, wie das für alle geltende Kommando beim Turnen nicht auf den einzelnen zugeschnittene Feinarbeit (λεπτουργεῖν 294d) sein kann, sondern notwendigerweise παχύτερον ... ὡς ἐπὶ πολὺ καὶ ἐπὶ πολλούς gegeben wird[5], ebensowenig bei dem für alle zusammen geltenden Gesetz das ἀκριβῶς ἑνὶ ἑκάστῳ τὸ προσῆκον ἀποδιδόναι erwarten darf[6]. Auch das Gesetz wird nur das auf die Mehrzahl der Menschen und Fälle Passende enthalten können und damit Einzelfälle ziemlich grob behandeln. Das Gesetz ist eben nicht das Richtigste ,,ὀρθότατον''[7].

Der aristotelische Gedanke von der mit den menschlichen Handlungen und den Situationen des Menschenlebens gegebenen, nicht

für den Angeklagten erbeten, Sache der γνώμη ist es zu bestimmen, ob jene wirklich am Platze ist. Daß der Richter sein ,,ὀρθῶς'' (*E. N.* 1137b 14) streng oder seinerseits wiederum mit einer Tendenz zur Milde nehmen kann, ist eine Komplikation, die Aristoteles in der Tat auch hier stillschweigend hineinbringt und ausnutzt; aber der Gedanke leidet darunter, wenn auch nicht in dem Maße, wie es der abscheuliche Zusatz von συγγνώμη an der verkehrtesten Stelle erscheinen läßt. Der antike Leser, der für ihn verantwortlich ist, war einfach nicht imstande, einem aristotelischen σημεῖον δέ· zu folgen.

[5] 294e, dazu 295a 4f. *E. N.* 1094b 20 heißt es παχυλῶς καὶ τύπῳ τἀληθὲς ἐνδείκνυσθαι καὶ περὶ τῶν ὡς ἐπὶ τὸ πολὺ καὶ ἐκ τοιούτων λέγοντας τοιαῦτα καὶ συμπεραίνεσθαι. Zu τύπῳ vgl. *Leg.* 876e.

[6] *E. N.* 1094b 24 τἀκριβὲς ἐπιζητεῖν.

[7] 294d. Vgl. *F. N.* 1137b 14ff. ὀρθῶς und 1143a 20ff. die κρίσις ὀρθή (oben S. 169 Anm. 4).

genau zu erfassenden ὕλη hat sich als ein platonischer erwiesen. Bei Platon sind wir davor sicher, daß die Zuständigkeit des Wissens auch nur auf Momente gefährdet erscheinen oder daß ein Hang zur Nachgiebigkeit die Klarheit des Denkens trüben[8] könnte. Hier sind wir auf festerem Boden, auf dem also | eigentlich auch Aristoteles steht, und zwar, wie es nun zunächst scheinen möchte, für das καθόλου der Gesetzgebung fast ohne Vermittlung durch seine eigene allgemeine Entwickelung. Und doch war Kuypers im Recht, wenn er den Gedanken der Entwicklung des Aristoteles auch hier in Rechnung gesetzt wissen wollte. Denn

> „Anders lesen Knaben den Terenz,
> Anders Grotius".
> Mich Knaben ärgerte die Sentenz,
> Die ich nun gelten lassen muß.

1822 hat Goethe so geschrieben. Aristoteles hat nur die Sechzig erreicht, aber auch das genügt wohl, um in dieser einen Beziehung ihn und nicht Platon, der nie ein Frühfertiger und nie ein Spätvollendeter war und der für sich vom Lesen nicht viel hielt, mit Goethe zu vergleichen. Ein rettender Zufall der Überlieferung hat es gefügt, daß wir übersehen können, wie der jüngere Aristoteles aus demselben platonischen *Politikos* ganz anderes herausgelesen hat als der ältere.

Jaeger hat in seinem „Aristoteles" (91) das 10. Kapitel von Jamblichs *Protreptikos* (= Aristoteles' *Protreptikos*) zum Zeugnis für einen so scheinbar orthodox sich unterordnenden Glauben an „die" Ideenlehre aufgerufen, wie er eigentlich schon durch Platons spätere Dialoge — das deutet Jaeger 96f. an — zum Anachronismus geworden sein mußte. Auf den ersten Blick liest sich das Kapitel wie eine wilde Klitterung aus einer ganzen Reihe von platonischen Schriften: mindestens der *Phaidros*, *Philebos*, mehrere Partien des *Staat*es und auch der *Kratylos* und vor allem der *Politikos* haben Gedanken oder Gedankenteile beisteuern müssen. Gleichwohl schließt die Originalität nicht sowohl der Einzelzüge wie vielmehr des Ganzen den Gedanken an einen andern Verfasser als Aristoteles sicher aus; darin stimme ich Jaegers Ausführungen zu. Die benutzten platonischen Stellen haben das Gemeinsame, daß in allen von dem, was nur durch Philosophie zugänglich wird, die Rede ist. Aber im *Phaidros* ist das die φύσις (270a) und die ἀλήθεια (259e und weiterhin), was dort zunächst auf Psychologie (in einem ganz modernen Sinne) | und das, was man wissen muß, um technisch vollendet lügen zu können, hinweist, aber mit tieferem Hintergrund, so daß hier das ἓν διὰ δυοῖν, das der *Protreptikos*

---

[8] Vgl. *Leg.* 875d—876e, wo das Platonische über den Spielraum für das Ermessen des Richters steht.

zu im einzelnen unverbindlicher Bezeichnung des Gegenstandes der Philosophie auch sonst (Jambl. *Protr.* 54, 4 Pistelli) hatte, sachlich vorgebildet war. Die benutzte Stelle des *Philebos* (55c—59c, besonders zu beachten 56b) läuft auf die „reine" Wissenschaft hinaus. Im *Staat* ist es das φύσει δίκαιον, καλόν, σῶφρον usw. (501b), Ruhe und Ordnung, kurzum das Göttliche im Gegensatz zum wüsten Menschentreiben, an dem die Handwerkskunst des Philosophen orientiert sein würde, falls die Welt von ihr Gebrauch machen wollte (500b—501e). Aus einer anderen Stelle des *Staat*es (596b) zusammen mit *Kratylos* 389b gewinnen wir unmittelbar freilich nur etwas, woran sich der wirkliche zünftige Handwerker orientiert, nämlich den zweckbestimmten Begriff eines Gebrauchsgegenstandes, aber der ist unter anderm Vorläufer gewesen sowohl der von Aristoteles so bitter bekämpften auf Naturdinge bezogenen Ideenlehre, wie des aristotelischen τέλος im Rahmen der aristotelischen Physik und weist jedenfalls stets über sich selbst hinaus. Endlich im *Politikos* ist αὐτὸ τὸ ἀληθέστατον ἐκεῖνο, das nachgeahmt wird, aber selbst nicht μίμημα ist (300e), das äußerlich unbeschränkte an Wissen und Gerechtigkeit orientierte Schalten und Walten des königlichen Mannes zum Nutzen der Bürger seines Staates, das freilich in der nicht ganz zu umgehenden Gesetzgebung zu notwendigerweise unzulänglichen Festsetzungen von δίκαια und ἄδικα, καλά und αἰσχρά, ἀγαθά und κακά durch ihn selbst (295e) führt.

W. Theiler hat darauf aufmerksam gemacht[9], daß die von Jaeger als entscheidend genommenen Ausdrücke, soweit sie im *Politikos* vorkommen, dort von Platon selbst nicht im Sinne der Ideenlehre verwandt sind: das αὐτό und das ἀκριβές, die μίμησις und die μιμήματα. Denn das Handeln des echten Politikers ist keine Idee, sondern tritt — überraschenderweise, so gibt es Platon einmal (300d/e) selbst — in dieser Welt unmittelbar in Erscheinung. Und allgemein gedacht und unwandelbar, oder hier | vielmehr: starr zu sein, ist in diesem Zusammenhang eine Eigentümlichkeit nicht des αὐτό, sondern einer besonderen Art μιμήματα (300c), nämlich der Gesetze und gesetzähnlichen, schriftlichen oder nichtschriftlichen Festlegungen[10]. Für die Ideenlehre bleiben im *Politikos* von den erwähnten Ausdrücken höchstens die ὅροι (293e) oder der ὅρος (296e) der rechten Staatsführung oder -verwaltung: alle ihre Handlungen geschehen nach Maßgabe von Wissenschaft und Gerechtigkeit zum wahren Nutzen der Bürger. Den

---

[9] Zur Geschichte der teleologischen Naturbetrachtung bis auf Aristoteles, Zürich 1925, 2. Auflage Berlin 1965, 87f.

[10] Auch für diese Sorte Allgemeinheit gebraucht Aristoteles das Wort καθόλου z. B. *Pol.* 1269a 11, 1286a 10, *E. N.* 1137b 13, Das wird pikant, wenn man Plat. *Leg.* 875d τάξιν τε καὶ νόμον ἃ δὴ τὸ μὲν ὡς ἐπὶ τὸ πολὺ ὁρᾷ καὶ βλέπει, τὸ δ᾽ ἐπὶ πᾶν ἀδυνατεῖ danebenhält. Auf welche Seite gehört eigentlich *E. N.* 1135a 6—8?

wahren πολιτικός, der so handelt, kennen wir nun aber schon aus dem *Gorgias* 521 d, und der *Gorgias* hat da, wo später die Ideen stehen, durchweg entweder οὐδὲν ποικίλον ἀλλ᾽ ὥσπερ οἱ πολλοί (491 d, vgl. 488 e), oder aber Weltanschauung von ungesuchter Diesseitigkeit (508 a). Es ist für Platon charakteristisch, daß dieser autonome Politiker, der eigentlich ein autonomer Kritiker war[11], für ihn etwas Primäres ist, von einer ganz andersartigen Echtheit und Lebendigkeit als das erschlossene a priori der Ideen und der nach Wunsch gebildete Staat: sein Handeln gab es und gibt es auf Erden, einerlei, ob der Wunschstaat und dessen Erziehungswesen da ist oder nicht: *Rep.* 592 a/b. Sokrates *handelte* exakt und *forderte* das Wissen, eine Forderung, | die unter Umständen um so unangenehmer klingen mußte, als in seinen Erörterungen darüber die primitive Forderung der Gerechtigkeit überraschend zur Geltung kam. Diese eigenartig sokratischen Beziehungen zwischen Handeln, Wissen und Gerechtigkeit kehren in den Formulierungen des *Politikos* wieder; die Vermittlung zwischen einst und jetzt stellte der im *Phaidros* neubegründete Begriff des lebendigen λόγος (276 a) und einer das zu fordernde Wissen enthaltenden lebendigen Technik her. Denn Platon hat sich zeitlebens nie soweit in „Theorie" verloren, daß er nicht, wenn es nötig wurde, ohne weiteres mit dem lebendigen λόγος und dem souveränen freien Denken (*Leg.* 875 c/d) allen zugleich unlebendigen und illiberalen Spuk, mochte er von außen[12] oder im Innern drohen, hätte verscheuchen können.

---

[11] Wenn man sich an ihn und an Platons scharfes Denken und Empfinden gewöhnt hat, verliert man den Geschmack an dem gepriesenen autonomen σπουδαῖος des Aristoteles (Stellen bei Jaeger 89), der, wenn man die etwas zu modernen Ausdeutungen seiner heutigen Erklärer ernst nehmen wollte, sogar eine üble contradictio in adiecto würde. Denn das rational Unbestimmbare als Quelle des Genauen scheidet für Aristoteles aus, wie schon einmal bemerkt ,und dann würde ,,das im erkenntnistheoretischen Sinn durchaus nicht ,exakte' autonome Gewissen der sittlich durchgebildeten Persönlichkeit" (Jaeger 89, Anm. 1) hohl. Richtig aber ist, daß sich Aristoteles keine Mühe mehr gibt, ordentlich abzugrenzen, was nicht exakt sein kann; Platon macht das mit Leichtigkeit: *Pol.* 294 d—295 b, *Leg.* 875 d ff. Aristoteles dagegen richtet in der *Nikomachischen Ethik* einleitungsweise für seine Theorie einen Spielraum scheinbar auch da ein, wo es kein Spielen gibt, nämlich im Moralischen. Wir müssen es lateinisch bezeichnen, weil die aristotelische Ethik schließlich zu lässig und in der Tat zu gelassen vornehm war, es gesondert zu bestimmen. Freilich braucht der Kampf des platonischen *Gorgias* nicht alle Tage ausgefochten zu werden.

[12] Im ,,Staat" wird die beste πόλις mit Ausdrücken wie ἡ ἐν λόγοις κειμένη (dies 592 a) bezeichnet, womit etwas aller Praxis Überlegenes gemeint ist (473 a) und doch ohne inneren Widerspruch kein Anspruch auf mehr als spielerische Ausführung (z. B. 501 e) erhoben wird. Man braucht nur daran zu denken, wie leicht die λόγοι, ,,in" welchen die Stadt ihre ,,Lage" hat, mit dem, was in Platons Buch schwarz auf weiß steht, zu verwechseln waren, um zu erkennen, weshalb im *Phaidros* der lebendige λόγος gegen *alles* Geschriebene ausgespielt werden mußte.

Auch im *Politikos* merkt man an der einen, übrigens gedanklich
völlig korrekt gehaltenen Stelle (300e) noch den Ruck, mit dem Platon
in dieser Schrift dem *Handeln* des Wissenden trotz seiner Erdennähe
die Exaktheit gewahrt hat. — Aber die Schriftstücke, die der Wissende
ergehen läßt, können wegen ihrer Steifheit in keinem guten Verhältnis
zu ihrem Gegenstand stehen (294c). Ziemlich unverkennbar wird im
Folgenden gelegentlich auf die eventuelle Schriftstellerei des Wissenden
angespielt, so wie der *Phaidros* nebenbei mit der Gesetzgeberei und
dem rhetorischen Lehrbuch (275c vgl. 266d) gespielt hatte. Das ist
vielleicht das Einzige, worin Platon eine bedenkliche Analogie, von
der sich die Gedanken des *Politikos* bis zu einem gewissen Grade
haben leiten lassen, nicht offen eingesteht. Natürlich stammt der
Gegensatz zwischen Schriftstücken und (lebendiger) Technik (*Pol.*
299e) aus dem *Phaidros*. Aber im *Phaidros* versagt die geschriebene
Rede hauptsächlich dem Höheren gegenüber, während der wahre
Techniker sie in Menschendingen, wenn er Lust hätte, sogar höchst |
raffiniert würde handhaben können. Dagegen im *Politikos* versagt
die geschriebene Rede (und jede ungeschriebene starre Institution),
wenn es sich darum handelt, menschliche Dinge erschöpfend und dauernd zu regeln. Über die hier gelassene Unklarheit hinaus führt es,
wenn Platon zuletzt für die Darstellung und Vermittelung des Höheren
auch den lebendigen λόγος beinahe versagen läßt. Das διὰ τὸ τῶν
λόγων ἀσθενές im *7. Brief* 343a geht in erster Linie auf die gesprochene
Sprache. Wenn der Funke überspringen soll, müssen noch sehr viele
andere Bedingungen erfüllt sein, die nur die Akademie geben kann,
ganz abgesehen von der nötigen Begabung. Aber dies alles gilt nun
nicht für das Niedere; dem fühlt sich Platon immer ohne weiteres gewachsen: *7. Brief* 343c, so, wie es Sokrates gewesen war. — Deshalb
konnte die von Aristoteles mehrfach genutzte Partie des *Politikos* geradezu das Widerspiel der Ideenlehre werden.

Für Aristoteles, und zwar den jungen wie den alten, ist es bezeich-
nend, daß er dieses und nicht jenes andere zum unmittelbaren Anschluß wählt. Schon damit wird es vielleicht nicht persönlich, wohl
aber sachlich ziemlich bedeutungslos, ob der junge Aristoteles noch nicht
klar genug sah, um zu merken, auf welchen Boden er sich mit dieser Wahl
stellte. Es kommt aber noch etwas hinzu. Vielleicht hat Aristoteles
wirklich bei Platon den Glauben an den Grundsatz, daß mit Wissen
und Gerechtigkeit zum wahren Nutzen der Bürger regiert werden soll,
auf Grund dessen, was im *Staat* daraus geworden war und was er natürlich hinzudenken mußte, wenn er den *Politikos* las, als Ideenlehre
angesprochen und im Übrigen ohne langes Kopfzerbrechen genommen,
was ihm zusagte. Das ist dann aber immer noch nicht *die* Ideenlehre,
die er so bitter bekämpft hat. Dieser Kampf galt dem späteren Sta-

dium, das Platon im *Parmenides* als solches abgehoben hat, mit den eventuellen Ideen von Mensch, Feuer, Wasser usw. Damit hatte das frühere Stadium, das es zugestandenermaßen nicht für nötig hielt, Ideen von Dingen anzusetzen, wenig mehr als eine äußere Ähnlichkeit der Fragestellung gemein. Auch wenn man es Ideenlehre nennen will und darf, bedeutet der Satz des *Protreptikos* αὐτῶν γάρ ἐστι θεατής, ἀλλ' οὐ μιμημάτων in seinem eigenen Zusammenhang genommen sachlich nicht mehr, | als daß der Begriff des Rechts nicht lediglich roh empiristisch aus den gegebenen positiven Rechtsbestimmungen abgeleitet, sondern philosophisch gewonnen wird. Damit verträgt sich bei vielen Menschen ein von vornherein mehr oder weniger deutlich sich geltend machender Horror vor dem αὐτοάνθρωπος und dergl. sehr wohl.

Es gibt hier nicht so gar viel zu streiten, und wir wenden uns nun dem zu, was Jaeger (78) mit Recht hochinteressant genannt hat, der früharistotelischen Vorstellung einer ernstlich praktisch gemeinten „Politik auf wissenschaftlicher Grundlage". Hochinteressant ist sie für uns deshalb, weil, wie das von Jaeger genannte 2. Buch der *Politik* und insbesondere noch dessen Einleitungssatz zeigt, die „wissenschaftliche Grundlage" vorbestimmt war, bei Aristoteles verhältnismäßig früh die Gestalt eines Vorlesungsmanuskripts anzunehmen, das, wieder und wieder umgearbeitet, schließlich mit einer Einleitung versehen wurde, in der der resignierte Verzicht auf mehr als private Wirksamkeit dasteht (*E. N.* 1180a 26ff.), obwohl der Anspruch des Vortragenden, die Philosophie der Sache geben zu müssen, weil sie nirgendwo anders zu finden wäre, aufrechterhalten wird (1181b 13).

Wie war es möglich, daß für Aristoteles die „wissenschaftliche Grundlage" der Politik auch dann noch ihren Sinn behielt, als die Hoffnung auf wesentliche Gestaltung der Praxis gar nicht mehr ernsthaft galt, und daß damit der geistreiche Denker ein Treiben initiiert hat, das die Achtung vor der Wissenschaft mehr gefährdet als alle Dummheit der Verächter des Geistes zusammengenommen? Auch daraufhin wollen wir uns den uns kenntlichen ersten Einsatz betrachten. An allen platonischen Stellen spielt das Handwerk eine Rolle. Nach dem *Staat* würde der Philosoph kein schlechter Handwerker sein (500d)[13]. Im *Phaidros* nimmt | er das Handwerk nicht ernst, kann aber, wenn

---

[13] Wir wissen anderweitig, der Philosoph will eigentlich gar nicht, sondern er würde müssen. Aber unter staatspädagogischen Gesichtspunkten betrachtet, verwandelt sich der Philosoph ohne weiteres in den zünftigen Handwerker. Die Natur der Dinge hat für ein Analogon in der Familie gesorgt. Der schlechte Vater will erziehen; der gute Vater will nicht, aber er muß; und der beste Vater, der nicht zu erziehen braucht, ist keine Idee und kein Ideal, aber, wie es scheint, in der Praxis so selten, daß er für die Theorie nicht in Betracht kommt.

er will, viel bessere Arbeiten liefern als alle sogenannten Zünftigen. Im *Kratylos* (389b) und an der entsprechenden Stelle des *Staates* ist das Interesse bei dem Geheimnis, das heute den echten Techniker vom Monteur scheidet; und am sonderbarsten ist es im *Philebos*. Hier werden wir auf diejenigen Handwerke aufmerksam gemacht, die Meß-instrumente verwenden und deswegen Arbeiten liefern, die alle andere Handarbeit an Exaktheit übertreffen. Diese Handwerke sind hier eine Vorstufe im Aufstieg zur reinen Wissenschaft, die sich mit dem rein Geometrischen, rein Arithmetischen und noch Reinerem beschäftigt, sich hier aber einmal freiwillig und ausdrücklich (58b—d) aller An-sprüche auf praktischen Nutzen begibt.

Natürlich geht es nicht mit rechten Dingen zu, wenn es Aristoteles gelungen ist, gerade den Gedanken an die Meßinstrumente in die ent-gegengesetzte Richtung zu wenden. Freilich sagt Platon selbst, wenn man das Zählen, Messen und Wiegen streichen wollte, dann bliebe nicht viel brauchbare Technik übrig (55e). Aber er setzt als wesent-lichen Gesichtspunkt ein, daß z. B. der Kaufmann rechnen kann, ohne vom Arithmetiker abhängig zu sein (56e), faßt das Handwerk also gerade nicht als ,,angewandte Wissenschaft''. Der rettende Gedanke für Aristoteles' Zwecke ist, daß die Meßwerkzeuge, die exakte Arbeit garantieren, auf Grund von *Natur*gegebenheiten[14] erfunden sind. Das muß herhalten zum Vergleich mit der φύσις αὐτή und der ἀλήθεια, von der der Politiker die ὅροι hat zur Bestimmung dessen, was praktisch δίκαιον und καλόν und συμφέρον ist (vgl. *Pol.* 295e); das Ergebnis dieser Bestimmung ist ein νόμος κάλλιστος, weil μάλιστα κατὰ φύσιν κείμενος. Dieser sehr vage Gebrauch von φύσις wird nachträglich re-dressiert, und wir bekommen jetzt mit einem Male die πρῶτα, δεύτερα usw., die auch Platon am Ende so nennt (59c), aber natürlich ohne sich eines Taschenspielerkunststückes schuldig gemacht zu haben. Aristoteles eskamotiert das Arithmetische und das Geometrische und erreicht die Täuschung, ein Kriterium des praktisch Guten, Schönen und Gerechten als für gute politische Arbeit unerläßliches Meßinstru-ment aufgewiesen zu haben. Es | soll nicht bestritten werden, daß sich im Ganzen der, man möchte sagen, unerwartet gute Sinn ergibt, daß zur rechten Politik eine Theorie gehört, die nicht an irgendwelchen fertig vorgefundenen Staaten und Gesetzen und irgendwelchen vorbildlichen Handlungen, sondern unmittelbarer an den elementaren Grundbegriffen orientiert ist[15]. Aber mit der Umbiegung des Gedankens des *Philebos*

---

[14] Wieso, das soll uns nicht aufhalten, leider ist die Stelle (S. 54, 22ff. Pistelli) korrupt.

[15] Von der Idee des Staates liest man auch bei Platon nichts, ebensowenig von der Idee des Politikers. Hierauf und auf die daraus sich ergebende Problematik ener-gisch hinzuweisen, sah sich K. v. Fritz im Gnomon 12, 1936, 123ff. veranlaßt.

in die Gedanken des *Politikos* ist nun auch von diesen letzteren das
Scharfe und Entscheidende preisgegeben.

In Platons *Politikos* wird das Handwerk des Politikers, das Regieren, bitter ernst genommen; gerade deswegen können dessen eigene
Gesetze nur sekundäre Leistungen, inexakte μιμήματα seines eigenen
lebendigen Regimes sein[16]. Wir haben bereits gesehen, daß Aristoteles
später gerade die Theorie der zugleich notwendigen und unzulänglichen Allgemeinheit und Starre aller Gesetzesbestimmungen aufgegriffen hat. Dem Verfasser des *Protreptikos* war sie gleichgültig. Obwohl das Nebeneinander von Gesetzen und Handlungen (55, 18 und
25 Pistelli) die unmittelbare Benutzung des platonischen *Politikos* außer
Frage stellt, wird hier der Philosoph derjenige Handwerker, der, an
der Natur und dem Göttlichen (dies nach *Rep.* 500c) orientiert, allein
dauerhafte, feste (!) Gesetze und rechte und schöne Handlungen liefert,
und insofern, obwohl ihm eine lediglich theoretische, d. h. um ihrer
selbst willen getriebene Wissenschaft zu eigen ist, gleichwohl maßgebend für alles andere Handwerk. Das wäre trotz des hübschen Ver-
gleichs von Wissen und Sehen kein geschlossener Sinn, wenn es uns
nicht unbenommen oder vielmehr geboten wäre, bei den νόμοι βέβαιοι
und den πράξεις ὀρθαί καὶ καλαί an Leben, Lehre und politische Schrif-
ten des | Mannes zu denken, ὃν οὐδ᾽ αἰνεῖν τοῖσι κακοῖσι θέμις. *Staat* und
Gesetze Platons stehen hier nicht anders als im zweiten Buch der
Politik neben und vor denen der Lakedaimonier und Kreter, nur daß
von Kritik am platonischen Staat hier noch nichts zu merken ist.
Wenn nach erwachter Kritik auch diese Bücher in eigenen Vorlesungen
ganz dieselbe Rolle spielen werden wie die wirklichen Staaten, dann
sind die Bedingungen dafür da, daß die politische Theorie in der Auseinandersetzung mit den Vorgängern oder in der sachlich interessierten
Aufnahme empirischen Stoffes zu leben glaubt, auch wenn sie totge-
boren ist, weil sie von vornherein die politische Praxis nicht gewollt
hat, was wir von Aristoteles eben durch seinen *Protreptikos* genau so
sicher wissen, wie für Platon das Gegenteil feststeht.

Für die Politik verwechselt Aristoteles von vornherein Theorie und
Praxis, während er in der Ethik nur schließlich sich keine Mühe gab,
das Wesentliche gesondert zu bestimmen, weil es sich da für ihn von

---

[16] Das Leben und die Gesetze aller anderen Staaten sind ihrerseits Nachahmungen
des Regimes des Wissenden unter Verwendung seiner Schriftstücke (297d). Auf
diese zweite Klasse von μιμήματα gehe ich nicht ein. Sie sind dadurch charakterisiert, daß sich die selbstverständliche Verfassungslosigkeit in das Postulat
unbedingter Verfassungstreue verwandelt, damit wenigstens das ganz Heillose
vermieden wird. Dies und die ebenfalls unmißverständliche Lehre vom Verfassungs-
bruch verträgt sich mit allem, was wir von der derzeitigen Realpolitik Platons
wissen, vollkommen; aber wir können das beiseite lassen.

selbst verstand, wie sich das für den geborenen Theoretiker praktisch, meint Platon, gehört (*Phd.* 68bff., *Rep.* 485dff.).

Politische Theorie ist ihrem *ursprünglichen* Sinn nach gegen die gewöhnliche und auf eine neue Praxis gerichtet. Was den Kampf betrifft, so ist bei Platon alles einfach und natürlich. Hier bedeutet auch der Verzicht auf schriftliche Fixierung durchaus nicht den Verzicht darauf, der gewöhnlichen Praxis ein für alle Mal die Wahrheit zu sagen wie im *Gorgias*, oder das Wesentliche über sie in allen ihren Formen restlos auszusprechen wie im *Politikos*; nur das Unwesentliche entzieht sich aus leicht begreiflichen Gründen der erschöpfenden Darstellung. Auch dann geschieht nichts Widersinniges, wenn die Theorie imstande ist, neue praktisch gangbare Wege zu zeigen; hier hat die Theorie freie Bahn, darf sich ruhig über Einzelheiten hinwegsetzen und kann es getrost einer späteren Zeit, die diese Wege gegangen sein wird, überlassen — etwa im Falle des staatlichen Erziehungswesens oder des Staatsbeamtentums —, auf Grund ihrer Erfahrungen nachträglich den Vergleich zwischen Theorie und Praxis anzustellen. Daß in der Praxis nicht alles so schön gehen wird, wie vorher darüber gesprochen wurde, versteht sich von selbst | und macht den richtigen Plan nicht zu etwas weniger Wahrem, als die Wirklichkeit ist, im Gegenteil! Das sonderbare Wort, das Platon im *Staat* beim Übergang zu dem, was ihm das Entscheidende ist, spricht und das uns nun zum Schluß doch noch eine Übersetzung unseres Begriffspaars ins Platonische liefert, hat zunächst trotz seines paradoxen Klanges einen ungefährlichen Sinn: ἆρ' οἷόν τε πραχθῆναι ὡς λέγεται ἢ φύσιν ἔχει πρᾶξιν λέξεως ἧττον ἀληθείας ἐφάπτεσθαι κἂν εἰ μή τῳ δοκεῖ; (473a) es wird im Dialog auch einfach zugegeben. Aber plötzlich, alle Wünsche in eins zusammennehmend und geschickt die wirklich nur vorgetäuschte Deckung durch diesen Satz benutzend, tut der Philosoph seinen berühmten Gewaltstreich, nach dem es, ihn vorausgesetzt, eigentlich nur noch eine einzige praktische Schwierigkeit zu geben scheint: die vorgefundenen menschlichen Schwächen. Aber da macht der Philosoph reine Bahn, oder er tut überhaupt nicht mit (501a). ὃ οὐ πάνυ ῥᾴδιον. Es ist keineswegs leicht. Aber die „Bildung" (500d) und das staatliche Unterrichtswesen (502cff.) nach vorhergegangener radikaler Säuberung (501a) werden es schon schaffen. Damit ist das geborene Athenertum, das so stolz war auf sein αὐτοφυῶς und οὔτι πλαστῶς (*Leg.* 642c/d), preisgegeben. Platon hat es in der Theorie als erziehungstechnisch ersetzbar (500d) behandelt, wenigstens bis zum Alter von 50 Jahren. Nur das urwüchsig Volkstümliche des Demagogen, für Platon unverkennbar das genaue Gegenteil des guten Athenertums, ist nach einer wenig beachteten These des platonischen *Gorgias* durch keine Technik zu ersetzen (*Grg.* 513b). In so hohem Grade verdrängt das Utopische, das sich

schon im *Gorgias* in dem radikalen Kampf nach allen Seiten anmeldet
und in das uns der Gewaltstreich des platonischen Staats hinein-
zwingen will, zeitweise die einfachere Wahrheit (*Rep.* 485d), daß vor
allem echte Menschengröße jeder Art sich frühzeitig und unbefangen
selbst bestimmen[17] muß.

Platon hat nichts zurückgenommen. Und doch sieht im *Politikos*
so vieles ganz anders aus. Hier rechnet er, ohne sich und dem Denken
im mindesten etwas zu vergeben, nicht nur mit einer gewissen dauern-
den Zwiespältigkeit des gewöhnlich Menschlichen | (294b), die ein ein-
faches Regieren und Ethisieren (dies 306aff.) nicht zuläßt, sondern
auch damit, daß dem Regenten, als einem Menschen, die Allgegen-
wart fehlt (295b), und fängt sogar an, damit zu rechnen, daß die volle
unverantwortliche Gewalt auch im besten Fall die innere Kraft eines
Menschen übersteigen könnte (301c/d). In den *Gesetzen* wird dies das
die nunmehrige Theorie vorweg Bestimmende (691c/d, 874eff.). Das
andere ist zu selten, und es langt nicht (875d). In welchen Kreisen es
zu finden gewesen wäre, verrät ein Kompliment an anderer Stelle:
eben der Satz vom ohne Zwang gewachsenen guten Athenertum
(*Leg.* 642c).

---

[17] „Bilden" 500d ist zweideutig, μὴ πεπλασμένως 485d nicht.

Sokrates der Jüngere

1924

In den drei von Valentin Rose am Schluß seiner Fragmentausgabe von 1886 vereinigten Viten des Aristoteles überrascht die Nachricht, der 17jährige Aristoteles sei in Athen vor dem Beginn der 20 Jahre des Anschlusses an Platon zunächst eine kurze Zeit lang (so S. 427, 15f.; 3 Jahre S. 438, 12; S. 443, 9) Schüler des Sokrates gewesen, nämlich bis zu dessen Tode. Das ist entweder unkontrollierbarer Unsinn, wie er sich so auch in dieser Überlieferung sonst kaum findet, oder es hat sich bei der Nachricht ursprünglich um den jüngeren Sokrates gehandelt, den wir aus Platons *Theaetet, Sophistes* und *Politikos*, aus dem pseudoplatonischen *11. Brief* und vor allem aus einer Stelle der aristotelischen *Metaphysik* kennen: 1036b 24 καὶ ἡ παραβολὴ ἡ ἐπὶ τοῦ ζῴου, ἣν εἰώθει λέγειν Σωκράτης ὁ νεώτερος, οὐ καλῶς ἔχει· ἀπάγει γὰρ ἀπὸ τοῦ ἀληθοῦς usw. Da haben wir eine Berufung auf etwas, was Sokrates der Jüngere zu sagen pflegte, und an sich liegt die Auffassung nahe, daß Aristoteles das selbst von ihm gehört hat. Darf man etwas auf die Nachricht der Viten geben?

Für die Frage ihrer Herkunft scheiden die lateinische Vita (Rose S. 442), die aus den beiden anderen *dedita confusaque opera conflata est* (Rose a. a. O.), sowie die Vulgatfassung (Rose S. 437) von vornherein aus. Denn das Wenige, was die letztere gegenüber der ersten Fassung des Marcianus (Rose S. 426) an Eigenem bietet, scheint durchweg improvisiert[1]. Übrig bleibt nur | die Stelle bei Rose S. 427, 14: ἐτῶν δὲ γενόμενος ἑπτακαίδεκα τοῦ Πυθοῖ θεοῦ χρήσαντος αὐτῷ φιλοσοφεῖν [παρ'] Ἀθήνησι φοιτᾷ Σωκράτει καὶ συνῆν ⟨αὐτῷ τὸν⟩ μέχρι τελευτῆς αὐτοῦ χρόνον πλὴν ὀλίγον ὄντα. μετὰ δὲ τοῦτον φοιτᾷ (φοιτᾶν

---

[1] So der „Makedone" Aristoteles 437, 2: die 3 Jahre bei Sokrates 438, 12; die Gegengründung des Lykeion gegen Platon erschlossen ἐκ τοῦ ἐν πολλοῖς ἀντιλέγειν Πλάτωνι 438, 22 vgl. 428, 8; 431, 20; das „wörtliche" Platonzitat 438, 28 vgl. das verfälschte Zitat aus der *Nikomachischen Ethik* 433, 16; das Distichon 439, 8 siehe Jaeger, Aristoteles S. 108 A. 1; Aristoteles' Rückkehr nach Makedonien 440, 19; endlich zum Schluß 441, 21 die Aufrechnung der 63 Jahre von Aristoteles' Leben: 17jährig zu Sokrates, 3 Jahre bei ihm, 20 bei Platon, 23 nach Platons Tod. Hier greift man, daß die bestimmte Zahl der 3 Jahre bei Sokrates eingesetzt ist, damit trotz des aus der Vorlage übernommenen Fehlers: 23 Jahre nach Platons Tod (die stehen auch S. 428, 6 und 17) doch 63 Jahre herauskommen. Selbständig ist die Vulgatfassung nur in der Einordnung des angeblich von Aristoteles mitge-

cod.) Πλάτωνι καὶ συνῆν τούτῳ τὸν μέχρι τελευτῆς αὐτοῦ χρόνον εἰκοσαετῆ τυγχάνοντα², ὡς αὐτὸς ἐπιστέλλων Φιλίππῳ λέγει. An sich wäre es möglich, daß dies Zitat aus einem Briefe an Philipp in der biographischen Tradition nur die Rolle eines Selbstzeugnisses für die treue Anhänglichkeit an Platon gespielt hätte; aber man muß doch wohl mit Rose dessen Fragment 653 (Julian. *or.* 7, S. 309 Hertlein) hinzunehmen: φησὶ γὰρ καὶ αὐτὸς (ὁ Ἀριστοτέλης) εἶναι Πύθιον οἴκοι παρ' ἑαυτῷ, ὅθεν αὐτῷ καὶ ἡ ὁρμὴ πρὸς φιλοσοφίαν ἐγένετο³. Und damit kommt man für das Ganze auf denselben Boden; denn wenn Anfang und Ende dem Brief an Philipp entstammten, so ist nicht einzusehen, woher der Sokrates nachträglich eingedrungen sein sollte. Daß der Ge-| danke an eine Korruptel aus Isokrates unwahrscheinlich ist, hat Wilamowitz, Aristoteles u. Athen I S. 318 mit Recht betont, weil wir das dann auch anderweitig hören würden, und das gleiche gilt für Xenokrates, an den man auch gedacht hat. Aber für Sokrates war, nachdem man ihn nicht mehr als den ὁμώνυμος erkennen konnte, in der Tat gerade in besseren biographischen Arbeiten kein Platz mehr. Überdies wurde das Zitat als Ganzes unbrauchbar, wo man Aristoteles sich bei Lebzeiten Platons selbständig machen ließ⁴.

machten Alexanderzuges, der daher in ihrer Vorlage, die man im übrigen der ersten Fassung des Marcianus ziemlich gleichsetzen kann (eine Kleinigkeit wie 441, 15 verglichen mit 435, 1 etwa ausgenommen), noch nicht eingearbeitet gewesen zu sein scheint. Die Vulgatfassung erfindet dazu einen zweiten Aufenthalt in Makedonien nach der Vertreibung aus Athen, während die erste Fassung des Marcianus die Teilnahme am Alexanderzuge irgendwie vor die Rückkehr nach Athen fallen läßt, beides noch deutlich als sekundärer Einschub zu erkennen.

² „εἰκοσαετὴς τυγχάνων (sic) cod., sed corr. in marg. εἰκοσαετοῦς τυγχάνοντος cf. (D. L. 5, 9) Dionys. Hal. opp. rhet. p. 728 [= I 262 Us.-Rad.] χρόνον εἰκοσαετῆ διέτριψε σὺν αὐτῷ" Rose im Apparat. Durch die Lesung εἰκοσαετὴς τυγχάνων des Marcianus und durch das Hysteronproteron bei Diog. La. καὶ διατρῖψαι παρ' αὐτῷ εἴκοσιν ἔτη, ἑπτὰ καὶ δέκα ἐτῶν συστάντα gerät man in Versuchung, die drei Jahre vor dem Verkehr mit Platon gelten zu lassen und eine falsche Beziehung der dann ursprünglich das Lebensalter des Aristoteles beim Beginn des Anschlusses an Platon bezeichnenden Zahl 20 zu vermuten (vgl. Zeller, Die Philosophie der Griechen II, 2¹ S. 8 Anm.), aber das Abhängigkeitsverhältnis der Viten spricht dagegen, zumal sich verstehen läßt, wie die Vulgatfassung zu der Zahl 3 gekommen ist (siehe die vor. Anm.), und außerdem gerät man bei weiterer Verfolgung der Möglichkeit mit der Autorität Apollodors in Konflikt. Apollodor wird, falls er, wie zu vermuten, die Briefstelle seiner Chronologie mit zugrunde legte, die unbestimmt kurze Dauer des Verkehrs mit Sokrates als für chronologische Zwecke nichts ausgebend übergangen haben. Dabei müssen wir uns beruhigen, denn um zu entscheiden, wie sich in Wirklichkeit der Unterricht bei Sokrates mit den 20 Jahren vertrug, dazu fehlt uns die Kenntnis des Wortlauts der Briefstelle.

³ Zur Sache vgl. Wilamowitz Ar. u. Ath. I, 317.

⁴ Kombiniert findet sich dies doch irgendwie mit den 20 Jahren bei Platon unter Benutzung der Kenntnis von Platons sizilischen Reisen in der am besten in der syrisch-arabischen Tradition faßbaren Biographie des Ptolemaios Chennos (siehe

Die Distinktion ὁ νεώτερος hat offenbar in dem Brief, dessen Echtheit sich, soviel ich sehe, weder aus äußeren noch aus inneren Gründen wird bestreiten lassen, von vornherein gefehlt. Sehr begreiflich, daß Aristoteles, wo er von seinem Leben erzählte, den Zeitgenossen nicht besonders als solchen bezeichnet hat; der Zusatz war hier ebenso überflüssig, wie er in der *Metaphysik* notwendig war. Übrigens ist in dem pseudoplatonischen *11. Brief* ja auch nur von ,,Sokrates" die Rede. Das Gegenstück dazu ist die Erwähnung des alten Sokrates im echten *7. Brief* 324e φίλον ἄνδρα ἐμοὶ πρεσβύτερον Σωκράτη[5]; die Erinnerung an den jüngeren Sokrates war eben damals noch lebendig genug, um ihm seinen Platz neben dem großen Träger desselben Namens zu wahren.

So dürfen wir also wohl das Vakuum, das schon wegen Platons zweiter sizilischer Reise zwischen der Ankunft des 17jährigen Aristoteles in Athen (um 367) und dem Eintritt des engeren Verhältnisses zu Platon anzusetzen war, ausfüllen. An den jüngeren Sokrates hat er zuerst Anschluß gefunden, und er hat die Tatsache trotz der kurzen Dauer des Verkehrs später für bedeutend genug gehalten, um sie in dem Brief an Philipp zu erwähnen. Sokrates starb bald; daß seine letzte Krankheit in Platons spätere Lebens|zeit fiel, war dem Verfasser des *11.* platonischen *Brief*es noch geläufig. Dazu stellt sich zwar nicht mit Sicherheit die Erwähnung im platonischen *Theaetet* (147d), wohl aber nun *Sophistes* 218b (Theaetet spricht) καὶ τόνδε παραληψόμεθα Σωκράτη, τὸν Σωκράτους μὲν ὁμώνυμον, ἐμὸν δὲ συνηλικιώτην καὶ συγγυμναστήν, ᾧ συνδιαπονεῖν μετ᾽ ἐμοῦ τὰ πολλὰ οὐκ ἄηθες sowie *Politikos* 257c bis 258a und die ganze Rolle des jüngeren Sokrates in diesem Dialog. Schwerlich hätte Platon das so eingerichtet, wenn nicht nach Theaetets Tod inzwischen auch der jüngere Sokrates gestorben und nunmehr die wenigstens äußerliche Parallelisierung der beiden, wie wir annehmen müssen, lebenslangen Freunde geradezu das Gegebene geworden wäre.

Die Erwähnung des jüngeren Sokrates im *Z* der *Metaphysik* verdient noch besondere Behandlung, da ihr Verständnis nicht ganz an der Oberfläche liegt.

καὶ ἡ παραβολὴ ἡ ἐπὶ τοῦ ζῴου, ἣν εἰώθει λέγειν Σωκράτης ὁ νεώτερος, οὐ καλῶς ἔχει · ἀπάγει γὰρ ἀπὸ τοῦ ἀληθοῦς καὶ ποιεῖ ὑπο-

---

Baumstarks Übersetzungen in ,,Syrisch-arabische Biographien des Aristoteles", 1898, S. 40—43). Statt dessen und wohl dagegen gerichtet hat die erste Vita des Marcianus, die S. 435, 17 den Ptolemaios in ihrem Text erwähnt, den gelehrten, aber jetzt konfusen Abschnitt 428, 6—429, 9.

[5] Was man schwerlich mit Howald ,,einen mir sehr lieben älteren Freund, den Sokrates" übersetzen kann. Das sprachlich einfachste, aber ein wenig philosophiegeschichtlich anmutende Σωκράτη τὸν πρεσβύτερον (wie etwa Aristoteles sagt Σ. ὁ γέρων, ὁ πρεσβύτης) wird man für den Stil des *7. Brief*es nicht fordern dürfen.

λαμβάνειν ὡς ἐνδεχόμενον εἶναι τὸν ἄνθρωπον ἄνευ τῶν μερῶν, ὥσπερ ἄνευ τοῦ χαλκοῦ τὸν κύκλον. τὸ δ᾽ οὐχ ὅμοιον· αἰσθητὸν γάρ τι τὸ ζῷον, καὶ ἄνευ κινήσεως οὐκ ἔστιν ὁρίσασθαι, διὸ οὐδ᾽ ἄνευ τῶν μερῶν ἐχόντων πως. (οὐ γὰρ πάντως τοῦ ἀνθρώπου μέρος ἡ χείρ, ἀλλ᾽ ἡ δυναμένη τὸ ἔργον ἀποτελεῖν, ὥστε ἔμψυχος οὖσα· μὴ ἔμψυχος δὲ οὐ μέρος) (dazu *de an.* 413a 5f.). „Und der Vergleich ἐπὶ τοῦ ζῷου, den Sokrates der Jüngere zu sagen pflegte, ist nicht in Ordnung. Denn er führt von der Wahrheit ab und bewirkt, daß man sich einbildet, als sei es möglich, daß der Mensch ohne seine (materiellen) Teile sei, wie der Kreis ohne das Erz. Aber das läßt sich nicht parallelisieren. Denn das Lebewesen ist Gegenstand der sinnlichen Wahrnehmung und läßt sich nicht ohne Bewegung definieren, also nicht ohne daß ein bestimmtes Verhalten seiner (materiellen) Teile angegeben wird"[6].

Was ist ἡ παραβολὴ ἡ ἐπὶ τοῦ ζῷου? Aristoteles setzt sie offenbar als bekannt voraus, denn aus dem, was hier gesagt wird, läßt sich ihre Absicht nicht rekonstruieren. Das Einfache, was man | zunächst gern herauslesen möchte, Sokrates hätte die Unabhängigkeit des εἶδος von „Lebewesen" oder von „Mensch" durch die Analogie der Unabhängigkeit des Begriffes „Kreis" von dem Erz (des ehernen Modellkreises) erläutert, würde Aristoteles auch einfach ausgedrückt haben. Richtig ist allerdings, daß seine mit den Worten τὸ δ᾽ οὐχ ὅμοιον beginnende Widerlegung sich auf die Aufdeckung der Unzulässigkeit dieser Parallele beschränkt. Aber wenn wirklich Sokrates' Weisheit in nichts weiterem bestanden hätte als in dem etwas dürftigen Gedanken ἐνδέχεται εἶναι τὸν ἄνθρωπον ἄνευ τῶν μερῶν ὥσπερ ἄνευ τοῦ χαλκοῦ τὸν κύκλον, wozu dann die seltsame Ausdrucksweise zu Beginn? Wer nur zu sagen hat: „Es ist nicht wahr, wie Sokrates der Jüngere zu vergleichen pflegte, daß der Mensch ohne seine Teile sein kann, wie der Kreis ohne das Erz", kann der überhaupt anfangen: „Und der Vergleich ἐπὶ τοῦ ζῷου, den Sokrates der Jüngere zu sagen pflegte, ist nicht in Ordnung; denn er führt von der Wahrheit ab und bewirkt, daß man sich einbildet, als wäre es möglich usw."? Soviel dürfte von vornherein klar sein, daß Aristoteles mit ποιεῖ ὑπολαμβάνειν das Bedenkliche *in* Sokrates' Gedankengang anrührt, nicht aber dessen Ziel angibt, sondern dieses vielmehr durch die Worte ἡ παραβολὴ ἡ ἐπὶ τοῦ ζῷου ausreichend mitbezeichnet hat. Ehe man sich entschließt, Aristoteles dies nur für den eigenen Gebrauch notieren oder aber ihn die Aufstellung des Sokrates als allgemein bekannt voraussetzen

---

[6] Zu ἐχόντων πως die Anmerkung: „Nicht unter allen Umständen ist die Hand Teil des Menschen, sondern nur die ist es, die ihre Aufgabe erfüllen kann, d. h. sie muß beseelt sein, unbeseelt ist sie nicht Teil." Was in unserm Aristotelestext dann folgt, schließt gedanklich gar nicht oder nur *sehr* lose an, „Nachtrag auf losem Blatt" Jaeger, Aristoteles S. 205 A.

zu lassen, sucht man natürlicherweise die Aufklärung in vorher Gesagtem.

1036 a 26 ἀπορεῖται δ᾽ εἰκότως καὶ ποῖα τοῦ εἴδους μέρη καὶ ποῖα οὔ, ἀλλὰ τοῦ συνειλημμένου. Daß nicht alles, was man „Teil" eines Dinges nennen kann, Teil des εἶδος oder seiner οὐσία im eigentlichsten Sinn ist und dementsprechend in deren Definition gehört, sondern daß daneben, in anderer Wortbedeutung, von „Teilen" eines Dinges gesprochen werden kann, die nur beim συνειλημμένον aus εἶδος und ὕλη vorkommen, davon war im ganzen vorhergehenden Kapitel 10 ausführlich geredet worden, und es sollte mit dieser Unterscheidung die künstlich zugespitzte Aporie bewältigt werden, daß zwar zugestandenermaßen die Definition der Silbe die der Buchstaben voraussetzt (vgl. Plat. *Theaet.* 202 d—206 b), der Definition des Kreises gegenüber aber die seiner Abschnitte, z. B. der Halbkreise, etwas Sekundäres ist, obwohl | doch der Kreis sich in diese Teile zerlegen läßt wie die Silbe in die Buchstaben, und daß ferner, wenn die Teile gegenüber dem Ganzen das Primäre sind, wie bei der Silbe, dann auch der spitze Winkel vor dem rechten und der Finger vor dem Menschen käme, während es offenbar umgekehrt ist. Wie weit es Aristoteles gelungen ist, hier mit seiner Unterscheidung εἶδος, ὕλη, συνειλημμένον die nach seinem eigenen Geständnis (1035 b 3) im ersten Anlauf nicht gewonnene Klarheit zu schaffen, stehe dahin, jetzt aber handelt es sich also um die Schwierigkeit der Bestimmung, wie die Teile des εἶδος im Gegensatz zu denen des συνειλημμένον beschaffen sind, oder mit andern Worten, so sieht es wenigstens zunächst aus, darum, ein Kriterium zu finden, das erlaubt zu sagen, dies ist Teil des εἶδος und gehört daher in die Definition, jenes dagegen ist *nur* Teil des συνειλημμένον, oder Teil nur in dem Sinne, wie es die Materie im Gegensatz zur Form ist, und gehört daher nicht in die Definition. Die Wichtigkeit einer Lösung der Aporie für die Möglichkeit des Definierens wird ausdrücklich betont, aber unsere Hoffnung, die scheinbar so klar gestellte Frage ebenso beantwortet zu finden, wird, wie nicht gerade selten bei Aristoteles, enttäuscht. Was wir tatsächlich lesen, erweist sich bei näherem Zusehen als ein schrittweises Vorgehen zu einer zwar nicht von Aristoteles, wohl aber von ihrem Urheber ernstgemeinten Behauptung über die Definition mathematischer Gegenstände, wonach zum Zweck der Definition von Kreis und Dreieck Begriffe wie Linien und Kontinuum abzustreifen und nur die reinen Zahlen übrigzulassen sind. Damit wird nach Aristoteles' Ansicht das Abstreifen der ὕλη denn doch zu weit getrieben, obwohl wenigstens nach den Ausführungen des Kapitels 10 nicht recht einzusehen ist, woher er eigentlich theoretisch die Berechtigung zu einem „Bis hierher und nicht weiter" nehmen will. Das Ganze ruht auf dem Gedanken: Beim Kreis ist die Absonderung von Stofflichem, wie Erz,

Stein, Holz leicht, weil man da das Auftreten der einen Form in den verschiedenen Stoffen *beobachten* kann; gäbe es nur eherne Kreise zu beobachten, so würde die Sonderung auch da eine Schwierigkeit für das Denken bedeuten. Nun steht aber nichts im Wege, daß es beispielsweise mit dem εἶδος des Menschen dieselbe Bewandtnis hat : *zu beobachten* ist dies εἶδος freilich nur ἐν σαρξὶ καὶ ὀστοῖς καὶ τοῖς τοιού-τοις | μέρεσιν: aber müssen diese ,,Teile'' deswegen von εἶδος und λόγος sein? Sind sie nicht vielmehr ὕλη, und nur wir sind nicht imstande zu sondern, weil das εἶδος an anderer Materie nun einmal nicht vorkommt? Und weil das letztere wenigstens als Möglichkeit anzuerkennen ist und man keinen Maßstab hat, wann diese Möglichkeit vorliegt, so, sagt Aristoteles, stellen nunmehr gewisse Leute dieselbe Frage auch beim Kreis und Dreieck in dem Sinne: es ist nicht in der Ordnung, daß Kreis und Dreieck durch Linien und Kontinuum definiert werden, sondern von all diesem ist nur in gleicher Weise (als zum Kreise gehörig) die Rede, wie von Fleisch und Knochen als zum Menschen und von Erz und Stein als zur Statue gehörig. ,,Und sie führen alles auf die Zahlen zurück und sagen, die Definition der Linie sei die der Zwei'' (1036b 12f.). Ähnlich Vertreter der Ideenlehre, was, nach Aristoteles' Darstellung, vollends zu Absurditäten führt (13—20). Nun erwarten wir eigentlich die Auflösung der Aporie, indessen Aristoteles bricht ab mit den etwas vagen Worten ὅτι μὲν οὖν ἔχει τινὰ ἀπορίαν τὰ περὶ τοὺς ὁρισμούς, καὶ διὰ τίν' αἰτίαν, εἴρηται, um daran zunächst nur die knappe Warnung anzuhängen: διὸ καὶ τὸ πάντ' ἀνάγειν οὕτω καὶ ἀφαιρεῖν τὴν ὕλην περίεργον· ἔνια γὰρ ἴσως τόδ' ἐν τῷδ' ἐστιν, ἢ ὡδὶ ταδὶ ἔχοντα. Unverkennbar ist hierin die direkte Beziehung auf den Zusammenhang von 1036b 12 καὶ ἀνάγουσι πάντα εἰς τοὺς ἀριθμοὺς und für den Gedanken unentbehrlich: Aristoteles konnte es gar nicht unausgesprochen lassen, wie er die Sache zurechtlegen will, da das in der Darstellung der Aporie gerade nicht herausgekommen war.

Damit ist, denke ich, die Erwähnung des jüngeren Sokrates in ihren Zusammenhang gerückt. Denn wenn es nun weitergeht καὶ ἡ παραβολὴ ἡ ἐπὶ τοῦ ζῴου, ἣν εἰώθει λέγειν Σωκράτης ὁ νεώτερος, οὐ καλῶς ἔχει, so kann man das unmöglich von dem Vorhergehenden trennen. Jetzt erfahren wir das Bedenkliche an dem Vergleich: ἀπάγει γὰρ ἀπὸ τοῦ ἀληθοῦς, καὶ ποιεῖ ὑπολαμβάνειν ὡς ἐνδεχόμενον εἶναι τὸν ἄνθρωπον ἄνευ τῶν μερῶν ὥσπερ ἄνευ τοῦ χαλκοῦ τὸν κύκλον. Das ist wörtliche Bezugnahme auf 1036a 34—b 7: ὅσα δὲ μὴ ὁρᾶται χωριζόμενα, οὐδὲν μὲν κωλύει ὁμοίως ἔχειν τούτοις, ὥσπερ κἂν εἰ οἱ κύκλοι πάντες ἑωρῶντο χαλκοῖ (οὐδὲν γὰρ ἂν ἧττον ἦν ὁ χαλκὸς οὐδὲν | τοῦ εἴδους), χαλεπὸν δ' ἀφελεῖν τοῦτο τῇ διανοίᾳ. οἷον τὸ τοῦ ἀνθρώπου εἶδος ἀεὶ ἐν σαρξὶ φαίνεται καὶ ὀστοῖς καὶ τοῖς τοιούτοις μέρεσιν· ἆρ' οὖν καὶ ἐστὶ ταῦτα μέρη τοῦ εἴδους καὶ τοῦ λόγου; usw. Und damit haben wir, was wir suchen mußten; denn nicht um seiner selbst willen stand hier das εἶδος ἀνθρώπου in Parallele mit dem vom Erz unabhängigen Kreis, sondern nur um die Brücke zu bilden zu dem Postulat für die mathematischen Definitionen[7]. Demnach ist Sokrates identisch mit den 1036 b 8 erscheinenden τινές[8] oder ist wenigstens einer von ihnen, und wir fassen seinen Gedanken: Es ist der bereits oben (S. 184f.) wiedergegebene. ἡ παραβολὴ ἡ ἐπὶ τοῦ ζῴου ist nicht der *für* das Lebewesen sondern der *an* ihm gebildete Vergleich, und Sokrates wollte gar nicht auf die Idee des Menschen hinaus, war überhaupt keiner der eigentlichen Vertreter der Ideenlehre, die 1036 b 13 noch besonders aufgeführt werden, sondern ihm kam es | darauf an, die mathematischen Definitionen in reine Zahlendefinitionen überzuführen und die Berechtigung dieser gedanklich schwierigen Forderung darzutun. Daraus hat sich dann Aristoteles seine Aporie zurechtgemacht, denn Sokrates selbst hatte es nicht als solche hingestellt, wie der Schluß von Aristoteles' Wiedergabe (1036 b 12f.) noch erkennen läßt.

[7] Von hier aus fällt nun auch Licht auf Aristoteles' seltsam abruptes Verfahren in den Zeilen 21—24. Woher nimmt er eigentlich theoretisch die Berechtigung zu der Ablehnung des Gedankenganges der Aporie? Er sagt: ,,Einiges ist eben wohl doch dies in dem, oder dieses sich so und so verhaltend", mit anderen Worten: Bei einigem gehört eben die ὕλη doch dazu! Man muß schon etwas guten Willen mitbringen, um ihn hier nicht mit sich selbst in Widerspruch geraten zu lassen, denn bisher haben wir immer nur gehört, daß für die ὕλη kein Platz in der Definition ist; und selbstverständlich fragt man: wie in aller Welt kann Aristoteles hier so platt einfach das Gegenteil behaupten oder zum mindesten die Sache plötzlich von der entgegengesetzten Seite ansehen, ohne darüber Rechenschaft zu geben? Daß eine solche Rechenschaftsablegung ihn in schwierige und hier höchst unwillkommene Erörterungen über die mathematischen Gegenstände und über die im Grunde relativen Begriffe ὕλη und εἶδος verwickeln würde, sieht man, und daß er dem ausweicht, ist begreiflich. Aber was ihm bei dem Gewaltstreich das gute Gewissen gibt, ist doch wohl der Umstand, daß er rein logisch genommen mit den ihm an dieser Stelle unmittelbar zur Verfügung stehenden gedanklichen Mitteln der Aporie zwar nicht spitz, wohl aber von der Seite kommen kann. Der Angriffspunkt ist die in der Aporie aller Unvorstellbarkeit zum Trotz erschlichene Möglichkeit, das ,,συνειλημμένον" ἄνθρωπος von seiner ὕλη so abzutrennen wie den Kreis vom Erz. Das kann Aristoteles ohne weiteres zurückweisen, und damit steht und fällt in der Tat die Behauptung, daß man sich durch die gedankliche Schwierigkeit der Zurückführung der mathematischen Definitionen auf Zahlen nicht schrecken lassen dürfe, mag nun in diesem letzteren Fall der Begriff ,,συνειλημμένον" anwendbar sein (vgl. 1043 a 33 f.) oder nicht. Aristoteles ist also logisch auf alle Fälle berechtigt, die seiner Meinung nach absurden Konsequenzen des Gedankenganges der Aporie auf sich beruhen zu lassen, weil er das Mittelstück sprengen kann. Auf Weiteres läßt er sich im Grunde gar nicht ein, und wir werden uns hüten, schärfer zupacken zu wollen, als er selbst getan hat.

[8] Mit den 1036 b 18 beiläufig zur Diskreditierung der Ideenlehre genannten Pythagoreern haben sie nichts zu tun.

Für die Geschichte der platonischen Ideenlehre bedeutet es kaum mehr als eine Illustration, wenn wir sehen, wie etwa um das Jahr 366 Sokrates mit dem von Fleisch, Knochen usw. zu sondernden εἶδος des Menschen für seine Zwecke operiert. Denn wir lesen ja noch in Platons wohl etwas früher geschriebenem *Parmenides* dessen eigene prinzipielle Anerkennung der Notwendigkeit, die Ideenlehre auf alle Naturwesen auszudehnen (*Parm.* 130 b—e; anders noch *Staat* 523 b—d, vgl. *Phaedr.* 263 a). Natürlich hatte Sokrates das aus der Akademie. Aber in der bestechenden Art, wie er zunächst die Schwierigkeit der Abstraktion im Falle des Menschen durch die Analogie des ehernen Kreises, von dem wir auch nur schwer das Erz würden sondern können, wenn es nur eherne Kreise gäbe, faßlich macht, um dann darauf sein Postulat für die mathematischen Definitionen zu stützen, kann etwas Eigenes liegen, und jedenfalls ist der Gedanke genügend ausgeprägt und geschlossen, um eine Vorstellung davon zu geben, wie der junge Aristoteles zuerst von „Ideen" mag haben reden hören[9].

[9] Auch das lehrt zumal nach Jaegers Zeichnung der Akademie beim Eintritt des Aristoteles („Aristoteles" S. 12 ff.), die mir noch gerade zur Hand kommt, nichts eigentlich Neues; aber ich denke, es paßt in das Bild.

Besprechung:

Hans von Arnim, Die drei aristotelischen Ethiken

1927

Durch eine besondere Gunst des Schicksals ist uns Aristoteles'
ethische Lehre großenteils in drei stark voneinander abweichenden
Fassungen erhalten. Die Verschiedenheit ist nicht nur formaler, sondern auch inhaltlicher und kompositioneller Art, und so erheblich, daß
die Zurückführung von allen drei Versionen oder auch nur von je zwei
auf ein und dieselbe Ethikvorlesung, die uns etwa nach der Urschrift
und einer bzw. zwei getreu sein wollenden Schülernachschriften gegeben wäre, untunlich ist. Gleichwohl ist es natürlich denkbar, daß
unsere Überlieferung in dem einen oder anderen Zweige nicht auf eine
Urschrift, sondern auf eine Schülernachschrift zurückginge, aber das
hätte keine weitreichenden Konsequenzen. Der unangenehmste Fall
wäre der, daß wir es mit der Umarbeitung einer sonst weder auf Grund
der Urschrift noch einer direkten Nachschrift erhaltenen Vorlesung
zu tun hätten; indessen hat sich die Berücksichtigung dieser Möglichkeit, so einladend sie auch für Kompromißversuche sein mag, bisher
noch stets als unfruchtbar erwiesen. Sehen wir davon ab, so liegt die
Sache so: ist Aristoteles selbst Urheber nur einer der drei Fassungen,
so sind die beiden anderen mehr oder weniger selbständige spätere Um-
arbeitungen von verschiedener Hand; kommt seine Autorschaft für
mehrere | in Frage, so haben wir es mit zu verschiedenen Zeiten ver-
schieden entworfenen und durchgeführten Vorlesungen zu tun. Solange man auf Differenzen des philosophischen Standpunktes bei
Aristoteles zu achten nicht gewöhnt war, haben gerade die Kenner
ersten Ranges wie Schleiermacher, Spengel, Bonitz die letztere Möglichkeit als unwahrscheinlich, ja geradezu des Aristoteles unwürdig
verworfen, und da trotz Schleiermacher die Echtheit der *Nikomachischen Ethik* unantastbar ist, so war damit das Vorurteil gegen die
beiden anderen Ethiken, die *Eudemische* und die sog. *Große*, gegeben;
nur im Sinne des Sichbeugens vor der Überlieferung wurden gegen
Spengels energisches Zupacken von dem einen oder anderen Vorsich-
tigen Einwendungen erhoben und in mehr oder weniger äußerlicher
Weise zu begründen versucht. Heute, wo wir nach Wilamowitz' Vorgang für die *Politik* und nach Jaegers allgemein als bahnbrechend an-

erkannten Arbeiten mit Schichten verschiedener Zeit und verschiedenen philosophischen Standpunktes sogar innerhalb der als scheinbarer Einheiten überlieferten Lehrschriften zu rechnen gelernt haben, ist die wissenschaftliche Situation umgekehrt. Wir sind darauf vorbereitet, Aristoteles ein und denselben Gegenstand wiederholt behandeln zu sehen, erwarten dann aber nicht ein im Grunde gleichgültiges Variieren der Gedanken und des Vortrages, sondern entwicklungsgeschichtlich zu begreifende Wandlungen, die fassen zu können und zu wollen, wo immer es geht, die Wissenschaft sich nicht mehr wird nehmen lassen.

Bisher war nur das Verhältnis der *Eudemischen* zur *Nikomachischen Ethik* einer Neuprüfung unterworfen worden, mit dem durch Jaegers „Aristoteles" sichergestellten Resultat, daß in der *Eudemischen Ethik* eine echt aristotelische frühere Bearbeitung fragmentarisch erhalten ist. Für die ‚*Große*‘ *Ethik* dagegen war man bei dem durch Trendelenburg, Ramsauer und andere bestätigten Ergebnis von Spengels grundlegender Abhandlung (Über die unter dem Namen des Aristoteles erhaltenen ethischen Schriften, in: Abh. d. Bayer. Ak. III 2, 1841, 437—496) geblieben, daß sie, „nur ein Auszug von beiden Werken aus später Zeit, am wenigsten Beachtung verdiene" (so formuliert von Spengel selbst, Aristotelische Studien I, in: Abh. d. Bayer. Ak. X 1, 1864, 7—175); nicht ohne Grund, denn selbstverständlich hat jeder, der sich an die Vergleichung der beiden anderen Ethiken wagte, immer wieder versucht, wenigstens in irgendeinem der heiklen Punkte Hilfe bei diesem dritten Zeugen zu finden, und wenn diese Hoffnung ebenso oft schnöde enttäuscht wurde, so schien auch das ein Beweis für die Richtigkeit von Spengels Einschätzung der *Großen Ethik*. Höchstens für fehlende Partien der *Eudemischen Ethik* schien sich bisweilen ein spärlicher und unzuverlässiger Ersatz zu bieten.

Hier setzt überraschend v. A.s Buch ein. Das Problem wird zunächst von außen formuliert: „Da sich bei der eudemischen Ethik Spengels An|sicht nicht bewährt hat, so ist wohl die Frage berechtigt, ob sein Nachweis für die Unechtheit der ‚großen Ethik‘ von seiner hinfällig gewordenen Beurteilung der *Eudemischen* soweit unabhängig ist, daß er auch jetzt noch stichhaltig bleibt". Es folgt eine vorläufige kurze Kritik der gegen die Echtheit vorgebrachten Gründe; v. A. vermißt einen strikten Beweis: im Grunde ruhe alles auf der inzwischen beseitigten Voraussetzung des nacharistotelischen Ursprungs der *Eudemischen Ethik*. Als Ziel der folgenden Untersuchung wird ausgesprochen: „Es wird nun möglich, die ‚große Ethik‘ als ein echtes Werk, und zwar als die früheste, der eudemischen noch vorausliegende Ethikvorlesung des Aristoteles zu erweisen". — In dieser Einleitung werden nicht alle Karten offengelegt. Eine Untersuchung mit dem bezeich-

neten Ziel kann nicht geradlinig an die neuen Verteidigungen der
Eudemischen Ethik, insbesondere nicht an Jaegers Behandlung an-
knüpfen. Denn all das, was Jaeger an der *Eudemischen Ethik* im Gegensatz zur *Nikomachischen* charakteristisch findet für die frühere Ent-
wicklungsstufe des ethischen Denkens, dürfte so nicht aufgefaßt werden, wenn die *Große Ethik* eine noch frühere Stufe bedeutet. Ich kann
das hier nur behaupten und werde auch nicht darauf zurückkommen,
da v. A. überhaupt vermieden hat, in dieser Hinsicht mehr als die
chronologische Außenseite seines Ergebnisses hervorzukehren. Sind
aber wirklich „die M. Mor. das früheste der drei Werke und gewissermaßen der Grundbau, der in den folgenden Fassungen weiter ausge-
baut, bereichert, vervollständigt und vervollkommnet wurde" (S. 14),
so hat die Geschichte der Entwicklung wenigstens von Aristoteles'
ethischer Lehre eine neue Grundlegung gefunden. In die von Jaeger
aufgezeigte Entwicklungsreihe: *Philebos, Protreptikos, Eudemische
Ethik, Nikomachische Ethik* (W. Jaeger, Aristoteles, Berlin 1923,
248) paßt die *Große Ethik* nicht hinein. Wir müßten *Philebos* und
Protreptikos beiseiterücken und an ihre Stelle vorneweg ein Werk
setzen, das zwar fast alle nicht nur in der *Eudemischen*, sondern auch
in der *Nikomachischen Ethik*[1] vorkommenden Dinge irgendwie berührt, nur vielfach unklarer, flacher und gedankenärmer (denn das ist
doch wohl der Gegensatz von „klarer, tiefgründiger und gedanken-
reicher" S. 95), das in seiner Anlage zwar den in der Folge weiter aus-
gebauten Grundplan darstellt, gleichwohl aber darauf verzichtet, diesen Plan irgendwie herauszuarbeiten, sondern statt dessen eine äußerlich anreihende Methode wählt, die nur „bei einigem guten Willen"
den Zusammenhang der einzelnen Kapitel | erkennen läßt (S. 46 ff.),
einen ersten Entwurf endlich, in dem nicht die Bedeutung der Sache
oder die Freude an der eigenen Denkbewegung maßgebend ist für die
Form der Darstellung, sondern diese vorsorglich dem etwas niedrigen
„Bildungsniveau des Hörerkreises" (S. 5) angepaßt wird, „sei es, daß
im Anfang des Schulbestandes oder auch später wegen mangelnder
Auswahl den Hörern nicht viel zugemutet werden konnte" (S. 18). —
    Die eigentliche Untersuchung gliedert sich in einen ziemlich um-
fangreichen ersten Teil (S. 6—96), der einen gründlichen Versuch der
Widerlegung der gegen die *Große Ethik* vorgebrachten Beanstandun-
gen enthält, und in einen kürzeren zweiten (S. 96—141), in dem ohne
Rücksicht auf die Argumente der Gegner der unversehens gewonnene
Echtheitsbeweis durch weitere Beobachtungen verstärkt und zum Ab-

---

[1] Darin findet v. A. keine Schwierigkeit: „Es kann nicht auffallen, wenn einzelne
nebensächliche Bestandteile dieses Grundbaues, die in den Eudemien, dem
früheren Ausbauversuch, beiseite gelassen worden waren, in den spätesten und end-
gültigen Ausbau wieder aufgenommen wurden" usw. (S. 14).

schluß gebracht werden soll (S. 95). Raumknappheit und ein vom Verfasser gegebener Wink[2] bestimmen mich, der Besprechung diesen zweiten Teil zugrunde zu legen und auch hier nur in der äußeren Reihenfolge des einzelnen dem wohlüberlegten Gang der Darstellung zu folgen.

I. Die Freundschaftsabhandlung (S. 96ff.). 1. In allen drei Ethiken ist, in der *Eudemischen* und *Großen* allerdings ohne Schluß, als ein in sich abgeschlossener Untersuchungskomplex (Jaeger, Aristoteles 247) eine Abhandlung über die Freundschaft erhalten. Da die *Große Ethik* schon die ähnlich isolierte, nur kürzere Behandlung der ἡδονή mit der Wendung ἐπειδήπερ ὑπὲρ εὐδαιμονίας ἐστὶν ὁ λόγος (1204a 19 und 27) und ebenso die noch kürzere der εὐτυχία (1206b 30) eingeleitet hat und auch unmittelbar vor der Freundschaftsabhandlung eine speziell die Eudaimonie betreffende Frage erörtert, so ist für sie, die an dieser Stelle alle sonstigen Einzelheiten erledigt hat und für die höchstens noch ein dem Schlußteil der *Nikom. Ethik* entsprechender Anschluß des Ganzen aussteht, die Einleitung 1208b 3 ἐφ᾽ ἅπασι δὲ τούτοις ὑπὲρ φιλίας ἀναγκαῖόν ἐστιν εἰπεῖν ... ἐπειδὴ γάρ ..., συμπαραληπτέα ἂν εἴη πρὸς τὴν εὐδαιμονίαν in der Ordnung. Die *Eudemische* und die *Nikom. Ethik* haben je eine ausführlichere Einführung, beide im Einklang mit der Eigenart der folgenden Abhandlung, aber das Wort εὐδαιμονία fällt nicht. Statt dessen hat die *Eud. Ethik* zu Anfang die Wendung περὶ φιλίας ... ἐπισκεπτέον οὐθενὸς ἧττον τῶν περὶ τὰ ἤθη καλῶν καὶ αἱρετῶν (1234b 18ff.) und die *Nik.* sagt vorneweg 1155a 1 ἔστι γὰρ ἀρετή τις ἢ μετ᾽ ἀρετῆς. Beachten wir, daß der Schlußteil der *Nik. Ethik* die Gesamtheit alles Vorausliegenden, das uns im wesentlichen nach der letzten Redaktion, freilich mit dem in dieser unerträglichen | Überschuß einer ersten ἡδονή-Abhandlung im *H*, erhalten ist, als τὰ περὶ τὰς ἀρετάς τε καὶ φιλίας καὶ ἡδονάς bezeichnet (1176a 30. 1179a 33), ohne uns durch jenen Überschuß beirren zu lassen, so ist ein passenderer Übergang von der ἀρετή in dem weiten Sinne, daß nicht nur ethische und dianoetische Tugenden, sondern auch ἐγκράτεια und καρτερία darunterfallen, zur φιλία wohl nicht gut denkbar. Von der *Eud. Ethik* wissen wir direkt nicht, was alles vorausging. Erschließen dürfen wir, daß sich an ihr Buch *Γ* zunächst die Behandlung der Gerechtigkeit anschloß und daß vor dem als letztem Buch erhaltenen Fragment nicht nur die Sonderbehandlung von ἀρετή und φρόνησις (danach disponiert die *Eud. Ethik*, Jaeger, Aristoteles 247) erledigt ist (1246b 37), sondern daß auch schon

---

[2] „Diese Beobachtungen waren es, die zuerst meinen Glauben an die herrschende Meinung erschütterten und mich zu meiner Untersuchung veranlaßten." Ein weiterer Fingerzeig S. 109 oben.

ein Abschnitt περὶ ἡδονῆς seine Stelle gefunden hat (1249a 17). Aber ob das Buch *H* mit der Freundschaftsabhandlung auch ursprünglich, wie in der Überlieferung, vor dem, wovon uns in *Θ* ein vorn und hinten verstümmelter Rest geblieben ist, gestanden hat, darüber ist die Entscheidung schwer, nachdem diese Reihenfolge auf Grund der *Großen Ethik* in Zweifel gezogen worden ist. Ich finde, abgesehen davon, daß sich die letzte Partie des *Θ* für den Schluß des Ganzen eignet und trotz naher Berührungen auch mit dem *Z* der *Nik. Ethik* doch mehr innere Verwandtschaft mit deren *K* hat, keinen weiteren Anhalt als eben die angeführte Eingangsformel der Freundschaftsabhandlung, die so aussieht, als hätte die *Eud. Ethik* die φιλία im Anschluß an den Hauptteil περὶ ἀρετῆς im engeren Sinne, also περὶ ἀρ. ἠθικῆς (vgl. 1220a 5ff.) behandelt, so daß wir hinsichtlich der Reihenfolge von *H* und *Θ* bei der Überlieferung bleiben müßten. — Bei dieser Sachlage scheint mir kein gegründeter Anlaß, uns über das Fehlen des ‚Schlagwortes' εὐδαιμονία in den Einleitungen der *Nik.* und *Eud. Ethik* zu wundern und umgekehrt sein Auftreten in der *Großen Ethik* unter Voraussetzungen, die es dem Verfasser der *Großen Ethik* in den Mund legen mußten, die aber in der *Nik. Ethik* sicher und in der *Eud.* wahrscheinlich nicht gegeben waren, mit v. A. für einen Beweis der Ursprünglichkeit zu halten.

I 2 (S. 98—108). Nach der Einleitung folgt in den drei Ethiken je eine Aufführung der Aporien. Am ausführlichsten ist dies Stück in der *Eud. Ethik*, die *Nik.* schließt sich dem Sinne nach ganz daran an, kürzt aber stark ab; ein Unterschied ist, daß sie die Frage des ποσαχῶς, die die *Eud. Ethik* in die Themastellung einbezieht (1234b 19), als Aporie nachbringt, so daß sie ein in der *Eud. Ethik* nicht erwähntes Argument der ἐν οἰόμενοι gleich als unzulänglich abtun kann. Zeitlich ist das Verhältnis der beiden eindeutig und im ganzen auch durch v. A. ins rechte Licht gesetzt. Für die *Große Ethik* wird richtig bemerkt erstens, daß der Verfasser die Aporien als drei Alternativfragen gibt, deren Lösung er, wie auch teilweise die Ausführung zeigt, als das wesentliche | seiner Aufgabe zu betrachten scheint, zweitens, daß ihm die methodische Überlegenheit, mit der Aristoteles in den beiden andern Ethiken die Ausweitung des Freundschaftsproblems auf die naturphilosophische Frage des Zueinanderstrebens von Gleichartigem oder Entgegengesetztem als unwissenschaftlich hinstellt, fremd ist. Letzteres ist gewiß das Harmlosere, ob das Ursprüngliche, ist fraglich. Eine Seltsamkeit der *Gr. Ethik* ist es, daß ihre zweite Aporie (Ist es schwer, Freund zu werden, oder leicht?) in der folgenden Abhandlung nicht mehr erwähnt wird, aber das mag als Nebensächlichkeit, die man allenfalls erklären kann, einmal hingehen. Bleiben also die beiden Alternativfragen 1. Liebt sich das Gleichartige oder das Entgegengesetzte? 2. Eignet sich der Schlechte zum Freund oder nicht? Geht man von

dieser begrenzten Fragestellung aus, so kann man über die *Eud. Ethik*
in Verwunderung geraten. Die der ersten Alternative entsprechenden
verschiedenen Meinungen führt sie allerdings an erster Stelle und hebt
sie deutlich ab, aber eben aus methodischen Erwägungen, die der *Gr.
Ethik* fremd sind, und dann werden „als ob sie nicht eine Alternative
bildeten" weitere Ansichten angeschlossen, zunächst drei, von denen
zwar die ersten beiden jener dritten Alternative der *Gr. Ethik* entsprechen, aber die letzte τοῖς δὲ τὸ χρήσιμον δοκεῖ φίλον εἶναι μόνον
(1235a 35) etwa den Ansichten der ersten Alternative der *Gr. Ethik*
hätte angereiht werden können, aber auch das nur, wenn jene „nicht
als eine Alternative bildend empfunden wurden". Endlich bringt die
Eud. Ethik nach der nun folgenden zweiten Alternative der *Gr. Ethik*,
übrigens wieder deutlich abgehoben, eine neue Aporie: Ist das ἡδύ
oder das ἀγαθόν das φιλούμενον? Daß letzteres um der nun folgenden
Untersuchung willen geschieht, ja eigentlich schon den Beginn der
Untersuchung bildet, ist klar und würde auch v. A. kaum stören; aber
das Schlimme ist also einmal, daß die Alternativfragen nicht als solche
herausgebracht werden, und dann vor allem das Auftauchen des
χρήσιμον 1235a 35. v. A. stellt es mit dem ἡδύ und ἀγαθόν auf eine
Stufe und meint: „Die drei neuen Antworten auf die Frage: τί τὸ
φίλον; die er den beiden der *M. Mor.* hinzufügt, χρήσιμον, ἀγαθόν, ἡδύ,
sind dieselben, die hernach in der allen drei Ethiken gemeinsamen Erörterung τί τὸ φιλητόν; allein in Betracht gezogen werden. Deswegen
hat er sie offenbar hinzugefügt und dadurch die Verwirrung verschul-
det." Ein Blick in den Text der *Eud. Ethik* lehrt, daß damit jedenfalls
des Rätsels Lösung nicht gefunden ist. Wenn dies das Motiv der Ver-
mischung der „Aufzählung von Ansichten über das φίλον mit der Aufzählung von Aporien (Alternativfragen) über die φιλία" war, bleibt
die Stellung des χρήσιμον unerklärt. Übrigens gibt der Text der *Eud.
Ethik* an sich kein Recht, in ihr ausschließlich nach jenen Alternativ-
fragen zu suchen. | Ihr kommt es darauf an, daß *mancherlei* ἐναντιώ-
σεις bestehen, nicht nur im Sinne jener Alternativen: 1235b 2—6; und
sie sucht eine Lösung, die möglichst alle vorhandenen Meinungen trotz
ihres scheinbaren Widerspruchs in ihrer jeweiligen Berechtigung zur
Geltung kommen läßt (1235b 13ff.). Dieser Standpunkt, der jedem
Kenner des Aristoteles geläufig ist, ist freilich etwas anderes als der
der *Gr. Ethik*, den v. A. so kennzeichnet: „Die Aporien in den *M. Mor.*
sind alle Alternativfragen. Je zwei entgegengesetzte Ansichten über je
eine die Freundschaft betreffende Frage sind mit Gründen vertreten
worden. Zwischen ihnen gilt es zu entscheiden." Hat wirklich Aristoteles so angefangen?

Glücklicherweise kommt Hilfe von außen. Was v. A. an der Problematik der *Eud.
Ethik* zu beanstanden hat und nur als sekundäre Verwirrung verstehen zu können

glaubt, ist unmittelbar aus dem platonischen *Lysis* herübergenommen. Da wird, nachdem die Vorfrage, ob das Liebende oder das Geliebte oder das Liebende und Wiedergeliebte ‚freund' sei (die die *Eud. Ethik* nicht als Aporie gelten läßt, sondern erst 1236 a 14 und 1236 b 3 als natürlich im letzten Sinne zu entscheiden aufnimmt), für den Dialog zu keinem Ergebnis geführt hat, 214a auf Dichter und Naturphilosophen rekurriert, die dem Gleichartigen einen Zug zum Gleichartigen verleihen, und dieser scheinbar so einleuchtende Satz dann sogleich dahin eingeschränkt, daß mit den Gleichartigen nur die Guten gemeint sein könnten, da das Böse wegen seiner Ungerechtigkeit und Unbeständigkeit weder freund noch überhaupt gleichartig sein könne. Aber auch dieser Satz, daß nur der Gute dem Guten wirklich freund sei, wird für den Fortgang des Dialogs sofort wieder umgeworfen durch Besinnung auf das Prinzip der Nützlichkeit (214e 4 χρήσιμος). Weder kann überhaupt das Gleichartige dem Gleichartigen etwas bieten, das dieses nicht schon in sich besäße, noch kann insbesondere der Gute dem Guten freund sein, weil er als Guter sich selbst genug ist, also nichts außer sich nötig hat und somit einen Freund unmöglich schätzen kann. Wieder müssen Dichter und ein ungenannter Philosoph heran, um ein umgekehrtes Freundschaftsprinzip, das der Gegensätzlichkeit, zu liefern, das dann aber ebenfalls nicht standhält, weil es Gegensätze gibt, die sich absolut nicht miteinander vertragen. Resultat: οὔτε ἄρα τὸ ὅμοιον τῷ ὁμοίῳ οὔτε τὸ ἐναντίον τῷ ἐναντίῳ φίλον. Und dann wird es mit dem οὔτε ἀγαθὸν οὔτε κακόν probiert, was Aristoteles in seiner Problematik wohlweislich nicht mitmacht, weil es sich nunmehr um spezifisch platonische Dinge, nicht allgemein δοκοῦντα handelt. Aber der Anschluß an das Vorhergehende ist, auch in Einzelheiten, unverkennbar und längst bemerkt.

Aristoteles hat nur die beiden ins allgemeine sich verlierenden naturphilosophischen Lösungsversuche vorweggenommen und dann das übrige folgen lassen: Einige glauben, die Schlechten können nicht freund sein, sondern nur die Guten (1235a 31); das ist einfach *Lysis* 214b—d. Ein unmittelbar aufsteigendes Bedenken gegen rigorose Anwendung des Satzes setzt er von sich aus hinzu (τοῖς δ᾽ ἄτοπον, εἰ μὴ φιλοῦσιν αἱ μητέρες τὰ τέκνα usw., vgl. übrigens *Lys.* 212e—213a), und dann kommt das χρήσιμον, dessen Auftreten an dieser Stelle aus dem Zusammenhang *Lys.* 214e—215b ohne weiteres erklärt ist. Die Ausführung des Gedankens ist selbständig; hier wird ein τόπος der Sokratik benutzt (Xen. *Mem.* 1, 2, 53—55. Pl. *Symp.* 205e. Diog. L. 2, 91. Stob. IV 611, 10 Hense). Übrig bleibt noch die Widerlegung des Prinzips der Gegensätzlich|keit, die *Lys.* 216a/b zugestandenermaßen eristisch gegeben war; sie bringt Aristoteles in der Gegenüberstellung 1235b 2—6 in nüchternerer Formulierung nach: καὶ τὸ ἐναντίον ἀχρηστότατον τῷ ἐναντίῳ· φθαρτικὸν γὰρ τοῦ ἐναντίου τὸ ἐναντίον. — Auf diesen Zusammenhang hat v. A. wohl im Interesse der Vereinfachung der Darstellung nicht eingehen wollen; da gerade er ihn sicher nicht übersehen hat, so kann sein Standpunkt nur der sein, den er später (S. 106) für eine Einzelheit (E. E. 1239 b 11 ∼ *Lys.* 214c/d) zu erkennen gibt, daß es sich nämlich in der *Eud. Ethik* um ein sekundäres Zurückgreifen auf den platonischen *Lysis* handele. Aber auch das verträgt sich kaum mit seiner Argumentation, und überdies braucht man es nur auszusprechen, und die Unwahrscheinlichkeit liegt auf der Hand.

Die Stellungnahme zum Folgenden wird dadurch erschwert, daß v. A. die Argumentation für die Priorität der *Gr. Ethik* mit der Beseitigung von Schwierigkeiten, die sich nur auf Grund dieser These erheben, verwoben hat. Ich muß versuchen, zu trennen.

Ausschlaggebend soll die Art sein, wie in der *Gr. Ethik* ihre erste und dritte Aporie — mit der zweiten gibt sie sich ja nicht weiter ab —

durch die folgende Untersuchung gelöst werden. In der Tat stürzt sie sich bei der ersten Gelegenheit (1209a 3) auf die Lösung der — dritten Aporie und verquickt sie mit der Unterscheidung der drei Freundschaftsarten, die in den beiden anderen Ethiken wie billig[3] das Wesentliche ist, und nimmt die ‚erste‘ auch 1210a 6 „in gutem Glauben" auf. Aber es ist eine Übertreibung, wenn die Lösung der beiden Aporien als die „eigentliche und hauptsächliche Aufgabe" der ganzen Freundschaftsabhandlung erscheinen soll. Eigentlich will doch auch sie die drei Freundschaftsarten herausbringen und weiteres sich anschließen lassen, und der speziellen Lösung der Aporien widmet sie hochgerechnet 4 von 16 Teubnerseiten, und dabei ist sie am Schluß unvollständig. Nur soviel kann man sagen, daß die Art und Weise, wie die Aporien aufgestellt werden, die folgende Darstellung bis zu einem gewissen Grade beeinflußt; aber daß der Verfasser der gr. Ethik bis zu einem gewissen Grade seinen eigenen Weg geht, hat noch nie jemand bestritten. Ein Beweis für die Echtheit und Priorität läßt sich so nicht führen. Und die ‚Gutgläubigkeit‘ in Sachen der ersten Aporie entspricht nur dem Gesamthabitus dieser Ethik, wonach man fast mit Sicherheit darauf rechnen kann, feinere Gedankenbestimmungen der beiden anderen übergangen oder durch eine Plattheit oder eine Verschrobenheit ersetzt zu finden.

An Einzelbemerkungen, die als Argumente gelten können, finde ich folgendes: S. 102 „Für die M. Mor. ist die Tugendfreundschaft die βελτίστη, für die Eud. die ἀληθινή und der Tugendhafte der ἀληθινὸς καὶ ἁπλῶς φίλος", in der nik. Ethik ist im eigentlichen Sinne (κυρίως) „ihm jetzt Freundschaft | nur die der Tugendhaften, die beiden andern nur καθ᾽ ὁμοιότητα und in Anbequemung an den Sprachgebrauch der Menge". Das soll ein stetiger Fortschritt sein. Ich finde soweit sachlich keinen Unterschied zwischen der *Eud.* und *Nik. Ethik* (κυρίως *E. E.* 1236a 20), in der *Gr.* nur den bekannten Mangel an Schärfe, und stelle gegenüber die Tatsache, daß die *Gr. Ethik* wie die *Nik.* die Tugendfreundschaft als τελεία bezeichnet (1210a 8. b 27. 1211a 3. παντελής 1209a 16), während die *Eud. Ethik* die πρώτη φιλία hat, die Jaeger, Aristoteles 254f. als das Ursprüngliche erwiesen hat. — S. 106: *E. E.* 1239b 24f. sollen die Beispiele Herr und Sklave, Mann und Weib ein Residuum der älteren Darstellung sein, weil nur die *Große Ethik* die καθ᾽ ὑπεροχὴν φιλία mit der κατ᾽ ἐναντιότητα identifiziert. Aber inwiefern die *Eud. Ethik* dadurch, daß sich nach ihrer Theorie dies beides nicht deckt, sondern kreuzt, an einer Exemplifikation aus dem gemeinsamen Bereich gehindert sein sollte, ist nicht einzusehen. Tatsächlich führt übrigens die *Gr. Ethik* an der entsprechenden Stelle (1210a 9) andere Beispiele auf (arm und reich, und seltsamerweise gut und schlecht); wenn sie dabei lediglich an die ὑπεροχή des einen Teils über den anderen zu denken scheint, so gibt das für die Interpretation der *Eud. Ethik* nichts aus. Denn für deren Gedanken kommt eben nicht die einseitige Überlegenheit des Herrn über den Sklaven und des Mannes über die Frau in Betracht, sondern die wechselseitig vorhandene Fähigkeit beider Teile, Dinge zu leisten, deren der andere bedarf. Verschiedene Gesichtspunkte für das Ver-

---

[3] Wie sie die Frage des ποσαχῶς in ihren Einleitungen behandeln, habe ich bei Gelegenheit bereits oben (S. 192) erwähnt.

hältnis von Mann und Frau gibt *E. N.* 1162a 16ff. an, ohne Rücksicht auf die ὑπεροχή. — S. 108 endlich findet v. A. in den beiden Sätzen über das ἐναντίον *E. N.* 1159b 12—15 und 19—23 ganz verschiedene und unvereinbare Anschauungen und erklärt das daraus, daß an der ersten Stelle ἐξ ἐναντίων δὲ μάλιστα μὲν δοκεῖ ἡ διὰ τό χρήσιμον γίνεσθαι φιλία, οἷον πένης πλουσίῳ, ἀμαθὴς εἰδότι· οὗ γὰρ τυγχάνει τις ἐνδεὴς ὤν, τούτου ἐφιέμενος ἀντιδωρεῖται ἄλλο die beiden Beispiele statt aus der *Eudemischen Ethik* „aus dem älteren Konzept, das die *M. Mor.* wiedergeben", genommen seien. Er interpretiert denn auch nach der *Großen Ethik*: „die Liebe des Armen zum Reichen, durch den er reich, und des Unbelehrten zum Wissenden, durch den er wissend zu werden hofft, ist nicht das Sichhingezogenfühlen zum Entgegengesetzten, das eigentlich ein Streben nach der richtigen Mitte ist". Hier zeigt sich, wohin man kommt, wenn man von der *Gr. Ethik* ausgehen will. Weder hofft in der *Nik. Ethik* nach dem Zusammenhang der Stelle der Arme durch den Reichen selbst reich zu werden, noch hofft der ἀμαθής wissend zu werden (so etwas bringt nur die *Gr. Ethik* hinein, 1210a 11 διὰ γὰρ τὴν ἔνδειαν τὴν τῆς ἀρετῆς, παρ' οὗ οἴεται αὐτῷ ἔσεσθαι, διὰ τοῦτο τούτῳ φίλος), sondern der Arme erhofft das Notwendige, und der ἀμαθής hofft von dem Wissenden in dem Sinne zu profitieren, wie beispielsweise der Kranke vom Arzt (Beweis: Pl. *Lysis* 215d!), und gibt dafür etwas anderes. Es ist also doch auch an die Wechselseitigkeit des Verhältnisses gedacht, wie in der *Eud. Ethik*, deren Beispiele v. A. hier günstiger zu beurteilen scheint als zwei Seiten vorher. Und da sich das Streben des Armen und des Ungelehrten, wie gezeigt, nicht auf das entgegengesetzte Extrem richtet, so schließen die Zeilen 19—23 ohne Bruch an. Richtig ist nur, daß die *Nik. Ethik* für den Gedanken ἔστι δέ πως καὶ ἡ τοῦ ἐναντίου φιλία τοῦ ἀγαθοῦ (*E. E.* 1239b 29, vgl. 1240b 18. 38f.) kein sonderliches Interesse mehr hat. In der großen Ethik ist er bis auf eine Spur (1210a 19—21) verwischt.

Schwierigkeiten macht in der besprochenen Partie für die These der Echtheit und Priorität der *Großen Ethik* einmal das Auftauchen des Terminus φιλητέον 1208b 38ff. Ihn bespricht v. A. auch schon im ersten Teil (S. 20ff.), weil man | darin einen Beleg stoischer Beeinflussung gesehen hat. Zuzugeben ist, daß der Gebrauch, den der Verfasser von ihm macht, nicht identisch ist mit der verglichenen Terminologie; man kann ja auch schwerlich erwarten, daß ein Peripatetiker mit einem Male anfinge, von λεκτά und κατηγορήματα zu reden. v. A. bestreitet jede Abhängigkeit und glaubt ein βουλητέον neben βουλητόν bereits in der Schulsprache der ältesten Akademie voraussetzen zu dürfen. Mag das ein erlaubter Notbehelf sein, jedenfalls ist dagegen zu protestieren, wenn S. 102 an dem „viel subtileren und verwickelteren" Gedankengange der *Eud. Ethik* (1235b 25ff.) das Fehlen der „Hauptbegriffe φιλητόν und φιλητέον" geradezu beanstandet wird. Der *Eud Ethik* scheint nach ihrem ganzen Verfahren ein Terminus nicht zur Verfügung zu stehen; die *Nik. Ethik* setzt das φιλητόν ein; in der *Gr. Ethik* haben wir überdies noch das φιλητέον: das sind die Tatsachen.

Untragbar für die These ist die Hauptschwierigkeit. Die *Eud. Ethik* bringt im Anschluß an die Erörterung der drei auf die drei verschiedenen Freundschaftsziele (ἀγαθόν, ἡδύ, χρήσιμον) sich gründenden Freundschaftsarten 1238b 15 die Unterscheidung von Freundschaften κατ' ἰσότητα und solchen καθ' ὑπερβολήν, wo einer der beiden Teile dem anderen hinsichtlich des jeweiligen Wertes erheblich überlegen ist, so daß (1239a 1) zwei Gruppen von je drei ‚φιλίαι' entstehen, wenn auch nur in der ersten Gruppe von ‚φίλοι' gesprochen werden kann (vgl. 1240a 7. 1242a 10). In der zweiten hat der überlegene Teil einen entsprechend höheren Anspruch auf das Geliebtwerden, was bei

1239b 2 erörtert wird. Es folgt, gut und deutlich abgehoben — von einer „Art von Nachtrag oder Anhang" zu reden hat keine Berechtigung —, die Stellungnahme zu den wieder als zu allgemein gekennzeichneten Sätzen, das ὅμοιον bzw. ἐναντίον sei φίλον, so, daß die Freundschaft zum Gleichartigen auf das ἀγαθόν und ἡδύ, die zum ἐναντίον zunächst auf das χρήσιμον, dann ‚in gewisser Weise' doch auch auf das ἀγαθόν zurückgeführt wird. Inhaltlich dasselbe hat die *Nik. Ethik* von 1158b 1 an, nur gleitet sie 1159b 1 über die Wendung, daß auch zwischen den (durch eine φιλία καθ᾽ ὑπερβολήν verbundenen) Ungleichen, falls das φιλεῖν nach Maßgabe der Würdigkeit geschieht, ein Ausgleich stattfinde, durch Gleichsetzung von ἰσότης und ὁμοιότης *unvermerkt* zum Problem der ὁμοιότης und ἐναντιότης über, wie v. A. S. 107 richtig hervorhebt. Eine direkte Rückverweisung steht erst beim Übergang zum folgenden, da allerdings unverkennbar (1159b 24 = 1155b 8). Das Verhältnis zwischen *Eud.* und *Nik. Ethik* ist wieder eindeutig; wir haben es zum Schluß mit einer aus einem Abflauen des Interesses zu begreifenden Änderung der Vortragsweise, nicht mit einer gedanklichen Diskrepanz zu tun. Der Verfasser der *Gr. Ethik* dagegen wirft von vornherein 1210a 6ff. ἰσότης — ἀνισότης (ὑπεροχή) einerseits und ὁμοιότης — ἐναντιότης andererseits durcheinander, so daß eine heillose Verwirrung entsteht, bei der auch v. A.s Verständnis aussetzt („Das ist wohl ein kleines Versehen" S. 104. | „Hier bleibt eine Unklarheit" S. 105) und die als urwüchsig erweisen zu wollen vergebliche Mühe ist.

Wer sich nicht bedingungslos dem Glauben an die Priorität der *Gr. Ethik* hingibt, der wird die Verwirrung sein lassen, was sie ist, zumal die Veranlassung zu greifen ist. Der Verfasser der *Gr. Ethik* hat bei seiner Vorbereitung auf ein neues Kapitel die entsprechende Partie der *Nik. Ethik* durchgelesen und hat dabei natürlich nicht 1159b 1, sondern erst bei dem deutlichen Übergang 1159b 24 haltgemacht, und so ist das Unglück geschehen, daß er zwei verschiedenartige Abschnitte ineinanderzog, was ihm, soweit er sich überhaupt darüber klar geworden ist, dann ja wohl als eine Verbesserung oder Vereinfachung erschienen sein wird. Nicht nur hier scheint ihn das Nebeneinander seiner beiden Vorlagen eher verwirrt oder leichtsinnig gemacht als gefördert zu haben.

II 3 (S. 109—124). Wir kommen zum Kernstück der v. A.schen Schrift. „Es ist die jetzt folgende Partie des Lehrganges, an der mir das Verhältnis der drei Ethiken zueinander zuerst klar und dadurch die Echtheit der M. Mor. sowohl wie der Eud. zur Gewißheit wurde."

Der Tatbestand, um den es sich handelt, ist einigermaßen kompliziert. In der *Eud. Ethik* folgt 1240a 8 auf die Erörterung der ὁμοιότης

und ἐναντιότης ein Abschnitt über die Liebe des einzelnen zu sich
selbst, in den einbezogen ist die Auseinandersetzung mit gewissen
dem Vortragenden und seinen Hörern aus dialektischen Übungen bekannten Freundschaftsmerkmalen, die sich untereinander nicht recht
zu vertragen scheinen: Freund ist 1. wer dem anderen Gutes oder vermeintlich Gutes nicht aus eigenem Interesse, sondern um jenes willen
wünscht, 2. wer die Existenz des anderen um dessentwillen wünscht,
3. wer das συζῆν mit dem anderen eben um dieses Verkehres willen
und nicht aus irgendeinem anderen Interesse sucht, 4. wer mit dem
anderen uneigennützig Mitleid und Mitfreude empfindet (diese vier
auch *E. N.* 1166a 1ff., in der *Gr. Ethik* 1210b 23—1211a 22 tritt
wiederholt neben die Existenz, das ζῆν, als fünftes noch das εὖ ζῆν).
Dann folgt die Behandlung der mit der Freundschaft verwandten Begriffe εὔνοια und ὁμόνοια, dann eine scheinbar isoliert stehende Aporie,
warum der Wohltäter größere Liebe zu empfinden pflege als der Be-
dachte, darauf 1241b 10 abgesetzt ein langer Abschnitt über das
δίκαιον in der Freundschaft (—1244a 36); zuletzt steht ein Nachtrag
(1244a 31—36, an passender Stelle aufgenommen E. N. 1164a 6ff.);
unmittelbar davor (1244a 20—30) in erkennbarem Anschluß an Vor-
hergehendes eine nochmalige Erwähnung jener Freundschaftsmerkmale — nicht berücksichtigt bei v. A. —, und dann folgen Abschnitte
περὶ αὐταρκείας καὶ φιλίας, περὶ πολυφιλίας, endlich einer über das Teil- |
nehmen- bzw. Nichtteilnehmenlassenwollen des Freundes an Glück
und Unglück. Die letzten drei Stücke bilden auch in der *Nik. Ethik*
den Schluß (1169b 3ff.), aber der Abschnitt über das δίκαιον ist nach
vorn gerückt (1159b 24—1165b 36 vor 1166a 1ff.), so daß jetzt die
vier Freundschaftsmerkmale nur einmal vorkommen, und zwar an
der Stelle, die jener zweiten Erwähnung der *Eud. Ethik* entspricht.
Hier hat eine bewußte Umgruppierung stattgefunden[4], und zwar liegt,
wie auch v. A. mit Recht hervorhebt, in der *Eud. Ethik* eine ältere An-
ordnung vor als in der *Nik. Ethik.* — Auch in der *Gr. Ethik* stehen die
Abschnitte περὶ αὐταρκείας, περὶ πολυφιλίας gegen Ende des Erhaltenen, aber darauf folgt, unter Übergehung des Abschnittes über
Teilnahme des Freundes an Glück und Unglück, der Anfang der Erörterung einer Frage, die nach den beiden anderen Ethiken in den Abschnitt über das δίκαιον gehören würde (in der *Gr. Ethik* selbst wäre
der Anschlußpunkt 1211b 17 gewesen, vgl. *E. E.* 1242a 19—1243b
14). Einen selbständigen Abschnitt über das δίκαιον hat die *Gr.*

---

[4] Zugleich eine gewisse Veränderung der Ausdrucks- und Anschauungsweise, indem
in der *Nik. Ethik* nicht mehr Freundschaft zu sich selbst, εὔνοια und ὁμόνοια als
etwa noch in Betracht kommende εἴδη φιλίας behandelt werden, sondern alles
unter dem Titel φιλικά ‚Dinge, die zur Freundschaft dazugehören' nachgebracht
wird.

Ethik überhaupt nicht, wohl aber zwei kurze Stücke (1211a 6—15.
1211b 4—20) in Verfilzung mit dem, was in der *Eud. Ethik* gesondert
davorsteht und in der *Nik. Ethik* gesondert folgt. Grob gesagt ist der
Tatbestand also der: Nach der Erörterung des ὅμοιον und ἐναντίον hat
in der *Eud. Ethik* ein Abschnitt, der mit der Liebe zu sich selbst und
den Freundschaftsmerkmalen beginnt, in der *Nik. Ethik* der Abschnitt
über das δίκαιον den Vortritt, in der *Gr. Ethik* aber wird gleich beides
in schwerverständlicher Weise durcheinandergemengt. v. A. glaubt
nun den Nachweis führen zu können, daß wir es gerade in der *Gr.
Ethik* „mit einem planvollen, aus dem Denken des Vortragenden er-
wachsenden Aufbau zu tun haben, nicht etwa mit zusammenhanglosen
Einzelabschnitten, die von einem ungeschickten und den Zusammenhang der Lehre selbst nicht begreifenden Kompilator aneinanderge-
reiht sind" (S. 113). Des weiteren hören wir, „daß die Gedanken des
Verfassers, als er diese Vorlesung entwarf, sich zum Teil noch in statu
nascendi befanden", und die Vergleichung der eud. und nik. Ethik soll
uns zeigen, „wie die in den M. Mor. noch unentwickelten Keime sich
entfaltet haben" (S. 116).

Dem ersten Blick bietet die *Gr. Ethik* fraglos ein Durcheinander. Zunächst
werden 1210b 23 die Freundschaftsmerkmale erwähnt; sie gehen bisweilen nicht
zusammen, und wir werden belehrt, daß man sie auf die vollkommene, die Tugend-
freundschaft, beziehen könne oder müsse, bei der fänden sie sich | alle. Dann wird
1210b 33 die Frage, ob es Freundschaft zu sich selbst gäbe, scheinbar nur aufgeworfen, um zurückgeschoben zu werden, findet aber gleichwohl, wenn auch in vor-
sichtiger Form, schon die Lösung, die an der späteren Stelle einfach wiederholt
wird, mit dem einzigen Unterschied, daß das zweite Mal das Resultat sicher ist
(1211a 24) und weiter ausgeführt wird. Fürs erste begnügt sich der Verfasser mit
der Feststellung, daß, wenn wir von den fünf Merkmalen redeten, wir dabei entweder auf die Freundschaft zu uns selbst oder auf die vollkommene Bezug nähmen,
bei beiden wären eben allesamt vorhanden. Dann kommt etwas anderes: vielleicht
könnte man glauben, wo es ein δίκαιον gäbe, da sei auch Freundschaft; also: wieviel
Arten δίκαια, so viele Arten Freundschaft. In Übereinstimmung mit einem Kapitel
aus der eigenen früheren Behandlung der δικαιοσύνη (1194b 5ff.) werden vier Arten
des δίκαιον aufgezählt und vorweg noch eine fünfte, das δίκαιον im Verhältnis des
ξένος zum πολίτης. Für die entsprechende Freundschaft hat der Verfasser aus irgend-
welchem Grunde eine Vorliebe (in der *Eud. Ethik* fehlt die ξενική, in der *Nik. Ethik*
hat, wie es scheint, jemand sie vermißt und an zwei Stellen unterzubringen versucht:
1156a 30f. 1161b 15f.); sie soll — das wird angeschlossen — die sicherste sein, was
mit einem eigenen Gedanken begründet wird. ‚Und im Anschluß hieran dürfte es
jetzt an der Zeit sein', so lesen wir, halb vorbereitet, halb verwundert, daß das so
schnell und gerade jetzt kommt, ‚die Frage zu entscheiden, ob es eine Freundschaft
zu sich selbst gibt.' Es folgt 1. die schon erwähnte Begründung mit dem diesmal
sicheren Resultat, 2. als Parallele (ὥσπερ καὶ .. 1211a 24) die im Kapitel über die
δικαιοσύνη behandelte Möglichkeit der Ungerechtigkeit gegen sich selbst, die auf dem
Vorhandensein *mehrerer* Seelenteile, die uneinig sein können, beruht, 3. in Form
einer Begründung (ἐπειδὴ γὰρ ... 1211a 31) unter Berufung auf die Redensart μία
ψυχή der Satz, daß Freundschaft zu sich selbst dann stattfinde, wenn die Seelenteile in Harmonie wären, so daß jetzt schnurrigerweise herauskommt: ὥστε μιᾶς

γενομένης (τῆς ψυχῆς) ἔσται πρὸς αὐτὸν φιλία[5]. Aber durch diese Wendung sind wir dann beim σπουδαῖος, bei dem allein es also eine Freundschaft zu sich selbst gibt, während beim Schlechten, der nie mit sich selbst einig ist, davon nicht die Rede sein kann. Wieder bricht es ab. Wir bekommen den Unterschied einer φιλία ἐν ἰσότητι und ἐν ἀνισότητι, von dem der vorhergehende Hauptteil in Vermischung mit dem Unterschied καθ' ὁμοιότητα und κατ' ἐναντιότητα handelte, noch einmal vorgesetzt, nur wird jetzt mit Beispielen exemplifiziert, die man als δικαίων εἴδη auffassen kann; insofern scheint Anschluß an das Stückchen 1211a 6—15 beabsichtigt; neu ergibt sich dann der ungeschickt eingeführte Satz, im Falle der ἀνισότης käme die zu fordernde Gleichheit dadurch zustande, daß dem Besseren mehr und dem Schlechteren weniger Gutes erwiesen würde. In den beiden anderen Ethiken entsprechen Kapitel über die möglichen Rechtsstreitereien im Falle der καθ' ὑπεροχὴν φιλία | (E. E. 1242b 2—21. E. N. Θ 16); daneben, in der Eud. Ethik dahinter, in der Nik. davor, steht je ein Kapitel über solche Schwierigkeiten bei der φιλία κατ' ἰσότητα, das könnte auch in der Gr. Ethik anschließen, kommt aber, wie schon bemerkt, erst ganz am Ende des Erhaltenen. Statt dessen führt ein seltsamer Übergang[6] zu der Aporie: Warum liebt der Vater den Sohn mehr als der Sohn den Vater? Die Lösung erfolgt im Einklang mit E. N. 1167b 17ff., überhaupt lenkt die Gr. Ethik von hier ab in das Fahrwasser der Nik. Ethik (wenn auch spezielle Anklänge an die Eud. Ethik nicht fehlen), nur daß die Aporie vor εὔνοια und ὁμόνοια zu stehen kommt, nicht wie dort dahinter.

Wenden wir uns v. A.s Deutung zu. Da nach ihm die gr. Ethik ihre eigentliche Aufgabe in der Lösung jener beiden Aporien gesehen haben soll, „so könnte man meinen, der Gegenstand wäre nun erschöpft". Aus dieser Erwägung heraus, die natürlich höchstens für die Gr. Ethik gilt, gewinnt er einen „Leitgedanken" für den mit 1210b 23 beginnenden Teil: es gilt die im ersten Teil entwickelte „Fundamentaltheorie" gegen mögliche Einwendungen zu sichern. Zu dem Zweck werden zunächst einige andere Formen der Freundschaft, „von denen man spricht und die man dafür hält", an die Fundamentaltheorie gehalten und zu ihr in ein Verhältnis gebracht. Das Stichwort (ὑπὲρ τῶν ἄλλων φιλιῶν τῶν λεγομένων καὶ δοκουσῶν) bringt allerdings erst der Übergang zur ὁμόνοια und εὔνοια (1211b 40, vgl. E. E. 1240b 38ff.), aber man muß

---

[5] In den beiden anderen Ethiken fehlt die Ableitung der Freundschaft zu sich selbst aus dem Vorhandensein der Freundschaftsmerkmale (1), weil umgekehrt die Freundschaftsmerkmale auf das Verhalten zu sich selbst zurückgeführt werden; die Möglichkeit der Freundschaft zu sich selbst wird lediglich aus der Annahme einer Mehrheit von Seelenteilen (2) erklärt (E. E. 1240a 13—21. b 28—34; in der Nik. Ethik zurückgedrängt 1166a 34), während der Gedanke der συμφωνία (3) diese Freundschaft auf die Guten beschränkt (E. F. 1240b 11ff. E. N. 1166a 10ff.). Nur so bleiben die Gedankenverbindungen natürlich, was der Verfasser der Gr. Ethik allerdings schwerlich würde einsehen wollen.

[6] ‚Von allen den genannten Freundschaften findet sich das φιλεῖν wohl im höchsten Maße bei der Freundschaft zwischen Verwandten (die direkt nicht genannt war), und hier wieder bei der, die der Vater zum Sohn hegt. Und wie kommt es nur, daß der Vater den Sohn mehr liebt' usw. (1211b 18ff.). Das Naheliegende, daß die größere Liebe des Vaters in einem auffallenden und der Erklärung bedürftigen Widerspruch zu dem unmittelbar vorhergehenden Prinzip des Ausgleichs bei der Freundschaft von Ungleichen steht, wird also nicht gesagt.

zugeben, daß, soweit der Verfasser der *Gr. Ethik* sich bei seiner Gedankenführung etwas gedacht hat — und etwas total Sinnloses wird ja niemand erwarten —, es in der dadurch gewiesenen Richtung liegt. Aber für die Frage der Ursprünglichkeit hängt nun alles daran, ob der Leitgedanke auch vorher schon einigermaßen deutlich und natürlich, wenn nicht zum Ausdruck, so doch zur Auswirkung kommt.

Zunächst wird die Erwartung befriedigt. Es paßt, wenn die Freundschaftsmerkmale statt auf Freundschaft überhaupt, was Schwierigkeiten macht, auf die τελεία φιλία bezogen werden[7]. Aber daneben | tritt die andere Möglichkeit, die fünf Merkmale auf das Verhalten des einzelnen zu sich selbst zurückzuführen. Der Verfasser beruhigt sich bei der Alternative (1211a 1—5). v. A. bemüht sich vergeblich, durch Supplierung von Gedanken zu zeigen, daß vorläufig alles in der Schwebe bleibe. Was in der Schwebe bleiben soll, sagt der Verfasser deutlich selbst: die Frage, ob es eine πρὸς αὑτὸν φιλία gibt. Daß es ein den fünf Merkmalen entsprechendes Wollen sich selbst gegenüber gibt, erkennt er an, und wenn er bei Aufstellung der Alternative gleichwohl den Ausdruck εἰς τὴν πρὸς ἡμᾶς αὑτοὺς φιλίαν wählt, so ist das eine durch die Verweisung auf das folgende nur entschuldigte Ungeschicklichkeit, die in beiden anderen Ethiken an entsprechender Stelle vermieden ist (*E. E.* 1240a 23 ἀπὸ τῆς πρὸς αὑτὸν ἕξεως. *E. N.* 1166a 2 ἐκ τῶν πρὸς ἑαυτόν). Wie es kommt, daß wir die fünf Verhaltungsweisen als Freundschaftsmerkmale zu betrachten gewohnt sind, ist erledigt: wir denken entweder an das Verhalten zu uns selbst oder an die vollkommene Freundschaft und übertragen, was in beiden Fällen gilt, auf Freundschaft überhaupt. Tatsächlich behandelt der Abschnitt 1211a 16—b 3 lediglich die Frage πότερον ἔστι πρὸς αὑτὸν φιλία ἢ οὔ, mit dem Endresultat, daß es sie nur beim σπουδαῖος gibt, wodurch wir *nicht* bei der τελεία (zwischen zweien) anlangen. Keine Spur von dem komplizierten Gedankenzusammenhang, durch den v. A. die einfache Vor- und Rückverweisung (1210b 34 und 1211a 16) glaubt ersetzen zu dürfen. Ich muß wenigstens den Schluß seiner Ausführungen (S. 114) hersetzen:

---

[7] Die ersten Zeilen 1210b 23—25 sind so unbestimmt und kurz, daß es wenig Zweck hat, darüber zu streiten. v. A. meint, es müßten gleich alle fünf Merkmale aufgeführt gewesen sein, und ergänzt entsprechend. Aber auch dann bleibt der Satz οὔκ ἐστιν δὲ ἡ ἐπὶ τούτων γινομένη φιλία πάντα ταῦτα (oder ταὐτὰ) ἔχουσα so vage ausgedrückt, daß er keine genaue Übersetzung verträgt. In Z. 26 ἀλλὰ ταῦτα πότερον φιλίας δεῖ εἰπεῖν ἢ τῆς τελείας φιλίας τῆς κατ᾿ ἀρετὴν πάθη; fasse ich trotz des Plurals τοιαῦται φιλίαι Z. 23, der durch die zwischenstehende Wendung ἡ ἐπὶ τούτων γινομένη φιλία schon verwischt ist, auch das erste φιλίας als gen. sing. (vgl. *E. E.* 1244a 20f.). Es kommt nicht viel darauf an, und ich will die Möglichkeit der Wiedergabe ,,diese sogen. Freundschaften will er nicht als wirkliche Freundschaften gelten lassen'' nicht unbedingt bestreiten.

„Es hatte sich aber daneben" — nämlich neben der Rückführung auf die τελεία — „die Möglichkeit geboten, jene fünf φιλικά aus dem Verhältnis des Menschen zu sich selbst abzuleiten. Wenn jeder Mensch in seinem Verhalten sich selbst gegenüber diese fünf Merkmale zeigte, dann wäre in der Tat bewiesen, daß sie mit Tugend nichts zu schaffen haben; und da die reine selbstlose, nur das Wohl des anderen um des anderen willen wollende Liebe auch auf das Streben nach Nutzen oder Lust nicht zurückgeführt werden kann, so wäre die Fundamentaltheorie widerlegt. Der Nachweis aber, daß nur der Tugendhafte sein eigener Freund ist und in seinem Verhalten zu sich selbst jene fünf φιλικά πάθη aufweist, macht diese Widerlegung zunichte und verwandelt sie in eine Bestätigung. Die Gefühle, die der Mensch sogar sich selbst gegenüber nur fühlen kann, wenn er tugendhaft ist, die kann er natürlich erst recht einem anderen gegenüber nur fühlen, wenn *dieser* gut und tugendhaft ist. Ὃς αὐτὸς αὑτὸν οὐ φιλεῖ, πῶς ἄλλον ἂν φιλοίη; Jene φιλικά der reinen selbstlosen Liebe sind also wirklich nur Attribute der vollkommenen Freundschaft, die nur zwischen Tugendhaften bestehen kann." |

Ich kann nur wiederholen, daß all dies in dem zu interpretierenden Text mit keinem Wort angedeutet ist.

Für die beiden mit den besprochenen so eigentümlich verschränkten Abschnitte 1211a 6—15 und 1211b 4—39 soll zugestanden werden, daß im ersten „eine ganze Reihe weiterer φιλίαι angeführt werden, von denen es nicht ohne weiteres klar ist, wie sie sich in die Fundamentaltheorie einordnen lassen" (S. 113), und es soll ebenfalls zugestanden werden, daß der zweite den ersten irgendwie weiterführen will. Aber v. A. gibt seinerseits zu, daß der Verfasser „leider versäumt, sich klar über ihr Verhältnis zu den drei Hauptarten der eigentlichen Freundschaft auszusprechen" (S. 115), und es wirkt alles andere als überzeugend, wie, um wenigstens eine Spur der Bezugnahme auf die Fundamentaltheorie zu konstatieren, die Worte 1211b 18 τῶν δὲ φιλιῶν ἁπασῶν τῶν εἰρημένων τούτων μάλιστά πως ἐγγίνεται τὸ φιλεῖν ἐν τῇ συγγενικῇ gepreßt werden: „Das φιλεῖν und ἀντιφιλεῖν gehört nach der Fundamentaltheorie zur φιλία. Wenn es also bei der hier behandelten Gruppe auf die συγγενική eingeschränkt wird, so heißt das: in den anderen Arten dieser Gruppe ist wenig oder kein φιλεῖν enthalten. Sie sind also nur λεγόμεναι καὶ δοκοῦσαι φιλίαι." Wieder steht, was man erwarten müßte, nicht im Text. Über die Anreihung der die Liebe von Vater und Sohn betreffenden Aporie bemerkt v. A.: „Dadurch kommt hier ganz beiläufig und gelegentlich ein für die Liebestheorie wichtiges allgemeines Gesetz zur Sprache, das wohl eine nicht bloß gelegentliche Erwähnung verdient hätte. Wir ersehen daraus, daß die Gedanken des Verfassers, als er diese Vorlesung entwarf, sich zum Teil noch in statu nascendi befanden." Ich würde das annehmbar finden, wenn wir es mit einer „gelegentlichen Erwähnung" in dem Sinn zu tun hätten, daß bei natürlicher Gedankenführung ein wichtiges Problem auftauchte, ohne erledigt zu werden. Es ist aber fast umgekehrt: der Übergang ist erzwungen und die Behandlung ist abschließend, nur wird allerdings das Problem nicht allgemein gestellt.

Obwohl es in der Tat für den Zweck der Untersuchung wichtig wäre einzusehen, daß wir es mit einem planvollen, aus dem Denken des Vortragenden erwachsenden Aufbau zu tun hätten (S. 113), so liegt an Tatsächlichem nur das Eine vor, daß von den vier untersuchten Abschnitten der erste durch den dritten und der zweite durch den vierten irgendwie weitergeführt wird, aber weder geschieht das im Sinne jenes „Leitgedankens", noch wird das Erstaunlichste, die sonderbare Verschränkung selbst, erklärt; man müßte sich schon dabei beruhigen, daß in statu nascendi die Gedanken noch etwas durcheinandergehen. Aber wo bleibt dann der planvolle Aufbau? |

Auf die entsprechenden Partien der beiden anderen Ethiken geht v. A. nur so weit ein, als er glaubt, für die Prioritätsfrage Entscheidendes nachweisen zu können, und wir werden uns dieser Beschränkung auf einzelne Punkte in freier Weise anschließen. Ich numeriere:

1. Wenn dem früheren Teil der *Eud. Ethik* 1240a 5—1241b 9 der spätere der *Nik.* 1166a 1—1168a 27, und dem späteren Teil der *Eud.* 1241b 10—1244a 36 der frühere der *Nik. Ethik* entspricht (S. 117), die *Große Ethik* aber beides, soweit sie es hat, ineinander verfilzt in einem Teil bringt, so kann ich, solange der Prioritätsbeweis nicht auf andere Weise geführt ist, darin nur eine Folge des Nebeneinanders jener beiden Vorlagen sehen, das einen Epigonen sowohl verwirren wie zu Eigenmächtigkeiten ermutigen konnte[8]. Aber v. A. meint, daß in der *Eud. Ethik* der Zusammenhang der drei Abschnitte ihres ersten Teiles (über die πρὸς αὑτὸν φιλία, über εὔνοια und ὁμόνοια, über die Liebe des εὐεργετήσας zum εὐεργετηθείς) nur erkennbar wäre, wenn man die *Gr. Ethik* zu Hilfe nähme. Indessen für die beiden ersten Abschnitte genügt ein Hinweis auf die Übergänge 1240a 5ff. 1240b 38ff., die an Deutlichkeit nichts zu wünschen übriglassen. Die Aporie 1241a 35—b 9 steht nur scheinbar isoliert. Da das Wort δίκαιον fällt (1241a 37), hat sie eine gewisse Beziehung zum Folgenden, wichtiger ist der Zusammenhang mit allem Bisherigen. Es handelt sich um eine auffallende Freundschaftserscheinung, für deren Erklärung man sich, wenn man nicht Aristoteles wäre, bei dem Nützlichkeitsprinzip beruhigen könnte (τοῦτο δ᾽ ὑπολάβοι μὲν ἄν τις διὰ τὸ χρήσιμον καὶ τὸ αὐτῷ ὠφέλιμον συμβαίνειν); dann paßte sie ohne weiteres in die Lehre von den εἴδη φιλίας. Nur für ihn selbst tut sie es nicht: wo sollte er das hinstellen, wenn er, wie seine Worte beweisen, sich des Zusammenhanges bewußt war? Ist die Stellung am Schluß unnatürlicher als jene „gelegentliche Erwähnung" in der *Gr. Ethik*[9]?

---

[8] Daß er sich ein klares Bild von dem Verhältnis ihrer jeweiligen Verschiedenheiten hätte machen sollen, wäre viel verlangt; die moderne Wissenschaft verbraucht nachgerade Zeit genug an der Aufgabe, das aufzuarbeiten; daß er, wenn er zwei Vorlagen hatte, die eine oder die andere hätte unberücksichtigt lassen sollen, wird man auch nicht fordern.

[9] Wer die *Nik. Ethik* als Vorlage der *Gr.* gelten lassen darf, für den löst sich das Rätsel, das letztere aufgibt, mit dem Kapitel *E. N.* 1161b 11ff. über die συγγενικὴ und ἑταιρικὴ φιλία. Denn hier führt die Untersuchung *zwanglos* auf die grundlegende Bedeutung der πατρικὴ φιλία und die größere Liebe der Eltern zu ihren Kindern. Das brachte den Verfasser der *Gr. Ethik* auf den Gedanken, die eigentlich selb-

2. v. A. muß behaupten, die Abschnitte *M. M.* 1211a 6—15. 1211b 4—17 (und 1213b 18ff., füge ich hinzu) seien die Keime, aus denen die *Eud. Ethik* zuerst die große Abhandlung über Recht und Freundschaft entwickelt habe. Das soll zur Gewißheit werden durch die Beobachtung, daß die *Eud. Ethik* „in der Vorrede des Freundschaftsbuches *H* 1234b 22—31 die politische Be|deutung der Freundschaft und die nahe Verwandtschaft der Begriffe φιλία und δικαιοσύνη so unverhältnismäßig stark" hervorhebt (S. 118). Hier brauche ich nur zu interpretieren. Die Beobachtung wird zum Argument, weil auch der Beweis der Priorität der *Eud. Ethik* vor der *Nik.* v. A. noch am Herzen liegt, zum Argument also für das ‚zuerst'; die Priorität der *Gr. Ethik* vor beiden ist dabei Voraussetzung. Denn die Vorrede der *Eud. Ethik* beweist weder allein noch mit der der *Nik. Ethik* zusammengenommen, daß eine andersartige Behandlung vorausgegangen wäre.

3. Die *Nik.* und die *Gr. Ethik* haben je einen Abschnitt über die φιλαυτία in gleicher Stellung und dispositioneller Funktion, der in der *Eud. Ethik* fehlt. v. A. bemüht sich zu zeigen, wie es kommen konnte, daß die φιλαυτία in der *Eud. Ethik* ausfiel, um dann in der *Nik. Ethik* wieder dieselbe Stellung zu bekommen wie in der *Gr. Ethik.* Aber er gerät dabei in Verteidigungsstellung: „Man darf also aus dem Umstand, daß die M. Mor., die im allgemeinen mehr Ähnlichkeit mit den Eud. zeigen, hier einmal mit den Nik. zusammengehen, nicht schließen, daß sie die beiden anderen Ethiken nebeneinander benützt haben, in welchem Fall der Verfasser nur ein nach Aristoteles' Tode schreibender jüngerer Peripatetiker gewesen sein könnte, sondern man muß als möglich anerkennen, daß der Philosoph, als er die Nik. schrieb, gelegentlich einmal über die Eud. hinweg auf noch ältere Aufzeichnungen zurückgreifen konnte." Dazu muß bemerkt werden, daß die Stellen, wo die *Gr. Ethik* gegen die *Eud.* mit der *Nik.* zusammengeht, zahllos sind, so daß man mehr „als möglich anerkennen" müßte, als hier zugegeben wird.

4. In der *Eud. Ethik* wären nach v. A. durch die Verselbständigung des Abschnittes über das δίκαιον in der φιλία zwei neue Fugen entstanden, 1241b 10 und 1244b 1. An der ersten Stelle ist mit dem besten Willen nichts auszusetzen. „Dagegen finden wir in der anderen Fuge einen sehr harten Übergang von einem Werkstück zum anderen 1244b 1: σκεπτέον δὲ καὶ περὶ αὐταρκείας καὶ φιλίας, πῶς ἔχουσι πρὸς τὰς ἀλλήλων δυνάμεις." Diese Beobachtung ist richtig. Wenn wie in der *Eud. Ethik* der Abschnitt über die πρὸς αὑτὸν φιλία vom Schluß der ganzen Abhandlung durch den Abschnitt über das δίκαιον getrennt war, dann war ein Hingleiten über die φιλαυτία zur αὐτάρκεια, wie man es in beiden andern Ethiken, wenn auch mit Störungen, finden kann, ausgeschlossen, es sei denn, man wollte vom Verfasser der *Eud. Ethik* verlangen, daß er den ganzen Schlußteil vor den Abschnitt über das δίκαιον hätte hinsetzen sollen, wo jetzt mit Recht nur die Aporie über die εὖ ποιήσαντες steht. Die Beobachtung bedarf aber der Ergänzung. Nur getrennt durch den Nachtrag 1244a 31—36 erscheinen in der *Eud. Ethik* vor der Fuge nicht ohne Anschluß an das Vorausgehende die vier Freundschafts-ὅροι zum zweiten Male (1244a 20—30). *Diesen* Dispositionsmangel erklärt v. A.s Hypothese nicht, denn der Stellung nach entspricht nur *E. N. I* 4. Es ergäbe sich also folgende Komplikation: infolge Verselbständigung des Abschnittes über das δίκαιον in der *Eud. Ethik* wäre ein ursprüng-

ständige Aporie an die Erwähnung der συγγενική anzuschließen; dabei schränkt sie sich entgegen den beiden anderen Ethiken auf das Verhältnis vom Vater zum Sohn ein, das bei der selbständigen Behandlung gar nicht die Hauptsache war, oder vielmehr eigentlich erst in die Lösung hineingehört: *E. E.* 1241a 34ff.; die *Nik. Ethik,* die das Verhältnis von Eltern zu Kindern ja bereits behandelt hat, erwähnt überhaupt bloß noch die Mutter 1168b 25.

licher Zusammenhang, der von der Selbstliebe über die Selbstsucht zur Selbst-
genügsamkeit geführt hätte, so zerrissen, daß die Selbstsucht ausfiel und die Selbst-
genügsamkeit unvermittelt auftreten mußte; zufälligerweise aber wäre das neue
Kapitel über das δίκαιον in eine Wiedererwähnung der Freundschaftsmerkmale aus-
gelaufen, wodurch die Wiederherstellung jenes ursprünglichen Zusammenhanges
zwar vorbereitet, aber noch nicht verwirklicht worden wäre. — Demgegenüber wird
die Möglichkeit, daß ein erster Entwurf an einer Stelle zu einer unvorhergesehenen
Wiedererwähnung und zu einem Abreißen des Gedankenfadens führt, nicht zu be-
streiten sein. Läßt man die *Große Ethik* | beiseite, so erklärt sich allein von hier aus
die Dispositionsänderung der *Nik. Ethik*, während man im anderen Falle zugleich
mit dem leidigen Rückgriff über die *Eud. Ethik* hinweg auf die angeblich noch ältere
Fassung rechnen muß.

5. Daß in der *Eud. Ethik* auch am Anfang der Besprechung der Selbstliebe der
Übergang sehr hart wäre (S. 121), kann ich nicht finden. 1240a 5 steht eine ziemlich
genaue Rekapitulation des Vorhergehenden πόσα μὲν οὖν εἴδη φιλίας, καὶ τίνες
διαφοραὶ καθ᾽ ἅς λέγονται οἵ τε φίλοι καὶ οἱ φιλοῦντες καὶ οἱ φιλούμενοι, καὶ οὕτως
ὥστε φίλοι εἶναι καὶ ἄνευ τούτου (vgl. 1239a 4. 1242a 10), εἴρηται, um so besser hebt
sich die πρὸς αὐτὸν φιλία, die doch kein gewöhnliches εἶδος φιλίας ist, ab, vgl. 1241b
10. Nur wenn man von der *Großen Ethik* herkommt und diese für das Ursprüngliche
hält, mag man sich wundern. Während die *Eud. Ethik* die Behandlung der Freundschaftsmerkmale der Selbstliebe unterordnet, geht die *Gr. Ethik* von einem auf die
Merkmale gegründeten problematischen Freundschaftsbegriff aus, um sich erst nachträglich der Selbstliebe zu erinnern; daß der Übergang *M. M.* 1210b 23 das Zusam-
menhangsbedürfnis besser befriedigte als *E. E.* 1240a 5—9, ist eine kühne Behauptung. Was die Verschiedenheit hervorgerufen hat, läßt sich fassen: es ist die Reduktion der Freundschaftsmerkmale auf die τελεία der Guten untereinander, mit der
die *Gr. Ethik* allein steht und die sie unvermittelt neben die Reduktion auf das Verhalten des Einzelnen zu sich selbst stellt. Damit hängt noch etwas weiteres zusammen.
Es ist nämlich kein Zufall, wie v. A. (S. 110) meint, daß die *Gr. Ethik* den Zusatz zu
den Freundschaftsmerkmalen ‚um des anderen willen, nicht aus Selbstsucht' entweder wegläßt oder durch ein sinnleeres, geradezu albern wirkendes μετ᾽ οὐδενὸς
ἄλλου 1210b 29, οὐκ ἄλλῳ τινί 1210b 32. 37 ersetzt; für ihn gibt nämlich die Reduktion auf die τελεία nichts aus. In der *Eud. Ethik* war er die Hauptsache: 1240a
24—1240b 1. Nur der Zusatz machte die aus der Dialektik (in aristotelischem Sinne)
herübergenommenen τρόποι τοῦ φιλεῖν zu einer Schwierigkeit für die aristotelische
Theorie. Es handelt sich um δοκοῦντα, also um ohne weiteres einleuchtende Sätze,
die besonders hohe Ansprüche an die Freundschaft stellen und sich gleichwohl untereinander nicht vertragen (μάχεται δὴ ταῦτα πάντα πρὸς ἄλληλα 1240a 30). Wie soll
man ihr Vorhandensein im allgemeinen Bewußtsein erklären? Die Theorie von der
πρώτη φιλία liefert keine brauchbare Erklärung[10], übrigens war sie schon für die
Aufstellung der drei Freundschaftsarten verbraucht (1236a 16ff. 1237b 8f. 1238a
30). So hat sich Aristoteles mit dem gescheiten Gedanken geholfen: ἅπαντα ταῦτα
ἀναφέρεται πρὸς τὸν ἕνα (1240b 3ff.), dem logisch alles andere nachgeordnet ist,
sowohl die Einschränkung als das Verhältnis des Guten zu sich selbst, wie auch der
Schlußgedanke ὥστε καὶ ἡ πρὸς αὐτὸν φιλία ἀνάγεται πρὸς τὴν τοῦ ἀγαθοῦ, den Jaeger
(Aristoteles 254) besonders gewürdigt hat und dessen Funktion innerhalb der *Eud.
Ethik* jedenfalls die ist, auch die Freundschaft zu sich selbst dem obersten Prinzip,

---

[10] Erstens wird es Aristoteles einfach nicht für wahr gehalten haben, daß die τρόποι
von der Freundschaft der Guten untereinander abgezogen seien, und zweitens
erführe der Zusatz ἐκείνου ἕνεκα nicht die unmittelbare Erhellung, die das Verhalten
des einzelnen zu sich selbst liefert.

der πρώτη φιλία, zu unterwerfen, wie der Übergang zum folgenden ausspricht; denn bei ὅτι πᾶσαι αἱ φιλίαι ἀνάγονται πρὸς τὴν πρώτην 1240 b 38 f. kann man nicht umhin, auch an 1240 b 18 zu denken. Das bedeutet natürlich nicht, daß die Selbstliebe auf die Liebe zweier σπουδαῖοι untereinander zurückzuführen wäre, sondern wir sind in der Tat in eine überpersönliche Sphäre geraten, zu der der spätere Begriff | der τελεία (oben S. 195) den Weg versperrt. — Von der *Gr. Ethik* her ist das alles nicht zu verstehen; v. A. findet die ganze Erörterung der *Eud. Ethik* von Unklarheit durchzogen. |

II. Die einzelnen ethischen Tugenden und das Zeugnis Theophrasts (S. 124—141).

Vorweg sei bemerkt, daß, wenn in der *Gr. Ethik* sich einzelne Anklänge an Theophrastisches finden (es gibt solche Beobachtungen), dies kein Beweis für rein aristotelischen Ursprung der *Gr. Ethik* sein muß. —

In den Zeilen, die bei Stobaeus 2, 140, 15 W. anschließend an die theophrastische Erklärung des μέσον πρὸς ἡμᾶς und ein Zitat der Tugenddefinition aus der *Nik. Ethik* stehen: εἶτα παραθέμενος τινὰς συζυγίας ἀκολούθως τῷ ὑφηγητῇ σκοπεῖν ἔπειτα καθ᾽ ἕκαστα ἐπάγων ἐπειράθη τὸν τρόπον τοῦτον· ἐλήφθησαν δὲ παραδείγματος [überl. -μάτων] χάριν αἵδε· σωφροσύνη, ἀκολασία, ἀναισθησία, πραότης usw. ist Subjekt von ἐπειράθη sicher Theophrast. v. A. setzt vor ἐλήφθησαν Anführungszeichen und nimmt das Folgende als wörtliche Anführung eines von Theophrast selber gebrachten Berichtes über eine aristotelische Vorlesung. Aber ἀκολούθως τῷ ὑφηγητῇ heißt nur ,im Anschluß an seinen Lehrer'; daß dieser Anschluß in einem auf Selbständigkeit verzichtenden Referat seinen Ausdruck gefunden hätte, kann man unmöglich heraushören. Außerdem gehört es lediglich zu παραθέμενος τινὰς συζυγίας[11], die unmittelbare Wiedergabe des „Berichtes" des Theophrast würde also nur in der Syzygienaufzählung oder, da für diese die direkte bzw. indirekte Wiedergabe irrelevant ist, eigentlich nur in dem Sätzchen ἐλήφθησαν — αἵδε bestehen; die Worte σκοπεῖν ... ἐπάγων ἐπειράθη τὸν τρόπον τοῦτον bereiten unter allen Umständen auf eine von Theophrast selbst unternommene Induktion vor und werden S. 141, 3 mit τούτων δὴ τῶν ἕξεων αἱ μὲν τῷ ὑπερβάλλειν ἢ ἐλλείπειν περὶ πάθη φαῦλαί εἰσιν, αἱ δὲ σπουδαῖαι, τῷ μεσότητες εἶναι δηλονότι in direkter Rede aufgenommen, also so, daß Arius dies noch von sich aus angibt, um dann den Einzelnachweis Theophrasts in indirekter Rede folgen zu lassen: σώφρονά τε γὰρ εἶναι usw. Aber davor mußten natürlich die Syzygien aufgezählt sein; also wird 140, 17 mit ἐλήφθησαν δὲ . . auf παραθέμενός τινας συζυγίας zurückgegriffen. Das ist doch ganz lebendig und verständlich, während die Beziehung des Aoristes ἐλήφθησαν auf Aristoteles als Handelnden nach dem von

---

[11] Schreibt man mit Spengel σκοπῶν ... ἐπάγειν, so wird die Beziehung unsicher, aber ein ἀκ. τῷ ὑφ. σκοπῶν vertrüge die Deutung auf ein Referat erst recht nicht.

Theophrast geltenden ἐπειράθη nicht einmal bei Setzung von Anführungszeichen unmiß|verständlich herauskommt. Das einzige, was m. E. für v. A.s Deutung spricht, ist die wörtliche Übereinstimmung mit *E. E.* 1220b 1 εἰλήφθω δὴ παραδείγματος χάριν, worüber man nicht besser referieren könnte als mit den Worten ἐλήφθησαν δὲ π. χ., aber schließlich kann Theophrast doch auch in eigener Darstellung eine ähnliche Wendung gebraucht haben, die dann bei Arius nachklingt. Das ἀκολούθως τῷ ὑφ. deutete Von der Mühll (De Ar. Eth. Eud. auctoritate, Gött. Diss. 1909, 28) so, daß er den Arius (oder dessen Vorlage) die Übereinstimmung mit der *Eud. Ethik* konstatieren ließ. Allenfalls möglich scheint die Annahme, daß Theophrast selbst sich für die beispielshalber vorweggesetzte Syzygientafel auf die Autorität des Aristoteles berufen hatte; er hatte da für die Darstellung einen leichten Vorteil vor dem Lehrer, der die διαγραφή zunächst ohne Beglaubigung hatte vorausschicken müssen. — Gibt man diese Interpretation zu, so hätten wir freilich für den Anschluß des Theophrast an Aristoteles sein eigenes Zeugnis, aber eine Sicherheit für rein aristotelischen Ursprung aller Besonderheiten der in Frage kommenden Partie bei Stobaeus ist nicht gegeben.

Die einzelnen ethischen Tugenden nebst den entsprechenden Fehlern oder nur die letzteren werden in der *Eud. Ethik* zusammen dreimal aufgeführt: 1. beides in der Tabelle 1220b 38—1221a 12; 2. nur die ὑπερβολαί und ἐλλείψεις in einer unmittelbar folgenden kurzen Erörterung 1221a 13—1221b 3; 3. beides in der ausführlichen Besprechung des dritten Buches. Auch die *Nik. Ethik* hat drei Reihen gehabt, aber in unsern Text ist die vom Verfasser vorausgesetzte διαγραφή (1107a 32f.) nicht aufgenommen; übrigens werden hier in der kurzen Erörterung auch die Tugenden geführt. Im Text der *Gr. Ethik* findet sich nur 3., dagegen bringt Arius bei Stobaeus aus Theophrast offenbar 1. und 2. — v. A. gibt zunächst eine tabellarische Zusammenstellung und sorgfältige Besprechung der möglichen Vergleichspunkte. Leider ist ihm bezüglich der *Gr. Ethik* ein Versehen passiert. 1190b 7 werden der Einzelbehandlung der ethischen Tugenden, zunächst der ἀνδρεία, vorausgeschickt die Worte ἐπεὶ δὲ μεσότητάς τινας τῶν παθῶν κατηριθμησάμεθα, λεκτέον ἂν εἴη περὶ ποῖα τῶν παθῶν εἰσιν. Hieran hat man angestoßen: „1185b 21—30. 1186a 17—35. b 5—32 plura attulit exempla, sed exempla afferre non est καταριθμεῖσθαι" F. Susemihl, Aristotelis quae feruntur Magna Moralia, Leipzig 1883, 125. Außerdem schien der Anfang des Kapitels über die ἀνδρεία verstümmelt. Es ist schwer zu entscheiden, ob man in der *Gr. Ethik* nicht beides sich einfach gefallen lassen muß. Wenn aber v. A. behauptet, wir müßten auf Grund der beiden anderen Ethiken „gerade an dieser Stelle des Lehrgangs" eine Tabelle der Tugendsyzygien erwarten, und dann weiterhin diese Tabelle vor dem be|anstandeten Sätzchen, das er für einen Rest des Ursprünglichen hält, und eine kurze Übersicht *hinter* ihm ausgefallen sein läßt, so ist die Grundlage falsch. Denn nach Analogie der beiden anderen Ethiken können wir an *dieser* Stelle nichts anderes erwarten, als was dazustehen scheint, einen kurzen mehr oder weniger abrupten Übergang (*E. E.* 1228a 23. *E. N.* 1114b 26); die Tabelle mit anschließender Übersicht müßte vor dem Abschnitt über ἑκούσιον und προαίρεσις gestanden haben: das tat sie aber sicher nicht, wie die von Susemihl zitierten Stellen beweisen.

Dagegen wird unumstößlich dargetan, ,,daß Theophrast nicht die Nik., sondern eine ältere, mehr den Eud. oder M. Mor. ähnliche Fassung der ethischen Vorlesungen des Aristoteles als Vorlage benützt hat" (S. 133). Genaueste Vergleichung soll dann erweisen, daß die Vorlage des Theophrast doch weder der eudemische Text[12] noch der der *Gr. Ethik*, sondern nur eine vierte Fassung der Ethikvorlesung, ,,wahrscheinlich die, die er selbst bei seinem Lehrer gehört hatte", gewesen sein könne. Das ruht auf der von mir in Zweifel gezogenen Prämisse, daß bei Stobaeus ein von Arius wörtlich zitierter ,,Bericht" des Theophrast stände, den wir seinerseits ,,als wörtliche Wiedergabe eines aristotelischen Textes anzusehen" berechtigt wären (S. 136), und mag, da es direkt für die These der Echtheit und Priorität der *Gr. Ethik* nichts ausgibt, dahingestellt bleiben. Aber inwiefern nun indirekt das Zeugnis des Theophrast doch die Echtheit der Gr. Ethik beweisen soll, darauf ist man nach den Vorbereitungen gespannt.

1. Der Verfasser der *Nik. Ethik* zeigt sich äußerst empfindlich gegen die Tatsache, daß ihm der Sprachgebrauch für eine ganze Reihe von ὑπερβολαί und ἐλλείψεις, die er der Theorie der μεσότης zuliebe aufstellen muß, einen festen Terminus nicht zur Verfügung stellt. Daher immer wieder die Betonung der Anonymie (πολλὰ δ᾽ ἐστὶν ἀνώνυμα heißt es entschuldigend bei erster Gelegenheit 1107b 1) und vorsichtigste Ausdrucksweise, wenn gleichwohl das eine oder andere einigermaßen passende Wort zur terminologischen Bezeichnung gewählt wird, was er andererseits doch nötig findet σαφηνείας ἕνεκα καὶ τοῦ εὐπαρακολουθήτου (1108a 18). Die *Eud. Ethik* macht allerdings nicht ganz soviel Aufhebens von der Anonymie, aber es ist doch dieselbe

---

[12] Eine Einzelheit: ,,Die theophrastische Darstellung ist der Form nach, trotz der inhaltlichen Ähnlichkeit, insofern von der *Eudemischen* durchgängig verschieden, als sie die Tugend von den schädlichen Extremen aus, die *Eudemische* dagegen die Laster von der richtigen Mitte aus erklären will" (S. 135). Das stimmt nicht: die *Eud. Ethik* bringt 1221a 15ff. lediglich die ὑπερβολαί und ἐλλείψεις, um in ihrem dritten Buch zunächst immer wieder aus deren Vorhandensein auf die richtige Mitte zu schließen (1228a 36. 1231a 35. 1231b 15. 1231b 33. 1232b 32), macht es also im Grunde genau wie Theophrast.

Art | und Weise. Daß die *Nik. Ethik* gegenüber der *Eud.* einiges Terminologische ändert, ist unter diesen Umständen nur zu erwarten. Die *Gr. Ethik* kennt solche Vorsicht nicht. Sie ist „noch frei" von solchem Schwanken, sagt v. A. (S. 137), „wie es bei der ersten Konzeption der Theorie natürlich ist". Es ist schwer, hier mitzudenken; bisher hat man die Sache immer umgekehrt angesehen. Aber das Bestimmende ist für v. A. offenbar, daß „auch das theophrastische Exzerpt unbedenklich überall die Ausdrücke der M. Mor. gebraucht". Schon vorher hat er als wichtigsten Punkt hervorgehoben, daß Theophrast „die ὑπερβολή der μεγαλοπρέπεια, wie die M. Mor., schlechtweg und ohne einen anderen Ausdruck zur Wahl zu stellen, σαλακωνία nennt". Sieht man sich den Text bei Stobaeus an, so fragt man sich vergeblich, wie darin ein Bedenken gegen die Wahl des Ausdrucks hätte Platz finden sollen. In der διαγραφή doch sicher nicht, und die nachfolgende Erörterung benennt lediglich die Tugenden, wo es kein Schwanken gab, während die ὑπερβολαί und ἐλλείψεις konsequent unbezeichnet bleiben, bis auf den ἀκόλαστος, der 141, 8 in einer Parenthese auftritt; der ἀνάλγητος 141, 12 ist Ergänzung Spengels. Also das zieht nicht, selbst nicht für den Fall, daß wirklich unmittelbar Aristoteles vorläge. Was bleibt, ist nur die mehrdeutige Tatsache, daß die *Gr. Ethik* und Theophrast mit ihrer σαλακωνία der *Eud. Ethik*, die den σαλάκων hat, näher stehen als der *Nik. Ethik*, die ihn nicht hat. Wenn übrigens v. A. mit der ἀναλγησία ähnlich argumentieren will wie mit der σαλακωνία, so muß er übersehen haben, daß die *Gr. Ethik* daneben auch den Terminus der *Nik.*, die ἀοργησία, hat: 1191b 25.

2. Aristoteles ist sich im 5. Buch der *Nik. Ethik* klar darüber, daß seine Theorie der δικαιοσύνη nicht ohne weiteres in die μεσότης-Lehre paßt. Wohl läßt sich das δίκαιον als ein Mittleres zwischen einem Zuviel und Zuwenig, und sogar die gerechte Handlung, die δικαιοπραγία, als Mitte zwischen ἀδικεῖν und ἀδικεῖσθαι bezeichnen, aber das ἀδικεῖσθαι ist dabei lediglich passives Korrelat zu ἀδικεῖν, und die δικαιοσύνη selbst steht nicht in der Mitte zwischen zwei fehlerhaften ἕξεις, von denen die eine durch übertriebenes und die andere durch zu schwaches Streben oder Empfinden charakterisiert wäre, sondern es steht ihr nur die ἀδικία gegenüber, bei der das Zuviel und Zuwenig gleichzeitig da ist, sofern eben zu jedem ἀδικῶν ein ἀδικούμενος gehört. Ist somit die δικαιοσύνη selbst kein Mittleres, so zielt sie immerhin auf ein Mittleres, und das erlaubt schließlich doch die Anwendung des Terminus μεσότης, wenn auch nicht ohne gedankliche und sprachliche Schwierigkeit. Aristoteles formuliert das so: 1133b 32 ἡ δὲ δικαιοσύνη μεσότης τίς ἐστιν, οὐ τὸν αὐτὸν δὲ τρόπον ταῖς ἄλλαις ἀρεταῖς, ἀλλ᾽ ὅτι μέσου ἐστίν· ἡ δ᾽ ἀδικία τῶν ἄκρων, 1134a 8 διὸ ὑπερβολὴ | καὶ ἔλλειψις ἡ ἀδικία, ὅτι ὑπερβολῆς καὶ ἐλλείψεώς ἐστιν. Es

ist klar, daß mit *dieser* ‚μεσότης' in der allgemeinen Theorie der ethischen Tugenden und der sie bekräftigenden Übersicht des zweiten Buches nichts anzufangen war, und deshalb scheidet Aristoteles sie dort (1108b 8) aus, mit nur vorläufiger Begründung (ἐπεὶ οὐχ ἁπλῶς λέγεται). — Dagegen wird im zweiten Buch der *Eud. Ethik* und bei Theophrast die δικαιοσύνη ruhig in der Reihe der anderen Tugenden mitgeführt und hat wie diese eine regelrechte ὑπερβολή und ἔλλειψις zur Seite (*E. E.* 1221a 4. b 23. Stob. 2, 141, 16)[13]. Freilich ist das nicht maßgebend für die Vorstellung, die wir uns von der auch in der *Eud. Ethik* ja schon nach hinten gerückten und jetzt verlorenen Sonderbehandlung der δικαιοσύνη zu machen haben, wie der Parallelfall der φιλία in ihr und in der *Nik. Ethik* beweist.

Was die *Gr. Ethik* in einer Tabelle und anschließender kurzer Erläuterung gehabt haben würde, falls sie das jemals gehabt haben sollte, wissen wir nicht. Jedenfalls stellt auch sie die Einzelbehandlung der Gerechtigkeit wie die beiden anderen Ethiken aus der Reihe heraus ans Ende. Aber innerhalb dieses Kapitels findet v. A. „folgerichtig die ethische Einstellung durchgeführt, die durch den Zusammenhang und Aufbau der Lehre gefordert wird", und meint, das sei das Ursprüngliche. Zum Beweis wird der Abschnitt 1193b 19—32 zitiert. Aber was v. A. heraushebt, 1. daß, wenn man sich vom Guten den größeren und vom Schlechten den kleineren Teil aussucht, dies ein ungleiches Verfahren ist und daß auf diese Weise Unrecht tun und Unrecht leiden zustande kommt, 2. daß das δίκαιον auf einer Gleichheit in der Sphäre des geschäftlichen Verkehrs beruht, 3. daß der Ungerechte vermöge seines Unrechttuns mehr und der Unrecht Leidende vermöge des Unrecht Leidens weniger hat, 4. daß der Gerechte das Gleiche haben will, sind Gedanken, die ebensogut in die *Nik. Ethik* hineinpassen und auch tatsächlich dastehen, nur in reicheren Zusammenhängen, und was wir als Kennzeichen einer besonderen ‚ethischen' Einstellung der *Gr. Ethik* brauchten, steht nirgends. Das ist nämlich der Mann, der aus Veranlagung und Gesinnung selbsttätig den kürzeren zieht, der ζημιώδης der *Eud. Ethik* und τὸ ἔλαττον ἑαυτῷ νέμων bei Stobaeus: Finden wir ihn durch den passiven ἀδικούμενος ersetzt wie hier (1193b 27 vgl. *E. N.* 1133b 30—32), so ist es um die Auffassung der Gerechtigkeit als einer μεσότης im Sinne der allgemeinen Lehre von den ethischen | Tugenden geschehen. Klar ist das dem Verfasser der *Gr. Ethik* vielleicht nicht ganz geworden, er drückt sich sonderbar aus ἡ δικαιοσύνη μεσότης τις ἂν εἴη ὑπεροχῆς καὶ ἐλλείψεως καὶ πολλοῦ καὶ ὀλίγου

---

[13] Zu beachten ist immerhin, daß in der Tabelle der *Eud. Ethik* abweichend vom übrigen nicht die δικαιοσύνη, sondern das δίκαιον und entsprechend κέρδος und ζημία erscheinen und in der theophrastischen Tabelle nur die δικαιοσύνη ohne die beiden Laster steht (vgl. Wachsmuths Bemerkung im Apparat zu 140, 20).

(1193b 25), was dann in dem Mehrhaben des Ungerechten vermittels des Unrechttuns und dem entsprechenden Wenigerhaben des Unrecht Leidenden eine Erläuterung finden soll; aber soweit hier ein Gedanke dahintersteckt, ist es der der *Nik. Ethik* ἡ δικ. μεσότης ἐστίν . . . ὅτι μέσου ἐστίν. Die Unfähigkeit der *Gr. Ethik*, feinere Unterscheidungen mitzumachen oder klar auszudrücken, bestätigt sich auch hier[14]. —

Damit sind die Dinge besprochen, von denen der gründliche, tief in die Schwierigkeiten der Sache hineinführende und daher auf jeden Fall dankenswerte Rehabilitationsversuch ausgegangen ist. Wer ihn durch vorstehende Ausführungen erschüttert findet, dem glaube ich versichern zu dürfen, daß eine genaue Prüfung des ersten Teils der Schrift zu keinem anderen Ergebnis führen würde. Es widerstrebt mir, nach eigener Wahl Einzelheiten herauszugreifen, wo ich anderes unter Berufung auf den Raummangel umgehen müßte. Dagegen halte ich für angebracht, zum Schluß noch die Argumente zur Sprache zu bringen, mit denen v. A. in der neusten Auflage von Ueberweg-Praechter, Grundriß der Geschichte der Philosophie I[12] 1926, 370 Anm. Anklang gefunden hat.

Da ist erstens die Erwähnung des Mentor 1197b 22. Es handelt sich um die Unterscheidung von φρόνησις und δεινότης. δεινὸς μὲν καὶ ὁ φαῦλος λέγεται, οἷον Μέντωρ δεινὸς μὲν ἐδόκει εἶναι, ἀλλ᾽ οὐ φρόνιμος ἦν. Das soll nur Aristoteles selbst haben sagen können, weil den Hörern eines späteren Peripatetikers dieses Beispiel ohne geschichtliche Erläuterung nichts besagt hätte, oder wie Praechter sagt: „Die Nennung des Mentor deutet auf eine dem Aristoteles ganz persönlich zu Herzen gehende Angelegenheit." Man könnte das in Aris|toteles' eigenem Munde auch für eine Geschmacklosigkeit halten, und jedenfalls scheint es mir nichts weniger als ausgeschlossen, daß in der peripatetischen Schule die vieldiskutierte Hermiasgeschichte genügend bekannt blieb, um eine gelegentliche Exemplifikation mit dem bösen Mentor zu erlauben. Erwähnt wurde die Weiberwirtschaft um Mentor von

---

[14] Besonderen Wert legt v. A. noch darauf, „daß die theophrastische Definition des δίκαιος als οὔτε τὸ πλεῖον ἑαυτῷ νέμων οὔτε τὸ ἔλαττον, ἀλλὰ τὸ ἴσον (τὸ δ᾽ ἴσον τὸ κατὰ τὸ ἀνάλογον, οὐ κατ᾽ ἀριθμόν) ihre genaueste Entsprechung, auch im Ausdruck, in der Stelle der *M. Mor.* 1193b 20 findet: ὅταν τῶν μὲν ἀγαθῶν τὰ μείζω αὐτοῖς νέμωσι", und schließt daraus, daß die von Theophrast benutzte Fassung der *Gr. Ethik* näher als die *Eud.* stehe, und daraus wieder auf die Echtheit der *Gr. Ethik*. Aber erstens wissen wir nicht, wie sich die *Eud. Ethik* in ihrem δικαιοσύνη-Kapitel ausgedrückt hat, und es ist unerlaubt *E. E.* 1221a 24f. als Ersatz zu brauchen, zweitens steht *E. N.* 1134a 3 διανεμητικὸς . . . οὐχ οὕτως ὥστε τοῦ μὲν αἱρετοῦ πλέον αὐτῷ, ἔλαττον δὲ τῷ πλησίον im Ausdruck nicht ferner, und drittens besteht eine inhaltliche Übereinstimmung nur zwischen der Stobaeusstelle und *E. E.* 1221a 23f.; hier stehen sich der ἑαυτῷ πλεῖον und der ἑαυτῷ ἔλαττον νέμων bzw. der κερδαλέος und ζημιώδης gegenüber, während in der Stelle der *Gr. Ethik* genau so wie in der von mir zitierten der *Nik. Ethik* das zweite Glied dieses Gegensatzes fehlt. — Der Vollständigkeit halber sei darauf hingewiesen, daß v. A. auf S. 37 auch die Zeilen 1194a 26—28 in seinem Sinne zu deuten versucht, ohne aber wohl selbst die Beweiskraft seiner Auslegung zu überschätzen.

Klearch im Γεργίθιος (Athen. 256d), und das 2. Buch der Ökonomik bringt sogar eine Probe seiner Raffiniertheit (1351a 33).
Zweitens die Erwähnung des Dareios 1212a 5 (v. A. S. 10f.). Man darf εὔνοια nicht einfach mit φιλία gleichsetzen. Denn vielfach werden wir jemandem bloß vom Sehen oder weil wir etwas Gutes über ihn hören (ἀπὸ τοῦ ἀκοῦσαί τι ὑπέρ τινος ἀγαθόν) gut (εὔνοι), aber es ist deshalb noch lange keine Freundschaft da. οὐ γὰρ εἴ τις ἦν Δαρείῳ εὔνους ἐν Πέρσαις ὄντι, ὥσπερ ἴσως ἦν, εὐθέως καὶ φιλία ἦν αὐτῷ πρὸς Δαρεῖον. Das läßt v. A. zu Lebzeiten des Dareios III. gesagt sein — den Ansatz nach 330 erlaubt ihm die Chronologie nicht —, ,,aber mit seiner Beliebtheit war es, wenigstens vorläufig, schon vorbei''. Wir hätten eine aktuelle ,,Anspielung auf politische Stimmungen des Tages'', ,,der Augenblickswirkung zuliebe'' im Manuskript vorgesehen (,,Ein Professor kann eine besonders lebendige Auffassung eines Satzes seines Lehrgegenstandes in den Hörern erzeugen, indem er auf aktuelle Verhältnisse, die seinen Hörern naheliegen, exemplifiziert'' S. 11). ,,Das ,Wohlwollen', das man in Athen für Dareios hegte, war durch die Hoffnung hervorgerufen, daß sein Sieg über Makedonien die Befreiung Griechenlands von der makedonischen Oberherrschaft herbeiführen werde. Jeder Erfolg Alexanders schwächte dieses Wohlwollen, jeder Mißerfolg verstärkte es.'' . . . ,,Als ,Freund des Dareios' zu gelten, war politisch gefährlich; Wohlwollen für ihn zu hegen, konnte man keinem verwehren.'' Diese Interpretation ist auch abgesehen von der befremdlichen Auffassung der Imperfekta unhaltbar. Sowohl der unmittelbare Zusammenhang als auch die Zeilen 1212a 9—12 (= E. E. 1241a 4—10, nur E. N. 1155b 34—36 treten die χρήσιμοι neben die ἐπιεικεῖς) verbieten den Gedanken an das politische Tagesinteresse, und überdies ist der Perserkönig doch nicht deshalb zur Illustration gewählt, weil man in Athen tatsächlich in Verdacht geraten konnte, ,Freund des Dareios' in v. A.s Sinne zu sein — erstens wäre das keine φιλία, und zweitens würde so nichts bewiesen —, sondern weil die Vorstellung eines Freundschaftsverhältnisses zu ihm etwas Absurdes hat. Das Beispiel ist schlagend, aber gemacht — daher das ὥσπερ ἴσως ἦν — und denkbar trivial, was freilich immer noch besser ist, als wenn der Augenblickswirkung zuliebe unpassende Anspielungen gemacht werden[15].

3. ,,Die Argumente für stoische Beeinflussung erweisen sich nicht als zwingend'' (Pracchter). Mag sein, aber die waren auch früher schon nicht für jeden das Ausschlaggebende: ,,Stoicorum rationem tum sententiae tum verba | rarissimi tantum atque leniter admodum et in rebus haud ita magni momenti modo sapiunt modo perstringunt'' Susemihl praef. S. XI. Noch zurückhaltender E. Zeller, Die Philosophie der Griechen II 2³, 942.

4. v. A. bemüht sich, die häufige Verwendung des Wortes ὁρμή und seine gleichzeitige Beschränkung auf die Bezeichnung seelischer Antriebe als Vorstufe des selteneren Vorkommens in der Eud. und ganz seltenen in der Nik. Ethik zu retten. Das Wort wird in den anderen Ethiken ohne terminologische Bindung für Bewegungsantriebe irgendwelcher Art gebraucht und tritt daher auch gerade dann auf, wenn

---

[15] Zum Ersatz darf ich vielleicht auf einen wirklichen chronologischen Anhalt aufmerksam machen, den der Vergleich von E. E. 1226a 29 mit E. N. 1112a 28 bietet: οὐ βουλευόμεθα περὶ τῶν ἐν Ἰνδοῖς wird ersetzt durch das auch in den zwanziger Jahren noch gewiß in jeder Beziehung unverfängliche οἷον πῶς ἂν Σκύθαι ἄριστα πολιτεύοιντο οὐδεὶς Λακεδαιμονίων βουλεύεται. — Die Gr. Ethik hat im gleichen Zusammenhang, nur an etwas anderer Stelle πολλάκις διανοούμεθα ὑπὲρ τῶν ἐν Ἰνδοῖς, ἀλλ' οὔτι καὶ προαιρούμεθα (1189a 20). Ich möchte behaupten, daß sich Aristoteles erst zur Zeit, als er die Eud. Ethik schrieb, und früher so nicht hätte äußern können und es zur Zeit der Nik. Ethik nicht getan haben würde; letzteres gilt auch für Top. 116a 36—38.

einmal die seelischen Erscheinungen mit dem bloß Körperlichen (E. N. 1102b 18—21) oder dem Unbeseelten (*E. E.* 1224a 15ff.) verglichen werden. Der Verfasser der *Gr. Ethik* kann sich umgekehrt 1185a 23ff. die Gedankenreihe leisten, daß das θρεπτικὸν μέρος der Seele, wenn man ihm schon eine ἀρετή zuschreiben wolle, doch deswegen für eine Mitwirkung bei der Eudaimonie nicht in Frage komme, weil ihm die ὁρμή fehle, was kurios bewiesen wird (anders *de an.* 416a 15), und weil, wo keine ὁρμή vorliege, auch von dem für die Eudaimonie wesentlichen Begriff ἐνέργεια nicht die Rede sein könne. Daß ein Kenner wie Trendelenburg hier mehr als einen Anstoß fand, ist begreiflich, und er machte bei dieser Gelegenheit darauf aufmerksam (A. Trendelenburg, Einige Belege für die nacharistotelische Abfassungszeit der Magna Moralia, in: Hist. Beiträge zur Philosophie III, 1867, 438), daß die *Gr. Ethik* auch schon vorher „in ihrer Weise, mit planen Beispielen bereit" etwas Eigenes hat: 1185a 13—23. Während nämlich in beiden anderen Ethiken das Vorhandensein eines vegetativen Seelenteiles Voraussetzung dafür ist, daß der Verfasser überhaupt auf ihn zu sprechen kommt, wird in der *Gr. Ethik* zunächst einmal dieses Vorhandensein bewiesen, wobei sie sich bewußt ist, etwas zu tun, was eigentlich nicht zur Sache gehört (μετὰ τοῦτο τὸ μέλλον λέγεσθαι οὔτε λίαν δόξειεν ἂν οἰκεῖον εἶναι τούτων οὔτε μακρὰν ἀπέχον). Der Beweis ruht darauf, daß keiner der drei platonischen Seelenteile (vgl. *de an.* 432a 24ff.) imstande ist, das τρέφεσθαι zu bewirken; vielmehr muß das ein anderer sein, und dafür haben wir keinen besseren Namen als ‚θρεπτικόν'. Man muß v. A. (S. 29. 37f.) zugestehen, daß dieser Verfasser sich nicht traut, seinen Hörern gegenüber ohne weiteres vom θρεπτικὸν μέρος zu sprechen, und daß er vorzog, um weiteren Komplikationen zu entgehen, nur die berühmten drei platonischen Seelenteile zu nennen, mehr aber auch nicht, denn die Unterstellung, daß die Benennung θρεπτικόν „*für ihn selbst*" noch einen fremden Klang" hätte, verträgt sich nicht mit den einleitenden Worten οἷον ἐπειδήπερ ἔστιν, ὡς δοκεῖ, μόριόν τι τῆς ψυχῆς ᾧ τρεφόμεθα, ὃ καλοῦμεν θρεπτικόν, die sich auf eine bereits bestehende Doktrin einschließlich Terminologie beziehen. Schwerlich verdient gerade dieses Argument, „die volle Herübernahme der platonischen Seelenteile mit Neueinführung des θρεπτικόν", die bei Praechter allerdings wohl durch den Zwang der Kürze bedingte Hervorhebung.

5. Mit der Deutung der Stelle 1183a 24ff. (v. A. S. 142) wird ausnahmsweise einmal die Schlauheit des Verfassers der *Gr. Ethik* unterschätzt. Um der Erörterung der Ideenlehre aus dem Wege zu gehen, hält er sich zunächst an den aristotelischen Gedanken, daß man das Bekanntere nicht aus dem Unbekannteren soll ableiten wollen (vgl. *E. E.* 1218a 15ff.), und es ergibt sich, daß, wenn jemand es unternimmt, über ‚das Gute' zu reden, das sich bereits vorher in dem besonderen Sinne des ἄριστον und zwar des ἡμῖν ἄριστον als Gegenstand der ‚Politik' herausgestellt hat, daß er dann nicht anfangen soll, von der Idee zu reden. ‚Freilich meinen sie, wenn sie von ‚dem Guten' sprächen, müßten sie von der Idee reden, weil man dann von dem, was im höchsten Maße gut ist, reden müßte, und weil αὐτὸ ἕκαστον im höchsten Maße τοιοῦτον, also (das αὐτοαγαθόν, also) die Idee des Guten im höchsten Maße gut sei; so meinen sie. | Dieser Gedankengang ist vielleicht ganz richtig (ὁ δὴ τοιοῦτος λόγος ἀληθὴς μέν ἐστιν ἴσως): aber das politische Wissen oder Können, das den Gegenstand der jetzigen Untersuchung bildet, hat es ja gar nicht mit diesem ‚Guten' zu tun, sondern mit dem ‚ἡμῖν ἀγαθόν' usw. Was an dem Einwand als vielleicht richtig anerkannt wird, ist gar nicht die Ideenlehre selbst, sondern die Forderung, daß man in einer Vorlesung ‚über das Gute' von der Idee zu reden habe. Dagegen schützt die eigene Aufgabestellung, die ja gerade keine ‚Vorlesung über das Gute' im Sinne Platons geben will, und so kommt der Verfasser nach Beseitigung des weiteren Einwandes, daß man die Idee vielleicht als Ausgangspunkt für die Besprechung des Einzelnen brauchen könnte, um jede direkte Auseinandersetzung mit

der Ideenlehre herum. Durch Aristoxenos (R. Westphal, Aristoxenes von Tarent. Metrik und Rhythmik des klassischen Hellenentums II 1893, 57) wissen wir ja glücklicherweise, welche Rolle die Erinnerung an Platons berühmte Vorlesung im peripatetischen Lehrbetrieb spielte, und einen Nachklang davon haben wir in der *Gr. Ethik* kurz vorher 1182a 27. Da wird es als der Fehler von Platons Ethik bezeichnet, daß er die Behandlung der ἀρετή in die πραγματεία über das Gute hineingebracht habe, obwohl die ἀρετή da gar nichts zu suchen hätte. Das stützt sich mit unserer Stelle auf das schönste, und so spricht doch wohl einiges für die Möglichkeit, daß „ein jüngerer Peripatetiker" sich „so ausgedrückt" hätte.

Daß ich die chronologischen Bedenken Praechters teile, ohne jedoch mit ihm in den Erwähnungen des Mentor und des Dareios nachträgliche Einfügungen in ein altes Konzept sehen zu können, brauche ich nicht auszuführen. Selbstverständlich halte ich ferner seinen Einspruch gegen die Art, wie v. A. die sprachlich-stilistische Form der *Gr. Ethik* zu retten sucht, für berechtigt. Aber wenn man sich bei der von Praechter vorgeschlagenen Kompromißlösung — die *Gr. Ethik* Überarbeitung einer ältesten Ethik „durch einen Schüler, der den schon durch seine Kürze sich zum Handbuch empfehlenden Entwurf repristinierte, indem er ihn in einen ihm geläufigen oder sonst als geeignet erscheinenden Stil umgoß" — beruhigen sollte, so wäre, fürchte ich, v. A.s zielbewußte Arbeit umsonst getan. Es ist ihr großer Vorzug, daß sie keine halbe, sondern eine ganze These mit wissenschaftlicher Strenge durchzuführen versucht; und wenn ich geglaubt habe, widersprechen zu müssen, so darf ich nun doch wohl auch die Überzeugung aussprechen, daß die erwünschte Weiterarbeit an der durch die Erhaltung der drei Ethiken gestellten Aufgabe zwar gewiß nicht bequemer geworden ist, daß sie aber in dem Maße wertvollere Ergebnisse liefern wird, als sie sich bis in alle Einzelheiten hinein mit den anregenden Beobachtungen und zu Ende gedachten Kombinationen des vorliegenden Buches auseinanderzusetzen gehalten fühlt.

Die Kategorienlehre in der aristotelischen Topik

1920

Die sogen. Kategorienlehre spielt in den verschiedenen Teilen der aristotelischen Philosophie eine mehr oder weniger bedeutsame Rolle und erscheint, abgesehen von der kleinen Schrift mit dem traditionellen Titel Κατηγορίαι, in den *Analytiken,* in der *Physik,* der Schrift über *Entstehen und Vergehen,* über die *Seele,* über die *Träume,* in der *Metaphysik,* der *Ethik* und der *Rhetorik.* Wenn gleichwohl der folgenden Untersuchung im Gegensatz zu den bisherigen Behandlungen nur ein einziges Werk, die *Topik,* zugrunde gelegt wird, so ist damit von vornherein auf Vollständigkeit verzichtet. Freilich glaube ich, daß diese Beschränkung der Aufgabe, wie die Dinge liegen, nicht nur äußere Vorteile mit sich bringt. Nahegelegt wird sie durch die bekannte, aber überhaupt noch wenig ausgenutzte Sonderstellung der *Topik* den größeren übrigen philosophischen Lehrschriften gegenüber, die m. E. allerdings zwingt, sie bis auf einzelne Zusätze (namentlich in BuchΘ) relativ früh anzusetzen, jedenfalls aber, da die Topik in erster Linie der Übung[1] dienen will, zu der Erwartung verhältnismäßig einfacher und durchsichtiger philosophischer Voraussetzungen berechtigt[2].

Am Schluß der *Topik* spricht Aristoteles aus, es sei sein Ziel gewesen, den bereits ausgebildeten Künsten auf dem Gebiet der Dialek-

---

[1] Wie sehr der dialektische Betrieb für den Verfasser der *Topik* das Gegebene ist, zeigt 101a 26:

ἔστι δὴ πρὸς τρία (χρήσιμος ἡ πραγματεία), πρὸς γυμνασίαν, πρὸς τὰς ἐντεύξεις, πρὸς τὰς κατὰ φιλοσοφίαν ἐπιστήμας. ὅτι μὲν οὖν πρὸς γυμνασίαν χρήσιμος, ἐξ αὐτῶν καταφανές ἐστι· μέθοδον γὰρ ἔχοντες ῥᾷον περὶ τοῦ προτεθέντος ἐπιχειρεῖν δυνησόμεθα. πρὸς δὲ τὰς ἐντεύξεις usw. Als erster Punkt wird also nicht etwa der Nutzen der Übung im ἐπιχειρεῖν περὶ τοῦ προτεθέντος — das ist erst unter Nummer zwei und drei mitzuverstehen —, sondern der für diese Übung mit einer Methode selbstverständlich in die Hand gegebene Vorteil hervorgehoben.

[2] Man könnte einwenden, daß nicht nur einfachere dialektische Termini wie z. B. γένος, ἴδιον, συμβεβηκός, διαφορά als auch ohne die nachträgliche genauere Bestimmung verständlich eingeführt werden (101b 17), sondern daß 101b 19 das berüchtigte τί ἦν εἶναι unvermittelt auftritt und ohne weiteres zur Bestimmung der Begriffe ἴδιον und ὅρος verwandt wird. Ich erblicke darin vielmehr eine Warnung, hinter dem *Ausdruck* τί ἦν εἶναι irgend welchen Tiefsinn zu suchen. τί ἦν εἶναι c. dat. ist die auf eine möglichst einfache und unmißverständliche Formel gebrachte Frage nach der Definition; man sieht leicht, was zu dieser Formulierung führte, wenn man sich vergegenwärtigt, daß auf die einfache Frage τί ἐστι,

tik, wo es keinerlei Vorarbeit gegeben habe, etwas Ebenbürtiges zur
Seite zu stellen. Insbesondere nennt er die Rhetorik, und wenn man
darauf achtet, so ist es sehr deutlich, wie er von dieser mit der Idee des
Ganzen zugleich die Richtlinien für seine Disposition — mutatis
mutandis, das versteht sich bei Aristoteles von selbst — und damit die
Möglichkeit, eines so eigenartigen Stoffes überhaupt Herr zu werden,
übernommen hat. Daher bietet die *Topik* eine unverächtliche Handhabe, das Bild der von Aristoteles' eigener ausgebildeter *Rhetorik*
unbeeinflußten rhetorischen τέχνη, deren Repräsentant für uns die
Rhetorik ad Alexandrum ist, zu ergänzen. In erster Linie aber kann
die Beachtung dieses Zusammenhangs natürlich der Erklärung der
Topik selber dienen.

Die Gegenstände der im tatsächlichen Gebrauch vorkommenden
Reden geben der Rhetorik den nächsten Anhalt für eine irgendwie
geordnete Darstellung ihres Stoffes; demgegenüber lehrt sie, woher
man über den betreffenden Gegenstand die nötigen reichlichen Worte
nimmt, und das ergibt einen zweiten Ordnungsbegriff. Der einfachste
Ausdruck für die beiden angedeuteten Gesichtspunkte ist in den Präpositionen περί und ἐξ (dazu ἐντεῦθεν, ὅθεν) gegeben. Belege bietet die
Rhetorik ad Alexandrum in Menge, z. B. 1422a 24: εὐπορήσομεν δὲ
περὶ τούτων λέγειν ἐξ αὐτῶν τε τῶν προειρημένων καὶ τῶν ὁμοίων
τούτοις usw. oder ganz einfach 1423a12: καὶ περὶ μὲν τούτων ἐντεῦθεν
εὐπορήσομεν. Ein gutes Beispiel findet sich auch in Isokrates' *Helena*
§ 15: ἔστιν δ᾽ οὐκ ἐκ τῶν αὐτῶν ἰδεῶν οὐδὲ περὶ τῶν αὐτῶν ἔργων ὁ
λόγος vgl. Busiris § 9. Natürlich ließ sich das Begriffspaar περὶ ὧν und
ἐξ ὧν verschieden wenden und verschieden scharf fassen, und man
kann annehmen, daß das auch vor Aristoteles[3] schon reichlich geschehen ist, aber die ganz elementare Bedeutung mußte überall durch-
scheinen.

selbst wenn sie ganz im richtigen Sinne genommen wurde, immer noch entweder
nur der Name des betreffenden Gegenstandes oder eine höhere Gattung zur Antwort gegeben werden konnte, was durch diese Wendung ausgeschlossen wird
(vgl. *Met.* 1029b 19 ἐν ᾧ ἄρα μὴ ἐνέσται λόγῳ αὐτό, λέγοντι αὐτό, οὗτος ὁ λόγος
τοῦ τί ἦν εἶναι ἑκάστῳ und *Top.* 146b 31 ἀπολείπων γὰρ διαφορὰν ἡντινοῦν οὐ
λέγει τὸ τί ἦν εἶναι). Die Schwierigkeit, die für uns in der Erklärung des Imper-
fektums liegt, wurde schwerlich empfunden, wie mir die Angleichung ἀληθὲς ἦν
εἰπεῖν *Anal. post.* 91b 3 direkt zu zeigen scheint. — Daß im τί ἦν εἶναι das schwie-
rigste Problem der ausgebildeten aristotelischen Metaphysik enthalten ist, steht
auf einem anderen Blatt; merkwürdig ist, wie sich hier das Verhältnis umgekehrt
hat und zur vorläufigen Bestimmung des τί ἦν εἶναι 1030a 6 der — doch wohl
inzwischen selbständig gewordene — Begriff ὁρισμός benutzt werden kann.
[3] In seiner eigenen *Rhetorik* sind 1360a 38 περὶ ὧν die gewöhnlichen Gegenstände
der politischen Rede, Finanzen, Krieg und Frieden, Landesverteidigung, Ein-
und Ausfuhr, Gesetzgebung, ἐξ ὧν demgegenüber die Lebensziele und -güter;
aber das ist eine Weiterbildung, die man für das unmittelbare Verständnis der

Nun heißt es in der *Topik* nach der zunächst gegebenen Bestimmung der Aufgabe des Unternehmens, seines Nutzens und seiner Grenze: πρῶτον οὖν θεωρητέον ἐκ τίνων ἡ μέθοδος. εἰ δὴ λάβοιμεν πρὸς πόσα 101 b 11 καὶ ποῖα καὶ ἐκ τίνων οἱ λόγοι, καὶ πῶς τούτων εὐπορήσομεν, ἔχοιμεν ἂν ἱκανῶς τὸ προκείμενον. ἔστι δ᾽ ἀριθμῷ ἴσα καὶ τὰ αὐτά, ἐξ ὧν τε οἱ λόγοι καὶ περὶ ὧν/οἱ συλλογισμοί. γίνονται μὲν γὰρ οἱ λόγοι ἐκ τῶν 15 προτάσεων· περὶ ὧν δὲ οἱ συλλογισμοί, τὰ προβλήματά ἐστι. πᾶσα δὲ πρότασις καὶ πᾶν πρόβλημα ἢ γένος ἢ ἴδιον ἢ συμβεβηκὸς δηλοῖ· καὶ γὰρ τὴν διαφορὰν ὡς οὖσαν γενικὴν ὁμοῦ τῷ γένει τακτέον. ἐπεὶ δὲ τοῦ ἰδίου τὸ μὲν τὸ τί ἦν εἶναι/σημαίνει, τὸ δ᾽ οὐ σημαίνει, διῃρήσθω τὸ 20 ἴδιον εἰς ἄμφω τὰ προειρημένα μέρη, καὶ καλείσθω τὸ μὲν τὸ τί ἦν εἶναι σημαῖνον ὅρος, τὸ δὲ λοιπὸν κατὰ τὴν κοινὴν περὶ αὐτῶν ἀποδοθεῖσαν ὀνομασίαν προσαγορευέσθω ἴδιον. δῆλον οὖν ἐκ τῶν εἰρημένων ὅτι κατὰ τὴν νῦν διαίρεσιν τέτταρα τὰ πάντα/συμβαίνει γίνεσθαι, ἢ ἴδιον ἢ ὅρον 25 ἢ γένος ἢ συμβεβηκός.

Daß sich für Aristoteles, wenn er das Begriffspaar περὶ ὧν und ἐξ ὧν aus der Rhetorik auf das Gebiet der Dialektik übertrug, erstere mit den προβλήματα, letztere mit den προτάσεις identifizierten, war in den Bedeutungen der Präpositionen gewissermaßen vorherbestimmt[4]. Aber nun ergab sich eine eigentümliche Schwierigkeit. In der Rhetorik lassen sich die Gegenstände aufzählen und bieten so einen einfachen Einteilungsgrund. Die Aufgabe, die die Dialektik stellte, aber war nach Aristoteles' Bestimmung μέθοδον εὑρεῖν ἀφ᾽ ἧς δυνησόμεθα συλλογίζεσθαι περὶ παντὸς τοῦ προτεθέντος προβλήματος ἐξ ἐνδόξων usw. (100 a 1), und für die Dialektik gibt es ohne weiteres wirklich weder grundsätzlich noch, wie in der Rhetorik, wenigstens tatsächlich, bestimmte ein verschiedenes Verfahren bedingende Gegenstände, die man hätte aufzählen und irgendwie für die Disposition zum Anhalt nehmen können. Die Kombination dieser Schwierigkeit mit einer zweiten brachte die praktische Lösung. Schon die eben angeführten Eingangsworte der *Topik* zeigen nämlich, daß Aristoteles auch für die Dialektik das Ziel vorschwebt, die eine ,,Methode'' zu finden, auf die man alle Schlüsse zurückführen könnte. Aber das ist ihm nicht gelungen und konnte ihm nicht gelingen, da in dem, was er unter Dialektik verstand, zum mindesten zwei in Wahrheit unvereinbare Tendenzen durcheinandergehen, das sophistische Streben, den Gegner durch lauter ἔνδοξα zum Zugeständnis eines ἀδοξότατον zu zwingen, und die im platonischen Sinne dialektischen Bemühungen um die Definition. Dem Verfasser

---

Topik wohl besser ebenso beiseite läßt wie die entsprechende Lehre der ausgebildeten Apodeiktik 76 b 21, 77 a 27 und etwa gar die Kuriosität, daß *Phys*, 195a 18 um der Präposition ἐξ willen die ὑποθέσεις zur Stoffursache, dem ἐξ οὗ, des συμπέρασμα gemacht werden.

[4] Für περὶ kann πρός (101b 12, 103b 3), neben ἐκ διά (103b 2) eintreten.

der *Topik* erschien beides als συλλογισμός[5], und das ließ sich wirklich nicht unter einen Hut bringen, denn wie er selbst sagt, bei der Definition und den verwandten Begriffen γένος und ἴδιον handelt es sich im Gegensatz zu dem bloßen συμβεβηκός, mit dem es nach einer hübschen Stelle der *Metaphysik* (1026b 15) der Sophist so gut wie ausschließlich zu tun hat, um mehr als nur darum, daß etwas von etwas behauptet wird (*Top.* 151a 28 ἐν μὲν γὰρ τοῖς ἄλλοις οὐ μόνον ὑπάρχον, ἀλλὰ καὶ ὅτι οὕτως ὑπάρχει, δεικτέον· ἐπὶ δὲ τοῦ συμβεβηκότος, ὅτι ὑπάρχει μόνον, ἱκανὸν δεῖξαι), und dieses Mehr bedingt zum mindesten eine andere Methode. Das ist der Standpunkt, mit dem sich die *Topik* zufrieden gibt[6]: freilich läßt sich, sagt sie (102b 27ff.), in gewissem Sinne die Behandlung von ἴδιον, γένος und συμβεβηκός der des ὁρισμός unterordnen: ἀλλ᾽ οὐ διὰ τοῦτο μίαν ἐπὶ πάντων καθόλου μέθοδον ζητητέον· οὔτε γὰρ ῥάδιον εὑρεῖν τοῦτ᾽ ἐστίν, εἴ θ᾽ εὑρεθείη παντελῶς ἀσαφὴς καὶ δύσχρηστος ἂν εἴη πρὸς τὴν προκειμένην πραγματείαν. ἰδίας δὲ καθ᾽ ἕκαστον τῶν διορισθέντων γενῶν ἀποδοθείσης μεθόδου ῥᾷον ἐκ τῶν περὶ ἕκαστον οἰκείων ἡ διέξοδος τοῦ προκειμένου γένοιτ᾽ ἄν (102b 35ff.). Daß in der so gewonnenen Vierteilung dem ὅρος als ursprünglich selbständig nur das συμβεβηκός gegenübersteht, wird im Anfang des vierten Buches besonders deutlich (120b 12ff.): μετὰ δὲ ταῦτα περὶ τῶν πρὸς τὸ γένος καὶ τὸ ἴδιον ἐπισκεπτέον. ἔστι δὲ ταῦτα στοιχεῖα τῶν πρὸς τοὺς ὅρους· περὶ αὐτῶν δὲ τούτων ὀλιγάκις αἱ σκέψεις γίνονται τοῖς διαλεγομένοις. Doch war, wenn die beiden Endglieder der Reihe einmal gegeben waren, die Vierteilung in der Tat wohl naheliegend; Aristoteles jedenfalls hielt sie für induktiv und deduktiv beweisbar: 103b 12ff.

So führte die Reflexion auf die Methode des συλλογισμός von selbst zu einer Einteilung, deren letzter Grund die verschiedenen Sphären sind, denen der nur scheinbar einheitliche Begriff entstammte. Damit war zugleich über die Schwierigkeit, den Gegenstand der Dialektik zu teilen, hinweggeholfen: περὶ ὧν sind entweder γένος oder ἴδιον oder

---

[5] Wir haben in der *zweiten Analytik* den Beleg dafür, daß er sich später bewußt von der Behauptung der *Topik*, auch die Definition lasse sich durch συλλογισμός gewinnen, losgemacht hat (A. Kantelhardt, De Aristotelis Rhetoricis, Gött. Diss. 1911, 51ff.; H. Maier, Die Syllogistik des Aristoteles II 2, 1900, 79f.).

[6] Die *eine* Methode alles Schließens zur Darstellung gebracht zu haben rühmt sich das erste Buch der *ersten Analytik* in sehr eindringlichen Worten (45b 36ff.), deren Verhältnis zur *Topik* genau dasselbe ist wie das in der vorhergehenden Anmerkung erwähnte der *zweiten Analytik* zu ihr betreffs der Möglichkeit, Definitionen durch ein Schlußverfahren zu gewinnen, mit dem es auch sachlich eng zusammenhängt. Daß 46a 28 auf die mehr ins Einzelne gehenden Anweisungen der *Topik* zurückverwiesen wird, steht dieser Auffassung nicht im Wege, denn für so überflüssig hat Aristoteles sie natürlich auch nach der Auffindung des „einen Weges" nicht gehalten, daß er sich nicht durch den Hinweis auf sie der Mühe, auf Einzelheiten einzugehen, hier hätte überheben können.

συμβεβηκός, wobei ἴδιον entweder ὅρος[7] oder eigentliches ἴδιον sein kann (101b17—23). Und teilte man den Gegenstand der Dialektik, also die προβλήματα, in dieser Weise, so waren die προτάσεις, also die ἐξ ὧν, ihrer Natur nach derselben Einteilung unterworfen und es ergab sich die der Rhetorik gegenüber allerdings auffallende Erscheinung, daß in dieser Disziplin die ἐξ ὧν τε οἱ λόγοι καὶ περὶ ὧν οἱ συλλογισμοί „an Zahl gleich und dieselben" sind.

Damit halte ich den Sinn der Stelle der *Topik*, von der wir ausgingen, und der für alles weitere grundlegenden Einteilung ὅρος, ἴδιον, γένος, συμβεβηκός im Wesentlichen für erklärt. Wenn es 101b26 noch mit Emphase heißt μηδεὶς δ᾽ ἡμᾶς ὑπολάβῃ λέγειν ὡς ἕκαστον τούτων καθ᾽ αὑτὸ λεγόμενον πρότασις ἢ πρόβλημά ἐστιν, ἀλλ᾽ ὅτι ἀπὸ τούτων καὶ τὰ προβλήματα καὶ αἱ προτάσεις γίνονται, so erscheint uns das als eine Selbstverständlichkeit; es ist aber zu bedenken, daß damals die Unterscheidung von Wort und Begriff einerseits und Satz und Urteil andererseits etwas Neues und Beachtenswertes war. Durch diese Bemerkung werden die vier Glieder der Einteilung als Prädikate charakterisiert, denn das ist etwa die Bedeutung von ἀπὸ τούτων γίνονται (vgl. *Top.* 103b5ff., 109b4, *Cat.* 3a34)[8]. Dementsprechend wird z. B. das γένος 102a31 als τὸ κατὰ πλειόνων καὶ διαφερόντων τῷ εἴδει ἐν τῷ τί ἐστι κατηγορούμενον definiert und kann dem „syllogistischen", d. h. hier deduktiven, Beweis der Vollständigkeit der Vierteilung 103b 7ff. der Begriff πᾶν τὸ περί τινος κατηγορούμενον zugrunde gelegt werden.

Unmittelbar an den genannten Beweis schließt sich nun das Kapitel an, das die Kategorienlehre einführt:

μετὰ τοίνυν ταῦτα δεῖ διορίσασθαι τὰ γένη τῶν κατηγοριῶν, ἐν οἷς 103b 20 ὑπάρχουσιν αἱ ῥηθεῖσαι τέτταρες. ἔστι δὲ ταῦτα τὸν ἀριθμὸν δέκα, τί ἐστι, ποσόν, ποιόν, πρός τι, ποῦ, ποτέ, κεῖσθαι, ἔχειν, ποιεῖν, πάσχειν. ἀεὶ γὰρ τὸ συμβεβηκὸς καὶ τὸ γένος καὶ τὸ ἴδιον καὶ ὁ ὁρισμὸς ἐν/μιᾷ 25

---

[7] Daß der ὅρος so zunächst als Unterabteilung des ἴδιον aufgeführt wird, hat wohl nur terminologische Gründe. Der Begriff ὅρος fällt ja dem Sinne nach eigentlich aus der Reihe heraus, aber εἶδος, das man neben γένος erwarten könnte, ist zu unbestimmt, und τί ἦν εἶναι selbst (vgl. Anm. 2) paßt der sprachlichen Form wegen nicht.

[8] Man würde sich nicht zu helfen wissen, sollte man bei der Erörterung der Anfänge der Logik auf die Anwendung der später gebräuchlich gewordenen einfachsten grammatischen und logischen Termini wie Begriff, Satz, Prädikat usw. verzichten. Solange es aber nicht auf Kritik abgesehen ist, wird man sich jeder Präzisierung derselben in modernem Sinne enthalten dürfen. Wenigstens geht man so der Gefahr aus dem Wege, daß gerade das zur „Erklärung" wird, was an ihnen nicht einmal zur Beschreibung taugt; und sollte darüber einmal der Hinweis auf den „grammatischen", „logischen", „ontologischen" oder „metaphysischen" Sinn versäumt werden, so braucht das für das unmittelbare Verständnis nicht immer ein Nachteil zu sein.

τούτων τῶν κατηγοριῶν ἔσται · πᾶσαι γὰρ αἱ ἀπὸ τούτων προτάσεις
ἢ τί ἐστιν ἢ ποιὸν ἢ ποσὸν ἢ τῶν ἄλλων τινὰ κατηγοριῶν σημαίνουσιν.
δῆλον δ᾿ ἐξ αὐτῶν ὅτι ὁ τὸ τί ἐστι σημαίνων ὁτὲ μὲν οὐσίαν σημαίνει,
ὁτὲ δέ ποιόν, ὁτὲ δὲ τῶν ἄλλων τινὰ κατηγοριῶν. ὅταν μὲν γὰρ ἐκκει-
30 μένου ἀνθρώπου/ φῇ τὸ ἐκκείμενον ἄνθρωπον εἶναι ἢ ζῷον, τί ἐστι
λέγει καὶ οὐσίαν σημαίνει · ὅταν δὲ χρώματος λευκοῦ ἐκκειμένου φῇ τὸ
ἐκκείμενον λευκὸν εἶναι ἢ χρῶμα, τί ἐστι λέγει καὶ ποιὸν σημαίνει. ὁμοίως
δὲ καὶ ἐὰν πηχυαίου μεγέθους ἐκκειμένου φῇ τὸ ἐκκείμενον πηχυαῖον
35 εἶναι ⟨ἢ ?⟩ μέγεθος, τί ἐστιν ἐρεῖ καὶ/ποσὸν σημαίνει. ὁμοίως δὲ καὶ ἐπὶ
τῶν ἄλλων · ἕκαστον γὰρ τῶν τοιούτων ἐάν τε αὐτὸ περὶ αὑτοῦ λέγηται,
ἐάν τε τὸ γένος περὶ τούτου, τί ἐστι σημαίνει. ὅταν δὲ περὶ ἑτέρου, οὐ
τί ἐστι σημαίνει, ἀλλὰ ποσὸν ἢ ποιὸν ἤ τινα τῶν ἄλλων κατηγοριῶν[9].

Eins ist hier meiner Meinung nach von vornherein klar: es ist ausgeschlossen, daß Aristoteles in diesem Kapitel mit dem Stamm des
Wortes κατηγορία bewußt einen wesentlich anderen Sinn verbunden
hätte als den in dem πᾶν τὸ περί τινος κατηγορούμενον des vorhergehenden Abschnittes steckenden; man ist ja sogar gezwungen, αἱ
ῥηθεῖσαι τέτταρες 103 b 21 durch κατηγορίαι zu ergänzen. Niemand
kann dem Zusammenhang der Stelle die Begründung für eine solche
Vermutung entnehmen, und, was bei der *Topik* besonders ins Gewicht fällt, keiner, der die Unterscheidung nicht schon mitbrachte,
hätte das verstehen können. Schon diese eine Stelle reicht aus, um die
an Bonitz anschließende Polemik Heinrich Maiers (Die Syllogistik des

---

[9] Damit schließt der Abschnitt: ὥστε περὶ μὲν ὧν οἱ λόγοι καὶ ἐξ ὧν, ταῦτα καὶ
τοσαῦτά ἐστι · πῶς δὲ ληψόμεθα καὶ δι᾿ ὧν εὐπορήσομεν, μετὰ ταῦτα λεκτέον. Dies
geht auf die ὄργανα, deren Behandlung von Kapitel 13 bis zum Schluß des Buches
reicht. Zwischengeschoben sind die Erörterungen der Begriffe πρότασις διαλεκτική,
πρόβλημα διαλεκτικόν, θέσις und die Einteilung der λόγοι διαλεκτικοί in die εἴδη
ἐπαγωγή und συλλογισμός. Unter den ὄργανα ist vieles untergebracht, was an
sich auch ebensogut anderswo stehen könnte oder etwas anders gewendet tatsächlich steht. Es herrscht eben die Art der rhetorischen Techne, die die Gesichtspunkte nimmt, wie sie kommen, wenn nur die verschiedenartigen Dinge
irgendwie kenntlich werden. Daß er in der *Topik* nicht mehr beabsichtigte, sagt
Aristoteles ja selbst 101a 19. Die Bücher *B—H* bringen dann die τόποι (τόπος
ist Substantiv zu ἐξ ὧν) und zwar *BΓ* für das συμβεβηκός, *Δ* für das γένος, *E* für
das ἴδιον, *ZH* für den ὅρος, am Ende von *H* wird die Schwierigkeit des ἀνασκευάζειν
und κατασκευάζειν von allen vieren verglichen. Den Schluß macht *Θ* mit Anweisungen für die Frage- und Antworttechnik und dgl., die nach Analogie der
Rhetorik zunächst dem Begriff τάξις untergeordnet werden — vgl. *Rhet. ad
Alex.* 1444b 8ff. —; bei der Frage geht das, bei der Antwort muß es aufgegeben
werden (159a 16). Die Disposition des ganzen ist so klar, daß ich die Andeutungen
Jaegers (Studien zur Entstehungsgeschichte der Metaphysik des Aristoteles,
1912, 151f.), der auch in der *Topik* die Selbständigkeit der Teile und ihren Mangel
an Zusammenhang evident findet, nicht verstehe. Das Buch περὶ σοφιστικῶν
ἐλέγχων ist nachträglich, aber, wie das berühmte Schlußkapitel zeigt, von Aristoteles selbst als Abschluß angehängt worden, vgl. unten S. 231.

Aristoteles II 2, 1900, 304A.) gegen Apelt, der mit Trendelenburg an der natürlichen Deutung des Namens κατηγορίαι festhält, als eine Verirrung zu kennzeichnen: ,,Schon der Ausgangspunkt der ganzen Auffassung ist bedenklich. Die technischen Ausdrücke ,κατηγορίαι' und ,κατηγορεῖν' sind beide Schöpfungen des Aristoteles. Welcher aber der frühere ist, können wir nicht einmal vermuten. Es ist also eine sehr gewagte Kombination, den technischen Ausdruck κατηγορία von dem technischen Ausdruck κατηγορεῖν abzuleiten. Und es ist recht wohl möglich, daß der Terminus κατηγορία zu einer Zeit geprägt wurde, als die technische Bedeutung von κατηγορεῖν sich noch nicht verfestigt hatte, m. a. W., daß die technischen Termini κατηγορία und κατηγορεῖν beide auf eine allgemeinere Bedeutung von κατηγορεῖν zurückgehen. Dieses ursprüngliche κατηγορεῖν hätte einen Sinn derart, daß es ebensowohl das Aussagen eines Prädikats von einem Subjekt im Urteil als das Aussagen eines Inhalts im Wort bedeuten könnte, und aus ihm hätten sich die beiden Termini κατηγορία (= Aussagen eines bestimmten Inhalts in einem Wort) und κατηγορεῖν (= prädizieren) entwickelt. Die Frage ist nur, ob sich diese Bedeutung von κατηγορία nachweisen läßt.'' Soll etwa die allgemeinere Bedeutung (weder Prädikat noch Nichtprädikat) an unserer *Topik*stelle noch vorliegen? Man müßte den Tatsachen gegenüber beide Augen zumachen, wenn man das für 103 b 7—19 gelten lassen wollte. Die Frage ist keineswegs nur, ,,ob sich diese Bedeutung von κατηγορία nachweisen läßt''[10], darauf hat wirklich Apelt schon im Voraus geantwortet (Beiträge zur Geschichte der griechischen Philosophie, 1891, 132ff.), — sondern vielmehr die, ob an den wichtigsten Stellen, in denen das Wort κατηγορία irgendwie zur Bezeichnung dessen, was *wir* Kategorien nennen[11],

---

[10] Übrigens sind die von Bonitz angeführten Stellen *Soph. el.* 181b 27, *Met.* 1004a 28, 1028a 28 nach seinen eigenen Erläuterungen in Wahrheit für seinen Zweck unbrauchbar. Wenn κατηγορία hier lediglich das ,,Aussprechen'' bedeutet, wenn es gewissermaßen einfach farbloses Substantivum zu λέγειν oder λέγεσθαι ist, was man sachlich immerhin gelten lassen kann, ohne freilich für die Erklärung dieses Gebrauches auf die eigentliche Bedeutung verzichten zu können, so liegt darin eben gerade n`cht, daß ,,ein Begriff *in bestimmter Bedeutung* ausgesprochen *oder ausgesagt* werde''. Sieht man genauer zu, so findet man hier bei Bonitz die unerfreulichsten Umbiegungen (vgl. die nächste Anm.), und etwas besseres hat H. Maier (Syll. II 2, 304 Anm.) auch nicht zu bieten. Dieser Methode, was zur Not irgendwie dem Zusammenhang entnommen werden kann (oder auch nicht!), in das harmlose Wort hineinzuprojizieren, mag ich nicht weiter nachgehen.

[11] Es steht mit den ,,Kategorien'' ganz ähnlich wie mit dem Wort Methode: was w`r Methode nennen, ist bei Aristoteles τρόπος τῆς μεθόδου (*de part. an.* 642b 2), oder aber der Zusammenhang schafft erst diesen Sinn (μία, ἴδιος, ἡ αὐτὴ μέθοδος), und was wir Kategorien nennen, sind ihm eigentlich γένη τῶν κατηγοριῶν oder σχήματα τῆς κατηγορίας. Der Bedeutungswandel ist leicht zu erklären, und man wird ihn auch zur Darstellung seiner Lehre ruhig übernehmen, aber man darf

gebraucht wird, der Zusammenhang darauf führt, an eine Bedeutung zu glauben, die in Worte zu fassen den Gegnern der nächstliegenden Auffassung kaum gelingt — man lese nur H. Maier S. 303 — und deren Hauptcharakteristikum darin besteht, daß sie zu der gewöhnlichen, Prädikat oder Prädizierung, im Gegensatz stehen soll. Mit einer der wichtigsten Stellen für das Verständnis der Kategorienlehre haben wir es hier in der *Topik* zu tun; ihre Antwort auf die gestellte Frage ist eindeutig.

Bonitz, mit dessen Deutung des Namens Kategorien sich diese *Topik*stelle so schlecht verträgt, geht gleichwohl im ersten Teil seiner Untersuchung, (Über die Kategorien des Aristoteles, Sitzungsb. d. K. Ak. Wien X, 1853, 591 ff.), wo er aus der Anwendung der Kategorien ihre sachliche Bedeutung erschließen will, von ihr aus. Den Vorteil, den der Zusammenhang in die Hand gibt, nutzt er in anderer Richtung aus. Zuerst nämlich teilt nach ihm (S. 595) Aristoteles „die Sätze, um deren Beweis oder Widerlegung es sich handelt, nach der Verschiedenheit der *logischen Bedeutung* welche sie in Anspruch zu nehmen haben; hiernach enthalten sie entweder die Aussage eines ὁρισμός oder eines γένος oder eines ἴδιον oder eines συμβεβηκός. *Diese* Einteilung ist vollkommen gleichgültig dagegen, welcher Art der *Gegenstand* ist, über den etwas ausgesagt wird; ... Daher tritt zur Ergänzung eine zweite Einteilung hinzu ... Diese zweite Einteilung kann nach dem Zusammenhang, nach den Worten, nach den unmittelbar darauf gegebenen Beispielen nichts anderes treffen, als die Arten dessen, *worüber* die Aussagen ergehen." Hiergegen erhebt sich zunächst ein sprachlicher Einwand. „Die Arten dessen, worüber die Aussagen ergehen" können durch die Worte γένη τῶν κατηγοριῶν nicht getroffen werden, und die Deutung des ihm unbequemen Ausdrucks, die Bonitz später (S. 622) ohne besondere Bezugnahme auf diese Stelle gibt, „τὰ γένη, nämlich αἱ κατηγορίαι" paßt nicht, denn dann erhält das Wort κατηγορίαι eben jene „technische" Bedeutung, gegen die wir uns bereits zu wehren hatten. Bedenklich ist auch der Schluß aus dem sachlichen Zusammenhang. Es ist allerdings tatsächlich richtig, daß die erste Art der Einteilung gleichgültig ist gegen die Art des Gegenstandes, über welchen etwas gesagt wird, während die zweite ihn irgendwie berücksichtigt. Aber da es an sich noch mehrere M⸳glichkei-

---

ihn doch nicht übersehen und auch bei ihm in den Terminus verlegen, was eigentlich nur im Zusammenhang liegt. Schuppe (Die aristotelischen Kategorien, Berlin 1871, 27 unten) hat gut darauf hingewiesen, daß die Anwendung, die Bonitz von *Met.* 1028a 28 ἐν τῇ κατηγορίᾳ τῇ τοιαύτῃ macht, eigentlich auf der Bestimmung τῇ τοιαύτῃ ruht und daß, „wenn auch verschiedene Formen des Aussagens als mehrere Aussagen, κατηγορίαι, bezeichnet werden können", daraus doch nicht folge, „daß auch der Singular κατηγορία schon Form der Aussage bedeutet".

ten gibt, die Sätze lediglich „nach der Verschiedenheit der logischen Bedeutung" zu teilen, so folgt die Eigentümlichkeit der zweiten Einteilung nicht unbedingt aus der ersten, zumal der von Bonitz zu Hilfe genommene Begriff des Formallogischen für Aristoteles nicht existiert. Und jedenfalls geben weder der Zusammenhang noch die gegebenen Beispiele eine Grundlage für die Wendungen, in denen Bonitz nun die zweite Einteilung beschreibt: „Das gesamte Bereich des Gedachten oder des Seienden — mit welchem dieser beiden Worte wir richtiger den Sinn des Aristoteles treffen, wird sich später ergeben — wird in zehn oberste Klassen eingeteilt, deren einer ein jeder Gegenstand unserer Vorstellung oder erfahrungsmäßiger Auffassung anheimfallen muß. Wenn wir irgend etwas vorstellen, so ist dies entweder ein Ding, oder eine Quantität, oder eine Qualität, oder eine Relation, oder ein Ort, oder ein Zeitpunkt, oder ein Haben, oder ein Beschaffensein, oder ein Tun, oder ein Leiden." Von dem Bereich des Gedachten oder des Seienden zu reden, zu sagen „wenn wir etwas vorstellen, so ist dies entweder usw.", dazu gibt der interpretierte Text durchaus keine Veranlassung.

Wir müssen nun noch eine eigentümliche Vorstellung Apelts[12] (Beitr. S. 119ff.) erwähnen, die er zur Erklärung von *Met.* Δ 7[13]

---

[12] Ich finde in Apelts Abhandlung (Beiträge zur Geschichte der griechischen Philosophie, 1891, III. Die Kategorienlehre des Aristoteles) das Treffendste, was seit Trendelenburg (Gesch. der Kategorienlehre, 1846) über die Kategorien bei Aristoteles gesagt ist. In seinen Ausführungen ist trotz der mir wenigstens unbehaglichen philosophischen Zutaten und trotz einzelner Fehlgriffe das Richtunggebende doch das Leben des Gegenstandes und nicht die Absicht der Konstruktion. Über Trendelenburg selbst vgl. Apelt 104. Die ebendort von Bonitz' Aufsatz gegebene Beurteilung, gegen den Apelt sich hauptsächlich wendet, ist meines Erachtens eher zu günstig. Freilich hat Bonitz die geistreiche Vermutung, mit der Trendelenburg die gerade von ihm deutlich gekennzeichnete Lücke unseres Wissens über den Ursprung der Kategorien eigentlich nur versuchsweise füllte — man beachte die vorsichtige Ausdrucksweise Tr.s Gesch. d. Kat. 208 —, mit Recht verworfen, auch mag man die Durchsichtigkeit der Darstellung und die Beherrschung des Stoffes hier wie anderwärts bewundern, aber daß Bonitz, wie Apelt selbst ausspricht, den Hauptpunkt verfehlen konnte, hat seinen Grund in umso bedenklicheren Erschleichungen. Demgegenüber ist eine scharf zugreifende Kritik wie die Schuppes (Die ar. Kategorien 24ff.) gar nicht so unnötig, wie Apelt findet; schade nur, daß die von Schuppe selbst vorgeschlagene Deutung — κατηγορίαι τοῦ ὄντος = Prädikate des (noch unbekannten, eben erst erkannten) Seins — die Sache wieder verwirrt.

[13] Die Schwierigkeit dieses Kapitels, dessen besondere Wichtigkeit für das Verständnis der Kategorienlehre bei Aristoteles Apelt mit Recht betont und H. Maier, für dessen Standpunkt es freilich unbequem ist, mit Unrecht leugnet, liegt in dem Satz 1017a 22 καθ' αὑτὰ δὲ εἶναι λέγεται ὅσαπερ σημαίνει τὰ σχήματα τῆς κατηγορίας· ὁσαχῶς γὰρ λέγεται, τοσαυταχῶς τὸ εἶναι σημαίνει. Apelt will, wenn ich ihn recht verstehe, καθ' αὑτὰ nach 1022a 27ff. als ὅσα ἐν τῷ τί ἐστι ὑπάρχει deuten und erklärt (S. 120):

braucht und zu deren Bestätigung er auch das vorliegende Kapitel dienen läßt. Nach Apelt ging Aristoteles aus von der Frage „was sind es für Seinsbestimmungen, die durch das ἐστι an das Subjekt herangebracht werden? Wieviele Arten derselben gibt es?" und antwortete: „offenbar so viele als es Arten von Prädikaten gibt" . . .

„Wie aber wird es möglich, diese Seinsbestimmungen oder Prädikate in ihre natürlichen Gattungen zu gliedern? Dadurch, daß man mit der Frage τί ἐστιν an die einzelnen Prädikatsvorstellungen herantritt. Denn diese Frage geht eben auf

„Die Antwort nämlich auf dies τί ἐστι führt von der niederen Art *unmittelbar*, d. h. ohne das Beiwerk der spezifischen Differenz, welche der Definition vorbehalten ist, durch die höheren Arten bis zur letzten Gattung. So viele letzte, d. h. mit der höchsten Gattung abschließende Antworten auf diese Frage es gibt, so viele Gattungen von Prädikaten, so viele ὄντα καθ' αὐτά oder κυρίως ὄντα (Met. 1027b 31) muß es geben."
Aber zu dem Sprung an der spezifischen Differenz vorbei *durch die höheren Arten* bis zur letzten Gattung gibt der Wortlaut nicht die mindeste Berechtigung. Es steht nur da, dem eigenen Wesen entsprechend gälte εἶναι von so vielem, wie die Formen der Aussage bezeichneten. Denn „sein" hätte gerade so viele Bedeutungen wie diese. Man kann die Stelle ganz einfach aus sich selber erklären. Fragt man, worauf bezieht sich eigentlich καθ' αὐτά, auf die Subjekte oder die Prädikatsnomina (falls vorhanden) der mit „ist" gebildeten Sätze, so erhält man schon durch die folgenden Beispiele ἄνθρωπος ὑγιαίνων ἐστίν (1017a 28) und ἄνθρωπος βαδίζων ἐστίν (29) die Antwort: auf letztere, denn auf erstere paßt es in keiner Weise, auf letztere aber unbedingt, da ja das ἐστί sich in seiner Bedeutung nach ihnen richtet. Das „sein" gilt von ihnen also wirklich καθ' αὐτά. Dabei ist zu beachten, daß καθ' αὐτό λέγεσθαι auch Ausdruck für den „eigentlichen" Gebrauch der Bezeichnung ist, wodurch die Stelle auf Griechisch einen sehr einfachen Sinn erhält. Also wenn, modern gesprochen, das „ist" die Bedeutung der Kategorie des Prädikatsnomens hat, dann ist „ist" von diesem καθ' αὐτό gesagt. Der Gegensatz des εἶναι καθ' αὐτό, das εἶναι κατὰ συμβεβηκός, muß folglich da seine Stelle haben, wo das „ist" nicht diese Bedeutung hat: daß diese Kennzeichnung für 1017a 8—22 stimmt, davon überzeuge man sich selbst. Und damit ist auch die nicht zu leugnende sachliche Unklarheit dieses Kapitels erklärt, daß nämlich das Prädikatsnomen eines Satzes wie ἄνθρωπός ἐστι λευκός beliebig zu den κατὰ συμβεβηκός wie zu den καθ' αὐτὰ εἶναι λεγόμενα gerechnet werden kann. Faßt man nämlich in einem solchen Satz Subjekt und Prädikat als ein κατὰ συμβεβηκὸς ἕν oder ταὐτόν (1015b 16ff., 1017b 27ff.), so daß sie beliebig vertauschbar sind, dann hat das „ist" keine innere Beziehung zum Prädikatsnomen, die es erst bekommt, wenn man das Verhältnis als nicht umkehrbar ansieht, also das Prädikatsnomen nach dem dem hier gebrauchten εἶναι καθ' αὐτό teilweise (nicht für die 1. Kategorie, die besonders zu beurteilen ist) parallelen Begriffsbestimmung von An. post. 1, 22 ein ἁπλῶς (μὴ κατὰ συμβεβηκός) κατηγορούμενον oder συμβεβηκός καθ' αὐτό (83b 19f.) sein läßt. — Die Termini κατὰ συμβεβηκός und καθ' αὐτό gehören bekanntlich vorzugsweise zu denjenigen bei Aristoteles, deren Bedeutung nur aus dem jeweiligen Zusammenhang zu bestimmen ist und sich nicht ohne weiteres von einer Stelle auf die andere übertragen läßt. Ihr Sinn in dem besprochenen Kapitel ist, wenn man es unbefangen hinnimmt, durchaus nicht etwa schwierig zu erfassen; das entspräche auch gar nicht dem Zweck des Kapitels. Bonitz verliert zu Apelts Verdruß kein Wort über die besprochene „Schwierigkeit", offenbar hat er sie nicht empfunden.

die *wesentlichen* Verschiedenheiten der Begriffe. Ihre Beantwortung fordert, daß jedes denkbare Prädikat selbst zum Subjekt eines Urteils gemacht werde, dessen Prädikat der dem Subjektsbegriff übergeordnete Art- und Gattungsbegriff bis zum letzten und höchsten hinaus ist."

Aber weder hier noch an der Parallelstelle *Met.* 1030a 17ff.[14] steht etwas von diesem eigentümlichen Verfahren, durch das Aristoteles die natürliche Gliederung der Prädikate herausbekommen haben soll. Tatsächlich steht da, und das ist allerdings wichtig genug, es sei ohne weiteres klar, das τί ἐστι könne bisweilen οὐσία, unter Umständen aber auch eine andere Kategorie sein, und zwar dann, wenn dergleichen von sich selbst, oder wenn von ihm das γένος ausgesagt würde; würde es aber von etwas anderem gesagt, so bezeichne es nicht τί ἐστι, sondern eben eine der Kategorien; oder nach der *Metaphysik*: das τί ἐστι hat zwei Bedeutungen, in der einen bezeichnet es οὐσίαν καὶ τόδε τι, in der andern jede Kategorie. Fragt man, welche Bedeutung gehört denn nun in die Zehnteilung der *Topik* hinein, so gibt sich die Antwort von selbst, denn unmöglich kann eine Bedeutung, die auf alle Glieder der Einteilung paßt, zugleich eins der Glieder sein. Also die erste Kategorie ist οὐσία, ja es hilft nichts: οὐσία καὶ τόδε τι, wenn wir die Ergänzung der *Metaphysik* gelten lassen wollen[15]. Da die andere Bedeutung des τί ἐστι wiederum, wie nicht ausgeführt zu werden braucht, die engste Beziehung hat zu einem Glied der Vierteilung, dem γένος, so steht die Unterscheidung beider Bedeutungen an ihrem natürlichen Platze.

[14] ἢ καὶ ὁ ὁρισμὸς ὥσπερ καὶ τὸ τί ἐστι πλεοναχῶς λέγεται· καὶ γὰρ τὸ τί ἐστιν ἕνα μὲν τρόπον σημαίνει τὴν οὐσίαν καὶ τὸ τόδε τι, ἄλλον δ' ἕκαστον τῶν κατηγορουμένων, ποσός, ποιὸν καὶ ὅσα ἄλλα τοιαῦτα. ὥσπερ γὰρ καὶ τὸ ἔστιν ὑπάρχει πᾶσιν ἀλλ' οὐχ ὁμοίως, ἀλλὰ τῷ μὲν πρώτως τοῖς δ' ἑπομένως, οὕτω καὶ τὸ τί ἐστιν ἁπλῶς μὲν τῇ οὐσίᾳ, πῶς δὲ τοῖς ἄλλοις. καὶ γὰρ τὸ ποιὸν ἐροίμεθ' ἂν τί ἐστιν, ὥστε καὶ τὸ ποιὸν τῶν τί ἐστι μὲν ἀλλ' οὐχ ἁπλῶς, ἀλλ' ὥσπερ ἐπὶ τοῦ μὴ ὄντος λογικῶς φασί τινες εἶναι τὸ μὴ ὂν οὐχ ἁπλῶς ἀλλὰ μὴ ὄν, οὕτω καὶ τὸ ποιόν. δεῖ μὲν οὖν σκοπεῖν καὶ τὸ πῶς δεῖ λέγειν περὶ ἕκαστον, οὐ μὴν μᾶλλόν γε ἢ τὸ πῶς ἔχει. διὸ καὶ νῦν, ἐπεὶ τὸ λεγόμενον φανερόν usw.

[15] Damit geraten wir freilich in einen zweiten Widerspruch gegen Apelt, nach dem τόδε τι nicht eigentlich, sondern höchstens unmittelbar erste Kategorie sein können soll und eigentlich erste Kategorie gerade der dem γένος der Vierteilung verwandte Begriff τί ἐστι (,,Anfang der Definition" S. 138) wäre. Schon Trendelenburg hatte gesagt: ,,Solange indessen für die Kategorie der Begriff des Prädikats, und zwar im eigentlichen und ursprünglichen Urteil, festgehalten wird, ist das Allgemeine des Geschlechts, also das τί ἐστιν in der oben angegebenen Bedeutung, das Wesentliche (Gesch. d. Kat. 43)." Es ist allerdings richtig, daß *Anal. post.* I 22 die Stelle der ersten Kategorie zu ganz bestimmtem Zwecke mit den ἐν τῷ ἐστι κατηγορούμενα (83b 1 ἢ γένος ἢ διαφορά) besetzt wird, und auch sonst gibt es Stellen, wo man mit der strengen Auseinanderhaltung nicht durchkommen würde (vgl. S. 288 ff.); aber an sich *paßt* das τί ἐστιν als Geschlecht gar nicht in die Reihe der Kategorien.

Auf der Vierteilung ruht der ganze Bau der *Topik*, die Zehnteilung wird, wie auch die Anwendung zeigt, nur gelegentlich herangezogen; daß sie nicht für die Zwecke der *Topik* gefunden ist, ist klar. Wir wenden uns jetzt einigen Anwendungen zu.

107a3. Aristoteles gibt Fragestellungen an, von denen aus man bestimmen kann, ob ein und dasselbe Wort verschiedene Bedeutungen hat:

107a 3 σκοπεῖν δὲ καὶ τὰ γένη τῶν κατὰ τοὔνομα κατηγοριῶν, εἰ ταὐτά
5 ἐστιν ἐπὶ πάντων. εἰ γὰρ μὴ ταὐτά, δῆλον/ὅτι ὁμώνυμον τὸ λεγόμενον, οἷον τὸ ἀγαθὸν ἐν ἐδέσματι μὲν τὸ ποιητικὸν ἡδονῆς, ἐν ἰατρικῇ δὲ τὸ ποιητικὸν ὑγιείας, ἐπὶ δὲ ψυχῆς τὸ ποιὰν εἶναι, οἷον σώφρονα ἢ ἀνδρείαν ἢ δικαίαν. ὁμοίως δὲ καὶ ἐπὶ ἀνθρώπου. ἐνιαχοῦ δὲ τὸ ποτέ, οἷον τὸ ἐν
10 τῷ καιρῷ ἀγαθόν· ἀγαθὸν γὰρ λέγεται/τὸ ἐν τῷ καιρῷ. πολλάκις δὲ τὸ ποσόν, οἷον ἐπὶ τοῦ μετρίου· λέγεται γὰρ καὶ τὸ μέτριον ἀγαθόν. ὥστε ὁμώνυμον τὸ ἀγαθόν. ὡσαύτως δὲ καὶ τὸ λευκὸν ἐπὶ σώματος μὲν χρῶμα, ἐπὶ δὲ φωνῆς τὸ εὐήκοον. παραπλησίως δὲ καὶ τὸ ὀξύ· οὐ γὰρ
15 ὡσαύτως ἐπὶ πάντων τὸ αὐτὸ λέγεται·/φωνὴ μὲν γὰρ ὀξεῖα ἡ ταχεῖα, καθάπερ φασὶν οἱ κατὰ τοὺς ἀριθμοὺς ἁρμονικοί, γωνία δ' ὀξεῖα ἡ ἐλάσσων ὀρθῆς, μάχειρα δ' ἡ ὀξυγώνιος.

σκοπεῖν δὲ καὶ τὰ γένη τῶν ὑπὸ τὸ αὐτὸ ὄνομα, εἰ ἕτερα καὶ μὴ ὑπ'
20 ἄλληλα, οἷον ὄνος τό τε ζῷον καὶ τὸ/σκεῦος. ἕτερος γὰρ ὁ κατὰ τοὔνομα λόγος αὐτῶν· τὸ μὲν γὰρ ζῷον ποιόν τι ῥηθήσεται, τὸ δὲ σκεῦος ποιόν τι. ἐὰν δὲ ὑπ' ἄλληλα τὰ γένη ᾖ, οὐκ ἀναγκαῖον ἑτέρους τοὺς λόγους εἶναι. οἷον τοῦ κόρακος τὸ ζῷον καὶ τὸ ὄρνεον γένος ἐστίν. ὅταν οὖν
25 λέγωμεν τὸν κόρακα ὄρνεον εἶναι, καὶ ζῷον ποιόν/τί φαμεν αὐτὸν εἶναι, ὥστ' ἀμφότερα τὰ γένη περὶ αὐτοῦ κατηγορεῖται. ὁμοίως δὲ καὶ ὅταν ζῷον πτηνὸν δίπουν τὸν κόρακα λέγωμεν, ὄρνεόν φαμεν αὐτὸν εἶναι· καὶ οὕτως οὖν ἀμφότερα τὰ γένη κατηγορεῖται κατὰ τοῦ κόρακος, καὶ ὁ λόγος αὐτῶν. ἐπὶ δὲ τῶν μὴ ὑπ' ἄλληλα γενῶν οὐ συμβαίνει τοῦτο·
30 οὔτε γὰρ ὅταν σκεῦος λέγωμεν, ζῷον λέγο/μεν, οὔτ' ὅταν ζῷον, σκεῦος.

Dazu 152a38. Hier handelt es sich darum, ob zwei verschiedene Worte dasselbe bedeuten oder nicht:

ὁρᾶν δὲ καὶ εἰ μὴ ἐν ἑνὶ γένει κατηγορίας ἀμφότερα, ἀλλὰ τὸ μὲν ποιὸν
b 1 τὸ δὲ ποσὸν ἢ πρός τι δηλοῖ. πάλιν εἰ/τὸ γένος ἑκατέρου μὴ ταὐτόν, ἀλλὰ τὸ μὲν ἀγαθὸν τὸ δὲ κακόν, ἢ τὸ μὲν ἀρετὴ τὸ δ' ἐπιστήμη.

Aus dieser Zusammenstellung geht sogleich hervor, daß Aristoteles ganz bestimmt unterscheidet zwischen γένος τῆς κατηγορίας und dem eigentlichen γένος, und damit wird die schon im Altertum gern gebrauchte Charakteristik der Kategorien als γενικώτατα, vermöge deren z. B. noch Zeller in seiner Darstellung den Übergang von der aristotelichen Logik zur Metaphysik findet, bedenklich. Hier jedenfalls kann man aus γένη τῶν κατηγοριῶν im Gegensatz zum einfachen γένη unmöglich die Bedeutung „höchste γένη" heraushören. Es mag sein, daß der Unterschied nicht so sehr in der Sache liegt als vielmehr in der Wendung, die Aristoteles der Sache gibt, und das ist kein Wunder, denn was hier gegeben wird, sind Fragestellungen, und natürlich kann man ein und dieselbe Sache verschieden anpacken. So wird bald nach 107 a 3 ff. ὀξύ unter die von der angeführten abweichende Frage σκοπεῖν εἰ τὰ ὑπὸ τὸ αὐτὸ ὄνομα ἑτέρων γενῶν καὶ μὴ ὑπ' ἄλληλα διαφοραί εἰσιν (107 b 21) gebracht und das λευκόν unter σκοπεῖν τῶν ὑπὸ τὸ αὐτὸ ὄνομα εἰ τὸ μὲν εἶδός ἐστι τὸ δὲ διαφορά (107 b 33). Aber uns interessiert gerade die Fragestellung, die auf die Kategorien führt. Daher werden wir uns mit dem angeführten Text noch etwas näher beschäftigen müssen.

αἱ κατὰ τοὔνομα κατηγορίαι 107 a 3 sind die von einem Subjekt mittelst des betreffenden Namens gemachten Aussagen; davon gibt es verschiedene Arten, d. h. sie können verschiedene Bedeutungen haben und zwar zunächst, wie das erste Beispiel vom ἀγαθόν zeigt, die in der Zehnteilung angegebenen. Aber darauf ist der Sinn des Ausdrucks τὰ γένη τῶν κατηγοριῶν in diesem Falle nicht beschränkt — glücklicherweise ist der Terminus noch nicht erstarrt: bei den Beispielen vom λευκόν und ὀξύ kann man *nicht* an die „Kategorien" denken. Um das γένος dessen, was ausgesagt wird, handelt es sich auch nicht, denn zwar χρῶμα, aber nicht εὐήκοον ist γένος von λευκόν, — vgl. die schon erwähnte Stelle 107 b 33—37 —, und ebensowenig ist das, worin der Unterschied der Bedeutung von ὀξύ zu Tage tritt, ihr γένος im Sinne der höheren Gattung, vielmehr sind es nach 107 b 19—26 die Gattungen, deren διαφοραί sie sind, was etwas anderes ist. Und gleichwohl ist gesagt, in diesen Fällen seien die γένη τῶν κατὰ τοὔνομα κατηγοριῶν nicht dieselben; was heißt das? Die Erklärung steht eigentlich da: οὐ γὰρ ὡσαύτως ἐπὶ πάντων τὸ αὐτὸ λέγεται (107 a 14). ὡσαύτως ist Adverbium und gehört zum Verbum, wirklich bezieht sich die Verschiedenheit auf das Sagen und nicht auf das Gesagte[16]: die Verschiedenheit kommt eben erst durch die Prädizierung von den betreffenden Subjekten heraus, und dementsprechend gliedern sich die Prädizierungen in verschiedene Arten der Prädizierung. In den Beispielen werden die Subjekte oder die Gebiete der Subjekte angegeben, damit die gesuchte Bedeutungsverschiedenheit ans Licht tritt.

Dagegen 107 a 18 ff. ist es einfach auf das γένος der unter das untersuchte Wort fallenden Dinge abgesehen, und das Verfahren ist nicht etwa so, daß man das untersuchte Wort von diesen Dingen aussagte, sondern daß man es, auf diese Dinge bezogen, definiert, um das γένος

---

[16] οὐ τὸ αὐτὸ ἐπὶ πάντων λέγεται wäre sachlich auch richtig, aber das ist eben nicht die technische Wendung, die Aristoteles der Sache gibt. Man könnte beinahe sagen: οὐ τὸ αὐτὸ ἐπὶ πάντων λέγεται, διότι οὐχ ὡσαύτως τὸ αὐτὸ ἐπὶ πάντων λέγεται.

zu finden; das untersuchte Wort wird dabei Subjekt, die γένη dessen Prädikate (107a25 und 28).

152a38—b2 lehrt demgegenüber nichts Neues, nur tritt besonders scharf hervor, daß für Aristoteles vom γένος keine Brücke zum γένος τῆς κατηγορίας führt. —

Buch Δ behandelt das γένος und gibt zunächst zwei allgemeine Erfordernisse an, die erfüllt sein müssen, wenn behauptet wird, B sei γένος von A (πρῶτον 120b15 und εἶτα b21 gehören zusammen, mit μάλιστα b30 beginnen die eigentlichen τόποι). Man muß 1) alles zur Klasse A Gehörige (συγγενῆ 120b16, genauer gesagt Zeile 20: was unter dasselbe εἶδος fällt) daraufhin ansehen, ob von einem darunter B nicht ausgesagt werden kann; Beispiel: εἰ τῆς ἡδονῆς τἀγαθὸν γένος κεῖται usw.; in dieser Hinsicht wird auf das συμβεβηκός zurückverwiesen[17]; 2) muß man zusehen, ob B von A μὴ ἐν τῷ τί ἐστι κατηγορεῖται, ἀλλ᾽ ὡς συμβεβηκός. Das ἐν τῷ τί ἐστι κατηγορεῖσθαι ist nach der Definition des γένος sein Charakteristikum und daher der eigentliche Gegenstand dieses Buches. Zwei Beispiele für den Verstoß dagegen werden gegeben: καθάπερ τὸ λευκὸν τῆς χιόνος, ἢ ψυχῆς τὸ κινούμενον ὑφ᾽ αὑτοῦ. Das wird erläutert:

120b23
25
οὔτε γὰρ ἡ χιὼν ὅπερ λευκόν, διόπερ οὐ γένος τὸ λευκὸν τῆς χιόνος, οὔθ᾽ ἡ ψυχὴ ὅπερ κινούμενον· συμβέβηκε/δ᾽ αὐτῇ κινεῖσθαι, καθάπερ καὶ τῷ ζῴῳ πολλάκις βαδίζειν τε καὶ βαδίζοντι εἶναι. ἔτι τὸ κινούμενον οὐ τί ἐστιν, ἀλλά τι ποιοῦν ἢ πάσχον σημαίνειν ἔοικεν. ὁμοίως δὲ καὶ τὸ λευκόν· οὐ γὰρ τί ἐστιν ἡ χιών, ἀλλὰ ποιόν τι δηλοῖ. ὥστ᾽ οὐδέτερον αὐτῶν ἐν τῷ τί ἐστι κατηγορεῖται.

Es sind zwei Wege, die Aristoteles zur Erläuterung einschlägt, der eine führt über das Wort ὅπερ, in dem die Sprache ein unübersetzbares Kriterium für das γένος in die Hand gibt, mit dem Gegensatz συμβεβηκός, der andere über τί ἐστι mit den Gegensätzen τι ποιοῦν, πάσχον, ποιόν. Im ersten Fall geht es durch die Sphäre der Vierteilung, im zweiten durch die der Zehnteilung. Aber so leicht man dort nachkommt, hier hat es seine Schwierigkeiten. Denn einerseits muß das τί ἐστι, das zu ποιοῦν, πάσχον, ποιόν gehört, bis zu einem gewissen Grade gleichbedeutend sein mit dem in ἐν τῷ τί ἐστι κατηγορεῖσθαι steckenden, sonst geht der Zusammenhang verloren, andererseits muß es doch wieder mehr bedeuten, sonst wird die Stelle sinnlos. Natürlich

---

[17] καθάπερ ἐπὶ τοῦ συμβεβηκότος 120b 17 gehört zu πρῶτον μὲν ἐπιβλέπειν. Es ist an den gewöhnlichsten und leichtesten Fall des διαλέγεσθαι über ein συμβεβηκός zu denken, daß θέσις ein allgemein bejahender Satz ist und dieser angegriffen wird; vgl. den Anfang von Buch B, wo auch gleich als erstes Beispiel πᾶσα ἡδονὴ ἀγαθόν auftritt, und 155b 33—36. Waitz zu 120b 17 „nam quod accidens est, id non simul de omnibus quae eidem generi subiecta sunt, praedicari debet" hat den Zusammenhang nicht erkannt.

denkt man sofort an die *Topik A* 9 angegebenen beiden Bedeutungen von τί ἐστι, und mit Recht, aber das Seltsame ist, daß hier die beiden Bedeutungen zugleich herausgehört werden müssen. Daß es Aristoteles bei der Sache nicht ganz wohl gewesen ist, darauf scheint die Wendung ἔτι τὸ κινούμενον οὐ τί ἐστιν, ἀλλά τι ποιοῦν ἢ πάσχον σημαίνειν ἔοικεν zu deuten. Das Mehr an Bedeutung, das hier in τί ἐστι steckt, erhält es durch die auch sprachlich unterstrichene Zusammenstellung mit τι ποιοῦν ἢ πάσχον. Wenn wir das wiedergeben wollen, so können wir nur sagen ,,,bewegt' bedeutet nicht Ding, sondern Tun oder Leiden''; daher können wir die Stelle eben nicht übersetzen. Aber was durch die Zugehörigkeit von τί ἐστι zu der Reihe ποιοῦν, πάσχον, ποιόν in seinen Sinn hineinkommt, ist unverkennbar: der Begriff des Dinges und damit zugleich die uneingestandene Voraussetzung dieses Weges der Erläuterung, daß nämlich Schnee und Seele Dinge sind.

Aus der doppelten Erläuterung wachsen die ersten beiden τόποι gewissermaßen von selbst heraus:

μάλιστα δ᾽ ἐπὶ τὸν τοῦ συμβεβηκότος ὁρισμὸν ἐπιβλέπειν, εἰ ἐφαρ- 120 b 30 μόττει ἐπὶ τὸ ῥηθὲν γένος, οἷον καὶ τὰ νῦν εἰρημένα. ἐνδέχεται γὰρ κινεῖν τι αὐτὸ ἑαυτὸ καὶ μή, ὁμοίως δὲ καὶ λευκὸν εἶναι καὶ μή, ὥστ᾽ οὐδέτερον αὐτῶν γένος ἀλλὰ συμβεβηκός, ἐπειδὴ συμβεβηκὸς ἐλέγομεν ὃ ἐνδέχεται ὑπάρχειν/τινὶ καὶ μή.   35

ἔτι εἰ μὴ ἐν τῇ αὐτῇ διαιρέσει τὸ γένος καὶ τὸ εἶδος, ἀλλὰ τὸ μὲν οὐσία τὸ δὲ ποιόν, ἢ τὸ μὲν πρός τι τὸ δὲ ποιόν, οἷον ἡ μὲν χιὼν καὶ ὁ κύκνος οὐσία, τὸ δὲ λευκὸν οὐκ οὐσία ἀλλὰ ποιόν, ὥστ᾽ οὐ γένος τὸ λευκὸν τῆς χιόνος οὐδὲ τοῦ κύκνου./πάλιν ἡ μὲν ἐπιστήμη τῶν πρός τι, 121 a 1 τὸ δ᾽ ἀγαθὸν καί τὸ καλὸν ποιόν, ὥστ᾽ οὐ γένος τὸ ἀγαθὸν ἢ τὸ καλὸν τῆς ἐπιστήμης· τὰ γὰρ τῶν πρός τι γένη καὶ αὐτὰ τῶν πρός τι δεῖ εἶναι, καθάπερ ἐπὶ τοῦ διπλασίου· καὶ γὰρ τὸ πολλαπλάσιον,/ὃν γένος 5 τοῦ διπλασίου, καὶ αὐτὸ τῶν πρός τί ἐστιν. καθόλου δ᾽ εἰπεῖν, ὑπὸ τὴν αὐτὴν διαίρεσιν δεῖ τὸ γένος τῷ εἴδει εἶναι· εἰ γὰρ τὸ εἶδος οὐσία, καὶ τὸ γένος, καὶ εἰ ποιὸν τὸ εἶδος, καὶ τὸ γένος ποιόν τι, οἷον εἰ τὸ λευκὸν ποιόν τι, καὶ τὸ χρῶμα. ὁμοίως δὲ καὶ ἐπὶ τῶν ἄλλων.

Hier heben sich Vierteilung (30—35) und Zehnteilung (36—121 a 9) aufs schärfste voneinander ab. Wir bemerken, daß als erstes Glied der letzteren οὐσία genannt wird, und zwar natürlich nicht in der nicht hineingehörenden mit γένος verwandten Bedeutung ,,Wesensinhalt, Wesensbestimmung'' oder wie man sagen will, sondern in der Bedeutung ,,Ding''. ,,Schnee und Schwan ist Ding, weiß aber nicht Ding, sondern Eigenschaft''. Jene andere Bedeutung gäbe überhaupt keinen Sinn, denn der Wesensinhalt kann auch einer anderen Kategorie angehören (vgl. z. B. 146 b 3). — Ferner ist bemerkenswert, daß, wie der Ausdruck ἐν τῇ αὐτῇ διαιρέσει zeigt, die Kategorienteilung dem Verfasser der *Topik* unter Umständen schlechthin ,,die Einteilung'' ist, was bekanntlich in der einfachen Benennung γένη anderwärts seine Parallele hat, hier aber dadurch erleichtert wird, daß tatsächlich schon 120b26 die Kategorienteilung eingeführt war. Trotzdem ist es kein Zufall, daß das Wort κατηγορία *hier* nicht verwendet wird. Denn während es sich 120b26ff. noch tatsächlich um Satzprädikate handelte, deren Bedeutung nach Anleitung der Zehnteilung bestimmt wurde, hört bei der Wendung, die Aristoteles in diesem Abschnitt derselben Sache gibt, diese bestimmte Beziehung auf. Denn nicht nur an das Prädikat, sondern auch an das Subjekt des zu untersuchenden Satzes wird in gleicher Weise die Frage gestellt, „in welches" oder auch „unter welches" der Glieder der Einteilung es gehöre. Die Glieder der Einteilung erscheinen als Titel, unter welche sich ohne weiteres Begriffe aller Art unterordnen lassen. Übrigens ist diese Unterordnung eine unmittelbare, und nichts deutet darauf hin, daß dazu der Weg über γένος, höheres γένος usw. führte[18]. Wie leicht der Übergang von einer Art der Verwendung der Zehnteilung zur andern war, wird an unserer Stelle sehr deutlich, aber auch, daß sich dieser Wechsel des Gesichtspunktes eigentlich nicht mit dem Terminus κατηγορία verträgt. Da jedoch dieser Standpunkt in der *Topik* nur gelegentlich eingenommen wird und nicht wie in der *Kategorien*schrift, auf die wir noch zu sprechen kommen werden, herrschend ist, so möchte ich die Frage, ob möglicherweise er der ursprüngliche sein könnte, einstweilen zurückschieben. —

In der Lehre von der Definition spielt die Unterscheidung von γένος und διαφορά eine Rolle. Obwohl eigentlich von letzterer das ἐν τῷ τί ἐστι κατηγορεῖσθαι ebenfalls gilt (122a17; 128a20 der bequemeren Darstellung zuliebe durch δοκεῖ τισι verklausuliert), braucht Aristoteles zu ihrer Unterscheidung vom γένος doch auch das Gegensatzpaar τί ἐστι — ποιόν:

122b15   οὐδενὸς γὰρ ἡ διαφορὰ γένος ἐστίν. ὅτι δὲ τοῦτ᾽ ἀληθές, δῆλον· οὐδεμία γὰρ διαφορὰ σημαίνει τί ἐστιν, ἀλλὰ μᾶλλον ποιόν τι, καθάπερ τὸ πεζὸν καὶ τὸ δίπουν.

128a20   ἐπεὶ δὲ δοκεῖ τισι καὶ ἡ διαφορὰ ἐν τῷ τί ἐστι τῶν εἰδῶν κατηγορεῖσθαι, χωριστέον τὸ γένος ἀπὸ τῆς διαφορᾶς χρώμενον τοῖς εἰρημένοις (121b11, 122b16, 123a7) στοιχείοις, πρῶτον μὲν ὅτι τὸ γένος ἐπὶ πλέον λέγεται τῆς διαφορᾶς, εἶτ᾽ ὅτι κατὰ τὴν τοῦ τί ἐστιν ἀπόδοσιν
25   μᾶλλον ἁρμόττει τὸ γένος ἢ τὴν διαφο/ρὰν εἰπεῖν· ὁ γὰρ ζῷον εἴπας τὸν ἄνθρωπον μᾶλλον δηλοῖ τί ἐστιν ὁ ἄνθρωπος ἢ ὁ πεζόν. καὶ ὅτι ἡ μὲν διαφορὰ ποιότητα τοῦ γένους ἀεὶ σημαίνει, τὸ δὲ γένος τῆς διαφορᾶς οὔ· ὁ μὲν γὰρ εἴπας πεζὸν ποιόν τι ζῷον λέγει, ὁ δὲ ζῷον εἴπας οὐ λέγει ποιόν τι πεζόν.

---

[18] Vgl. etwa 122a 3—7.

144a 9. Das ἀγαθόν ist nicht γένος sondern διαφορά als ἕξις ἀγαθή der insofern ganz richtig definierten ἀρετή. Der zweite Beweis dafür lautet: ἔτι ἡ μὲν ἕξις τί ἐστι σημαίνει ἡ ἀρετή, τὸ δ᾽ ἀγαθὸν οὐ τί ἐστιν ἀλλὰ ποῖον· δοκεῖ δ᾽ ἡ διαφορὰ ποιόν τι σημαίνειν.

Der in diesen drei Stellen theoretisch allein erlaubte Gegensatz ist nicht der von Ding und Beschaffenheit, sondern eben der von γένος und διαφορά, den zu verdeutlichen das Wortpaar τί ἐστι —ποιόν auch geeignet ist. Wie fast unvermeidlich es aber ist, den Gegensatz zu ποιόν als Ding zu nehmen, zeigt die letzte Stelle in eigentümlicher Weise. Während 122b 15 und 128a 20ff. die Beispiele den (unkorrekten) Nebenbegriff ‚Ding‘ erlauben würden, ist das hier durch das Beispiel ἀρετή ausgeschlossen. Dafür folgt als weiterer τόπος:

ὁρᾶν δὲ καὶ εἰ μὴ ποιόν τι ἀλλὰ τόδε σημαίνει ἡ ἀποδοθεῖσα διαφορά· 144a 20 δοκεῖ γὰρ ποιόν τι πᾶσα διαφορὰ δηλοῦν.

Aus dem Nebengedanken wird ein neuer τόπος, der ihn zu voller Geltung bringt, es ist fast genau das zwischen 120b 26—29 und 36ff. beobachtete Verhältnis. Es wird erlaubt sein, das τόδε mit dem τί ἐστι der Zehnteilung gleichzusetzen, da der andere Gegensatz der als ποιόν gefaßten διαφορά, τί ἐστι = γένος, nicht hineingehört. —

Mit Buch Θ wird die zu Anfang der *Topik* angekündigte πραγματεία sachlich zum Abschluß gebracht. Den formalen Abschluß bringt aber erst das Ende des unter dem Sondertitel περὶ σοφιστικῶν ἐλέγχων erhaltenen 9. Buches, das im übrigen offenbar erst nachträglich von Aristoteles verfaßt und in diesen Zusammenhang gebracht worden ist (Brandis, Handbuch II 2, 1, 345; H. Maier, Syll. II 2, 82, gegen dessen Unterscheidung von drei Schichten in der Topik aber Kantelhardts Einwände, De Aristotelis Rhetoricis 51ff., zu beachten sind).

Die Themastellung des Buches erklärt sich leicht, wenn man den Anlaß zu seiner Abfassung in einer wiederholt polemisch berücksichtigten fremden Bearbeitung dieses Gegenstandes sieht, in der Aristoteles eine unberechtigte Konkurrenz erblickte; vgl. besonders Kapitel 10 und darin den Ausfall 171a 1 ὅλως τε ἄτοπον τὸ περὶ ἐλέγχου διαλέγεσθαι, ἀλλὰ μὴ πρότερον περὶ συλλογισμοῦ usw.

Die Vierteilung erscheint nicht mehr, dagegen spielt die Kategorienteilung eine etwas größere Rolle als in den übrigen Büchern der *Topik*. Das hängt damit zusammen, daß eine der von Aristoteles aufgestellten 13 Arten des φαινόμενος συλλογισμός im engsten Verhältnis zur Kategorienlehre steht.

Die Stichworte dieser 13 Arten sind nach den Kapiteln 4 und 5:

I. (Kap. 4): παρὰ τὴν λέξιν: II. (Kap. 5): ἔξω τῆς λέξεως:

1) ὁμωνυμία   1) παρὰ τὸ συμβεβηκός
2) ἀμφιβολία   2) ἁπλῶς ἢ μὴ ἁπλῶς λέγεσθαι

3) σύνθεσις   3) ἐλέγχου ἄγνοια

4) διαίρεσις   4) παρὰ τὸ ἑπόμενον

5) προσῳδία   5) π. τὸ λαμβάνειν τὸ ἐν ἀρχῇ

6) σχῆμα λέξεως   6) π. τ. μὴ αἴτιον ὡς αἴτιον

                            7) πλείω ἐρωτήματα ἓν ποιεῖν.

In beiden Kapiteln folgen den Aufzählungen die Erklärungen. Uns interessiert die letzte der ersten Abteilung:

166 b 10   οἱ δὲ παρὰ τὸ σχῆμα τῆς λέξεως συμβαίνουσιν, ὅταν τὸ μὴ ταὐτὸ ὡσαύτως ἑρμηνεύηται, οἷον τὸ ἄρρεν θῆλυ ἢ τὸ θῆλυ ἄρρεν, ἢ τὸ μεταξὺ θάτερον τούτων, ἢ πάλιν τὸ ποιὸν ποσὸν ἢ τὸ ποσὸν ποιόν, ἢ τὸ ποιοῦν πάσχον ἢ τὸ διακείμενον ποιεῖν, καὶ τἆλλα δ᾽ ὡς διῄρηται
15 πρότερον./ἔστι γὰρ τὸ μὴ τῶν ποιεῖν ὂν ὡς τῶν ποιεῖν τι τῇ λέξει σημαίνειν. οἷον τὸ ὑγιαίνειν ὁμοίως τῷ σχήματι τῆς λέξεως λέγεται τῷ τέμνειν ἢ οἰκοδομεῖν· καίτοι τὸ μὲν ποιόν τι καὶ διακείμενόν πως δηλοῖ τὸ δὲ ποιεῖν τι. τὸν αὐτὸν δὲ τρόπον καὶ ἐπὶ τῶν ἄλλων.

Mit πάλιν wird die Kategorienlehre eingeführt und mit ὡς διῄρηται πρότερον auf A 9 verwiesen.

Entsprechend der etwas seltsamen, aber straff durchgeführten und daher leicht übersehbaren Disposition des Buches kommt jede der 13 Arten wenigstens noch dreimal zur Sprache, nämlich erstens bei der Zurückführung aller Arten auf τὴν τοῦ ἐλέγχου ἄγνοιαν Kap. 6, zweitens in dem Kapitel über die Entstehung der Täuschung (7), und drittens bei der Einzelbehandlung der λύσεις Kap. 18—32. Außerdem wird die Art παρὰ τὸ σχῆμα τῆς λέξεως noch mehreremal gelegentlich erwähnt.

Nach Kapitel 6 fallen drei der auf der Sprache beruhenden Paralogismen nicht unter die Definition des wirklichen ἔλεγχος wegen des in ihnen steckenden Doppelsinnes:

168 a 23   τῶν μὲν γὰρ ἐν τῇ λέξει οἱ μέν εἰσι παρὰ τὸ διττόν, οἷον ἥ τε ὁμωνυμία καὶ ὁ λόγος καὶ ἡ ὁμοιοσχημοσύνη (σύνηθες γὰρ τὸ πάντα ὡς τόδε τι σημαίνειν) . . . es folgen die andern drei. Die Erklärung σύνηθες — σημαίνειν hat schon Pseudo-Alexander Not gemacht, er bezieht sie auf ἀμφιβολία (hier durch λόγος bezeichnet); Waitz bezieht sie auf alle drei, und doch gehört sie, wie auch die noch zu besprechenden weiteren Stellen beweisen, allein zur ὁμοιοσχημοσύνη. Das διττόν in ὁμωνυμία und λόγος liegt nach den vorangegangenen Erklärungen auf der Hand, nicht so das in ὁμοιοσχημοσύνη, daher gibt Aristoteles die Erläuterung, es sei Sprachgebrauch[19], „alles" wie ein τόδε τι zu bezeichnen; daß das Betreffende in derselben Form wie ein τόδε τι gesagt wird und doch etwas anderes ist, das ist der von dem Sophisten ausgenutzte Doppelsinn.

---

[19] σύνηθες = εἰωθότες ἐσμέν vgl. 166a 17, 156b 26; σημαίνειν wie 166b 15 ἔστι γὰρ τὸ μὴ τῶν ποιεῖν ὂν ὡς τῶν ποιεῖν τι τῇ λέξει σημαίνειν.

Die Bestätigung dieser Auffassung gibt 170a15: soll aus dem scheinbaren ἔλεγχος ein wirklicher werden (d. h. einer, der mit Notwendigkeit aus den ausdrücklichen Zugeständnissen des Gegners sich ergibt), so muß man im Falle der ὁμοιοσχημοσύνη noch das Zugeständnis erlangen, daß das Betreffende lediglich τόδε bedeute:

ἂν μὲν γὰρ μὴ λάβῃ ὅ τε παρὰ τὸ ὁμώνυμον ἐν σημαίνειν καὶ ὁ παρὰ τὴν ὁμοιοσχημοσύνην τὸ μόνον τόδε τι σημαίνειν καὶ οἱ ἄλλοι ὡσαύτως, οὔτ᾽ ἔλεγχοι οὔτε συλλογισμοὶ ἔσονται[20].

Ausführlicher geht Aristoteles in dem Kapitel über die Entstehung der Täuschung auf den Fall ein. Die fünf anderen Arten παρὰ τὴν λέξιν sind kurz abgetan:

τῶν δὲ παρὰ τὸ σχῆμα διὰ τὴν ὁμοιότητα τῆς λέξεως (sc. ἡ ἀπάτη   169a 29 γίνεται). χαλεπὸν γὰρ διελεῖν ποῖα ὡσαύτως καὶ ποῖα ὡς ἑτέρως λέγεται (σχεδὸν γὰρ ὁ τοῦτο δυνάμενος ποιεῖν ἐγγύς ἐστι τοῦ θεωρεῖν τἀληθές, μάλιστα δ᾽ ἐπίσταται συνεπινεύειν), ὅτι πᾶν τὸ κατηγορούμενόν τινος ὑπολαμβάνομεν τόδε τι καὶ ὡς ἓν ὑπακού/ομεν· τῷ γὰρ ἑνὶ καὶ τῇ οὐσίᾳ 35 μάλιστα δοκεῖ παρέπεσθαι τὸ τόδε τι καὶ τὸ ὄν. διὸ καὶ τῶν παρὰ τὴν λέξιν οὗτος ὁ τρόπος θετέος, πρῶτον μὲν ὅτι μᾶλλον ἡ ἀπάτη γίνεται μετ᾽ ἄλλων σκοπουμένοις ἢ καθ᾽ αὑτούς (ἡ μὲν γὰρ μετ᾽ ἄλλου σκέψις διὰ λόγων, ἡ δὲ καθ᾽ αὑτὸν οὐχ ἧττον δι᾽ αὐτοῦ τοῦ πράγματος), εἶτα καὶ καθ᾽ αὑτὸν ἀπατᾶσθαι συμ/βαίνει, ὅταν ἐπὶ τοῦ λόγου ποιῆται τὴν 169b 1 σκέψιν· ἔτι ἡ μὲν ἀπάτη ἐκ τῆς ὁμοιότητος, ἡ δ᾽ ὁμοιότης ἐκ τῆς λέξεως.

Man merkt die Mühe, die es Aristoteles gemacht hat, diesen Fall einzuordnen, zugleich aber auch die Wichtigkeit, die er ihm beilegt, und zwar nicht sowohl für die Dialektik, sondern für die eigentliche Philosophie: das ist direkt ausgesprochen. Ein Satz aber muß uns vor allem auffallen: πᾶν τὸ κατηγορούμενόν τινος ὑπολαμβάνομεν τόδε τι καὶ ὡς ἓν ὑπακούομεν: „Jedes, was von etwas prädiziert wird, fassen wir als τόδε τι und hören das Einssein heraus." Bonitz hat bekanntlich die Frage nach der Bedeutung des Namens der Kategorien in folgender Weise zugespitzt (S. 616):

„Diese Bedeutung nun von κατηγορία, κατηγόρημα, κατηγορούμενον, daß nämlich diese Worte das Prädikat eines Urteils bezeichnen, paßt sehr gut für die neun Kategorien mit Ausschluß der ersten; denn die in diesen enthaltenen Bestimmungen nehmen in der Regel und ihrer Natur nach die Stellung des Prädikates in einem Urteil unmittelbar oder mittelbar ein. Wo wir von einer Eigenschaft, einer Größe, einer Beziehung, einer Orts- oder Zeitbestimmung, einem Tun oder Leiden, oder Verhalten u. s. f. reden, ist immer ein Gegenstand vorausgesetzt, welchem als dem Subjekte wir diese Eigenschaft u. s. f. als sein Prädikat beilegen. Anders aber verhält es sich mit der ersten Kategorie, ihr gehört im eigentlichsten und strengsten Sinne an τόδε τι, d. h. das Einzelding, und nur mittelbar auch diejenigen Allgemeinbegriffe, unter welchen wir ganze Arten und Geschlechter der Einzeldinge zusammen-

---

[20] Geraten wird das freilich kaum, vgl. Anm. 34.

fassen, als ἄνθρωπος, ζῷον u. a. m. Von dem Einzeldinge aber hebt Aristoteles nicht etwa allein in der Schrift über die Kategorien, sondern auch sonst an Stellen unbezweifelter Schriften hervor, daß es in der richtigen, nicht willkürlich verschobenen Form der Urteile *nie* die Stelle des *Prädikates* einnehmen kann, sondern *immer* ὑποκείμενον ist, d. h. zugleich *Subjekt*, welchem Prädikate beigelegt werden, und *Substrat*, welchem Accidenzen anhaften. Läßt sich nun auf diese Bedeutung von κατηγορία als Prädikat derjenige Sprachgebrauch des Aristoteles zurückführen, nach welchem derselbe κατηγορίαι fast durchweg zur Bezeichnung der obersten Geschlechter des Seienden anwendet?"

Bonitz findet Trendelenburgs Erklärungen, die man als Bejahung der gestellten Frage nehmen kann, in sich unbefriedigend:

„Aristoteles gibt den von ihm zuerst aufgestellten obersten Geschlechtern des Seienden einen von ihm selbst gewählten Namen, und soll diesen so gewählt haben, daß er wohl auf die übrigen Arten, nur gerade auf diejenige nicht paßt, welche mit vollstem Grunde von ihm *immer* und überall den übrigen *vorausgestellt* wird, oder auf sie wenigstens in ihrer eigentlichsten und wesentlichsten Bedeutung nicht paßt. Ich kann mich von einer solchen Ungeschicklichkeit des Aristoteles in der Wahl philosophischer Kunstausdrücke schlechterdings nicht überzeugen, sondern denke, *wenn* κατηγορίαι nichts anders bezeichnen kann als Prädikate, so hätte er, mag man Deutungskünste daran anwenden wie man will, damit nimmermehr diejenigen Geschlechter benennen können, deren erstes und wichtigstes er ausdrücklich dadurch charakterisiert, daß es *nicht* Prädikat werden kann."

Von dieser Aporie aus gelangt Bonitz zu seiner bereits erwähnten Deutung des Namens der Kategorien, und um sie dreht sich im Grunde der ganze Streit. Selbst Apelt hat sich nicht anders zu helfen gewußt, als dem unbequemen τόδε τι, das auch nach ihm nie Prädikat, sondern immer nur Subjekt sein können soll, mittelst der Statistik seine Stellung in der ersten Kategorie streitig zu machen. Und an unserer *Topik*stelle heißt es nicht nur, τόδε τι könne Prädikat sein, sondern wir hätten die Neigung, jedes Prädikat, „πᾶν τὸ κατηγορούμενόν τινος", als τόδε τι aufzufassen. Unmöglich kann bei der Wendung, die Bonitz der Sache gegeben hat, alles in Ordnung sein.

Was Aristoteles unter dem angeführten Satz verstanden hat, darüber belehrt das 22. Kapitel. Der Anfang lautet:

178a 4   δῆλον δὲ καὶ τοῖς παρὰ τὸ ὡσαύτως λέγεσθαι τὰ μὴ ταὐτὰ πῶς ἀπαντητέον, ἐπείπερ ἔχομεν τὰ γένη τῶν κατηγοριῶν. Hier ist die Kategorienteilung das ausschließliche Lösungsmittel. Wir müssen uns darein finden, daß damit die zu allererst gegebenen Beispiele für die Fehlschlüsse dieser Art (166b 11 οἷον τὸ ἄρρεν θῆλυ ἢ τὸ θῆλυ ἄρρεν, ἢ τὸ μεταξὺ θάτερον τούτων) unter den Tisch zu fallen scheinen[21]. Eine ernstliche Schwierigkeit aber macht, was nun kommt:

---

[21] Eine gewisse, freilich entfernte und rein sprachliche Beziehung gibt es. Eins der fünf Ziele im Wortkampf ist nach Kapitel 3 das σολοικίζειν ποιεῖν, das dann Kap. 14 behandelt wird. Zum Schluß zieht Aristoteles den belebenden Vergleich:

ὁ μὲν γὰρ ἔδωκεν ἐρωτηθεὶς μὴ ὑπάρχειν τι τούτων ὅσα τί ἐστι 178 a 6
σημαίνει· ὁ δ᾽ ἔδειξεν ὑπάρχον τι τῶν πρός τι ἢ ποσῶν, δοκούντων δὲ
τί ἐστι σημαίνειν διὰ τὴν λέξιν, οἷον ἐν τῷδε τῷ λόγῳ.

Daß hier im Hinblick auf A 9 τί ἐστι zur Bezeichnung der ersten
Kategorie gewählt wird — im weiteren Verlauf des Kapitels heißt es
τόδε und τόδε τι —, das ist ganz in der Ordnung. Aber man sollte doch
erwarten, daß in dem zunächst folgenden Beispiel die erste Kategorie
eine Rolle spielte und daß dies überhaupt ohne weiteres zu der vorhergehenden allgemeinen Erläuterung paßte. Das tut in Wahrheit aber
erst etwa 178 a 36: καὶ ὅτι δοίη ἄν τις ὃ μὴ ἔχει. οὐ γὰρ ἔχει ἕνα μόνον
ἀστράγαλον. Hier ist wirklich der Fall, daß der Gefragte zunächst
zugibt μὴ ὑπάρχειν τι τούτων ὅσα τί ἐστι σημαίνει und daß der andere
dann ein πρός τι aufzeigt, das aber sprachlich τί ἐστι zu bedeuten
scheint (178 a 38 ἢ οὐ δέδωκεν ὃ οὐκ εἶχεν, ἀλλ᾽ ὡς οὐκ εἶχεν, τὸν ἕνα.
τὸ γὰρ μόνον οὐ τόδε σημαίνει ... ἀλλ᾽ ὡς ἔχει πρός τι, οἷον ὅτι οὐ
μετ᾽ ἄλλου). Dagegen handelt es sich in den beiden Beispielen 178a

καὶ τρόπον τινὰ ὅμοιός ἐστιν ὁ σολοικισμὸς τοῖς παρὰ τὸ τὰ μὴ ὅμοια ὁμοίως λεγομένοις ἐλέγχοις. ὥσπερ γὰρ ἐκείνοις ἐπὶ τῶν πραγμάτων, τούτοις ἐπὶ τῶν ὀνομάτων
συμπίπτει σολοικίζειν· ἄνθρωπος γὰρ καὶ λευκὸν καὶ πρᾶγμα καὶ ὄνομά ἐστιν.
Was den Vergleich nahelegte, ja ihn zur Rechtfertigung der eigenen Einteilung
gewissermaßen forderte, war, daß die Erschleichungen von Soloikismen durchweg
auf der Verwendung des neutr. sing. eines Demonstrativums oder Relativums beruhen, gerade wie ein Teil der Fehlschlüsse παρὰ τὸ σχῆμα τῆς λέξεως. Der Unterschied ist, daß im ersten Fall durch ein τοῦτο eine verkehrte Kasusform wie λίθον
statt λίθος, im zweiten etwa durch ein ὅ ein verkehrter Sinn erschlichen wird. Nun
hat Aristoteles zur Bezeichnung des neutr. sing. eines Demonstrativums oder
Relativums nur den Ausdruck τόδε, der von τόδε τι in dem Sinne, daß es sich um
ein Ding handelt, um so weniger scharf getrennt werden kann, als dieser Sinn
meist gleichzeitig vorhanden ist. Für das τόδε bei der Erschleichung des Soloikismus ist es nun wesentlich, daß es für ein ἄρρεν oder θῆλυ eintreten kann, vgl.
173b 26ff. und Kapitel 32. — Übrigens sind diese Kapitel über den Soloikismus
gerade dafür charakteristisch, wie wenig sich Aristoteles durch den Mangel an
grammatischen Termini beirren ließ und wie gut er sich ihm zum Trotz dem klar
durchschauten sprachlichen Unfug gegenüber zu helfen wußte. So berechtigt der
Hinweis ist, daß für Aristoteles *unsere* Kategorien ,,grammatisch, logisch, meta-
physisch" nicht existieren, so bedenklich ist die namentlich von Steinthal getriebene Art der Aristoteleserklärung, die das Wesentliche ihrer Aufgabe darin
sucht, ohne weiteres überall naive Dunkelheit und Hilflosigkeit zu wittern. ,,Es
wird ganz unzweideutig gesagt, daß das Seiende (τὰ ὄντα) gesagt wird (λέγεται).
Uns in diese naive Dunkelheit zu versetzen, ist eine harte Zumutung; aber, wenn
wir sie nicht erfüllen, bleibt uns Aristoteles unverständlich" (Steinthal, Gesch.
der Sprachw., II, 1891, 215). Ich möchte bezweifeln, daß das von solchem Standpunkt aus für *Cat.* 1a 20ff. gewonnene Verständnis sehr adäquat ist. Freilich,
wenn man die Termini absolut nimmt und sich nicht darum kümmert, was im
jeweiligen Zusammenhang zum Ausdruck kommen soll! Das führt allerdings zu
Feststellungen wie S. 206: ,,Aristoteles scheint eben niemals zu einer abschlie-
ßenden Ansicht über den Sinn von κατηγορία und κατηγορεῖν gekommen zu sein"!

9 ff. um den Unterschied von ποιεῖν und πάσχειν. Es ist versucht worden, das durch Annahme einer Lücke zu erklären, aber man sieht nicht, was ausgefallen sein sollte. Wahrscheinlicher ist mir daher, daß diese Beispiele nur daran angehängt sind, daß διὰ τὴν λέξιν eine *verkehrte* Bedeutung, wenn auch nicht gerade die der ersten Kategorie, vorgespiegelt wird, denn um das anschaulich zu machen, dazu eignen sich Aktivum und Passivum des Verbums in der Tat besonders gut, und in dieser Funktion ist ersteres auch schon 166 b 15 ff. aufgetreten. Ja eigentlich wiederholt sich nur sehr auffallend das ungeklärte Verhältnis, das schon zwischen der gerade genannten Stelle 166 b 10 bis 19 einerseits und 168 a 25 f., 169 b 29 ff., 170 a 15 andererseits besteht; denn auch da läßt sich die ὁμοιοσχημοσύνη der Beispiele schwerlich unter den Sprachgebrauch, alles als τόδε τι zu bezeichnen, unterordnen, illustriert aber die Möglichkeit eines solchen trügerischen Sprachgebrauches vortrefflich. Ob doch irgendwie mitspielt, daß man jeden Satz unter die Formel τόδε εἶναι τόδε bringen kann, vermag ich nicht zu bestimmen. Jedenfalls ist der Stoff nicht ganz von der Darstellung durchdrungen; die nicht zu unterschätzende Schwierigkeit, eines so aller Ordnung widerstrebenden Materials überhaupt systematisch Herr zu werden, macht solche Unebenheiten begreiflich.

Bei der Besprechung der beiden ersten Beispiele legt Aristoteles wie häufig Wert darauf, das Verschweigen der falschen Prämisse festzunageln, durch deren ausdrückliche Aufstellung erst ein wirklicher Syllogismus zustande kommen würde. Dabei fällt die Wendung: τὸ δὲ λέγεται μὲν οὐχ ὁμοίως, φαίνεται δὲ διὰ τὴν λέξιν, die zeigt, daß ὁμοίως λέγεσθαι bei Aristoteles die Bedeutung „in demselben Sinne gesagt werden" haben kann, gerade wie es 107 a 14 hieß οὐ γὰρ ὡσαύτως ἐπὶ πάντων τὸ αὐτὸ λέγεται. Dagegen 178 a 4 heißt ὡσαύτως λέγεσθαι „in derselben sprachlichen Form gesagt werden". Doch das ist ganz durchsichtig, und gerade weil der Sinn entgegengesetzt ist, ist ein Durcheinandergehen dieser Bedeutungen ausgeschlossen. Ihnen entsprechen auf der einen Seite Ausdrücke wie σχῆμα λέξεως, ὁμοιοσχημοσύνη, auf der anderen γένη oder σχήματα τῆς κατηγορίας; das kommt schon nahe genug aneinander heran, πτώσεις kommt auf beiden Seiten vor: aber ich meine, man kann sich das Verfehlte von Trendelenburgs Versuch, den „Ursprung der Bezeichnung σχήματα τῆς κατηγορίας oder τῶν κατηγοριῶν zunächst nicht in den inneren Begrenzungen des Begriffs, sondern in der verschiedenen Gestalt des Ausdrucks, welche die verschiedenen Aussagen begleitet," (Gesch. d. Kategorienlehre, 1896, 8) zu fassen, nicht deutlicher machen, als wenn man sich überlegt, daß dies im Grunde dasselbe ist, wie wenn man die eine Bedeutung von ὡσαύτως λέγεσθαι als ursprünglich identisch mit der anderen nehmen wollte.

Von 178a29 an bis b36 folgt eine ganze Reihe weiterer Beispiele, die alle mittelst der Kategorienunterscheidung gelöst werden[22] und das Gemeinsame haben, daß der Doppelsinn nicht in dem, was wir Prädikat nennen, sondern in einem als Objekt auftretenden ὅ steckt. Die Lösung ist immer, daß dasjenige, was fälschlich unter dieses ὅ gebracht wird, οὐ τόδε σημαίνει, sondern eine der anderen Kategorien. Hieraus fällt ein Licht auf jenes πᾶν τὸ κατηγορούμενόν τινος. Denn wir müssen annehmen, daß Aristoteles dabei gerade auch diese zahlreichen Fälle im Auge gehabt hat. Also ist der Ausdruck κατηγορούμενον nicht so eng zu nehmen wie unser ,,Prädikat''. Aber ebenso klar ist, daß auch in diesen Fällen der Doppelsinn erst durch das tatsächliche Aussagen des einer mehrfachen Auslegung fähigen Ausdrucks in einem bestimmten Satz zustande kommt. Was den Doppelsinn herbeiführt, ist der Sprachgebrauch, der es nach 168a25f. erlaubt, πάντα ὡς τόδε τι σημαίνειν, d. h. alle ,,Kategorien'' in der Form der ersten auszudrücken; nämlich z. B. in solchen Fällen, wie sie in Kap. 22 angeführt sind; dahin bestimmt sich der Sinn der angezogenen Stelle von selbst.

Das Interessanteste bringt der Schluß des Kapitels:
καὶ ὅτι ἔστι τις τρίτος ἄνθρωπος παρ' αὐτὸν καὶ τοὺς καθ' ἕκαστον. 178b36
τὸ γὰρ ἄνθρωπος καὶ ἅπαν τὸ κοινὸν οὐ τόδε τι, ἀλλὰ τοιόνδε τι ἢ
πρός τι ἢ πῶς ἢ τῶν τοιούτων τι σημαίνει. ὁμοίως δὲ καὶ ἐπὶ τοῦ Κο/-
ρίσκος καὶ Κορίσκος μουσικός, πότερον ταὐτὸν ἢ ἕτερον· τὸ μὲν γὰρ τόδε 179a1
τι τὸ δὲ τοιόνδε σημαίνει, ὥστ' οὐκ ἔστιν αὐτὸ ἐκθέσθαι (cf. *Met.* 1003a
9ff.)· οὐ τὸ ἐκτίθεσθαι δὲ ποιεῖ τὸν τρίτον ἄνθρωπον, ἀλλὰ τὸ ὅπερ
τόδε τι εἶναι συγχωρεῖν. οὐ γὰρ ἔσται τόδε τι εἶναι,/ ὅπερ Καλλίας καὶ 5
ὅπερ ἄνθρωπός ἐστιν. οὐδ' εἴ τις τὸ ἐκτιθέμενον μὴ ὅπερ τόδε τι εἶναι
λέγοι ἀλλ' ὅπερ ποιόν, οὐδὲν διοίσει· ἔσται γὰρ τὸ παρὰ τοὺς πολλοὺς
ἕν τι, οἷον τὸ ἄνθρωπος. φανερὸν οὖν ὅτι οὐ δοτέον τόδε τι εἶναι τὸ κοινῇ
κατηγορούμενον ἐπὶ πᾶσιν, ἀλλ' ἤτοι ποιὸν ἢ πρός τι ἢ ποσὸν ἢ τῶν
τοιούτων τι σημαίνειν.

Hier handelt es sich nicht mehr um bloße Spielereien, wie ἆρ' ἐστί τι τῶν πάσχειν ποιεῖν τι; (178a11), ἆρ' ὃ μή τις ἔχει δοίη ἄν; (178b2) und ἆρ' ὃ βαδίζει τις πατεῖ (178b31). Der τρίτος ἄνθρωπος ist für Aristoteles notwendige Konsequenz aus der Ideenlehre, so daß die Widerlegung nur aus demselben Grunde geschehen kann wie die der Ideenlehre selbst; und auch hinter der Frage, ob Koriskos und ,,gebildeter Koriskos'' dasselbe oder verschiedenes sei, steckt für Aristoteles ein Problem, das um seiner prinzipiellen Wichtigkeit willen immer wieder gerade auch in wirklich philosophischen Erörterungen auftaucht. Wenn also 169a30 gesagt wurde, es sei schwierig auseinanderzuhalten, ποῖα

---

[22] Eine Ausnahme macht eigentlich das letzte 178b34, wo der Unterschied von Singular und Plural das Entscheidende ist.

ὡσαύτως καὶ ποῖα ὡς ἑτέρως λέγεται, und wer das könnte, der wäre so ziemlich an der Wahrheit selber[23], so werden wir das gerade auf diese Fälle beziehen, auf die andern paßt es gar nicht. Hier weist also die *Topik* über sich selbst hinaus auf die ernsthafte Philosophie, der diese Dinge eigentlich angehören, während sie in der *Topik* nur als Sophismen neben anderen Sophismen rubriziert erscheinen und nur andeutend[24] behandelt werden.

Die Erklärung des Textes ist zunächst dadurch erschwert, daß sich die Behandlung der Koriskosfrage in die des τρίτος ἄνθρωπος einschiebt. Sie selbst ist einfach. Die Frage, ,,Ist Koriskos dasselbe wie gebildeter Koriskos?'', kann man bejahen oder verneinen, in jedem Falle wird man dem Sophisten eine Handhabe bieten. Wie das gemacht zu werden pflegt, setzt Aristoteles als bekannt voraus; er gibt nur den Hinweis, daß Koriskos ein Ding, ,,gebildeter Koriskos'' aber so, wie es von dem Sophisten verwendet wird, nur eine Beschaffenheit bezeichnet, daß beides also nicht beliebig füreinander eingesetzt werden kann[25]. Dem Wortlaut nach würde man bei den Worten ὥστ' οὐκ ἔστιν αὐτὸ ἐκθέσθαι gerne auch noch an diesen Fall denken, ich sehe dazu aber keine Möglichkeit. Von der Feststellung, daß ,,Mensch'' und alles Allgemeine nicht Ding, sondern Beschaffenheit usw. bezeichnet, kommt Aristoteles darauf, daß dieser Gegensatz auch bei Koriskos und ,,gebildeter Koriskos'' vorliege, um dann an die auch hier zutreffende Erklärung τὸ μὲν γὰρ τόδε τι τὸ δὲ τοιόνδε σημαίνει ohne weiteres die Fortsetzung der Besprechung des τρίτος ἄνθρωπος anzuhängen. Aber auch wenn man das gelten und den Koriskos nunmehr ganz ausscheiden läßt, ist die Erklärung nicht ganz einfach. Wir werden gut tun, eine Darstellung des τρίτος ἄνθρωπος, die ausdrücklich für Aristoteles selbst bezeugt ist (fr. 188), zu Hilfe zu nehmen[26]:

[23] Aristoteles fügt noch hinzu: μάλιστα δ᾽ ἐπίσταται συνεπινεύειν, er versteht am besten im Gespräch mit einem andern Ja zu sagen, natürlich wo es am Platze ist, d. h. er ist die beste Kontrolle für ein Gespräch.

[24] Dies im Gegensatz zu dem sonstigen Verfahren (vgl. z. B. 177b 27ff., 178b 10ff., 179b 7ff.). Aber sich auf die philosophischen und nicht nur dialektischen Probleme einzulassen war die *Topik* eben nicht der richtige Ort.

[25] Aber auch nicht beliebig für verschieden erklärt werden kann, vgl. *Top.* 133b 31ff., wo dieselbe Sache in ganz anderen Ausdrücken behandelt wird: οὐκ ἔστιν ἕτερον ἁπλῶς τὸ ᾧ συμβέβηκε καὶ τὸ συμβεβηκὸς μετὰ τοῦ ᾧ συμβέβηκε λαμβανόμενον, ἀλλ᾽ ἄλλο λέγεται τῷ ἕτερον εἶναι αὐτοῖς τὸ εἶναι· οὐ ταὐτὸν γάρ ἐστιν ἀνθρώπῳ τε τὸ εἶναι ἀνθρώπῳ καὶ λευκῷ ἀνθρώπῳ τὸ εἶναι ἀνθρώπῳ λευκῷ. Die Identität der Sache in beiden Stellen ist eine der Voraussetzungen für die Verbindung der Kategorienlehre mit der Lehre von der Homonymie des Seins, die mir aber in der *Topik* nirgends vollzogen zu sein scheint. Trotzdem wird der Hinweis erlaubt sein, daß auch 133b 31ff. die zugestandene und durch Beispiele belegte Verschiedenheit der untersuchten Begriffe die von Prädikaten ist.

[26] Der von Pseudo-Alexander zu unserer Stelle angeführte λεγόμενος ὑπὸ τῶν σοφιστῶν λόγος paßt gar nicht und ist von ihm offenbar nur um dieser Bezeichnung willen, die er vorfand (vgl. Alex. zur *Metaph.* 990b 15), hier gewählt worden.

δείκνυται καὶ οὕτως ὁ τρίτος ἄνθρωπος. εἰ τὸ κατηγορούμενον τινῶν S. 151 Z. 5
πλειόνων ἀληθῶς καὶ ἔστιν ἄλλο παρὰ τὰ ὧν κατηγορεῖται κεχωρισμένον Rose
αὐτῶν· τοῦτο γὰρ ἡγοῦνται δεικνύναι οἱ τὰς ἰδέας τιθέμενοι, διὰ τοῦτο
γάρ ἐστί τι αὐτοάνθρωπος κατ᾽ αὐτούς, ὅτι ὁ ἄνθρωπος κατὰ τῶν καθ᾽
ἕκαστα ἀνθρώπων πλειόνων ὄντων ἀληθῶς κατηγορεῖται καὶ ἄλλος
τῶν καθ᾽ ἕκαστα ἀνθρώπων ἐστίν· ἀλλ᾽ εἰ τοῦτο, ἔσται τις τρίτος
ἄνθρωπος. εἰ γὰρ ἄλλος ὁ κατηγορούμενος ὧν κατηγορεῖται καὶ κατ᾽
ἰδίαν ὑφεστώς, κατηγορεῖται δὲ κατά τε τῶν καθ᾽ ἕκαστα καὶ κατὰ τῆς
ἰδέας ὁ ἄνθρωπος, ἔσται τρίτος τις ἄνθρωπος παρά τε τοὺς καθ᾽ ἕκαστα
καὶ τὴν ἰδέαν. οὕτως δὲ καὶ τέταρτος ὁ κατά τε τούτου καὶ τῆς ἰδέας καὶ
τῶν καθ᾽ ἕκαστα κατηγορούμενος, ὁμοίως δὲ καὶ πέμπτος καὶ τοῦτο
ἐπ᾽ ἄπειρον.

Danach ist die Tatsache, worauf sich die Ideenlehre stützt, daß der
Allgemeinbegriff wahr von den Einzeldingen ausgesagt werden kann
und gleichwohl, da dabei doch nicht etwa das Einzelding von sich
selbst ausgesagt wird[27], etwas anderes sein muß. Die Ideenlehre
nimmt nun dies eine, das von den Einzeldingen gesagt wird und doch
etwas anderes ist, und sondert es aus, als ein weiteres Einzelding,
behauptet Aristoteles, so daß man das Verfahren wiederholen kann
und so zum τρίτος ἄνθρωπος kommt. Dagegen erklärt *er*, das κοινόν
ist kein τόδε τι, sondern ein τοιόνδε, das man nicht aussondern kann.
Man kann nicht sagen, daß er hier vorzugsweise an das erste ἐκτίθεσθαι,
welches auf die Idee, oder an das zweite, welches auf den τρίτος ἄνθρωπος führt, dachte; die Kritik setzt zunächst daran an, daß überhaupt ein κοινόν, d. h. nach Aristoteles ein τοιόνδε oder πρός τι usw.,
ausgesondert würde, was unzulässig sei. Und dann wird schärfer zuge-
griffen und erklärt, der Fehler liege nicht eigenlich in dem Aussondern,
sondern in dem Zugeständnis, es handele sich um ein τόδε τι (cf.
An. pr. 49b 33ff.). Denn unmöglich könne ein τόδε τι sein, was Kallias
und was Mensch ist, d. h. was von ‚Kallias‘ und von ‚Mensch“ gesagt
werden kann (hier denkt man am bequemsten an die Voraussetzung
des zweiten ἐκτίθεσθαι fr. 188 S. 151 Z. 14 Rose: κατηγορεῖται δὲ κατά
τε τῶν καθ᾽ ἕκαστα καὶ κατὰ τῆς ἰδέας ὁ ἄνθρωπος). Das ἐκτίθεσθαι
eines τοιόνδε dagegen ist diskutabel (wenn es auch nicht unbedingt
akzeptiert wird): wollte jemand sagen, das ἐκτιθέμενον als solches
sei nicht τόδε τι, sondern ποιόν, so wäre es kein Einwand dagegen,

---

[27] Vgl. die Darstellung in fr. 187 (S. 150 Z. 5ff. Rose): εἰ ἕκαστος τῶν πολλῶν ἀνθρώπων ἄνθρωπός ἐστι καὶ τῶν ζῴων ζῷον καὶ ἐπὶ τῶν ἄλλων ὁμοίως, καὶ οὐκ ἔστιν
ἐφ᾽ ἑκάστου αὐτῶν αὐτὸ αὑτοῦ τι κατηγορούμενον, ἀλλ᾽ ἔστι τι ὃ καὶ πάντων
αὐτῶν κατηγορεῖται οὐδενὶ αὐτῶν ταὐτὸν ὄν, εἴη ἄν τι τούτων παρὰ τὰ καθ᾽
ἕκαστα ὄντα ὂν κεχωρισμένον αὐτῶν ἀίδιον· ἀεὶ γὰρ ὁμοίως κατηγορεῖται
πάντων τῶν κατ᾽ ἀριθμὸν ἀλλασσομένων. ὃ δὲ ἕν ἐστιν ἐπὶ πολλοῖς κεχωρισμένον
τε αὐτῶν καὶ ἀίδιον, τοῦτ᾽ ἐστιν ἰδέα· εἰσὶν ἄρα ἰδέαι.

daß dann jeder Unterschied zwischen Einzeldingen und κοινόν auf-
gehoben würde — an dieser Voraussetzung der Ideenlehre, daß das
von den Einzeldingen ausgesagte „Mensch" mit diesen nicht identisch
ist, wird unbedingt festgehalten —, vielmehr bleibe nach wie vor
τὸ παρὰ τοὺς πολλοὺς ἕν τι, nämlich das κοινόν ἄνθρωπος, aber eben
als ein nicht schlechtweg selbständig existierendes ποιόν. Das zum
Anfang stimmende Ergebnis, daß der eigentliche Fehler darin liegt,
daß das κοινόν als τόδε τι gefaßt wird, wird nachdrücklich hervorgehoben: φανερὸν οὖν ὅτι οὐ δοτέον τόδε τι εἶναι τὸ κοινῇ κατηγορούμενον ἐπὶ πᾶσιν, ἀλλ᾽ ἤτοι ποιὸν ἢ πρός τι ἢ ποσὸν ἢ τῶν τοιούτων τι
σημαίνειν.

Damit sind die wichtigsten Stellen, in denen die *Topik* die Kategorienlehre heranzieht, besprochen. Ich frage: besteht die mindeste
Veranlassung, ja besteht auch nur die Möglichkeit, angesichts dieser
Stellen entweder dem τόδε τι seine Stellung in der ersten Kategorie
streitig zu machen, oder aber in dem Wort κατηγορία, wie es in γένη
τῶν κατηγοριῶν (τῆς κατηγορίας), der einzigen eigentlichen Bezeichnung, die die *Topik* für die „Kategorien" hat[28], erscheint, eine besondere, von der gewöhnlichen auf den Satz oder das Urteil bezogenen
Bedeutung abweichende zu suchen? Daß wir diese gewöhnliche Bedeutung nicht ohne weiteres mit unserm sei es grammatischen, sei es
logischen Terminus Prädikat, Prädizierung identifizieren dürfen, ist
wirklich selbstverständlich; worauf es ankommt, ist, daß sie durch
keinerlei scharfe, auch für Aristoteles gültige Grenze davon geschieden
ist.

Daß für die erste Kategorie in der *Topik* der Begriff des τόδε τι,
des „Dinges" oder wie man sagen will, wesentlich ist, und daß auch τί
ἐστι nur, insofern diese Bedeutung darinsteckt, ursprünglich hineingehört, dafür glaube ich einfach auf die Besprechung der einzelnen
Stellen hinweisen zu dürfen. Und für die Bedeutung von κατηγορία
braucht man eigentlich auch nur die Frage aufzuwerfen, um wenigstens
die Richtung, in der die Antwort liegen muß, zu sehen. Wenn es
169a 33 heißt πᾶν τὸ κατηγορούμενόν τινος ὑπολαμβάνομεν τόδε τι καὶ
ὡς ἓν ὑπακούομεν, so denkt Aristoteles dabei, wie sich schon aus der

---

[28] Denn αἱ ἄλλαι κατηγορίαι ist von γένη τῶν κατηγοριῶν abhängig; ἐν τῇ αὐτῇ
διαιρέσει ist an sich nichtssagend. Einmal, 182b 30, heißt es nur ἐν τίνι γένει;
hier ergibt sich die Bedeutung γένος τῆς κατηγορίας mit ähnlicher Notwendigkeit
aus dem Zusammenhang (vgl. Anm. 22) wie etwa 168a 25 für λόγος die an
sich freilich noch viel weniger darin liegende: ἀμφιβολία. 146b 21 bezeichnet ἡ
κατὰ τὰς ἄλλας διαφοράς, obwohl vorher drei „Kategorien" aufgeführt sind, nicht
die „übrigen Kategorien", sondern die übrigen in den betreffenden Fällen in
Frage kommenden unterscheidenden Merkmale, wie b 30, wo ὑπὸ τίνος hinzutritt
und in den beiden folgenden Zeilen ganz deutlich wird (vgl. Bonitz, Ind. 378a 43).

unmittelbar vorhergehenden Hervorhebung der Wichtigkeit dieses Punktes für die Erkenntnis der Wahrheit, aber auch aus der Betonung des ἕν ergibt, unter allen Umständen auch an die für die Auseinandersetzung mit der Ideenlehre fundamentale Trennung von κοινόν und τόδε τι. Dann dürfen wir uns den Sinn des Wortes κατηγορούμενον, das in dem κοινῇ κατηγορούμενον ἐπὶ πᾶσιν 179a9 wiederkehrt und von dem die γένη τῶν κατηγοριῶν 178a5 unmöglich zu trennen sind, unbedenklich aus der angeführten aristotelischen Darstellung des τρίτος ἄνθρωπος erläutern: κατηγορεῖσθαι liegt also z. B. vor, wenn ein Allgemeinbegriff von einem Einzelding ausgesagt wird, also in: Καλλίας ἐστὶν ἄνθρωπος. Daß Aristoteles hier wirkliche Sätze oder Urteile im Sinne hat, zeigt der Zusatz ἀληθῶς zu κατηγορεῖται: auf das Zugeständnis der Wahrheit solcher Sätze stützt sich die Ideenlehre; wahr und falsch sein findet sich nur im Satz (vgl. z. B. *Cat.* 2a 4—9). Immerhin bleibt die Bedeutung von κατηγορεῖσθαι so weit, daß, wie wir sahen, beispielsweise das Objekt ὅ in ἆρ' ὃ μή τις ἔχει δοίη ἄν; darunter geordnet werden kann. Auf der andern Seite aber beruhte die scharfe und wie selbstverständlich gemachte Unterscheidung von γένος und γένος τῆς κατηγορίας darauf, daß letzteres erst da herauskommt, wo es sich um ein wirkliches Aussagen, ein Aussagen im Satze, handelt; an einer Stelle, wo diese Beziehung nicht aufrechtzuhalten ist, fehlte das Wort κατηγορία.

Es ist nicht ganz unberechtigt, wenn Bonitz die „jedem Leser des Aristoteles, namentlich der logischen Schriften des Philosophen" bekannte Bedeutung von κατηγορεῖν, κατηγορία, κατηγόρημα für die Erklärung des Namens der Kategorien nicht gelten lassen will. Denn man denkt allerdings unwillkürlich an die schärfere Ausprägung der Bedeutung, die nur die in der Schlußlehre der *Analytiken* vorkommenden Prädikate trifft und die in einem ganz bestimmten Verhältnis zu dem Begriff ‚Einzelding‘ steht. In der aristotelischen Schlußlehre gibt es kein ‚Ding‘ als Prädikat, und Aristoteles hat innerhalb ihrer ausdrücklich die Bedeutung des Terminus κατηγορεῖσθαι so bestimmt, daß er für Einzeldinge höchstens κατὰ συμβεβηκός gilt: *An. pr.* 1, 27, *post.* 1, 22. Danach können im eigentlichen Sinne prädiziert werden nur 1) τὰ ἐν τῷ τί ἐστι κατηγορούμενα (d. h. γένος und διαφορά), 2) ὅτι ποιόν, ποσόν, πρός τι usw. Dagegen von den Einzeldingen heißt es 43a25: (ἁπάντων δὴ τῶν ὄντων τὰ μέν) ἐστι τοιαῦτα ὥστε κατὰ μηδενὸς ἄλλου κατηγορεῖσθαι ἀληθῶς καθόλου, οἷον Κλέων καὶ Καλλίας καὶ τὸ καθ' ἕκαστον καὶ αἰσθητόν, κατὰ δὲ τούτων ἄλλα· καὶ γὰρ ἄνθρωπος καὶ ζῷον ἑκάτερος τούτων ἐστί und weiterhin 32 ὅτι μὲν οὖν ἔνια τῶν ὄντων κατ' οὐδενὸς πέφυκε λέγεσθαι, δῆλον· τῶν γὰρ αἰσθητῶν σχεδὸν ἕκαστόν ἐστι τοιοῦτον ὥστε μὴ κατηγορεῖσθαι κατὰ μηδενός, πλὴν ὡς κατὰ συμβεβηκός· φαμὲν γάρ ποτε τὸ λευκὸν ἐκεῖνο Σωκράτην εἶναι καὶ τὸ προσιὸν Καλλίαν. Auf *dieses* Verhältnis des Begriffes ‚Ding‘ zu κατηγορεῖσθαι kann man den Namen der Kategorien allerdings nicht zurückführen, aber es hat sich, denke ich, bereits gezeigt, daß man für die Erklärung der *Topik* damit nicht auskommt. Erweitern muß man die uns geläufigere Vorstellung wirklich bis zu einem gewissen Grade, wenn man den Namen der Kategorien verstehen will, aber man darf darüber nicht gleich jede Beziehung zum Satz oder Urteil verwerfen.

Was an Bonitz’ Behauptung, das τόδε τι könne kein κατηγορούμενον im gewöhnlichen Sinne sein, Richtiges ist, sagt die *Topik* selbst (179a8): φανερὸν οὖν ὡς οὐ δοτέον τόδε τι εἶναι τὸ κοινῇ κατηγορούμενον ἐπὶ πᾶσιν. Aber dieser Satz setzt die Möglichkeit, daß unter Umständen ein κατηγορούμενον ein τόδε τι ist, voraus, denn er wendet sich ja gerade gegen den doch nur dieser Möglichkeit entstammenden Sprachgebrauch, „*jedes*“ κατηγορούμενον als τόδε τι zu fassen.

Welcherlei Sätze mit τόδε τι im Prädikat für die erste Kategorie übrigbleiben, scheint danach klar: solche, in denen das Prädikat kein κοινῇ κατηγορούμενον ist; und ich glaube auch, daß man damit den unmittelbaren Sinn der *Topik*stelle trifft[29]. Aber schwer einzusehen ist, wie Aristoteles gleichzeitig aus solchen immerhin besonders gearteten Sätzen den Ursprung des Scheines, der in „allen“ Prädikaten ein τόδε τι erblicken läßt, herleiten kann. Damit wird auch fraglich, ob der Ursprung der ersten Kategorie selbst ausschließlich auf Sätze

---

[29] Es klingt allerdings ganz plausibel, wenn unter Berufung darauf, daß Aristoteles selbst das Prädizieren eines Einzeldings als ein uneigentliches bezeichnet habe, behauptet wird, daß diese Art des Prädizierens für die Kategorienlehre unter allen Umständen außer Betracht zu bleiben habe. Dabei klammert man sich im Grunde daran, daß Aristoteles, eben um diese Unterscheidung machen zu können, die aus Bequemlichkeitsgründen auch anderwärts (vgl. περὶ ἐνυπνίων 458b 10ff.) gebrauchte Formulierung τὸ προσιόν ἐστι ... oder eine ähnliche wählt. Wo bleiben aber bei der darauf gegründeten Unterscheidung Sätze wie „Dies ist Kallias“? Die liegen in Wahrheit in einer ganz andern Richtung und können von Sätzen wie „Dies ist ein Mensch“ (wo durch das κοινόν Mensch ja gleichwohl ausgedrückt wird, daß es sich um ein τόδε τι handelt) nicht getrennt werden. Solche Sätze liegen auf dem Wege, der Aristoteles zu seiner Unterscheidung von ὕλη und οὐσία geführt hat, deren Konsequenz τὰ μὲν γὰρ ἄλλα τῆς οὐσίας κατηγορεῖται, αὕτη δὲ τῆς ὕλης (*Met.* 1029a 23) man ebenfalls für die Deutung der Kategorienlehre nicht in Betracht ziehen lassen will. Zugestanden, daß es sich hier um eine Weiterbildung handelt, die z. B. in der *Topik* höchstens im Keime vorhanden sein könnte, so darf doch wohl daran erinnert werden, daß in dieser Weiterbildung τόδε τι zwar Einzelding ist, daß aber dasjenige, wodurch ein wirkliches Einzelding ist, die οὐσία und nicht etwa, was uns näher läge, die ὕλη ist und insofern τόδε τι auf Seiten der οὐσία, die ausgesagt werden kann, steht. — Für die Erklärung des *Ursprungs* der Kategorienlehre halte ich die Heranziehung von Sätzen der besprochenen Art nicht unbedingt für erforderlich, aber ihre Berücksichtigung überhaupt zu verbieten scheint mir eine ganz willkürliche Einseitigkeit.

dieser Art zurückzuführen ist. Wir müssen versuchen, das Verhältnis der Stelle zur Kategorienlehre noch weiter aufzuklären.

Die Widerlegung des Sophismas vom dritten Menschen ist die philosophisch bedeutsamste Anwendung der Kategorienteilung innerhalb der *Topik*. Den von Aristoteles selbst gegebenen Hinweis, daß es sich bei der Fehlerquelle der Schlüsse παρὰ τὸ σχῆμα τῆς λέξεως um einen Punkt von unter Umständen größter Schwierigkeit und besonderer philosophischer Wichtigkeit handele, mußten wir auf den Zusammenhang des τρίτος ἄνθρωπος mit der Ideenlehre beziehen. Da nun ohnedies die ganze Art und Weise, wie in der *Topik* die Kategorienlehre herangezogen, übrigens aber gar nicht voll ausgenutzt wird, unverkennbar macht, daß sie nicht für die Zwecke der *Topik* gefunden ist wie jene Vierteilung, so liegt die Vermutung nicht fern, in der Bestreitung der Ideenlehre wenn nicht den „Grund des Entwurfs", so doch den Punkt zu treffen, an dem der Entwurf der Kategorienlehre ansetzt. Aber das ist so schwerlich richtig. In der *Topik* wenigstens finden wir auch hier nur eine Anwendung, nicht den Ursprung der Kategorienlehre. Das äußert sich in einem eigentümlichen Widerspruch, zu dem die Anwendung führt. Ich muß hier noch einmal auf das Kapitel *A* 9 zurückgreifen. Dort wird nach Aufstellung der Zehnteilung ausgeführt, daß die Aussage des τί ἐστι bisweilen οὐσία, bisweilen aber auch ποιόν oder eine der anderen Kategorien sei[30]. Das Beispiel für ersteren Fall lautet: ὅταν γὰρ ἐκκειμένου ἀνθρώπου φῇ τὸ ἐκκείμενον ἄνθρωπον εἶναι ἢ ζῷον, τί ἐστι λέγει καὶ οὐσίαν σημαίνει. Die Aussage, die hier gemacht wird, ist offenbar: „Dieses" oder „es ist ein Mensch, ein Lebewesen". Durch diese Aussage wird also die οὐσία bezeichnet und zwar, wie aus dem Zusammenhang hervorgeht, nicht etwa nur in dem Sinne der Wesensbestimmung, sondern es muß gemeint sein, daß es sich um ein selbständiges Ding (also ein τόδε τι) und nicht nur um eine Eigenschaft, eine Größe usw. handelt. Diese Bedeutung muß man aber doch auch für den Satz „Kallias ist ein Mensch" im Gegensatz etwa zu „Kallias ist weiß" gelten lassen: das γένος τῆς κατηγορίας ist auch hier τί ἐστι im Sinne von οὐσία, τόδε τι. Dagegen ruht die Bestreitung des Sophismas vom τρίτος ἄνθρωπος darauf, daß „Mensch" und jedes einen Allgemeinbegriff bezeichnende Wort nicht τόδε τι, sondern τοιόνδε oder πρός τι usw. bezeichnet. Ein

---

[30] Bei diesen, also den Gliedern 2—10, kommt die Kategorienbedeutung nach 103b 35—39 nämlich nur heraus, wenn sie „von etwas anderem" gesagt werden. Für das erste Glied gilt das nicht. Daß οὐσία und τόδε τι nicht von etwas anderem gesagt werden, nur sie selbst „sind", wird ausgesprochen *An. post.* 73b 5: (καθ' αὑτὰ λέγω) ἔτι ὃ μὴ καθ' ὑποκειμένου λέγεται ἄλλου τινός, οἷον τὸ βαδίζον ἕτερόν τι ὂν βαδίζον ἐστὶ καὶ λευκόν, ἡ δ' οὐσία καὶ ὅσα τόδε τι σημαίνει, οὐχ ἕτερόν τι ὄντα ἐστὶν ὅπερ ἐστίν.

sachlicher und dem Verständnis Schwierigkeit bereitender Widerspruch ist das nicht, denn es ist klar, daß der letztere Sinn sich dann ergibt, wenn man dem κοινόν die Beziehung auf ein bestimmtes Subjekt nimmt und vielmehr an die Möglichkeit denkt, es zahlreichen verschiedenen Subjekten beizulegen. Aber ebenso klar ist, daß ursprünglich nur entweder dieses oder jenes in die Kategorienteilung hineinpassen kann. Der Name der Kategorien paßt nur zu der ersten Bedeutung: es ist gar keine „Art der Aussage" mehr, wenn ein κοινόν von der Klasse ἄνθρωπος als τοιόνδε gefaßt wird, sondern von der Aussage von einem bestimmten Subjekt muß gerade abgesehen werden, damit diese Bedeutung einleuchtet.

Zugleich faßt man, was wesentlich mitspielt, wenn Aristoteles zur Erklärung des „Scheines", es handele sich um ein τόδε τι, sagen kann πᾶν τὸ κατηγορούμενόν τινος ὑπολαμβάνομεν τόδε τι und σύνηθες γὰρ τὸ πάντα ὡς τόδε τι σημαίνειν. Freilich hört man aus dem Satz „Kallias ist Mensch" im Gegensatz etwa zu „Kallias ist weiß" heraus, Kallias sei οὐσία, τόδε τι, und nicht etwa, Kallias habe die und die Eigenschaft; aber das ist doch kein falscher Schein, sondern führt geraden Wegs zur ersten Kategorie. Zum Schein wird es erst, wenn man die Beziehung auf das bestimmte Subjekt ignoriert, durch welche diese „Art der Aussage" allerdings erst herauskommt.

Und damit bin ich auch zu der Deutung des Namens der Kategorien gekommen, die sich mir wenigstens aus den behandelten Stellen der *Topik* zu ergeben scheint, wenn man sie zu vereinigen sucht, aber nach Möglichkeit vermeidet, Fremdes hineinzutragen. Daß dabei hinter einen Teil des Gegebenen zurückgegangen werden muß, will ich nicht bestreiten, denn schon in der *Topik* decken sich Ursprung und Anwendung der Kategorieneinteilung, die zu den frühesten philosophischen Leistungen des Aristoteles gehören muß, nicht völlig. Ursprünglich sind γένη τῶν κατηγοριῶν die Verschiedenheiten der Bedeutung, die der einen sprachlichen Form des Aussagens von einem bestimmten Subjekt in einem Satze unmittelbar innewohnen und durch diese Form verdeckt werden können, solange die Aufmerksamkeit nicht gerade auf sie gerichtet wird. Umgekehrt aber, wird diese Bedingung erfüllt, so braucht man nur mehrere solcher Bedeutungen in die gleiche sprachliche Form, also etwa in die durch Platons *Sophistes* (263a) nahegelegte Grundform des einfachen Satzes mit persönlichem Subjekt zu bringen[31]: „Sokrates ist Mensch", „Sokrates ist

---

[31] Dazu kann man die Stelle *Soph.* 251a 8ff. geradezu als Anleitung nehmen: λέγομεν ἄνθρωπον δήπου πόλλ᾽ ἄττα ἐπονομάζοντες, τά τε χρώματα ἐπιφέροντες αὐτῷ καὶ τὰ σχήματα καὶ μεγέθη καὶ κακίας καὶ ἀρετάς, ἐν οἷς πᾶσι καὶ ἑτέροις μυρίοις οὐ μόνον ἄνθρωπον αὐτὸν εἶναί φαμεν, ἀλλὰ καὶ ἀγαθὸν καὶ ἕτερα, καὶ τἄλλα δὴ κατὰ τὸν αὐτὸν λόγον οὕτως ἓν ἕκαστον ὑποθέμενοι πάλιν αὐτὸ πολλὰ καὶ

weiß", „Sokrates ist fünf Fuß hoch", „ist größer", „geht" usw., dann
springen diese Arten der Aussage von selbst heraus[32]. Aber sie tun es
eben nur in wirklichen Aussagen, daher der Name.

Es handelt sich hier um eine sehr einfache Unterscheidung, die
freilich zunächst eine ganz bestimmte Richtung der Aufmerksamkeit
voraussetzt, aber, einmal gemacht, gar nicht mehr zu übersehen ist
und in alle möglichen Gedankengänge eintreten kann. Eben deshalb
läßt sich schwer bestimmen, welcher tatsächliche Gedankengang
zu dieser eigenartigen logischen Entdeckung geführt hat. Daß Vor-
stufen und Anlässe — insbesondere doch wohl in eristischen Fang-
schlüssen — vorhanden waren, wissen wir, und für die Hälfte der
Glieder gab ja die Sprache in ihren gewöhnlichsten Frageworten (τίς,
ποῖος, πόσος, ποῦ, πότε, vgl. auch *Met.* 1026a 36 *Rhet.* 1385b 5)[33] ohne

πολλοῖς ὀνόμασι λέγομεν. Aber für Platons eigenen Gedankengang kommt nicht
die Verschiedenheit der Bedeutungen der vielen möglichen Prädikate untereinander in Betracht, sondern lediglich, daß sie bis auf ἄνθρωπος allesamt etwas anderes sind als das eine „ὑποκείμενον", wie der Ausdruck ὑποθέμενοι ohne weiteres zu
sagen erlaubt. Zu beachten ist, daß das Aussagen der verschiedenen Prädikate
noch als ein Benennen mit verschiedenen Namen gefaßt ist (πολλοῖς ὀνόμασι
προσαγορεύειν unmittelbar vorher, vgl. 252c, *Phileb.* 13a); den Begriff des Prädizierens hat Platon selbst erst eben durch die Behandlung des Satzes im *Sophistes* geschaffen (vgl. besonders 263a—d). Es ist kein Zufall, daß sich die *Kategorien*schrift durch die Wahl des Terminus προσαγορεύειν jenem in gewissem
Sinne also vorplatonischen Standpunkt wieder annähert (*Cat.* 1a 8, 3b 14, anders
z. B. *Top.* 110a 17, 109a 31). Darüber unten S. 250.

[32] Man hat sich häufig den Kopf darüber zerbrochen, wie Aristoteles eigentlich mit
gutem Gewissen seine Kategorientafel hatte aufstellen können. Auch in dieser Beziehung gibt die *Topik* einen Hinweis. Sie rechnet nämlich die Erschleichungen
παρὰ τὴν λέξιν zu denjenigen, die keine ausdrückliche Frage vertragen: 169b 33:
ὃ γὰρ μὴ ἐρωτηθεὶς οἴεται δεδωκέναι, κἂν ἐρωτηθεὶς θείη. πλὴν ἐπί γέ τινων ἅμα
συμβαίνει προσερωτᾶν τὸ ἐνδεὲς καὶ τὸ ψεῦδος ἐμφανίζειν, οἷον ἐν τοῖς παρὰ τὴν
λέξιν καὶ τὸν σολοικισμόν. Das sind also Unterschiede, auf die man nur aufmerksam gemacht zu werden braucht, um sie nicht mehr übersehen zu können. —
Was bei der Kategorienlehre ursprünglich behauptet wird, ist die *Verschiedenheit*
der Glieder der Einteilung gegenüber dem Schein der Einerleiheit; diese Verschiedenheit ist, unter dem richtigen Gesichtspunkt zur Geltung gebracht, unmittelbar einleuchtend; einen Gegner aber, der demgegenüber die Vollständigkeit der
Einteilung bestritte, gibt es für diesen Standpunkt zunächst gar nicht. Auf die
Vollständigkeit der Einteilung kommt es erst an, wenn, um mit Bonitz (vgl. oben
Anm. 11) zu reden, „das gesamte Bereich… eingeteilt wird". Wäre das der *Ursprung*
der Kategorienlehre gewesen, so wäre das Fehlen der Reflexion auf die Vollständigkeit bei Aristoteles und überhaupt seine an den meisten Stellen, wo die Kategorienlehre benutzt wird, zutage tretende Gleichgültigkeit gegen die Zahl der
Kategorien unbegreiflich.

[33] Nur πῶς, das die Stoa mit ihren πὼς ἔχοντα später gerade aufgriff, ist zu unbestimmt und paßt zu dem hier eingenommenen Standpunkt auch nicht recht, da
die Antwort darauf nicht unmittelbar als Bestimmung eines Subjektes, sondern
als die eines Prädikates erscheint. 178a 38 ist ein ὡς als πρός τι, 166b 18 ein

weiteres die adäquaten Bezeichnungen an die Hand. Aber gegeben war der Gesichtspunkt nicht. Trendelenburg hat es ausgesprochen, daß wir Aristoteles „in dem wesentlichsten Punkt, in dem ersten Ansatz" nicht nachrechnen können (Gesch. d. Kategorienlehre 180). Ich glaube ja, daß man etwas weiterkommen kann, als Trendelenburg dachte; aber die Anhaltspunkte für eine ernsthafte Beschreibung des faktischen „ersten Ansatzes" scheinen mir in der Tat zu fehlen[34].

Die als Ausdruck der „Arten der Aussagen" unmittelbar gewonnenen Glieder der Reihe: τί ἐστιν, ποσόν, ποιόν usw. machen den Eindruck von sehr allgemeinen, ja von allgemeinsten Begriffen, weil nicht darüber hinauszukommen ist und weil man, wenn man will, alles mögliche irgendwie in ihnen unterbringen und nach ihnen ordnen kann, wozu die Zehnteilung schon in der *Topik* tatsächlich gelegentlich benutzt ist. Aber der Ursprung verrät sich dauernd darin, daß sie zu den eigentlichen, durch Klassifikation gewonnenen γένη in kein rechtes Verhältnis treten wollen: sie stehen einfach daneben. So mannigfach die Anwendung der Kategorienlehre bei Aristoteles auch sein möge, das γένος τῆς κατηγορίας bleibt im Grunde immer wie in der *Topik* dem echten γένος gegenüber ein verschiedener Ausgangspunkt, der Sache beizukommen, ein verschiedener ‚τόπος'.

Die Verbindungen, in denen die Kategorienlehre in den übrigen aristotelischen Schriften auftritt, liegen außerhalb des der vorliegenden Arbeit gegebenen Rahmens. Nur die kleine Schrift mit dem Titel Κατηγορίαι verlangt wegen ihrer offenkundigen Beziehungen zur *Topik* und ihrer merkwürdigen Abweichungen, die übrigens meines Erachtens in gleicher Weise die Echtheit mindestens des ersten Teiles verbürgen[35], noch einige Worte.

(διακείμενόν) πως als ποιόν gefaßt. Bei der Frage nach der Kategorie der Adverbien ταχέως, ἡδέως, λυπηρῶς 178b 1—7 (οὐ τόδε, ἀλλ' ὧδε), ταχύ b 31 (οὐχ ὅ, ἀλλ' ὡς) gerät man in Verlegenheit.

[34] Der letzte ausführlich dargestellte Versuch nach dieser Richtung hin reizt nicht zur Nachfolge. H. Maier (II 2, 288ff.) bringt die Tatsache, daß im platonischen *Sophistes* die διαίρεσις eine große Rolle spielt, mit der andern, daß, um die Möglichkeit falscher Urteile zu erweisen, auf die Entstehung des Urteils aus ὄνομα und ῥῆμα eingegangen wird, in eine sehr künstliche Verbindung, so daß daraus wird, der διαίρεσις sei im *Sophistes* die Aufgabe gestellt, die Möglichkeit von Urteilen zu erweisen. Im Gegensatz zu dieser Unzulänglichkeit der platonischen Argumentation soll es Aristoteles nun klargeworden sein, daß „eine Diairesis, die den Zweck hat, das Urteil sicherzustellen, nur den Seinscharakter der Begriffe zum unmittelbaren Einteilungsobjekt nehmen dürfe" usw.

[35] Das Zeitverhältnis beider Schriften ist schwer zu bestimmen. Daß sie im Ganzen derselben Epoche angehören, scheint mir sicher. Eine ganze Reihe von Stellen der *Topik* setzt die Existenz gerade solcher Bestimmungen voraus, wie sie in der *Kategorien*schrift gebracht werden. Aber Hambruch (Logische Regeln der Platonischen Schule in der Aristotelischen Topik, Berl. Progr. 1904) hat gezeigt, daß

Zu Anfang der Schrift werden einige Bestimmungen nebeneinandergestellt, die das Gemeinsame haben, daß sie im Verlauf der Behandlung der „Kategorien" selbst irgendwie zu deren Charakteristik oder ihrer Abgrenzung gegeneinander dienen. Vorangestellt sind sie offenbar, um den Verlauf dieser Behandlung, wo sie gebraucht werden, nicht zu stören.

Uns interessiert der Anfang von Kap. 2:

τῶν λεγομένων τὰ μὲν κατὰ συμπλοκὴν λέγεται, τὰ δ᾽ ἄνευ συμ- 1a 16 πλοκῆς. τὰ μὲν οὖν κατὰ συμπλοκὴν οἷον ἄνθρωπος τρέχει, ἄνθρωπος νικᾷ· τὰ δ᾽ ἄνευ συμπλοκῆς οἷον ἄνθρωπος, βοῦς, τρέχει, νικᾷ.

Dies wird sogleich bei der ersten Aufstellung der Zehnteilung verwendet, um eine Bezeichnung und einen Hinweis darauf, was eigentlich eingeteilt wird, zu gewinnen:

τῶν κατὰ μηδεμίαν συμπλοκὴν λεγομένων ἕκαστον ἤτοι οὐσίαν 1b 25 σημαίνει ἢ ποσὸν ἢ ποιὸν ἢ πρός τι ἢ ποῦ ἢ ποτὲ ἢ κεῖσθαι ἢ ἔχειν ἢ ποιεῖν ἢ πάσχειν.

Die Beziehung der Glieder der Einteilung auf den Satz wird also offen verneint. Das wird nach Anführung der Beispiele noch ausdrücklich ausgeführt:

ἕκαστον δὲ τῶν εἰρημένων αὐτὸ μὲν καθ᾽ αὑτὸ ἐν οὐδεμιᾷ καταφάσει 2a 4 λέγεται, τῇ δὲ πρὸς ἄλληλα τούτων συμπλοκῇ κατάφασις γίνεται. ἅπασα γὰρ δοκεῖ κατάφασις ἤτοι ἀληθὴς ἢ ψευδὴς εἶναι· τῶν δὲ κατὰ μηδεμίαν συμπλοκὴν λεγομένων οὐδὲν οὔτε ἀληθὲς οὔτε ψεῦδός ἐστιν, οἷον ἄνθρωπος, λευκόν, τρέχει, νικᾷ[36].

es mit derartigen „logischen Regeln" eine besondere Bewandtnis hat, die nicht erlaubt, lediglich mit der Möglichkeit eines einfachen Abhängigkeitsverhältnisses zu rechnen; zudem wird man sich schwer entschließen, die *Kategorien*schrift vorne vor den Anfang der „langen Zeit", die Aristoteles nach seinem eigenen Zeugnis an der *Topik* gearbeitet hat, zu setzen. Von gewissen Eigentümlichkeiten der *Kategorien*schrift findet sich in der *Topik* kaum eine Spur. Aber offenbar will die *Kategorien*schrift anderen Zwecken dienen als die *Topik*. Sie gehört zu dem ernsten philosophischen Betriebe, auf den die *Topik* ja selbst oft genug hinweist. Charakteristisch in dieser Hinsicht ist es, wenn die *Topik* 142a 31 an eine etwas diffizile Bestimmung, mit der sich die *Kategorien*schrift besondere Mühe macht (8a 28ff.), die ähnlich auch vorher schon gebrauchte (140b 7, 142a 13), den praktischen Zweck in Erinnerung bringende Bemerkung anhängt: γνωρίζειν μὲν οὖν δεῖ τὰ τοιαῦτα πάντα, χρῆσθαι δ᾽ αὐτοῖς ὡς ἂν δοκῇ συμφέρειν.

[36] Diese Gegenüberstellung des Satzes und seiner Bestandteile, die Erkenntnis, daß erst durch Verbindung der Satzbestandteile die eigentümliche Beziehung des Satzes auf die Wirklichkeit herauskommt, deren Konsequenz ist, daß der Satz entweder wahr oder falsch sein kann, geht bis in die Einzelheiten offenkundig auf die Partie des platonischen *Sophistes* zurück, in der die Entstehung des Satzes aus seinen Teilen vorgeführt und diese Beziehung auf die Wirklichkeit gewissermaßen experimentell nachgewiesen wird. Der Zusammenhang dieser Partie mit antisthenischen Aufstellungen ist bekannt. Aber etwas Wichtiges scheint mir übersehen zu werden. Bei Diogenes Laertius 6, 1, 3 steht von Antisthenes: πρῶτός

Während man es auf dem Boden der *Topik* geradezu als das Charakteristikum der Zehnteilung bezeichnen könnte, daß die Gegenstände der Einteilung nicht als unverbundene Einzelvorstellungen oder Einzelbegriffe, sondern als Behauptungen von etwas gefaßt sind, die mit dem Anspruch wahr zu sein auftreten oder auftreten können, steht hier das Gegenteil. Was damit erreicht wird, ist leicht zu sehen: eine außerordentlich einfache und zugleich wesentlich erweiterte Fragestellung, die dieser ganzen Behandlung der Kategorien ihr Gepräge aufdrückt und der Schrift den eigentümlich grundlegenden, man kann auch sagen propädeutischen Charakter verleiht, dem sie ihren Vorzugsplatz und zugleich ihre außerordentliche historische Bedeutung verdankt.

Nach Aufstellung der Zehnteilung wird zunächst das erste Glied, οὐσία, besprochen. An der Spitze steht die bekannte Einteilung in erste und zweite οὐσία. Die erste οὐσία, die nur in der *Kategorien*schrift als wirklicher Fundamentalbegriff auftritt[37], hat das Charakteristikum, daß sie μήτε καθ᾽ ὑποκειμένου τινὸς λέγεται μήτ᾽ ἐν ὑποκειμένῳ τινί ἐστιν (2a12). Beide Bestimmungen waren bereits im zweiten Kapitel zum Zwecke dieser Charakteristik aufgestellt. Für die erste verwendet die *Kategorien*schrift speziell auch den Ausdruck ὡς καθ᾽ ὑποκειμένου κατηγορεῖσθαι 1b10 oder einfach κατηγορεῖσθαι 1b13, 22[38]. Bei dieser Bedeutung von κατηγορεῖσθαι ist es eine Selbst-

τε ὡρίσατο λόγον εἰπών· λόγος ἐστὶν ὁ τὸ τί ἦν ἢ ἔστι δηλῶν. Das hat man schon im Altertum unklar irgendwie mit dem aristotelischen τί ἦν εἶναι zusammengebracht und darin eine Definition der Definition oder dergl. gesehen. Aber wenn es eine These des Antisthenes war ὀνομάτων συμπλοκὴν εἶναι λόγου οὐσίαν (Pl. *Theaet* 201e—202c, besonders 201b 4/5), wenn andererseits bei Platon im *Sophistes* vorgeführt wird, wie durch die συμπλοκή der λόγος entsteht und damit zugleich die Bedeutung herauskommt, daß etwas ist, war oder sein wird: δηλοῖ γὰρ ἤδη που τότε περὶ τῶν ὄντων ἢ γιγνομένων ἢ γεγονότων ἢ μελλόντων, καὶ οὐκ ὀνομάζει μόνον ἀλλά τι περαίνει, συμπλέκων τὰ ῥήματα τοῖς ὀνόμασι. διὸ λέγειν τε αὐτὸν ἀλλ᾽ οὐ μόνον ὀνομάζειν εἴπομεν, καὶ δὴ καὶ τῷ πλέγματι τούτῳ τὸ ὄνομα ἐφθεγξάμεθα λόγον (262d, vgl. das ἔστιν ἢ ἦν ἢ ἔσται bei Aristoteles περὶ ἑρμηνείας 16b 3, 17a 11), so kann man meiner Meinung nach das antisthenische λόγος ἐστὶν ὁ τὸ τί ἦν ἢ ἔστι δηλῶν, obwohl hier das Futurum fehlt, unmöglich in einem andern Sinne verstehen. Antisthenes bestritt die Möglichkeit der Definition dadurch, daß er sie unter den wohl wirklich von ihm zuerst erfaßten Begriff des als Behauptung notwendig eine Vielheit unterschiedener Bestandteile einschließenden Satzes oder Urteiles brachte: τὸν γὰρ ὅρον λόγον εἶναι μακρόν (Ar. *Met.* 1043b 26); durch das geflügelte Wort wird zugleich das Verfehlen des Zweckes angedeutet, darauf scheint nun wieder Plato *Soph.* 263a 2 μῶν μὴ μακρὸς ὁ λόγος anzuspielen.

[37] In der *Metaphysik* ist sie etwas Sekundäres, übrigens der besonderen Erörterung gar nicht Bedürfendes: ὑστέρα γὰρ καὶ δήλη heißt es 1029a 31. Dazu stimmt, daß auf der anderen Seite in der *Kategorien*schrift der Begriff ὕλη nicht einmal angedeutet und εἶδος nur in ziemlich trivialem Sinne verwendet wird.

[38] Daß der Name von solchem, was ἐν ὑποκειμένῳ ist, κατηγορεῖται τοῦ ὑποκειμένου, wird 2a 29 fast als Ausnahme aufgeführt, obwohl doch in Wirklichkeit zahllose

verständlichkeit, wenn 3 a 36 festgestellt wird: ἀπὸ μὲν γὰρ τῆς πρώτης οὐσίας οὐδεμία ἐστὶ κατηγορία· κατ᾽ οὐδενὸς γὰρ ὑποκειμένου λέγεται. Mit der Bezeichnung γένος τῆς κατηγορίας in der Bedeutung, die wir auf Grund der *Topik* behaupten zu müssen glaubten und die nach unserm Ergebnis gerade auch die Eigentümlichkeit der πρώτη οὐσία, das Dingsein traf, verträgt sich diese Terminologie schlechterdings nicht, wenn sie auch sachlich nicht die geringste Schwierigkeit macht.

Überhaupt sind es zum Teil nur terminologische Unterschiede, welche hier die *Kategorien*schrift von der *Topik* trennen, das Sachliche stimmt sogar überraschend gut. So wenn es von den εἴδη und γένη zur Rechtfertigung der Bezeichnung δεύτεραι οὐσίαι heißt:

μόνα γὰρ δηλοῖ τὴν πρώτην οὐσίαν τῶν κατηγορουμένων. τὸν γὰρ 2 b 30 τινα ἄνθρωπον ἐὰν ἀποδιδῷ τις τί ἐστι, τὸ μὲν εἶδος ἢ τὸ γένος ἀποδιδοὺς οἰκείως ἀποδώσει καὶ γνωριμώτερον ποιήσει ἄνθρωπον ἢ ζῷον ἀποδιδούς· τῶν δ᾽ ἄλλων ὅ τι ἂν ἀποδιδῷ τις, ἀλλοτρίως ἔσται ἀποδεδωκώς, οἷον λευκὸν ἢ τρέχει ἢ ὁτιοῦν τῶν τοιούτων ἀποδιδούς. ὥστε εἰκότως τῶν ἄλλων ταῦτα μόνα οὐσίαι λέγονται. Daß es sich bei der ersten Kategorie um ein Ding handelt und daß eine Aussage davon wie ἄνθρωπος oder ζῷον, obwohl ein κοινόν, gleichwohl im Gegensatz zu den anderen Aussagen eine besondere Beziehung zu diesem Ding hat, indem sie eben mitbezeichnet, daß es sich um ein Ding handelt, war etwas, worauf wir bei der Erklärung der *Topik* Gewicht legen mußten, und das finden wir hier fast vollständig zum Ausdruck gebracht.

Noch mehr fällt die sachliche Übereinstimmung mit der *Topik* in folgendem Abschnitt in die Augen:

πᾶσα δὲ οὐσία δοκεῖ τόδε τι σημαίνειν. ἐπὶ μὲν οὖν τῶν πρώτων 3 b 10 οὐσιῶν ἀναμφισβήτητον καὶ ἀληθές ἐστιν ὅτι τόδε τι σημαίνει (ἄτομον γὰρ καὶ ἓν ἀριθμῷ τὸ δηλούμενόν ἐστιν), τῶν δὲ δευτέρων οὐσιῶν φαίνεται μὲν ὁμοίως τῷ σχήματι τῆς προσηγορίας τόδε τι σημαίνειν, ὅταν εἴπῃ/ἄνθρωπον ἢ ζῷον, οὐ μὴν ἀληθές γε, ἀλλὰ μᾶλλον ποιόν τι 15 σημαίνει· οὐ γὰρ ἕν ἐστι τὸ ὑποκείμενον ὥσπερ ἡ πρώτη οὐσία, ἀλλὰ κατὰ πολλῶν ὁ ἄνθρωπος λέγεται καὶ τὸ ζῷον. οὐχ ἁπλῶς δὲ ποιόν τι σημαίνει, ὥσπερ τὸ λευκόν. οὐδὲν γὰρ ἄλλο σημαίνει τὸ λευκὸν ἀλλ᾽ ἢ ποιόν. τὸ δὲ/εἶδος καὶ τὸ γένος περὶ οὐσίαν τὸ ποιὸν ἀφορίζει· ποιὰν 20 γάρ τινα οὐσίαν σημαίνει.

Also ganz dieselbe auffallende Feststellung, daß, was zunächst ohne weiteres unter die erste Kategorie zu gehören (1 b 27 lauteten die Beispiele ἄνθρωπος, ἵππος) und τόδε τι zu bezeichnen schien, nur scheinbar ein τόδε τι und in Wahrheit ein ποιόν τι ausdrückt. Wenn wir

---

Aussagen darunter fallen. Aber die *Kategorien*schrift hat ihre besonderen Gesichtspunkte. Das äußert sich z. B. auch darin, daß γένος und εἶδος fast nur als δεύτεραι οὐσίαι. d. h. als γένος und εἶδος von Dingen erscheinen.

hören, daß es sich dabei aber doch nicht um ein gewöhnliches ποιόν handelt, so nehmen wir das als eine dankenswerte und sehr notwendige Ergänzung der Lehre gern an. Der Unterschied, daß die *Topik* neben ποιόν noch einige andere Kategorien nennt, fällt nicht ins Gewicht. Aber die Terminologie ist eine ganz andere. Der Begriff πρώτη οὐσία erscheint neu, an Stelle der Ausdrücke πᾶν τὸ κατηγορούμενόν τινος und ἄνθρωπος καὶ ἅπαν τὸ κοινόν treten die δεύτεραι οὐσίαι, und zur Bezeichnung der ὁμοιοσχημοσύνη werden die Worte gebraucht φαίνεται μὲν ὁμοίως τῷ σχήματι τῆς προσηγορίας[39] τόδε τι σημαίνειν gegenüber πᾶν τὸ κατηγορούμενόν τινος ὑπολαμβάνομεν τόδε τι. Doch dies letzte ist kein bloß terminologischer Unterschied mehr, sondern hängt damit zusammen, daß als Beispiel nicht ein κατηγορούμενόν τινος, das nur in einem Satz vorkommen kann, sondern ein einzelnes Wort (ὅταν εἴπῃ ἄνθρωπον ἢ ζῷον) gewählt wird und in Übereinstimmung mit der anfänglichen Bestimmung der Zehnteilung als Einteilung der κατὰ μηδεμίαν συμπλοκὴν λεγόμενα auch nur gewählt werden kann. Dagegen würde das entsprechende Beispiel für den Standpunkt der *Topik* nach 103 b 29 ὅταν γὰρ ἐκκειμένου ἀνθρώπου φῇ τὸ ἐκκείμενον ἄνθρωπον εἶναι ἢ ζῷον zu bilden sein.

Nach all diesem kann es nicht überraschen, daß die *Kategorien*schrift im Gegensatz zu ihrem jetzigen, natürlich nicht maßgebenden Titel, für die Glieder ihrer Zehnteilung die Bezeichnung γένη τῶν κατηγοριῶν oder eine ähnliche *vermeidet*: faßt man die Glieder als Einteilung der ἄνευ συμπλοκῆς λεγόμενα, so ist jener Name tatsächlich nicht zu gebrauchen. Nur an einer einzigen Stelle, weit entfernt vom Anfang, der doch in den Gegenstand der Erörterung einführen muß, und in einem Zusammenhang, wo es sich tatsächlich um Prädizierungen und nur um die Glieder 2—10 handelt, erscheint der Ausdruck αἱ ἄλλαι κατηγορίαι:

10 b 17   (zur Charakteristik des ποιόν) ἔτι δὲ ἐὰν τῶν ἐναντίων θάτερον ᾖ ποιόν, καὶ τὸ λοιπὸν ἔσται ποιόν. τοῦτο δὲ δῆλον προχειριζομένῳ τὰς ἄλλας κατηγορίας, οἷον εἰ ἔστιν ἡ δικαιοσύνη τῇ ἀδικίᾳ ἐναντίον, ποιὸν δὲ ἡ δικαιοσύνη, ποιὸν ἄρα καὶ ἡ ἀδικία· οὐδεμία γὰρ τῶν ἄλλων κατηγοριῶν ἐφαρμόσει τῇ ἀδικίᾳ, οὔτε τὸ ποσὸν οὔτε τὸ πρός τι οὔτε ποῦ οὔθ᾽ ὅλως τι τῶν τοιούτων οὐδέν, ἀλλ᾽ ἢ ποιόν. ὡσαύτως δὲ καὶ ἐπὶ τῶν ἄλλων τῶν κατὰ τὸ ποιὸν ἐναντίων.

Ich glaube, das ist wirklich eine der Ausnahmen, die die Regel bestätigen; wer die Dinge unbefangen ansieht, kann unmöglich aus dieser Stelle das, was die *Kategorien*schrift eigentlich will, erklären, noch aber auch diesen Ausdruck aus dem, was die *Kategorien*schrift tatsächlich treibt, ableiten wollen.

---

[39] Vgl. Anm. 33.

Meiner Meinung nach läßt der Sachverhalt nur eine einzige Deutung zu: wenn in der *Kategorien*schrift die Zehnteilung als eine Einteilung der ἄνευ συμπλοκῆς λεγόμενα eingeführt und im weiteren entsprechend behandelt wird, so ist hier dieselbe Sache tatsächlich unter einen Gesichtspunkt gerückt, den wir freilich auch einmal in der *Topik* antrafen (s. oben S. 229 f) der aber wesentlich verschieden ist von demjenigen, von dem aus allein der Name γένη τῶν κατηγοριῶν und die übrigen Einzelheiten der Behandlung der *Topik* erklärbar sind. Aus allgemeinen Gründen wird niemand bestreiten können, daß Aristoteles die unter einem Gesichtspunkt gefundene Einteilung unter den andern bringen konnte, und faktisch sehe ich keine andere Erklärungsmöglichkeit.

Damit ergibt sich das Problem, welcher Gesichtspunkt ist der ursprüngliche? Ist die primitive, einen so durchsichtigen Eindruck machende, für die Darstellung so bequeme und die Anwendung über die Grenze der bestimmten Behauptung hinaus auf alle Vorstellungsgegenstände erweiternde Fragestellung der *Kategorien*schrift älter oder diejenige, die der Behandlung in der *Topik* zugrunde liegt, ohne freilich ganz so offen an die Oberfläche zu treten? Mit andern Worten, erneut wird die Frage brennend, ob die Kategorienteilung ursprünglich eine innere Beziehung zum Urteil hat oder nicht. Ins Gewicht fällt hier zunächst die Tatsache, daß die *Topik* die Bezeichnung γένη τῶν κατηγοριῶν offenbar anderswoher nimmt und daß sie oder eine verwandte in andern Schriften gewöhnlich ist (selbst die *Kategorien*schrift verrät ja an einer Stelle ihre Bekanntschaft damit); ich wüßte das nicht zu erklären, wenn der Standpunkt der *Kategorien*schrift der älteste wäre. Viel wichtiger und vollkommen ausschlaggebend ist aber der Charakter der Einteilung selbst. Auffallen muß schon, daß die wichtigste Unterscheidung, die die *Kategorien*schrift zu bringen hat, nämlich die von ersten und zweiten οὐσίαι, einen dicken Strich mitten durch das erste Einteilungsglied macht und zwar so, daß die eine Hälfte in gewisser Hinsicht unter das zweite Einteilungsglied fällt. Und wie will man z. B. vom Standpunkt der *Kategorien*schrift erklären, daß die Begriffe Raum und Zeit unter ποσόν und nicht mit ποῦ und ποτέ zusammenfallen?[40]) Aber hier kann ich mich auf getane

---

40 Es hat nicht nur äußere Gründe, daß die ausführliche Behandlung der sechs letzten Kategorien in der *Kategorien*schrift fehlt. Man überlege nur einmal, was nach ihrer Methode wohl Bedeutsames darüber zu sagen gewesen wäre, wenn nicht ganz neue Begriffe hätten eingeführt werden und die Sache sehr komplizieren sollen. Die letzten Kategorien passen gar nicht so ohne weiteres für alle möglichen Standpunkte, und das „usw.", das sie ja auch sonst bei Aristoteles alle oder zum Teil zu ersetzen pflegt, ist kein Zufall. Die Leistung der *Kategorien*schrift liegt nicht in der Aufstellung der Zehnteilung, sondern in der ihr eigentümlichen Heraus-

Arbeit berufen. Denn den Nachweis, der sich durch Apelts ganze Abhandlung in freilich teilweise seltsamer Entwicklung hinzieht, daß die Einteilung nur getroffen ist ,,vom Standpunkt des Urteils und in Beziehung auf dasselbe" (S. 127 der Abh.), kann man zwar wie H. Maier ignorieren[41], aber nicht widerlegen. Freilich halte ich das Einswerden der Kategorienteilung mit der Lehre von den verschiedenen Bedeutungen des Seienden nicht, wie auch Apelt tut, für das erste Stadium; jedenfalls findet es sich weder in der *Topik*[42] noch in der *Kategorien-*

arbeitung der ersten Glieder, insbesondere der οὐσία und da wieder der πρώτη οὐσία, zu philosophischen Fundamentalbegriffen. Die Neigung des Aristoteles, solche Begriffe nicht an den Grenzen der Spekulation, sondern zunächst in der ganz gewöhnlichen Erfahrung zu suchen, kommt so stark zur Geltung, daß die vielfach geäußerten Zweifel an der Echtheit begreiflich sind; es ist wirklich eine ganz andere Philosophie, was hier geboten wird, und hat ja auch als solche gewirkt. Aber während die besondere Bedeutung der Schrift für die Geschichte der Philosophie des Mittelalters anerkannt ist, ist meines Wissens die Aufgabe, ihren Standpunkt als eine Vorstufe der ausgebildeten aristotelischen Metaphysik zu begreifen, vollkommen hinter die Echtheitsfrage zurückgetreten.

[41] Nach ihm soll umgekehrt der ,,Eintritt der Kategorienlehre ins Urteil", obwohl zugleich behauptet wird, daß das ursprüngliche Motiv ,,nach dieser Richtung" liege, eine sekundäre Übertragung sein, wodurch nach Maiers eigenem Ausdruck ,,ein verhängnisvolles Durcheinander für die Forschung" geschaffen wurde. Der Gedanke, daß nicht alle Anwendungen der Kategorienlehre gleich ursprünglich und auf dieselbe Ebene zu stellen sind, ist richtig; aber der Eindruck des verhängnisvollen Durcheinander — modifizierte Gestalten und ursprüngliche Fassung der Theorie nebeneinander, bald so, bald so (II 2, 325) — entsteht doch wohl erst, wenn sich die Forschung nicht die Mühe nimmt, jedes einzelne zunächst nur an seinem Ort und in seinem Zusammenhang gelten zu lassen und zu verstehen, sondern von vornherein alle möglichen Stellen unmittelbar der eigenen Konstruktion dienen läßt oder danach beurteilt. — Daß in Apelts Darstellung (von der philosophischen Orientierung ganz abgesehen) mancherlei zu beanstanden ist und daß auch H. Maier einzelne berechtigte Einwendungen erhoben hat, bestreite ich nicht. Aber es ist wirklich keine Widerlegung, wenn Maier 308 Anm. zeigt, daß Apelts Kategorienlehre einen großen Teil der ihr von Maier a priori gestellten ,,erkenntnistheoretischen und metaphysischen Aufgabe" nicht erfüllt.

[42] Περὶ σοφιστικῶν ἐλέγχων Kap. 33 wird gesagt, daß die Schwierigkeit, einen Fehler der Paralogismen zu entdecken, auch innerhalb derselben Klasse von Fehlschlüssen sehr verschieden sein könne. Zum Beleg wird ausgeführt, daß es unter den Paralogismen παρὰ τὴν ὁμωνυμίαν, also in der gewöhnlichsten Klasse, der so gut wie alle ,,Witze" angehören, solche gebe, die die erfahrensten Leute nicht zu durchschauen vermöchten: σημεῖον δὲ τούτων ὅτι μάχονται πολλάκις περὶ τῶν ὀνομάτων, οἷον πότερον ταὐτὸ σημαίνει κατὰ πάντων τὸ ὂν καὶ τὸ ἓν ἢ ἕτερον· τοῖς μὲν γὰρ δοκεῖ ταὐτὸ σημαίνειν τὸ ὂν καὶ τὸ ἕν· οἱ δὲ τὸν Ζήνωνος λόγον καὶ Παρμενίδου λύουσι διὰ τὸ πολλαχῶς φάναι τὸ ἓν λέγεσθαι καὶ τὸ ὄν. (vgl. 170b 21) ὁμοίως δὲ καὶ περὶ τοῦ συμβεβηκότος καὶ περὶ τῶν ἄλλων ἕκαστον οἱ μὲν ἔσονται ῥᾴους ἰδεῖν οἱ δὲ χαλεπώτεροι τῶν λόγων· καὶ λαβεῖν ἐν τίνι γένει, καὶ πότερον ἔλεγχος ἢ οὐκ ἔλεγχος, οὐ ῥᾴδιον ὁμοίως περὶ πάντων. Mit λαβεῖν ἐν τίνι γένει können in diesem Zusammenhang unbedingt nur die Paralogismen παρὰ τὴν ὁμοιοσχημοσύνην, also mit γένος nur das γένος τῆς κατηγορίας gemeint sein: man sieht, die Homonymie

schrift. Aber das Wesentliche von Apelts Darlegungen wird dadurch nicht berührt; und wie gesagt, dies liegt eben jenseits der Grenze, die ich mir gesteckt habe.

des ὄν gehört für die *Topik* unter eine andere Rubrik. Genau so steht es mit dem Unterschied von ἁπλῶς und τι εἶναι, vgl. 166b 22, 166b 37ff. (167a 2 εἶναί τέ τι καὶ εἶναι ἁπλῶς), 168b 11ff., 169b 10, 180a 23ff. (180a 37 τὸ εἶναί τι καὶ εἶναι sc. ἁπλῶς). Daß unter den näheren Bestimmungen des μὴ ἁπλῶς auch ποῦ, πότε und πρός τι erscheinen, reduziert die Unterscheidung nicht auf die Kategorienteilung.

Syllogistik

1931

Unter Syllogistik haben wir nach Aristoteles' am Anfang der *Topik* und der *1. Analytik* zugrunde gelegter und auch für die Schrift περὶ σοφιστικῶν ἐλέγχων und für die *2. Analytik*, also für seine sämtlichen logischen Hauptschriften maßgebender Definition des Syllogismus seine Lehre von derjenigen Rede zu verstehen, in der nach gewissen Setzungen etwas anderes als diese Setzungen eben durch die Setzungen zwangsweise sich ergibt. Die Lehre von diesem Syllogismus überhaupt bringt die *1. Analytik* (zwei Bücher 24a 10—52b 34, 52b 38—70b 38 der Bekkerschen Ausgabe); ihr hat Aristoteles selbst die *2. Analytik* (zwei Bücher: 71a 1—89b 20, 89b 23—100b 17), nämlich die Lehre von der Apodeixis, d. i. dem Wissen schaffenden Syllogismus, als das Besondere gegenüber dem Allgemeinen nachgeordnet und angeschlossen (25b 26—31, 99b 15f.). Neben dem wissenschaftlichen Syllogismus steht als andere Hauptart der dialektische Syllogismus, dem die acht Bücher *Topik* (100a 18—164b 19) gewidmet sind. Weiter nennt der Anfang der *Topik* noch den eristischen Syllogismus (100b 23) und bereitet damit auf die von Aristoteles selbst der *Topik* angehängte Schrift περὶ σοφιστικῶν ἐλέγχων (164a 20—184b 8) vor, außerdem noch eine eigentümliche Art von Paralogismen, die aus definitorischen Gründen gesondert geführt werden mußte, übrigens keine besondere Behandlung verlangte (101a 5—17 vgl. 171b 12ff.). Endlich werden die rhetorischen Syllogismen der allgemeinen Lehre vom Syllogismus unterworfen (68b 11ff., entsprechend an mehreren Stellen der *Rhetorik*) καὶ ἁπλῶς ἡτισοῦν πίστις καὶ ἡ καθ᾽ ὁποιανοῦν μέθοδον (ebendort), ein ‚und überhaupt‘, das deutlich zeigt, wie in den logischen Schriften Gegenstand und Anwendungsgebiet der Syllogistik nicht außerhalb eines irgendwie kunstmäßig geübten Argumentierens gedacht sind. Freilich wird das Argumentieren ‚bis zu einem gewissen Grade‘ nichtkunstmäßig schon von ‚allen‘ unternommen (172a 30ff., danach *Rhet*. Anfang); aber Aristoteles denkt nirgends daran, sich für seine Theorie etwa an dieser Vorstufe zu orientieren. |

Die *1.* und *2. Analytik* sind, wie schon erwähnt, von Aristoteles selbst in die überlieferte Aufeinanderfolge gebracht worden; die Schrift π. σ. ἐλ. hat ebenfalls er selbst mit der *Topik* zusammengefaßt, aber diese Gesamttopik hat er einfach *neben* den *Analytiken* stehen lassen.

Trotzdem sie in der *1. Analytik* mehrfach primär zitiert wird, blieb dem Urheber der überlieferten Anordnung kaum etwas anderes übrig, als sie nach dem von Aristoteles 25 b 29 angegebenen Prinzip des Vorantretens des Allgemeinen vor das Besondere auf die beiden *Analytiken* folgen zu lassen. Vorausgeschickt sind den *Analytiken* in unserm Corpus die beiden kleinen Schriften mit den (unaristotelischen) Titeln κατηγορίαι und περὶ ἑρμηνείας; das Anordnungsprinzip ist hier offensichtlich das des Fortschreitens vom Einfachen zum Zusammengesetzten, das sich in der traditionellen Logik in der Reihenfolge ,Begriffe, Urteile, Schlüsse' darstellt; aber die *Kategorien*schrift ist keine Lehre vom Begriff in diesem Sinne, und wenn sich die Schrift π. ἑρμ. auch als Lehre vom Urteil bezeichnen läßt, so setzt doch die *1. Analytik* eine derartige gesonderte Lehre *nicht* voraus, und es gibt keinerlei Anzeichen, daß Aristoteles die jetzige Anordnung jemals sollte intendiert haben.

Die Befreiung von der traditionellen Reihenfolge der logischen Schriften des Aristoteles ist die Voraussetzung für eine genetische Erklärung der Syllogistik. Schon 1833 hat Chr. Aug. Brandis in seiner ganz knapp gehaltenen Berliner Akademieabhandlung ,Über die Reihenfolge der Bücher des aristotelischen Organons' nicht nur das Problem meisterhaft formuliert, sondern mit einer Reihe von im einzelnen fast unscheinbaren Beobachtungen die Grundlage geschaffen, auf der man heute noch arbeiten muß. Denn seine These, ,,daß die Topik früher als die Analytiken und diese wiederum früher als die Abhandlung vom Urteil abgefaßt wurde'' und auch seine Einschätzung der Schrift über die Kategorien kann im ganzen als unerschüttert gelten. Leider hat Brandis selbst in seinem Handbuch II 2, 1, 151, 1853 die Frage: ,,in welcher Abfolge hat Aristoteles diese Schriften abgefaßt oder sind die ihnen zugrunde liegenden Vorträge von ihm gehalten und von Schülern aufgezeichnet worden (um auch diese Möglichkeit nicht außer acht zu lassen)?'' zugunsten der weniger förderlichen, aber allerdings der herkömmlichen Betrachtungsweise näherstehenden: ,,in welcher Abfolge würde er etwa zu eindringlichem und übersichtlichem Studium der Logik sie zusammengereiht haben, wenn er zu einer Gesamtausgabe derselben gekommen wäre?'' zurückgestellt, und Prantl ging in seiner ,Geschichte der Logik im Abendlande', 1855, über jene erste Fragestellung kurzerhand hinweg (I 92: ,,über die zeitliche Abfolge, in welcher die Bücher des Organons von Aristoteles verfaßt sein mögen, wird sich infolge der so mannigfachen Wechselbeziehungen kaum ein unbestreitbares Resultat erzielen lassen''), um sich ungestört an die sog. ,wissenschaftliche Reihenfolge' halten zu können. Auch in dieser Hinsicht bedeutete Heinrich Maiers Werk ,Die Syllogistik des Aristoteles' 1896—1900, eine entschiedene Wendung zum Bessern. Zwar sagt er | im Vorwort des ersten Teils (S. VI): ,,auf die

Chronologie der aristotelischen Schriften gehe ich nicht genauer ein, da diese Frage, die sich durch äußere Gründe nicht mit Sicherheit entscheiden läßt, für meinen Zweck ziemlich bedeutungslos ist. Im Inhalt selbst liegt keinerlei Aufforderung zu einer genetischen Darstellung der aristotelischen Logik, und eine solche zu geben, ist unmöglich"; aber er fährt fort: „wo gleichwohl innere Gründe auf eine chronologische Verschiedenheit, bzw. auf eine Entwicklung hinweisen, werde ich nicht versäumen, das hervorzuheben". Tatsächlich bringt er im zweiten Teil, 2. Hälfte 78ff. eine seitdem vielbenutzte lange Anmerkung, in der er Brandis' grundlegende Beobachtungen in dankenswerter Weise weiterzuführen versuchte. — Inzwischen hat sich auf dem Gebiet der Aristotelesstudien die Philologie zum Worte gemeldet. Nach dem Erscheinen von Jaegers ‚Studien zur Entstehungsgeschichte der Metaphysik des Aristoteles‘, 1912, und vor allem seines ‚Aristoteles‘, 1923, darf sie glauben, in der Aufdeckung von Schichten verschiedenen Alters in der Gesamtmasse sowohl wie auch in den einzelnen redaktionellen Einheiten der uns erhaltenen aristotelischen Schriften den Schlüssel zu lebendigem Verständnis gefunden zu haben. Während nun in Jaegers Darstellung gerade die logische Leistung des Aristoteles noch als etwas eigentümlich Selbständiges und Einheitliches neben oder eigentlich vor allem übrigen bestehen blieb (Aristoteles 44f.), hat sein Schüler Friedrich Solmsen nunmehr auch die aristotelische Logik der schon nach den Vorarbeiten von Brandis und Maier allerdings ganz unvermeidlichen ‚entwickelungsgeschichtlichen Fragestellung‘ unterworfen in seinem Buch ‚Die Entwickelung der aristotelischen Logik und Rhetorik‘ (1929, dazu sein Aufsatz ‚Platons Einfluß auf die Bildung der mathematischen Methode‘, Studien zur Geschichte der Mathematik Bd. 1 H. 1, 93—107). Damit ist der schwere Schritt, die eigentlich philologische Diskussion im ganzen und im einzelnen zu eröffnen, endlich getan. — Nur an H. Maiers Versuch, auch innerhalb der *Topik* selbst Schichten verschiedenen Alters und Standpunkts aufzuweisen, schließt Gohlkes Aufsatz ‚Untersuchungen zur Topik des Aristoteles‘ (Hermes 63, 1928, 457—479) an, in dem sein Verfasser Brandis' fruchtbare Erwägung, „daß die Topik anders ausgefallen sein würde, wenn Aristoteles nach vollendeter Analytik sie ausgearbeitet hätte", die H. Maier auf die Schrift π. σ. ἐλ., also auf die Gesamttopik ausgedehnt hatte, nur noch für die Bücher *Topik II—VII* scheint gelten lassen zu wollen. Derselbe erhebt Einwendungen gegen Solmsens Buch in seiner Rezension Berl. Phil. Woch. 49, 1929, 1505—1516. —Zu dem Werk von Guido Calogero ‚I fondamenti della logica Aristotelica‘, 1927, hat Solmsen DLZ 1929, 467—474 Stellung genommen.

Die Frage nach Herkunft und Sinn der für die Geschichte der Logik so eminent wichtig gewordenen Syllogistik der *ersten Analytik* ist solange mit nicht eigentlich in der Sache liegenden Schwierigkeiten belastet, als in der modernen Logik sei es die Fortführung der mit ihr beginnenden Tradition, sei es der Gegensatz dazu eine Rolle spielt. | Da das heute noch vielfach der Fall zu sein scheint und da die rein philologische Betrachtung noch in den Anfängen steht, so wird es erlaubt sein, an dieser Stelle, wo sich Einzeluntersuchungen ohnehin verbieten, von Problemen auszugehen, die sich aus gewissen modernen Vorstellungen von ‚Logik' ergeben und die ihre Aktualität verlieren dürften, wenn einmal die Entstehungsgeschichte der aristotelischen Logik auf philologischem Wege sichergestellt sein wird. Vollständigkeit bei Anführung moderner Äußerungen über die aristotelische Logik, sei es auch nur im Sinne der Anführung des Allerwichtigsten, ist aber von dem Verfasser dieses Artikels nicht angestrebt; auch für die allgemeinen historischen Voraussetzungen, wie sie im Rahmen einer Geschichte der Logik zu zeichnen wären, darf er sich begnügen, auf die reiche Orientierung, die der Art. *Logik* bietet, hinzuweisen. Der Wechsel in der Person des Bearbeiters bringt es mit sich, daß die Syllogistik nun nur auf schmalerer Basis, als dort angelegt, und in Beschränkung auf Aristoteles und das durch das Stichwort gegebene Thema behandelt werden kann.

Kants immer wieder zitierter Äußerung in der Vorrede zur zweiten Auflage der Kritik der reinen Vernunft darf man die Gleichung entnehmen: aristotelische Logik = traditionelle Logik = formale Logik: als solche etwas verhältnismäßig früh und leicht Erreichbares und tatsächlich schon bei Aristoteles im wesentlichen fertig Geleistetes, von dauernder wissenschaftlicher Geltung und dementsprechend ziemlich unverändert an einer bestimmten Stelle im philosophischen System unterzubringen.

Ganz anders Hegel. Bei ihm findet sich ein viel aufrichtigerer Respekt vor Aristoteles als wirklichem Philosophen, als wenn Kant etwa von dem ‚scharfsinnigen Mann' redet. Aber dieser Respekt Hegels gilt der ganzen geistigen Haltung und inhaltlich der Metaphysik und nicht der aristotelischen Logik. Letztere unterscheidet auch er ihrem Inhalt nach nicht so recht von der traditionellen und von der formalen Logik und für die, und insbesondere für ihr Kernstück, den bejahenden Schluß in der ersten Figur, hat er nur die gründlichste Verachtung übrig. Eine Aufzeichnung aus der Jenenser Periode in ‚G. W. F. Hegels Leben' von K. Rosenkranz, 1844, 538 lautet:,,Zur historischen Logik. Es wird versichert, daß wir urteilen: das Gold ist gelb. Diese Versicherung ist wahrscheinlich. Aber nicht ebenso wahrscheinlich ist, daß wir schließen: alle Menschen sind sterblich: Cajus ist ein Mensch, also ist er sterblich. Ich wenigstens habe nie so plattes Zeug gedacht. Es soll im Innern vorgehen, ohne daß wir Bewußtsein darüber haben.

17 Kapp, Ausgew. Schriften

Freilich, im Innern geht viel vor, z. B. Harnbereitung und ein noch
Schlimmeres, aber wenn es äußerlich wird, halten wir die Nase zu.
Ebenso bei solchem Schließen." Über die Tatsache, daß sich nun doch
gerade Aristoteles in der ersten Analytik mit solchen Dingen befaßt
hat, half sich Hegel weg, so gut es ging. Z. B. ‚Encyclopädie' 2. Ausg.,
1827, 174: die drei Figuren des Schlusses hätten einen sehr gründlichen
Sinn, aber die gewöhnliche Art, sie nur nebeneinanderzustellen, hätte
zum leeren Forma|lismus geführt. „Welche Bestimmungen sonst die
Sätze, ob sie universelle, u. s. f. oder negative sein dürfen, um einen
richtigen Schluß in den verschiedenen Figuren herauszubringen, dies
ist eine bloß *mechanische* Untersuchung, die wegen ihres begrifflosen
Mechanismus und innern Bedeutungslosigkeit mit Recht in Vergessen-
heit gekommen ist. — Am wenigsten kann man sich für die Wichtigkeit solcher Untersuchung und des Verstandesschlusses überhaupt
auf Aristoteles berufen, der freilich diese, so wie, fast möchte man sagen,
unzählig andere Formen des Geistes und der Natur beschrieben und
ihre Bestimmtheit aufgesucht und angegeben hat." Also Aristoteles
hat freilich gelegentlich auch so etwas wie formale Logik getrieben,
aber er hat das nicht in dem Sinne für etwas Wichtiges gehalten wie
seine Nachtreter; das Wichtige — führt er aus — und schließlich alles
Beherrschende ist im Gegensatz zu den Verstandesgesetzen der
‚*speculative* Begriff'.

In dieser Richtung ging es zunächst weiter. Wenn man Aristoteles
hochschätzt und die traditionelle Logik wegwirft, dann ist es schon
besser, wenn Aristoteles selbst an dem verachteten Treiben überhaupt
unschuldig ist. So haben die Sache Trendelenburg und Prantl in
Ordnung bringen wollen. Beide bestreiten der formalen Logik ener-
gisch das Recht, sich aristotelisch zu nennen, und behaupten, die echt
aristotelische Logik sei nur von ihrer metaphysischen Orientierung her
zu verstehen. Zu bemerken ist, daß diese Auffassung namentlich in der
extremen Darstellung Prantls (Geschichte der Logik im Abendlande,
1. Bd. 1855) offensichtlich unhaltbar ist. Bei ihm ist alles derart auf
den sog. ‚schöpferischen Begriff' gestellt, daß jedes Verhältnis zu dem
aristotelischen logischen Text aufhört. Das gute Gewissen bei dieser
Art Ausdeutung gibt eigentlich nur eine Homonymie, die man längst
bemerkt hat und bemerken mußte, von deren Mißbrauch man sich aber
bis heute noch nicht immer freihält. Man mag immerhin das τί ἦν
εἶναι der aristotelischen Metaphysik als ‚schöpferischen Begriff' bezeichnen, aber schon ὅρος = Definition ist damit nicht identisch, und
jedenfalls hat *der* Ausdruck ὅρος, der in den Analytiken gleich ‚Terminus einer Prämisse' vorkommt, schlechterdings nichts mit dem τί
ἦν εἶναι zu tun; denn zu dem Gebrauch der Analytiken bot sich das
Wort lediglich deshalb, weil es in der Proportionslehre im Anschluß an

musikalische Terminologie das Glied einer Proportion bezeichnete (das Richtige neben dem Falschen schon z. B. bei Trendelenburg, Elementa Logices Aristoteleae § 22; im wesentlichen richtig, doch nicht erschöpfend Cauer, Rh. Mus. 73, 1920/24, 169—173). Alle Darstellungen der aristotelischen Logik, die im ὅρος der Schlußlehre direkt den aristotelischen Begriff und etwa weiterhin die platonische Idee suchen, sind, sofern sie sich bewußt (Prantl 271) oder unbewußt auf diese Homonymie stützen, falsch. Das Extremste in dieser Hinsicht — auch im Ton — ist Prantls Darstellung, aber die Auffassung des ruhig urteilenden und vornehm redenden Trendelenburg lag in derselben Richtung. Da andererseits sich wenigstens | Prantls Übertreibungen nicht übersehen ließen, so drohten an die Stelle der Frage: ‚Ist die aristotelische Logik formale Logik oder nicht?‘ dauernd Erörterungen zu treten, inwieweit sie formal, und inwieweit sie metaphysisch oder noch etwas anderes wäre. Das führt schwerlich weiter. Dagegen wird es interessant, wenn man die Frage so stellt, wie es die moderne geistesgeschichtliche Betrachtung tut. Gibt man nämlich in der aristotelischen Logik echt und berechtigt Formallogisches zu, so springt für sie ein ernsthaftes Problem heraus. Mit dem metaphysisch Gebundenen wird heute die Geistesgeschichte grundsätzlich leicht fertig; aber wie kommt es bei Aristoteles zu formaler Logik? Unter diesen Gesichtspunkt hat Stenzel den Artikel ‚Logik‘ gestellt. Nach ihm ist es die Aufgabe, die bei Aristoteles vorliegenden formallogischen Regeln als abschließende Leistungen griechischer Abstraktion zu verstehen, und als Produkte einer im Verlauf der Geschichte der griechischen Philosophie ganz allmählich und stetig sich vollziehenden Ablösung des Logischen aus dem Mythischen und Metaphysischen. Es fragt sich, ob die große Schwierigkeit, gerade auf diesem Wege zum Tatbestand des Formallogischen bei Aristoteles zu kommen, überhaupt überwindbar ist.

Einen weiteren Gesichtspunkt, unter dem die aristotelische Logik problematisch wird, liefert der moderne Kampf der Logik gegen Übergriffe der Psychologie auf ihr Gebiet. Bei diesem Kampf pflegt es zu einigermaßen subtilen Erörterungen zu kommen, und wenn er auch im ganzen heute zugunsten einer reinen Logik entschieden sein dürfte, so darf man doch unterstellen, daß heutzutage die Notwendigkeit empfunden wird, einen gewissen gedanklichen Aufwand zu machen, um der Logik ihr spezielles Gebiet zu bestimmen. Und natürlich beruft sich nun der Antipsychologismus für seine Forderung, die Logik psychologiefrei zu halten, auf Aristoteles als Eideshelfer. Die Logik von der Psychologie geschieden zu haben wird in solchem Zusammenhang als eins der entschiedensten Verdienste des Aristoteles, wenn nicht sein größtes, hervorgehoben, so z. B. von Riehl in seiner kurzen Darstellung der Logik in der Teubnerschen ‚Kultur der Gegenwart‘

17*

(I. Abt. VI, 1907), vor allem aber in H. Maiers ,Syllogistik des Aristoteles'. In der Einleitung sagt er, die Arbeit werde nicht lediglich aus historischem Interesse unternommen, sondern ,,Wer über die Aufgabe der Logik, ihre Untersuchungsmethode, ihre Stellung im System der Philosophie und ihr Verhältnis speziell zur Psychologie und Metaphysik sich klar werden will, der wird an dem ersten Versuch zur Lösung dieser Fragen, der in der Geschichte aufgetreten ist, nicht vorübergehen dürfen. Die Richtung, die Aristoteles der Logik gewiesen hat, ist prinzipiell die richtige, so verfehlt die Ausführung im ganzen oder wenigstens an vielen Punkten sein mag . . .'' Und am Schluß der ganzen, umständlichen und im Vertrauen auf den Segen der Gründlichkeit durchgeführten Untersuchungen lautet das Ergebnis: ,,Es ist nicht zu leugnen: die aristotelische Logik bedarf einer umfassenden Umgestaltung. Eines jedoch kann und muß der moderne Logiker von Aristoteles lernen, und das ist für die Logik | grundlegend und richtunggebend: daß *die logische Betrachtung nicht die psychologische* ist.'' Ein paar Seiten vorher hieß es mit Beziehung auf das Verdienstliche an Aristoteles' Leistung: ,,So wird *die Logik von der Psychologie emanzipiert*'' (II 2, 388. 375).

An diesem Punkte mag hier angesetzt werden. Wörtlich darf man das Lob der Emanzipation der Logik von der Psychologie nicht nehmen; denn wie es vor Aristoteles überhaupt keine Logik im modernen Sinne gegeben hat, so hat es natürlich auch keine psychologistische Logik gegeben; Aristoteles hatte also keine Veranlassung, die Logik zu emanzipieren, aber so wörtlich ist es auch nicht gemeint. Immerhin, wenn der moderne Logiker gerade hier von Aristoteles lernen kann und muß, so ist doch wohl die Voraussetzung, daß Aristoteles sich selbst prinzipiell einigermaßen im klaren über das gewesen ist, was von ihm gelernt werden kann und muß, und daß seine Gründe für die eigentümliche Gebietsabgrenzung der Logik einigermaßen dem entsprechen, was sich der moderne Logiker denkt, wenn er sie in seiner Nachfolge ebenso vollzieht; denn andernfalls wäre die Zumutung für das Selbstbewußtsein des modernen Logikers zu stark. Und das ist nun jedenfalls ein Problem. Nämlich es kann allerdings kein Zweifel darüber bestehen, daß die aristotelische Logik psychologiefrei, rein auch im Sinne des modernen Logikers ist. Bedenklich machen können nur etwa der Schluß des 2. Buches der *2. Analytik* und der Anfang der Schrift περὶ ἑρμηνείας, deren genauere Betrachtung zeigt, daß Aristoteles, wenn es die Gelegenheit mit sich bringt — aber das kommt eben kaum je vor — durchaus nicht den Horror des modernen Logikers vor einem psychologischen Unterbau logischer Gegebenheiten empfindet. Aber im übrigen sind seine logischen Erörterungen allerdings derartig frei von psychologistischen Tendenzen, daß er von dieser

Eigentümlichkeit seiner Betrachtungsweise überhaupt nicht spricht. Waren ihm also diese Dinge, die uns heute zugestandenermaßen erhebliche Schwierigkeiten machen, bis zu dem Grade geläufig und selbstverständlich, daß er ihnen kein auch noch so bescheidenes Wort gönnt? Davon kann im Ernst nicht die Rede sein. Wenn ihm aber solche Gedankengänge fremd waren, wie konnte er dann mit solcher Sicherheit das Gebiet abstecken, das in diesem Fall erst die modernen Logiker in seiner Eigenart erfaßt und bestimmt hätten? Man wird also fragen, warum sind Aristoteles' logische Interessen im allgemeinen frei von jeder psychologischen Neugier für den im Einzelsubjekt sich vollziehenden Denk- und Erkenntnisvorgang, wie geht es zu, daß die aristotelische Logik reine Logik ist, obwohl wir nicht den mindesten Anhalt haben, die modernen Gedanken zur Gebietsbestimmung der Logik auch bei ihm vorauszusetzen?

Gegenstand der aristotelischen Logik ist das συλλογίζεσθαι, Fundamentalbegriff also der Syllogismus, etwas Unübersetzbares, wofür aber der Bequemlichkeit halber der uns geläufige Ausdruck ‚Schluß‘ ruhig mit unterlaufen mag. Diese Tatsache, wonach die aristotelische Logik in ihrer | Eigenart nur vom Begriff des Syllogismus her faßbar sein kann und woraus sich ohne weiteres die Einseitigkeit ihrer Lehre vom Urteil und das gänzliche Fehlen einer logischen Lehre vom Begriff erklärt, ins gebührende Licht gerückt zu haben, ist wohl das Hauptverdienst von H. Maiers Werk, dem er deshalb mit Recht den Titel ‚Die Syllogistik des Aristoteles‘ gegeben hat, obwohl darin ursprünglich alles, was irgend ins Gebiet der aristotelischen Logik gezogen werden kann, behandelt werden sollte.

Eine Definition des Syllogismus gibt Aristoteles am Anfang der *1. Analytik* und am Anfang der *Topik*, ferner wird in der Schrift π. σ. ἐλ. Gebrauch von ihr gemacht, und auch in der *Rhetorik* 1356b 16 kommt sie vor. Der Wortlaut ist nach der 1. Analytik: συλλογισμός ἐστι λόγος ἐν ᾧ τεθέντων τινῶν ἕτερόν τι τῶν κειμένων ἐξ ἀνάγκης συμβαίνει τῷ ταῦτα εἶναι. „Ein Syllogismus ist eine Rede, worin bestimmte Sätze gesetzt werden und etwas anderes als diese Sätze mit Notwendigkeit sich ergibt eben auf Grund dieser Sätze.“ Will man sich eine Vorstellung von einem solchen Syllogismus machen, so orientiert man sich selbstverständlich zunächst an der im ersten Buch der *1. Analytik* gegebenen Lehre von den Schlußfiguren, und hier natürlich wieder in erster Linie an dem allgemein bejahenden Schluß in der ersten Figur:

A gilt von jedem B

B gilt von jedem C

A gilt von jedem C.

Von je her hat die Kritik der aristotelischen Logik daran angesetzt,
daß dieses ihr Hauptstück keinen Erkenntnisfortschritt bedeute (Sext.
Empir. *Pyrrh. Hyp.* 2, 195f.: Prantl 502). Dazu muß man Prantl
hören (265): „In der Causalität des Begriffs allein, welche allerdings
sehr bald nach Aristoteles in stets sich steigerndem Grade eine Ver-
kümmerung erfuhr, besitzt Aristoteles die treibende Kraft des Syllogismus, und wir werden sehen, wie gerade der Mittelbegriff es ist, in
welchem das Leben aller Syllogistik sich konzentriert; sobald aber
diese Realität und ontologische Macht des Mittelbegriffes mißkannt
wurde, konnte es im Zusammenhange mit der allgemeinen und gänzlichen Korruption, welche die Logik unter den Händen der blödsinni-
gen Stoa erfuhr, dazu kommen, daß der Skeptizismus sich gegen das
Prinzip aller Syllogistik mit der ebenso pöbelhaften als einfältigen Bemerkung kehrte, daß ja der Schlußsatz nichts anderes enthalte, als
was schon vorher in den Prämissen gestanden war; dieses Andere oder
dieser Überschuß aber, welchen der Schlußsatz über den Inhalt der
Prämissen besitzt, ist gerade der Begriff als Mittelbegriff oder die
durch ihn bedingte begriffliche und notwendige Einheit. Mit Recht
aber muß jene Behauptung der Skeptiker jeden Augenblick gegen die
Syllogistik der formalen Logik gewendet werden, weil dieselbe gleichfalls keinen Begriff vom Begriffe hat, und daher an Sinnlosigkeit dem
Stoizismus gleichsteht, an Eitelkeit aber denselben wo möglich noch
überbietet, insoferne sie sogar heutzutage noch als unweigerliche Vor-
halle der philosophischen Spekulation sich präsentieren möchte.‘‘
Ähnlich versuchte Riehl zu interpretieren (Kult. d. Gegenw. I, | 6, 78):
„Das Neue, ,das andere als das bereits Vorliegende‘, . . . ist nicht eine
ohne den Syllogismus unbekannt bleibende Erkenntnis tatsächlicher
Art, sondern die Einsicht in den Grund oder die Ursache des im Schluß-
satze ausgedrückten Sachverhaltes.‘‘ Diese Deutungen sind aus der
Apodeiktik der *2. Analytik* hergeholt, aber mit der allgemeinen Definition des Syllogismus vertragen sie sich schlechterdings nicht, es
kann gar keine Rede davon sein, daß Aristoteles selbst das ἕτερόν τι
τῶν κειμένων je in diesem Sinne verstanden hätte. In dem Syllogismus
A—B, B—C/A—C sind die beiden Vordersätze A—B, B—C die κείμενα,
und das durch den Syllogismus gewonnene ἕτερον, das andere als das
bereits Vorliegende, ist und bleibt unweigerlich der einfache Schlußsatz A—C. Unter diesen Umständen scheint nichts übrigzubleiben,
als doch im lebendigen Denken den mit dem Schlußsatz getanen
Fortschritt aufzuweisen. Aber wohin man geraten kann, wenn man
den aristotelischen Syllogismus als ein Prinzip des lebendigen Gedankenfortschrittes fassen will, zeigt das Beispiel H. Maiers. Er bemüht
sich gegenüber den alten Einwendungen gegen den aristotelischen
Syllogismus zu erweisen, „daß selbst den beiden Prämissen gegenüber

der aus der Synthese entspringende Schlußsatz einen Erkenntnisfortschritt bedeutet, daß er, wie die Definition des Syllogismus es verlangt, wirklich ein ἕτερον τῶν κειμένων ist" (II 2, 175). Hauptstütze des
Beweises ist eine Stelle des 2. Buches der *1. Analytik* (67a 33), wo
Aristoteles buchstäblich sagt: ,,Nichts hindert es, daß man einerseits
weiß, A gilt von jedem B, und andererseits, B gilt von jedem C, und
daß man sich doch einbildet, A gälte nicht von C." Leider läßt Maier
hier das von Aristoteles selbst gegebene Beispiel beiseite: Es ist z. B.
nicht unmöglich, daß jemand weiß ,jedes Maultier ist unfruchtbar',
und daß er ebenfalls weiß ,dieses ist ein Maultier', und daß er sich doch
einbildet, dieses Maultier würde ein Junges bekommen. Er hat dann
nämlich nicht das (aktuelle) Wissen, daß A von C gilt, wofern er die
beiden Prämissen getrennt läßt und sie nicht zusammen zum Bewußtsein bringt (μὴ συνθεωρῶν τὸ καθ' ἑκάτερον). Man sieht, die Fälle, an
denen nach dieser Auslegung der Erkenntniswert des Syllogismus
zutage tritt, sind ziemlich eigenartig. In Wahrheit denkt aber Aristoteles in dem schwierigen Zusammenhang der angeführten Stelle, über den
man sich gut bei Maier II 1, 360ff. orientieren kann, nicht daran, beweisen zu wollen, daß der Schlußsatz auch den vorhandenen Prämissen
gegenüber noch etwas Neues bedeute. Vielmehr braucht er die Tatsache, daß ich z. B. wissen kann, daß alle Dreiecke die Winkelsumme
2 R haben, und es zugleich auch wieder nicht wissen kann von einem
bestimmten irgendwo existierenden Dreieck, das ich gar nicht kenne.
In dergleichen Fällen liegt kein realer Widerspruch, lehrt Aristoteles,
und um die Sache auf die Spitze zu treiben, konstruiert er den extremsten Fall, wo bei einem ,Wissen' von beiden Prämissen eines Syllogismus doch noch eine Täuschung über den damit eigentlich gegebenen
Schlußsatz möglich ist; aber er rechnet dabei ausdrücklich *nicht* mit
bewußtem Zusammenrücken von | beiden Prämissen, wie es die Defi-
nition des Syllogismus natürlich voraussetzt. Einen Moment zu statuieren, in dem zwar die beiden Prämissen schon zusammen aktuell
im Bewußtsein vorhanden sind, aber noch nicht der Schlußsatz, liegt
Aristoteles hier fern, und somit hat das Ganze für ihn mit der Frage
nach dem Erkenntnisfortschritt im Syllogismus überhaupt nichts zu
tun.

　　Schon der Mangel an aristotelischen Zeugnissen für Verteidigungs-
versuche in dieser Richtung zeigt, daß Aristoteles selbst sich um die
Frage, inwiefern im Syllogismus seiner fertigen Schlußlehre der Schlußsatz den Prämissen gegenüber etwas ,Neues' bedeute, gar nicht ge-
kümmert hat. Er hatte auch wenig Veranlassung dazu. Denn das ziemlich stark betonte praktische Ziel seiner *1. Analytik* ist nicht, zu lehren,
wie man auf Grund gegebener Prämissen den Schritt zum Schlußsatz
zu tun hat, sondern die praktische Aufgabestellung ist die: Wie kann

ich zu einem gegebenen Schlußsatz die zum Beweise nötigen Prämissen finden? wozu auf Grund der Lehre von den Figuren 43a 20ff. ausführliche besondere Anweisung gegeben wird. Bei einer solchen Auffassung des Syllogismus, wonach die Kenntnis des Schlußsatzes dem Finden der Prämissen, man kann auch sagen dem Finden des Syllogismus, vorhergeht, braucht die Frage, inwiefern der Schlußsatz seinerseits den Prämissen gegenüber etwas Neues wäre, gar nicht brennend zu werden. Aber in der Tat, der Syllogismus ist dann auch kein Prinzip des Gedankenfortschrittes, sondern eher ein Prinzip des Gedankenrückschrittes, oder besser gesagt: im Syllogismus ist die zeitliche Folge von Gegebenem und Gesuchtem auf den Kopf gestellt. Im Rahmen der *1. Analytik* wird also von der Definition des Syllogismus gerade der Teil, der allein der gewöhnlichen Auffassung vom Syllogismus als einem Prinzip des Gedankenfortschrittes eine Stütze bieten kann, nämlich die vier Worte vom Schlußsatz als ἕτερόν τι τῶν κειμένων, und zugleich die Reihenfolge der Gedanken im Schema des Syllogismus problematisch.

Nicht so in der *Topik*. Sie ist in ihrem Hauptteil, den jetzigen Büchern 2—7, Sammlung einer Fülle von dialektischen Einzelanweisungen. Umrahmt wird diese Sammlung von den das Ganze zusammenhaltenden Büchern 1 und 8, von denen das erstere in ziemlich straffer Disposition die nötige methodische Einleitung und das letztere mit Anweisung über Aufstellung und Anordnung der dialektischen Fragen einerseits, sowie über die Rechte und Pflichten des Antwortenden andererseits den entsprechenden Abschluß gibt. Erster und selbstverständlicher Nutzen der ganzen Pragmatik ist nach 101a 25ff., daß mit ihr die von Platon begründete philosophische Gymnastik (wichtigste Stelle bei Platon *Parm.* 135c/d) eine Methodik erhält, wie es sie vor Aristoteles nicht gab (184b 1—3, vgl. 159a 36f.). Ganz falsch sagt Maier II 2, 384A., dieser erste Punkt (πρὸς γυμνασίαν) hätte neben dem zweiten (πρὸς τὰς ἐντεύξεις) keine selbständige Bedeutung. Es ist im Gegenteil fundamental für das Verständnis der ganzen Topik, daß die philosophische Gymnastik etwas ist, womit Aristoteles ohne weiteres rechnet. |

Bei dem philosophischen Übungsgespräch, für das Aristoteles die Regeln geben will, geht es nach der Darstellung der Bücher 1 und 8, grob charakterisiert, folgendermaßen zu: Es sind zwei Personen da, ein Frager und ein Antworter. Der Frager setzt dem andern ein Problem vor, z. B. ‚Ist ζῷον πεζὸν δίπουν Definition von Mensch oder nicht?‘ Der Antworter wählt eine der beiden möglichen Seiten des Problems zu seinem Standpunkt, dann ist die Aufgabe für den Frager, diese Aufstellung zu widerlegen, er muß den Antworter zu dem entgegengesetzten Zugeständnis zwingen. Dieser Satz, zu dem der Antworter gezwungen werden soll, wird etwa προκείμενον, häufig auch τὸ ἐν ἀρχῇ *(principium)* genannt. Der Zwang auf den Antworter, diesen ‚Anfangssatz‘, der das Gegenteil der von ihm gewählten These ist, zuzugestehen, wird durch Fragen ausgeübt, die nicht die problematische, sondern die Form der einfachen ein Ja oder ein Nein erwartenden Frage haben sollen. Das sind die προτάσεις, das was ich dem Gegner hinstrecke, oder, etwas anders gewendet, das, womit ich ihm zu Leibe rücke. Den durch eine Reihe von solchen Fragen gewonnenen Schlußsatz — τὸ συμπέρασμα —, der mit dem ‚Anfangssatz‘ identisch ist, *muß* der Antworter zugeben, und daher empfiehlt es sich nicht, ihm hier durch die Frageform noch eine Chance zum scheinbaren Entwischen zu geben (158a 7—13) Wir kennen Ähnliches aus den platonischen Dialogen zur Genüge; und wir können uns schwerlich eine übertriebene Vorstellung davon machen, mit welchem Eifer und welchen Hoffnungen solche praktischen philosophischen Übungen getrieben worden sind. Bedürfte es außer den platonischen Dialogen und den väterlichen Mahnungen des alten Platon zur philosophischen Gymnastik eines Beweises, so ist die aristotelische Topik selbst Beweis genug; unmöglich hätte Aristoteles die Geduld zu seiner Sammlung von dialektischen Regeln aufbringen können, wenn man das nicht wichtig genommen hätte. Auch der Stolz, mit dem er einmal nach Abschluß des Ganzen sein uns glücklicherweise erhaltenes Schlußwort (183a 27—b 8) gesprochen hat, redet deutlich genug.

Im Rahmen dieses Werkes gewinnt nun die Definition des Syllogismus ein ganz anderes Gesicht. „Ein Syllogismus ist eine Rede oder vielmehr, wie wir hier ruhig sagen dürfen, ein Syllogismus ist ein Gespräch, in dem etwas gesetzt wird — die προτάσεις — und etwas anderes als das Gesetzte — nämlich das προκείμενον, τὸ ἐν ἀρχῇ, das, worauf der Frager hinauswill und der Antworter nicht will — erzwungen wird eben mittels des Gesetzten (διὰ τῶν κειμένων 100a 26, 165a 2).“ Diese Definition ruht *nicht* auf einer festen Vorstellung vom inneren Bau eines Syllogismus, wie sie für uns durch den Gedanken an die Lehre der *1. Analytik* unwillkürlich mitgegeben ist — diese Lehre gibt es für die *Topik*, abgesehen von einzelnen späteren Zusätzen, überhaupt noch nicht. Sondern die Definition gibt von außen her eine Beschreibung der zu fordernden Leistung eines Syllogismus, und zwar gilt diese Beschreibung nicht einem Vorgang des einsamen Denkens, sondern dem auf zwei Personen verteilten Hin und Her des Gesprächs. Sie ist nichts | anderes als eine Formulierung der in der dialektischen Übung dem Angreifer (Frager) gestellten Aufgabe, den Antworter durch geschickt gewählte Fragen zur Anerkennung eines von ihm zunächst abgelehnten Satzes zu *zwingen*. Natürlich ist der diskutierte Satz auch hier von Anfang an gegeben, und er wird ja geradezu der

Anfangssatz genannt, aber — das ist der Witz der Sache — der Gegner lehnt ihn zunächst ab, und nun wird der Satz durch Fragen, die der Gegner *nicht* ablehnen kann, erzwungen: hier *ist* der Schlußsatz etwas ‚Anderes' — nicht: ‚Neues' — und natürlich im Verlauf der Ausführung des Syllogismus auch etwas später Kommendes als die Prämissen. Das läßt sich entweder so formulieren: der Angreifer hat die Aufgabe, durch bestimmte Fragen, die ihm zugestanden werden, ein anderes zu erzwingen, und so, der zeitlichen Reihenfolge bei der Ausführung entsprechend, lautet die gewöhnliche Definition des Syllogismus. Aber es läßt sich natürlich auch umkehren: die Prämissen müssen korrekterweise etwas anderes sein als der Schlußsatz. Auch diese Wendung findet sich. So in der von Aristoteles der *Topik* angegliederten Schrift π. σ. ἐλ. 167a 23ff. bei der Definition des ἔλεγχος, der sich vom Syllogismus dadurch unterscheidet, daß in seinen Begriff noch die anfängliche Gegenbehauptung des Antworters eingeschlossen ist, so daß herauskommt, daß dieser gezwungen wird, sich selbst zu widersprechen. Die Sache soll vor sich gehen ἐκ τῶν δοθέντων ἐξ ἀνάγκης, μὴ συναριθμουμένου τοῦ ἐν ἀρχῇ: der Widerspruch muß sich aus den Zugeständnissen mit Notwendigkeit ergeben, und zwar so, daß in die Reihe dieser Zugeständnisse der Anfangssatz (das ist zugleich der Schlußsatz des Syllogismus) nicht eingerechnet wird. Dies ist nichts anderes als das bekannte Verbot der petitio principii, deren Name sich ja von hier aus ohne weiteres erklärt. Die Bestimmung der gewöhnlichen Definition des Syllogismus, wonach er auf ein ἕτερόν τι τῶν κειμένων hinauslaufen soll, ist mit diesem Verbot identisch. Sie hat also einen sehr einfachen und guten, aber einen lediglich dialektischen, keinen erkenntnistheoretischen und erst recht keinen psychologischen Sinn.

Mit diesen Erwägungen dürfte die Frage, auf welchem Gebiet Aristoteles urprünglich seinen Syllogismus aufgegriffen hat und woran er sich orientiert hat, als er seine Definition aufstellte, entschieden sein: auf dem Gebiete derjenigen Syllogistik, die das 1. und 8. Buch der *Topik* und die Schrift π. σ. ἐλ. anschaulich machen, also im Bereich des Zwiegespräches, nicht aber in dem des einsamen Denkens oder Forschens. Von hier aus erschließt sich ein Zugang in die ganze aristotelische Logik. Grundsätzlich ist für Aristoteles der wissenschaftliche Syllogismus, sofern er Syllogismus ist, dasselbe wie der dialektische Syllogismus: der Unterschied beruht für ihn auf dem verschiedenen Wahrheits- und Seinsgehalt der Prämissen; der syllogistische Zwang aber ist in allen Fällen ein und derselbe. Auch in der späteren Fortbildung und Erweiterung des Anwendungsgebietes hat die aristotelische Syllogistik ihren Ursprung aus der Dialektik nicht verleugnet. Das beweist schon die Terminologie. Die Prämissen heißen dauernd προτάσεις, sie bleiben etwas, das | einem anderen hingehalten wird, damit

er zugreift, und ganz unbefangen tritt auch in den *Analytiken*
für ,eine Prämisse setzen' gelegentlich das Wort ἐρωτᾶν auf.
Und wo einmal zwischen dem Fragen des Dialektikers und dem
,Nehmen' des Wissenschaftlers unterschieden wird, bleibt doch die
Vorstellung bestehen, daß der Syllogismus bestimmt ist, einer zweiten
Person vorgesetzt zu werden; sie beherrscht die gesamte aristotelische
Logik. πᾶσα διδασκαλία καὶ πᾶσα μάθησις διανοητικὴ ἐκ προυπαρ-
χούσης γίνεται γνώσεως lauten die Anfangsworte der *2. Analytik.*
,Lehren und Lernen', damit ist tatsächlich das Gebiet der wirklichen
Vorgänge umschrieben, auf welche die aristotelische Wissenschaftslehre reflektiert, so weit sie an der Syllogistik orientiert ist; das selbständige Forschen und Erkennen fällt unter den Tisch. Will man den
aristotelischen Syllogismus als ein Prinzip des Erkenntnisfortschrittes
betrachten, so kommt höchstens die künstlich vermittelte Erkenntnis
des Schülers beim deduktiven Unterricht in Frage: die Erkenntnis des
Lehrenden ist immer schon vorausgesetzt. Diese eigentümliche Einseitigkeit der *2. Analytik,* soweit sie Syllogistik ist, dürfte in der Tatsache, daß Aristoteles' syllogistisches Interesse zunächst nicht dem
wissenschaftlichen Betrieb im engeren Sinne, sondern der dialektischen
Übung und der Eristik gegolten hat, und daß er von da her die Rich-
tungslinie für die Auffassung jedes ,Syllogismus' mitbrachte, ihre volle
Erklärung finden. Die Tatsache nun ist, wie gesagt, eigentlich schon
von Brandis 1833 bewiesen, und man würde wohl längst aus ihr her-
ausgeholt haben, was sie bedeutet, wenn man diesen Ursprung des
,Logischen' nicht für mehr oder weniger absurd und kompromittierend
hielte. Als Heinrich Gomperz sich in einer Besprechung von Maiers
Werk im Archiv für Geschichte der Philosophie Bd. 19, 1906, 550
äußerte: ,,Daß dieses Prinzip (der Syllogismus) durch die ,Reflexion
über das *empirische Schließen* gewonnen', daß ,die syllogistische
Funktion zuletzt aus der *lebendigen Bewegung des Denkens selbst*
herausgehoben' wurde, wie M. (II 2, 77) meint, möchte ich bezweifeln,
denn ich glaube nicht, daß je irgendwer in Syllogismen gedacht hat.
Und M. selbst bemerkt ja S. 233f. sehr richtig: ,Die aristotelische
Methodologie ist nicht aus der Reflexion auf den faktischen Betrieb,
auf die wirklichen Methoden des wissenschaftlichen Denkens hervor-
gewachsen'. Viel eher glaube ich, daß der Syllogismus von der eristischen Praxis abstrahiert ist", schallte es zurück: ,,ob Gomperz selbst
in Syllogismen denkt, weiß ich natürlich nicht. Für die andern logisch
denkenden Menschen aber wird sich das schwerlich mit Erfolg bestreiten lassen" (ebendort 20, 1907, 52). Also hier scheint man mit
Vorurteilen rechnen zu müssen. Im allgemeinen ist es schon das Maxi-
mum an historischer Unvoreingenommenheit, wenn man, wie Maier,
das Suchen nach einem logischen Mittel, vermöge dessen der Fragende

den Partner zur Zustimmung zwingen kann, wenigstens zu einem
selbständigen Teilmotiv beim Ursprung der Syllogistik macht. In dieser Hinsicht bedeutet Solmsens Buch schwerlich einen Fortschritt,.
denn wenn darin (195) | das entstehungsgeschichtliche Ergebnis für die
aristotelische Dialektik so formuliert wird: „Bereits beim frühen
Aristoteles hat sie ihren eigentümlichen diäretischen Charakter gegen
eine syllogistische Form eingetauscht, ist also zu einem Analogon der
apodeiktischen Methode geworden. Noch aber ist sie, wenn auch im
Grundgedanken abhängig, so doch in dessen Durchführung selbständig; sie tritt als autonome syllogistische Theorie neben die Apodeiktik,.
mit der sie lediglich die Begriffsbestimmung des Syllogismus gemein
hat. Im Stadium der *Analytica Priora* ist auch diese Selbständigkeit
geschwunden: die dialektischen Schlüsse sind jetzt nur noch eine ge-
ringwertige Kopie der analytischen, diese Erscheinungsformen der
ἀπόδειξις", so muß man entweder die Begriffsbestimmung des Syllogismus unbesehen hinnehmen, oder es ist hier die Abhängigkeit im Grundgedanken verkehrt herum konstruiert.

Es fragt sich nunmehr, ob und inwieweit noch darüber hinaus die
fertige Syllogistik der *1. Analytik* von dem dialektischen Ursprung her
bestimmt ist. Der Verfasser der *Analytiken* führt alle eigentlichen
Syllogismen auf das in der 1. Figur ausgedrückte einfache Schlußprinzip zurück und mißt an ihm verwandte Operationen (Dihairesis-
verfahren, Epagoge). Obwohl nun Aristoteles die Syllogistik der *Topik*
nie von Grund aus umgeschrieben hat, sondern sie bis zuletzt *neben*
den *Analytiken* hat bestehen lassen, wie nicht nur die *Rhetorik* (für
die an dieser Stelle nur auf Solmsens Buch verwiesen sei), sondern z.
B. auch die schwierige Stelle *An. Pr.* 46a 28—30 beweist, galten ihm
doch die Gesetze der ersten *Analytik* ebenso für den dialektischen wie
für den wissenschaftlichen Syllogismus; und in dem Kapitel *An. Pr.*
1, 30 (46a 3ff.) ist direkt ausgesprochen, daß mit der Syllogistik der
1. Analytik jener *eine* Weg alles Schließens gefunden ist, der ihm schon,.
als er das 1. Buch der *Topik* schrieb, vorschwebte, den aber anzugeben
er sich damals außerstande sah (102b 35—103a 1).

Daß für Aristoteles die Syllogistik der *1. Analytik* auch die Krö-
nung seiner Bemühungen um den dialektischen Syllogismus bedeutet,
steht somit außer Zweifel. Aber andererseits stellt sich in dem von
Aristoteles selbst geschaffenen Zusammenhang der *1.* und *2. Analytik*
(24a 10ff., 25b 26—31; 99b 15—19) die reine Syllogistik vor allem als
Grundlage der Lehre vom wissenschaftlichen Beweis dar, und es wird
von Aristoteles betont, daß seine erste Figur die Form wäre, in der die
mathematischen und überhaupt alle auf Begründung ausgehenden
Wissenschaften ihre Beweise brächten (79a 17ff.), so daß die Annahme
nahe liegt, „daß das Interesse an der Apodeixis den nächsten Anstoß.

zur Ausbildung der syllogistischen Theorie gegeben hat" (Maier II 1,
2). Will man so konstruieren, so empfiehlt sich als Ausgangspunkt die
platonische Dihairesismethode, die von Aristoteles selbst als einzige
Konkurrentin an seiner Syllogistik gemessen wird; und die Verwandtschaft einer ὅροι-Reihe wie Lebewesen-Mensch-Einzelmensch mit
Dihairesisstufen ist gar nicht zu verkennen, wie im Art. ‚Logik' ausgeführt ist (S. 1010), wo aber gleichzeitig mit Recht betont ist, daß die
Formalisierung der aristotelischen Syllogistik von Platon | weder er-
reicht noch angestrebt ist. Nun sind wir aber für die Frage, wie diese
Dinge für Aristoteles vor der Aufstellung des Schlußprinzips der *1. Analytik* lagen, nicht ganz auf Vermutungen angewiesen.

Wichtig ist hier zunächst eine Stelle der *Kategorien*schrift. Auf die
Vorgeschichte und den ursprünglichen Sinn der Kategorienlehre kann
hier nicht eingegangen werden; daß sie zu den ältesten philosophischen
Errungenschaften des Aristoteles gehören muß, wird jetzt meist anerkannt, und was die *Kategorien*schrift betrifft, so wird die Echtheit und
Unvollendetheit des 1. Teils (bis 11b 8) durch das Flickstück 11b
9—14 geradezu direkt bezeugt. Dieser Hauptteil kann dann aber aus
mancherlei Gründen, deren Darlegung hier ebenfalls unterbleiben muß,
nur in frühe Zeit gehören; ein ἐν Λυκείῳ ist kein eindeutiges Zeitindiz
(vgl. Gohlke, Hermes 63, 1928, 476). Am Anfang der Schrift erscheint
nun unter den vorausgeschickten Bestimmungen, die dann zur Charakteristik der ersten Glieder der berühmten Zehnerreihe benutzt werden,
der Satz: ὅταν ἕτερον καθ᾽ ἑτέρου κατηγορῆται ὡς καθ᾽ ὑποκειμένου,
ὅσα κατὰ τοῦ κατηγορουμένου λέγεται, πάντα καὶ κατὰ τοῦ ὑποκειμένου ῥηθήσεται, οἷον ἄνθρωπος κατὰ τοῦ τινὸς ἀνθρώπου κατηγορεῖται,
τὸ δὲ ζῷον κατὰ τοῦ ἀνθρώπου· οὐκοῦν καὶ κατὰ τοῦ τινὸς ἀνθρώπου
κατηγορηθήσεται τὸ ζῷον· ὁ γάρ τις ἄνθρωπος καὶ ἄνθρωπός ἐστι καὶ
ζῷον (1b 10—15). Aus den Anwendungen 2a 14ff., 3b 2ff. wird das
Hervorgehen des Satzes aus dem platonischen Dihairesisschema klar;
die *Topik* beweist ihre Bekanntschaft mit dieser ‚logischen Regel'
durch Stellen wie einerseits 127b 1—4, andererseits 121a 25f., 122a
3ff. Für uns sieht der Satz dem Schlußprinzip der 1. Analytik ähnlich, aber mit Recht hat sich Maier (II 2, 155) gegen den Versuch gewendet, darin eine ‚Charakteristik der syllogistischen Funktion' zu
sehen. Darüber hinaus ist zu sagen, daß von der platonischen Dihai-
resislehre aus weder der Anstoß zu weiterer Formalisierung noch zur
Ausbildung einer Syllogistik oder gar der Lehre von den 3 Figuren
gegeben war.

Dagegen erschließt sich aus einigen Stellen der Schrift π. σ. ἐλ. eine
ungemütliche logische Situation, über die erst die spätere Aufstellung
des Schlußprinzips der *1. Analytik* hinweghelfen konnte. Die Schrift
π. σ. ἐλ. muß, um sich gegen gewisse Fehlschlüsse, die sie παρὰ τὸ

συμβεβηκός nennt, zu wehren, eine dialektische Regel aufstellen, die wir etwa so wiedergeben können: es ist *nicht* notwendig, daß, wenn man irgendwie ‚A ist B‘ sagen kann, daß dann wegen dieser scheinbaren Identität in jeder anderen Aussage, in der A vorkommt, B statt dessen eingesetzt werden kann und umgekehrt (166b 28—36; 168a 34—b 10; 169b 3—6; 179a 26—b 6). Die hier in Frage kommenden Fehlschlüsse sehen so aus:

Koriskos ist ἕτερον ἀνθρώπου
Koriskos ist ἄνθρωπος
———————————————
Koriskos ist ἕτερος Κορίσκου

Koriskos ist etwas anderes als Sokrates
Sokrates ist Mensch
———————————————
Koriskos ist etwas anderes als Mensch |

Das Dreieck hat die Winkelsumme 2 R
Das Dreieck ist Figur
———————————————
(Jede) Figur hat die Winkelsumme 2 R

Das μέλλον ἐρωτᾶσθαι ist Dir unbekannt
Das μέλλον ἐρωτᾶσθαι ist τὸ ἀγαθόν
———————————————
τὸ ἀγαθόν ist Dir unbekannt

Das Verhüllte ist Dir unbekannt
Das Verhüllte ist Koriskos
———————————————
Koriskos ist Dir unbekannt

Der Herankommende ist Dir unbekannt
Der Herankommende ist Koriskos
———————————————
Koriskos ist Dir unbekannt.

(Die von Aristoteles hinzugenommenen Fehlschlüsse von dem Typus ‚Der Hund ist Dein Vater‘, mögen der Einfachheit halber hier beiseite bleiben.)

     Diese Fehlschlüsse gründen sich wie alle Fehlschlüsse auf Fälle, in denen scheinbar dieselbe Folge von Sätzen einen richtigen Schluß ergibt. Als zweifellos richtig nennt Aristoteles 179a 37 nur die Fälle, wo ‚A ist B‘ vollständige Wesensidentität bedeutet (vgl. 152b 25—29; Phys. 202b 14—16). Im übrigen ist es unbestimmt, wann man so schließen darf und wann nicht; in einigen Fällen glaubt man es zu dürfen, in anderen nicht; und so wird man sich gegen Fehlschlüsse dieser Art ganz allgemein mit dem Einwand ‚Es ist nicht notwendig‘ wenden können. Man muß freilich Beispiele zur Hand haben (179a

27—31). Theoretisch wird die Sache also nicht weiter ins Reine gebracht, so daß sogar ein Schluß wie

> Mensch ist Lebewesen
> Sokrates ist Mensch
> _____
> Sokrates ist Lebewesen

unter den ungeklärten Fällen bleibt, obschon nicht die Beispiele, wohl
aber die Formulierung 179 a 27 f. und 36 f. zeigt, daß Aristoteles vorzugsweise an Schlüsse der Form: ‚B ist C, A ist B / A ist C' denkt.

In dem Moment, in dem Aristoteles die hier gelassene und offen
ausgesprochene Unklarheit mit jener Regel der Kategorienschrift zu-
sammenbrachte, mußte die Frage πότε λεκτέον ἐπὶ τοῦ πράγματος,
ὅταν ἐπὶ τοῦ συμβεβηκότος ὑπάρχῃ (179 a 27) zu weiterer Untersuchung
und zu Experimenten führen, die in die Syllogistik der *1. Analytik*
auslaufen konnten. Nimmt man diesen hier exempli gratia vorgebrachten Ansatz an, so wird anschaulich, wie trotz des aus den platonischen
Bemühungen um γένος und εἶδος vermittels der Dihairesismethode
stammenden Einschlages doch in der fertigen aristotelischen Logik
sowohl die Richtung auf eine Syllogistik überhaupt, wie das rein formale Schlußprinzip und die Lehre von den drei Figuren in der dialektischen Syllogistik der *Topik* und der Schrift π. σ. ἐλ. die gegebenen
Vorbedingungen hat.

Man kann freilich versucht sein, das Schlußprinzip der *1. Analytik*
und ihre 1. Figur unmittelbar aus dem mathematischen Beweisverfahren herzuholen, weil Aristoteles behauptet, die mathematischen
Wissenschaften führten ihre Beweise in der 1. Figur, und man kann
sich dafür auf das Beispiel |

> Alle Dreiecke haben die Winkelsumme 2 R
> _____
> Das ἰσοσκελές ist ein Dreieck
> Das ἰσοσκελές hat die Winkelsumme 2 R

berufen, mit dem die *2. Analytik* experimentiert (wobei es zu einer so
unnatürlichen Annahme bzw. Formulierung wie 86 a 26 καὶ εἰ μὴ οἶδε
τὸ ἰσοσκελὲς ὅτι τρίγωνον kommen kann). Indessen sieht ein echter
mathematischer Gedankenfortschritt doch wohl anders aus, und
sucht man dahinter nur die Anwendung eines bekannten allgemeinen
Satzes auf ein bestimmtes ohne weiteres darunterfallendes Einzelsubjekt, so ist das einmal nichts spezifisch Mathematisches, und zum
andern ist es unwahrscheinlich, daß hier der Tatbestand des aristotelischen Syllogismus aufgefunden wäre und nicht vielmehr erst hinein-
gedeutet worden ist. Von dem wirklich interessanten mathematischen
Beweis über die Winkelsumme im Dreieck aber muß Aristoteles zu-

geben, daß es schwer ist, das Schema der 1. Figur auf ihn anzuwenden (48a 29—39); kaum denkbar, daß ihr Prinzip gerade auf diesem Gebiet zuerst gefunden wäre.

Erst mit der anderweitigen Entdeckung des Schlußprinzips der *1. Analytik* wird sich für Aristoteles der wissenschaftliche Syllogismus als ein Betätigungsfeld der Syllogistik eröffnet haben. Jedenfalls setzt die ausgebildete Lehre der *2. Analytik* von ἐπιστήμη und ἀπόδειξις die formale Syllogistik der *1. Analytik* mit ihren Grundzügen voraus, wie schon ein Vergleich mit dem Anfang der *Metaphysik*, wo die Nutzbarmachung der Lehre vom Syllogismus noch fehlt, beweisen kann. Aber diese Dinge müssen hier unerörtert bleiben. Gerade nach Solmsens für die historische Erschließung des Gehalts der *2. Analytik* bahnbrechendem Vorgehen wird es noch viel vorsichtiger und glücklicher Einzelinterpretation bedürfen, um hier klar zu sehen. Nur eine Illustration aus der weiteren Geschichte des Syllogismus bei Aristoteles sei noch gebracht, weil sie charakteristisch ist und weil sie eine Waffe derer zu sein scheint, die den Syllogismus im Verlauf des lebendigen Denkens glauben aufweisen zu können. In der Tat, auch Aristoteles stellt sich gelegentlich das Denken des Einzelnen als in der Form seines Syllogismus verlaufend vor. In den *Analytiken* freilich werden die Syllogismen kaum unter den Begriff des Denkens, des νοῆσαι, gebracht, da geschieht die Orientierung am dialektischen Gespräch und am διδάσκειν und μανθάνειν. Wohl aber finden wir Aristoteles selbst auf diesem Wege in der Schrift περὶ ζῴων κινήσεως (701a 7ff.) und in der *Nikomachischen Ethik* (1146b 36ff. 1147a 24ff.). Es geht um die Frage, wie es vom Denken zum Handeln kommt. Das ist so ähnlich wie beim theoretischen Denken und Schließen, sagt Aristoteles (701a 8); es müssen zwei Prämissen zusammenkommen: Denkt einer beide Prämissen, so denkt er sofort auch den Schlußsatz (ὅταν γὰρ τὰς δύο προτάσεις νοήσῃ, τὸ συμπέρασμα ἐνόησε καὶ συνέθηκεν); nur daß beim praktischen Denken an die Stelle des Schlußsatzes die Handlung tritt. Und eine selbstverständliche Prämisse wird eventuell gerade wie beim Fragen — die Dialektik tritt ihm unwillkürlich doch wieder neben das Denken (701a 25 und 31) — einfach unterschlagen. Z. B. ‚Jetzt ist | eine Situation, wo alle Menschen gehen müssen‘: da denkt man nicht lange ‚ich aber bin ein Mensch‘, sondern geht eben los. Weitere einfache Beispiele für den praktischen Syllogismus sind: ‚Ich muß trinken‘, sagt die Begierde; ‚dies ist ein Getränk‘ schiebt die Wahrnehmung oder die Vorstellung der Vernunft unter: sofort trinkt er. ‚Alles Süße muß man kosten, hier aber ist etwas Süßes‘ (*E. N.* 1147a 29): sofort greift man zu, falls man kann und falls nicht eine entgegenstehende Maxime stärker ist. Damit sind Aristoteles' Erörterungen, zu denen diese und kompliziertere Beispiele gehören, nur angedeutet,

aber so viel ist gerade bei den einfachen und durchsichtigen Beispielen deutlich: die Analogie des praktischen Syllogismus im theoretischen Denken ist eine irgendwie von außen ins Spiel gesetzte, dann
aber zwangsweise verlaufende Mechanik; etwas Freies und Lebendiges
sind beim Handeln in dieser Darstellung höchstens die etwaigen, aus
der Gespaltenheit der menschlichen Seele (1147a 35) erklärbaren
Gegenmaximen, die es nicht zum Vollzuge eines solchen praktischen
Syllogismus kommen lassen: aber da hört die Analogie des theoretischen Syllogismus auf, denn der zwingt immer. So dürfte der praktische
Syllogismus etwas Ungeeignetes sein, um die Auffassung zu stützen,
der aristotelische Syllogismus wäre ein Prinzip des *lebendigen* Denkens,
das mit *innerer* Notwendigkeit zum Schlußsatz triebe, und der Schlußsatz selbst wäre als eine besondere Tat des Denkens abzuheben. Gegen
diese Weise, dem spezifisch Ungeistigen die Prädikate des Geistigen
zuzuschieben, wird Hegels o. S. 257 f. gebrachte Äußerung immer recht
behalten.

Es ist nicht *das* Denken, das im einzelnen *lebt*, wo der aristotelische
Syllogismus seine Heimat hat, und wo er von Aristoteles gesucht und
gefunden worden ist. Von vornherein steckt in ihm etwas, was sich
einerseits dem psychologischen Zugriff entzieht und was ihn andererseits zum Skandalon für die Philosophie des Geistes macht. Dieses
Etwas stempelt nun aber Aristoteles auch nicht zu einem rätselhaften
Vorgänger der modernen reinen Logiker. Für Aristoteles rückt der
Syllogismus nicht aus der Welt des greifbaren Geschehens hinaus, er
kann ruhig als wirklicher Vorgang angesehen werden — es bedarf da
für Aristoteles keiner Distinktionen —, nur eben als ein Vorgang, zu dem
im Grunde immer 2 Personen, A und B, gehören. Der Schlußsatz ist
von vornherein da, er wird nicht gesucht und nicht gefunden, sondern
was gesucht und gefunden wird, sind die Prämissen, und zwar werden
sie nur von der Person A gesucht. Für dieses Aufsuchen der Prämissen
gibt Aristoteles sowohl in der *Topik* wie auch noch in einem Abschnitt
des 1. Buches der *1. Analytik* ausführliche praktisch gedachte Anweisungen. Aber das Aufsuchen der Prämissen verläuft natürlich in entgegengesetzter Richtung wie der Syllogismus selbst. Erst nachdem A die
Prämissen gefunden hat, tritt der Syllogismus in Erscheinung; und für
die andere Person B ist nun die Reihenfolge der Gedanken die der
Definition des Syllogismus, also von den Prämissen zum Schlußsatz hin.
An dieser Reihenfolge aber ist die Person B, die sich ihrem Zwange hingeben | muß, ganz und gar unschuldig; ohne die Person A, die den Syllogismus auf umgekehrtem Wege gefunden hat, ihn nun aber fertig mitbringt und ihn B vorsetzt, würde es für B gar nicht zum Syllogismus, d. h.
zu dem tatsächlichen Fortschreiten von den Prämissen zum Schlußsatz
kommen. Der Vorgang, der in der Definition des Syllogismus beschrieben

wird, findet sich also tatsächlich in der Person B als psychisches Erlebnis; aber er ist nichts aus ihrem psychischen Eigenleben und nichts in lebendigem Denken mit *innerer* Notwendigkeit Erzeugtes.

Danach müssen alle Versuche, den aristotelischen Syllogismus aus den Gesetzen des psychischen Einzellebens zu deuten oder ihn in die Tatbestände des eigentlich Geistigen einzuordnen, verfehlt sein. Andererseits bedarf es nur der Besinnung auf die historische Tatsache der durch Sokrates in die Welt gebrachten und von Platon als *des* Mittels philosophischer Erweckung gepriesenen und praktisch in den Unterricht eingeführten Dialektik und ihrer Konkurrentin, der Eristik, um zu verstehen, warum der Gründer der Logik seinen Gegenstand in der Sphäre des Zwiegesprächs fand, von wo aus er ihn mit so überraschender Sicherheit bestimmen konnte.

Etwas wirklich Lebendiges, ein Gebiet der neuen Entdeckungen, ist die Dialektik und die an sie anschließende philosophische Gymnastik auch im Altertum nur kurze Zeit geblieben. Seit Anaximander haben die Philosophen Bücher geschrieben; Sokrates unterbricht das in Athen, und Platon hat es zeitlebens nicht wahr haben wollen, daß ein Buch die geeignete Vermittlung philosophischer Erkenntnis sein könnte. Die Geschichte ist darüber hinweggegangen, und Aristoteles selbst fixiert für sich und andere seine Erkenntnisse wieder auf zahllosen Rollen, zu denen auch seine logischen Schriften gehören. Aber diese neue Buchwissenschaft, die Logik, hat zu ihrem ursprünglichen Gegenstand nicht das einsame Denken gehabt, das dann im Buch seinen Niederschlag findet, sondern aufgebaut hat Aristoteles sie in der Orientierung an der in der Geschichte unserer Philosophie nur einmal rein verwirklichten Form der Dialektik, in der ihm in jungen Jahren die wahre Philosophie sich dargeboten hatte. Eben darum mußte diese Logik rasch veralten und teilweise unverständlich und verkehrt angelegt erscheinen. Tatsächlich hat in den nächstfolgenden Jahrhunderten des Altertums auch nicht sie, sondern die den gewöhnlichen Voraussetzungen näher stehende stoische Logik das Bewußtsein der Gebildeten beherrscht.

Die *stoische Logik* will wirklich das nach Anaxagoras und Demokrit (Vors. 59 B 21 a) vom Bekannten und Offenbaren zum Unbekannten und Verborgenen fortschreitende Erkennen einfangen. Für das Grundsätzliche ihrer Behandlung der ἀπόδειξις sehen wir hinlänglich klar. Stoische Definitionen der ἀπόδειξις sind: λόγος διὰ τῶν μᾶλλον καταλαμβανομένων τὸ ἧττον καταλαμβανόμενον περαίνων (Diog. Laert. 7, 45 = St. fr. II 235. Cic. *Ac.* 2, 26 *ratio quae ex rebus perceptis ad id, quod non percibiebatur, adducit* = St. fr. II 111) und λόγος δι' ὁμολογουμένων λημμάτων κατὰ συναγωγὴν ἐπιφορὰν ἐκκαλύπτων ἄδηλον (Sext. Emp. *adv. math.* 8, 314 = St. | fr. 266) oder λόγος κατὰ συναγωγὴν διά τινων φαινομένων ἐκκαλύπτων τι ἄδηλον (Sext. Emp. 8, 385). Deutlich kommt hier die Forderung zum Ausdruck, daß der Syllogismus, um wissenschaftlichen Wert zu haben, um ἀπόδειξις zu sein, im Schlußsatz einen extensiven Zuwachs an Erkenntnis bringen müsse; etwas, das vorher noch unklar war, wird mit dem Schlußsatz ‚enthüllt‘. Sextus Empiricus hat in seinen Kapiteln über das σημεῖον und die ἀπόδειξις (adv. math. 8, 141ff. 300ff. Hyp. 2, 97ff.) nähere Erörterungen über die Natur eines solchen durch σημεῖον oder ἀπόδειξις (was in dieser Behandlung keinen Unterschied macht: Hyp. 2, 134) zu erfassenden ἄδηλον erhalten. Danach handelt es sich vor allem um Wesenheiten, die, der unmittelbaren sinnlichen Wahrnehmung unzugänglich, wie beispielsweise unsichtbare Hautporen, der unendliche leere Raum außerhalb des Kosmos, die Seele oder auch die göttliche Vorsehung, doch mit bestimmten wahrnehmbaren Dingen oder Vorgängen in einem derartigen Zusammenhang stehen, daß sie aus diesen erschlossen werden können. Musterbeispiel (Hyp. 2, 140): εἰ ἱδρῶτες ῥέουσι διὰ τῆς ἐπιφανείας, εἰσὶ νοητοὶ πόροι· ἀλλὰ μὴν ἱδρῶτες ῥέουσι διὰ τῆς ἐπιφανείας· εἰσὶν ἄρα νοητοὶ πόροι. Entsprungen scheint diese unverächtliche Apodeiktik dem Zusammenlaufen zweier historischer Linien, deren eine von Demokrit über Epikurs Erkenntnistheorie und deren andere von der aristotelischen Syllogistik über Diodoros Kronos' συνημμένα-Lehre (Sext. Emp. adv. math. 1, 309f., 8, 115, Hyp. 2, 110) führte.

Aristoteles kennt die entsprechenden Beweise natürlich auch, und sie lassen sich in die von ihm gefundene Schlußform umsetzen, aber wer die 2. Analytik gelesen hat, weiß, daß für ihn solche Schlüsse etwas Menschlich-Minderwertiges sind, und daß hier eigentlich nicht das ‚Neue‘, sondern das bekannte Faktum den Schlußsatz zu bilden hat. Aber es ist dann schon im Altertum die Auffassung, der aristotelische Syllogismus hätte wie der stoische vom Bekannten zum Unbekannten vorwärts zu führen, in die Aristoteleserklärung eingedrungen, was durch Aristoteles' Unterscheidung des uns Menschen Offenbaren und des an sich Offenbaren (der ἡμῖν γνώριμα und ἁπλῶς γνώριμα) erleichtert und verschleiert wurde. Man vergleiche Alexanders Kommentar zu dem ἕτερόν τι τῶν κειμένων der aristotelischen Definition des Syllogismus (Comm. in Ar. Gr. 2, 1, 18, 12): πάνυ δὲ καλῶς τὸ δεῖν ἕτερον τῶν τεθέντων εἶναι τὸ συμπέρασμα προσέθηκεν. ἄχρηστον γὰρ καὶ συλλογιστικῆς χρείας φθαρτικὸν τὸ τὸ ὁμολογούμενον καὶ κείμενον ἐπιφέρειν. —— ὅτι δὲ οὐ χρήσιμον τὸ τοιοῦτον εἶδος, μάθοιμεν ἄν, εἰ ἐπέλθοιμεν τὰ εἴδη τοῦ συλλογισμοῦ καὶ ἐξετάσαιμεν, τίνι αὐτῶν οἰκεῖον τὸ τῶν κειμένων τι ἐπιφέρειν. πότερον γὰρ τῷ ἀποδεικτικῷ; ἀλλ' οὗτός γε τὸ ἄδηλον πειρᾶται διὰ τῶν φανερῶν καὶ γνωρίμων ἐκκαλύπτειν καὶ τὸ ὕστερον διὰ τῶν πρώτων. ἀλλὰ τῷ διαλεκτικῷ; ἀλλὰ καὶ οὗτος, ὃ μὴ βούλεται συγχωρεῖν ὁ προσδιαλεγόμενος, τοῦτο πειρᾶται διὰ τῶν ἐνδόξων καὶ ὧν συγχωρεῖ δεικνύναι εἰς ἀντίφασιν περιάγων. ἀλλὰ τῷ ἐριστικῷ; ἀλλὰ καὶ τούτῳ πρόκειται καὶ αὐτῷ ἢ εἰς ἀντίφασιν ἢ εἰς φαινομένην ἀντίφασιν περιαγαγεῖν τὸν ἀποκρινόμενον, ἐξ ὧν δίδωσιν· οὐχ ὃ δίδωσι γοῦν συμπεραί|νεται, ἀλλ᾽ ἐξ ὧν δίδωσιν, ὃ οὐ βούλεται δοῦναι· δῆλον οὖν ὡς ἄλλο τι τοῦ δεδομένου ἐποίσει. Was hier über den dialektischen und eristischen Syllogismus gesagt wird, ist durchaus richtig; vgl. o. S. 266. Dagegen die Worte über den apodeiktischen Syllogismus sind nur durch die Zufügungen καὶ γνωρίμων und καὶ τὸ ὕστερον διὰ τῶν πρώτων an die aristotelische Logik angeglichen, fallen aber im übrigen heraus und setzen in Wahrheit nicht die aristotelische, sondern die stoische Syllogistik voraus. Die moderne Auffassung der aristotelischen Logik ist offenbar und begreiflicherweise von dem Prinzip der stoischen Logik, das schließlich aus der großen antiken Naturphilosophie stammt, nicht unbeeinflußt geblieben. Aber es ist für das Verständnis der aristotelischen Logik nötig, sich davon freizumachen. In der Geschichte der Logik sitzt der aristotelische Syllogismus gewissermaßen verkehrt herum. Hier ist eine Stelle, wo gerade die vorsichtige geistesgeschichtliche Betrachtungsweise, die sich das Ablösen des Logischen aus dem Mythischen und Metaphysischen nur ganz allmählich und stetig glaubt vorstellen zu können, *einen* Schritt nicht tun kann. Man kommt auf diesem Wege bis zur platonischen διαίρεσις, über deren metaphysische Gebundenheit heute kein Wort mehr zu verlieren ist. Und dann glaubt man gewonnenes Spiel zu haben, denn Aristoteles selbst hat seinen Syllogismus mit der διαίρεσις-Methode verglichen und sie als so etwas wie eine unvollkommene Vorstufe des Syllogismus charakterisiert. Man darf auch vermuten, daß sie bei der für Aristoteles' *Topik* und *1. Analytik* wichtigen Vorstellung von *einem* zu vielen Dingen hinführenden logischen Weg mitspielt. Aber wie sie zuletzt am Syllogismus gemessen wird, ist doch deutlich etwas Unnatürliches und Nachträgliches, und in Wahrheit geht keine gerade Linie über die διαίρεσις-Methode zum aristotelischen Syllogismus. Denn auch jene will, freilich in ganz besonderer Weise, vorwärts vom Bekannten zum Unbekannten, zu Erjagenden führen (vgl. Speusippos frg. 30, Art. *Speusippos* 1660 — beim aristotelischen Syllogismus ist das Bild der Jagd direkt nur auf die Prämissen, nicht auf den Schlußsatz anwendbar, 46a 11); sie ist für Platon eine erst aus dem letzten Stadium seiner Ideenlehre gewonnene Konsequenz und keineswegs aus der Reflexion auf *die* dialektische Technik erwachsen, die wir aus seinen früheren Dialogen in voller Anschaulichkeit kennen. Die Reflexion auf *diese* Technik, die praktisch inzwischen durch Platon selbst zur philosophischen Gymnastik geworden war, ist Aristoteles' Verdienst, für das es keine Vorstufe gab, wie er selbst gerühmt hat. Damit ist etwas Besonderes in die Philosphie hineingekommen, was sich neuerdings als formale, metaphysikfreie und als reine, psychologiefreie Logik darstellen kann, ohne doch über das einfache Geheimnis seines historischen Ursprungs immer ganz im klaren zu sein und ohne sich ganz davon freimachen zu können. Denn das hat die aristotelische Syllogistik vor aller späteren Logik voraus, daß sie ihren Gegenstand ursprünglich weder aus fertig vorliegenden theoretischen Gedankengebilden zu destillieren hatte noch ihn durch ad hoc anzustellende Gedankenexperimente erst ge|winnen mußte, sondern daß er sich ihr in einer viel geübten Praxis darbot, bei der Erfolg, Scheinerfolg und Mißerfolg dem technischen Zugriff ohne weiteres offenlagen.

Casus accusativus

1956

Schon auf der Schule haben manche von uns gelernt, den *accusativus* als eine Falschübersetzung des griechischen Terminus αἰτιατική (πτῶσις) zu belächeln; dieser sei nämlich nicht vom Verbum αἰτιᾶσθαι 'beschuldigen' abgeleitet, sondern hänge mit dem aristotelischen αἰτιατόν 'das Bewirkte' zusammen[1]. Später ist wohl jedem von uns die Sache gelegentlich etwas unheimlich geworden: immerhin hat schon Varro den *casus accusandi*; und wer schon die Erklärung für richtig hält, sollte vielleicht doch eher von einer auch für Griechen irreführenden Terminologie statt von einem zu bemitleidenden (römischen?) Mißverständnis reden. Aber wenn man dann zur wissenschaftlichen Literatur geht, wird man mit so seltener Einmütigkeit der Zustimmung auf Trendelenburg (Acta Soc. Graecae Lipsiensis 1, 1836, S. 123) verwiesen, daß man sich leicht wieder beruhigt. Ich habe vor sehr langer Zeit Trendenlenburgs Aufsatz einmal nachgeschlagen, habe ihn aber jetzt nicht zur Hand und halte mich der Kürze und Klarheit halber ausschließlich an Wackernagels Besprechung des „merkwürdigsten Kasusnamens" auf S. 19 der ersten Reihe der Vorlesungen über Syntax.

Während nach Wackernagel die γενική πτῶσις, und ihre Übersetzung *genetivus*, ähnliche Schwierigkeiten macht wie der *accusativus*, akzeptiert er die Übersetzung *dativus* als „unbestreitbar richtig" und die griechische Benennung als „adäquat": „Man kann viele durch eine Dativform ausgedrückte Kasusbeziehungen auf die Handlung des Gebens zurückführen; auch die indischen Sprachlehrer haben als Hauptfunktion des Dativs das Geben bezeichnet." Könnte man *viele* durch eine Akkusativform ausgedrückte Kasusbeziehungen auf die Handlung des Anklagens zurückführen, so würde offenbar nach Wackernagels Auffassung auch der Terminus *accusativus* genügend adäquat sein, um seine Einführung zu verstehen. Aber es geht nicht: „Nun wird ja allerdings bei *accusare* der Angeklagte im Akkusativ gegeben. Aber | es gibt ja Hunderte von Verben, die ebenfalls transitiv

---

[1] An sich könnte αἰτιατόν auch das ungefähre Gegenteil, nämlich das, was beschuldigt wird oder werden kann, bedeuten, cf. ἀναιτίατος, Ion (trag.) bei Phot. 113, 3 Reitz. Aber an der Bedeutung ‚bewirkt, verursacht' bei Aristoteles (*An. Post.* 76a 20 μὴ αἰτιαταὶ αἰτίαι und 98a 36, b 3 τὸ αἰτιατόν entgegengesetzt dem αἴτιον als das οὗ αἴτιον τὸ αἴτιον) kann allerdings nicht gezweifelt werden.

sind, und es ist ganz unverständlich, warum ein so spezieller Begriff wie der des Anklagens als Beispiel sollte gewählt sein."

Ehe wir weitergehen, erhebt sich die Frage, ob wirklich die Griechen — von den Indern kann ich nicht sprechen — anfänglich in dieser Weise nach Kasusbezeichnungen gesucht haben, daß sie sich für jeden einzelnen Kasus nach etwas Einheitlichem umsahen, auf das sich wenn nicht alle, so doch jedenfalls viele der durch die betreffende Kasusform ausgedrückten Beziehungen zurückführen ließen.

Wir wissen zufällig, daß es für Genetiv und Dativ noch andere ältere griechische Benennungen gab, die erst im Laufe der Zeit verdrängt worden sind. Für den Dativ gab es den Terminus ἐπισταλτική, der direkt nur diejenige Wortform bezeichnet, die man im Briefkopf für den Adressaten brauchte. So speziell diese Bezeichnung auch ist, ein so bestimmter Dativ genügt völlig, die unbestimmt große assoziative Reihe aller Dative, die die griechische Sprache zur Verfügung stellt, zu kennzeichnen; auf mehr kann es anfänglich kaum angekommen sein; denn schließlich muß man doch die im Sprechen vorkommenden „Dative" als solche erkennen und irgendwie bezeichnen können, ehe man nach einer möglichst vieles umfassenden einheitlichen Funktion überhaupt suchen kann. Auch was die δοτική betrifft, kann man sich unschwer vorstellen, daß der bloße Dativ eines Personennamens, z. B. Σωκράτει, oder auch eines Götternamens, an eine von einem solchen Dativ begleitete Gabe erinnerte und daß dann dieser nun benennbare und damit festgelegte Dativ zur Erkennung und Bezeichnung aller anderen „Dative" diente. Es soll aber nicht bestritten werden, daß früher oder später die Bezeichnung δοτική im Vergleich mit ἐπισταλτική auch einem Griechen adäquater vorgekommen sein mag.

Es erübrigt sich wohl, für die überlieferten Benennungen des Genetivs — πατρική, κτητική, γενική — Ähnliches auszuführen. Zum mindesten die Benennung πατρική kann wirklich nicht den Anspruch erheben, daß sich *viele* durch eine Genetivform ausgedrückte Genetivbeziehungen auf das Vatersein zurückführen ließen. Es kann nur gemeint gewesen sein: eine πτῶσις wie die, die z. B. in Θουκυδίδης ὁ Ὀλόρου als Vatersname erscheint.

Mit solchen Erwägungen ist das Rätsel des Akkusativs natürlich noch nicht gelöst. Niemand wird leicht glauben, daß irgendwer im Altertum zufälligerweise einen Satz wie αἰτιῶμαι Ἀρίσταρχον[2] gewählt hätte, um zu zeigen, | welche πτῶσις er meinte, und daß dann er

---

[2] Nicht ganz zufälligerweise erscheint dies Beispiel in einem konfusen Scholion zu Dionysios Thrax (232, 3 Hilg.): κατ' αἰτίαν φησὶν ἤτοι αἴτησιν ἢ καὶ αἰτίασιν, ἐπείπερ αἰτούμενοι λαβεῖν τι ἢ αἰτιώμενοί ⟨τινα⟩ ταύτην προφερόμεθα, ὡς ἂν εἴποις „αἰτοῦμαί σε δοῦναί μοι βιβλίον"· τὸ γὰρ σέ καὶ τὸ βιβλίον αἰτιατικῆς εἰσι πτώσεως. καὶ πάλιν· „αἰτιῶμαι Ἀρίσταρχον."

selbst oder ein Schüler aus diesem zufälligen Beispiel einen Terminus gemacht hätte. Die πατρική und die ἐπισταλτική sind offenbar nicht so erfunden, sondern hier wie dort handelt es sich um eine besonders wohlbekannte, gewissermaßen institutionelle Verwendung des betreffenden Kasus. Es bleibt also dabei, daß der Terminus αἰτιατική nicht lediglich deshalb auf das Verbum αἰτιᾶσθαι zurückgeführt werden kann, weil αἰτιᾶσθαι ein transitives Verbum ist.

Aber ein von αἰτιᾶσθαι abhängiger Akkusativ braucht nicht notwendig ein gewöhnlicher Objektsakkusativ zu sein. Wenn er mit einem Infinitiv zusammengeht, bleibt zwar der oder das durch den Akkusativ Bezeichnete Objekt der Beschuldigung, wird aber zugleich als αἴτιος oder αἰτία dessen, was im Infinitiv ausgedrückt wird, gedacht. Dies kommt der allbekannten Konstruktion des *accusativus cum infinitivo* nach Verben des Sagens oder Behauptens zum Verwechseln nahe. In dieser Konstruktion ist für das Sprachgefühl ein Σωκράτη εἶναι dasselbe wie der entsprechende Nominativ mit dem entsprechenden Verbum finitum — der Akkusativ wird entweder als Subjekt oder als Prädikatsnomen zum Infinitiv empfunden —, nur daß die Akkusativkonstruktion ohne weiteres herausbringt, daß dies „indirekte Rede" ist; ein Verbum dicendi braucht gar nicht immer dabeizustehen, z. B. in der indirekten Erzählung; erinnern darf man wohl auch an den substantivierten Infinitiv mit Artikel, wo „der Agens des Inf. normalerweise durch den Akkusativ ... ausgedrückt" wird (Schwyzer, Gr. Gr. II 369).

Wenn wir an solche Akkusative denken dürften, dann würde an dem von αἰτιᾶσθαι abgeleiteten Terminus αἰτιατική wenig auszusetzen sein; denn daß αἰτιᾶσθαι auch in gewöhnlicher Rede in neutralem oder gutem Sinne gebraucht werden konnte, entnimmt man dem Wörterbuch; daß beim ersten, unbefangenen Reflektieren auf Subjekt und Prädikat das Subjekt als Agens gedacht wird, beweist Platons *Sophistes* 262a; daß endlich bei terminologischer Verwertung der unangenehme Beigeschmack des Anklagens, Beschuldigens ganz verlorengehen kann, würde der Parallelfall des von Aristoteles allerdings für andere Zwecke verbrauchten κατηγορεῖν belegen[3]. Für den Akkusativ der indirekten Rede, verglichen mit dem Nominativ der direkten, den er ersetzt, wäre αἰτιατική, von αἰτιᾶσθαι abgeleitet, eine genügend adäquate Bezeichnung. Aber die Frage ist nun natürlich, ob man im Altertum so früh auf diesen Akkusativ aufmerksam geworden ist, daß er dann für die grammatische Terminologie aufgegriffen werden konnte.

Es trifft sich, daß derselbe Aristoteles, von dem sich Trendelenburg sein αἰτιατόν holte, in der Schrift περὶ σοφιστικῶν ἐλέγχων gezwungen

---

[3] Eine Ausnahme, die die Regel bestätigt: π. σ. ἐλ. 167b 12.

war, sich | zur Auflösung einer besonders albernen Art von Trug-schlüssen gerade mit diesem Akkusativ und seinem Verhältnis zum entsprechenden Nominativ zu befassen.

Worum es sich handelt, ist das scheinbare dialektische Erzwingen eines Sprachfehlers, eines Soloikismos[4]. Die für uns und, wie seine Be-handlung zeigt, auch für Aristoteles interessantesten „Syllogismen" dieser Art sehen wie folgt aus:

182a 10: ἆρ' ὃ λέγεις ἀληθῶς, καὶ ἔστι τοῦτο ἀληθῶς; φὴς δ' εἶναί τι λίθον· ἔστιν ἄρα τι λίθον.

182a 28: ἆρ' ἀληθές ἐστιν εἰπεῖν ὅτι ἔστιν αὕτη ὅπερ εἶναι φὴς αὐτήν; εἶναι δὲ φὴς ἀσπίδα· ἔστιν ἄρα αὕτη ἀσπίδα.

182a 31: (οὐδ') εἰ ὃ φὴς εἶναι τοῦτον, ἔστιν οὗτος, φὴς δ' εἶναι Κλέωνα, ἔστιν ἄρα οὗτος Κλέωνα· (οὐ γὰρ . . .).

In unserer Sprache kurz ausgedrückt besteht der Kniff darin, daß, nachdem der Wahrheitsgehalt von indirekter und direkter Rede iden-tifiziert ist, dann vermittels eines fälschlich auf eine Akkusativ*form* bezogenen τόδε, τοῦτο, oder ὅ, ὅπερ ein Akkusativ aus der indirekten Redeform in die direkte hinübergeschmuggelt wird, so daß da ein Nominativ einen Akkusativ zum Prädikat erhält[5].

Zur Beschreibung und Auflösung des Unsinns konstatiert Aristote-les folgende sprachliche Fakten:

1. Ein τόδε oder τοῦτο (ὅ und ὅπερ gleich τοῦτο ὅ, τοῦτο ὅπερ) kann sich auch auf ein männliches oder weibliches Wesen, und auch auf eine Sache, die sprachlich durch ein Maskulinum oder Femininum ausgedrückt wird, beziehen (173b 28—31).

2. Beim Maskulinum und Femininum haben alle verschiedenen Kasus verschiedene Form, aber nicht beim Neutrum, da sind nur manche verschieden, andere nicht: τοῦ μὲν οὖν ἄρρενος καὶ τοῦ θήλεος διαφέρουσιν αἱ πτώσεις ἅπασαι, τοῦ δὲ μεταξὺ αἱ μὲν αἱ δ' οὔ (173b 37). |

3. Mit ἔστι geht οὗτος, mit εἶναι geht τοῦτον usw. (173b 31) (s. unten S. 283).

Erläuternd sei bemerkt, daß Aristoteles das Wort πτῶσις, auch wo es sich um Sprachliches handelt, in verschiedenen Bedeutungen und Bedeutungsnuancen braucht. Die Dinge waren noch im Fluß, und man darf nur nach dem jeweiligen Zusammenhang interpretieren. In der

---

[4] Hauptstellen π. σ. ἐλ. 173b 17—174a 11 und 182a 7—b 5. Nach 182a 7 war der Inhalt des früheren Abschnittes gewesen παρ' ὅτι φαίνονται (οἱ σολοικισμοί); nunmehr soll kommen: ὡς δὲ λυτέον. Ich versuche, nur das zum Verständnis Unerläßliche zur Sprache zu bringen, halte mich nicht an die aristotelische An-ordnung und zitiere überdies das Griechische oft nur, soweit es mir zur Kontrolle nötig scheint.

[5] Etwas komplizierter vielleicht 182a 11 beim Übergang von φὴς δὲ εἶναί τι (subj.) λίθον (präd.) zu ἔστιν ἄρα τι λίθον, wo man wohl τι λίθον zusammen als Subjekt auffassen soll.

hier zu besprechenden Partie von π. σ. ἐλ. sind die verschiedenen
Deklinationskasus in unserem Sinn gemeint; der Nominativ wird
mitgerechnet[6]. Übrigens kann hier mit dem Wort sowohl eine der verschiedenen Deklinations*formen* als auch einer der verschiedenen syn-
taktisch geforderten Kasus bezeichnet werden; und der Schein, der
entstehen kann, wenn zwei verschiedene Kasus dieselbe sprachliche
Form haben, wird so ausgedrückt: φαίνεται δὲ παρὰ τὸ τὴν ἀνόμοιον
πτῶσιν τοῦ ὀνόματος ὁμοίαν φαίνεσθαι (182a 26). „Der Schein entsteht dadurch, daß ein verschiedener Kasus nicht verschieden aussieht."

Bei einem Neutrum, wo Nominativ und Akkusativ gleichlauten,
kann sich offenbar kein Soloikismos wie in den drei oben S. 281 zitierten
Beispielen ergeben, das zeigt Aristoteles an dem Beispiel εἰ ὃ λέγεις
εἶναι, ἔστι τοῦτο, ξύλον δὲ λέγεις εἶναι, ἔστιν ἄρα ξύλον (182a 17). Wie
in den anderen Fällen der Soloikismos zustande kommt, beschreibt er
in einer Weise, die schwer wiederzugeben ist, weil für ihn einerseits
das Neutrum τοῦτο das Mittel ist, mit dem der täuschende Schein
hervorgerufen wird, andererseits die Kasusformen von οὗτος, αὕτη
zur Bezeichnung der Einzelkasus dienen müssen und weil er für das,
worauf es ihm ankommt, keinen Unterschied zwischen Subjekt und
Prädikatsnomen zu machen braucht. Er sagt etwa: τοῦτο kann beides
bedeuten, den entsprechenden Nominativ, oder auch den entspre-
chenden Akkusativ | (173b 36). Oft, wenn zugestanden ist τοῦτο, d. i.
der mit dem ἔστι der Fangfrage gehende Nominativ, ziehen sie den
Schluß, als wäre damit τοῦτον gesagt, d. i. der zu λέγεις oder εἶναι φής

---

[6] Anders Περὶ ἑρμηνείας 16a 32—b 5. In dieser Schrift sind ὄνομα und ῥῆμα von
   vornherein als Subjekt und Prädikat jeder entweder wahren oder falschen Behauptung (ἀποφαντικὸς λόγος) ins Auge gefaßt; ὄνομα ist also eo ipso Nominativ.
   Demgegenüber sind hier τὸ Φίλωνος ἢ Φίλωνι καὶ ὅσα τοιαῦτα οὐκ ὀνόματα, ἀλλὰ
   πτώσεις ὀνόματος. Der Unterschied wird scharf bestimmt: (eine πτῶσις ὀνόματος)
   μετὰ τοῦ ἔστιν ἢ ἦν ἢ ἔσται οὐκ ἀληθεύει ἢ ψεύδεται· τὸ δ' ὄνομα ἀεί, z. B.: mit
   Φίλωνος ἔστιν ἢ οὐκ ἔστιν ist noch nichts Wahres oder Unwahres gesagt — οὐδὲν
   γάρ πω ἀληθεύει ἢ ψεύδεται. Was fehlt, ist offenbar das Subjekt, das „ὄνομα". Der
   nicht als Beispiel angeführte Akkusativ wird ja wohl in καὶ ὅσα τοιαῦτα mitge-
   meint sein, obwohl er zu ἔστι usw. direkt nicht gehören kann, mit einem εἶναι
   aber, wie wir sehen werden, auch für Aristoteles etwas bedeuten würde, das sehr
   wohl entweder wahr oder falsch ist. Die vielzitierte Stelle *Poetik* 1457a 18—21
   scheint auch Singular und Plural als πτώσεις ὀνόματος zu führen (mit dem Beispiel im *Nominativ*: ἄνθρωποι ἢ ἄνθρωπος), ist aber, wenn korrekt erhalten, so
   unscharf ausgedrückt, daß man nicht zugreifen kann. Den Akkusativ führt sie
   aber ebenfalls nicht an. — Alle Kasus werden aufgeführt *An. Pr.* 48b 39—49a 5,
   und zwar so, daß zunächst der Nominativ eine Sonderstellung hat, dann aber
   auch als letzter vor einem „und was es sonst noch geben mag" in der Reihe der
   πτώσεις erscheint, was den beiden Funktionen, in denen er hier vorkommt, genau
   entspricht.

gehörige Akkusativ (auf den sich ja in der Tat der ausgesprochene oder — bei ὅ, ὅπερ — zu denkende Nominativ τοῦτο bezieht), vgl. die Beispiele S. 281. Solange nicht ausdrücklich zwischen Form und Inhalt der in direkter und indirekter Rede inhaltlich identischen Aussage oder, anders ausgedrückt, zwischen der Akkusativform und ihrer Funktion, in indirekter Rede Subjekt bzw. Prädikatsnomen dieser Aussage zu sein, unterschieden wird, läßt sich, was passiert, wohl nicht klarer ausdrücken.

Etwas der zu fordernden Unterscheidung Entsprechendes bringt Aristoteles selbst 174a 5ff. in einem interessanten Vergleich nach: „In gewisser Weise ist die Erschleichung eines Soloikismos den Widerlegungen vergleichbar, die sich darauf gründen, daß verschiedener Inhalt in *nicht* verschiedener Form ausgedrückt werden kann" — καὶ τρόπον τινὰ ὅμοιός ἐστιν ὁ σολοικισμὸς τοῖς παρὰ τὸ τὰ μὴ ὅμοια ὁμοίως λεγομένοις (λέγεσθαι γινομένοις?) ἐλέγχοις. „Dort ergibt sich ein sachlicher, hier ein sprachlicher Unsinn" — ὥσπερ γὰρ ἐκείνοις ἐπὶ τῶν πραγμάτων, τούτοις ἐπὶ τῶν ὀνομάτων συμπίπτει σολοικίζειν· ἄνθρωπος γὰρ καὶ λευκὸν καὶ πρᾶγμα καὶ ὄνομά ἐστιν. Folgen wir diesem Wink, so erhalten wir, umgekehrt: „Die Erschleichung eines (sprachlichen) Soloikismos gründet sich darauf, daß nicht verschiedener Inhalt in verschiedener Form ausgedrückt wird." Man könnte es nicht besser sagen. Unglücklicherweise formuliert aber Aristoteles die Möglichkeit des scheinbar erzwungenen Soloikismos mehrfach gerade umgekehrt, z. B. wie schon erwähnt (S. 282), 182a 26: φαίνεται δὲ παρὰ τὸ τὴν ἀνόμοιον πτῶσιν τοῦ ὀνόματος ὁμοίαν φαίνεσθαι. Schwerlich korrekt. Die eigentliche Irreführung besteht m. E. darin, daß ein τοῦτο, einerlei ob Nominativ oder Akkusativ, sich in der Tat auf irgendeine Kasusform beziehen kann, aber nicht weil Nominativ und Akkusativ des Neutrums gleich aussehen, sondern so, daß man statt der Sache die Wortform, durch welche die Sache in einem verschieden konstruierten Satz bezeichnet wird, aufgreift, z. B. — dies ist eins der uns anderweitig hier nicht interessierenden Beispiele — ἆρ᾽ οὗ ἐπιστήμην ἔχεις, ἐπίστασαι τοῦτο; ἐπιστήμην δ᾽ ἔχεις λίθου· ἐπίστασαι ἄρα λίθου (182a 38). — Zureichend erklärt die Tatsache, daß beim Neutrum Nominativ und Akkusativ nicht verschieden aussehen, nur, wieso in den Paralogismen, in denen statt einer Nominativform eine Akkusativform erschlichen wird, mit einem Neutrum ein Soloikismos *nicht* erzielt werden kann (vgl. das Beispiel 182a 17, oben S. 282).

Sei dem wie es wolle, richtig ist es auf jeden Fall, wenn Aristoteles im Zusammenhang seiner anfänglichen Erörterung konstatiert, 173b 36ff.: Ein | τοῦτο, das (syntaktisch) mit einem ἔστι geht, kann nicht, wie wenn es mit εἶναι geht, einen Akkusativ, sondern muß, in richtiger Zuordnung, einen Nominativ bedeuten: δεῖ δ᾽ ἐναλλὰξ σημαίνειν,

μετὰ μὲν τοῦ ἔστι τὸ οὗτος, μετὰ δὲ τοῦ εἶναι τὸ τοῦτον, οἷον ἔστι Κόρισ-
κος, εἶναι Κόρισκον (173b 36). Dies gilt auch für weibliche Namen —
ἐπὶ τῶν θήλεων — und für durch ein Maskulinum oder Femininum bezeichnete Sachen; deshalb unterscheidet sich auch hier in derselben
Weise ἔστι und εἶναι: διόπερ καὶ ἐπὶ τῶν τοιούτων ὡσαύτως τὸ ἔστι καὶ
τὸ εἶναι διοίσει (174a 4).

Der Akkusativ, der „bei verschiedenem Agens" mit dem Infinitiv
der oratio obliqua geht, ist also dank den voraristotelischen sophistischen Spielereien verhältnismäßig früh aufgefallen[7] und stand so der
beginnenden grammatischen Terminologie zur Verfügung. Es brauchte
nur der Kasus, den die Sprache statt des Nominativs forderte, wo eine
Beschuldigung (Behauptung, Erzählung) indirekt wiedergegeben wurde, durch einen passenden Namen fixiert zu werden, um damit alle
Akkusativformen greifbar zu machen. Daß dies der Weg war, auf dem
es zu dem Terminus αἰτιατική gekommen ist, halte ich bei der großen
Unsicherheit, die auf diesem Gebiet noch herrscht, für nicht mehr als
eine beachtenswerte Möglichkeit, lasse mich aber gern belehren, wenn
es weniger sein sollte.

---

[7] Auch die Konstruktion „bei gleichem Agens" mit dem Nominativ war diesen
Spielereien dienlich. 166a 10 finden wir sie mit der Konstruktion bei verschiedenem Agens gleichlautend und fälschlich identifiziert, und das Resultat ist ein
‚sachlicher' Unsinn: ἆρα ὃ σὺ φῂς εἶναι, τοῦτο σὺ φῂς εἶναι; φῂς δὲ λίθον εἶναι· σὺ
ἆρα φῂς λίθος εἶναι, vgl. 174a 5ff. (oben S. 283).

Besprechung:

Philodemus, On Methods of Inference
A Study in Ancient Empiricism

Edited with translation and commentary by Phillip Howard DeLacy
and Estelle Allen DeLacy

1957

According to a still widely held opinion, which is propagated even by Bertrand Russell in his *History of Western Philosophy* (1945), Aristotle's logic, although quite an achievement in its time, failed to initiate a continual progress towards the "discoveries of modern logic" and was "followed by over two thousand years of stagnation" (Russell, *op. cit.*, 195). The adherents of this simplified view of the history of logic still believe in the necessity of fighting Aristotle's doctrine of the syllogism (*ibid.*); and, since through Sextus Empiricus (*Pyrrh. Hyp.* 2, 195—197) we know of the arguments that were used by critics of Aristotle's logic in later antiquity, one may say that at least a stagnation of the views of Aristotle's opponents in this field for, cautiously speaking, over 1800 years can be taken for granted. The example for the alleged main function of the Aristotelian syllogism is still an allegedly deductive inference from what is true of "all men" (e. g., "all men are mortal'") to a human individual ("Socrates is a man, therefore Socrates is mortal"); and it is still pointed out reprovingly that our belief in Socrates' mortality is not strictly and in a merely deductive way derived from a major premise that would include every single actual case (which Aristotle never asserted); and furthermore it is still emphasized that we believe in this general proposition "on the basis | of induction" (as if such premises were objectionable). At the same time Russell states that the question of our knowledge of general propositions is a very difficult one and that there are different types (according to him merely verbal ones and those based on induction). This is indeed beyond the reach of Sextus Empiricus' mind, as his examples indicate. But one can hardly say that Aristotle himself was not aware of such differences and that he was generally not able to see the difficulties of the question of the *katholou*. Many of the inadequacies of ancient and modern criticisms of Aristotle's syllogistic derive, in the opinion of this reviewer, from the constant and almost exclusive use of the example of the mortal Socrates or Cajus or "Mr. Smith" (Russell). It might well be worth while to ask why Aristotle himself never discussed the problems that even in the dullest mind arise immediately whenever *this* example, which never occurs in Aristotle's writings, is used as if it were a typical Aristotelian syllogism.

But however this may be, it should come as a pleasant surprise to many critics of Aristotle's logic when, in the publication under review, they find documentary evidence that in later antiquity the waters of logic were stirred a little and that at least after Aristotle's time the issue of the mortality of "all men" and similar problems were indeed discussed at lenght and along lines that are not far removed from modern expectations. "And further" — this is the argument of an Epicurean philosopher of probably the first century B. C. in the editor's translation (pp. 101 ff.) — "the Stoics err in so far as they have not taken the trouble to understand the right method of analogical inference. Whenever we say,

Since things in our experience are of such a nature,
Unperceived objects are also of this nature *in so far as* things in our experience are of this nature,
we judge that there is a necessary connection between an unperceived object and the objects of our experience. For example,

Since men in our experience *as men* are mortal,
If there are men anywhere,
They are mortal.

"There are four things that the words 'as such', 'according as', and 'in so far as', signify:

"First ... Second ... Third ... Fourth ...

"... But those who attack the inference from analogy do not indicate the distinctions just mentioned, namely, how we are to take the 'according as', as in the statement, for example,

Man as man is mortal.

"Hence they say that if the 'according as' is omitted, the argument will be inconclusive; if it is admitted, the method of contraposition is used. But we Epicureans take this to be necessarily connected with that from the fact that this has been observed to be a property of that in all cases that we have come upon, and because we have observed many varied living creatures of the same genus who have | differences in all other respects from each other, but who all share in certain common qualities (e. g., mortality). According to this method we say that man according as and in so far as he is man is mortal, on the ground that we have examined systematically many diverse men, and have found no variation in respect to this characteristic and no evidence to the contrary . . ."

I have had to quote at least part of one of many most interesting passages from the remnants of Philodemus' best preserved book on a subject of logic (Herculanean papyrus No. 1065). For this should make it clear at once that if we still busy ourselves with turning over and over the notorious syllogism concerning the mortal individual we are dealing with problems that have had the full interest of Stoic and Epicurean logicians, but, for some reason, were not the problems of Aristotle's logic. Under present conditions, that is, so long as the history of ancient logic has not been rewritten, the new editors of these remnants, which are the basis of their "study in ancient empiricism", cannot be blamed for extolling the importance of their subject, not even when they quit the solid ground of the evidence in venturing a guess like: "Had the Epicurean method had more influence on subsequent philosophy, the progress of empirical method in both philosophy and science might have been much accelerated" (Foreword, p. viii).

The pitifully short story of modern research concerning this most illuminating, though difficult, ancient document of non-Aristotelian logic is adequately told by the editors in the following few lines (p. 10): "The Greek text was published by Th. Gomperz in 1865, and subsequently improved in many passages by R. Philippson. It has been the subject of two German dissertations, and it has received passing notice in a few works of a more general nature. On the whole, however, it has remained practically unknown, especially in America.[1]" For many reasons, which will be fully realized only after a study of the whole book (and which, incidentally, caused this reviewer to delay his promised review almost beyond excuse), the task of getting acquainted with these Stoic-Epicurean controversies is hard indeed. But the authors have done everything in their power to provide their readers with badly needed help. In addition to the Greek text there are two introductory chapters; the authors' translation and their commentary (III); three "supplementary essays": The Sources of Epicurean Empiricism (IV); The Development of Epicurean Logic and Methodology (V); The Logical Controversies of the Stoics, Epicureans and Sceptics (VI); and a valuable Bibliography and two

---

[1] Perhaps the interesting article "Epicurean Induction" by J. L. Stocks (Mind 34, 1925, 185—203) should be mentioned in particular, because the author states: "My treatment can claim no special novelty; it is in the main only an attempt to show that the tract deserves much more attention than it has hitherto received from students of ancient philosophy."

Indices. If this document of ancient logic should now actually reach more of those whose interests are concerned, the credit will have to go to the authors of the present new edition.

Of course, there are limitations. The presentation of the Greek text could not be final, since a reëxamination of the papyrus was, in | 1941, only a hope for the future. This could not be helped and we should be glad that it has not led to an indefinite postponement of a publication of so much actual interest. But, though it may seem ungrateful, one thing must be mentioned here. The philologically trained reader cannot help feeling very uneasy, where dotted letters (α̣) occur. In this edition the dots mark "letters whose reading is uncertain." But one look at R. Philippson's article in Rh. Mus. 64, 1910, 1—38, shows that, used this way, the dots cover uncertainties of very different degrees. In a case like p. 28, Col. III, line 8 even the understanding of the authors' own critical apparatus is made extremely difficult by this usage of the dot. On p. vii of the "Foreword" the authors remark: "The obscure and technical language of Philodemus' treatise has required a rather lengthy commentary." In order to avoid disappointment, the philological reader must be warned not to expect any kind of grammatical or syntactical explanation of the given Greek text beyond what may be implied in the translation and the generously repeated paraphrases. He will understand that the authors' reticence in this respect was due to regard for the largest part of the hoped-for audience, and he will resignedly suspend judgment in many actually or seemingly desperate cases, unless he has access to the older publications.

The English translation and the corresponding paraphrases and explanatory notes seem to me very readable, but the danger is, naturally, the necessary use of many traditional or modern philosophical technical terms. Epicurus' important Greek term ἐπιλογισμός (see Kurt v. Fritz, Gnomon 8, 1932, 71ff.) should not have been translated by "inductive inference." An ἐπιλογισμός is preceded by an inference (or somebody else's "opinion"); but, as the authors state correctly on p. 141, "inferences concerning that which is not directly or completely experienced may be true or false." Therefore a methodical verification is required in order to decide definitely whether the preliminary inference (or given "opinion") can be established as true or not. Clearly ἐπιλογισμός is the mental activity that is concerned with checking up on an "inductive inference", and in so far it may be called an indispensable *part* of a "scientific" induction; but it is not itself an inductive inference, it comes "after" or "in addition to" it. The ἐπι- is identical with the ἐπι- in ἐπιμαρτύρησις, but has nothing to do with the ἐπ- in ἐπαγωγή. Worse, though less important, is the translation of ἀναλογισάμενος (Col. XXVI, 23) by "using analogies" and of ἀναλογιζόμενος (Col. XXVI, 39) by "forming the analogy." Though ἀναλογία, ἀναλογέω go back to ἀνὰ λόγον, the verb ἀναλογίζεσθαι does not. It means simply "to reckon up, sum up" or "to calculate, consider", as the dictionary says.

The most questionable part of the authors' achievement is their attempt to present their practically new logical material "historically." It could hardly have been otherwise; for in this field the ground is simply not yet prepared for more than provisional constructions. According to their preface, which presumably represents a last stage of their reflections on the subject, they have chosen the terms "empirical" and "rational" in order to determine the "Epicurean position advanced by Philodemus", though, as they cautiously remark, these terms "name procedures which need not be | opposed or completely distinct." On the one side there would have been "the absolutism of Plato and Aristotle", on the other side the "rampant individualism and scepticism of the Sophists and Pyrrhonists." But they believe they have discovered in the remnants of later Epicurean epistemology ("together with the critical additions of the Empirical Sceptics") at least an implicit recognition of a *via media*, on which "truth is neither necessary and absolute once and for all, nor is it wholly unattainable." This attempt to bring Epicurean methodology close to the views of "modern empiricists" seems to me to be in no way substantiated by Philodemus' treatise. Throughout all its now available sections we see the Epicurean logicians striving to prove against their Stoic opponents that their own favored method of analogical inference grants *necessary* conclusions; and has there ever been an orthodox member of the Epicurean school who would have conceded to anyone that the truth reached by Epicurus was *not* "absolute once and for all"?

The authors believe in the possibility of presenting their material "historically" while strictly claiming: "No attempt is made to give a critical evaluation of the philosophical issues involved" (p. vii). To this reviewer it seems, on the one hand, that their presentation of the material is strongly influenced by a certain (perhaps not critical) predilection for a certain kind of "empiricism"; and on the other hand it is his conviction that in the field of philosophy a definite advance towards historical understanding will be possible only when those who have access to the primary sources abandon their strange reluctance to face with their own mind the "philosophical issues involved." For instance, one might say that the Epicurean logicians were rather good in dealing with the problem of the mortality of "all men" (though exaggerating the "necessity" in such cases), but that they were not so good when they tried to reduce the

19 Kapp, Ausgew. Schriften

necessity in a case like εἰ ἔστι κίνησις, ἔστι κενόν to their favored epistemological principle and obscured the issue by a clever use of the equivalent term "inconceivability." Then, of course, one would ask why Epicureans were so intolerant of rational necessity, and why, on the other hand, the Stoic logicians felt bound to attack the respectable part of Epicurean logic, the existence of which obviously cannot be denied any longer. Or, considering what is characteristic of both Stoic and Epicurean logic, namely "the common view that appearances are the signs of the unperceived"[2], one would ask, who it was who for the first time saw the logic of the syllogism, Aristotle's invention, one-sidedly from this angle, and in what connection he thus originated the belief that a syllogism to be useful must reveal in its conclusion something unperceived or unknown before. In later antiquity this belief invaded even the interpretation of Aristotle's logic (Pauly-Wissowa-Kroll-Mittelhaus, R.-E., *s. v.* "Syllogistik", IV A, cols. 1065f.), but Aristotle was not responsible for this. Was it Nausiphanes? Or a Stoic philosopher? And what was the part of Diodorus Cronos? When Anaxagoras coined his famous ὄψις τῶν ἀδήλων τὰ φαινόμενα, he did so, in my opinion, in sharp reply to some stupidly sceptical remark against trying to know the imperceptible, and it was this that impressed Democritus (Gnomon 12, | 1936, 167f.). But even if both men wanted only to express the modest belief that "appearances may be used as indications of the imperceptible" (the De Lacys, 124), it is still a long way from there to "the real issue between the Stoics and Epicureans", namely "the validity of inference from appearances to the unperceived", which is ably presented by the authors in their last chapter (157ff., the quotation from 160f.). The numerous questions that here arise for us are undeniably relevant to a historical understanding, but they cannot even be asked without some attempt at "critical evaluation of the philosophical issues involved." And, in conclusion, I might add to my already lengthy comment, I doubt whether this complex of problems can be discussed adequately in terms of "empirical", "rational", and *"via media"*.

---

[2] Bromios in Philodemus' book, Col. XXVII, 30f.: τὸ κοινὸν ὅτι τὰ φανερὰ τῶν ἀδήλων ἐστὶ σημεῖα.

Deum te scito esse?

1959

I. Im zweiten Kapitel des dritten Buches der aristotelischen *Rhetorik* folgt auf den grundlegenden Abschnitt über die ἀρετὴ λέξεως (oder τοῦ ῥητορικοῦ λόγου, 1404b 1—37) eine Bemerkung über die Nutzbarkeit von Homonymien und Synonymien[1]. Überliefert ist sie wie folgt: τῶν δ᾽ ὀνομάτων τῷ μὲν σοφιστῇ ὁμωνυμίαι χρήσιμοι (παρὰ ταύτας γὰρ κακουργεῖ), τῷ ποιητῇ δὲ συνωνυμίαι, λέγω δὲ κύριά τε καὶ συνώνυμα οἷον τὸ πορεύεσθαι καὶ τὸ βαδίζειν· ταῦτα γὰρ ἀμφότερα καὶ κύρια καὶ συνώνυμα ἀλλήλοις.

Zweierlei fällt auf: 1. Da scheinbar nur vom Sophisten und vom Dichter die Rede ist, so ist nicht einzusehen, wieso diese Bemerkung in einen Zusammenhang gehört, in dem es um den Stil der Prosarede geht; 2. auf die Dichtkunst bezogen ist die Einschränkung auf κύριά τε καὶ συνώνυμα einfach falsch; man braucht nur z. B. an γλῶτται zu denken. Das Richtige war längst gesehen: Bernays (Rhein. Museum 8, 1853, 585 Anm. 1) hatte vorgeschlagen, λέγω δὲ in λόγῳ δὲ zu ändern. Das einfache Wort λόγος für Prosarede erscheint nämlich in diesem Teil des dritten *Rhetorik*buches schon 1401b 5 und ebenso wenige Zeilen nach der Bemerkung über Homonymien und Synonymien 1405a 6. Es ist also 1404b 39 zu lesen . . . λόγῳ δὲ κύριά τε καὶ συνώνυμα οἷον . . ., womit die Bedenken schwinden. Leider hatte Bernays die richtige Konjektur mit einer überflüssigen gekoppelt; er wollte nämlich am Anfang des Satzes τῶν δ᾽ ὀνομάτων durch τῶν δὲ ῥημάτων ersetzen[2] und machte es so für Spengel leichter, in seinem Kommentar zu 1405a 1 das Ganze mit einem schnöden *sine causa* abzulehnen. Es spielte aber wohl bei dieser Ablehnung noch etwas anderes mit.

Lichtenberg hat einmal den Einfall notiert: ,,Er las immer Agamemnon statt ,angenommen‘, so sehr hatte er den Homer gelesen."[3]

---

[1] Die Termini sind hier auf die Wörter bezogen, so daß Homonymie den Fall bezeichnet, daß ein Wort zwei verschiedene Bedeutungen hat, dagegen Synonymie den Fall, daß zwei verschiedene Wörter ein und dieselbe Bedeutung haben.

[2] 1404b 26 stehen freilich ὀνόματα und ῥήματα nebeneinander, aber wenn es sich um Wortwahl (κύρια, γλῶτται usw.) handelt, werden auch Verba einfach als ὀνόματα bezeichnet (z. B. *Poet.* 1458b 20) und können keinesfalls als im Gegensatz zu ὀνόματα stehend behandelt werden.

[3] Jahre später (Frühjahr 1792) auch den folgenden: ,,Seitdem er die Ohrfeige bekommen hatte, dachte er immer, wenn er ein Wort mit einem O sah, als Obrigkeit pp, es hieße Ohrfeige" (J 903 bei Leitzmann).

Das ist gewiß eine nur erdachte Beobachtung; aber den Spaß verstehen und sich darüber freuen kann nur, wer aus eigener Erfahrung weiß, daß gewisse Fehllesungen eine | spezifische Voreingenommenheit zur psychologischen Voraussetzung haben. Der Schreiber, der das λέγω δὲ in die Aristotelesüberlieferung hineingebracht hat, hatte offenbar den Aristoteles immerhin „so sehr gelesen", daß sich ihm diese gut aristotelische Phrase vor das nicht erwartete λόγῳ δὲ schob. Das ist nur natürlich. Aber daß einem so scharfen Kritiker wie Leonhard Spengel dieselbe Voreingenommenheit den Blick für das gefundene Richtige trüben konnte, zeigt darüber hinaus, wie hartnäckig sich solche Korruptelen, einmal entstanden, in den Texten halten können.

II. Zu Anfang der philosophischen Diskussion des Schönen im (doch wohl echt-)platonischen *Größeren Hippias* macht der Verfasser ausgiebigen Gebrauch von dem heute sogenannten „substantivierten Neutrum singularis als Prädikativ" beim Femininum:

287e 3 ἔστι γὰρ, ὦ Σώκρατες, εὖ ἴσθι, εἰ δεῖ τὸ ἀληθὲς λέγειν, παρθένος καλὴ καλόν.

288b 8 θήλεια δὲ ἵππος καλὴ οὐ καλόν, ἣν καὶ ὁ θεὸς ἐν τῷ χρησμῷ ἐπήνεσεν;

288c 6 εἶεν . . . τί δὲ λύρα καλή; οὐ καλόν;

288c 10 τί δὲ χύτρα καλή; οὐ καλὸν ἄρα; e 4 οὐκοῦν καὶ χύτρα . . . καλὴ καλόν;

Die Wahl dieses Neutrums hat zunächst den Zweck, Hippias' verfehlte Antwort auf die Frage nach dem Schönen wenigstens dem Klange nach erträglich zu machen; und das übrige schließt sich dann scheinbar zwanglos so an, wie es Sokrates zu bringen für gut befindet. Moderne Grammatiker zitieren in dem betreffenden Syntaxkapitel[4] mit Vorliebe nicht die erste, sondern die zweite der angeführten Stellen — θήλεια ἵππος καλὴ οὐ καλόν; — offenbar weil sie da das Genus femininum direkt ausgesprochen finden.

Glücklicherweise ist es nicht nötig zu diskutieren, ob der Übergang von der παρθένος καλή zu der θήλεια ἵππος καλή etwas befremdend oder besonders ansprechend ist und wie ,das' Orakel betreffend die schöne Stute gelautet haben könnte. Denn aus Hippias' Antwort 288c 4 ἀληθῆ λέγεις, ὦ Σώκρατες· ἐπεί τοι καὶ ὀρθῶς αὐτὸ ὁ θεὸς εἶπεν· πάγκαλοι γὰρ παρ' ἡμῖν ἵπποι γίγνονται ergibt sich m. E. mit Sicherheit, daß der von Sokrates vorgeschobene unbequeme Frager und der Gott im Orakel nicht von einer θήλεια, sondern von einer Ἠλεία ἵππος καλή gesprochen haben.

---

[4] Z. B. Kühner-Gerth I 59, Schwyzer-Debrunner II 605.

Es ist natürlich ein Zufall, daß in einem durch den unmittelbaren Zusammenhang eigentlich gesicherten Text eine abwegige[5] Gedankenverbindung: παρθένος | -θήλεια ἵππος und eine Buchstabenähnlichkeit zweier Wörter von ganz verschiedener Bedeutung: ΗΛΕΙΑ-ΘΗΛΕΙΑ in gleicher Richtung zielen[6] und zu einer nicht nur syntaktisch, sondern bis zu einem gewissen Grade auch inhaltlich möglichen Fehllesung führen konnten. Die Dauerhaftigkeit einer solchen Fehllesung ist dann aber sozusagen die Probe auf das Exempel, indem dieselben Assoziationen, die die Korruptel verursachten, ihre Aufdeckung hinausschieben.

III. Ein ähnlicher Fall findet sich gegen Ende von Ciceros *Somnium Scipionis*, unmittelbar vor dem aus Platons *Phaidros* übersetzten Unsterblichkeitsbeweis und auf ihn hinleitend. Doch die beiden bisher besprochenen griechischen Textstellen waren inhaltlich nicht von besonderer Bedeutung, und jedenfalls geht mit den vorgeschlagenen Textänderungen nichts verloren, das irgend jemand schmerzlich vermissen könnte. Lassen wir aber in diesem dritten Fall der Kritik denselben Spielraum wie dort, so muß in Frage gezogen werden, was Macrobius, dem wir den Text des *Somnium* verdanken, in seinem Kommentar (2, 12, 5) geradezu als *praesentis operis*[7] *consummatio* bezeichnet. Da alles auf den Gedankenzusammenhang ankommt, so setze ich den ganzen ciceronischen Passus her:

Tu vero enitere et sic habeto non esse te mortalem sed corpus hoc, nec enim tu is es quem forma ista declarat sed mens cuiusque is est quisque, non ea figura quae digito demonstrari potest. d e u m   t e   i g i t u r   s c i t o   e s s e, s i   q u i d e m   e s t   d e u s   q u i   viget qui sentit qui meminit qui providet qui tam regit et moderatur et movet id corpus cui praepositus est quam hunc mundum ille princeps deus; et ut mundum ex quadam parte mortalem ipse deus aeternus, sic fragile corpus animus sempiternus movet. nam quod semper movetur ... (= τὸ γὰρ ἀεικίνητον ... Plat. *Phdr.* 245 c 5).

---

[5] Das von einem Adjektiv begleitete Wort für Pferd (ἵππος καλή) ist im Griechischen ja ohne den Zusatz ‚fem.' als weiblich zu erkennen; vom Autor beabsichtigt war das im Orakel gelobte Elische Pferd um des ξένος ᾽Ηλεῖος (287 c 1) willen. Bei dem Orakel denkt man nun natürlich an das Megarerorakel und die Rolle, die dort die Thrakischen oder Thessalischen Stuten spielen. Nach Analogie davon könnte das Lob „der" Elischen Stute allenfalls so gelautet haben: ᾽Ηλείαν ἵππον, Λακεδαιμονίαν δὲ γυναῖκα/ἀνδρῶν δ᾽ οἳ ... (Für die Akkusative vgl. Kritias, Vorsokr.[6] 88 B 8.)

[6] Es kommt vielleicht noch hinzu, daß in der *Ilias* (Λ 680f.) und in der *Odyssee* (δ 635f.) tatsächlich wertvolle ἵπποι θήλειαι aus oder in Elis erwähnt werden; was betont wird, ist allerdings ihr Wert für Pferde- bzw. Mauleselzucht.

[7] So nennt er das *Somnium* auch schon gelegentlich am Anfang des Kommentars: 1, 4, 1 *propositum praesentis operis*.

In den von mir gesperrten Worten sieht Macrobius (2, c. 12) die Offenbarung eines nur dem ganz vorgeschrittenen Menschen mitteilbaren Geheimnisses, das Cicero in wunderbarer Kürze — *miro compendio* — durch das eine Wort *deum* in ‚*deum te scito esse*‘ ausgesprochen haben würde.

Ich gehe auf diese Art der Erklärung nicht weiter ein, obwohl wenigstens Macrobius' Kapitel durchaus verdient gelesen zu werden. Aber alles was von Macrobius und Späteren an vorplatonischem, platonischem, ciceronischem und neuplatonischem Gedankengut herangezogen ist oder hätte herangezogen werden können, kann zwar zeigen, daß es unendlich viele Gedankenverbindungen gibt zwischen dem Begriff Gott und dem des Göttlichen in der Menschenseele, kann aber schlechterdings nicht hinreichen, das Auftauchen des Begriffes *deus* an dieser Stelle der Gedankenfolge zu rechtfertigen. ,,Nicht Du bist sterblich, sondern dieser Dein Körper; Du bist ja doch nicht der, den Dein Äußeres | erkennen läßt, sondern der Geist eines jeden, das ist ein jeder und nicht die Gestalt, die mit dem Finger aufgewiesen werden kann. Wisse, daß Du also ein Gott bist, wenn anders Gott ist, wer . . .‘‘ und nun folgt eine Reihe von Prädikaten, die einschließlich des ersten Vergleiches mit dem höchsten Gott ohne weiteres vom Menschengeist oder der Menschenseele behauptet werden könnten; dagegen ist nicht zu verstehen, wie das, wovon alle diese Prädizierungen gelten, ohne weiteres Gott sein soll, was doch die Wendung *si quidem est deus qui* . . . bedeuten müßte. Im zweiten Vergleich mit der Gottheit, in dem die Unsterblichkeit behauptet wird[8], ist, was den Menschen betrifft, ohnehin nur von *animus* — wie anf nglich nur von *mens* — die Rede; der Mensch als *deus* wäre schon wieder vergessen. Die Worte *si quidem est deus* können schwerlich etwas anderes sein als eine nachträgliche Interpolation, die die Form einer Argumentation vortäuscht, genauer betrachtet aber hier keinen haltbaren Sinn gibt. Läßt man das weg, so bleibt *deum te igitur scito esse qui viget qui sentit* . . . aber nun schwebt der durch das Wort *deum* ausgesprochene Begriff vollkommen in der Luft. Ich schlage also vor zu lesen *eum te igitur scito esse qui* . . .: ,,Wisse, daß Du also (nämlich weil, wie gesagt, Du nicht Dein Körper sondern Dein Geist bist) der bist, der *viget* etc.‘‘ Ich hoffe, ich brauche keine Worte mehr darüber zu machen, wie es schon vor Macrobius zu der Fehllesung *deum*, die dann eine Interpolation nach sich zog, kommen und wie beides sich bis auf den heutigen Tag in den Texten halten konnte; jedenfalls ergibt *eum te igitur scito esse qui* . . . den einfachen Sinn, den der Zusammenhang verlangt.

---

[8] *animus sempiternus* entspricht der These des platonischen Unsterblichkeitsbeweises: ψυχὴ πᾶσα ἀθάνατος (*Phdr.* 245 c 5). Der Beweis schließt sich bei Cicero wie bei Platon unmittelbar an.

Die Identifizierung des *menschlichen* Ich oder Du mit der Seele und ihren höchsten Funktionen unter Ausschluß des sterblichen bzw. gestorbenen Körpers stammt aus Platons *Phaidon* 115 c ff. Cicero kennt die Stelle aus erster Hand und zitiert sie teilweise *Tusc.* 1, 102f. im Zusammenhang mit der Frage der Bestattung, so wie sie im *Phaidon* steht[9]. Er kennt die Identifizierung aber auch aus zweiter Hand, nämlich, wie im pseudoplatonischen ‚ersten' *Alkibiades* 129 a ff., verkoppelt mit dem delphischen γνῶθι σεαυτόν, *Tusc.* 1, 52: „... *praeceptum Apollinis quo monet ut se quisque noscat. Non enim credo id praecipit, ut membra nostra aut staturam figuramve noscamus; neque nos corpora sumus, nec ego tibi haec dicens corpori tuo dico. cum igitur ‚nosce te' dicit hoc dicit: ‚nosce animum tuum'. nam corpus quidem quasi vas est aut aliquod animi receptaculum; ab animo tuo quidquid agitur id agitur a te"*. Auch hier folgt, nach ausgewechselter Überleitung, der Unsterblichkeitsbeweis aus dem *Phaidros* mit Ciceros eigener Rückverweisung auf das *Somnium:* „... *illa ratio Platonis quae a Socrate est in Phaedro explicata, a me autem posita est in sexto libro de re publica"*.

---

[9] Vgl. auch Plat. *Leges* 959 a/b, erwähnt von Cicero *De Legibus* 2, 68, Ende des Paragraphen.

Besprechung:

Giorgio Pasquali, Preistoria della poesia romana

1936

Dies Buch will einer neuen Hypothese nicht über das Wesen, wohl
aber über Ursprung und Vorgeschichte des saturnischen Verses Geltung verschaffen. Im Vorwort rechtfertigt der Verfasser den scheinbar
mehr oder anderes versprechenden Titel mit dem Bedürfnis nach Einfachheit und Kürze; der Berichterstatter darf aber wohl gleich vorweg
hinzufügen, daß auch derjenige, der nach dem Titel mehr und anderes
erwartet als eine metrische Untersuchung, in seinen Erwartungen nicht
enttäuscht wird. Friedrich Leo[1] hat für den Anfang seiner bekannten
Abhandlung über die metrische Natur des Saturniers den Satz geprägt:
„Es ist viel mehr als eine metrische Frage; vielmehr recht sehr eine
metrische Frage, insofern die Frage nach den metrischen Formen eines
Volkes ins Herz seiner Geschichte reicht." Aber dieser Satz hatte in
Leos Abhandlung nur die Funktion, über die Länge und Umständlich-
keit der metrischen Erörterung hinwegzutrösten. Denn für Leo lagen
die Dinge noch so, daß ihm nur die zu bekämpfende These vom ‚akzentuierenden‘ Saturnier aufregende Konsequenzen für die Geschichte
des römischen Geistes zu haben schien. Ist es nicht interessant, daß
Pasquali, dem die abstrakt metrischen Identifikationen Leos noch
heute die Evidenz zu haben scheinen, die ihnen Leo vor 30 Jahren zu-
schrieb, | in allem Historischen ganz andere Wege zu gehen sich ge-
zwungen sieht? Hier geht er zur Freude des Lesers Wege, die, an den
neuesten Gesichtspunkten und Ereignissen der sprachgeschichtlichen
und archäologischen Forschung orientiert, auch dem nach P. (S. 70)
noch in der Einfalt der Unwissenheit weiterlebenden Nurphilologen
neue und bestimmte Vorstellungen von den modernen Problemen der
römischen Frühgeschichte vermitteln können. Aber der Nurphilologe
muß mit dem Metrischen beginnen und, wie wir sehen werden, das
Historische auf sich beruhen lassen,

I. P.s erstes Kapitel, *Saturnio, metrica greca e metrica indoeuropea*,
schließt in der Beurteilung der metrischen Natur des saturnischen
Verses so ohne weiteres an Leo an, daß die Vertreter einer abweichen-

---

[1] Der Saturnische Vers, Abh. Gött. Ges. N. F. VIII 5, Berlin 1905.

den Grundansicht, die schon bei Leo kaum zu Worte kamen, hier mit
einem Satze mundtot gemacht werden. Es sei unvorstellbar, daß ein
und derselbe Dichter, Livius Andronicus, seine Verse nach zwei verschiedenen Prinzipien sollte gedichtet haben. Ich glaube nicht, daß
dem Inhalt von Leos erstem Abschnitt mit dieser kurzen Zusammen-
ziehung Wesentliches genommen wird, muß aber, aus einem bestimmten Grunde, hier ausführlicher werden als Pasquali. Zweifellos reicht
die auch von Leo anerkannte Tatsache der Berücksichtigung des Wortakzentes im lateinischen Bühnenvers allein nicht aus, um daraus die
akzentuierende Natur des Saturniers zu folgern. Aus dieser Unmöglichkeit eines zwingenden Schlusses wurde für Leo das Fehlen jeden
Anhaltes für die gegnerische Behauptung infolge einer die theoretischen Möglichkeiten stark einengenden These. Ausschlaggebendes und
einziges Kennzeichen für den fundamentalen Unterschied zwischen
akzentuierenden und quantitierenden Versen sollte nämlich das Vorkommen einer den Wortakzent tragenden kurzen Silbe als ‚Vershe-
bung' im akzentuierenden, und das Verbot eines solchen Vorkommens
im quantitierenden Verse sein. Dann gab es freilich nur eine einzige
Möglichkeit, Spuren eines ‚akzentuierenden' Saturniers in der sonstigen
römischen Metrik zu finden: es „müßte eine kurze betonte Silbe, d. h.
eine kurze Stammsilbe oder Innensilbe, als Hebung im Verse erscheinen können; aber es gibt kein *dábunt* in der römischen Metrik". Alles
Weitere in diesem grundlegenden Abschnitt von Leos Buch, auch die
nicht unbedenkliche Art, wie die Gegner (Keller, Thurneysen, Lindsay)
von vornherein in eine hoffnungslose Stellung gedrängt werden, läuft
auf die Behauptung hinaus, es wäre schlechterdings unvorstellbar, daß
ein Volk, in dessen urtümlicher Metrik ein *dábunt* vorkommen konnte,
sich jemals in der Weise wie die Römer es getan hätten, an eine |
Metrik hätte gewöhnen können, in der ein *dábunt* nicht so vorkommen
konnte, oder daß ein und derselbe Dichter, Livius Andronicus oder
Naevius, nach beiden Prinzipien so hätte dichten können, wie er es
getan hätte.

Der Grund, aus dem ich diese Dinge hier berühren muß, ist folgender. Leo betont, wenn es sich um Römer handelt, den jede Vermittlung und Kuppelung ausschließenden Unterschied zwischen akzentuierenden und quantitierenden Versen. Sein Kennzeichen für
diesen Unterschied ist sehr einfach: „das Entscheidende, der kurze
Vokal als Träger der Hebung" (S. 5); und er kann die Streifrage ver-
mittelst der Bentleyschen Iktuszeichen graphisch darstellen; was er
bestreitet, ist die Behauptung, „daß eine Wortgruppe *malum dabunt
Metelli* jemals habe *málum dábunt Metélli*, daß sie jemals anders als
malúm dabúnt Metélli im Verse haben klingen können" (S. 4f.). Leo
kann das als Iktusgläubiger. Pasquali glaubt nicht an den Iktus, er

setzt keine Iktuszeichen und ist sich auch vollkommen bewußt, daß
er dem Terminus Hebung keine sachliche Bedeutung beilegen darf
(S. 9 A. 2, S. 16). Es erhebt sich die Frage, was nunmehr, auf lateinische Verse angewendet, der Unterschied zwischen akzentuierender
und quantitierender Versbildung bedeuten soll, und wieso ein histori-
sches Nach- und Nebeneinander der beiden Prinzipien bei den Römern
absurd und unvorstellbar sein soll.

Eine Antwort auf diese Frage gleich zu Anfang wäre um so nötiger
gewesen, als der nächste Schritt, den P. tut, zwingt, für das Gebiet
der von ihm nunmehr ausschließlich berücksichtigten ,quantitieren-
den' Versbildung dieselbe Sache noch einmal zur Sprache zu bringen.
Thurneysen[2] hatte darauf hingewiesen, daß man bei rein quantitierender Deutung des Saturniers zur Annahme großer Willkür in der
Weglassung oder Setzung der Thesis gezwungen ist, ,,wie sie sich in
andern quantitierenden Versen, etwa den griechischen, kaum wird
nachweisen lassen''. Auch Leo (S. 71) spricht von dem ,,bunten Bild''
der nach seiner Theorie innerhalb der einen Form des saturnischen
Verses ,,durch unterdrückte Senkungen, umgebogenen Rhythmus,
Verkürzung vorhandener Reihen'' herbeigeführten Variationen, und
auch er ist der Ansicht: ,,die Analogie muß bei den Griechen gesucht
werden''; aber im Gegensatz zu Thurneysen glaubt er sagen zu können:
,,und da findet sie sich reichlich''. Nicht freilich in der Metrik er- |
haltener griechischer Gedichte, sondern — und damit erklärt sich die
Diskrepanz in den Äußerungen der beiden Gelehrten — in den zur
Erklärung des Vorhandenen vor allem von Wilamowitz immer weiter
geführten versgeschichtlichen Konstruktionen, die schon 1905 alles
Nötige zu liefern schienen. Es ist hier nicht der Ort, auf die Fragwürdig-
keit dieser Konstruktionen auch für das Griechische einzugehen; jedenfalls stehen und fallen sie mit der Anwendbarkeit des Terminus ,He-
bung' für bestimmte Längen im Verse und ruhen auf einer Vorstellung,
die ,,vom ,Iktus' nicht loskommt'', wozu wir Wilamowitz' Eingeständ-
nis noch aus dem Jahre 1921 haben: Gr. Verskunst 88f. Nun sehen
die Längen- und Kürzenfolgen der erhaltenen Saturnierkola immer
noch viel variabler aus als selbst die in Wilamowitz' Versgeschichte
und Versdeutung für möglich gehaltenen Kolavariationen; und wenn
Leo fragt: ,,Wo hat dies bunte Bild seine Einheit?'', so möchte man
am liebsten antworten: in den mit Iktus versehenen ,Hebungen', die,
mit Wilamowitz zu reden, ,,das Knochengerüst, sozusagen'', auch
dieser ,quantitierenden' Verse bilden sollen. Es scheint mir nicht zu
bestreiten, daß ohne diejenige Art der metrischen Vorstellung, die vom

---

[2] Der Saturnier und sein Verhältnis zum späteren römischen Volksverse, Halle
1885, 3.

‚Iktus' nicht loskommt, auch Leo nicht zu seinen Identifikationen der Saturnierkola untereinander und mit gewissen griechischen Kola gekommen wäre.

Pasquali glaubt nicht an den Iktus, aber er glaubt, daß Leo seine Identifikationen bewiesen hätte. Oder vielmehr, er glaubt es nicht ganz, sondern hält es für nötig, Leos Argumentation durch einen eigenen Beweis zu ergänzen, den er bei Leo vermißt (S. 2 A. 2). Dieser Beweis ist tatsächlich iktusfrei, und damit kommt die Diskussion auf eine neugeschaffene Grundlage. Was wir stillschweigend zugestehen müssen, können wir billigerweise nicht verweigern: lediglich die Möglichkeit, daß die beiden Saturnierkola, jedes für sich genommen, mit gewissen griechischen Verskola identisch sein *könnten*. Für den Fall nun, daß ein und dasselbe griechische Kolon, das für die Identifikation in Aussicht genommen ist, in einer größeren Zahl untereinander verschiedener Gestaltungen auftritt, die den Variationen des betreffenden Saturnierkolons so genau entsprechen, wie man es nur verlangen kann, für diesen Fall hält P. Zufall für ausgeschlossen und eine historische Identität für gesichert, für die dann, abstrakt genommen, noch zwei Möglichkeiten bleiben: Urverwandtschaft oder römische Entlehnung aus dem Griechischen. Der Beweis des ausgeschlossenen Zufalls wird mit großer Zuversicht für den iambischen Dimeter und das erste Saturnierkolon geführt, mit derselben gedanklichen Klarheit, aber weniger großer | Zuversicht für das zweite Saturnierkolon, weil hier auf griechischer Seite und dann also auch auf lateinischer mit wahlweisem Eintritt verwandter Kola füreinander gerechnet werden muß. Ich muß mich auf Besprechung des Beweises für das erste Saturnierkolon beschränken, nicht nur der Kürze wegen und weil P. selbst ihn im Notfall für ausreichend hält, sondern weil wir in diesem Fall auf griechischem Gebiet sicheren Boden unter den Füßen haben, während wenn, wie im zweiten Fall, mit Äquivalenz von Ithyphallikus und iambischem Dimeter, mit sehr wechselnden Gestaltungen eines und desselben ‚Reizianum' und schließlich mit Äquivalenz aller drei Kola untereinander gerechnet werden muß, auch im Griechischen noch *alles* problematisch ist.

Mit zwei Hilfsannahmen über lang für kurz bzw. kurz für lang lassen sich die Folgen von Längen und Kürzen, welche die erhaltenen ersten Saturnierkola aufweisen, umsetzen in solche Folgen von Längen und Kürzen, wie sie sich in ähnlicher Fülle der Variation z. B. in iambischen oder choriambisch-iambischen äschyleischen Liedern finden, und wie man sie jedenfalls, wenn sie irgendwo in griechischer Poesie gegeben wären, ohne Bedenken als iambische Dimeter ansprechen würde. Der Beweis hierfür ist, wie P. zeigt (S. 3ff.), in der Tat leicht zu führen. Ob dies aber zugleich der Beweis des ausgeschlossenen

Zufalls ist, hängt nicht nur an der Berechtigung jener Hilfsannahmen, sondern auch daran, ob es möglich ist, die ratio, die im Griechischen hinter der Variantenfülle steht und sie erklärt, auf den saturnischen Vers zu übertragen, und zwar — damit wird P. einverstanden sein — ohne auf den Iktus zu rekurrieren.

Bei iambischen (und trochäischen) Liedern der von P. angezogenen Art, wo der Worttext nicht stets für eine *anceps-* oder *breve*-Stelle eine besondere Silbe bietet, geht es nicht an, den Grund der in die Augen fallenden silbischen Vielgestaltigkeit zu verschmähen, der uns durch die Reste der aristoxenischen Rhythmik, das Seikiloslied und Pap. Ox. 9 an die Hand gegeben wird. Hier wissen wir, was wir sonst nicht wissen und meist auch gar nicht vermuten dürfen, daß lange Silben nicht nur ein Längezeichen, sondern auch ein $\times$ — oder $\cup$ — des rhythmischen Schemas überdecken konnten, daß also die vorhandene Einheit des Maßes in den Silbenfolgen der gesungenen Worte allein *nicht* in Erscheinung treten konnte; mit andern Worten, solche Verse hatten ein rhythmisches Maß, aber nur wenn sie gesungen wurden.

Saturnier sind uns direkt nur als Inschriften-, Sprichwort- und epische Verse bekannt; aber wenn die Verwandtschaft ihres ersten Kolons mit den wegen ihrer variablen Silbenfolge ins Auge gefaßten | griechischen Dimetern zu Recht bestehen soll, dann war dieses Kolon ursprünglich auch im Lateinischen für den musikalischen Vortrag bestimmt und wurde erst sekundär zum ersten Teil eines Rezitationsverses. Einen solchen Vorgang sich vorzustellen macht für Leo und E. Fraenkel (Iktus und Akzent, 355 A.) deswegen keine Schwierigkeiten, weil sie an den iktustragenden Silben genügend festen Halt haben. Ohne Annahme eines Iktus liegt die Sache aber anders; die Umwandlung eines Singkolons der besprochenen Art in ein Sprechkolon unter Wahrung der ihm eigenen Vielgestaltigkeit der Silbenfolgen ist dann unvorstellbar und hat im Griechischen nicht stattgefunden. Sie für das Lateinische gleichwohl zu postulieren, ist um so bedenklicher, als hier die Bedingungen dafür, daß man aus den fraglichen Silbenfolgen beim bloßen Sprechen noch etwas (quantitierend) Versartiges hätte heraushören können, noch ungünstiger lagen als im Griechischen. Denn — das ist eine der Hilfsannahmen, ohne die sich die Identifizierung mit griechischen Kola nicht durchführen läßt — das Schema des lateinischen ‚iambischen Dimeters‘ zerstört so ziemlich den Rest von rhythmischem Zwang, dem im Griechischen die Silbenfolgen unterworfen waren, den Zwang nämlich, die Stelle zwischen den zwei *longa* eines Metrons, falls sie mit einer besonderen Silbe besetzt wurde, mit einer kurzen Silbe zu besetzen. Soviel scheint mir sicher: der Sinn und der Grund der Vielgestaltigkeit der *erhaltenen* ersten Saturnierkola kann nicht identisch sein mit dem Sinn und dem Grund der Vielgestaltigkeit der von P. vorzugsweise in Betracht gezogenen — übrigens nicht gerade volkstümlichen — gesungenen iambischen Dimeter; und P.s Beweis des ausgeschlossenen Zufalls, dessen Vorzug es ist, mit bereitliegendem, nicht erschlossenem Material zu arbeiten, muß als mißglückt angesehen werden.

Wenden wir uns nun mit P. dem Beginn der historischen Deutung der behaupteten metrischen Identität der Saturnierkola mit bestimmten griechischen Liedkola zu! Daß ein und derselbe Dichter erfolgreich zugleich akzentuierend und quantitierend gedichtet haben sollte, daß ein und dasselbe Volk erfolgreich von akzentuierender zu quantitierender Metrik übergegangen sein sollte, das hielt Leo für unglaublich. Aber Leo dachte nicht daran, dem Prinzip der Unvereinbarkeit der beiden Metriken über die Grenzen der erhaltenen römischen und griechischen Literatur hinaus Geltung zu geben; und so können in seiner historischen Konstruktion (Geschichte der römischen Literatur 14ff.) Saturnier und die „ursprünglichsten Formen der griechischen Lyrik" in friedlicher Urverwandtschaft „mit den Hauptmaßen der anderen sprachverwandten Völker" (z. B. | dem Nibelungenvers) auftreten. Ich fürchte den Überdruß des Lesers, aber ich muß darauf hinweisen, daß die iktustragenden Hebungssilben die Vermittlung darstellen. P., für den es diese Vermittlung nicht gibt, macht den Gegensatz zwischen quantitierender und akzentuierender Metrik *radikal*: und Leos historische Vorstellungen erscheinen mit einem Schlage derart unzulänglich und zwiespältig, daß er sich veranlaßt sieht, der Aufdeckung des Widersinns (S. 15) eine psychologische Erklärung vorauszuschicken (S. 13f.).

Wenn Gleichungen zwischen akzentuierenden und quantitierenden Versen verboten werden, dann liefert die vergleichende indogermanische Metrik zur Konstruktion derjenigen Metrik, die die gemeinsame Urahne von Saturniern und griechischen Kola gewesen sein könnte, z. Z. nur die Gleichungen zwischen vedischen und äolischen Versen. Aber die hieraus rekonstruierbaren Urverse sind als silbenzählend nicht nur keine brauchbaren Ahnen für die Saturnier, sondern sie machen es lediglich durch ihr wahrscheinliches Vorhandengewesensein unwahrscheinlich, daß es daneben überhaupt noch andere quantitierende indogermanische Urverse gegeben haben sollte, aus denen man die Saturnier ableiten könnte. Damit wird es für P. wahrscheinlich, daß die ersten römischen Vorgänger der Saturnier oder der Saturnierkola nicht indogermanisches Erbe, sondern Entlehnungen aus dem Griechischen gewesen sind, und zwar um so mehr, als er ihre Eigentümlichkeit, für eine Länge zwei Kürzen setzen zu können, innerhalb des indogermanischen Sprachgebietes für einzelgriechische, genauer jonische oder jonisch-attische Neuerung, möglicherweise nichtindogermanischer Herkunft, hält. —

II. Im ersten Kapitel war die Möglichkeit einer indogermanischen Vorgeschichte des Saturniers diskutiert und von P. abgelehnt worden. Das zweite Kapitel *Cola saturnii lyrici* arbeitet lediglich mit römischem Material und ohne daß die metrische Deutung eine entscheidende Rolle spielte. Knapp und klar wird die These aufgestellt, daß der rezitative saturnische Vers eine römische Vorgeschichte gehabt habe, in welcher seine Kola als Liedkola noch nicht notwendig zum quasistichischen Verse zusammengeschlossen waren. Die Entstehung des rezitativen Verses wird, unromantisch, einer bewußt schaffenden römischen Persönlichkeit spätestens des 4. Jahrhunderts beigelegt.

III. *Il saturnio e il senso ritmico romano.* Während der Referent den Erwägungen des zweiten Kapitels nur folgen könnte, wenn die Identität der lyrischen Saturnierkola insbesondere mit (nur singbaren) iambischen Dimetern preisgegeben würde, gewinnt P., daß er den rezitativen saturnischen Vers nicht als Ganzes von den Griechen | herübergeholt sein zu lassen braucht, was, wie er einleuchtend darlegt, seine Bedenken hätte. Unbedenklich scheint ihm Folgendes, was ich lieber in seinen eigenen Worten gebe: „Chi primo trasportò a Roma il dimetro catalettico, l'itifallico e il reiziano, conobbe antichissima poesia greca, sacrale insieme e popolare; e seppe che quei metri avevano tendenza ad associarsi tra loro. Chi regolò una determinata forma di associazione, una strofa distica nella quale al dimetro giambico seguiva più raramente un altro dimetro, normalmente o un itifallico o un reiziano, aveva tanta conoscenza e tanto senso di ritmi greci da sentire che i due ultimi membri erano particolarmente adatti quale clausola" (S. 39).

Sehr romantisch geht es in der Vorgeschichte der römischen Poesie nicht zu. Nicht der Volksgeist, sondern „große Unbekannte" (S. 73 questo grande ignoto) schaffen Neues. Dem Philologen, dem die Vorstellung schwerfallen sollte, daß schon im 6. Jahrhundert „un Romano, sentendo il bisogno di una forma ritmica per *naeniae* e canti nuziali e canti trionfali, la desumesse da carmi greci uditi nell' Italia Meridionale, probabilmente a Cuma; che il ritmo di questi carmi egli imitasse in suo linguaggio", wird später (S. 70) im Kapitel über die Kultur des archaischen Rom derartig über den Mund gefahren, daß ich es ratsam finde, vom Metrischen abgesehen die historische Möglichkeit einer solchen ersten Rezeption von griechischen Kola einfach zuzugeben. Und wie er sich die Tat des zweiten Unbekannten denkt, der aus schon römisch gewordenen lyrischen Kola, doch nicht ohne Orientierung am Griechischen, spätestens im 4. Jahrhundert den rezitativen Saturnier schuf, das weiß P. so hübsch an der Schaffung des *versus Reizianus* durch Plautus oder einen unmittelbaren tragischen oder komischen Vorgänger anschaulich zu machen, daß man auch da nicht remonstrieren mag. Was einmal möglich war, kann schließlich 100 und mehr Jahre früher auch schon so ähnlich passiert sein.

Daß die Geschichte der römischen Verskunst in manchen Dingen ihre Vorgeschichte wiederholt, glaubt P. noch in einem andern, grundsätzlich wichtigen Sinn, und damit sind wir erst wirklich beim ‚senso ritmico romano‘, den dies interessante Kapitel in seinem vielversprechenden Titel trägt. Über den rhythmischen Sinn der Römer in seinem Gegensatz zu dem der Griechen können wir etwas wissen, weil die römischen Bühnenverse so wesentlich anders aussehen als ihre griechischen Vorbilder. Aber es ist schwer, dieses Wissen in eine Präsumption für das ursprüngliche Wesen des Saturniers umzusetzen, wenn darum gestritten wird, ob dieses ursprüngliche Wesen identisch mit dem Wesen griechischer | Verse gewesen sei. Denn die Befürworter der ursprünglichen metrischen Identität setzen die bekannten Differenzen zwischen den römischen und griechischen Bühnenversen zu ihren Gunsten in Rechnung und erreichen dadurch eine erhebliche Ausgleichung des Unterschiedes im Aussehen der erhaltenen Saturnier und der in Betracht gezogenen griechischen Kola. So macht es auch Leo[3], bei dem es aber ohne die iktustragenden Hebungssilben historisch gar nicht vorstellbar ist[4]. P. bringt eine andere Hypothese. Wenn wir ohnehin mit zwei bis drei, freilich durch Jahrhunderte getrennten, Rezeptionen griechischer Metrik in Rom zu rechnen haben, dann ist es eine Möglichkeit, und zwar eine imposante Möglichkeit, daß das römische rhythmische Gefühl über die Jahrhunderte hin konstant blieb und in souveräner Selbstsicherheit jeweils das Griechische in derselben

---

[3] Nicht ohne petitio principii, wenn er z. B. im Verlauf eines scheinbar induktiven Verfahrens neben zweite Saturnierkola wie *Naevio poetae* solche wie *insece versutum* stellt und *ehe* er seine ratio für die metrische Gleichwertigkeit — die erstaunliche „Dihärese“, s. nächste Anmerkung — bringt, erklärt: „Es kann gar kein Zweifel sein, daß alle dem *insece versutum* gleich oder ähnlich gebildeten Kola die zweite Hebung durch eine Kürze bilden, die als Länge behandelt wird. So sicher die Beobachtung ist, so wenig hilft sie uns weiter, wenn ihre ratio nicht zu finden ist“ (S. 20). Daß die Schlußkürze von *insece* eine metrische Hebung wäre und daß sie als Länge behandelt würde, ist doch keine Beobachtung, sondern eine das Wesentliche vorwegnehmende Deutung.

[4] Ohne Iktusvorstellung ist es ein Unding, daß ein quantitierender Sprechvers von lyrischer Variabilität, der lang für kurz setzt, wo die Griechen es nicht vertrugen (in gewissen ‚Senkungen‘), und kurz für lang, wo es für Griechen absurd gewesen wäre (nämlich in ‚Dihäresen‘ mit der Wirkung von Vers- oder Periodenschluß, die ganze drei bis vier Silben vom Kolonanfang entfernt liegen), entweder seit Urzeiten ein Vers gewesen oder nach einer eventuellen Umwandlung noch einer geblieben wäre. — Die Annahme des Iktus macht umgekehrt die griechischen Sonderregelungen zu im Grunde überflüssigen, nur möglichen Empfindlichkeiten, die das Wesen und die Erkennbarkeit des Verses nicht berühren; man kennt das aus Wilamowitz' versgeschichtlichen Konstruktionen und metrischen Deutungen.

Weise umsetzte. Aber die unerwartete Konsequenz ist, daß wir in Betreff der Eigentümlichkeiten dieses rhythmischen Gefühles über den uns ohnehin bekannten Unterschied zwischen römischen und griechischen Bühnenversen hinaus aus den erhaltenen Saturniern — *nichts* lernen können und daß diese Eigentümlichkeiten als ein unerklärtes Rätsel dastehen[5], wenigstens solange man nicht reumütig zum Iktus zurückkehrt. |

Anders lägen die Dinge, wenn doch die Saturnier den Bühnenversen gegenüber eine hierhergehörige Besonderheit aufwiesen. Wenn wir Leos Theorie zugrunde legen, dann gibt es in der Tat eine solche Diskrepanz, die freilich nicht Leo, sondern E. Fraenkel ins Licht gerückt hat (Iktus u. Akzent 12ff., 355 A.): die Lagerung der Wortakzente. P.s Verzweifelung darüber, daß Fraenkels Untersuchungen über Iktus und Akzent im lateinischen Sprechvers im Ganzen ein Resultat gehabt haben, das auch auf Sophokles paßt (S. 16), hätte ihn nicht zu hindern brauchen, sich um diese Diskrepanz zu kümmern. Denn um die Tatsache der Berücksichtigung des Wortakzents im plautinischen Sprechvers anzuerkennen und zu verstehen, bedarf man nicht der Vorstellung eines Iktus, eines von der Natur der Dinge bestimmten Stellen eines abstrakten Versschemas beigegebenen Intensitätsakzentes; man bedarf fürs erste nicht einmal einer Annahme über die genaue Natur des lateinischen Wortakzentes. Von Versen, in denen wie im griechischen Vorbild Längen und Kürzen und Wortenden bis zu einem gewissen Grade geregelt sind, mußte infolge des lateinischen Akzentgesetzes die große Mehrzahl wenigstens an gewissen Stellen zu gleichem Wortakzentklang neigen. Auch wenn die Römer im Übrigen unter genau denselben Bedingungen gedichtet hätten wie die Griechen, würden sie gleichwohl in ihren lateinischen Versen eine gewisse Eintönigkeit, die über das Griechische hinausging, nicht haben überhören können. Sie dichteten aber unter wesentlich anderen Bedingungen, wie ihre bekannte Unempfindlichkeit gegen den Unterschied von *anceps* und *breve* im Schema iambischer und trochäischer Verse beweist. Hier erhebt sich von selbst die Frage, wie sie der bei ihnen erlaubten Folge von mehr als drei Längen diejenige rhythmische Qualität gaben, die eine solche Silbenfolge im Griechischen gerade nicht haben konnte, und diese erste Frage erweitert sich wiederum von selbst zu der Frage, wie sie überhaupt solche Verse hörten. Es ist kein kühner und ein durch den tatsächlichen Befund bestätigter Gedanke, hier den ohnehin in

---

[5] „Jenes Überwiegen langer über kurze Silben in der lateinischen Sprache, das bekanntlich der archaischen Metrik ein besonderes Kolorit gegeben hat" (P. S. 3 A. 3), mag erklären, warum die Römer gewisse Dinge änderten, aber es erklärt nicht, wieso das, was dabei herausgekommen ist oder wäre, noch Verse sein konnten.

lateinischen Versen nicht ganz zu überhörenden Wortakzentklang (d. h. zugleich auch Cäsuren) subsidiäre Funktion übernehmen zu lassen; denn irgend etwas zum Ersatz dessen, was den Rhythmus des griechischen Vorbildes gewahrt hatte[6], müssen wir fordern, und was sollte es | sonst sein? Aber es besteht keine Veranlassung, die Regelung des Wortakzentes im lateinischen Bühnenvers über das ungezwungen Beobachtbare hinaus auszudehnen, oder doch, wie es seit Bentley meist geschah, eine leider durch die Natur der Sprache vereitelte Tendenz zur restlosen Durchführung wie selbstverständlich von vornherein[7] vorauszusetzen.

E. Fraenkels Vergleich des ersten Saturnierkolons mit dem zweiten Kolon von iambischen Septenaren (Iktus und Akzent 12ff., 355 A.; beim Senaranfang spielt die Cäsur eine von Leo betonte Rolle) beweist, daß sich hinsichtlich der Lagerung der Wortakzente das erste Saturnierkolon völlig anders verhielt als die Dialogmaße des Dramas, *falls* es ein iambischer Dimeter war; es nahm nämlich dann trotz seiner über alles griechische Maß hinaus gesteigerten Variabilität, auch nachdem es rezitativ geworden war, keine Rücksicht auf die Wortakzente, und wer nicht an den Iktus glaubt, fragt sich vergeblich, wie es als iambisches Kolon charakterisiert gewesen sein soll.

Auf Grund dieser Erwägungen wird die Identität des ersten Saturnierkolons mit einem iambischen Dimeter vollends (vgl. oben S. 300f.) so problematisch, wie sie überhaupt nur werden kann. Es wird aber noch viel mehr problematisch, nämlich die ganze Problemstellung, unter der insbesondere Leo und P. arbeiten: das Entwederoder akzentuierend — quantitierend.

Erstens, die lateinische Sprache lieferte keine Worte, in denen man rein quantitierend dichten konnte, nämlich so, daß der Wortakzent dem Rhythmus gegenüber eine freie Melodie bildete wie im Griechischen; sie zwang beim Versuch zu Regulierungen, die der modernen Hebungs- und Senkungsrhythmik parallel ausfallen konnten, wie im Bühnensprechvers, aber nicht mußten, wie Hexameter und Pentameter beweisen. Zweitens, die lateinische Sprache lieferte ebensowenig Worte, bei denen der Akzent eine kurze Silbe in eine metrische Länge, d. h.

---

[6] Nämlich *ancipitia* und *brevia* in diesem ihrem Unterschied. Es gibt keinen Grund für Wilamowitz' Annahme, daß in einem iambischen Trimeter Stimmverstärkungen irgendwelcher Art, „guter Taktteil", „Ikten" oder „Schwanzikten", die Funktion gehabt hätten, „nicht nur die sechs Hebungen, sondern auch die drei Metra" hörbar zu machen (Gr. Versk. 88f., 294 A. 2); vielmehr haben wir Anlaß, statt dessen die sonst rätselhaften Ancepsstellen an den Grenzen der Metra in iambischen und trochäischen Versen als den Rhythmus markierend aufzufassen.

[7] Ich will nicht bestreiten, daß Übung und Gewöhnung die Anfangsposition verschieben konnten; aber die wissenschaftliche Fragestellung muß sich zunächst auf die Anfangsposition richten.

eine das *longum* eines quantitierenden Versschemas füllende Silbe
hätte verwandeln können: diese Forderung Leos (s. oben S. 296f) will
Unmögliches von einer Sprache, in der der Wortakzent abhängig ist
von dem bestimmt ausgeprägten Unterschied von langen und kurzen
Silben. Mit andern Worten, die lateinische Sprache stellte dem Vers- |
bildner, „um den Rhythmus in Erscheinung treten zu lassen" (Leo,
passim) als natürliches Material nicht Silben mit dem Unterschied kurz
oder lang, und auch nicht Silben mit dem Unterschied betont oder
unbetont zur Verfügung, sondern eine Anzahl verschiedener Typen von
ganzen Worten, in denen, wie das lateinische Akzentgesetz zeigt, Quantität und Wortakzent eine unlösliche Verbindung eingegangen waren[8].
Was für eine Art von Rhythmus mochte wohl natürlicherweise diesen
mit der Sprache gegebenen Bedingungen entsprechen? Aber vielleicht
ist es Romantik, eine natürliche Entsprechung zwischen Sprache und
Metrik für den Saturnier zu erwarten. Jedenfalls meine ich, im Gegensatz zu P. und Leo, aber im Anschluß z. B. an Lindsay (AJPh. 14,
1893, 164), daß die Bahn durchaus frei ist für unvoreingenommene
Untersuchung. Wie soll man beginnen?

„Gehen wir zuvörderst vom Äußerlichsten aus! Überfliegt man
die obige Zusammenstellung" — Aufzählung der überlieferten Saturnier — „mit dem Blicke, so bietet sich sofort eine ganze Reihe von
Versen dar, die aus fünf Wörtern bestehen; von diesen gehören gewöhnlich drei der ersten Vershälfte, zwei der zweiten an." „... in
über der Hälfte aller Saturnier wird der erste Halbvers durch drei
Wörter (54 mal), der zweite durch zwei (64 mal) gebildet. Was kann
das bedeuten? ... Dagegen[9] hat in der Sprache jedes Wort — mit
sofort zu besprechenden Ausnahmen — auf einer seiner Silben einen
Hauptaccent, seinen Wortton. Also darin stimmen die zuletzt genannten Saturnier überein, daß sie fünf Wortaccente enthalten und
zwar drei in der ersten, zwei in der zweiten Vershälfte." So, und zwar
mit den hier wiedergegebenen Sperrungen, begann vor über 50 Jahren
Thurneysen seine von Lindsay aufgenommene Untersuchung. Ich
hebe diesen ersten Schritt auf einem m. E. glücklich beschrittenen
Wege deshalb hervor, weil das von Thurneysen zum Ausgangspunkt

---

[8] *Worte* mit dem Unterschied steigenden oder fallenden Akzentes weist als Material
  der Saturnierbildung nach Lindsay AJPh. 14, 1893, 307. Natürlich ist damit die
  Untersuchung unter diesem Gesichtspunkt nur begonnen. Nimmt man aber
  Lindsays und Thurneysens sonstige Feststellungen hinzu, dann ist im Grunde die
  Untersuchung der dem Saturnierdichter zur Verfügung stehenden Worttypen mit
  Rücksicht auf ihre Verschiedenheit, Gleichwertigkeit und Kombinationsfähigkeit
  im Saturnier nicht nur begonnen, sondern ziemlich weit fortgeschritten.

[9] Über die Adversativpartikel bitte ich einstweilen hinwegzusehen, ich komme in
  der übernächsten Anmerkung darauf zurück.

genommene „Äußerlichste" genau dasjenige ist, wozu nach Ciceros Zeugnis (*de or.* 3, 198) ein natürliches, später als primitiv empfundenes | Gefühl schon die Römer früher Zeit anhielt, freilich nicht wenn sie dichteten, sondern wenn sie redeten:

Itaque illi veteres, sicut hodie etiam nonnullos videmus, cum circui-
tum et quasi orbem verborum conficere non possent — nam id quidem
nuper vel posse vel audere coepimus — terna aut bina aut nonnulli
singula etiam verba dicebant; qui in illa infantia naturale illud, quod
aures hominum flagitabant, tenebant tamen, ut et illa essent paria, quae
dicerent, et aequalibus interspirationibus uterentur[10].

Cicero spricht in einem Zusammenhang, der § 195 beginnt, von einem natürlichen, bis auf seine Zeit lebendigen rhythmischen Gefühl des ungebildeten *römischen* Publikums, das die Redner älterer Zeit zu einer eigenartigen Vortragstechnik veranlaßt und das dem modernen Redner die Sicherheit gibt, daß auch seine Finessen verstanden werden. Das Ältere war ein *numerus* der *Worte*, man kann es kaum anders nennen, während der moderne Periodenrhythmus von Cicero selbst — theoretisch wenigstens — als *numerus* der Silben dargestellt wird. Der von Cicero gekennzeichnete Sprechrhythmus der älteren Redetechnik wird beim freien Sprechen wohl bis zu einem gewissen Grade Wortwahl, Satzbau und Wortstellung beeinflußt haben; dagegen ist in der geschriebenen Prosaliteratur, auch z. B. Catos Reden, schwerlich irgend etwas davon festzustellen gewesen. Die Sache ist an sich nicht so unglaublich und sonderbar, wie sie zunächst klingt; davon kann man sich durch Erfahrungen und Experimente in unserer deutschen Sprache | überzeugen. Aber als Zeugnis für das rhythmische Gefühl der Römer fällt sie allerdings derartig aus allem Gewohnten

---

[10] Daß es sich bei Cicero nicht um Übertragung griechischer Theorie ins Römische handelt, beweist der Konflikt, in den die hier behauptete Tatsache mit der gewöhnlichen historischen Konstruktion gerät, vgl. § 175, 182. — *illi veteres* kann nach dem Zusammenhang nicht wohl das zurückweisende *veteres illi* sein, denn dann stellte Cicero schwer beweisbare Behauptungen über die Redner aus der Zeit des Numa und des Salierliedes auf; gemeint sind einfach die älteren Redner, die noch nicht periodisieren konnten; der Relativsatz ist unter den Tisch gefallen, weil derselbe Satzinhalt unmittelbar darauf in kausaler Funktion auftreten mußte. — *aut nonnulli singula etiam*: daß in einem Atem auch nur *singula verba* gesprochen werden konnten, wird glücklicherweise durch das zutretende *etiam* als Ausnahme gekennzeichnet; das zwischen *aut* und *singula* sich einschiebende *nonnulli* kann eigentlich nur bedeuten, daß auch die Leute, die sich dies erlaubten, eine Ausnahme bildeten. Sachlich einfacher, aber deswegen nicht unbedingt von Cicero gemeint, wäre *aut nonnulla singula etiam*. — *naturale illud quod* . . . war ausführlicher geschildert in § 181; es ist gerade *nicht* das Äußerste, wo einem der Atem ausgeht und man eine Pause macht, weil man muß, gerade nicht das, was § 175 zum Charakteristikum des *ignarus dicendi* machte und was § 182 *modus naturae* nennt.

heraus, daß man einem Cicerointerpreten schwerlich verdenken könnte, wenn er auf die Saturniertechnik als auf eine parallele Äußerung
dieses selben natürlichen rhythmischen Gefühles der Römer hinwiese.
Denn daß die Saturniertechnik auf den ersten Blick — und nicht nur
auf den ersten Blick — denselben Aspekt bietet, das ist seit Thurneysens Abhandlung mehr nur geleugnet als bestritten worden. Ich sehe
nicht, daß der hier zu dem Thema ,,il saturnio e il senso ritmico romano'' von mir in umgekehrter Richtung gegebene Hinweis auf die
Cicerostelle wesentlich gewagter sein könnte. Nur, daß es in diesem
Falle notwendig ist, eine Voraussetzung auszusprechen, die im andern
Falle als selbstverständlich gelten könnte, daß es sich nämlich bei der
archaischen rednerischen Vortragstechnik nur um eine vergleichsweise
sehr rohe Äußerung des fraglichen rhythmischen Gefühles gehandelt
haben kann, während seine dichterische Ausgestaltung zu den von
Thurneysen und Lindsay untersuchten, keineswegs rohen positiven
und negativen Regelungen führte, deren erste gleich die Konstituierung
eines zweiteiligen, die Kola differenzierenden, auf *drei* plus *zwei* Wort-
akzenten ruhenden Verses war[11]. —

IV. ,Italische' Saturnier vertragen sich so schwer mit P.s Hypothese, wie sie gut in Leos Vorstellungen paßten. P. ist begreiflicher-
weise nicht gut auf sie zu sprechen. Da das Material zu unsicher ist,
um allein eine Entscheidung zu geben, werden allgemeinhistorische
Erörterungen über den Begriff ,italisch' notwendig, denen man mit
großem | Interesse folgt. Die schon durch das Fragezeichen im Titel
dieses Kapitels *Saturnii italici?* ausgedrückten Zweifel P.s sind gewiß
berechtigt.

V. ,,*La cultura di Roma arcaica*''. Dies ist meines Erachtens das
beste Kapitel des kleinen, aber vielfach zum Fortschritt zwingenden

---

[11] ,,Gerade die Ungleichheit beider Vershälften scheint mir die wesentliche Eigentümlichkeit des Saturniers zu sein'' Thurneysen S. 24, 1. — Die Ausnahme, das
Kolon aus *einem* Wort, kann im Saturnier nur an zweiter Stelle erscheinen, das
Wort ist dann fünfsilbig: Thurneysen S. 30, 45. — Thurneysen lenkte die Fragestellung gleich anfangs von der Wortzahl auf den Wortton ab, mit der von mir
in dem oben zitierten Text ausgelassenen Begründung: ,,Daß die *Wortzahl* bei der
Poesie eines indogermanischen Stammes eine Rolle spiele, ist von vornherein
nicht wahrscheinlich; eine solche Annahme würde hier auch sofort widerlegt
durch alle übrigen Verse, welche aus mehr oder weniger als fünf Wörter bestehen.''
Hier muß ich nun nachträglich widersprechen, denn nach Ciceros Zeugnis ist das
Prinzip *terna aut bina aut ... singula etiam verba* sogar in roher Anwendung
geeignet, *paria* zu schaffen. Daß beim Saturnier die Gleichheit zwischen 3 und 2,
und zwischen 2 und 1 (die zwischen 3 und 1 scheidet für den Saturnier aus) durch
Doppeltonigkeit vier- und mehrsilbiger Worte zustande kam, bleibt aber natürlich
möglich; und für die Behandlung der Verse, welche aus ,,mehr als fünf Wörtern'',
oder der Kola, die aus mehr als drei bzw. aus mehr als zwei Wörtern bestehen,
ergibt sich wohl nicht einmal theoretisch eine Differenz.

Buches. Um die nach den bisher verbreiteten Anschauungen unerwartet frühe Rezeption griechischer Metrik in Rom als historisch möglich zu erweisen und zugleich chronologisch näher zu fixieren, weist P. eindrucksvoll auf, was wir heute von der Kultur des archaischen Rom und seinen schwankenden Beziehungen zur griechischen Welt wissen sollten. Ich kann im Einzelnen nicht kritisieren, sondern nur mich belehren lassen, müßte aber gleichwohl das Ziel der Erörterungen unter kritischen Vorbehalt stellen. Da mit einem so den Zusammenhang mit dem eigentlichen Gegenstand des Buches preisgebenden Referat hier wohl niemandem gedient wäre, begnüge ich mich mit der dringenden Empfehlung, gerade auch dies Kapitel zu lesen. —

VI. Aus dem Wort *carmen* hat sich die klassische Philologie einen Terminus geschaffen, um eine von ihr heute geglaubte besondere Form altlateinischer mehr oder weniger gebundener Rede zu bezeichnen. In seinem Schlußkapitel *Il carme allitterante, Celti e Germani* bringt P. zunächst eine glänzende Charakteristik dieser Form, die man in seiner eigenen Darstellung lesen möge (S. 75ff.). Westphal und Norden wollten die Rhythmik solcher *carmina* in direkte Beziehung zum Saturnier bringen. Hier erhebt P. Einspruch: „Connessione diretta è impossibile: il saturnio è un verso quantitativo, tali *carmina* mostrano isocolia e nulla più. Questo è un abisso incolmabile" (S. 78). Außerdem hebt er, und dies gewiß richtig, hervor, daß im Saturnier die Allitteration nur dekoratives, nicht konstitutives Element ist (vgl. Lindsay AJPh. 14, 1893, 308), und daß im Saturnier jede stilistische Überfülle und jeder Synonymenluxus fehlt. In direkter Beziehung stehe das *carmen* vielmehr zu den ältesten literarischen Formen des keltischen und des germanischen Stammes, wozu die sprachlichen Beziehungen der Formenlehre und des Lexikons eine Parallele bilden. D e gemeinsame Allitteration ruhe auf der gemeinsamen Anfangsbetonung, diese erkläre sich aus gemeinsamem Substrat oder, eher noch, aus Wanderung von einem Stamme zum andern. Bei den Römern wäre durch das Eindringen lyrischer Kola aus der griechischen Welt die natürliche Entwickelung gehemmt oder abgeschnitten worden. — S. 83 bringt eine für den Schluß aufgesparte Überraschung. In gewissem Sinne führt doch eine Brücke über den | ‚abisso incolmabile': die Zwei- bzw. Viergliedrigkeit des Saturniers ist aus der Form des *carmen* hinübergetragen und darf z. B. mit dem Nibelungenvers verglichen werden.

Nach meinen obigen Ausführungen über das Prinzip des radikalen Unterschiedes zwischen akzentuierenden und quantitierenden Versen in seiner Anwendung auf das Lateinische brauche ich meine Zweifel an der Tiefe des *abisso incolmabile* nicht besonders auszuführen. Übrigens glaube ich, daß es P. gelungen ist, einen greifbaren Unterschied zu statuieren. Im Anschluß an seine und ältere Darlegungen bin ich sehr

einverstanden, die uns kenntliche Form der *carmina* in die vorhistori-
sche Zeit, in welcher die Anfangssilbe ihre bekannte Sonderfunktion
ausübte, zurückreichen zu lassen; dagegen scheint die uns kenntliche
Form des Saturniers, zumal nach den Untersuchungen von Thurneysen
und Lindsay, nicht nur äußerlich der Zeit der fast unumschränkten
Herrschaft des Dreisilbengesetzes anzugehören[12]. Wenn sich der Gedanke der inneren Zusammengehörigkeit von Saturniertechnik und
historischer Dreisilbenbetonung durchführen läßt, dann haben wir
einen Anhalt mehr, einmal für Betrachtungen über die gestört oder
ungestört früh sich bewährende Originalität der römischen Sprach-
kunst, und zum andern zur Entscheidung der auch praktisch wichtigen
Frage, inwieweit die Saturniertechnik geeignet ist, etwas über das unge-
zwungene sprachrhythmische Gefühl der Römer historischer Zeit zu
lehren.

---

[12] Es gäbe die Möglichkeit, auch das lateinische Akzentgesetz und nicht nur die
Saturnierkola auf frühen griechischen Einfluß zurückzuführen (Literaturnachweis
bei Leumann, Lat. Gr. 188f.); aber dazu scheint auch P. keine Neigung zu haben.

Bentley's Schediasma
"De metris Terentianis" and the Modern Doctrine of Ictus in Classical Verse[1]

1941

Let me for the sake of brevity begin with a rough definition. What I call the "Modern Doctrine of Ictus in Classical Verse" is the assumption that Greek and Latin poets composed their lines for singing or reading with a stressed accent at definite points of each metrical line, and that we are correct in marking with Ictus-signs any set of long and short syllables that was an ancient verse. Stressed Ictus is regarded as a general principle ruling Greek as well as Latin versification and even the Saturnian metre, while the question whether or not the metrical Ictus coincided with the usual prose accent is left open for further consideration in a special discussion of the different kinds of verse. As far as we know, a theory of universal Ictus was not established in ancient times — certainly there is no express ancient testimony, which would settle the matter without argument — but in our times the theory has had its devoted followers and its ardent opponents. Even to-day, as Prof. Sturtevant stated fifteen years ago, "the disagreement is as complete as ever".

Whoever is convinced that his own theory is the right one, may state his arguments directly and is not usually obliged to bother about an historical or psychological explanation of how the right theory came about; at any rate, if it is the simple truth, it cannot be made clearer by accidental details. But if you oppose a doctrine, the case is different: a false theory calls for such explanations. Thus, it is only natural that we find especially the opponents trying to account for its origin. They do it by assuming that English, German and American scholars are prejudiced in favor of the sound of verses in their own languages and lack the imagination to con|ceive of other possibilities. This explanation seems plausible enough, though some misgivings are left, because, if it is true, the first of these narrow-minded, naive, Anglo-Teutonic modern metricians must have been of all men Bentley.

---

[1] A short abstract of this paper has appeared in Volume 69 of Proceedings of the American Philological Association.

But more astonishing is this: even adherents of the universal Ictus-theory are inclined now to share this somewhat condescending view of Bentley's naivety. When ten years ago Eduard Fraenkel published an elaborate book on Ictus and Accent in Latin dialogue verse (a book whose aim would be vain, according to its author's words, unless the general Ictus-theory can now be taken for granted), he stated Bentley's contribution as follows: Bentley's main intention, when he invented and introduced a sign for metrical ictus, was a pedagogical one, but it cannot be denied that he and his early followers believed in the reality of a stressed metrical ictus, and that they did so without sufficient reason. When Madvig, Nietzsche, and others urged the difference of modern and ancient languages and verses, they were quite right in their time. Only more recent examination decided the question in favor of Ictus. Here Fraenkel mentions especially two American scholars, Prof. Hendrickson and Sturtevant, and also Prof. Von der Mühll of Basel.

Certainly according to this view Bentley's part in establishing the theory of Ictus seems a little mysterious and one is reminded of Gottfried Hermann, who invented the ambiguous praise that the metrician Bentley felt the rhythm of ancient verse most adequately, but did not give an explanation of his feeling. So much is surely true: Bentley could neither anticipate Hermann's peculiar reasons for accepting Ictus — because Kantian philosophy is required for their understanding — nor could he be aware of modern psychological experiments or presumptions, and of Usener's or Wilamowitz' speculations on the prehistory of ancient verses, which now are alleged as arguments for Ictus.

A Bentley relying on sense without reason is not a very familiar Bentley, but judging from that part of modern metrical literature to which I have already referred, it seems as if we have to acquiesce in Hermann's statement that metrics was the "una res, in qua Bentleyus sensui omnia, iudicio prope nihil tribuit", and as if we could discuss only whether, in the case of Ictus, Bentley withheld judgement "singulari cum fructu literarum" as Hermann said, or by | a deplorable gap in his critical alertness, as opponents might put it.

But the case is more complicated. In modern metrical and grammatical literature Henri Weil is occasionally quoted as having been the first to object to the metrical doctrine of Bentley and his English and German followers, on the ground that they took for granted generally what is only a special feature of English and German versification. Now Weil was himself an adherent of the theory of Ictus, and what he made Bentley responsible for was not the Ictus-theory as such but his assumption of regard for word-accent in Latin versification. So here we have to face another riddle. On one side all modern adherents of Ictus agree with Weil that metrical Ictus and regard for accent are separable from each other not only in theory but in ancient practice also: otherwise the theory of Ictus could not be applied to classical Greek verse, where manifestly there was no regard for accent. On the other side there is this disagreement as to what Bentley initiated: whether it was the general theory of Ictus, or the assumption of regard for accent in certain Latin verses. Of course there are other possibilities besides this alternative, but it is useless to mention them beforehand. It seems time for me now to turn to Bentley's short dissertation "de metris Terentianis" itself. Bentley called it a σχεδίασμα and so we have his word that it was extemporized for his edition of Terence's plays; but then it is perhaps the most remarkable of all philological extemporizations. While it is true that on many points its statements are only provisional, yet the whole development of future metrical research was not only initiated but as it were predestined by the Schediasma, and without it modern metricians never will be fully aware of what they are doing.

For our present purpose I need to pick out only a few of Bentley's many observations and suggestions, and since Bentley's very peculiar way of sketching does not allow direct shortening, I arrange them quite differently from that order of facts and ideas, in which they are found in the Schediasma.

According to Bentley the sign of accentus acutus was chosen by him for marking the real pronunciation of ancient verses and corresponded to a stress-accent laid on the marked syllable by ancient actors and readers, and of course intended by the poets themselves. In hexameters the single words had Ictus in the places of their | usual prose accents; and it was Bentley's opinion that thus, immediately and without dislocation of stress, the words constituted the rhythm of the whole line; here schoolboy-scanning was heartily despised by Bentley. He sets down the first four lines of the *Aeneid* with his Ictus-signs, thus:

> *'Arma virúmque cáno, Trójae qui prímus ab óris*
> *Itáliam fáto prófugus Lavínaque vénit*
> *Lítora; multum ílle et térris jactátus et álto*
> *Vi súperum saévae mémorem Junónis ob íram,*

and he adds: "Qui perite et modulate hos versus legat, sic eos, ut hic accentibus notantur, pronuntiabit; non, ut pueri in Scholis, ad singulorum pedum initia,

> *'Italiám fató profugús Lavínaque vénit,*

sed ad rhythmum totius versus." You see, whatever adherents of the general theory of Ictus may claim now as possible or impossible, we cannot mistake the fact that Bentley was conscious of feeling that the rhythm of Latin hexameters comes out by stressing the word-accents. Bentley adhered to a tradition of pronunciation of hexameters which has lived beside mechanical scanning from ancient times till to-day, at least in Italy, where the living language protects Latin word-accents from abuse.

On the other hand Bentley curses schoolteachers for boring and maltreating their pupils since the t me of the Renaissance in order to teach them "dactylica", a kind of verse which the English language abhors, and for neglecting "Terentiana metra", of which English boys have an unconscious knowledge from English poetry. No doubt, the dead science of metrics was aroused to new life when all of a sudden it appeared that the "Trochaicus Tetrametrus Catalecticus" was not only a frequent "metrum Terentianum", but at the same time a very common English line, and modern metricians cannot be too grateful for that ingenious turn. But we must not overlook the fact, that, in giving it, Bentley himself established for Latin dramatic verse the very thing he despised when dealing with hexameters, namely reading them with a regularly recurring stress, even against and instead of natural prose accent. This differentiation is accounted for so far, and so far only, as the iambic and trochaic | lines of Plautus and Terence lend themselves to this way of scanning more easily than Latin hexa- meters do; indeed they are the only kind of classical verse that shows a peculiar affinity, however incomplete, to modern English and German versification. Thus Bentley founded the modern doctrine of regard for accent in Latin verse, but only when applying it to iambic and trochaic lines did he make a beginning upon a modest and limited sort of Ictus- theory.

Since Bentley's times things have changed greatly. We are ac- quainted now with a general theory of Ictus, extended to hexameters too, and including Greek verse of all kinds. Is it true then that Bentley had little or nothing to do with its origin? Here I come at the main point of this paper. The truth is that Bentley himself extended his assumption of a regular Ictus to Greek iambic and trochaic verse in spite of the fact that the traditional Greek word-accents do not encour- age the attempt, whereas the Latin word-accents in such verses certain- ly do. How could he do this? Are we here discovering that gap in his critical alertness which moderns unanimously assume? I myself am convinced that here we have found the origin of so much t ouble in modern metrics, but it is not Bentley who must be held responsible for the lack of clearness.

As is well known, he concludes the Schediasma by stating that Latin poets were compelled, by the nature of their language to have words like *omnes, malum* mispronounced as *omnés, malúm* at the beginning and end of iambic trimeters. For this statement, which comes rather late and is given with some reluctance, he appeals to the use of Greek poets in Greek trimeters: "Nimirum aures vel invitae patienter id ferebant, sine quo ne una quidem in Fabula Scaena poterat edolari. Quin et Graecos ipsos eadem tenuit necessitas, eadem passa est indulgentia. Cum Aristophanes dixit,

Δουλόν γενεσθαι πάραφρονουντος δέσποτου,

cum Euripides,

Ηκώ νεκρων κευθμώνα και σκοτού πυλας,

idem admiserunt in Δουλόν et Ηκώ, quod noster in Malúm et Omnés: ipsi enim alibi priorem acuunt, Δούλον et ῞Ηκω."

Notice that he does not appeal simply to Ictus against word-accent in the beginning of the two Greek verses, but only to the assumption that in other verses the same poets had the first syl|lables of the two words δουλον and ἥκω stressed by Ictus, so that by inference either in this case or in the other the word-accents must have been neglected. Clearly Bentley avoided referring to the traditional Greek word-accents. Certainly the alternative arrived at by inference served his immediate purpose just as well, but then he seems surprisingly cautious about a trifle while shamelessly begging the question as to Ictus in Greek verse.

This puzzling passage of Bentley I have been considering for a long time, but never dreamt of its easy explanation till my friend Bruno Snell, whom I bothered with it, called my attention to Prof. Drerup's two volumes: "Die Schulaussprache des Griechischen von der Renaissance bis zur Gegenwart", published in 1930 and 1932. There I found ample evidence for a curious fact in the development of modern classical studies which has been almost forgotten but which after Drerup's painstaking work must not be overlooked any longer.

In Bentley's time Greek verse spoken with Greek accentuation sounded badly to the ears of men who were better acquainted with Latin verse, especially hexameters, and felt, or believed they felt, the aesthetic value of Latin accentuation. Now the Erasmian contempt for modern Greek pronunciation of certain vowels and consonants was already becoming widespread, and in a literal sense it was certainly right to assert that Greek accentuation was a comparatively late invention too. Under these conditions it may well have appeared questionable whether the Byzantine accentuation system represented the real accents of classical times; to oppose the claim would seem only the next step in the r ght direction; and amongst the men who yielded to the temptation, the most prominent was Bentley. What they claimed for classical Greek versification were word-accents that gave to Greek metrical lines the same aesthetic impression which they received when hearing the corresponding Latin verses; in other words, they claimed for the classical Greek language something quite or nearly like the Latin accentuation system. The practical result of this claim has been that till now many teachers and pupils in many countries pronounce Greek words with Latin accentuation, and in this survival Drerup became interested when in 1923 he went from Germany to a Dutch university. I am dealing only with the theoretical consequence which this | strange theory of Greek accentuation enforced on its believers as long as it could be defended. It was clearly this: that the relation of ancient word-accents and ancient versification could be studied adequately only in Latin lines, where the true accents were supposed to be preserved, but that nevertheless observations, made in Latin lines, might constitute a true theory of Greek versification also.

I have no time to enlarge on this point and must beg to conclude my remarks on the Schediasma with the statement that Bentley's assumption of Ictus in Greek trimeters was founded on considered disbelief in the traditional Greek word-accents and not in a naive belief in Ictus everywhere.

Instead of revising Bentley's view on metrics with reference to Greek word-accents, modern metricians preferred to take it for granted generally that the theory of Ictus might be extended to ancient verses in which it is not supported by the distribution of word-accents; and going on to apply the theory to hexameters, they seemed to find by the way good reason for maintaining the old schoolboy practice of scanning Latin hexameters, against Bentley and against history. For, this practice can be traced back to late antiquity, when *"scande versum"* with reference to a line of Vergil was a part of their grammatical exercises (Priscianus, Partitiones duodecim versuum Aeneidos principalium, Gramm. Lat. III 459ff.). Scanning consisted of speaking (and writing) separately the syllables of each single foot of a metrical line, and in Latin hexameters inevitably led to pronouncing as Bentley said "ut pueri in Scholis, ad singulorum pedum initia". But in its origin the scansion of hexameters clearly presupposed the other way of pronunciation as the obvious and natural thing.

Disbelief in Greek word-accents was shared by Bentley but was justly attacked or justly neglected during the 18th century, and in the course of the 19th century comparative linguistics soon put an end to the discussion. But as things had already begun to be mixed up, modern metricians did not notice the collapse of this sole tangible support of Ictus in Greek poetry. The first to defend their practice by developing a general theory of Ictus was Gottfried Hermann. Whoever is inclined to suspect some naivety at the bottom of the modern doctrine of Ictus should study the phil|osophical part of Hermann's metrics; the naivety of his pseudo-philosophic reasoning is exempted from criticism only by its indescribable absurdity.

Still Hermann mixed up only two incompatible things, hexameter-scanning and Bentley's Ictus; for the fact that he followed Bentley in accepting a bad use of the ancient word ἄρσις did not do much harm and is hardly worth mentioning to-day. After Hermann the theory took in two more ingredients of different origin and dubious compatibility, namely the "temps fort" of modern music, which vain efforts to trace are now being made in Aristoxenos' rhythmical fragments, and the "Hebung" of pure Germanic poetry, which is certainly a different thing from regularly recurring Ictus and from musical "temps fort". This difference, as well as the inconsistency of Bentley's metrical views with simple scanning were appreciated properly by Weil and Benloew who expounded the principles of scansion and of "temps fort", and urged the musicality of ancient accents some 80 years ago. Their very clear and consistent general theory of Ictus left no room for any Teutonic elements. I am far from believing that this somewhat mechanical theory interferes with Bentley's observation of regard for accent in Latin verse and with the successfull criticism founded on it; but I mention Weil and Benloew's theory specially, first because it is free from the carelessness with which other adherents of Ictus confuse at least three or four incompatible things, and secondly because even this purified theory of Ictus goes back via August Boeckh to Gottfried Hermann, and so to a misunderstood Bentley; that is, to an illegitimate belief in Ictus even in Greek verse. No wonder, then, that when the metrical chapter in Weil and Benloew's book "Théorie générale de l'accentuation Latine" was eagerly consulted later on by adherents and opponents of the theory of Ictus, it supplied arguments to both sides, and, instead of clearing up the situation, only made confusion worse confounded. If we want to see things clearly, we have to go back as far as Bentley's Schediasma "de metris Terentianis".

Nachwort der Herausgeber

Der Leser, der in diesem Buch die Inhaltsübersicht mit dem Schriftenverzeichnis von Ernst Kapp vergleicht, wird feststellen, daß von seinen früher veröffentlichten Arbeiten nur wenige nicht aufgenommen wurden. Es handelt sich im wesentlichen um diejenigen, die gesondert publiziert worden waren und in dieser Form zugänglich sind: die Dissertation, das in den USA erschienene Buch „Greek Foundations of Traditional Logic" und seine deutsche Übersetzung und die gemeinsam mit Kurt v. Fritz gleichfalls in den USA veröffentlichte Übersetzung und Erklärung von Aristoteles' Schrift über den Staat der Athener. Andererseits konnten in diese Sammlung — dank der Hilfe des Verfassers und des Verlags — zwei bisher nicht publizierte Arbeiten aufgenommen werden: Kapps Habilitationsschrift und seine Untersuchung über die Ideenlehre in Platons früheren Dialogen. Wer nachrechnet, wird also durch Addition und Subtraktion zu dem Ergebnis kommen, daß der Umfang von Kapps bisher veröffentlichtem Oeuvre, rein quantitativ betrachtet, nicht allzu groß ist, — zumal wenn man es an der heute vielfach ausgebrochenen Schreibseligkeit mißt. Daß es so ist, erklärt sich vor allem aus der großen Selbstkritik Ernst Kapps, die ihn immer erst nach gründlichsten und vorsichtigsten Überlegungen an die Niederschrift gehen ließ. Es erklärt sich aber auch aus dem Gang seines Lebens, der auf der Höhe seiner Schaffenskraft durch die politischen Katastrophen unserer Zeit hindurchführte. Das ist auch der Grund dafür, daß die Schriftensammlung dieses deutschen Gelehrten mehrere Arbeiten in englischer Sprache enthält.

Ernst Kapp, geboren am 21. Januar 1888 in Düsseldorf, wandte sich nach dem Abitur dem Studium der Klassischen Philologie und der Philosophie zu und promovierte 1912 in Freiburg. Nach dem ersten Weltkrieg habilitierte er sich 1920 in München. 1927 wurde er als Ordinarius für Klassische Philologie nach Hamburg berufen, wo er auf Kollegen und Studenten gleich anregend wirkte. So war es für alle, die mit ihm zusammen gearbeitet hatten, ein harter Schlag, als ihm 1937 aus politischen Gründen der Lehrstuhl entzogen wurde. 1939, vor Ausbruch des Krieges, übersiedelte er in die USA. Hier war er seit 1941 an der Columbia University, und zwar seit 1948 als Professor of Greek and Latin tätig. 1955 kehrte er nach Deutschland zurück und lebte hier zunächst wieder in Hamburg, seit 1959 in München.

Während seines Studiums verband ihn enge Freundschaft mit
Tycho v. Wilamowitz-Moellendorff. Nachdem dieser im Kriege gefallen war, gab Kapp aus seinem Nachlaß die für die Tragödien-Inter-
pretation so bedeutsam gewordenen Untersuchungen zur Dramatischen Technik des Sophokles heraus. Dadurch trat er auch zu Ulrich
v. Wilamowitz, der dem Werk seines Sohnes ein letztes Kapitel über
den Oedipus auf Kolonos hinzufügte, in nahe Verbindung. Eine solche
bestand auch zu Eduard Schwartz, der Referent seiner Dissertation
war. Diese Verbindung mit führenden Vertretern der großen deutschen Philologen-Generation aus der Zeit um 1900 wird viel zu der
interpretatorischen, dem historischen Zusammenhang sich verpflichtet
fühlenden Gewissenhaftigkeit beigetragen haben, die Kapps Arbeiten
auszeichnet; seine geistige Selbständigkeit hat sie nie beeinträchtigt.

Kapps Dissertation (Nr. 1 des Schriftenverzeichnisses) beschäftigt
sich mit dem Verhältnis der Eudemischen zur Nikomachischen Ethik.
Werner Jaeger nennt sie eine „scharfsinnige und vorsichtige Arbeit"
... „die weitaus das Beste ist, was in den letzten Jahren über die
Eudemische Ethik und ihre philosophische Stellung geschrieben worden ist" (Aristoteles, 1923, 240). Ihr Ergebnis, daß es sich um eine
ältere und weniger vollständige Ethik-Vorlesung des Aristoteles gegenüber der Nikomachischen Ethik handelt, ist durchweg anerkannt.
Kapp hat es in seiner Besprechung von Arnims Ethik-Abhandlung (5)
mit neuen Argumenten bekräftigen und die Andersartigkeit der Magna
Moralia als einer von der Nikomachischen Ethik abhängigen, nicht
aristotelischen Schrift überzeugend darlegen können.

In seiner Habilitationsschrift blieb Kapp Aristoteles treu; aber er
wandte sich jetzt von der Ethik der Logik zu und erschloß sich damit
ein Arbeitsgebiet, auf dem er sich jahrzehntelang betätigt hat. Die
Reihe reicht von der Habilitationsarbeit über die Kategorienlehre in
der aristotelischen Topik (2) über den RE-Artikel „Syllogistik" (8)
bis zu dem Buch „Greek Foundations of Traditional Logic" (14), das
inzwischen auch ins Deutsche und in andere Sprachen übersetzt wurde,
und zur Besprechung der Philodem-Ausgabe von Ph. H. und E.
A. De Lacy (16). Der Kreis der behandelten Phänomene erweitert sich
also von der Lehre einer logischen Frühschrift des Aristoteles über ein
bestimmtes logisches Verfahren bis zu den Grundlagen der „traditionellen" europäischen Logik und ihrer möglichen Kritik in Antike und
Neuzeit. Im Mittelpunkt steht aber immer wieder die Antwort auf eine
Frage: wie war für Aristoteles der Aufbau einer Logik möglich, die im
eigentlichen Sinn „formal" und ebenso frei von Metaphysik wie von
Psychologie ist? Die Antwort darauf findet Kapp in dem Streben, in
der Logik eine „Gymnastik" auszubilden, die den Adepten der Philosophie der Auseinandersetzung mit der Sophistik gewachsen sein läßt,

insbesondere der Beantwortung sophistischer Fangfragen. Den Grund zu dieser philosophischen Gymnastik hat Platon in seinen Dialogen gelegt; sie führte bei ihm weiter zur Antwort auf die Frage τί ἐστιν; d. h. zur Möglichkeit der Definition. Diese Logik ist ihrem Ursprung nach notwendig an die Form des philosophischen Gesprächs gebunden; sie muß mißverstanden werden, wenn sie samt ihrem Beweisverfahren zu einer „Buchwissenschaft" wird, wie es in der stoischen Logik der Fall war.

Platons Reaktion auf die Sophistik zeigt also, daß ihm schon früh daran gelegen sein mußte, den Fang-Charakter sophistischer Fragestellung zu enthüllen und zu einer Frageform zu kommen, die eine sachgerechte Definition als Antwort zuließ. Im Dienst dieses Strebens steht nach Kapps Überzeugung von Anfang an auch die platonische Idee; sie gehört als ‚Begriff‘ zunächst in die Logik bzw. Dialektik und nicht in die Metaphsyik.

Schon in seinen Logik-Untersuchungen hat Kapp sich gegen Versuche gewandt, dieses Verhältnis umzukehren, so vor allem gegen Stenzels Versuch einer Gleichsetzung der platonischen Idee mit einer Vorstellung von Areté. Zu unserer Freude können wir jetzt das, was sonst nur in gelegentlichen Andeutungen anderer Schriften steht, in einer eigenen, umfassenden Abhandlung „The Theory of Ideas in Plato's Earlier Dialogues" (15) vorlegen. Kapp hat sie bald nach seinem Logikbuch in den USA niedergeschrieben und an einigen Stellen später überarbeitet. Wir bringen sie in der Fassung, wie sie in Kapps Manuskript jeweils als abgeschlossen gelten kann; nachträgliche Änderungen würden der Konzeption den Charakter der Einheitlichkeit nehmen.

Wenn Kapp im Titel dieser Abhandlung von Platons „earlier dialogues" spricht, so meint er damit diejenigen, die die Sprachstatistik der großen „ersten Gruppe" zugewiesen hat. Denn nur die Einteilung in drei Gruppen erkennt Kapp als sicheres Ergebnis der Sprachstatistik an. Einer Anwendung ihrer Methoden zwecks einer weiteren chronologischen Differenzierung steht er mißtrauisch gegenüber und meint, daß eine solche nur mit Argumenten aus dem Inhalt der Dialoge möglich sei. Derartige Argumente sucht er aus der gedanklichen Entwicklung in den Dialogen in Übereinstimmung mit den Nachrichten über Platons Leben zu gewinnen. Dafür ist ihm der wertvollste Zeuge der siebente Brief, von dessen Echtheit er überzeugt ist.

So sondert Kapp zunächst eine Gruppe von drei frühen Dialogen ab, in denen die Ideenlehre, auch in Andeutungen, noch keine Rolle spielt (Apologie, Kriton, Gorgias). Sie sind nach seiner Überzeugung vor Platons erster sizilischer Reise geschrieben. Platon zeigt in ihnen Sokrates im Kampf um ein anständiges, gerechtes Verhalten des

Staatsbürgers. Besonders eindrucksvoll ist Kapps Interpretation des Gorgias als einer Auseinandersetzung mit den „feinen Leuten" (Repräsentant Kallikles), die die athenische Demokratie zwar nicht billigen, sich aber doch an dem in ihr geübten Unrecht beteiligen. So sei der Gorgias in der — natürlich schon durch den Prozeß des Sokrates verursachten — Verzweiflung Platons an den moralischen Möglichkeiten der athenischen Demokratie geschrieben, die ihn zur ersten Reise nach Sizilien und Italien veranlaßte. Die Erfahrungen, die er mit den noch viel verhängnisvolleren Zuständen in jenen Tyrannen-Staaten machte, ließen ihn aber den Plan endgültiger Auswanderung aus Athen aufgeben und brachten ihn zur Rückkehr in die Vaterstadt, um einen Versuch zur moralisch-politischen Erziehung junger Menschen zu machen. Diese Absicht veranlaßte ihn zur Gründung der Akademie, die in allen späteren Dialogen der „ersten Gruppe" vorausgesetzt wird. Als Zeugnisse eines solchen neuen Appells an Athen sieht Kapp Dialoge wie Menexenos, Protagoras und Menon an, als Zeugnisse der Bemühungen der frühen Akademie „Definitions"-Dialoge aus dem Gebiet des Moralischen wie Laches, Charmides, Euthyphron. Einen Schritt weiter geht der Phaidon, in dem die Idee zuerst als etwas Transzendentes erscheint, und dann das Symposion, in dem die Idee als Erklärungsprinzip nicht nur für die moralische Welt, sondern auch für die Kosmologie gefordert wird. Damit ist in der Ideenlehre der entscheidende Schritt von der Logik zur Metaphysik getan. Eine weitere Entfernung von der ursprünglichen Konzeption der Idee bedeutet das Postulat von Ideen für materielle Dinge (Mensch, Feuer, Wasser, Haar, Schlamm, Schmutz usw.), wie es zuerst im Parmenides erwogen wird.

Kapp sieht in dieser Entwicklung einen Rückzug der platonischen Philosophie von der ursprünglichen Absicht, zu einer klaren Begründung des menschlichen Verhaltens in Staat und Gesellschaft zu kommen, auf eine stärkere Exklusivität des philosophischen Denkens und seiner Zielsetzung. Diese Entwicklung entspringt der Resignation hinsichtlich der Möglichkeiten, auf die Zustände in Athen aus wissenschaftlicher Einsicht heraus einwirken zu können. Diese Resignation birgt aber zugleich die Gefahr in sich, daß der Philosoph — im Bedürfnis nach Kompensation — sich in eine „akademisch-vornehmtuende Staatsphilosophie" zurückzieht. Verständlich und berechtigt ist ein solches Verhalten nur als Provisorium, nicht als Dauerzustand. Als solcher droht er vor allem in der aritotelischen Ethik fixiert zu werden.

Kapp stellt diese Gefahr vor allem in dem Vortrag „Platon und die Akademie" (10) und in dem Aufsatz „Theorie und Praxis bei Aristoteles und Platon" (12) dar. Beide sind in den dreißiger Jahren entstanden, und das ist gewiß kein Zufall. Kapp bekennt in der sehr offenen und bewegten Einleitung zum „Akademie"-Vortrag, es liege ihm

fern zu behaupten, ,,wir Philologen könnten aus den Vorgängen unserer
eigenen Zeit und unseres eigenen Landes nichts lernen; im Gegenteil:
manche Seiten des antiken Lebens, über die man sonst hinwegsah,
können plötzlich in ungeahnter Weise verständlich werden". Was er
— ebenso deutlich — ablehnt, ist die Forderung, aus den Ergebnissen der
eigenen Wissenschaft etwas anzubieten, das diese Vorgänge der eigenen
Zeit und des eigenen Landes (!) etwa rechtfertigen könnte. Es ist er-
staunlich, daß dieser mutige Vortrag noch 1935 nicht nur in Amersfoort
in Holland, sondern auch vor der Deutsch-Griechischen Gesellschaft
in Hamburg gehalten werden konnte.

Kapp hatte aus den Vorgängen jener Zeit, die ihn auch selbst noch
hart genug betreffen sollten, ,,gelernt" — man darf wohl sagen: auf
dem Wege der Anamnesis; denn er stellte jetzt nur emotionaler und
engagierter heraus, was er grundsätzlich schon vorher gewußt hatte.
So nimmt er etwa in der Rezension von Langerbecks Demokrit-Buch
(9) vor allem Stellung gegen die Auffassung von der Inkommensurabilität vorsokratischen und modernen Denkens in der geradezu klassischen Formulierung: ,,Es ist das Vorurteil des Verfassers, daß das
archaische Denken ein für uns Moderne eigentümlich schwieriges
Denken gewesen sei, und es ist das Vorurteil des Rezensenten, daß man
das archaische Denken so lange nicht als Denken verstanden habe, als
es sich nicht als ein einfaches und natürliches Denken auch für uns erwiesen hat." Kapp befürchtet, daß man etwas Unbegreiflich-Irratio-
nales in das frühgriechische Denken hineinschaue und sich dabei be-
ruhige, bevor man sich ernstlich bemüht hat, die Vorgänge dieses
Denkens, die zu dem jeweils vorliegenden Resultat geführt haben,
gründlich nachzuvollziehen. Bemühung um wirkliche Einsicht war
immer das Ziel von Kapps Interpretationen, und so erkannte er es
auch — bis zum zwingenden Beweis des Gegenteils — den Gegenstän-
den seiner philologischen Bemühungen zu. So ist es auch keineswegs
zufällig, daß er in der Besprechung von Schadewaldts Thukydides-
Versuch (7) im thukydideischen Methodenkapitel den Willen zur
Vermittlung der Einsicht in die Wahrheit, nicht von Hinweisen zur
praktischen Nutzanwendung für den Politiker ausgesagt findet.

Ernst Kapp hat sich in seinen Schriften wie im akademischen Unterricht immer um den Nachvollzug dessen bemüht, was der antike
Autor dachte und aussagte. Er versuchte, der geistigen Situation gerecht zu werden, von der jener ausging und in die er weiterhin in der
Konsequenz seines Denkens geriet. Daß philosophische Schriftsteller
besonders zu einer solchen Behandlung auffordern, ist klar. Aber Kapp
hat diese Methode in Vorlesungen auch an Autoren ganz anderer Art
bewährt, etwa an Homer, Aristophanes oder Kallimachos, und für
ein weit abliegendes Gebiet liegen uns auch gedruckte Zeugnisse vor:

für die römische Metrik (11. 13). Hier hat er einen kühnen Vorstoß im alten Streit um Iktus und Wortakzent, um akzentuierendes und quantitierendes Prinzip unternommen, indem er darauf hinwies, daß im Lateinischen nicht die Silbe, sondern der Worttyp Grundlage des Versbaus sei und daß der Wortakzent für den Klang des lateinischen Verses sehr wohl eine „subsidiäre Funktion" übernehmen konnte. Charakteristisch ist für Kapp wieder, daß er im zweiten dieser Beiträge die Frage stellt, wie Bentley zu seiner Lehre von der Aussprache des lateinischen und des griechischen Verses kam, und sie auf eine schon vor seiner Zeit verbreitete Auffassung zurückführen kann, wonach die Wortakzentuierung im Griechischen im wesentlichen dem lateinischen Dreisilben-Gesetz entsprochen hätte.

Wir sind überzeugt, daß diese Sammlung von Kapps Schriften einen Überblick vermittelt, der nicht nur sachlich, sondern zugleich auch methodisch lehrreich sein wird. Wir danken dem Verlag und seinem zuständigen Mitarbeiter, Herrn Professor Wenzel, dafür, daß die Sammlung zu Ernst Kapps 80. Geburtstag erscheinen konnte.

Kiel, im Januar 1968   Hans Diller   Inez Diller

Verzeichnis der Schriften von Ernst Kapp

1. Das Verhältnis der Eudemischen zur Nikomachischen Ethik des Aristoteles. Dissertation Freiburg/Br. 1912.
2. Die Kategorienlehre in der aristotelischen Topik. Habilitations-Schrift München 1920. Zuerst gedruckt: diese Sammlung.
3. Sokrates der Jüngere. Philologus 79, 1924, 225/233.
4. Artikel: Sokrates 6). Pauly-Wissowa, Real-Enzyklopädie III A, 1927, 890/891.
5. Besprechung: H. v. Arnim, Die drei aristotelischen Ethiken. Gnomon 3, 1927, 19/38 und 73/81.
6. Πισθέταιρος. Philologus 84, 1929, 259/261.
7. Besprechung: W. Schadewaldt, Die Geschichtsschreibung des Thukydides. Gnomon 6, 1930, 76/100.
8. Artikel: Syllogistik. Pauly-Wissowa, Real-Enzyklopädie IV A, 1931, 1046/1067.
9. Besprechung: H. Langerbeck, Δόξις ἐπιρυσμίη. Studien zu Demokrits Ethik und Erkenntnistheorie. Gnomon 12, 1936, 65/77 und 158/169.
10. Platon und die Akademie. Mnemosyne III 4, 1936, 227/246.
11. Besprechung: G. Pasquali, Preistoria della poesia romana. Gött. Gel. Anz. 198, 1936, 477/492.
12. Theorie und Praxis bei Aristoteles und Platon. Mnemosyne III 6, 1938, 179/194.
13. Bentley's Schediasma „De metris Terentianis" and the Modern Doctrine of Ictus in Classical Verse. Mnemosyne III, 9, 1941, 187/194.
14. Greek Foundations of Traditional Logic. New York 1942. (Deutsche Übersetzung von Elisabeth Serelman-Küchler: Der Ursprung der Logik bei den Griechen. Göttingen 1965.)
15. The Theory of Ideas in Plato's Earlier Dialogues. Niedergeschrieben nach 1942. Zuerst gedruckt: diese Sammlung.
16. Besprechung: Ph. H. and E. A. De Lacy, Edition of Philodemus: On Methods of Inference. Am. Journal of Philology 68, 1947, 320/325.

17. Aristotle's Constitution of Athens and Related Texts. Translated with an Introduction and Notes by K. v. Fritz and E. Kapp. New York 1950.

18. Casus Accusativus. Festschrift Bruno Snell 1956, 15/22.

19. Deum te scito esse? Hermes 87, 1959, 129/132.

Herausgeber:

     T. v. Wilamowitz-Moellendorff, Die dramatische Technik des Sophokles. Philologische Untersuchungen 22, Berlin 1917.

REGISTER

Namen und Sachen

Wörter

Stellen

Anaxagoras VS 59 B 21a:
 51. 274
Alexander Aphrodisiensis
 Comm. in Ar. Gr. 2, 1,
 18, 12: 275
Aristophanes
 Av. 162. 339 430. 545 ff.
  627–645: 53
  631 ff.: 54
  1565 ff.: 162
 Nub. 112: 86 A.39
  694 ff.: 119
 Pax: 8
 Ran. 1431: 16
Aristoteles
 Cat. 1a 8: 245 A.31
  1a 16: 247
  1a 20 ff.: 235 A.21
  1b 10–15: 269
  1b 10. 13. 22: 248
  1b 25: 247
  1b 27: 249
  2a 4–9: 241
  2a 12: 248
  2a 14 ff.: 269
  2a 29: 248 A.38
  2b 30: 249
  3a 34: 219
  3a 36: 249
  3b 2 ff.: 269
  3b 10: 249
  3b 14: 245 A.31
  8a 28 ff.: 247 A.35
  10b 17: 250
  11b 9–14: 269
 Int. 16a 32–b 5: 282
  A. 6
  16b 3. 17a 11:   248
  A. 36
 APr. 24a 10 ff.: 268
  24a 13 ff. b 18: 261
  25b 26–31: 254f. 268
  25b 37: 261
  43a 20 ff.: 264
  43a 25. 32: 241
  45b 36 ff.: 218 A.6
  46a 3 ff.: 268

46a 11: 276
46a 28 ff.:   218 A.6.
 268
48a 29–39: 272
48b 39–49a 5:   282
 A. 6
49b 33 ff.: 239
67a 33 ff.: 44. 263
APo. 71a 1 ff.: 266
73b 5: 243 A.30
76a 20: 278 A.1
76b 21: 217 A.3
77a 5: 51. 61
77a 27: 217 A.3
78a 6–10: 51
79a 17 ff.: 268
83b 1: 225 A.15
83b 1–16: 241
83b 19f.: 224 A.13
86a 26: 271
91b 3: 216 A.2
98a 36. b3: 278 A.1
99b 15 ff.: 254. 268
Top. 100a 1: 217
100a 26: 265
101a 19: 220 A.9
101a 25 ff.:   215 A.1.
 264
101b 11–26: 217
101b 12: 217 A.4
101b 17: 215 A.2
101b 17–23: 219
101b 19: 215 A.2
101b 26: 219
101b 30: 264
102a 31: 219
102b 27ff. 102b 35ff.:
 218
103a 1: 268
103b 2–3: 217 A.4
103b 5ff. 7ff.: 219
103b 7–19: 221
103b 12 ff.: 218
103b 20: 219
103b 21: 220
103b 29: 250
103b 35–39: 243 A.30

107a 3ff.: 226f.
107a 14: 227. 236
107a 18ff.: 227
107a 25–28: 228
107b 19–26. 33: 227
109a 31: 245 A.31
109b 4: 219
110a 17: 245 A.31
116a 36–38: 212A.15
120b 12ff.: 218
120b 15f.: 228
120b 17: 228 A.17
120b 21. 23: 228
120b 30: 229
120b 36ff.: 231
121a 25ff.: 269
121b 11: 230 A. 18.
 269
122a 17: 230
120b 15ff.: 230f.
123a 7: 230
127b 1–4: 269
128a 20ff.: 230f.
133b 31ff.: 238 A.25
140b 7. 142a 13. 31:
 247 A.35
144a 9. 20: 231
146b 3: 229
146b 21: 240 A.28
146b 31: 216 A.2
151a 28: 218
152a 38ff.: 226. 228
152b 25–29: 270
155b 33–36: 228 A.17
156b 26: 232 A.19
158a 7–13: 265
159a 16: 220 A.9
159a 36f.: 264
SE 165a 2: 265
166a 10: 284
166a 15ff.: 232 A.19
166b 10: 232. 236
166b 11: 234
166b 15ff.: 236
166b 18: 245 A.33
166b 28–36: 270
167a 2: 253 A.42

PAUL FRIEDLÄNDER

Platon

3 Bände. 3., durchgesehene und ergänzte Auflage. Groß-Oktav. 1960/1964.
Ganzleinen je DM 38,—

PAUL FRIEDLÄNDER

Opuscula humaniora

Kleine Schriften

Groß-Oktav. Etwa 650 Seiten. 1968. Im Druck

NICOLAI HARTMANN

Platos Logik des Seins

2. Auflage. Groß-Oktav. XII, 512 Seiten. 1965.
Ganzleinen DM 42,—

GEROLD PRAUSS

Platon und der logische Eleatismus

Groß-Oktav. 226 Seiten. 1966. Ganzleinen DM 38,--

RAINER MARTEN

Der Logos der Dialektik

Eine Theorie zu Platons Sophistes

Groß-Oktav. VIII, 260 Seiten. 1965. Ganzleinen DM 52,—

DIETRICH MANNSPERGER

Physis bei Platon

Oktav. Etwa 290 Seiten. 1968. Etwa DM 32,—

Walter de Gruyter & Co · Berlin 30

Aristotelis Opera

Ex Recensione Immanuelis Bekkeri.
Edid. Academia Regia Borussica
Accedunt Fragmenta Scholia Index Aristotelicus.
Editio Altera.
Addendis Instruxit Fragmentorum Collectionem retractavit Olof Gigon.

Quart. 5 Vols. Ganzleinen.

I. XXIV, 789 Seiten. 1960. DM 98,—

II. XVII, Seite 791—1462. 1960. DM 84,—

III. Fragmente. In Vorbereitung

IV. Scholia in Aristotelem. Collegit Christianus A. Brandis.
Supplementum Scholiorum: Syriani in metaphysica commentaria.
Edid. Hermannus Usener. Accedit Vita Marciana. Edid. Olof Gigon.
LI, 955 Seiten. 1961. DM 120,—

V. Index Aristotelicus. Edid. Hermannus Bonitz.
XII, 878 Seiten. 1961. DM 110,—

Willy Theiler

Zur Geschichte der teleologischen Naturbetrachtung bis auf Aristoteles

2. Auflage. Groß-Oktav. XII, 109 Seiten. 1965.
Ganzleinen DM 20,—

Cicero — Ein Mensch seiner Zeit

Acht Vorträge zu einem geistesgeschichtlichen Phänomen

Herausgegeben von Gerhard Radke
Oktav. Etwa 300 Seiten. Mit 4 Tafeln. 1968. Etwa DM 28,—

Klaus Holzkamp

Wissenschaft als Handlung

Versuch einer neuen Grundlegung der Wissenschaftslehre

Groß-Oktav. XII, 390 Seiten. 1968.
Ganzleinen DM 48,—

Walter de Gruyter & Co · Berlin 30

EUROPA

Studien zur Geschichte und Epigraphik der frühen Aegaeis

Festschrift für ERNST GRUMACH

Herausgegeben von WILLIAM C. BRICE

Groß-Oktav. XII, 338 Seiten. 28 Tafeln. 1968.
Ganzleinen DM 120,—

KURT VON FRITZ

Die Griechische Geschichtsschreibung

3 Text- und 3 Anmerkungsbände. Groß-Oktav.

Band I. Von den Anfängen bis Thukydides.
Textband. XII, 823 Seiten. Anmerkungsband. IV, 423 Seiten. 1967.
Ganzleinen DM 148,—

KURT VON FRITZ

Platons Verwicklung in der sizilischen Politik und das Problem der Philosophenherrschaft

Oktav. Etwa 145 Seiten. 1968. Etwa DM 14,—

WERNER JAEGER

Paideia

Die Formung des griechischen Menschen

3 Bände. Groß-Oktav. 1959. Ganzleinen DM 50,—

Band I. 4. Auflage. X, 513 Seiten. DM 19,80
Band II. 3. Auflage. 418 Seiten. DM 16,80
Band III. 3. Auflage. VIII, 462 Seiten. DM 18,80

Walter de Gruyter & Co · Berlin 30